Sharkbait

A FLIGHT SURGEON'S ODYSSEY IN VIETNAM

Guy S. Clark, M.D.

Weeping Willow
Books

This is a work of nonfiction. The events and experiences detailed herein are all true and have been faithfully rendered as the author has remembered them, to the best of his ability. Some names, identities, and circumstances have been changed in order to protect the privacy and/or anonymity of the various individuals involved.

ISBN 978-0-99656-393-2
Weeping Willow Books
Santa Barbara, California

These writings are dedicated to the pilots of the 12th Tactical Fighter Wing, with whom I flew. I am especially grateful to Maj. Roland X. "Chico" Solis for teaching me to fly the magnificent F-4C Phantom and to Col. Wilbur T. McElvain (deceased), commanding officer of the 12th Tactical Fighter Wing Hospital at Cam Ranh Bay, Vietnam.

I also want to acknowledge Dr. William Simmons, flight surgeon (killed in action); Dr. Al Aleckna, fight medical officer (deceased); the 557th Tactical Fighter Squadron, the 558th TFS, the 559th TFS, and the 391st TFS; and my private pilot's license instructor, Russ Tyler, who taught me to "just fly the airplane!"

Special thanks go to my high school speech teacher, Miss Julia Elliot, of Griffin, Georgia, and Dr. Edwin T. Martin, my then-chairman of the Department of English at Emory University.

For her editorial guidance and assistance, I am grateful to Marcia Meier, editor and publisher of Weeping Willow Books.

INTRODUCTION

Several years ago, while cleaning out a closet in my study, I stumbled on an entire footlocker of handwritten notes from my tour of duty in Vietnam, a half century earlier. These notes were maintained as a daily diary during a single year of my life, 1966-1967, as a U.S. Air Force flight surgeon stationed in Vietnam. My first impulse was to dispose of the entire lot.

You haven't looked at these during the past forty and some odd years. What makes you think they have any value at all? ....But, once they are gone, they are gone forever..., I thought.

These notes are a time capsule of what I did and what I thought at age twenty-eight; meticulously documented for that one year of my life. No other period of my life, before or since, is or will be so well-documented. All other writings of my life will be second-hand history, from memory. Only these "on line" notes are all that remain of the man I was at that age. These are the words and thoughts, written at a specific time in history, by a person whose personality and thoughts had been molded in Southern military tradition by ancestors from colonial Virginia and New England, who wrote the history of this country by their deeds in war and peace.

A man is a complex product of the society and times that produce him. Having been born in 1938, my most formative years were encompassed by seven years of World War II, from 1938-1945. My father served in the Pacific Theater on Guadalcanal against Japan, as did my uncle and mother's brother. Another uncle served with Gen. George C. Patton in

Europe. Other uncles by marriage were pilots in the U.S. Navy and U.S. Army Air Corps, respectively. In summary, in the formative years of youth, all male members of my family had served in the U.S. armed forces. Since the earliest colonial days, my ancestors fought in every conflict to create this country. Sam Houston, who defeated Mexican Gen. Santa Ana for Texas independence, is from my mother's side. Gen. "Vinegar" Joseph Stilwell is also of mother's side. Gen. John Bell Hood from my paternal grand-mother's side lost the battle of Atlanta during the War Between the States.

In my unjaded, youthful perception of life, fighting for your country was the honorable fulfillment of duty for every man. However, Vietnam was a distant land and thus differed from other wars of this country. I was fortunate to enter the Vietnam conflict before the American citizenry reacted against the war. Morale was universally high and there was no conflict about our presence. From the perspective of a physician at the largest Air Force hospital in Vietnam, I never heard of a case of marijuana or other drug use. Our country had called and we had answered the call.

These writings are recordings of events, emotions and reactions during that one year of my life. During that time, I experienced more adventure than most men experience in ten lifetimes. Now, as I peer through the rear-view mirror of fifty years, I feel blessed beyond all measure.

During my nearly eighty years of life I have known many persons from every rank and file. I can state, without reservation, that the pilots with whom I flew and their support personnel were the finest men I have ever known. They were of the highest moral integrity and all served their country honorably. Let no critique of the conflict or of political decisions at any time cast shadows on the men who fought this terrible war.

As far as our nation and its leadership, I am not so sanguine. We continue to interfere in the affairs of other countries, with an arrogance that seems blind to the lessons of history. I can only attribute this ignorance to greed. The greatest human fortunes are made during times of war. Since wars are relatively short, as an investment, the financial return is enormous. After Rotterdam, Holland was bombed into near extinction during the Second World War; investors purchased distressed properties for pennies and later resold them for enormous gains. Great Britain used British troops to protect property of the Hudson Bay Company in North America.

The United States is a relatively new country and since its earliest inception, this country has been involved in various conflicts. Every form of new life, whether it is a creature or a nation, must always struggle to find its way against the old order. In every struggle, once the "Dogs of War" are unleashed, survival is the only goal, not amenable to philosophical cogitation from the cloistered comfort of a future armchair.

It is axiomatic that those who have known combat rarely talk about it, while those who talk of combat have rarely known it. These writings are an attempt to bridge the gap between the observer and the observed. My position was unique. My role as a physician was never compromised or questioned. My role as a fighter pilot was learned on the job. I lived two lives, each role complementing the other.

For me, the year in Vietnam was the astrologic perfect alignment of planets and stars that permitted me to fly these magnificent aircraft. I have held a lifelong abhorrence for "authorities" from scholarly backgrounds who pontificate on the life led by others, divorced from the realities of life experience. I do not believe it possible for any man or woman to comprehend the impact that combat has on an individual, unless he or she has walked in the same shoes as the airman, sailor or soldier.

And, yet from 1966-1967, I participated in more than eighty-six combat strike missions in the supersonic F-4C Phantom II as a crewmember and co-pilot. This participation was counter to the official policy of the United States Air Force. However, during war, rigid interpretation of regulations may impair the combat potential of a unit. In recognition of this, the ultimate decision about allowing flight surgeons to fly on combat missions was, therefore, relegated to the Wing commander, since mission success or failure rests completely on his shoulders.

Our Wing commander believed that the rapport between pilots who flew the missions and the flight surgeon was enhanced by the participation of physicians on the same combat missions, with the same risks experienced by the pilots. I agree.

But, there was more to my flying than contributing to rapport between doctor and patient.

My childhood was spent in solitude with nature. I was never more at home than when I was alone in a deep Southern swamp, surrounded by the forces of running streams and creatures of the forest. I knew perfect freedom. I give my father so much credit for this. He never tried to push me toward an arbitrary path or goal. He never offered unsolicited advice except on two occasions. Because of this, I followed his recommendations and am grateful for it. The first occasion occurred in high school. He recognized that I was at home with the creatures of the forests and swamps and less so with my own species. As such, I lacked verbal skills to communicate comfortably with others of my species. I mumbled and was uneasy in group conversations. He recommended that I take high school speech, with the comments that Regardless of how smart you are, if you can't communicate your knowledge by writing and speaking, it is all for naught. He was correct. In fact, I enjoyed public speaking so much that I became a ham and continued in high school dramatics.

His second recommendation was on the college level at Emory. Business and economic matters were very low on my list of interests. I wanted a life that was rich in experiences, not wealth or property. He informed me that business and economics are fundamental ingredients of life, for any person, regardless of his other interests. I took Economics 101 and have always been grateful. It was difficult for me and I didn't enjoy it. But the principles have stood with me all of my life.

While growing up, I was appalled by the lack of intellectual curiosity that surrounded me in the South. As a compulsive reader, my thirst for knowledge and wisdom was unquenchable. From the limited horizon offered by the Southern perspective, a medical doctor represented the "top of the mountain" in intellectual achievement. Many linked the degree with financial success, but this had no role in my life. I never regarded financial success as a primary, or even a secondary, goal in my life. Financial success had no more attraction for me than a bale of hay would tempt a carnivore. Because of my origins in the Old South and Protestant Fundamentalism, there was also a deep grain of anti-intellectualism ingrained in my soul. Academic achievement without application and experience in life is no more than intellectual masturbation.

More than anything else, I longed for a life of high adventure…a life that followed no one's previous path or track. In the words of Jack London, "Man was meant to live, not simply to exist…."

The only option that seemed viable for both passions was to be a medical missionary. Like Albert Schweitzer, I longed to tread new paths in the jungle, but from aposition of intellect, not provincial trailblazing. Therefore, my first goal was to become a physician and missionary. However, the depth of my commitment ended abruptly with a single radio announcement on October 4, 1957. On that date I was returning to college at Emory University, after a weekend with my family in Griffin, Georgia. My automobile radio announced the successful launch of Sputnik I by the Soviet Union. I was electrified! Pulling the car over to the shoulder of the highway, I listened, mesmerized by the details, while instantly reorganizing my priorities and future horizons.

It was obvious! Space was The Unknown Frontier, far vaster than man had ever envisioned on this planet. This would be my future. The cloak of missionary surgeon fell from my shoulders with the felicity of a snake shedding its skin. I chose a different route that encompassed a doctor of medicine degree. My visual acuity was not sufficient to qualify for military pilot training. But this could be worked around. Operating the spacecraft was less important to me than the exploration of unknown vistas of human adaptation to the space environment and space travel. The doctor of medicine degree would provide me entrée to conduct scientific and medical research in the entirely new universe of space exploration. I reasoned that future requirements change to meet changing mission demands. Besides it would be much easier to train a doctor to fly than to train a pilot to be a doctor.

Few men fulfill their childhood dreams during their short lifetime. As I review my life, I am overwhelmed with a profound sense of gratitude for the blessings of freedom that I have enjoyed. I have always believed the most perfect freedom is the privilege of choosing your own master. The aspirations, dreams and passions of my childhood have been fulfilled.

PROLOGUE

Ensconced in my beautiful home in the nirvana of Santa Barbara, California, memories return. I usually go to bed at 11 p.m. or midnight. By this time I am weary from the daily activities of diagnostic dilemmas, paperwork, and the stresses of responsibility imposed on a physician caring for other humans. Usually I fall asleep readily and sleep soundly.

But, occasionally, after midnight, I awaken to the sound of high-performance U.S. Navy jets high in the skies, above the coastal fog that envelops the area, as they perform night maneuvers. They are from Port Hueneme or Point Mugu or from the Top Gun schools in Fallon, Nevada. And, like an old warhorse long out to pasture who hears a distant trumpet, I sit up in bed to listen. Waking my wife, I ask her to listen as well.

The sounds have little meaning for her, but for me, the muted scream of distant turbines and the roar of supersonic jet aircraft are like jolts of adrenaline infused into my veins. I smile at memories long assumed to be lost. As the sounds recede into the distance, I return to my pillow.

As my body falls deeper into sleep, my dreams soar higher into the night sky. I am once more in the old Phantom, climbing through the fog, into the night sky, like a child racing to join his playmates to soar and gambol through the heavens like an eagle. Without ordnance and tip tanks, the drag on the Phantom is minimized. With full afterburner, I should be able to achieve Mach 2. Perhaps this will be fast enough for me to join up with the newer F-15s and F-18s...

CHAPTER 1

Orders to Go to Vietnam

WHEN I RECEIVED MY ORDERS TO GO TO VIETNAM, I was relatively comfortable.

I had finished my medical internship at Wilford Hall USAF Hospital in San Antonio in 1964, and was assigned to the School of Aerospace Medicine at Brooks Air Force Base for the Primary Course in Aviation Medicine. Following graduation, I was designated as flight medical officer and assigned to Bergstrom Air Force Base near Austin, Texas. During the course of the next two years, I had the privilege of flying on B-52 bombers and KC-135 Stratotankers for air-to-air refueling. I also attended the Advanced Aerospace Medicine Program at the School of Aerospace Medicine. Another duty was to provide aeromedical support for President Lyndon Baines Johnson whenever he was in the Texas area.

My wife, Elaine, was enrolled as a doctorate-level graduate student in molecular biology at the University of Texas in Austin. My schedule at Bergstrom was regular enough to allow mostly free evenings and weekends to explore the Texas Hill Country and surrounding communities. Working through the base aero club, I obtained my private pilot's license and flew a number of small Cessna and Piper single-engined aircraft.

But, as the poet stated, "All good things must come to an end." In early spring 1966, I received orders for reassignment to Vietnam. I was to report to the 12th Air Force Hospital at Cam Ranh Bay, RVN, as flight medical officer, leaving the United States on June 10. (My designation from flight medical officer to flight surgeon required 200 hours of flight time. This would be achieved after a short period.) This established my DEROS (date of expected return from overseas) as 10 June 1967.

Before embarking for Vietnam, I was assigned to Hamilton AFB in California for two weeks TDY (temporary duty) for combat training. This involved familiarization with the M-16 rifle and the M-60 machine gun. We were instructed in marksmanship and field-stripping of weapons. Grenade-launching with the M-16 was another part of the curriculum. The usual basic training exercises of learning rapid fire in response to pop-up targets as we walked through an open field were reviewed. Marksmanship with the M-16 was conducted at 300 yards. These exercises were standard for basic training in the Army, but as a physician entering the Air Force, I had never encountered any of this military training before. Many years later, I reflected on the fact that I had never encountered another physician in the Air Force who had this experience. Having been raised in the South, I had grown up with guns and hunting. Most of my boyhood had been spent in para-military games in Southern forests and swamps. With the exception of different weapon types, there was little new in this training. But, why I was the only physician subjected to this training remains a mystery many years later.

I formally protested the assignment to Vietnam. The protest had no direct influence on my assignment, but according to Air Force regulations, if an assignment were performed under protest, the individual was eligible for discharge at the completion of that assignment. This kept my options open. Without a statement of protest, on my return to the CONUS (Continental United States) I would simply receive another assignment to another facility, at the discretion of the Air Force.

After finishing the training at Hamilton, Elaine and I spent the few remaining days in Carmel, California, before I left for Vietnam. My memory of the events at this time is clouded. I had received the usual abundance of immunizations for infectious diseases and responded with a fever of 104 degrees during much of this time. The twenty-four hours before I departed for Vietnam were equally clouded by a wife who spent the entire night in intractable weeping. After spending the previous week with a high fever and the last night with a weeping wife, it was a relief to board the plane for Vietnam. Some things in life are worse than war.

11 June 1966

At the San Francisco Airport, I placed Elaine on her flight back to Austin, Texas, while I continued on to Travis Air Force Base, California. At Travis, I boarded a Boeing 707 commercial airliner that had been contracted by the Department of Defense for transporting military personnel to Vietnam. After the standard delay that seemed inherent in all airline departures, we finally took off, turning our wings west over the Pacific Ocean, heading for Honolulu International Airport.

Traveling with me were 170 other military personnel, from all services and of all ranks. Historical concepts of preparation for combat and transportation to a combat zone are deprivations of passage that attend all wars from every age. But, in 1966, the transportation was different. With classical music flowing through stereophonic headsets, I was served delicious food by attractive and courteous flight attendants. And all of this was at an altitude of 35,000-plus feet, above the weather and other tempests that tossed lower earth. A current movie was shown for those interested. I cannot help reminiscing at what a far cry this was from the troop ships and trains of World War I, WW II and Korea. It stands in even greater contrast to the forced marches through Gaul by Caesar's Roman Legions and interminable hours in the saddle endured by the cavalry of Alexander. While war continues to be best described by Gen. Sherman's statement, "War is hell," none can deny that enlightenment and technology have refined both the mode and methods of transporting men to war.

After four hours of flight, we landed at Honolulu International Airport. The delay, however, was for only fifteen minutes. Even this brief glimpse of the airport was impressive. The air was warm, dry and heavily laden with the perfume of tropical flowers. Pearl Harbor and the monument to the USS Arizona were visible relics of WWII. My thoughts were for Elaine and a very intense desire to share these tropical beauties with her. Someday we must return to this island paradise.

A few minutes later we again took off. And, for the next ten hours the vast Pacific Ocean unrolled beneath us like an endless carpet as we followed the sun westward. Daylight prevailed for eight of the ten flight hours. The next stop was Andersen Air Force Base in Guam. The layover at Andersen was also brief and we were confined to the airport. It was immediately obvious that Guam represented a different world from Hawaii. The weather was hot and the air steamy with humidity. It is a relief to seek the air-conditioning of altitude (35,000 feet). The final leg of our journey, from Guam to Vietnam, was slightly more than two and a half hours.

As we approached Vietnam, the first indication that we were entering a combat zone was the pilot's request to extinguish all reading lights. Then we were given the usual pre-landing instructions to fasten seatbelts and make sure all seats were "fixed in the upright position." The second indication of entering a combat zone was the pilot's next announcement, saying we would be making a "drop descent" with a straight-in approach to the runway. He explained that the standard gradual, prolonged descent, with approach to landing, opens the door for Viet Cong to surmise our flight path and open fire on the aircraft. This sudden sharp descent elicits soft gasps of surprise from some of the passengers. I was familiar with this procedure since it was a standard operation of basic flight training to land over an obstacle, as required to clear trees, buildings or other terrain features that obstruct the approach end of the runway.

With all lights out, we touched down at Saigon International Airport. Air Traffic Ground Control directed our aircraft to that portion of the airport that had been designated Tan Son Nhut Air Force Base. Tan Son Nhut was formerly a Republic of Vietnam Air Force facility. It had been usurped by the U.S. military as the main airport of the U.S. Air Force in the Saigon area.

Later as I reflected on these events, there seemed something quite unreal about the entire episode. Flying to a war zone in the comfort of a luxurious aircraft was irony enough. It became all the more so when I looked around to see young men of the Army, Navy and Air Force, many of whom seemed fresh out of high school or only recently removed from the home nest.

I was all too aware that many of these men would not make the return flight home or hear the classical music and view the current movies a year from now. Looking at their youthful faces, I thought with some bitterness of the intellectuals and beatniks at home. I deplored the editorials condemning all youth for its frivolity and lack of social responsibility. Some volunteered for military duty, but just as many were drafted and preferred not to be here. But, from all that I have seen of American youth, they will do their duty, not so much for "King and Country," but for the person who serves beside them…the bond that spontaneously forms between men in battle. War is comparable to the wilderness. American pioneers rapidly learned that "the wilderness breeds friendship." Survival depends on such bonds. Older generations decry the degeneracy of the younger generations. Heroes and brave men are always acknowledged in the past tense. But, I am confident that the youth of every generation will do their duty when called upon.

This quotation from "Idylls of the King" by Alfred Lord Tennyson comes to mind:

> *Though much is taken, much abides*
>
> *And though we are not now that strength*
> *which in olden days moved earth and heaven*
> *That which we are, we are...*
> *One equal temper of heroic minds*
> *Made weak by time and fate...*
> *But strong in will to strive*
> *To seek, to find and not to yield.*

CHAPTER 2

Arrival in Saigon

SAIGON HAD BEEN THE CENTER OF BUSINESS AND COMmerce in Southeast Asia for decades and was known as the "Pearl of the Orient" and "Diamond of the East." When I arrived in 1966, there was little evidence of Saigon's previous cosmopolitan grandeur. Before descending the stairs from the aircraft, I stood in the doorway and gasped at the change in air quality. Actually, the word "air" is a misnomer. The word "steam" is a more accurate description. But, it was not simply a matter of humidity! The fecal stench that immediately filled my lungs and threatened to drown me compared to that of an open, raw sewer.

The previous air-conditioned and sanitized splendor of our aircraft was replaced by air that slapped me in the face with the intensity of a steaming hot mop that has been dipped in garbage. In contrast to Honolulu, the perfume of flowers in the air had been replaced by the stench of human and other organic excrements. The odor was so putrid and omnipresent that I repeatedly stopped to look at the soles of my shoes, thinking that surely I had stepped into a pile of dung. I watched as our luggage was taken from the baggage compartment of the plane. Stored in the cargo bay, the luggage was cool and dry during long hours of transit at high altitude. Now, water condensed spontaneously from the steamy air onto the cooler surfaces of baggage and cargo. The parcels and luggage were instantly coated with a film of water droplets that coalesced into rivulets that dripped and finally streamed to the ground.

We had definitely arrived in Vietnam! Somewhere and somehow we lost an entire day by crossing the International Dateline. It was approximately 4 a.m. on 13 June 1966.

The scene that surrounded me was far removed from any of my previous experiences. When all around you is strange, a person searches for some familiar scene or object to reaffirm contact with previous reality.

I looked up to the sky. Screening out the cacophony of strange sounds, sights and odors, I saw the same familiar constellations in the night sky that I have known and loved throughout my boyhood. Spread above me in all of its majesty was the same Milky Way that I admired through a boyhood of camping under open skies. And within that cosmic sphere were my old friends, the familiar constellations of Orion, Ursa Major, Ursa Minor, Cassiopeia and the Pleiades. Despite having different locations in the sky, they were the same as I once viewed from a mountaintop in northern Alabama while studying for my Astronomy Merit Badge in the Boy Scouts. Nor were they different in appearance from when I viewed them while camping out on the banks of the Flint River in Georgia, or from the skies above the Ocklawaha River in Florida. The constellations were the same old friends I searched for in medical school while peering through the smoke and smog of Chicago's North Lakeshore Drive. And they were the same constellations I admired with greater clarity when flying at 40,000 feet above Kansas in a KC-135 Stratotanker during midnight refueling exercises with a B-52. It is an emotion that defies all reasoning. There was a measure of consolation in seeing these same old friends in the skies over

Vietnam. Regardless of the distance traveled, my friends were there to reassure me that I was still on my home planet.

From the airport we boarded buses transporting us to the visiting officer's quarters in Saigon. They were standard school buses with bars and wire screens stretched over the windows, meant to discourage someone from tossing hand grenades into the bus. Our sleeping quarters were in a wooden barracks-type building, enclosed by metal screens and barbed wire. We were to remain there for processing into the country and for briefing on our respective assignments. Following this we retired to another hooch-type barracks with assigned bunks. The bunks were two-tiered and each had mosquito netting. It was about 0530 hours (5:30 a.m.) and I collapsed onto my bunk, taking care to secure the mosquito netting behind me. Serenaded by the incessant roar of jets from the nearby flight line, I finally fell into a fitful sleep.

About two hours later I was awakened by a "swish, swish" sound from beneath my bunk. To my chagrin, the noise was caused by a straw broom, wielded by a hunched-over, elderly Vietnamese woman (Mama San)[1]. I got up and headed for the latrine and showers, which were in an open bay, similar to those in a high school boy's locker room. All showers were empty and I chose the closest. I had hardly turned the water on and begun to lather up when the high-pitched musical chatter of women's voices suddenly filled the room. Before I knew what was happening, three to four women gathered only two to three feet from me in the adjacent shower and squatted socially around the drain to wash clothes. I didn't have a stitch of clothing on and quite frankly didn't know which way to run. It was obviously my problem and not theirs. None of them even looked up as they

---

1 "Mama" is slang for mother. "San" denotes a position of authority. Originally, "San" was used to connote respect, but G.I. slang during the Vietnam War corrupted it to a person who worked in a brothel or bar. Without G.I. corruption, Mama San loosely translated into grandmother. Papa San referred to an elderly man.

continued chattering and washing their clothes. Ultimately my Puritanical ancestry decided the matter. Modestly draping my wet torso in a towel, I quickly retreated from the room and finished dressing in my quarters.

After these preliminaries, I attended the formal Air Force processing for entry into the country. It consisted of a lecture against importing personal weapons into the country. Now, as a descendant of colonial America, I firmly believe that every person has the inalienable right to bear arms for personal defense. I willingly acknowledged that firearms furnished by the U.S. Air Force may or may not be adequate. To provide an extra margin of safety, I had a newly purchased Smith & Wesson .357 Magnum pistol in my luggage and chose to ignore the warnings of the lecture. I depend on myself for survival…not the principles of the Geneva Convention that define a physician as a "non-belligerent." I firmly believe that during war, everyone is a belligerent.

Second, we were required to exchange all United States currency for military script. All financial negotiations were to be performed with this military script. Any transactions with the Vietnamese people or merchants were to be conducted exclusively in "piasters," the Vietnamese currency unit. The exchange rate was 118 piasters to one dollar. A further breakdown of the currency was that one piaster equaled 10 dongs. Because of a very strong black market in Vietnam for U.S. currency, it was strictly forbidden to pay a Vietnamese in anything but "P's," G.I. slang for piasters.

I learned one advantage of being in Vietnam; no postage was required for letters home!

I spent the remainder of the day looking over the city of Saigon. The temporary officer's quarters where I was staying was adjacent to the flight line at the airport. The Base Exchange and Officers Club were about three miles away, with a shuttle bus every fifteen minutes. The Officers Club was less elaborately decorated than in the United States, but it was functional and comfortable. There were advantages in eating there. It served edible food imported from the U.S. at fairly reasonable prices.

13 June 1966

The volume of air traffic at Tan Son Nhut AFB was astounding. The roar of aircraft, of every type and description, was incessant, and issued from every direction for aircraft, either taking off or landing.

Saigon and the surrounding areas were virtually armed camps. The military presence was everywhere. Every hotel and public building was surrounded by a sandbag barricade with soldiers and machine guns. Entrances to every building were guarded by both Vietnamese and United States Military Police with machine guns and automatic weapons. Every Jeep had a machine gun mounted on the hood. There was no such thing as an unguarded intersection. Every street and byway had some evidence of fortification and defense. Although I saw no positive evidence of enemy activity, the tension of war filled the air. According to the report of an acquaintance, during a thunderstorm that afternoon, every patron of a bar vanished beneath the tables with a single clap of thunder. Standing and walking in the hordes of push/pull rickshaws, bicycles, motor scooters and clamoring people was always encumbered by the knowledge that a knife may be thrust between your ribs in the jostle of the crowd. We were warned that every person was suspected of being a Viet Cong. It is estimated that 25 percent to 30 percent of the Vietnamese employees on the military installations in Vietnam are Viet Cong or VC sympathizers.

14 June 1966

Yesterday, in an attempt to get to the Base Exchange, I took the wrong G.I. bus. Two hours later, I arrived in downtown Saigon and quickly became lost. The traffic was unbelievable. Each avenue was like a giant parking lot crammed with bicycles, rickshaws, motor scooters and autos, all moving independently in defiance of any pattern or flow of traffic. There was no traffic control or discernible right of way.

As a farm boy from rural Georgia, Saigon unnerved me. And yet, without the impact of this war, I realized that Saigon probably differed little from other busy Asian and European cities. The crowds of people and traffic were difficult for me to cope with, especially when anyone who passed you on the street may cut your wristwatch from your wrist or cut your finger off to steal a ring. There was no effective security or authority there.

Despite this, I was hesitant to attribute all petty thieveries to enemy agents in this war. I was sure many of the petty thefts were committed by poor people, who earned their livelihoods by preying on rich foreigners, regardless of whether they were civilian tourists or military personnel. I also felt sure that Saigon had no exclusive rights on poverty-stricken people, who try to survive for generation after generation during the social disruptions of every war-torn land. As evidence, one need only read Charles Dickens and his writings about the poor in London during the Victorian period. The poverty of many was so extreme they had everything to gain and nothing to lose by robbing strangers.

Many of the U.S. Air Force officers stationed at Tan Son Nhut lived in hotels in downtown Saigon. Time magazine reported brigades of Viet Cong infesting the city to prey on Americans. While there may have been some truth in these statements, I was confident that many of the reports were grossly exaggerated by the news media. It makes good press to sell more magazines!

Finally, after finding my way back to the base officers quarters (BOQ) at 4 p.m., I crawled into my bunk and did not awaken until 6 a.m. the next day. I felt much better after a decent night's sleep. The seasonal monsoon rains had arrived. The rain fell in torrents both night and day, with an occasional break in the clouds by midafternoon. When the sun emerged for a short time, it was an open question as to whether you would be baked by its rays or boiled in the humidity. The humidity was far worse than I had ever experienced in Florida, Georgia, Alabama and Texas. When you awoke in the morning, your boots and clothing from the day before were coated with mildew.

I was scheduled to depart from Tan Son Nhut at 3 p.m. on a C-130. The flight was scheduled to stop at Phan Rang before continuing to Cam Ranh Bay for my assignment with the 12th Air Force Hospital. The 12th Air Force Hospital was the largest Air Force hospital in Vietnam. At 7th Air Force Headquarters in Saigon, Colonel Randall was the surgeon in charge of all Air Force medical officers in Vietnam. He was vice commander at the School of Aerospace Medicine, Brooks Air Force Base, Texas, whom I had met during my previous meetings with Colonel Ellinson. Colonel Randall was a very impressive individual, who seemed a notch above most career military physicians I have encountered.

While waiting for my flight, I had the chance to observe the masses of military humanity as they also waited for transportation. My fellow passengers were a colorful lot. American Army Special Forces were dressed in dirty fatigues that reeked with body odor and cheap Vietnamese beer. Their Green Berets had been replaced by fatigue caps or steel helmets, but they retained their constant companion of the M-16 rifle. Everyone wore a .38- or .45-caliber pistol with cartridge belt strapped around his waist.

U.S. Air Force Air Policemen wore black berets and certain U.S. Army airborne troops wore a maroon beret with unit insignia. All had the appearance of sunburned veterans, who either cursed with each other in profane English or spoke in Pidgin-English-Vietnamese to the small Vietnamese children. The "cowboys" are also present. These are young Vietnamese pilots who wear their newly won wings ostentatiously pinned on their blouses. They all wear silk scarves around their necks and shiny pistol belts around their waists, with accompanying M-16 rifles. Their dandified appearance was incongruous when contrasted with the motley appearance of most soldiers in the crowd.

Troops from the Republic of Korea (ROK) stood out as distinct from the more diminutive and frail Vietnamese military. The Korean soldiers and Marines had a very stocky and muscular appearance. Their uniforms were dark camouflaged fatigues and they were usually armed with M-14 rifles and .45-caliber pistols. The Koreans formed small cliques and were usually very quiet compared to the Vietnamese military personnel, who seemed to chatter constantly among themselves. Presumably, the Vietnamese felt more relaxed in their home country than did the Koreans. But, the very silence of the Koreans cloaked them in an aura of restrained ferocity.

Many of these men were returning to their field units after a weekend off-duty in Saigon. Some were American military advisers who usually lived alone or in small groups of two to three in small outlying villages. These men subsisted on a diet of rice, fish and rice wine/beer. They were a rugged group who had adapted to the impoverished and isolated conditions of their hosts. They lived from day to day, since any night their host might slit their throats if the political tide shifted the balance of power to the Viet Cong.

CHAPTER 3

Cam Ranh Bay

I ARRIVED AT CAM RANH BAY AFB AT 2000 HOURS (8 p.m.) for my assignment with the 12th Air Force Hospital. The flight over the mountains from Saigon was bumpy until it finally smoothed out for our descent to landing. Stepping from the plane onto the aluminum-mat runway, I was greeted by a scene of arid pandemonium. Even though it was twilight, the entire area was lit by floodlights for work that continued around the clock. It was obvious why Bob Hope dubbed Cam Ranh "Sahara West." The Cam Ranh Peninsula was barren, covered with white sand and more white sand. The Vietnam mainland, in the background, was covered by deep green mountainous jungles, while in the foreground were the bright blue waters of the South China Sea. On our approach to landing, the austerity of the white sand stood in sharp contrast to the verdant green background of the jungles and the softer blue of the ocean. Once on the ground, the ocean was barely visible from the base.

Initially, my senses were overwhelmed by the scene. The area was filled with aircraft of every type, while heavy equipment of every type and dimension plowed through the sands. Both air and land united in a collage of sound, sand and wind, sustained by swarms of humanity and its machines.

Everything and everyone was engaged in a frenzy of chaotic activity. As a new observer, I wondered how, where and if it would be possible for me to fit into this maelstrom of gargantuan forces and energies, all of which so desperately exceeded the bounds of my life experience and former reality.

The noise level was nearly deafening, with a resonance that not only filled the air but sent tremors through the ground. The unorchestrated cacophony of sound and vibrations united to concuss people and machines alike. On every side, planes were coming and going. The banshee screams of F-4C jet turbines, erupting into full afterburner as they scrambled ("scramble" is the Air Force term for an urgent takeoff) for takeoff, combined with the deafening roar of huge cargo aircraft, as each and all competed to land or take off on the single runway. Overhead, countless helicopters eschewed any semblance of a runway and simply rose, like so many dragonflies, from unmarked lily pads, fluttering up toward the mountains, north up the coast and south down the coast.

At every junction were heaped mountains of construction materials, munitions and supplies, either waiting to be stored or delivered elsewhere. Bulldozers and other heavy construction equipment crowded the taxiways and filled every spare corner as they waited either for shipment elsewhere or to be used on base.

The "buildings" were tents, Quonset huts and "white elephants." These white elephants were inflatable warehouses for temporary storage of anything and everything. They stood erect only by the energies of giant fans that constantly blew to maintain their inflation. Another row of cargo extended for 100 yards or more past the hooches and white elephants. It contained stacks of huge wooden crates, each the size of an automobile.

Every crate had large stenciled letters, that firmly stated, "↑This Side Up ↑," but this can only be read by standing on your head. Hundreds of these huge cartons are stacked on top of each other, and they are all upside down.

An oily, odiferous blanket of JP-4 (jet propulsive fuel-4) exuded over the landscape. The origin of these fragrant aromatics could be traced to the raw vapors that escape while refueling aircraft or from the exhausts of countless jet engines, excreting incinerated hydrocarbon residues, while sitting idle, or while straining at their leashes during "run up" to takeoff.[2] Thankfully, the all-pervasive organic fecal stench of Saigon was absent.

Sand was everywhere. It peppered your face, penetrated your clothing and filled your nostrils with each breath. Stepping from the safety of the steel matting runway, I was immediately up to my ankles in sand. The combined rumbles of bulldozers, tractors and other heavy equipment blended with the cacophony of the decrescendo-a-crescendo of jet aircraft either taking off or landing. This maelstrom would surely put Dante's Inferno to shame.

For a moment I had to smile, thinking of Dorothy's line from "The Wizard of Oz": "Toto…we're not in Kansas anymore." I thought of my own origins: "This is a long, long way from Orchard Hill, Georgia, and Tater Creek."

The nicknames for this desert peninsula, in the midst of a jungle-ocean oasis, were as descriptive as they were true. Bob Hope called it "Sahara West." The troops called it "LBJ's Cat Box." It is rumored that after the first women nurses arrived at the 12th Air Force Hospital, the men changed the name from Cam Rahn Bay to "The Bay of Pigs." After a short while, my appraisal is taken from an old Texas expression, "Cam Ranh Bay

---

2 In aviation parlance, the term "run-up" refers to a series of last-minute checks performed by pilots on their aircraft prior to takeoff.

is so dry that the trees are following the dogs around." But this was not Texas and there were no trees and there were no dogs.

I have always been impressed with the direct relationship between time and distance. The further one is removed from a location, the longer it seems since leaving that location. Although it had been less than ten days since I left the United States, it seemed as if ten years had passed. It was almost as if all of my previous life in the land of my birth, and of my colonial ancestors, was but a single chapter that now lay behind me.

The page had turned to begin this new chapter, toward a new volume with a new beginning. Now there was only Vietnam. And, now, there was only Cam Ranh Bay and Vietnam. All else was prelude… all else was history.

At Cam Ranh Bay, there was only the sand, wind and the incessant roar of aircraft. The average daily temperature was more than 100 degrees F, with intermittent periods during which temperatures exceeded 140. The remote austerity of Cam Ranh was amplified by the lack of vegetation and ubiquitous white sand, which both reflected the heat and defined its barrenness.

Despite all of these uncomplimentary descriptions, Cam Ranh Bay may well have been the blessing that accompanied the curse of war in Vietnam. By its location on a peninsula, Cam Ranh was a fortress, surrounded on three sides by the South China Sea and isolated from the treacheries of the Vietnamese population as well as from the conflicts on the mainland. Up to this time, it had been completely secure from enemy attack. There was also one other very positive attribute: There were no insects or mosquitoes there. Regulations urged all military personnel to take anti-malarial medications weekly, but the threat of malaria is nil when there are no mosquitoes. The most eloquent description of Cam Ranh's landscape was of a land so barren that even insects couldn't survive. That condition alone was sufficient to describe and summarize the atmosphere.

Another attribute was that, in 1966, Cam Ranh was one of only two bases in Vietnam totally controlled and manned by U.S. forces. Other bases were jointly managed and manned with the South Vietnamese military or with forces from the Republic of Korea.

At the time, the war in South Vietnam was fundamentally a ground war, fought against the Viet Cong and North Vietnamese Army troops who had infiltrated the country. The aerial component of the United States and its allies was supportive of these ground forces. Thus far, there had been no foreign aircraft to oppose Allied Forces in South Vietnam. However, in terms of jet travel time, North Vietnam was not so remote. Prudently, Cam Ranh and its facilities were guarded by surface-to-air missiles. The missile batteries were installed at Cam Ranh Bay in 1966 by Battery C of the 71st Artillery Unit to become the first fully operational HAWK[3] unit in Vietnam.

Cam Ranh Bay Air Force Base is on Cam Ranh Peninsula, which protrudes into the South China Sea. In 1965, the Civil Engineer Corps of the U.S. Navy, in conjunction with civilian contractors, constructed the airfield at Cam Ranh Bay. It was then turned over to the USAF Pacific Air Force Command on November 8, 1965.

As recently as 1946, the French were engaged in open warfare in Indochina with a Communist-backed nationalist coalition of guerrillas known as the Viet Minh. The struggle was intense, but at the time, the focus of United States' attention was on Europe and not Asia. In 1945, at the conclusion of World War II, our former ally, the Soviet Union, stood high on the list of priorities for a future enemy. The U.S. military mindset

---

3 The MIM-23 Hawk (*Homing All the Way Killer*) is a U.S. medium range surface-to-air missile. The Hawk was initially designed to destroy aircraft and was later adapted to destroy other missiles in flight. The missile entered service in 1960. It was finally phased out of U.S. service in 2002, the last U.S. users, the U.S. Marine Corps replacing it with the man-portable infrared-guided visual range FIM-92 Stinger.

was that of "overwhelming force" to demolish a foe, as exhibited in WWI and WWII. Wars fought for containment and without a goal of clear-cut victory were never considered by U.S. military planners or politicians. In short, wars were fought to victorious conclusions and not to a compromise for preserving the peace. This was America's mindset toward war in 1945.

Not until the Communist triumph of Mao Tse-tung in China were U.S. policymakers jolted into extending the ongoing containment of Communism in the Far East. Several events followed swiftly. Nothing startled U.S. military and political planners as much as the invasion of South Korea by North Korea in 1950. The United States was psychologically unprepared for partial war. By necessity, entry of the United States into the Korean conflict was accompanied by massive assistance for South Korea. Finally, the defeat of the French by the Viet Minh at Dien Bien Phu occurred on May 7, 1954. These events finally captured the attention of U.S. military planners. The pendulum switched from exclusive focus on Europe and the Soviet Union to a nearly hypnotic myopia on the Far East. The buzzwords changed from cataclysmic war with the Soviet Union to thwarting the "domino effect" of a Communist takeover in Asia.

After WWII, the geographic area formerly recognized as Indochina was divided into four parts: Laos, Cambodia, North Vietnam (Democratic Republic of Vietnam-DRV), and South Vietnam (Republic of Vietnam-RVN).

The significance of the Communist victory in Indochina was that now there were two Vietnamese states—the Democratic Republic of Vietnam (DRV) in the North and the State of Vietnam in the South (later to become the Republic of Vietnam). Initially there was a semblance of national unity in South Vietnam that inspired the United States to provide considerable financial and military support. A U.S. military assistance group took over the equipping, training and advising of the South

Vietnamese armed forces, all of which enabled the French military to withdraw completely by early 1956.

However, all was not well with the fledgling RVN. Infiltration of South Vietnam by Communist guerrillas from the north increased. Ultimately, a National Liberation Front was organized in the south to provide an organizational structure for the Communists. The Viet Cong were military personnel of the National Liberation Front. It became readily apparent that Ho Chi Minh and other leaders in North Vietnam were committed to bringing South Vietnam under their control.

In November 1963 a coup took place in South Vietnam, during which President Ngo Dinh Diem was slain. A parade of inept successors inflicted political chaos on the struggling state and the military situation worsened. In the meantime, U.S. military strength increased from 685 advisers in 1961 to more than 17,000 by 1964. The Gulf of Tonkin incident on 2 and 4 August 1964 resulted in Congress passing the Gulf of Tonkin Resolution. This granted President Lyndon B. Johnson the authority to assist any Southeast Asian country whose government felt jeopardized by Communist aggression.

The U.S. Air Force Tactical Air Command (TAC) began deploying a buildup of jet aircraft to Southeast Asia for temporary duty (TDY) in Operation Two Buck. In March 1965, the tempo of bombing over North Vietnam escalated substantially when air strikes by the U.S. Navy and Air Force initiated Operation Rolling Thunder.[4]

During these early years, the air war in Vietnam was not what the Air Force planners had envisioned in 1945 as the next conflict after World War II. Thinking in terms of a massive nuclear exchange with the Soviet Union, the airmen planned, equipped, and trained for nuclear war. This

---

4 "Operation Rolling Thunder" was a gradual and sustained aerial bombardment against North Vietnam by combined air forces of the U.S. Air Force, U.S. Navy and the Republic of Vietnam Air Force. It encompassed the period from 2 March 1965-1 November 1968.

was not illogical considering the standoff between the free world and the Soviet Union at the end of World War II. But, the intensity of this focus resulted in neglect of other factors. With the Vietnam conflict, the U.S. Air Force was called upon to perform tactical missions of close air support for ground troops, a task for which two decades of doctrine, force procurement and training had not prepared it. The previously directed worldwide strategic posture was only partially applicable. Now, it was being asked to continue maintaining this posture of holding the Soviet Union at bay on a strategic level, while at the same time, adapting to the new role of close ground support in the jungles of Southeast Asia.

With the prospect of conflict, there was immediate controversy between authorities on the choice between the uses of jet aircraft versus propeller aircraft in Vietnam. This controversy persisted throughout the war. Contemporary high performance jet aircraft were designed for atomic age aerial combat situations. The most conspicuous example of this was the B-52 bomber. Before nuclear submarines with Intercontinental Ballistic Missiles armed with nuclear warheads were developed, the B-52 bomber was the sole bastion of American defense against the Soviet Union. On my previous assignment as flight surgeon with the Strategic Air Command at Bergstrom Air Force Base in Texas, I flew missions on this giant aircraft that were specifically designed and mission-planned to deliver the hydrogen bomb against the strategic targets of the Soviet Union. But there were few targets of strategic value in the jungles of South Vietnam. There were strategic targets in the industrial and port facilities of Hanoi and Haiphong in North Vietnam, but aerial warfare in North Vietnam was conducted more on a political basis than a military basis. Because of these factors, extensive modifications of the B-52 bombers were accomplished to permit transporting large quantities of standard iron bombs for carpet bombing in South Vietnam, North Vietnam and Laos.

Another example of inappropriate aircraft designed to match the needs of aerial combat in this new environment was the McDonnell Douglas F-4C Phantom II. Originally the F-4C Phantom II was designed without an inboard gun. Old-fashioned dogfights and aerial gunnery were considered anachronistic for supersonic aircraft. Instead of being equipped with machine guns and cannons, the Phantom was fitted with rockets without an inboard gun. However, it became obvious that rockets were not always appropriate against the greater agility of older and slower MIGs. Nor were aerial rockets appropriate for strafing enemy ground forces. Almost as an afterthought, the Vulcan Cannon, comparable to the Gatling gun of the Civil War, was attached to hard points beneath the fuselage. The Republic F-105 Thunderchief was specifically designed to fight a nuclear war at high speeds and low altitudes. In the Vietnam War, it earned the nickname, "Thud" because of its high accident and crash rate in North Vietnam.

The U.S. Air Force entered the Vietnam War with the same free-fall, iron "Dumb Bombs," that were employed during World War I and continued through World War II and the Korean War. Most of my eighty-six strike missions in the F-4C Phantom II, from 1966-1967, used only Isaac Newton's gravity and pilot-directed ordnance. During my tour of duty, the sophistication of future precision-guided munitions (PGM) was unknown. These would arrive later. But, until that time, accuracy in dive-bombing depended on the skill of the pilot, the nature and geographic location of the target, local weather, and enemy defenses.

In 1964, before the explosion of manpower and materials signaled full-force American intervention in Vietnam, there were only three airports in South Vietnam capable of handling jet aircraft. These were Tan Son Nhut, Bien Hoa and Da Nang. All were under the domain of the South Vietnamese Air Force. Attempts by U.S. military to share these facilities created a chaos of over-congestion. Because of this limited capacity, plans were laid for three new, jet-capable landing fields to handle the vast influx of American airpower. The sites chosen were Cam Ranh Bay, Qui Nhon and Phan Rang.

Between June and September 1965, Army engineers prepared the Cam Ranh area by building thirty miles of roads and setting up quarries. In addition to this, they erected fuel storage areas, constructed a motor pool area and lengthened a pier that had been constructed two years earlier. In September 1965, the airfield at Cam Ranh was built by the U.S. Navy Civil Engineer Corps, in conjunction with the civilian firm RMK/BJR, which took over construction activities in 1965. Within fifty days, the AM-2 aluminum plank runway was ready for use and a week later aprons and taxiways were complete. At the same time, living quarters and supply buildings were ready for occupancy. It was officially turned over to the Pacific Air Force Command on November 8, 1965.

Plans for the other two jet airports were frustrated. A multitude of problems prevented establishment of satisfactory runways at both Qui Nhon and Phan Rang. At Phan Rang, the shortage of aluminum matting was compounded by heavy rains and unanticipated amounts of earth to be moved. The situation at Qui Nhon was even worse. Since the ground area around Qui Nhon was not yet secured from enemy forces, the original survey was accomplished from the air. Finally, when ground assessment was possible, engineers discovered that it was necessary to move more than three million cubic feet of earth. Additional factors were the necessities of spending months preparing the soil for aluminum matting plus additional months to prepare for the addition of a concrete runway. These changes would add $3 million to $4 million to the original cost.

Because of these difficulties, Cam Ranh Bay was the only one of the improved jet aircraft bases, proposed in April, that was combat ready by the end of the year in 1965.

Operations at Cam Ranh Bay, however, were not without obstacles. Although four F-4C Phantom II squadrons were operating out of Cam

Ranh at the beginning of 1966, problems were encountered with the temporary aluminum taxiways and runways. A 23-inch rainfall in December 1965 flooded the runways. Emergency drainage measures were required. Rain made the runways slick and forced all landings to be made with drogue chutes. At the first sign of rain, barrier crews and crash recovery personnel took positions near the runway, strobe lights were turned on, and decisions had to be made instantaneously as to whether the aircraft should land or be diverted.

With the advent of the dry season, the challenge of shifting runways arose. Dry sand under the aluminum moved with the wind, while the runway shifted in the direction of landing aircraft. During the first three months of 1966, a constant north wind pushed the taxiway three feet south, while the runway edged north under the weight of the planes landing from the south. Landing the air traffic to the south for three weeks moved the runway back. Daily stress measurements were required to determine the periodic changes of direction from shifting conditions to establish the proper orientation for air traffic. The moving sand created bumps and dips that required construction crews to continually replace sections of aluminum runway to smooth out the sand foundation.

After these first three months, Cam Ranh Bay assumed its rightful position as the major airfield for incoming and departing aircraft during the war. The 12th Tactical Fighter Wing and its four squadrons of F-4C Phantom IIs performed a vital role in the aerial war over North Vietnam as well as serving as a base for strike missions for ground support in South Vietnam and interdiction over the Ho-Chi-Minh Trail in Laos. Expansion of the U.S. Naval port facilities ensured that Cam Ranh would remain the dominant port for importing supplies and patrolling the coastal and inland waterways.

My primary assignment was to the 12th Air Force Hospital. The hospital, however, as with all medical support facilities, was subordinate to the 12th Tactical Fighter Wing. The wing commander was the highest-ranking officer on base, that of "Bird/Full Colonel" (symbolized by the same rank as the hospital commander). But, as a supportive organization, the Air Force medical corps was subordinate to the wing command. The primary mission of the Air Force was to oppose the enemy, and the primary tool was the organization of pilots and aircraft that formed the fighter wing.

The 12th Tactical Fighter Wing was composed of four squadrons of F-4C Phantom II aircraft. From the wing perspective, the flight surgeon's office has the singular purpose of providing medical support for the pilots who fly or personnel who support these four squadrons. A squadron is the smallest formally organized fighting unit in the Air Force. It is usually commanded by a lieutenant colonel. F-4 squadrons normally have twenty-four aircraft assigned to them. A "wing" is a self-sustaining combat unit that is composed of one or more squadrons. Personnel permitting, a flight surgeon is assigned to each squadron. I was assigned to the 391st Tactical Fighter Squadron (TFS).

As the base expanded to accommodate other aircraft types, the flight surgeon's office also had to expand its services to serve all flying organizations.

The day after I arrived, I reported to the flight surgeon's office. While being introduced to the office personnel, I glanced into one of the adjacent offices. I couldn't believe my eyes! Sitting with his feet propped on the desk was Al Aleckna, sporting a full handlebar moustache. Al was a year behind me at Northwestern University Medical School in Chicago and a Phi Chi Medical fraternity brother. As I stood in the doorway, staring at him in disbelief, Al looked up from his French grammar textbook and his eyes widened in amazement.

"Clark! What are you doing here?" he exclaimed.

"Al Aleckna, what are you doing here?" I responded, and he laughed.

Al was a standup comic. He had a natural elegance that blended with a slight indeterminate European accent. As a confirmed bachelor, he was studying French in order to become a "ski-bum" in Europe after he got out of the Air Force and before starting a residency in urology. I was delighted to see him. I couldn't ask for a better friend and companion than Al.

The other staff physician in the flight surgeon's office was Bill Simmons. Bill had been at Cam Ranh for eight months, while Al had been there six months. Bill Simmons had seniority over Al, and thus, was chief of aviation medicine.

However, shortly after I reported to the flight surgeon's office, the senior non-commissioned officer, Senior Master Sergeant Calidine, pulled me aside to inform me that I outranked Bill. My date-of-rank was earlier than his, meaning I was promoted to captain before he was. Now, I had absolutely no desire or cause to "pull rank" on him. He was a congenial and honorable person, who was totally dedicated to his work. He had been there for eight months and was familiar with the personnel, office routines and wing procedures. I had much to learn from him.

After working in the flight surgeon's office for a short time, an additional attribute of Bill's became obvious and guaranteed that I would never challenge his authority. He actually enjoyed paperwork! In fact, he jealously guarded every particle of paperwork as being subject to his review and signature. But, more important was the fact that he was very committed to excellence involving all paperwork. This suited me to a "T," since paperwork was the bane of my existence. I detested it. Bill actually reveled in it! For no other reason than this, I would never consider challenging him about the position of chief. A less passionate position for me is that the majority of all paperwork is the domain of the non-commissioned officers. They are trained with backgrounds specifically for this purpose. The NCOs are the administrative backbone of the Air Force. Both at Bergstrom and in Vietnam, I was extremely impressed with their dedication and commitment. I trusted them and they knew that I trusted them. I can't even imagine running a flight surgeon's office without them. (In a broader statement, I can't imagine running the U.S. Air Force without them.)

Details such as rank were rarely brought into question between physicians. Medical credentials, rather than military rank, dominated the associations and interpersonal relationships between physicians in the Air Force. Rarely were physicians addressed by their rank. Below colonel, you were most often addressed by "doctor," or more informally yet, by your first name.

I faced the same situation when I arrived at the flight surgeon's office at Bergstrom AFB in Texas. The doctor acting as chief of aviation medicine was Dr. Michael Rangle. Just as at Cam Ranh Bay, I was pulled aside by the NCOIC, MSgt. Cruz Valdez, to inform me that I outranked Dr. Rangle. I discounted the issue, but the other office staff did not. Courtesies and small favors were showered on me in preference to Dr. Rangle. I encountered the same situation in Vietnam. All of these subtleties of rank might have been ignored or discarded by me, but they were neither ignored nor discarded by the non-commissioned officers. These professional military men long learned that their survival depended on knowing precisely where the bottom-line of power lies. In the Air Force, commissioned officers may technically hold the titular power of command, but the non-commissioned officers are the mechanisms through which commissioned officers exercise their command. Woe to a junior officer who believes that his higher rank as a commissioned officer provides the last word in implementing a decision that involves a non-commissioned officer.

Bill Simmons had been chief of the flight surgeon's office since Cam Ranh Air Force Base first opened, when his stateside squadron was assigned to Vietnam. Bill had an interesting history. His stated reason for quitting private practice in favor of joining the Air Force was that private practice was all-consuming and he wished to have more time for his family. He graduated from the School of Aerospace Medicine at Brooks Air Force Base three months after I did. Just as I did, on graduation, he received the designation of FMO or flight medical officer. Bill's first assignment was to MacDill AFB in Florida as FMO. During that assignment, Bill's flying duties were primarily with the 557th TFS.

When the 557th TFS was deployed from MacDill to Cam Ranh Bay in October 1965, Simmons was left behind. However, through determined efforts of wing officials and multiple pilot friends, Bill was finally deployed from Florida to Cam Ranh Bay. After arriving in Vietnam, he was informed that, as a physician, he would not be able to fly on combat missions. It just so happens that the 557th Tactical Fighter Squadron, that he so ardently wished to accompany to Vietnam, has the singular purpose of flying combat missions. After all, Vietnam is a war zone. The types of missions might vary from strike missions to support ground troops or MIG-Cap over Hanoi, but every mission flown by the F-4C Phantom II is a combat mission.

In 1965-1966 the overall command authority of Pacific Air Force (PACAF) issued regulations that specifically prohibited doctors (i.e. flight surgeons) from flying on combat missions. On a more local level of command, the 7th Air Force surgeon's office in Saigon had also specifically issued a directive that prohibited doctors from flying on combat missions. This directive, of course, was primarily aimed at flight surgeons. However, there was a loophole within the ruling that left the final decision about physicians flying combat to the local wing commander. The argument for flight surgeons flying combat missions was that it bolstered rapport between the flight surgeon and the pilots under his care.

By the time I arrived at Cam Ranh, the issue had long been settled. The fact that Bill Simmons and Col. Levi R. Chase, wing commander, were longtime close friends provided support against both the PACAF ruling and the 7th Air Force ruling. When I arrived, both Bill Simmons and Al Aleckna were flying strike missions on a regular basis in the F-4C Phantom II. It was assumed that I would also fly strike missions.

Nothing could have pleased me more! The principle that stands for flight surgeons flying combat missions with pilots under his care seems entirely logical to me. I don't believe it is possible to appreciate the duties of another man until you have flown with him and have experienced the same risks and successes that he encounters on a daily basis. Were it not for the previous intervention of Simmons and Colonel Chase, I would not have had the privilege and wealth of experiences in flying combat that comprise these writings. I must also express my appreciation for the continuing support of my hospital commander, Colonel Wilbert McElvain, for endorsing this policy.

The workweek was seven days a week from 7:30 a.m. to 6 p.m. The hours, however, are misleading. The work load is very light since the pilots are thoroughly committed to flying and refuse to seek medical advice about any minor condition, such as a upper respiratory infection or blocked Eustachian tube, that might disqualify them from flying. For the pilots I encountered, being unable to fly for any reason was equivalent to moral decrepitude. For a fighter pilot to report on sick call was rare.

In addition to patient care, a flight surgeon must be available to respond to crash calls at all times. The flight surgeon on call carried the radio and had the office Jeep. The remainder of the time was spent flying on missions, giving lectures and visiting other areas that provided aeromedical support. Helicopters responsible for medical evacuation (MedEvac) sat on the ramp at the ready. Teaching methods of emergency treatment to the aeromedical corpsmen that fly on Med-Evac and rescue missions was a regular part of our duties. Anything that contributed to the health and well being of aircrew members was within our domain.

In addition to our duties in the flight surgeon's office, we also had staff duty at the hospital. This involved rotating MOD, or medical officer of the day, duty with other staff physicians every seven to eight days. On those nights, we slept at the hospital and treated anything and everything that came through the emergency room.

Types of Missions Flown by Flight Surgeons

The majority of strike missions were flown against enemy ground troops, in support of our ground troops. These missions were flown and coordinated with "Forward Air Controllers" (FACs) that flew at low altitudes and locally directed the strike mission. Since friendly and enemy forces were frequently in juxtaposition with each other, the delivery of napalm, bombs, and anti-personnel weapons had to be precisely directed. Other missions frequently flown and which will be defined later were: Sky Spot; missions over Laos and Cambodia… "Out of Country"; intercession of supplies and reinforcements over Ho Chi Minh Trail; and destruction of enemy supply depots, ammunition depots and weapon storage areas.

Types of ordnance carried on the Phantom for close ground support included the Vulcan cannon, or Gatling gun, for strafing; bombs of varying weights; napalm; and CBUs (cluster bomb units/anti-personnel weapons).

Thoughts on Being a Flight Surgeon

For the flight surgeon, there are additional benefits derived from our association with the pilots and air crewmembers. The flight surgeon's office at Cam Ranh was physically well-appointed. Located on the flight line adjacent to Base Operations and headquarters, the flight surgeon's office was isolated physically and spiritually from the hospital and other medical facilities. This relationship accordingly raised the flight surgeons' status and accommodations to a level far above that of other physicians at the hospital. Unfortunately, the status separation did not always lead to cordial relations between flight surgeons and other doctors. Everything in the Air Force favored the pilots and those who directly supported them. As a result, privileges that extended to pilots also extended to flight surgeons. Rank in the Army and Marines was based on the number of troops under an officer's command. In the Air Force, rank was a function of responsibility for very expensive aircraft. It was the same in the Navy, except "ships" may be inserted for "aircraft."

For the hospital at Cam Ranh, all specialty physicians on staff had their independent on-call schedules. There was internal medicine call, general surgery call, ear, nose and throat (ENT) call, radiology call, pathology call, orthopedic surgery call and psychiatry call. The flight surgeon's office also has its own call schedule that was independent from other physicians at the hospital. Beyond these on-call duties, the flight surgeon's office enjoyed autonomy unknown to other physicians.

The status of a flight surgeon on base, however, was not inherent. Much depended on the perspective of the hospital commander and the wing commander. If the hospital commander was a physician with the usual medical credentials and no particular interest in aviation, the flight surgeon was viewed as just another doctor, another subspecialist, who confined his practice to treating pilots and aircrew members. This type of hospital commander and physician would progress in rank and ultimately be given command of a larger hospital with more staff physicians.

My previous two years' experience at Bergstrom taught me that nothing is more tedious than the practice of clinical military medicine during peacetime. The military has only one reason to exist and that is to defend the nation during wartime. To be a military physician during peacetime is comparable to being an obstetrician in a geriatric hospital. During peacetime, military medicine marches to the metronomic drumbeat of drills, simulated emergencies, mind-numbing paperwork, inspections and constant mediations between quarrelsome physicians on the hospital staff. From the perspective of the professional military physician, scoring points on all of these routines was critical for promotion to higher rank. Promotion to the ultimate higher rank of brigadier general allowed a physician the privilege of supervising and conducting inspections on multiple hospital commanders, who marched to the same drumbeat. The usual hospital commanders were physicians who were satisfied with higher rank, administrative duties and who practiced limited clinical medicine. After a while they took pride in their rank and promotions for Excellence-in-Repetitious-Tedium. This description applied to the hospital commander who was in command when I arrived at Cam Ranh. He was a physician and not a pilot.

However, if the hospital commander is both a pilot and physician, chances are that he would "rather be flying" than sitting behind a desk settling grievances between other physicians…or preparing for the next disaster drill. And, if the hospital commander is also a pilot, the flight surgeon is a "favored son," who also loves to fly and has a special place in his heart for pilots and their airplanes.

During my tour in Vietnam, it was my great privilege to have a hospital commander who was both a military pilot and a physician. Col. Wilbert H. McElvain and I possessed the same maverick streak. Regardless of the differences in our ranks, it was obvious that garrison medicine was not our preferred duty. Both Colonel Mack and I would rather be flying. This was war and the golden opportunity for all things involving military aviation, the time when the veneer of garrison regulations and the tedium of peacetime medicine were shed…and we flew!

For the first time in my medical career, the person who outranks and commands me is of the same temperament as I. Colonel Mack and I were cut from the same bolt of cloth. I saluted him because I respected him.

With no disrespect to my biological father, if I were asked to choose a "surrogate father," I would choose Colonel Mack...that is, if he would have me.

Each flight surgeon was assigned to one of the four squadrons of F-4Cs, both for flying duties as well as for billeting (sleeping quarters) purposes. For the flight surgeon, there were definite advantages to this arrangement. Regardless of rank, flight surgeons lived much better than the average doctor at the hospital. Those with rank of colonel, as with Colonel Mack, had double-occupancy, air-conditioned trailers.

The flight surgeon's office was in a Quonset hut on the flight line next door to Base Operations, with air-conditioning and mahogany-paneled walls. The mahogany paneling was flown in from the Philippines on C-130s that regularly shuttle between the Philippines and Vietnam. On the return leg to Vietnam, the aircraft were frequently empty, and anything was possible when mahogany paneling was dirt cheap and air shipment cost nothing.

Pilots slept on bunks in air-conditioned Quonset huts and flight surgeons who treated them also slept in air-conditioned Quonset huts. In contrast, the only other air-conditioned areas in the 1,000-bed hospital were the intensive care unit and the operating/surgical tent. All medical clinics and work areas were housed in tents with only the offshore breezes for ventilation.

Other physicians slept on canvas cots in tents under mosquito netting, where ventilation was obtained by raising the tent flaps at night and praying for a breeze. Since mosquito netting didn't filter out blowing sand, those physicians frequently were forced to sleep with goggles over their eyes to keep the sand out.

The pilots and flight surgeons had hot and cold running water for shaving and showers, whereas other doctors of equivalent and higher rank had only cold water.

Other physicians walked, while the flight surgeon's office had a Jeep and its own portable radio for communications.

While many of these amenities were courtesy of Colonel Chase and his rapport with Bill Simmons, many items of furniture and personal comfort were donations from the pilots who flew cargo aircraft throughout Southeast Asia. This mal-distribution of wealth was not conducive to harmonious relations with other physicians. However, since contact with hospital and clinic physicians was so limited, friction rarely arose. The flight surgeon's call schedule was to cover aerial emergencies, which took precedence over hospital medical duties.

My reason for becoming a flight surgeon had nothing to do with these unanticipated luxuries. I became a flight surgeon because I love airplanes and I love to fly. As flight surgeon, I had the privilege of flying in the fastest and most advanced jet fighters in the world. Before my assignment in Vietnam, I was fortunate enough to fly in the Boeing B-52 bomber while stationed at Bergstrom. (I also had the great honor of being part of the aeromedical detail that served President Lyndon Johnson. Frequently, Johnson would fly in Air Force One to Bergstrom before continuing to his ranch in nearby Johnsonville by motorcade. But, occasionally he would fly directly to his ranch in the smaller Air Force One Jet Star. Requisite to the policy of assuring the president's safety was the provision of medical support whenever and wherever he landed, whether at the ranch or at Bergstrom. This medical support was considered aeromedical by design, and thus, the prerogative of a flight surgeon. At that time, there were two of us in the flight surgeon's office, but I was the only physician cleared for "Top Drawer" presidential support. The screening process was so intense that the Secret Service interviewed my kindergarten teacher in Griffin, GA, about my moral character at age five.)

Now, at Cam Ranh Bay, I had the double privilege of flying in the hottest jet fighter-bomber in the world, the F-4C Phantom II…not as an observer or as a passenger, but as an active crewmember. The overriding reason to become a flight surgeon is the privilege of flying. And, there is no higher privilege than in flying combat missions as a co-pilot in the extraordinary F-4C Phantom II.

After graduating from high school in 1956, I attended Emory University in Atlanta, Georgia, for my pre-medical education. I aimed for medical school during all of my studies. But, my motives were not pure. Through a quirk of genetics, I was blessed or cursed with a thirst for knowledge and an equal set of passions for high adventure. The very thought of practicing routine clinical medicine within closed office spaces would have prompted me to "fall on my sword."

I was intellectually oriented, but obtaining a doctorate degree did not satisfy an equally important life goal. Academic distinction rarely accompanies high adventure. Also, in the process, I had to make a contribution to humanity. When Sputnik soared overhead on 4 October 1957, my medical missionary goals were shed with the readiness of autumn leaves falling from the tree. Space was the greatest frontier that mankind had ever faced. I had to be part of its exploration. In 1959 I entered medical school at Northwestern University in Chicago for the sole purpose of using my degree as a back door entrée into the U.S. space program. I enlisted in the Air Force during my senior year at Northwestern Medical School. My subsequent Air Force internship was the first step toward entry into the Aerospace Medicine Residency Program. This was, in turn, the first step to prepare for the medical/scientific position in the Manned-Orbiting-Laboratory (MOL) program that was being planned as the first manned satellite of the United States. This program was jointly sponsored by NASA and the Air Force.

But, reality intervened. As I observed the increasing numbers of Vietnam casualties flowing through the emergency room, it was obvious that we were becoming involved in a war. This triggered a reassessment of my life goals. To be totally objective about a goal that had driven me through college and medical school was not easy.

My reasoning was thus: the MOL/Manned-Orbiting Laboratory program was a joint sponsorship between the Air Force and NASA. NASA was a publicly funded agency that depended on the good will of the public for its support. There had never been a war in history that was popular with everyone. In contrast, the primary duty of the Air Force was to fight our wars. I reasoned that the marriage between NASA and the Air Force, as required for the MOL project, could not last during a war. Not wishing to devote my life to a project that was preordained to fail, I resigned from the program. This decision was not made lightly. A considerable amount of time and effort had been spent in seeking Air Force sponsorship of my training. I had finally received endorsement from the Secretary of the Air Force, Eugene Zuckert, to enter the residency in aerospace medicine. And, in one of the most difficult decisions of my life, I chose to resign.

I discussed my reasoning with the two other candidates, Wayne Anderson and Chet Davies, both of whom were jet-rated pilots in the Air Force and Navy, respectively. During our internship, the three of us had achieved a certain degree of celebrity status in Air Force circles because of our goals. They heard me out but disagreed with me and planned to continue in the Aerospace Medicine Residency. I well remember their farewell comments: "Sorry that we won't see you on the moon, Clark…!"

For various reasons, the MOL program was not funded. The Air Force then considered both Wayne and Chet as persona non grata since they represented participation in a "failed project." Both of them resigned from the aerospace medicine residency after two years of additional training, during which they incurred additional years of pay-back obligation to the Air Force. They were not allowed to practice medicine or to fly. Chet told me they were considered an embarrassment to the Air Force and were transferred to an isolated base in the Arizona desert to run a dog lab. They bitched and kvetched so much that eventually they were sent to a small, remote base in Vietnam, simply to shut them up.

I found all of this out when Chet dropped into the flight surgeon's office at Cam Ranh Bay one day and told me the entire story. Personally embittered, he acknowledged that I had made the correct decision. Now, here I was, chief of aviation medicine for the largest Air Force base in Vietnam, working from a mahogany-paneled, air-conditioned office and regularly flying combat missions as a crewmember in the F-4C Phantom II.

I felt bad for both Chet and Wayne, but was very grateful for quitting the program when I was "on top." That night I said a thank-you prayer to the Good Lord for allowing me to make the correct decision.

I didn't get to orbit the Earth or to walk on the moon, but being able to fly combat missions as co-pilot in the F-4C Phantom II was certainly the next best choice. How could I be so fortunate?

When I arrived at Cam Rahn Bay, I was assigned to the 391st Tactical Fighter Squadron (TFS). Therefore, I bunked in the barracks with pilots of the 391st TFS and usually flew with them on their missions. Later, when I became chief of flight medicine, and represented all squadrons, I continued to bunk with the 391st TFS, but flew with all squadrons of the 12th TFW and other squadrons that were stationed at Cam Ranh.

For sleeping purposes, each squadron occupied its own Quonset hut, which was partitioned to allow four to eight bunks in each room. I was assigned a bunk that had recently been vacated by an F-4C pilot who with his co-pilot had been shot down by ground fire while making a bomb run just a week before my arrival. The details are unclear, but it apparently occurred when they released a bomb on their first pass and initiated a pull out over the target. As they were pulling out, the aircraft exploded in mid-air, killing both men. Either their plane was struck by ground fire or their bomb ricocheted off the water and exploded at the height of their aircraft.

Observers reported only that after they dropped their bombs, the entire plane was engulfed by flames.

And, if this weren't bad enough, before I arrived, the two F-4C pilots who bunked directly across the room from me were killed in a U.S. Navy C-130 crash that occurred near Nha Trang. The C-130 exploded in mid-air, killing all on board. A staff sergeant from Cam Ranh was also killed on the flight. The two pilots were taking a couple of days off for R&R. The reason for the crash was under investigation. Their deaths were tacitly acknowledged by their squadron mates, but it was not open for discussion and no one dwelled upon the circumstances. There was none of the theatrical mourning and histrionics depicted in Hollywood movies. No disrespect was intended. All of these pilots court death on a daily basis with each mission. All recognize this fact and are aware of their mortality. But, they have a job to do and there is no point dwelling upon the obvious. All efforts are concentrated on simply surviving the events that unfold from day to day.

When calls for air strikes arrive at Base Operations, the missions are rotated between the four squadrons. Each squadron has a lieutenant colonel squadron commander and vice commander. And each consists of approximately 300 enlisted airmen and forty officers. Of these forty officers, thirty-five are fliers/pilots and five are administrative.

The 12th Tactical Fighter Wing was the first Air Force Combat Wing selected for conversion to the new F-4C Phantom II. It was also the first Air Force unit to be stationed at Cam Ranh Bay. Thus, the 12th TFW represented the first permanently assigned F-4C Phantom II wing in Southeast Asia. After conversion to the F-4C, and throughout 1965, the wing was under the overall command of PACAF (Pacific Air Force Command). Initially, squadrons operated by rotating combat tours quarterly through Naha Air Base, Okinawa. The 557 TFS moved to Cam Ranh Bay in November 1965. On its arrival, strike missions were promptly initiated to provide close air support, interdiction, and combat air patrols over North Vietnam, South Vietnam and Laos.

Within a short period of time, the F-4C Phantom II assumed the bulk of heavy tactical bombing over both North and South Vietnam. From Cam Ranh Bay, squadrons of the 12th Tactical Fighter Wing conducted close air support of allied ground troops in South Vietnam. At the same time, Cam Ranh-based squadrons of F-4Cs were active in interdicting enemy forces and supplies that flowed from North Vietnam to South Vietnam over the Ho-Chi-Minh Trail through Laos and Cambodia.

"Tactical" implies action against the enemy on the field of battle. It implies mobility to intervene against enemy forces as required to counter a constantly changing combat situation. This is in contrast to the term "strategic," which implies action against a fixed major target, as represented by the dominant cities of Moscow and/or St. Petersburg, (also known as Leningrad and Stalingrad during the Cold War with the Soviet Union). The Strategic Air Command or SAC had B-52 bombers and KC-135 refueling tankers to carry hydrogen bombs for delivery against these strategic targets.

The extraordinary expansion of the Cam Ranh Bay facility was accomplished to accommodate a multitude of other aircraft types and missions that would soon arrive. In 1966, Lockheed C-130 Hercules from the 315th Air Division squadrons, based in Okinawa and Japan, begin "shuttle" missions out of Cam Ranh Bay. C-130s and C-123s from Tan Son Nhut and Nha Trang also made cargo pickups at Cam Ranh.

16 June 1966

I have finally settled into the squadron barracks. The more I see of the pilots, the more I am awed by the workload they bear. They fly two to three sorties a day, seven days a week, on very dangerous missions. The close air support required for each strike mission demands that they dive-bomb in mountainous jungle terrain against an enemy they rarely see, pulling out before striking a mountain or a tree, all while being subjected to the physical forces of 6-7 Gs. Or they drop napalm while flying at an altitude of 50-200 feet above the ground and traveling at 500-600 miles an hour, desperately avoiding ground fire or striking friendly troops. There is always the possibility that the napalm or bombs they were dropping against the enemy might engulf them during its eruption. When the aircraft is hurtling toward the ground or skimming over the terrain, the difference between accurately striking the target and destroying yourself might hinge on the precision of a single second in timing. And, yet, they continue, day-in and day-out, tempting fate…and defying death!

When I am not attending to matters on the flight line, I spend most of the day and much of the night in the office. It permits me to be centrally located in "off-duty" hours, in case of flight line emergencies. Besides, there is no other place to escape the heat and the sand. During the daytime, the barracks are darkened for pilots attempting to sleep after they have flown all night. However, to conserve electricity, there is no air conditioning in the Quonset huts during the day. There are fans, but the fact that the pilots are able to sleep despite the heat is testimony to their degree of exhaustion.

If I went to the barracks at night, the noise level of poker players, hi-fi music and loud renditions of the daily activities made sleep impossible. Quiet cool evenings in the office created the perfect environment for writing.

From the fundamental level of practicing medicine, the clinical workload is trivial. The pilots are healthy young men for whom a physical complaint is equivalent to moral degeneracy, unworthy of a fighter pilot. They are well aware that even the slightest complaint might decide whether they are fit to fly. The term DNIF or "Duty-Not-Involving-Flying" means that if you have a cold or upper respiratory infection that might interfere with flying duties, you will be temporarily assigned to a paperwork detail. This process was initiated by the flight surgeon. To be grounded is worse than the kiss-of-death for these young Turk fighter pilots. Their "macho" attitudes are a family joke as each accuses the other of standing in front of the mirror for an excessively long time when shaving...to nurture their narcissism!

Overall, the U.S. public is really quite ignorant of the war situation in Vietnam. Planes take off in the morning and return after missions that involved dive-bombing, napalming and strafing, yet few pilots ever saw the enemy, whether it be Viet Cong or North Vietnamese regulars. And, despite the size of its domain, the 12th Air Force Hospital at Cam Ranh receives relatively few casualties, except malaria, diarrhea and gonorrhea. Of course, there is the occasional incident in which a trigger-happy air policeman mistakenly shoots a G.I. who has wandered out of his barracks during the night.

From my short period of observation, the powers that be in Washington must be expecting an expansion of the war. The hospital facility and numbers of professional personnel are expanding at an enormous rate. However, I believe that most of the new physicians will wind up twiddling their thumbs and/or searching for a cool spot. I just learned from our cardiologist, Dr. Strickland, that my former professor and mentor in hematology from Wilford Hall Hospital, Lt. Colonel Buck Cantor, is supposed to arrive here in August. Dr. Cantor was an excellent physician and teacher. It seems a shame to place a person with his academic credentials over here. The only hematology-related diseases that I have seen here are related to malaria. Most of the patients with this diagnosis are air-evacuated back to the States for continuing care.

There is no morale problem at Cam Ranh. In contrast to the Army, Air Force personnel are all volunteers and not draftees. The enlisted men, non-commissioned officers (NCOs) and officers, of all job descriptions, are enthusiastic and dedicated to their work. Everyone firmly believes in his job and is dedicated to filling a vital role in defense of his country. Of course, there is the standard amount of G.I. bitching, but it is more of a military institutional joke rather than an expression of disgruntlement.

Most of the enlisted men keep a string of beads, not because they are Catholic…but as a method of keeping track of time. The official name for them is "DEROS beads." (DEROS means Date of Expected Return from Over Seas.) The string starts with fifty-two beads. Since the work-week is all day, seven days a week, it is easy to lose track of time. One day merges seamlessly into another. The problem is solved by the string of beads. Depending on how compulsive you are, each bead represents a day or week. At the end of each day/week, a bead is removed. The shorter the string of beads means that a person is closer to going home. That is why those who have only a month or two remaining before they leave Vietnam are known as "short-timers." When I first walked into the flight surgeon's office, several wisecracks were made that I should be careful: My string of beads was so long I might trip over it!

I am grateful for the footlocker of books that I shipped over. They were books I'd wanted to read all of my life, yet never seemed to find the time for doing it. Perhaps I could convert the "eternities of boredom" that accompany every war into a sabbatical for catching up on my education. Or I might wind up being the most educated "psycho" at Cam Ranh Bay! Time will tell…

CHAPTER 4

Back in the Air!

18 June 1966

C-130 Hercules flight

A flight surgeon is required to maintain a minimum of four hours' flight time each month. Because of my dislocation from Texas to Vietnam, I am behind on my flight time. To catch up, I start with a C-130 mission. The C-130 Hercules is a four-engine cargo plane and workhorse for logistical support in Vietnam. However, this particular aircraft had a number of write-ups on items that required repair and/or replacement. This mission was initially fragged (scheduled) to be a round-robin flight up the coast. Unfortunately, the aircraft developed an oil leak in the number two engine when we landed at a small landing strip in the middle of a flat, desert-like plateau. We sat there most of the day until mechanics could be flown in for repair. A delightful lunch of C-Rations was enjoyed by all as we sat in the shade under the wings while waiting for repairs. We were ten hours away from Cam Ranh Bay, but seven of the ten hours were spent on the ground and only three hours of flying time were recorded. It was a rather frustrating day. As Sherman said, "War is hell"...

Apparently, the newspapers in the States have leaked word that missions in Vietnam are compromised by a "bomb shortage." This has been vehemently denied by McNamara and all the other politicians. But onsite observation leaves no doubt about the shortage. The F-4C Phantom II is capable of carrying a bomb load that is twice the capacity of a B-17 bomber of World War II and as great a bomb load as the B-29 bombers and the Avro Lancaster bombers of World War II. What's more, it does this while flying at a cruise speed of 500-600 mph, compared to the cruise speeds of 170 mph for the B-17 and 357 mph for the B-29.

Lately, however, I have seen many planes taking off for missions while armed with only two 250-pound bombs. The absurdity of this is obvious. Lately, the usual flight consists of four aircraft, with each aircraft armed with only two 250-pound bombs. To appreciate the significance of this, one must know that a single aircraft, flown by two pilots, can easily carry eight bombs without risking the lives of six additional pilots and three additional airplanes valued at $2 million each.

So why is flying with inadequate armaments done? The only logical explanation is that the Air Force must compete with the Navy for the number of sorties flown. Financial appropriations for the Air Force and Navy are based on the number of missions flown and the number of aircraft involved. In order to keep the number of sorties on a par with the Navy, the Air Force is willing to fly four woefully unarmed aircraft on a mission that could easily be accomplished by a single aircraft carrying the same bomb load.

Yesterday a plane loaded with generals, Pentagon officials and political aficionados from Washington arrived on base. I was unaware of this fact when performing my routine, morning drive around the flight line.

When I arrived at the revetment area of parked aircraft, I was astonished to note the change that had occurred during the past twelve hours. There had been an enormous increase in the amounts and types of armaments loaded onto each aircraft since the day before. Each F-4C was loaded to the teeth with six to eight iron bombs, Side-Winder Missiles, Sparrow Missiles, napalm canisters and cluster bomb units, (CBUs, a type of anti-personnel weapon). As I drove around, I thought, "My Gosh, maybe we are going to war!" Several hours later, after the brass had left, the planes were promptly stripped of their full ordnance.

The Air Force is willing to risk the lives of six additional pilots and the costs of three additional aircraft (valued at over $6 million) plus an additional $14,616 in mission expenses, and to what purpose? The response cliché that higher command provides to any question or criticism is, "You don't have the big picture." By the way, these numbers do not reflect any of the indirect costs such as aircraft depreciation, staff support costs, three additional "starter units" for the additional aircraft, etc.

Quite frankly, I don't need to "have the big picture." My knowledge of grade school arithmetic is quite sufficient to add the cumulative costs and risks of this "smaller picture."

There have been recent articles in Time magazine about demonstrations and burning of embassies in cities such as Hue. However, when you talk to men who are stationed in these areas, they have absolutely no idea about the reported events…except vague rumors, obtained from Time magazine!

The young men who fly the F-4C Phantom aircraft are a different breed of cat from the pilots who fly the B-52 bombers and the KC-135 tankers for the Strategic Air Command (SAC). Before I left Bergstrom, a number of the younger B-52 pilots approached me on several occasions to request that I say a good word for them to get out of SAC and follow me to a fighter base. These young men are the cream of America's manhood. Most will leave the Air Force and not degenerate to the chronic level of dissatisfaction seen in so many SAC pilots. It is painful to see them become such political pawns to enhance the scorecards of the civilian and military politicians.

18 June 1966

C-130 flight from Cam Ranh to Qui Nhon to Da Nang to Hue/Phu Bai to Cam Ranh

Again, I am trying to catch up on my flight time with a C-130A flight from Cam Ranh Bay to Qui Nhon to Da Nang and then on to the Hue/Phu Bai area before returning to Cam Ranh Bay. Unfortunately, engine trouble develops at Hue (pronounced "Whay") and we are forced to remain there for several hours.

While we are sitting on the runway, a Vietnamese civilian drives up in a Jeep, accompanied by a stocky, powerfully built Asian who is clothed in camouflage fatigues and combat boots. Noting that my rank is higher than anyone else in the crew, the civilian approaches and introduces the male Vietnamese as Captain Nyguen. He states that Captain Nyguen wishes to transport members of his company from Hue to Saigon via Cam Ranh Bay. I direct them to the aircraft commander, 1st Lieutenant Luger, who has the authority to authorize the transportation and inform them of the estimated departure time.

Just why the civilian, who accompanies the Vietnamese captain, acts as intermediary, I have yet to understand. Every word of Lieutenant Luger is intercepted by the civilian and then repeated, in perfect English, with slight gesturing, to Captain Nyguen. Captain Nyguen, quite obviously, has no problem in understanding English or in comprehending all that is taking place. But, there is another aspect of the conversation that seems almost humorous. Captain Nyguen smiles constantly and salutes repetitiously with nearly every word. He salutes Lieutenant Luger and then salutes the co-pilot as well as me. After a few minutes of this, my right arm begins to grow weary of returning the snap salutes.

The encounter begins to assume a farcical depiction from a Charlie Chaplin movie. Since I am already a bit paranoid about the loyalty of these people, my imagination begins to run rampant. I began to wonder if he might be testing my reflexes, since the slightest movement, cough or fidget elicited a flash of salute…which once initiated had to be returned. If perchance he happens to catch my eye, the hand rapidly salutes…and I respond. I decide that if you can't beat them, join them. It becomes a game, and I will not be bested. I learn to catch him slightly off guard and anticipate his move. Before he can act, I snap a salute…to which he has to respond. I am now on the offensive and not the defensive. Quietly, I begin to peer into the bushes surrounding the runway, to assure that no Viet Cong are lurking and waiting for a lapse in my attention that might catch me off guard while I play allegiance roulette with the captain.

At last, the Vietnamese civilian takes his leave and drives away in his Jeep. Shortly thereafter, Captain Nyguen also departs by backing up with a volley of well-aimed salutes to each member of our party. He drives off. After he has disappeared I ask a U.S. Air Force sergeant, who is stationed in Hue, just why the captain wanted to transport his men to Saigon. The sergeant responded with a shrug and said he never has any idea what these people want or why.

Shortly after this encounter, three open trucks covered with tarpaulin arrive. When the tarp is raised, it reveals a motley bunch of scrawny Vietnamese soldiers and Marines, all armed with automatic weapons. They sit docilely on each side of the truck while two other Vietnamese stand over them with an M-60 machine gun trained at their heads. In one truck are two women, an ancient gnarled relic of a woman and a younger woman, dressed in what appears to be white pajamas.

With much chattering and gesturing with weapons, the "guards" shepherd the people from the trucks onto the ground. Here they squat in small groups. Captain Nyguen is nowhere to be seen. I wonder, "Exactly who are these people? Are they captured Viet Cong?" I learn later that one of the men, robed in black, is a Buddhist monk. This is significant since, in the political chaos of this country, there have been numerous examples of self-immolation by the Buddhists. This type of protest is running rampant in both Saigon and Hue.

I watch the Vietnamese soldiers and Marines of questionable identity and loyalty board the C-130 aircraft for transportation to Saigon, via Cam Ranh Bay. There is nothing to guarantee that the Buddhist monk or any one of the disheveled military personnel might not pull a flask of gasoline from beneath his cloak and ignite the plane in protest of some unknown grievance. We are certainly outnumbered. We are immensely vulnerable to anyone who is willing to destroy himself/herself in the process of destroying us. Once we are at altitude, efforts to extinguish the disaster of fire in the cargo bay would likely be an exercise in futility. This C-130 would become an instantaneous meteorite.

I express my concerns to Lieutenant Luger. He heartily agrees with me. By radio, we contact a number of American and Vietnamese officials in an effort to clarify the situation with these people...but all that we receive are bland reassurances that all is well. I, however, am unconvinced.

Captain Nyguen appears and begins to herd the sundry group into the cargo bay of our aircraft. He screams a name from the roster and grabs the man by the shoulder, literally throwing him aboard. It is apparent why he is captain. He is bigger and stronger than anyone else. As the plane fills with people, I have very mixed emotions. I have no desire to remain in this riot-torn city, but neither do I relish boarding the aircraft with the present company. Finally, against my better judgment and after an appeal to Zeus and other gods of the sky that might be listening, we board the aircraft.

Routinely, in this aircraft, the loadmaster remains with the passengers and manages the cargo. However, on this flight, he had one very dedicated flight surgeon to help him. With M-16 across my lap and pistol in hand, I position myself in the forward part of the passenger bay to maintain constant vigilance for any disturbance or trouble-maker. Just what I could have done if someone pulled a hand grenade from their bundle, I do not know. I have no idea what response would be appropriate and the thought terrifies me. Eventually, the co-pilot comes back to relieve me while the pilot transfers to the co-pilot seat and ushers me into his seat. He relinquishes control of the aircraft to me and tells me to fly us back to Cam Ranh. Entering the downwind leg for landing was a great relief and pure pleasure. That blast furnace of this base never looked so good. When I finally stood on the runway, I had to restrain myself from kissing the ground. After thanking Lieutenant Luger for his kindness in allowing me to fly, I leave the flight line, to slog my way through the sand to the squadron barracks, where I promptly fall into my bunk for a long night's sleep.

19 June 1966

Each day blends into the next, so seamlessly that all track of time is lost in a continuum of heat and sand. I have been in the office all day, clearing out paperwork. Someone said that today is Sunday, but it seems irrelevant since every day is the same. The temperature outside has been in excess of 132 degrees F. in the shade. Several "old timers" have informed me that the hottest months are yet to come.

I have just finished rereading a number of works by Thomas Paine. These, of course, were written during the American Revolution against Great Britain, but their relevancy spans the centuries.

"These are times that try Men's souls. The summer soldier and the sunshine patriot will in this crisis, shrink from the service of his country. Tyranny, like Hell, is not easily conquered; yet we have this consolation with us that the harder the conflict, the more glorious the triumph. Heaven knows how to put a proper price upon such goods; and, it would be strange indeed, if so celestial an article as freedom should not be highly rated."

It is all too easy to focus on the devastation and horrors that accompany every war in every age. But it is a self-inflicted wound to allow the tragedies and horrors of mankind to blind us or cause us to ignore the grandeurs of Nature that surround even the bleakest domain and garrison. When I walked out of my office this evening, the sun was setting on the mountains of the distant mainland. Above the mountains was the usual evening buildup of great cumulus clouds. An occasional shard of lightening pierced the clouds and a distant roll of thunder boomed to cascade through the silence. When viewed from the air, the entire panorama of white sand and crystal clear ocean waters is cast against a background of deep green jungle mountains, capped by towering clouds.

The military show of force in this small, beautiful country is awesome. Day and night, the skies are split with the scream of jets and the cut...cut...cut...of helicopters fluttering back and forth, like dragonflies soaring over a dry creek bed. From every direction, the rumble of bulldozers, tractors and trucks fills the air of this desert, jungle and mountainous land. At night, the dull thump, thump of distant mortars lulls you to sleep. And, you are awakened at 4 or 5 a.m. by the dawn takeoff of a flight of four Phantoms, loaded with bombs and/or napalm for the first air strike of the day.

It is impossible for one not to muse on the vast contrasts in mankind's nature. The ability of an individual to recognize celestial grandeur and cosmic magnificence… to a degree that exceeds his potential to explain or to fathom… must be contrasted to the insensibility of armies that swarm and destroy each other. Yet, both of these are features of the same men and the same mankind.

Leo Tolstoy expresses these sentiments with greater eloquence in War and Peace:

"Every man has a twofold life: One side is his personal life, which is free in proportion as its interests are abstract; the other is life as an element, as one bee in the swarm; and here a man has no chance of disregarding the laws imposed upon him. The higher a man stands on the social ladder, the more men he is connected with, the greater the influence he exerts over others-the more evident is the predestined and unavoidable necessity of his every action.

"Every one of their actions, though apparently performed by their own free will, is, in its historical significance, out of the scope of volition, and is correlated with the whole trend of history; and is, consequently, preordained from all eternity."

It is also impossible to convey these emotions to another in letters. After seven to ten days, when the letter is received, the emotions of the writer will have faded or disappeared, removed from the context of the moment. Regardless of a writer's skill, the context of a moment can never be entirely recaptured or adequately recorded for appreciation by the person who reads the letter and has never experienced the original circumstances. Life experiences are derived from living. The ultimate challenge for a writer is to convey those experiences to the reader with such fidelity that the reader relives the emotions of the experience, transcending all differences in time and place. Something will always be lost in transmission. Comprehension of another person's writing must always be grounded on the life experiences of the reader. There are times when any attempt to communicate the essence of life with another human being is damned to failure before it begins. Aleksandr Solzhenitsyn expressed these sentiments in One Day in the Life of Ivan Denisovich, published November 1962 in the Soviet literary magazine Novy Mir:

"It is impossible for a warm man to understand how a cold man feels."

Perhaps, this impossibility is the challenge that drives me. Only my compulsion to write demands that I try.

21 June 1966

C-130 flight

Route: Cam Ranh to Bien Hoa to Da Nang to Bien Hoa to Phan Rang to Cam Ranh

Flight Time: 5 hrs 10 mins

This is a rather dull, extended flight over the mountains and Central Highlands to Bien Hoa AFB. Bien Hoa is in the midst of a huge marshland/ swamp. From altitude, the entire landscape below is a patchwork of rice paddies and farmers with water buffalo.

Bien Hoa Air Base is a Vietnam People's Air Force (Khong Quan Nhan Dan Viet Nam) military airfield in South-Central South Vietnam about twenty miles (thirty kilometers) from Saigon. The base is a major facility of the U.S. Army, Navy and Air Force. It also continues to be in active use by the Republic of Vietnam Air Force. With its close proximity to the International Airport at Saigon, Bien Hoa Air Base is the most accessible tactical air base to be reached by visiting news reporters. Because of this it receives the greatest amount of news and photographic coverage during the war.

As we land to unload cargo, I note that the entire area has a peculiar musty odor. I have no idea what gives the air such an odor unless it is the stagnated water in the rice paddies and human excrement known as "night soil" that is used for fertilization. I can't even imagine the number of mosquitoes that must thrive in this miasma. Whenever I see large quantities of stagnant fresh water, my childhood memories of battling mosquitoes while camping in Florida swamps, always return. I am happy to be flying back to the arid, mosquito-free sands of Cam Ranh Bay.

For the first time, I am beginning to recognize a significant amount of animosity directed by hospital-based physicians against the flight surgeon's office. Certainly, the differences in our life styles and work conditions are in striking contrast with each other. I can't blame them for being disgruntled at the inequality of wealth, but it does not elevate a person to put another man down.

Today, I received confirmation that Dr. Buck Cantor will soon arrive on base. Dr. Guillebeau, the pathologist from Wilford Hall, will also be arriving soon. I have no idea what they will do over here.

I have learned very little medicine while here, but I have learned a great deal about the human creature…and, perhaps, that is the most valuable knowledge of all.

There is one exception to the last comment. I have learned one pearl of knowledge about radiology. Beetle Nut Juice is radiopaque and gives a marvelous esophagogram…even better than a barium swallow!

My immediate boss is the director of aeromedical services, Major John Bettancourt. He has a reputation for being quite eccentric. Age-wise, he is in his mid- to late thirties, and is extremely friendly and affable. If I had to summarize his appearance, I would characterize him as looking and acting like an overly eager and friendly basset hound. His background is that of an Air Force-sponsored residency in obstetrics-gynecology. After completing this residency, he decided that he didn't like the specialty. At this point, the Air Force didn't know what to do with him. Therefore, he was sent to flight surgeon school to become a glorified flight surgeon. He later completed the residency in aerospace medicine.

His wife and better half is a practicing pediatrician. I hope she has a practical vein that supersedes his free-floating abilities. He spends his entire day chasing mosquitoes, trapping rats and picking fleas off the sentry dogs. He also spends much of his time sorting through the garbage dump. All of these activities are performed under his title of chief, military public health. I can't obtain a clear answer from him as to what he is seeking...but he enthusiastically and intensely assures me that his activities are critical for "our mission"...whatever that is.

He is very big on missionary medicine and goes into the local Vietnamese villages "to help suffering humanity." I have heard that he is subject to temper tantrums and generally exhibits all of the characteristics of a cyclothymic personality. He likes to talk. That is the polite expression for this trait. Perhaps a less polite but more pointed expression is that he has "verborrhea," which is defined as having "diarrhea of the mouth and constipation of the brain." Today, he told me, "Vietnam brings out the quality in a doctor that originally brought him to medical school, while it activates forces to keep him inspired."

Now, I must admit that my sentiments on arrival in Vietnam were similar to the emotions that I experienced when I arrived in Chicago to enroll in Northwestern Medical School. I have also raised questions here that were comparable to questions that I asked when I enrolled in medical school. These sentiments and questions were primarily about my basic sanity, such as, "I can't believe that I actually competed for admission to medical school," "Why the Hell am I here?" and "What have I done to deserve this?" Or "Who have I sinned against to warrant such retribution?"But, perhaps, he is referring to something else that escapes me...who knows? In retrospect, if I were given the choice of attending medical school or fighting in this war, I wouldn't hesitate…I would rather fight in the war! At least you know who the enemy is!

In truth, I have had no significant difficulty with Major Bettancourt and I don't anticipate any. It is a large world, capable of embracing many personalities and opinions…or so the philosophy books say. But, I truly hope that he doesn't throw a temper tantrum in my office. I have a profound intolerance for lack of personal control concerning any issue. And even worse is that I have great difficulty in suppressing my intolerance of this. I have heard that he begins to stomp his feet and pound on the table, in addition to a juvenile tendency of throwing any object in his reach. I simply cannot tolerate that behavior in a grown man. But, I have one saving grace! How can they punish me for any infraction? They can't threaten to send me to Vietnam. But, if they really became aggressive, they might threaten to send me back to Chicago! Now, that would be a very real threat!

Since several G.I.s have been attacked by sharks while swimming, the beaches have been closed to swimming. This is unfortunate for the G.I.s but fortunate for the sharks and waters. Without the pollutions of civilization the waters are of pristine purity. The beach sands are the whitest and purest I have ever seen. Another perspective is that, if I were a shark, the last thing I would desire is a hoard of dirty G.I.s polluting these beautiful waters.

Regardless of the geographic natural beauty, everyone seems to spend their off-work hours in the Officers Club, NCO Club or Airmens Club, drinking and talking for hours with others, who like to drink and talk for hours on end, into oblivion. So many of the men are accustomed to bright lights, loud music and noisy urban environments that they have severe emotional problems here, where clean white sand has replaced asphalt and where the sounds of traffic on urban highways have been replaced by the sound of the wind and the roar of aircraft.

A number of the corpsmen in the office complain about the "isolation" of this base. I have great difficulty in defining what they mean by "isolation." How one can feel isolated when he/she is surrounded by 10,000-12,000 G.I.s on a relatively small peninsula?

While acknowledging that this is not home, I certainly have no sense of isolation. Of course, there are many things that I miss by being stationed here. I miss the South. I miss the sound of mockingbirds at midnight and the sound of breezes blowing through the pine trees. I miss whippoorwills and hoot owls calling to each other in a Southern cypress swamp. I miss the nightly chorus of Nature, the frogs, crickets and cicadas. But, we have the beach, the sky and birds, tide pools and countless other blessings of Mother Nature that are the same as in the South. There is so much beauty everywhere that to deny it anywhere must be an affront to the Almighty.

I am fortunate. Thus far, despite all of the problems, this promises to be a sabbatical year for me. I am removed from the urgency of studying for exams. I am free to write and to read books that I have longed to read for many years. And…I have moments of high adventure in flying combat missions in the fastest fighter-bomber in the world. Cam Ranh Bay is safer than any other place in Vietnam. I make my own schedule for working, flying and studying. No one tells me what I can do or what I cannot do. I can climb on any of many types of aircraft to fly to any destination in Southeast Asia, Japan, Bangkok and Hong Kong as part of my flying duty. I feel satisfaction in my work and have time to meditate and cogitate about why we are in this war and about life in general. Now, suddenly, as I am writing this, it dawns upon me that,

"I actually sound happy!"

I have also been blessed by having a speech teacher at Griffin High School, in Griffin, Georgia, by the name of Julia Elliot. She inspired me to search for greatness and beauty and not to hesitate in expressing these emotions. Poems that she pointed me toward have followed me all of my life.

One of my favorite quotes is by Robert Lovelace (1618-1657).
Stone walls do not a prison make,
Nor iron bars a cage;
Minds innocent and quiet take
That for an hermitage;
If I have freedom in my love,
And in my soul am free,
Angels alone that soar above
Enjoy such liberty.

Elaine asks my perspective of the Vietnam War, gleaned from the short time that I have been here.

I tell her I do not believe we can win this war unless we unloose the fetters imposed by politics and resort to unrestricted nuclear war. This would neither be wise nor appropriate in the eyes of history. I believe that this war is primarily a civil war and that we have allied ourselves with the wrong side. Of course, there is no "correct" or "incorrect" side. That decision must be settled by the Vietnamese themselves. But regardless of the loyalty of factions, South Vietnam is in a state of chaos. The Communist government of North Vietnam will not allow such chaos to continue without taking advantage of it. Therefore, North Vietnam will aggrandize the chaos in South Vietnam to its advantage. Ultimately, North and South Vietnam will be incorporated into one country and government. Communism will prevail, but the country will ultimately decide which form of government they wish, communism, theocracy or democracy. It is also somewhat of a replay of the Korean War in which there was no victory to be sought...only the stalemate of containment. However, I am not sure that our efforts to "contain" communistic takeover will be successful. Mentally, emotionally and material-wise, the United States is not prepared to fight a prolonged war against guerrilla forces any more than the British accepted a prolonged war on North America during the American Revolution. More and more, we are using citizen-soldiers and not professional military. The American public will only tolerate losses for so long before it says, "Enough! Either win the war or get out!" For a Western nation, any war in Asia is a sinkhole for men and materials. There are so many billions of poor humans in Asia that the worth of an individual is nothing. Lenin once stated that, "The death of an individual is a tragedy, while the death of 10,000 individuals is merely a statistic."

My previous flying and piloting experience had been limited to subsonic aircraft. When stationed at Bergstrom from 1964-1966, I obtained my private pilot's license through the Aero Club on base. As a private pilot, my flying experience was limited to single engine land (SEL) aircraft represented by Cessna 150, Cessna 172 and Piper Cherokee aircraft. The speeds of these aircraft were less than 200 mph.

After graduation from the Air Force School of Aerospace Medicine at Brooks Air Force Base, I was qualified as a flight medical officer (FMO). This rating is advanced to flight surgeon after 200 hours of flying time. My flying duties as flight medical officer at Bergstrom were to fly in KC-135 Stratotankers and B-52 bombers. During these flights, my hands-on experience in flying these large aircraft was occasional, when weary pilots and co-pilots invited me to give them a break by taking over the controls. My limited experience of "taking over the stick" required no special expertise or knowledge beyond steering the huge bomber or tanker through clear skies at high altitude. Despite their size, the speed of these giant aircraft was decidedly in the subsonic range of 450-500 mph range. Their flight paths were largely predetermined and flying was essentially a matter of following a compass heading and generally "keeping the car on the road." This required no unusual abilities or flying skills.

Both the B-52 and the KC-135 aircraft are large, complex aircraft that are manned by multiple air crewmen who accomplish the specialized and varied duties required to fulfill mission demands.

The primary mission of the B-52 is to carry four hydrogen bombs to the Soviet Union in times of war. The B-52 mission is accomplished by coordinated team work of the pilot and copilot flying the aircraft, guided by the navigator who directs the flight to the target and the bombardier who drops the bomb, all while the tail gunner fends off any opposition approaching from the tail position. The highest-ranking officer is the pilot, with descending ranks for the other duties. But, regardless of rank, no single person can accomplish all mission requirements. This is not a simple aircraft. The B-52 requires team effort, not individual prowess in flying.

In the KC-135 Stratotanker, the crew consists of pilot, copilot, navigator and loadmaster/boom operator. In the KC-135 Stratotanker, the highest-ranking officer was also the pilot, again with descending ranks for the other duties. However, for the KC-135, there is a difference. The pilot flies the aircraft to the general location for refueling. The loadmaster/boom operator is an enlisted man, usually a non-commissioned officer. His task is as critical for mission success as the pilot's. Air-to-air refueling of other aircraft involves inserting the male refueling nozzle from the KC-135 into the female receptacle of the aircraft receiving the fuel. The refueling nozzle is suspended on a boom that is fitted with a pair of winglets. These winglets allow the boom operator to "fly" the refueling boom toward the receiving aircraft and guide the probe into the female receptacle of the receiving aircraft. Ultimately, the success or failure of the mission depends on the skill of this non-commissioned officer.

These air crewmen were all dedicated men and each duty is vital for the mission, but my role as flight medical officer was not critical. It was interesting to observe these highly trained and skilled men as they performed their necessary duties, but, the mission would have been accomplished with or without my presence. I had enough skill to steer the aircraft and give the pilots a break from prolonged hours of mission time, but it was not a critical role for mission success. The average mission for the KC-135 was four to five hours in duration and usually flown late at night or in the early morning hours. We flew over the entire Western U.S.A to rendezvous with multiple airplane types for refueling. There was a clear Plexiglas panel through which the boom operator visually flew the boom to connect with the receiving aircraft. This panel was open at all times and provided a panoramic view of the night sky, the country below and the entire refueling process.

The work was fascinating in terms of observing the various refueling processes for different types of aircraft, and on cold, clear nights, there was always a magnificent high altitude view of the entire Western United States.

But, frequently, I felt somewhat guilty about being simply an observer and not having a specific job to perform like the other aircrew. Overall, airmen are as superstitious as sailors. A flight surgeon on board is considered a talisman for "good luck." Their goodwill allowed me the privilege to observe and participate in events that are rarely experienced by other men. The aircrew members could not have been more cordial or appreciative of my flying with them, but I always felt more like an honored guest than a critical member of the crew.

I longed to fly a faster aircraft, with greater maneuverability and for which I had a more personal and active role in flying. In many ways, flying these subsonic behemoths compared to steering a moving van for long distances over aerial freeways at high altitude. This was obviously my personal perspective, and did not reflect on the dedicated crews of these large aircraft. I longed for personal control of an agile, fast aircraft. It took me some time to accept the fact that flying the B-52 did not test my skill as a pilot. This huge aircraft is not merely an "aircraft" in the usual sense of the word. The B-52 is a weapons platform flown and armed by a team of highly skilled airmen!

My assignment to the 12th Tactical Fighter Wing and the 391st Tactical Fighter Squadron at Cam Ranh Bay fulfilled all of my flying aspirations. After flying the most powerful bomber in history, how could I now be fortunate enough to fly the fastest, most powerful fighter in the world… and as an active aircrew member?

CHAPTER 5

Flying the Phantom

EVER SINCE I ARRIVED AT CAM RANH BAY, I HAVE watched as the wicked-appearing supersonic F-4s take off and land. When a formation of four aircraft returns to base, its break-away approach to landing is as exquisitely choreographed as any ballet. During landings a drogue chute is routinely deployed to break the length of the landing roll after touchdown. Part of my daily office routine involves driving around the flight line to familiarize myself with the general layout and to look more closely at these aircraft as they stand parked in concrete and steel revetments. I marvel at how much these formidable aircraft resemble birds of prey as they crouch on the tarmac to be refueled or to be rearmed with bombs, rockets and napalm. These early appraisals were more an issue of satisfying my curiosity than for any personal involvement with the aircraft. This detached perspective, however, was short-lived before I became much more personally involved.

My formal introduction to the F-4C Phantom II occurred in the middle of my first week on base. One day, shortly after lunch, Lt. Col. Jack

Doerty stopped by the flight surgeon's office to say hello. Colonel Doerty is squadron commander of the 391st TFS, to which I am assigned for flying and sleeping quarters. He had just returned from R&R and this was our first meeting. I liked him immediately. After our introduction and a short chat, he presented me with a two to three-inch-thick operations manual for the F-4C Phantom II and politely advised me to learn everything in it before my first flight in one week!

After he left, I was more than a little taken aback when I thumbed through 400-plus pages of bewildering charts, circuits, OMG-graphs (Oh, My Gawd Graphs) and technical information of the F-4Cs hydraulic and engineering systems. All I could do was laugh at the thought of digesting this enormity of technical, engineering data in one week before my first flight. Laughter is cheaper than despair and safer than anger. My previous training is in biology, physiology, chemistry and medicine. I consider myself to be a reasonably competent private pilot, but I am not an engineer, mathematician or military jet-rated pilot.

The first Phantom was delivered to the Air Force on 1 February 1965. Thus when I entered the war in June 1966, the F-4C Phantom was a relatively new aircraft. In 1966, the Phantom II was regarded as the most advanced combat aircraft in the Air Force inventory.

My missions in the F-4C Phantom II will be flown from the back seat pilot position. In the Air Force, the rear seat pilot is officially known as a PSO or pilot systems operator. To avoid such formality, the back seat pilot is euphemistically known as the GIB or "guy in back." In the Air Force, the backseat pilot of a Phantom functions as the co-pilot. At first, I was honored that they had named the back seat pilot position for me. However, my egocentric balloon was promptly deflated when I learned that despite "Guy" being my first name, the GIB ("guy in back)" designation is generic.

14 June 1966

"Feathers shall raise men even as they do birds towards heaven: That is by Letters written with their quills." — Leonardo da Vinci, from Leonardo da Vinci's Note-Books, English translation by Edward McCardy

My first, physical, face-to-face introduction to the Phantom occurred on 14 June 1966, when Maj. Roland X. Solis (Nickname: Maj. "Chico" Solis) and I walked out to the revetment containing the parked aircraft. Major Solis was the most highly regarded pilot in the squadron, and probably in the wing. He is to be my mentor and will be aircraft commander while I try to learn the back seat, co-pilot position. This visit is my first opportunity to physically inspect this large fighter-bomber. The steel revetment provides a protective enclosed space between parked aircraft. In case of attack by air or by land, each aircraft is isolated and partitioned from other aircraft, thus preventing a chain-reaction of destruction during an enemy attack.

As we enter the flight line area, the mere presence of Major Solis is sufficient to attract the ground maintenance team, who follow, in tow, for inspection of the aircraft. While we walk around the huge fighter, prominent features of the aircraft are pointed out, such as the Vulcan Cannon suspended in the midline beneath the fuselage, Sparrow Missiles, snuggled into grooves under the fuselage, bombs, hanging on racks beneath the wings and Side-winder Missiles attached to hard points beneath the wing-tips. Other aircraft in the area are armed with general-purpose iron bombs of 250, 500, and 1,000 pounds. A few of the aircraft have silver canisters of napalm, suspended from hard points beneath the wings.

On this introductory visit, the details of different types of weaponry are beyond my immediate concern. The focus of my attention is on the fundamental aspects of my duties while flying from the backseat pilot position and how to eject. After our introductory "walk-around," Major Solis briefs me on duties of the back seat position. The co-pilot is responsible for the inertial navigation system, radio communications and radar guidance. The aircraft commander in the front seat also has a radarscope that is below the gun sight. This allows him to monitor the activities of the GIB, but he cannot determine what to scan. The same is true for the inertial navigation system. The commander can read the output, but the GIB controls the system. Other duties include monitoring and calling out altitudes during dive-bombing, monitoring air speeds and observing for enemy groundfire.

When missions are flown over regions defended by enemy aircraft, the usual tasks of the back seat pilot are to operate the weapons systems for air-to-air combat. Since none of my missions will be flown in "MIG-exposed" airspace, and will be predominately air-to-ground support, I didn't need to learn these more complex procedures. These missions over North Vietnam were flown by highly trained, select crews who are experienced in dog-fighting MIGs and flying cover for other aircraft during their bombing missions. I am more than happy to have this portion of the curriculum omitted since I am rapidly beginning to feel overwhelmed by a seemingly endless list of other duties that are required of the GIB.

The Phantom is a twin-engined, all weather, long-range supersonic jet fighter/bomber that was originally developed by the U.S. Navy in 1960. It's is a large aircraft that stands approximately 16 feet tall. The cockpits are approximately 12 feet above the ground and are entered by climbing a ladder propped against the side of the aircraft. The aircraft commander sits in the forward seat position, while the GIB sits in tandem behind him. My indoctrination continues with a visit to the cockpit. However, the significance of my being allowed to fly in the Phantom can only be appreciated by some background knowledge of this aircraft.

The F-4C Phantom II is a magnificent fighter-bomber that in 1966 had no parallel in any country. As this is written in 2013, the value of hindsight is appropriate. The Phantom is the second only in numbers of aircraft produced to the North American F-86 Sabre.

Overall, the F-4C Phantom II is considered to be one of the most versatile jet fighters ever built. It carries a bomb load that exceeds the B-17, B-29 and Avro Bombers of World War II, yet it excels as an air-to-air interceptor and fighter. During the Vietnam War, it was responsible for shooting down nearly 80 percent of all MIGs destroyed.

Early F-4Cs had problems with leaking wing fuel tanks that were so serious that the tanks had to be carefully resealed after each flight. The radar had a tendency to malfunction far too easily in the humid air of Southeast Asia. I can bear witness to this malfunction of radar in one of my mission descriptions.

Early F-4Cs also had problems with cracked ribs and stringers on the outer wing panels. Later F-4Cs were equipped with a heavier stringer and an additional wing rib. These modifications were retrofitted to earlier F-4Cs.

Unfortunately, the belief that dogfighting was obsolete had also infected pilot training, and for the time being, many Phantom pilots really didn't know how to make effective use of their machines in air-to-air combat. Thus in Vietnam, the Phantom had to engage in dogfighting against enemy aircraft for which it had not been designed and flown by pilots who had not been trained in the type of air-to-air combat encountered over the skies of Hanoi and Haiphong. The Air Force continued taking high rates of loss against the older MIGs, but the Navy recognized the deficiencies in training and established the "Top Gun" training programs for their pilots. Graduates quickly reversed the rate of loss ratio against older, slower MIGs.

The gun issue was addressed in 1966 with initial deliveries of Vulcan 20 mm cannon pods to the war zone. These Vulcan cannons were little more sophisticated than the Gatling guns from the American Civil War. Like an afterthought, they were attached to a hard point under the middle of the Phantom's fuselage and were in use when I arrived at Cam Ranh in June 1966. The addition of a SUU-16A gun pod on the under fuselage centerline compensated for the lack of a gun, but it seriously degraded overall performance and in addition made the aircraft somewhat unstable and difficult to recover from a spin.

The Phantom II was the first fighter aircraft to be completely self-contained and able to rely on its own radar and detection systems, rather than depending on ground-based fighter control and navigation aids.

During the Vietnam War, F-4C crews claimed the destruction of twenty-two MiGs with Sidewinders, fourteen with Sparrows, four with gunfire, and two by causing the MiGs to crash while maneuvering.

The Phantom's performance was such that it was the first airplane to be flown simultaneously by the Navy Blue Angels and the Air Force Thunderbirds. By January 1962, it was flying with three branches of our military services, the Navy, Air Force and Marine Corps.

Standard armaments for the F-4C Phantom II were four AIM-7 Sparrow air-to-air missiles that were recessed beneath the fuselage. AIM-9 Sidewinder Missiles were attached to mounts beneath the wings. The Sidewinders were heat-seeking, short-range air-to-air missiles.

The AIM-7D/E Sparrow was carried in the ventral trays. In principle, the Sparrow gave the Phantom a range beyond visual capability at distances of up to twenty-eight miles. However, such launches were very rarely permitted under the restrictive terms of engagement in Vietnam, lest a friendly plane be hit by mistake. When used at closer ranges, the Sparrow turned out to be virtually useless against fighter-sized targets, especially at low altitudes.

The AIM-9B/D Sidewinder was usually the weapon of choice. The AIM-9D had a range of up to twelve miles, but it was generally effective only in close stern engagements in good weather and at high altitudes. In bad weather or at low altitudes, the results were less impressive; the

Sidewinder often lost its lock on the target as a result of interference from rain or from clouds. It also had a tendency to lock onto the sun or onto reflections in lakes or ponds. Ultimately, the Sidewinder scored more aerial victories in the Vietnam War than any other weapon.

On July 24, 1965, an F-4C of the 47th Tactical Fighter Squadron was downed by a surface-to-air missile. It earned the aircraft the honor of becoming the first American warplane to be downed by a SAM. SAMs actually claimed only 5.7 percent of all U.S. aircraft shot down in the Vietnam War, but they forced American aircraft down to lower altitudes where ground-based anti-aircraft artillery (AAA) and even small arms fire were much more lethal.

In the first two years of combat in Vietnam, the casualties among the first F-4C squadrons reached almost 40 percent, for a total of fifty-four aircraft. Most were lost to AAA, but a few were lost in stall/spin accidents at low altitude. During close-in dogfights, when pulling high-Gs or when at steep angles of attack, it was very easy to lose control of an F-4C, especially if it was carrying a centerline store. Recovery from a spin at an altitude below 10,000 feet was essentially impossible, and the only option for survival was generally for the crew to eject.

The F-4C Phantom II in which I flew approximately 90 combat missions was "off-the-shelf" except for adaptations that were specific for the Air Force.

After climbing up the ladder to the cockpit height, I turn right toward the rear cockpit position and then swing my leg over to drop down two to three feet into the rear seat well. Major Solis stands on the wing outside the cockpit to point out pertinent instruments, circuit breakers and how to eject. Without strapping myself in, I try to absorb the bewildering array of switches glowing lights and dials of the instrument panel. At the same time I am confronted by countless circuit breakers and niceties of the inertial navigation system. Major Solis demonstrates clearly how to eject by using both the overhead rungs and the under-seat alternate ejection ring. The usual positions of the control stick and throttles are referenced. All of these "routine duties" are listed rather matter-of-factly by Major Solis.

It should be noted that the usual Air Force preparation for the back-seat pilot position is six weeks of F-4C ground school, followed by five months of flight training. The usual curriculum includes approximately thirty missions. During these missions, exercises include flying high-G maneuvers, slow flight, stall characteristics and landing. Other exercises include air-to-air combat with dogfight maneuvers and counter-ma-neuvers; aerial gunnery, ground weapons delivery, which includes guns, bombs, napalm and CBUs. In addition, the usual training for this position consists of a significant program of night flying.

Obviously, within the past hour, I have received my "six-weeks of ground school" for this position. The remaining "five months of flight training" will be learned on the job.

The Phantom was originally designed by the U.S. Navy to intercept enemy aircraft at long range. Because of this, the back seat position in the Navy version of the Phantom is manned by the radar intercept officer, who is not a pilot. The Navy version, therefore, has neither a stick nor throttle in the rear seat position; only the pilot in the front seat can fly the aircraft.

When the Air Force adopted the aircraft, the back seat position was employed to train young pilots. The rear cockpit of the Air Force Phantom is, therefore, equipped with control stick, throttles and rudder pedals for flying. The back seat pilot gains experience in operating the radar, weapon systems and navigation, as well as experience in learning to fly the Phantom. The back seat pilot can take off, land and fly the Phantom. The landing gear and flaps can only be raised or lowered by the pilot in the front seat. The other exclusion from the back seat position pertains to the use of afterburners.[5] The afterburners can only be engaged from the front seat position by pushing the throttles full-forward and outboard. Thus, the rear seat is a valid position for training new pilots to eventually fly as aircraft commander (AC). I have known a number of the younger pilots who have flown in the backseat position for the first year of their assignment in Vietnam and then who requested an additional tour of duty in Vietnam to serve as aircraft commander in the front cockpit.

The GIB is responsible for calling out the altitudes during dive-bombing, observing for enemy ground fire or anti-aircraft artillery and monitoring air speeds. During penetrations and/or descents through cloud layers, the GIB should report to the pilot every 5,000 feet change in altitude, when flying above 5,000 feet and each 1,000 feet change when below 5,000 feet, until the desired altitude is achieved.

Today as I look into the backseat cockpit, I am confronted by countless switches, circuit breakers and blinking lights, not only on the front instrument panel, but also on both side instrument panels. As GIB, I am responsible for initiating and coordinating these instruments with the aircraft commander. The aircraft commander focuses on delivering his ordnance on target, while counting on the GIB to perform these additional operations. My indoctrination lasts somewhat less than an hour, but by the time we finish the session my brain is aching with overload at the multitude of new tasks and responsibilities that have just fallen on my shoulders.

Prior to this indoctrination, I had discussed the back seat position with other pilots as well as with Bill Simmons and Al Aleckna. The majority of the information I received emphasizes the hazards of dive-bombing

---

5 **Afterburner** is a component utilized by military supersonic aircraft to provide additional thrust, usually for supersonic flight. Afterburning injects additional fuel into the jet pipe after the turbine. This advantage significantly increases thrust; the disadvantage is the high rate of fuel consumption and inefficiency. It is usually used only for short periods of time, such as take-off or in dogfighting.

in a supersonic aircraft, with very few practical pointers. In so many terms, I was led to believe that unless I lost consciousness from excess G-forces, became hysterically terrified with mission dangers, or at least vomited once or twice on this first mission, I would not be normal. I am well aware that the first flight or combat strike mission is a time-honored rite-of-passage in aviation, a ritual to initiate rookies like me. I am determined to prove them wrong!

My subconscious has been ruminating on what lies before me. I have never flown in a supersonic aircraft nor have I been subjected to the G-forces and aerobatic contortions of aerial combat maneuvers and situations. It sounds reasonable to be overloaded with the technicalities of my duties as GIB, but my dominant concerns and apprehensions about flying in the F-4C Phantom have nothing to do with the dangers of combat or even my ability or inability to perform duties required of the back seat pilot.

My primary concern involves the primitive reptilian portion of my brain, rather than the cerebrum of higher brain functions. My concern is vertigo and motion sickness, with vomiting, during radical aerial maneuvers while pulling Gs. A short spin in the human centrifuge years ago was okay. My only other experience was a rollercoaster ride at the Georgia State Fair when I was in high school. There were no problems there either. But my anatomy and physiology have never been subjected to the panoply of G-forces and gyrations of inverted flight, barrel-rolls, high speed turns and the 5-7 G pullout after dive bombing…and all while flying at one to two times the speed of sound. The thought of vomiting my head off on my first combat mission is not reassuring. To face the ground crew chief after we land, with the rear cockpit and instrument panels coated with vomitus, is more than my ego can endure. Nor will such a scenario be reassuring for pilots in the 391st TFS to have a squadron flight surgeon who is unable to fly on routine strike missions because of motion sickness.

At this point in my medical career, I have enough knowledge and experience to appreciate the autonomic nervous system as having a mind of its own, a mind that will not be subjugated by reason, self-control or willpower. In fact, it has long been axiomatic that all the willpower in the world cannot control diarrhea. During violent aerial maneuvers, over-stimulation of the ear's labyrinthine system can provoke nausea and vomiting to a degree that defies all conscious efforts to suppress or control it. At the time of this writing in 2013, during the early stages of space flight, astronauts continue to be plagued by it. Better men than I have succumbed to airsickness when first introduced to high performance aircraft. Gen. Chuck Yeager, the first man to break the sound barrier and World War II Ace, experienced airsickness with vomiting on his first flight in high performance aircraft. Col. Clarence E. "Bud" Anderson, World War II Triple Ace, had the same experience on his first flight. More remote chronicles of human experience with symptoms of motion sickness date back to Hippocrates, Julius Caesar, Lawrence of Arabia, and Admiral Horatio Nelson, all of whom suffered bouts of motion sickness.[6]

Antihistamines such as Dramamine and Benadryl may help, but they have very undesirable side effects of drowsiness and dulling of the senses. These side effects were prominent in causing increased casualties for soldiers who crossed the English Channel in ships prior to the World War II D-Day invasion of Normandy. For those troops who were transported by glider or others who parachuted into Europe from a C-47, the results were the same. Groggy paratroopers, doped up with increased doses of antihistamines, were barely able to stand or walk after landing. The most prominent war correspondent of World War II, Ernie Pyle, witnessed these events firsthand and described his impression of the enormously reduced fighting efficiency of soldiers and sailors due to sea sickness and medications for

---

6 Reason, J.T., & Brand, J.J. (1975), Motion sickness. New York: Academic Press.

sea sickness. He reported that the landing occasioned, "... the greatest mass vomiting ever known in the history of mankind...."[7]

I abided by my guiding philosophy concerning unclear circumstances in medical practice: "If forced to choose between more medication or less medication, always choose less...or...no medication." And so, my choice is to take a chance without any medication. Axioms, however, are fine for philosophers and textbook practitioners, but reality is another matter. Philosophic wisdom, both current and past, may occasionally crash on the rocks of reality. Therefore, to be on the safe side I tuck a plastic bag into my trouser pocket...just in case. As the Good Book says, "The spirit may be willing but the body is weak."

The day of this first mission begins as a fine summer morning. The sky is clear and a gentle breeze flows in from the ocean. It is early enough in the day to be pleasantly warm, in contrast to predictions for later in the day when temperatures will increase to well over 110 degrees F. The beauty of Nature on this magnificent day complies with the age-old saying, "God is in his Heavens and all is Right with the World." Unfortunately, the current war and today's mission is testimony to the contrary.

With the vertigo-vomiting issue haunting me, I have a very light breakfast and attend to paperwork in the flight surgeon's office before having a very, very light lunch. After lunch, I walk from the mess hall to Base Operations to meet Major Solis in one of the small conference rooms that are reserved for pre-flight intelligence briefings.

---

7 Money, K.E. (1972). Measurement of susceptibility to motion sickness. In M.P. Lansberg (Ed), AGARD Conference Proceedings No. 109: Predictability of Motion Sickness in the Selection of pilots. Nueilly-sur-Seine, France: Advisory Group for Aerospace Research and Development.

A typical strike mission consists of four aircraft, each of which may have the same or different weaponry, depending on mission demands. All aircraft are armed with the externally mounted Vulcan cannon. The 391st TFS mission call sign is "HAMMER." In military aviation, the term "sortie" is used to indicate the total usages of individual aircraft, so that today's mission, involving four aircraft, will tally four sorties. Our mission call signs are Hammer 41, 42, 43 and 44. These four aircraft compose a single flight. Since Major Solis is the flight leader, his aircraft, with me in the back seat position, is Hammer 41. The usual routine is for the four aircraft to take off in sequence with flight leader Hammer 41 taking off first. The other three aircraft take off in sequence, climbing to the agreed altitude for "join up" into the pattern formation for continuing the mission.

For this mission, each plane is armed with two 500-pound, general-purpose iron bombs. Takeoff is scheduled for 1400 hours (2 p.m.).

Formation flying requires maintenance of exquisite order between the aircraft. The flight leader is the "pack leader" in the first aircraft to take off. He shepherds the other three aircraft to the target area and dictates any changes that develop en route, in the target area and on our return flight to base.

Today, in addition to his duty as flight leader, Major Solis has the responsibility of flying the aircraft and teaching me, a rookie, non-pilot, flight surgeon, in his backseat pilot's position. I am grateful that this very skilled pilot has accepted the task of instructing and initiating me into the wonders of supersonic combat flying.

In formation flying, the position of each aircraft is determined by reference to the lead aircraft. The lead is responsible for all aspects of the flight from preflight briefing to post flight debrief. It's generally agreed that the lead should be the best pilot in the formation and should definitely have the most formation flight experience. The lead is responsible for all aspects of the flight profile, such as weather, communications, aircraft positions during flight and directing the attack on target. He is also responsible for the flight route, maneuver profile and all emergencies that develop on the mission. Feeling very insecure about my capabilities as a co-pilot, I began to be very sympathetic toward Major Solis for having me in the back seat. At 1200 hours, we meet in the Wing briefing room for our pre-flight briefing before takeoff at 1400 hours. As usual, the intelligence officer opens the briefing by providing information on the target area, such as a description of the target and its significance to justify the air strike. He discusses intelligence reports of enemy activity and defenses that we may encounter.

The target's location is defined in degrees and minutes of longitude and latitude and I carefully write the coordinates down. As the backseat pilot, navigation is my primary responsibility and these coordinates are the basis for my entry into the INS (Inertial Navigation System) that will guide us to and from the target area. In this primitive jungle country, none of the usual ground navigation aids, usually relied on for flying in the States, is available. Without sophisticated navigational instruments, flying over trackless jungle mountains to seek a small target can rapidly become an exercise in futility. The F-4C Phantom II is the first American aircraft to be equipped with the Inertial Navigation System[8] and it has been a godsend for precise aerial navigation in the primitive areas of Southeast Asia.

Today's target is fragged/programmed as a Viet Cong village and weapons storage area 250 miles northeast of Cam Ranh. Intelligence reports that AAA (anti-aircraft artillery), automatic weapons and possibly

---

8 An Inertial Navigation System (INS) is an aid to navigation that uses an onboard computer, motion sensors known as accelerometers and rotation sensors/gyroscopes to continuously calculate via the position, orientation, and velocity of the aircraft without the need for external references. It incorporates Schuler tuning as a modification to the electronic control system to account for the curvature of the earth. Schuler tuning describes the modifications that keep the inertial platform always pointing 'north', 'east' and 'down',

SAMS (Surface to Air Missles) guard the target area. Small-arms fire of many types has been experienced by other missions into this area. In fact, while flying at low altitudes, small-arms fire is ubiquitous anywhere over Vietnam.

The terrain of the target area is mountainous. This means that a steep approach for dive-bombing must be used, followed by a steep pullout after the bombs have been dropped. Today's intelligence briefing includes further discussion of what to do if hit by ground fire. This involves a review of damages that may be incurred by the airframe and/or loss of control features that render continuing flight hazardous. Further reviewed are the flight paths for leaving the target area, both after a satisfactory bomb drop, as well as for the quickest and most expeditious flight path out of the area of danger. Further discussion also offers advice about the safest route out of the target area if forced to eject. If the aircraft is disabled and it is necessary to eject, every attempt is made to get as far from the target area as possible before ejecting.

An Air Force policy manual emphasizes that it is considered undesirable to eject and be captured by the same people that you have just bombed! Even I can understand that...

The next speaker is the meteorologist with his report of local, en route and target weather conditions. Local ceiling at Cam Ranh Bay is 3,000 feet with scattered clouds, 10,000 feet scattered, high broken. Visibility at Cam Ranh is ten miles with surface winds at 090 degrees at 10 knots. Weather en route from Cam Ranh to the target area is 2,000 feet with scattered

---

in order to give correct directions on Earth. As this is written in 2011, it is difficult to emphasize the revolutionary nature of this equipment in 1966. Today, countless navigational computers or GPS (Global Positioning Systems) may be held in the palm by hikers or contained in automobiles. Portable cell phones, weighing several ounces, are complete with this equipment.

clouds, 12,000 feet scattered variable broken, 30,000 feet thin broken. Target weather conditions are 2,000 feet with scattered clouds, 30,000 feet scattered with visibility of ten-plus miles. Return conditions are the same.

Radio frequencies en route are given as well as the radio frequency for contacting the FAC when we approach the target area. Guard frequencies for emergencies are reviewed. Fuel shortage should not be a problem on today's mission, but for other flights, the "Bingo" fuel state is a minimum quantity of fuel at which the mission should be terminated with return to base using normal means. "Bingo" fuel is not an emergency situation. It simply means "go no further and return to base or obtain fuel from an aerial tanker."

Since we are flying in South Vietnam instead of North Vietnam, encounters with enemy aircraft are not usually an issue, but today we are briefed about measures to take if we are jumped by MIGs. Neither the intelligence officer nor the other pilots consider this possibility as out of the question for this target and location.

After weather and intelligence briefings, Major Solis takes the podium to review emergency procedures and to grill some of the younger pilots on emergency procedures. "Captain Wilkinson, what actions to take in the event of a single-engine flameout? ... Lieutenant Hardison, what measures to take in case of partial hydraulic failure? ... Lieutenant Spurling, what to do if your oil line is struck by ground fire? What to do in the case of hung bomb?" He continues with a review of what remedies to take for a variety of other problems.

After the briefing, Major Solis and I walk over to base operations and supply to gather our flight gear. Before every mission, all personal effects and credentials such a driver's license, credit cards and any personal correspondence are removed from our persons. This is to deny the enemy any vital information that might be used for propaganda purposes beyond name, rank and serial number on our dog tags in case we are captured or killed. My serial number is FV-3126200. Each pilot provides a personal recognition code to identify him in case of ejection that is followed by radio communication with the rescue parties. This is usually a question whose answer is known only to the pilot. The reason for this is simple. There are many cases in which the radio of a dead pilot has been captured by the enemy, who in turn use known emergency frequencies to lure rescue aircraft and helicopters into a trap. I use my mother's maiden name.

The flight gear is fitted over the basic flying suit worn by all pilots and the other flight surgeons. This is a single piece garment, comparable to a light fabric overalls with multiple pockets. For a reason that I cannot explain, I was never comfortable in this garment and choose to wear the standard issue heavier cotton fatigue shirt and trousers. The flight suit is lighter and has fire retardant qualities. While heavier than the flight suit, fatigues are cotton, which is an excellent absorbent for perspiration. And once soaked with sweat, it serves as an automatic air-conditioning unit that cools by evaporation. In a jungle environment, the thicker fabric also affords greater protection from snakes, briars and insects than the thinner fabric of the flight suit. Flight suits are the standard dress for pilots and are fashionable in allowing you to stand out in a crowd of non-aviators. I am less concerned about sartorial splendor than surviving while flying or during escape and evasion if shot down. Wilderness survival skills were ingrained in my brain at an early age. From childhood, as a Boy Scout and Explorer Scout in Florida, Georgia and Alabama, I have been steeped in games and principles of survival in swamps and mountains. For me, the jungle is what the briar patch was for Brer' Rabbit.

Instead of the lightweight Vietnam jungle combat boots, I also choose to wear the heavier standard all-leather combat boots. Jungle warfare usually involves walking through water in rice paddies, marshes and streams. This means getting your feet wet. The lightweight boots are mostly fabric and thin leather with perforations to allow water to exit when you walk on dry land. This construction has more of a utilitarian benefit by being lighter and in drying your feet quicker. Their cooler and thinner construction, however, sacrifices the protection afforded by heavier leather. Once again, my boyhood experience of catching rattlesnakes in the Big Scrub region of Central Florida persuades me to choose the heavier leather boots, both for support and for protection from snakes. The heavier leather also provides greater protection from punji stakes with razor-sharp points that have been planted in the mud and coated with dung to penetrate your foot when stepped on. I learned long ago that coating the leather with wax provides adequate waterproofing. Treated thusly, it was unusual for my feet to remain wet for protracted periods. For me, the added protection of heavier leather boots is more than worth the minor advantages of the lighter boot types. Officially there is no regulatory conflict since both flight suits and fatigues are in compliance with Air Force regulations. Boot type is also optional as far as regulations were concerned.

My G-Suit fits over this standard uniform. Under ordinary conditions at sea level, the effect of gravity causes blood to pool in veins of the legs and pelvis. Only by a complex system of reflexes, muscle activity and valves does blood from legs and abdomen return to the heart and hence to the brain. Veins are thin walled, elastic vessels that return blood to the heart. They stretch easily and have no inherent properties to contract or to propel blood back to the heart. The milking action exerted by leg muscles on the veins is the mechanism by which blood is returned to the heart and lungs. Without this milking action, veins become flaccid, like a previously inflated balloon, allowing blood to pool in the legs. The "milking" action that muscles exert on veins during walking prevents blood from pooling in the legs. This milking action is augmented by valves that prevent backflow and aid in propelling blood back to the heart. Soldiers standing immobile on parade grounds for prolonged periods of time may pass out as a result of blood pooling in the leg veins and not returning to the heart, lungs and brain.

However, under the greater G-forces experienced by pilots of modern high-performance aircraft, these usual mechanisms are inadequate to keep blood in the chest and head. Inadequate blood flow to the brain creates a condition known as G-LOC. G-LOC is the loss of consciousness that occurs when increased G-forces prevent blood from returning in adequate quantities to the brain. To maintain blood flow to the chest, coronary arteries and brain, a device known as a G-suit is required to prevent blood from pooling in the abdomen and legs.

The G-suit is a series of inflatable rubber bladders that are sewn into pockets of a corset-like garment that fits around the abdomen and legs. G-suits maintain blood flow to the brain, lungs and heart by retarding the accumulation of blood in the abdomen and legs. These rubber bladders are interconnected by a series of tubes and valves that plug into an outlet in the cockpit that receives bleed air from the engine compressors. In the Phantom, inflation of the bladders is triggered by acceleration of the aircraft in excess of pre-determined velocities. In the Phantom, this increasing velocity is triggered when the aircraft imposes a G-load of 2.5 Gs on the airframe. (Trotti, John, *Phantom Over Vietnam*, Presidio Press 1984).

While pulling Gs, the bladders inflate automatically in proportion to the G-forces being pulled. The G-suit provides protection for approximately 1-2 Gs over that of human tolerance. The greater the acceleration and the G-forces imposed on the aircraft/pilot, the greater the volume of air that inflates the bladder of the calves, thighs and abdomen. Pull out during typical dive-bombing accounts for G-forces that average 6.5 Gs. This means the human body weighs 6.5 times its sea-level weight. The inflation pressure around the abdomen is considerable.

To function optimally, the garment is laced on and drawn tight in order for the bladders to inflate and apply pressure on the legs and abdomen.

During a typical dive bomb attack, with subsequent pull out, it is common for the aircraft and the pilots to pull 6.5-7.0 Gs. This means that every portion of the human body increases in weight by six to seven times. Thus a man who usually weighs 175 pounds at sea level will increase in weight, under the G-load, to 1,138-1,225 pounds. When pulling out of a dive-bomb attack, the sudden G-load of 6-7 Gs inflates the abdominal bladder so dramatically that it makes you gasp. But 1-2 Gs are the limitations on the protection offered by G-suits to pilots. And even the Phantom has its limitations. The G-meter records the highest G-load imposed on the aircraft during a mission. At 9 Gs or greater, the aircraft must be inspected for structural damage to the airframe.

The "torso harness" fits over the G-suit. It is designed for use with the Martin-Baker MK-H5 ejection seat. As a rookie pilot, I considered it of utmost importance to understand the combination and functions of the torso harness and the ejection seat. Once airborne, the only method of safely getting out of the Phantom is by ejection. The torso harness is a collection of heavy web straps, with thin padding under the shoulder straps for comfort. This harness locks you into the ejection seat of the aircraft. In case of an emergency, there will just be the three of us, torso harness, ejection seat with parachute and me. In addition to confinement, the harness distributes body weight over a large area to lessen the shock of ejection and parachute opening. The Air Force uses a harness that is equipped with three closure buckles and rings, one for each crotch strap and one for the chest strap. Each crotch strap and chest strap may be unhooked to permit greater comfort and mobility before entering the aircraft. The leg restraints must be buckled below the knee to each leg. They function primarily to draw the legs tightly into the seat, restraining them during ejection. The leg restraints permit the legs to clear the instrument panel and forward canopy arch during ejection, holding them securely until the seat separates and parachute deploys. The final piece of equipment is my flight or crash helmet. Composed of impact resistant fiberglass, it is white and fits comfortably. Fittings for my oxygen mask with built-in microphone are on both sides of the helmet, near the angle of the jaws. A sun visor is also built into the helmet. It is easily lowered for protection from sun and/or wind blast in the event of a bail out. However, I rarely use it during flying, preferring sunglasses instead. The signature letters of the 391st Tactical Fighter Squadron are carefully stenciled on the front of each helmet:

KTRB translates to "KILL THOSE RED BASTARDS"

After all, this is war...

CHAPTER 6

================================

Preparing for Flight in the Phantom

PREPARATIONS FOR FLIGHT INVOLVE THE USE OF PRO-
tective clothing and equipment to extend physiologic tolerance to G-forces
and supersonic flight. But, there must also be lifesaving equipment to
extract a pilot from a supersonic aircraft that is no longer capable of flying.
Although the aircraft is expensive, the pilot's life is of greater value. The
ejection seat is there to protect the pilot's life.

The popular perspective of a pilot "bailing out" of a stricken aircraft
with only his parachute lingers from World War II. Stories and movies
popularized this version of emergency exit. Movies depict pilots climbing out of the cockpit of a stricken aircraft before plunging into the air,
pulling the "rip-cord," and safely floating down beneath the silk canopied
parachute. The parachute was strapped to the back of the aviator in readiness for such an exit. There were other depictions of pilots who inverted
their stricken airplanes, opened their canopies, and fell effortlessly from
their aircraft, after which they pulled the "rip-cord" and floated safely to
earth. But, with modern high-performance jet aircraft, the hypersonic

speed of today's jets does not permit such "leisurely" escape. With supersonic aircraft, the airspeed alone is sufficient to make a simple "bail-out" impossible. For a pilot attempting to escape from a crippled supersonic aircraft, jumping clear from a stricken plane that is writhing uncontrollably through space is virtually impossible. Instead, the pilot must be forcefully ejected from the aircraft while flying at airspeeds ranging from subsonic to supersonic. By remaining in the ejection seat the pilot is protected from the forces of the slip stream outside the cockpit and from the forces required to blast him out of the cockpit. Obviously, these conditions demand a device to forcefully expel the pilot from a stricken aircraft without incurring a severe injury.

After World War II, early ejection seats used a solid propellant charge to eject both the pilot and the seat by igniting a charge inside a telescoping tube attached to the seat. As aircraft speeds increased still further, this method proved inadequate to get the pilot sufficiently clear of the airframe. But, increasing the amount of propellant risked damaging the occupant's spine. These circumstances resulted in experiments with rocket propulsion. Every aspect of the ejection seat should be handled with the same precautions taken for handling a loaded gun. There are safety pins to protect against untimely firing of the ejection seat. Ground crew members and pilots have been killed or seriously injured by the ejection mechanism engaged by accident during inspection or maintenance work. These issues are addressed during the exterior inspection of the aircraft before flight begins. It is significant that the first three items of the F-4 pilot's Preflight Checklist relate to the ejection seat:

Face curtain and seat-mounted initiator safety pins – INSTALLED

Canopy interlock cable & interdictor link safety pin assembly – INSTALLED CORRECTLY & ATTACHED TO CANOPY

Lower ejection handle guard – UP

The following items of the front cockpit interior check involve the injection seat:

Leg restraint lines – BUCKLED & SECURED

Harness and personal equipment leads – FASTEN

Ejection seat height – ADJUST

Face curtain & seat-mounted initiator safety pins – REMOVED

The ejection seat has seven safety pins, all of which must be removed for the seat to fire. During periods when the F-4 is not occupied by its crew, before, during and after a flight, the ground crew always assures that all seven safety pins are inserted. The purpose of these pins is to prevent the accidental firing of the seat. When a crewmember arrives at the airplane before a flight, the crew chief usually has already removed six of the seven safety pins. These six pins and the nylon line attached to the pins are placed into a pouch and laid on the top of the seat.

At the time of entry into the rear cockpit, before I sit in the ejection seat, I always confirm that all six of the pins have been removed. I do not remove the last safety pin (the face curtain pin) until I am completely strapped into the seat. In recognition of my neophyte status, the ground crew chief usually finalizes my being strapped in and pulls the last safety pin. Once seated, to get strapped in, the following activities are required:

I connect the two D rings on my parachute harness to the two snap connectors on the seat survival kit to connect the kit to me. The survival kit has a radio, water, food and other survival items in case of ejection.

My lap belt is then connected to strap me into the seat.

Both leg restraints are then connected. Each leg has two garters – one that encircles the calf above the boot and the other that encircles the thigh above the knee. These four garters are connected to two nylon lines that are attached to the bottom of the ejection seat. During an ejection the seat pulls the nylon lines tight, thus locking both legs against the seat. This prevents the legs from flailing in the wind stream at high speeds.

The parachutes in the F-4 are built into the top of the ejection seats. This requires the pilots to attach their parachute harness to the parachute risers.

After completing the four steps listed above, I, or the crew chief, pull the seventh pin out of the face curtain and inserts it into the pouch with the other six pins. I then count to make sure all seven pins are in the pouch. After confirming the number of pins, the pouch is stowed until I land. After landing, I will replace the seventh pen into the top of the seat to assure no accidental ejection occurs while I am climbing out of the cockpit.

The F-4 ejection seat system is designed to prevent the seat from firing if the canopy is attached to the airframe. A steel cable is permanently attached to the back of the canopy and the other end is attached to a safety pin into the banana links on the top of the seat. The seat will not fire unless that safety pin is removed. Normally when an ejection is initiated the first thing to happen occurs when the canopy thrusters on the bulkhead just below the canopy push up and open the canopy. As soon as the front of the canopy opens enough to permit the air-stream to wedge itself underneath the front of the canopy, the massive amount of air causes the canopy to rapidly open and be ejected from the airframe, taking the steel cable and safety pin with it.

For this, my first mission, I place special emphasis on the concept of "egress" or ejection from this aircraft. I am not a jet-rated military pilot, with extensive past training in this aircraft. My two minimum requirements for functioning as the back seat pilot are:

Being able to perform my flying duties appropriately for the mission, and…

Being able to escape from this supersonic aircraft when and if necessary…

Ejection is demanded for anything that disables the Phantom II and makes it unsafe to continue flying. The standard ejection system operates in two stages. In the Phantom, the pilot initiates the ejection process by a hefty jerk on the primary ejection rings over his head or by pulling the secondary ejection ring under his seat.

The first stage jettisons/removes the entire canopy above the cock-pit by an explosive charge that separates it from the aircraft. This, in turn, triggers the second stage in which an explosive charge or rocket motor launches the ejection seat containing the pilot through the now open cock-pit. As the seat rides up the guide rails, the leg-restraint system is activated. Usually, the ejection process consumes no more than four seconds. This is an average time since body weight of the pilot, aircraft speed, aircraft atti-tude and other variables must be considered. The seat, parachute and sur-vival pack are all ejected from the plane along with the crewmember. After the seat and crewmember have cleared the cockpit, this rocket continues to lift the crewmember another 100 to 200 feet, depending on the crew-member's weight. This added propulsion allows the crewmember to clear the tail of the plane. Once clear of the plane, a drogue gun in the seat fires a metal slug that pulls a small parachute, called a drogue parachute, out of the top of the chair. This slows the person's rate of descent and stabilizes the seat's altitude and trajectory. After a specified amount of time, an altitude sensor causes the drogue parachute to pull the main parachute from the pilot's chute pack. At this point, a seat-man-separator motor fires and the seat falls away from the crewmember. The person falls back to earth as with any parachute landing.

Ejection is not a gentle process. It is a desperate action with only one purpose: pilot survival. During ejection, the pilot typically experiences an explosive acceleration of 12-14 Gs as he rockets out of the cockpit. This equates to an instantaneous velocity of 262-306 mph from a zero start. Viewed from the perspective that the metal and rivets of the 50,000-pound

Phantom must be inspected for structural damage after 9 Gs, there is little wonder that the frailty of human muscle and bones are subject to injury when ejected at forces of 12-14 Gs.

In pulling out of a dive-bomb attack, it is fairly common for a pilot to experience 6-7 Gs. If a force of 4-6 Gs is sustained for more than a few seconds, the resulting symptoms range from visual impairment to total blackout. The use of a G-suit will add 1-2 additional Gs protection to this tolerance.

Proper support of the head is essential during extreme acceleration in order to avoid swelling of the sinuses and severe headaches. From my experience, there is greater concern for the torticollis or wry neck that impairs movement for the novice during G-forces. During the course of my year in Vietnam, I cared for many pilots shortly after ejection and during rescue situations, but I have rarely observed a pilot who used the secondary ejection ring beneath the seat without experiencing a compression fracture of the lumbar spine. By subjecting the lower lumbar spine to the sudden impact of ejection forces while in a position of complete spinal flexion, there is instantaneous transmission of these forces to the lumbar spine during its most vulnerable position. Utilization of the primary ejection rings overhead is slightly more benign. Vertebral fractures are a recurrent side effect of ejections. Their severity ranges from transitory to career-ending to fatal. Elemental survival is the ultimate determinant of success in any mechanical system. The bottom line is that most ejections allow the pilot to survive.

The next gear to be attached is my survival vest, which is donned over the other layers of clothing. The standard issue Smith & Wesson .38-caliber pistol is issued to all officers. The survival kit includes fifty additional rounds of ammunition. This contains two survival radios. I check both of these for adequate battery power before leaving central supply. To be doubly safe, I add two more fresh batteries to my bulging pockets. Other items included are: compass, signaling mirror, two smoke flares, hunting knife, fishing gear, fire starters, flexible saw, First Aid kit, water purification tablets, NoDoz tablets, canteen, water bag, mosquito head net, tweezers, amphetamine tablets, escape & evasion map, casualty/space blanket, folding razor blade, nylon cord and two condoms. I never quite comprehended this latter survival article unless it is to pay allegiance to the lyrics of a popular song that state, "Love is where you find it." There are a number of other hooks and rings for pistol belt, canteen, flashlights and flotation gear. All of which rapidly fill up the rear cockpit.

For today's flight, Major Solis comes resplendent with yellow silk scarf around his neck and yellow kid gloves. Major Solis is a dark complexioned and handsome man of my height and weight, with a dash of romanticism borne by fighter pilots of yore. He has the slight swaggering attitude and gait of the quintessential fighter pilot in his garb from World War I. Smiling at his flare, I recall stories of the legendary Manfred Albrecht Freiherr von Richthofenthe, known as the Red Baron, during aerial duels with the British Sopwith Camel biplane over the Western Front in 1917.

Initially, I considered the yellow silk scarf as simply another exhibition of narcissistic splendor, so characteristic of fighter pilots of every age. But I learned there is a practical twist to the scarf. Elemental survival of a fighter pilot depends on seeing the enemy before he sees you. In the early days of aviation, there was no radar. The only method of detecting the enemy before he detected you was visual. To do this requires eternal vigilance by constantly twisting and turning the head to look in every direction, as part of the ongoing search for enemy aircraft. Standard military clothing of shirts with collars provides constant friction to chafe the neck. This flamboyant silk scarf prevents this, and thus became the defining feature and symbol to validate fighter pilots for all future generations.

But, sartorial splendor aside, Major Solis is considered the finest pilot in the squadron, if not in the Air Force. Major Solis is from Pennsylvania. He does not fly for a living; he lives to fly. Without any reservation, I can say that he is the finest pilot I have ever known. I have subsequently learned that he is recognized as one of the finest fighter pilots, not simply in the U.S. Air Force, but in the world. Today he will complete 100 combat missions in the F-4C Phantom. He has 141 combat missions in Korea to his credit. He is known as somewhat of a daredevil, but he takes no unnecessary chances. He is good and he knows he's good. The younger pilots regard him with awe and the paradigm of all aerial virtues. It is significant that when General White (four stars) requested an introductory flight in the back seat of the Phantom, he chose "Chico" as the pilot in command. He is a master of his trade and I feel extremely fortunate to begin my experience in this high performance aircraft with a man of this caliber.

Standing beside the aircraft in the revetment[9] is an electric start cart. As we finish our "walk-around," the crew chief starts the motor to the cart. This is an added power supply that furnishes both electrical power and provides the aircraft with a large volume of compressed air. Both electrical power and compressed air are required to activate the multitude of electrical components, as well as to spin the engines to start the two jet engines.

When it starts, the sound is a soft hum. This rapidly increases to a shrill whine. With activation of the engines in the aircraft, the whine changes to a dull roar. This roar increases in intensity as both engines engage. Now with the noise of the start cart motor in my ear, I clamber up the ladder to the level of the cockpits and then drop down into the rear cockpit as Major Solis climbs into the front cockpit. Before situating myself, however, I check the seat pins to assure a proper ejection sequence, as well

---

9 Revetment is a protected parking place for aircraft and helicopters on an airfield. These are protective compartments, partitioned by steel or concrete walls to enclose parked aircraft, to shield the aircraft from mortar shrapnel.

as to prevent being ejected by a miss-fire during the process of climbing into the cockpit. Before strapping myself in, I begin my checklist. First, I check the INS (inertial navigation system); dialing in the longitude and latitude coordinates for the target area. Next, I adjust the radar scope and tune in the frequency for ground control on the radio.

Then I begin the process of strapping myself into the aircraft. The first procedure is to secure the lower leg straps, then the groin straps and finally the lap belt. I plug my G-suit into the cockpit pressure receptacle at my lower left side.

This sequence of events is necessary since further strapping renders me totally immobile and unable to finish other preflight chores and adjustments. Next I connect the seat-lock harness and then connect the parachute risers to my parachute harness. Approaching the end of my checklist, I hook-up the aircraft oxygen to my oxygen mask. Finally, I plug my microphone into the aircraft communications system. By this time, the only parts of my body capable of movement are my head, arms and hands…but only to a limited degree, since movement is restricted by the cockpit size. This multitude of procedures is critical during flight to prevent you from being tossed, flailing and uncontrollably, about the cockpit during violent flight maneuvers.

The outside power booster and starter respond to the "power-on" switch in the front cockpit, and suddenly, with a hum and throb, the winged creature beneath me suddenly awakens and comes to life. Once the power is on, I continue my checklist that involves a myriad of switches, check-lights and instrument read outs.

The voice of Major Solis crackles crisply over the intercom, "All right, Doc?" I answer to the affirmative, while simultaneously touching the primary ejection rings over my head and the secondary ejection ring beneath my seat…all for good luck! The twin jet engines throb beneath us, pulsating like a giant, living creature. I go through my "Before Taxi Checklist."

Generator control switches—ON

Warning Lights—OUT

Vertical Gyro cut-out (VGI) switch—NORMAL

Remote attitude Indicator (VGI)—SET

Radios—TR +G

Tacan—T/R

Altimeter—SET

Clock—SET

Radar Power Switch—STANDBY

Report—"READY FOR TAXI"

At this point, the crew chief removes the chocks from the wheels and the brakes are released. Power is applied until engine sound increases to a dull roar, as the aircraft begins to move forward slowly. Taxiing slowly out of the steel revetment, we turn left onto the taxiway and continue until we are just short of the active runway. Holding at this point, I make further adjustments in the INS. We continue holding short of the runway while the Number 2 aircraft of our element pulls ahead of us and onto the active runway, ready for takeoff. Ordinarily the Number 1 or Lead Aircraft has priority for takeoff. But I am flying in the Number 1 aircraft and assume that the second aircraft is given preference for takeoff in deference to me. Since this is my first flight, the slight delay will allow more time for me to set up instruments and to adjust the INS. Following my checklist, I check to assure that all circuit breakers are "IN" and that other items listed on the checklist have been completed.

As we pause for run-up, the ambient temperature on the runway is already recorded at 140 degrees F. For this reason, we continue to leave the Plexiglas canopy open for ventilation. Plexiglas creates a greenhouse effect that may increase the temperature inside the cockpit by 50 to 60 degrees. If this is added to the outside temperature of 140 degrees, the temperature in the cockpit rapidly becomes intolerable. The Number 2 (Hammer 42) aircraft pulls around us and turns to the active runway for takeoff. When this occurs, the exhaust of Number 2 creates a huge blast of scorching air, sand and jet turbulence to slap me in the face.

Even before this clears, we are pulling onto the active runway. The voice of Major Solis is transmitted crisply over the intercom, advising me to close the canopy. Major Solis calls the tower for permission to take off on Runway 02.

While this exchange is taking place, the throttle is being advanced. Beneath me, the dull murmur of the twin engines increases to a guttural growl that progresses to a high-pitched whine before erupting into a deafening roar that launches us down the runway. The impact of this sudden acceleration catches me totally by surprise. While my body is fixed in position by the torso harness, I cannot say the same for my head and neck. This volcanic eruption of acceleration, with its attendant G-forces, slams my head forward and down, jamming my chin onto my chest. Under the pressure and weight of increasing G-forces, my arms are also pinned down and I am completely immobilized. With my head jammed down, my only view is of the cockpit floor. My head weighs a ton, and I am unable to lift my arms or wrists to grasp my nose and pinch my nostrils to clear my ears.

By now, it seems that we are approaching orbital velocity to depart planet Earth, but this is only the beginning! At a critical moment, Major Solis rams the throttles full forward and to the outboard left to ignite the Phantom's full afterburners.[10] Then at approximately 150 knots/172 mph we lift off… and, in an instant we are airborne… while my head continues to be jammed further down into my chest and my only view is the floor of the cockpit. The pressures in my sinuses and middle ears increase as the

---

10 An afterburner injects additional fuel into the jet pipe downstream of the turbine. Afterburning significantly increases the thrust. The disadvantage is very high fuel consumption and inefficiency. It is useful in takeoff and in aerial combat situations.

barometric pressure of sea-level air expands in response to the decreasing atmospheric pressure of increasing altitude. Rising G-forces progressively immobilize and nearly overwhelm me. Although unable to look out of the aircraft, from the corner of my eye, I watch the altimeter needle spin at a dizzying speed, winding upward… In desperation, I try to clear my ears by Valsalva maneuver of pinching my nostrils, closing my mouth and forcefully exhaling…all to no avail.

The same G-forces that force my head down now inflate my G-suit. My legs are caught in the vice-grip of expanding air bladders around my calves and thighs. The air bladders around my abdomen expand like a tourniquet, encircling and strangling my mid-section in a vice-grip. By preventing my diaphragm from descending with inhalation, the constriction makes it impossible to take a deep breath. At the same time efforts to inhale are thwarted even more by the G-forces sitting on my chest. My knowledge of body mechanics informs me that the simple act of flexing my head downward decreases the vital capacity of my lungs by 10 percent. Overall, the entire effort of breathing is increased by several hundred percent. Oxygen flowing through my oxygen mask, however, assures that my tissues are adequately oxygenated. But, regardless of the intellectual explanations, I realize that all the ingredients for hyperventilation are present. And I constantly warn myself, "Don't hyperventilate!"

As we continue to climb at a dizzying rate and the G-pressures continue to increase, I find it impossible to lift my arms high enough to pinch my nostrils closed. Every portion of my body feels like lead. I keep telling myself, "Hang on…just hang on… this can't last forever."

We remain in afterburner at a climb rate of 0.9 Mach. Despite being unable to raise my head, the Mach meter is visible from the corner of my eye. I watch the needle spin up to 1.25 Mach (1.25 times the speed of sound) for a short time as we approach the other three aircraft of our element. At last we reach the predetermined altitude of 10,000 feet. And here, finally, the acceleration and the G-forces begin to subside as we go out of afterburner and level off with the other three aircraft at 0.9 Mach. The time to achieve this altitude, by a Civilian Standard Rate of Climb of 500 feet per minute, would be twenty minutes. Today, climbing in the Phantom from ground zero on the runway to 10,000 feet altitude is achieved in 0.58 minute.

The speed of sound depends on the ambient temperature, which decreases with increasing altitude. Thus the speed of sound from the runway to altitude depends on the average temperature between the ground and our target altitude of 10,000 feet. With considerations for the decrease in ambient temperature from the runway to 10,000 feet, the average speed of sound during our ascent approximates 805 mph. And, that is the speed that propelled us up from sea level to 10,000 feet.

Now, I can raise my head to speak...

"Gee, Major, this thing really moves out, doesn't it?"

His answer says it all, "Yeah, it does, Doc, but just remember this... it comes down just as damn fast as it goes up!"

At last, with my head lifted off of my chest, I ask myself: Major Solis is subject to the same forces of gravity as I. He is no more/less human or immune to gravity than I am...How does he do it? Looking into the front cockpit, I note that Major Solis has anchored his head to the left, partially wedging it between the back of his seat and the aircraft canopy. By forcefully fixing his head into this crevice between seat and canopy, he prevents the sudden application of G-forces from catapulting his head down toward the floor.

My next obvious question is: "Why the hell didn't one of the other guys tell me about this?"

Well, no one has to tell me now! This is the price that a rookie aviator must pay on his first flight!

Finally we are in formation with the other aircraft and assume the lead position. Only now do I have the luxury of observation, to look outside the cockpit... and the beauty of it all is overwhelming. Up to this point, it has been impossible to appreciate our speed...until now... as we occasionally streak through a small patch of cumulus clouds, and then our speed through the air is truly phenomenal.

On both sides and to the rear of our plane, the other aircraft have reformed, aligning their positions with the wings of our aircraft. To our right is the azure blue of the South China Sea, while the lushness of green jungle peaks stretches to the left of our aircraft. Occasionally, we pass between towering pillars, mountains of white, cumulus clouds. The earth tones, brown and green shades of our aircraft camouflage, stand out in beautiful contrast to the puffy white clouds. The entire panorama of jungle, clouds and distant ocean unrolls in splendor beneath us...a magnificent tapestry that is constantly being renewed as we wing toward the distant horizon.

Ten thousand feet below and off our left wing tip is a large, beautiful green valley, wedged between the coastal mountain range and the larger inland mountains. And then, directly, before my eyes, the beauty and grandeur of this valley are suddenly interrupted by a chain of silent explosions that seem to extend throughout the entire length of the valley, a distance of several miles. From our altitude, there is no sound, but the visual effects are striking. Great clouds of flame and dust erupt, billowing into the air like a chain reaction that extends throughout the entire length of the valley. The scale of these events is enormous.

What can inflict such devastation over such a large area? And, then, I look around. Far above us is the familiar silver silhouette of a single B-52 bomber. At an altitude of 35,000-40,000 feet, the giant bomber appears tiny. From this ethereal altitude it soars serenely and silently, immune to all weather and ground fire. Immune to opposition, its bombs destroy the magnificent valley below.

Before Vietnam, my duty assignment was as flight surgeon for the Strategic Air Command at Bergstrom AFB. I had many hours of flight time in B-52s on long missions that carried the hydrogen bomb. Mercifully, these were never used. But, I have never seen this giant aircraft "fire a shot" in anger before today. Today's observation is a real eye-opener. Nor could I have appreciated the devastation wrought by the enormous capacity of a single aircraft, armed with unsophisticated, conventional iron bombs… This is its first use of non-nuclear weapons in actual combat. I can't even imagine the horror of being on the ground during such an attack. I learn later that this type of bombing by the B-52 is part of the Combat Skyspot bombing system, whereby ground radar control units direct the big bombers over an enemy target and indicate the exact moment for bomb release. Most of these aircraft are based on Guam. No one else in our flight makes any comment or even notes the event over the radio. I too remain silent, but I will never forget the scene of that magnificent valley, being so suddenly enveloped and completely devastated by that single aircraft.

At our cruise speed of 600-700 mph, both the B-52 and the destroyed valley are soon left behind. After another thirty minutes of flight time, we make radio contact through "Air Patch[11]" with our "Bird Dog" or Forward Air Controller (FAC). Several minutes are consumed in exchanging recognition codes to ensure proper identification. He informs us of his location in the region of a river that lies below. Our target is a village revealed by intelligence to contain an ammunition supply depot of the Viet Cong. He warns us to be prepared for an encounter with anti-aircraft artillery.

Although we have radio communication with the FAC, no one in our flight has sighted him. We continue to orbit the area several times, searching for the tiny silver Cessna, knowing that somewhere below he is

---

11 Air Patch is an air-to-ground radio relay system for voice communications.

floating above the jungle canopy at treetop level. Finally, someone in our flight sights the fragile plane off our left nose. The cry rings out over the radio, "Tally Ho!" Far below, the tiny Cessna is visible, skimming over the jungle canopies, like a small, dainty butterfly, wafting on a spring breeze.

Overhead, we follow him toward a bend in the river, where a small brown patch of earth stands in contrast to the surrounding jungle and swamp. We continue orbiting the area at an altitude of between 9,000-10,000 feet while observing and communicating with our Bird Dog. At this point, the Bird Dog fires his Willie Pete (white phosphorus) rocket to mark the target, and then floats gracefully out of our dive path.

Major Solis leads our four aircraft into the pattern of a rotating wheel above the target area. There are obvious problems in attacking a fixed target in a highly defended area. It is important to avoid a single flight path for all aircraft to dive on the target. The "wheel pattern" is used to throw enemy ground fire off guard. The general flow of aircraft around and over the target is circular, corresponding to the rim of a wheel, with the hub representing the target, while the spokes represent the attack paths.

While the lead aircraft makes his initial run along one of the spokes, the second aircraft continues on around the rim to approach the target along the spoke that represents one quarter of the circumference. Continuing on around, the third aircraft flies on a heading that is approximately the reciprocal flown by the leader, while the fourth aircraft approaches on a heading about 180 degrees opposite that of the second aircraft. This approach to the target requires close radio contact and critical spacing between aircraft. Before any one of the pilots can strike, he must make sure that the preceding aircraft is off the target and that he has the FAC in sight. The purpose of all this is to have continuous bombardment of the target. When the aircraft carry different types of ordnance, they alternate between high and low angles of attack to further confuse the enemy artillery and ground fire.

This allows each plane adequate time to peel off in sequence for each dive-bomb attack, time to drop his bombs, time to climb back up into formation, and time to resume his position in the wheel for the next go-round.

As the lead aircraft, we are the first to go. Banking the plane sharply to the left, we continue our roll over until completely inverted. At this instant, Major Solis growls, "Here we go!"

With ferocity of energies finally unleashed, the nose points straight down at an angle of 70-80 degrees and we plunge screaming to the earth at a speed of more than 700 feet per second (500 mph). I call off the altitudes at intervals of 1,000 feet. At 5,000 feet, Major Solis yells, "Pickle," and releases the bombs.

The only indication that our bombs have been released is a slight "bump" or "give" in the aircraft. Now, we begin the task of pulling out of the dive. In the few seconds between bomb release and pull out, we have continued to dive toward the ground at a speed of 700 feet per second. Not until we have descended to an altitude of 1,250 feet above the ground does full throttle with full afterburner finally kick in. The pull-out begins! With full afterburner, the huge fighter literally stands on its tail and rockets straight up.

Now, it is the same struggle all over again…G-forces snap my head down, ramming my chin into my chest and totally immobilizing me. Every portion of my body is weighted with lead. Automatic inflation of the G-suit is a tourniquet that crushes and strangles my abdomen while squeezing the calves of my legs and thighs. As before, I am unable to clear my ears by raising my arms to pinch my nose…until, finally with a super-human effort, I force my arms and hands up to pinch my nose in Valsalva maneuver and clear my ears. What a relief, as the air in my middle ear equilibrates with the atmospheric pressure.

By this time, we have recovered from the first dive-bomb attack and have re-entered the wheel to orbit and watch the performance of other aircraft in our flight. Now, fully inverted, I look straight down with a God's-eye-view from a front-row-center seat to the drama and devastation beneath us. Inversion to begin the next bomb run permits the target area to remain in sight at all times. The small brown patch that represented our target is no longer visible. Now, there is only fire and smoke.

Part of my duty as GIB is to "watch for ground fire against us." Ground fire is indicated by flashes of fire from the muzzles of machine guns and anti-aircraft artillery from the surrounding jungle. I would be less than honest if I didn't acknowledge my performance in this regard. My energies have been totally devoted to remaining conscious and alert enough to read the instrument panel as per my checklist. Quite frankly, I have been preoccupied with surviving the G-forces, clearing my ears and paranasal sinuses from the aerodynamic insults of dive-bombing, while enduring all other aspects of supersonic warfare. As a result, most of my attention has been devoted to gazing intensely at my boot lacings and at the floor of the cockpit, with occasional glimpses of the altimeter and other instruments. Thank goodness, Major Solis is quite capable of flying the aircraft without my humble assistance. Hopefully, the bombs deterred ground fire, but that is no credit to my powers of observation. In point of fact, I feel like a meteorite that has struck the earth a glancing blow and then yo-yo's back up in a cyclic pattern between earth and sky.

We make two more such passes and dives to release our bombs. As we finally pull off target, the FAC reports by radio that our bombing had been pinpoint in accuracy.

The FAC is the only close observer of these events. From treetop level, he is familiar with the terrain and recognizes enemy activity within his domain. Moving at our speed from the higher altitude makes it impossible for anyone in our aircraft to obtain a clear picture of a target obscured by trees, smoke, explosions and darkness. On most strike missions, ground follow-ups of the results are rare, particularly in the enemy-occupied areas of war Zones C and D north of Saigon. This absence of quantifiable battle damage assessment (BDA) allows for differences of opinion between advocates of propeller aircraft and those who favor jets.

There has been little conversation between Major Solis and me beyond the cryptic comments previously noted. Dive-bombing is all-consuming action, with no time wasted in conversation. Finally, after we have pulled off target, returned to altitude and regrouped in formation, Major Solis asks over the intercom how I am doing. I promptly reply, "Fine."

Despite my difficulties in learning how to deal with G-forces, I have remained somewhat functional throughout, with no nausea, vomiting or blackout. Major Solis turns control of the aircraft over to me as we fly back to Cam Ranh in formation.

This is my first attempt to fly this aircraft…and, it is quite obvious. With the throttles in my left hand and the control stick in my right hand, I encounter difficulties in maintaining my position in formation. By my position in the lead aircraft, it is the responsibility of the other aircraft to follow my lead. My FAA civilian private pilot's license provides little experience to enhance my flying a supersonic jet fighter-bomber. But, I try. While I focus intensely on maintaining altitude and position in formation, I didn't realize how much I was porpoising through the sky until I glance out of the cockpit to observe spacing of other aircraft in our formation.

The other three aircraft are porpoising through the sky in perfect synchrony with me, as one should expect, since all aircraft must follow the lead aircraft. My chagrin is expressed over the radio as, "Aw, come on guys…give me a break!"

We all have a good laugh at my amateurism. As we approach Cam Ranh, I turn the controls back over to Major Solis for landing.

My previous experience in single-engine, propeller-driven aircraft led me to expect a prompt response for each input into the controls, whether in speed or in aileron control. In an automobile, if you turn the wheel right, the car immediately goes to the right. In other words, the pilot has direct feedback, reflected by aircraft performance as he flies the aircraft. The Phantom does not yield so easily to the reins. There is a lag between advancing the throttle and the response of the aircraft to go faster. In other words, the pilot must "stay ahead" of the airplane. If you wait for a response to correct through the controls, it is too late.

My problem was linked to the throttle. Remaining in formation during level flight demands constant small adjustments of the throttle. When I advance the throttle and nothing happens, I advance it further. This increases the speed too much and I back off on the throttles. Thus, I was over controlling the aircraft one moment and under controlling it in another. The pitch or movement of the airplane through the air is comparable to a porpoise undulating in and out of water.

(For our formation, under my lead, the action was comparable to four porpoises undulating synchronously in and out of water.)

Now, on final approach back at Cam Ranh, we are in the landing pattern with Cam Ranh tower approach control. Airspeed decreases to 250 knots as landing gear is lowered and wing flaps are down. With slight rotation of the nose up, our airspeed slows to 125 knots as we gently touch down and roll out down the runway. Slight braking is applied as the drogue chute blossoms behind us to further slow the aircraft and permit taxing back toward the revetment area.

After landing, there are the post-flight and shutdown checklists:
From my back-seat position, I assure that the lower ejection handle guard is UP.
Ejection Seat is raised to gain clearance for insertion of rocket motor safety pin.
Radar: Perform Bits/OFF
Tacan: STANDBY
OXYGEN: OFF

UHF/COMM-OFF

Destruct Circuit Manual Arm Switch –SAFE (Safety pin inserted)

AN/ALQ-91 function selector switch-OFF

All checklist procedures for "shut-down" have been accomplished.

Only now can we get out of the aircraft, climb down the ladder to the ground and report to Base Operations for our post-mission debriefing.

As Major Solis and I open the door to enter the hallway of Base Operations, I can't believe my eyes! The entire hallway is filled with a huge crowd of pilots from our squadron who have congregated and are now standing expectantly outside the debriefing room, shoulder-to-shoulder. I can't believe it! They are all waiting for me! I am nearly overwhelmed. Obviously, the word has spread. Half of the squadron pilots cluster around me to ask how it was, etc. Many of these younger pilots recall all too well their first flight.

Their facial expressions border on incredulity that I have survived the test of this, my first strike mission. Apparently, this particular mission was billed as a difficult flight, even for veteran pilots. A novice on his first ride was not expected to return intact and remain capable of standing upright.

I must admit that it is a point of some satisfaction for me…an issue that requires some time for me to appreciate. I have passed muster and performed my duties to the satisfaction of Major Solis. But as much as anything else, I take greater pride in not sullying the cockpit with vomitus. I have learned an additional lesson in human physiology. Surges of adrenaline override the otic labyrinths and autonomic nervous system to a point that totally dispels any conscious or unconscious nausea! Probably my labyrinthine system was in such a state of shock that my autonomic reflexes were paralyzed during our maneuvers.

Both Bill Simmons and Al Aleckna are gregarious and fit the extrovert roles expected of fighter pilots. On the other hand, I am more introverted…

so much so that, when I was introduced to one of the senior nurses as "the new flight surgeon," she replied rather dryly, "Oh, so you're the quiet one." The gravity of her facial expression reminded me of a mother counseling her daughter, with the warning to "Watch out for the quiet ones…" But, perhaps, I was over-reading it. One thing is for sure. Today this "quiet one" greatly appreciates the New England Whalers, who in the 1800s experienced their first "Nantucket Sleigh Ride" after harpooning a whale.

I have survived my first combat mission in the F-4C Phantom II. It is a good feeling. For a reason that I cannot explain, recognition by the pilots of my squadron means more to me than any academic accolade from a book-bound professor. Intellect, isolated from physical reality, can carry you only so far. At some point in life, you must prove yourself as a man competing against other men in the pragmatism of performing meaningful duty. I have done this in the practice of medicine, but for some reason, I derived little satisfaction from it. Today is different. I feel that I have accomplished something else today…it is difficult to define, but it is a source of great satisfaction to me.

I remember a quote from Capt. Edward V. Rickenbacker during World War I: "There is a peculiar gratification on receiving congratulations from one's squadron for a victory in the air. It is worth more to a pilot than the applause of the whole outside world. It means that one has won the confidence of men who share the misgivings, the aspirations, and the trials of aeroplane fighting."

Today, my victory in the air was over myself and not over the enemy…and, perhaps, that is of equal or greater importance than anything else, if you live to tell it.

CHAPTER 7

======================================

First Strike Missions

26 June 1966

Today, I am scheduled to fly one strike mission in the morning and another mission in the afternoon. In the future, I will try to avoid this tight scheduling since it interferes with the routine flow of paperwork and patient care in the flight surgeon's office. But, because of scheduling issues, today is an exception.

The weather is fair and the day is pleasantly warm at 5 a.m. A soft breeze blows from the South China Sea and it promises to be a lovely day in this tropical land. After a light breakfast in the "chow hall," I report to Base Operations for our pre-mission briefing by weather and intelligence. Take-off is scheduled for 8 a.m. Our primary mission is to provide air support for the ground operation known as Operation Nathan Hale.

The target area lies on the coast, approximately seventy-five miles north of Cam Ranh Bay and slightly south of Tuy Hoa. Our armaments are napalm and rockets. Intelligence informs us that we can expect anti-aircraft artillery as well as intense ground fire from many sources. We are informed that a large battle, involving all military services, is raging in this area and we are not disappointed. Our preflight briefing provides coordinates of the target area as well as weather conditions there. Radio frequencies for contacting our FAC en route are also given.

En route, we are informed that a small village called Trung Luong has multiple trench works that are being used for cover by the Viet Cong. These trench works are being destroyed by U.S. Army artillery and by large guns from offshore Navy cruisers and destroyers. We arrive over the target area at 10,000-12,000 feet altitude, orbiting over the battleground, to watch the smoke and fire belch up from the battle below. The entire region is VERY HOT! The airspace above the target is filled with a multitude of aircraft types from all of the military services that vary from armed helicopters to various fixed-wing aircraft. These are represented by both propeller fighter-bombers and jet fighter-bombers.

Offshore to our right are multiple landing craft and support vessels of the Navy. The cruisers and destroyers are holding off shore to pound the entrenched enemy forces with their large guns. When these ships turn broadside to fire, the recoil or "kick back" from their guns rolls the entire ship backward. By the time that the ship rolls back to its original position, another salvo is released to start the cycle all over again. I can only imagine what sailors must experience during the blasts and concussions of the big guns as they wallow back and forth in the water.

There are also landing craft, either standing offshore or heading toward shore, to establish a beachhead landing for the troops. I would guess that these landing craft are LCI's (Landing Craft Infantry) and LST's (Landing Ship Tank). I am somewhat familiar with these ships since my father, George Warren Clark, Jr., was stationed on an LST during WWII, in the South Pacific, during the Battle for Guadalcanal. For a moment through the smoke and mists, I see what appears to be a large aircraft carrier farther out to sea. The entire bay is filled with ships and boats; all of which are either firing toward land or scurrying back and forth between ships and the beaches.

We remain at an altitude of 10,000 feet, awaiting clearance from the FAC to begin our strike. Beneath us, closer to the ground, the air swarms with Huey helicopters, firing machine guns and rockets, or disgorging troops into multiple LZ's (landing zones). Through the low-flying Hueys, a multitude of aircraft types are stacked up at varying altitudes, including F-100 Supersaber Jets and propeller-driven Douglas A-1 Skyraiders…waiting to plunge in and out, piercing the smoke. Like deadly wasps and angry hornets, they swoop down to strafe, bomb, napalm or to sow anti-personnel bomblets…before climbing back up to begin another run.

We continue orbiting above the battleground at this higher altitude for several minutes before given clearance by the FAC to begin our run on the target. These few moments in orbit provide me with a God's-eye view of the holocaust erupting on the earth below. It greatly exceeds the scale of any Hollywood attempt to synthesize the panorama of war.

Finally, we are given clearance to begin our attack. Landmarks are related to us by the FAC to maintain our bearing. The corridor for our attack is extremely narrow and requires pinpoint precision…since our troops are in close apposition with enemy troops. A slight overshot or undershot will consume our own troops in the fiery holocaust intended for the enemy. From 10,000 feet, we dive at an angle of 70-80 degrees to an altitude approaching 1,000 feet above ground level. I am busy calling out altitudes of 1,000-foot intervals for Major Solis. Finally at an altitude of 100 feet, we level off to begin our napalm run. At our speed, the run is short. At this altitude, we drop our napalm canisters to smear and splatter the target area with flames, snuffing out all life within its radius. Other aircraft of our formation fire rockets into enemy positions.

During our run in, I make fleeting glances to the left and right of the cockpit to observe masses of winking and blinking red, orange and white lights, sparkling like countless fireflies and Roman candles from both sides of the jungle as we pass. These are muzzle blasts from ground fire, directed against us. Our best protection is our speed. It is not so easy to hit a target that is moving at nearly 700 mph, with bullets that are moving only slightly faster. The enemy troops aim directly at our aircraft, but when the bullet arrives, we are no longer there. Obviously, there are no duck hunters among the enemy, or we would not be so fortunate. Part of my job as backseat pilot is to inform the aircraft commander of ground fire and anti-aircraft artillery. Over the intercom, I state tersely, "Keep it moving, Major, we're taking fire…!"

He acknowledges with a single word, "Roger," as he continues the pullout by jinking[12] back to our orbit altitude.

Again, the pullout is steep as we steer clear of other aircraft and helicopters that are also diving into or exiting from the fray. I am improving in my ability to handle the sudden onset of G-forces, but on today's pullout, my head is once more slammed down onto my chest and I am partially immobilized by the 6.5-7 Gs registered on my G-meter. But, I am no longer ignorant of what to expect. This will not happen again! As the old adage states, "Fool me once…Shame on you… Fool me twice…Shame on me!"

The flight back to Cam Ranh is uneventful. Once again, Major Solis turns the stick over to me, allowing me another attempt to practice flying this extraordinary aircraft. This is my first mission during which I was able to recognize being fired upon. It's reassuring to make this statement in the past tense.

---

12 JINKING is a defensive action of rolling from side to side and weaving from right to left through an area of active anti-aircraft artillery to evade Weapons Lock by enemy gunners.

From a broader perspective, any exposure to enemy fire that we experience while zooming down and away from a target can in no way compare to the incessant exposure that ground troops experience on a daily and nightly basis. For those who fight this war on the ground, battles are fought on an individual basis of man against man. If we are hit, the chances of survival are complicated by ejecting at low altitude or being killed by enemy capture. However, if I survive, I can anticipate a warm shower in our Quonset hut and a hot meal in the Officers Club after the mission. I can also plan on working in the air-conditioned flight surgeon's office at a clean desk for reading and writing. To close out the day, I return to a comfortable bed in the air-conditioned squadron Quonset hut...all secure from the dangers off base.

On the other hand, Marines and Army ground troops live from moment to moment, from day to day and from night to night, sleeping in mud through rain, mosquitoes and vengeful enemies in the surrounding jungle, hoping to avoid death from countless sources...hoping only to survive...from minute to minute, from hour to hour, or from day to day, simply to exist as long as fate and luck are on your side. There are no gradations to survival. The modern concept of "quality of life" is meaningless. Life is measured by its presence or absence. There is only the contest between the two fates, life or death.

The ground forces are the true heroes of this war and of all other wars. A brave man is not the one who has no fear. A brave man is the person who is terrified of conflict, yet continues to perform his duty...day in and day out.

The Air Force and the Navy provide aerial support, but they are simply complements to the efforts of the ground forces. I frequently think of the quote from Julius Caesar by William Shakespeare:

"A coward dies a thousand deaths. A brave man tastes of death but once..."

War casts a different perspective on life. This perspective can only be experienced; it cannot be learned from a book. And, having once experienced war, a person's perspective of life can never be the same.

CHAPTER 8

<hr>

Strafing Targets—and Meeting Sally

26 June 1966

"When once you have tasted flight, you will forever walk the earth with your eyes turned skyward, for there you have been, and there you will always long to return."[13]

This is my third mission and second strike mission of the day in the F-4C Phantom.

My tutor and aircraft commander is Major Solis.

Flight time: 1 hour 30 minutes

Our target is a small village with fifteen hooches, or buildings that are buried within a mountain valley and nestled in an inaccessible niche of a river canyon. Our armament is napalm, to be released in four passes from

<hr>

13 Widely attributed to Leonardo da Vinci including Smithsonian publications and Washington Post newspaper. Authorities on the writings of da Vinci refute that he was the author.

an altitude of 75-100 feet. At this altitude, the Phantom flies, screaming in full afterburner, below the level of tree-tops, hills and ledges at nearly 600-700 mph. From our arrival altitude of 9,000 feet, we push over to enter our dive and at a critical moment, barely 200 feet above the ground and before colliding with a mountain ledge, Major Solis rams the throttle full-forward and to the left outboard, to kick in with after-burner, while bringing the stick back into a hard left climbing turn, which slams me against the seat with a force of 6.5-7 Gs.

However, this time, I am prepared for both the dive and the pullout. I have no difficulty keeping my head erect and clearing my ears, while at the same time, observing our flight path and the entire action of the mission. As we pull out, I watch our napalm consume the flimsy wooden hooches in a holocaust of flames. From all sides of the jungle, there is heavy groundfire and muzzle blasts are directed at us. Fortunately none of our planes are hit.

This same napalm run is repeated four times on the target. After we have expended our napalm ordinance, we receive a request by radio for us to return to the battle scene of this morning. When we arrive, the local FAC directs us to strafe a village and trench works, where a regiment of Viet Cong is entrenched.

We start our run on target by descending from 9,000-10,000 feet to an altitude of 100-200 feet above the ground. At this altitude, we make several passes over the assigned area with our Vulcan cannon/Gatling gun. When it fires, at a rate of 6,000 rounds a minute, the sensation is comparable to sitting on top of a massive, rusty dental drill.

While we are pulling off target, I note that several secondary fires have been started from our strafing attack. These represent ammunition dumps in the area and are an added bonus for our mission. After we finally regroup and reform at altitude, the FAC informs us that our strafing was a complete success. Later we are informed by troops on the ground that a minimum of five Viet Cong were considered to be KBA (killed by air) from our attack. This paltry number of enemy troops killed hardly seems worth the effort or the expense of our ordinance and the risk to our pilots and aircraft. Accurate body counts are virtually impossible to perform in the midst of a large battle. Body counts do not include the numbers of enemy who were KBA and consumed in the exploding ammunition dump.

On the flight back to Cam Ranh, I continue to be impressed with Major Solis. I have nothing but lasting respect for his judgment and his abilities. It is a rare privilege to learn from him. As usual, he turns the controls of the aircraft over to me for flying back to Cam Ranh. With each time, I am improving.

We land uneventfully back at Cam Ranh. And, after shutting down the aircraft, I accompany Major Solis back to Base Operations for mission debriefing. I close out this third mission by thanking him for putting up with my performance in the back seat. Leaving the debriefing room, I turn to go back to the flight surgeon's office and close out the day's paperwork.

As I am leaving the Base Ops building, Major Solis follows me into the hallway and calls out, "Hey, Doc!"

I pause and turn…

"I've seen enough to know that you can handle the back seat…"

I am totally unprepared and taken aback by this statement. I manage to blurt out a somewhat awkward reply of, "Thank you, Sir."

In retrospect, I hadn't realized just how intensely my performance had been scrutinized. From the perspective of the 12th Tactical Fighter Wing and the 391st Tactical Fighter Squadron, Major Solis is considered the ultimate arbiter of pilot competence. It is reassuring to have his very positive endorsement of my performance after only three missions. I am not so naïve as to think I have mastered the position. My sense of insecurity in learning this position far exceeds any confidence that Major Solis expresses in me. There are obviously huge gaps in my knowledge and abilities, in terms of air-to-air combat, air-to-air refueling and surface-to-air missile avoidance, as well as countless other aspects of aerial combat.

As of today, at least, I have survived three combat strike missions in the fastest and most powerful fighter aircraft in the world.

But, something else more personal has occurred during the short course of these three missions. I have always been a loner. I have never found satisfaction in being a "team player." My life has been devoted to personal survival in the wilderness. I am comfortable alone in any environment. But, now, for the first time in my life, I am swept by a deep sense of satisfaction in being a team player. My squadron, the 391st TFS, is the team and I feel honored to be accepted as a team member.

26 June 1966

I have learned that Cam Ranh Bay is being developed as one of three air-evacuation and medical-evacuation centers in Southeast Asia. It will also be the largest port for incoming supplies for troops and combat materials for the entire country. The rate of expansion for all facilities on this giant base is phenomenal. With the increase in aircraft types and the facilities to manage these aircraft, the flight surgeon's office must also expand.

29 June 1966

F-4C flight

Time: 1:35

Aircraft Commander: Captain Thorkelson

Take Off Time: 1300 hours

Today's target is approximately 350 miles northwest of Cam Ranh Bay, in "Tiger Hound Country" of Laos. This is my first strike mission that is "out-of-country," meaning outside of Vietnam. Operation Tiger Hound was formulated as a covert aerial campaign conducted in southeastern

Laos from 5 December 1965 to 11 November 1968. Laos was considered a "neutral" country. The term "covert" means that the United States does not openly admit its presence or responsibility in the interdiction of supplies being transported from North Vietnam to South Vietnam. It is also "covert" in the sense that the North Vietnamese government does not admit any role in transporting supplies through Laos, a "neutral" country. The missions were initially controlled by the U.S. 2nd Air Division until that headquarters was superseded by the 7th Air Force and the U.S. Navy task force on 1 April 1966. A certain, unspoken veil of secrecy pervades all flying against targets in this region. Even on base, no one mentions flying missions in Laos or Cambodia. The generic designation for missions in these areas is simply "out of country." Many restrictions have been placed on U.S. pilots and personnel about speaking of any flights over "neutral" Laos. Even, while on base at Cam Ranh, we speak only of "Tiger Hound," "Tally-Ho," or missions "out of country," but never of Laos.

The purpose of the operation is to interdict the flow of supplies for the People's Army of Vietnam (PAVN) along the Ho Chi Minh Trail (or the Truong Son Strategic Supply Route according to the North Vietnamese), from North Vietnam, through southeastern Laos, and into the northern provinces of South Vietnam.

Today's mission is to napalm a Viet Cong bivouac and storage area in the mountains of Laos. With the exception of the weather conditions, our takeoff and flight to the target area is rather non-eventful. For the majority of the flight, we are in very dense clouds. Certain concessions must be made when flying in formation through heavy cloud cover. To avoid mid-air collisions, the formation of four Phantom aircraft closes into a tight formation during hard-core instrument conditions and for cloud penetration. Formation is maintained by visual reference to the wings of other aircraft, which position themselves relative to the lead aircraft. While maintaining this tight formation, the distance between wingtips is only two to three feet.

This allows each pilot to see his wingmate at all times and avoid mid-air collisions. All of this is accomplished while flying between 500-600 mph.

As we approach the target area, we descend from an approach altitude of 10,000 feet to an altitude of 2,000 feet above the highest mountain peaks.

Altitude can be measured two ways – MSL (above Mean Sea Level) – the height of an aircraft or terrain above sea level – or AGL (Above Ground Level) – the height of an aircraft above the ground directly below it.

The F-4 is 5,000 feet above Mean Sea Level (MSL) but only 2,000 feet Above Ground Level (AGL). A jungle canopy of trees may extend from 150-300 feet above ground level. Many aerial maps do not reflect this added protrusion of trees into the airspace and cause the pilot to misjudge his clearance altitude. Many crashes in Vietnam and Laos were the result of this discrepancy.

We continue descending through the clouds and finally break out in a jungle valley at an altitude of 1,500-2,000 feet above the ground. On all sides, the mountains tower majestically above us while the green valley below has the appearance of a veritable Garden of Eden. In the background, standing out like giant scars on the mountainside, are white limestone karsts. This is my first mission over Laos and my first appreciation of these white cliffs. It will not be my last mission into this region. Little do I realize how deeply the sight of those white karsts (formations of limestone) will be forever etched into my memory. While penetrating the stratum of clouds, radio contact is established with the FAC. As we break through the overcast, the FAC is readily seen as a tiny silver plane skimming above the floor of the jungle valley. A small clump of trees on the distant hillside is the target, which has been marked by his Willie Pete rocket. No persons or structures are visible to us. This fact is not surprising since all intelligence reports have noted heavy camouflage of everything throughout the area.

Aiming on the puff of white smoke, each aircraft makes two napalm runs in sequence according to flight order. With the drop of each silver canister, bright red and yellow flames combine with black smoke to burst and boil against the hillside, obliterating all features of the terrain. As we are pulling off target and climbing out to regroup, the FAC radios that we were 100 percent on target. Several hooches, filled with supplies and armaments, were destroyed. Throughout the strike, no one in our flight had seen either a person or a building.

This target is part of vast network of footpaths, vehicular roads and staging areas that has been dubbed, "The Ho Chi Minh Trail" by American military. It originates in North Vietnam in a number of places from Mu Gia Pass down to the DMZ, winding through Laos to enter South Vietnam in the vicinity of Khe Sanh and several more southerly points.

The terrain through which it runs is a spectacular panorama of rugged mountains that exceed 5,000 feet, all of which are interspersed with wide river valleys. From the floors of those valleys jagged limestone formations, called karsts, rise hundreds of feet straight up. Ordinarily, the limestone substrata are cloaked in dense triple-canopy jungle, but daily bombing has stripped away the greenery to reveal cliffs of white limestone that now stand naked in the sun. The main roads, with a few exceptions, are visible from the air, but the footpaths and way stations are hidden under the density of the forest canopy.

Now, many years' later, more than any other missions, I remember the denuded jungle with white limestone cliffs shining in the sun. The amount of opposition, anti-aircraft artillery and ground fire that we consistently received during our air strikes in this region are indelibly imprinted on my memory. The scenarios of anti-aircraft artillery reaching skyward to destroy us with red and white fingers of liquid-lead and explosives were typical and characteristic of every mission.

Pilots of World War II remember the White Cliffs of Dover as a welcome sign that they had survived their mission against Germany when returning home to England. But my memories of those limestone karsts are never welcome and they seem never to fade. Nearly a half century later I close my eyes and see them suddenly loom above the horizon as we approach at 10,000-12,000 feet. They stand before our flight, gleaming like an apparition in the Laotian sun. While approaching targets on these missions, it is possible to displace thoughts about what lies ahead. But, that luxury vanishes at the first sight of white cliffs rising above the plain to dispel all neutral thoughts. While writing of these events a half-century later, the same tightness arises in my chest and the same knot contracts in my abdomen. These white cliffs do not welcome me home. Like Harpies, they beckon to lure us closer, where the scorching fingers of artillery and ground fire rise eagerly ever upward, to destroy us. But today, we accomplish our mission and survive!

Climbing out of the valley, we detour slightly from our direct flight path back to Cam Ranh. Each F-4C squadron at Cam Ranh has "adopted" one of the Army Special Forces camps to support for morale purposes. This is a gallant gesture to men who live deep in the jungle, with little access to the world beyond the paths of their bivouac. They live in a world surrounded by the enemy and are haunted by death every moment of every day and night as it lurks behind every tree and every shadow. To ease their sense of isolation, we frequently perform a low fly-by over their camp when we return from a strike. This time, the bivouac is a hooch, buried deep in the jungle, with only a narrow, single-lane dirt road for access. The jungle runs up to their doorstep, with essentially no buffer space from the enemy infested morasses that surround them. Supplies are routinely flown in by helicopter to a rudimentary landing pad, hacked from the jungle. This is Dac Thu[14], a good place not to be.

For those men, the sudden, deafening roar of four Phantoms flying only a few feet over their heads is a gesture of recognition by their country that they are neither alone nor forgotten. As we roar over, shaking the walls of their bivouac, the roof is packed with men, waving their shirts, cheering and shouting at us. Many of these troops have never been as close to such supersonic aircraft as during our fly-by. Their appreciation is obvious. But the appreciation is mutual. It gives us greater appreciation for them and the conditions that they contend with day in and day out. Our return flight to Cam Ranh is relatively uneventful. Much of the flight is again through dense clouds. The visibility at Cam Ranh is less than a mile with a ceiling of 500 feet. We terminate the flight with a Ground Controlled Radar Approach (GCA) to landing. After the usual debriefing, I thank the crew for permitting me to fly with them. Next, I head to the flight surgeon's office to work on the mountain of paperwork that has accumulated in my absence.

Captain Thorkelson is the only other Phantom pilot with whom I have flown after Major Solis cleared me for the back seat position. But, based on this limited experience, it is impossible not to compare the performance of these two pilots. There is a marked contrast between them and the manner in which they handle the aircraft. Both are very competent pilots. In a tight situation, Major Solis would be more daring than Captain Thorkelson. Certainly, Captain Thorkelson is a good, safe pilot.

The general medical officers stationed at the hospital have a rather jaundiced view of flight surgeons. This is expressed subliminally and limited to snide remarks by the hospital physicians about the flight surgeons. There is an ongoing tendency to slough off any dirty work from the clinics

---

14 Dac Thu: I have been unable to confirm that this was the correct name of this camp. Regardless of the name, however, it does not detract from the men who lived and died in that area.

to the flight surgeon's office, based on the premise that "flight surgeons don't have anything to do." The general medical officers hold sick call from 9-12 in the morning. From 1-2 p.m., they hold specialty clinics, leaving one person to cover the clinic. The other six general medical officers head for the beach or immerse themselves in alcohol at the Officers Club. In the flight surgeon's office, we have an air-conditioned office that we staff from 7:00-7:30 a.m. until 6 p.m. or sometimes later to monitor all crash calls and for as long as there are planes in the air. I suppose the air-conditioning and our Jeep rubs them the wrong way.

I saw an airman in clinic today who had his fifth case of gonorrhea within the past thirty days. Morals in every country are different. I have heard from several sources that all of the prostitutes in the Vietnam cities are licensed and have numbers assigned to them. Many of the American officers in the cities have rented an apartment and keep a woman in full time attendance. The absence of these amenities at Cam Ranh Bay and the fact that there are no towns nearby seems to be a sore point among some of the men stationed here.

A small number of Vietnamese women are transported onto the base each morning by truck. They are employed for housekeeping, laundry and cleaning tasks. At the end of the day they are transported back out to their homes or villages. One of these ladies cleans the Operations building, where the flight surgeon's office and intelligence office are located. These women don't speak English very well and very few Air Force personnel speak Vietnamese. Women are generically addressed as Mama San, while the men are generically spoken of as Papa San.

A few days ago, one of our corpsmen was kidding the cleaning lady by making a play on words. He said, "Mama San, Papa San…Where is Baby

San?" This corpsman is a clean-cut young man from the Midwest with a great sense of humor. Even though she doesn't speak English, this woman can participate in conversations by gestures, facial expressions and body language. Today she boldly enters the office, specifically seeking this young corpsman by holding up two fingers to indicate two stripes for his rank, airman second class. She parades into the office searching for him and after much haggling, she announces why she is here; she is offering her Number 1 daughter (age sixteen) to the friendly airman second class for the bargain basement price of 250 piasters (approximately $2.50). She repeatedly emphasizes that this is a special price for him and him only. Everyone else must pay the going rate of 500 piasters ($5). This very nice young man is caught off guard and speechless. She is serious and impresses upon him that the offer is really a very great bargain. He wriggles and squirms before all of us until he is able to talk himself out of the situation, while trying desperately not to unduly offend the lady's generosity.

This seems very strange to most citizens of Western civilization, and especially, those of the United States. But when you see these women, stooped and deformed by age forty or fifty, with gray hair, laboring with a shovel in the burning sun, as they dig ditches for a few cents a day or a bit of rice, it is easier to see why they turn to prostitution. There is no consideration of the "quality of life." The only distinction is between "life" and "death."

The runway situation at Cam Ranh has reached a critical point. We continue to have the single runway with only steel and aluminum mats laid out on the sand. This is inadequate to handle larger planes. Not only is it too short, but it will not support the weight of larger aircraft, such as a Boeing 707 or C-141 cargo and troop carrier aircraft. A new concrete runway is under construction and should be complete by early fall. I believe that Cam Ranh will become the primary port of embarkation and debarkation for the entire country. Three Vietnam locations to be used for medical evacuation to the U.S. are: Cam Ranh Bay, Da Nang, and Tan Son Nhut

31 June 1966

C-130 flight from Cam Ranh Bay to Pleiku

Pilot in Command: Capt. James Morgan

Since I provide medical support for pilots and aircrew of both the Phantom fighters as well as for the C-130 pilots and aircrews, I fly various missions on different aircraft. The missions have different requirements and impose different demands on the crew. Varying aircraft types mold their pilots no less than the pilots fly the aircraft.

I don't believe that one can learn of life from books. Life can only be experienced by living. Without experiencing the travails inherent in different aircraft, and having some knowledge of the pilots and airmen who fly them, no person can comprehend the life of another. Today's flight is from Cam Ranh Bay to Pleiku, a town and Air Force Base in the Central Highlands region of South Vietnam. The aircraft is a C-130 Hercules, whose task today is to haul cargo from Cam Ranh to other bases as needed to support the war effort.

Before 1962, Pleiku Air Base was little more than an undeveloped airstrip when the South Vietnamese Air Force designated it Air Base 62. However, as North Vietnamese infiltration increased within and along the Laotian and Cambodian borders, the importance of Pleiku Air Base increased, and base facilities were pushed to improve and expand. Subsequently, American Army and Air Force civil engineering units resurfaced and extended the runway to 6,000 feet. Now the base is jointly used by the Vietnamese Air Force and the U.S. Air Force.

This is monsoon season and the Central Highlands are lashed daily by deluges of rain. If a single descriptive term were chosen for the Pleiku area, the word would be "wet." And there is nothing made by man that escapes the torrential monsoon rains that sweep the area. While the weather may be perfectly clear a few miles on the other side of the mountains, dark, dirty clouds always seem to settle 600 feet or lower over the city of Pleiku. This lowered ceiling is always challenging for aircraft attempting to land. The clouds, however, do not remain static, as they vary from minute to minute and hour to hour. Beneath those glowering clouds, Pleiku huddles and cowers in the mud like a creature seeking refuge from its assailant; no less than one might summon an arsonist to extinguish a fire.

Today, as we approach, the ceiling is even lower than the average 600 feet. However after a great deal of maneuvering, and with the assistance of ground controlled approach, we finally sneak under the clouds to land. There is no local control tower to advise aircraft about taxi instructions. But, finding our way is not difficult. There is only one building in sight…Base Operations. Nor is there anything in sight to lure the tourist or to entice the innocent wayfarer to linger longer. In fact, Pleiku offers little at this time of the year to attract tourists or even the curiosity of a drifting sojourner. The airport runway can barely be defined from the adjacent muddy turf. In fact, before the aircraft engines shut down and the propellers cease to turn, one is tempted to take off again and look for something better.

The so-called Base Operations building consists of little more than a small, dirty hooch that squats in the middle of a large mud puddle. Inside the single room, the tin roof leaks and water drips with metronomic regularity onto the counter. The entire floor is wet, but luckily there are ample cracks in the planked floor to permit good drainage and thus prevent puddles of water from accumulating. The Base Ops counter is littered with an assortment of dirty, half-empty coffee cups and spoons of various sizes. The dregs of coffee, left in the cups, are coated over by a pale green mold that is rimmed by a purplish sheen on its margins. Further down the counter, the raindrops are slowly diluting smears of spilled coffee, sugar and powdered cream, while the entire mixture drips to the floor. One may view the scene philosophically. These events represent the first step in the long journey of transporting all ingredients back to the distant ocean, that ultimate Unity, where all things begin and finally end.

Out of the line of foot traffic, a yellow mongrel puppy, with mange, is stretched out and sleeping peacefully on a rubber mat, seemingly grateful for the small favor of being out of the rain and having a mostly dry corner.

A grizzled staff sergeant by the name of Sgt. Bong, stands behind the counter and replies in monosyllabic phrases when questioned about the cargo that we are supposed to transport out of here. The bulge in his right cheek can only be a quid of chewing tobacco or a dip of snuff since tobacco stains line his lower lip and run down the front of his shirt. His eyes appear weary and unfocused as he pauses, before responding to a question, by loudly squirting a stream of tobacco juice toward a No. 10 tomato can behind the counter. The tobacco juice ricochets off the rim of the can, splatters onto the wall and drips onto the floor. The juice mingles with the cleansing raindrops until all forms a stream to run out of a crack in the floor and finally disappear beneath the building.

Our loadmaster, Staff Sergeant Meyers, chooses the wrong place to stand. Before he can move a salvo of raindrops from the leaky roof drips onto his cap. Sergeant Meyers is a fastidious man, and both Sergeants Meyers and Bong wear the same rank on their sleeves. Somewhat disgustedly, he peers around the room with a horrified expression on his face. He then turns to Sergeant Bong with the facial expression of someone chastising a "bad dog" as he makes an astute comment about the leaky roof.

In reply, Sergeant Bong passively mumbles: "Yeah, we've got to do sumpin' about it…sometime…" before his voice trails off.

Turning away, I am suddenly distracted by a series of muffled bumps, squeals and grunts from beneath the floor. Occasionally, there is a plop of mud and the slosh of water being displaced. Obviously, something very alive is beneath the plank flooring. I try desperately to look casual and nonchalant about these events as I direct an inquiring look at Sgt. Bong. With a bored expression he states simply, "Oh, that's only Sally with her brood."

I nod my head knowingly, but obviously no wiser. This is a strange world and I take nothing for granted. Sgt. Bong turns away to another task and I move to another area of the room to consider the noises that are issuing from "Sally and her brood." I ask myself, "Who or what the hell is Sally?"

If Sally is the madame of a concealed, muddy bordello, far be it from me to create an expose of innocent airmen. My mind is torn between curiosity and a sense of propriety. Curiosity wins. I walk with an absent-minded expression on my face around the room, trying to look bored and unconcerned, while strolling nonchalantly and aimlessly around the room...searching for a crack in the floor that might permit a glimpse of "Sally and her brood."

My conscience kicks in. I am beginning to feel like a Peeping Tom or voyeur. I gaze cautiously around the room to make sure that I am not being observed. Finally, through a large knothole, I look under the floor, almost afraid of what I will find. There is motion below and the same muffled squeals and grunts. As my eyes adapt to the partial darkness, I can make out the shape of a monstrous gray sow, weighing perhaps 250-300 pounds, comfortably ensconced in mud. Clustered around her underside are six to eight suckling pigs, all rooting for position of advantage for a favored teat. Occasionally one of the piglets is rooted away from his teat by another. Squeals from one or both fill the air. Their mother, Sally, looks supremely contented and grunts approval of her brood. As I watch, she tires of the effort to grunt, closes her eyes and with the casualness of a large balloon that ultimately deflates, simply exhales a prolonged sigh of relief.

Apparently, there is some indeterminate delay in off-loading our cargo and no place to stand aside and wait. Before I have the opportunity to suggest that we return to our aircraft and await the cargo, someone points outside to a wall tent about twenty feet removed from Base Ops. Over the entrance is a faded sign, "Crew Lounge." We slosh through the small muddy lake that stands between the "Crew Lounge" and Base Ops. Before we have waded less than half the distance, the rain has increased to a blinding intensity. In fact, it is nearly impossible to see as we stagger over to draw the tent flaps and enter the single room.

By Pleiku standards, the furnishings are tasteful, but I find less consolation at what I see. I am preoccupied by looking wistfully toward the runway, where our aircraft sits in the state of tidy perfection and interior cleanliness demanded by our loadmaster, Sergeant Meyers...

Furnishings in the room are simple. An old automobile seat is propped up on one side while a badly worn cushioned stool occupies the opposite side of the tent/room. A couch with torn cover and cotton batting, hanging from rips in the fabric, sits on the other side of the tent. A number of plain wooden chairs are scattered throughout the tent. On a small table with three and a half legs are scattered several dog-eared copies of very outdated Reader's Digests. Surprisingly the pages are only slightly soggy. Being a compulsive reader, I pick up a copy, shake off the loose water and begin to flip through the pages. When I reach for the magazine, I disturb a small green and brown lizard that flees under the table.

Other members of the crew are veterans of these flights and conditions. Taking everything in stride, they curl up on the old car seat and couch and promptly fall asleep. But, none of this is totally new to me. I have seen worse in the South and in the slums of Chicago, but in neither of those places, did I ever truly acclimate.

Looking around for a place to sit, I am ever mindful of my medical school days and nights spent delivering babies out of the Chicago Maternity Center for Home Delivery. Most of the home deliveries were performed in the slums of Chicago. How well I remember the 1st Cardinal Rule about Home Delivery: Never sit on stuffed furniture! Cushioned furniture offers an inviting, nest place for countless rodents and other denizens of slum apartments. I am sure that the warmth of dry cotton stuffing is no less attractive in Pleiku than in Chicago. Having no desire to endanger the local wildlife by sitting on a cushioned chair, I choose a plain, wooden chair with four nearly intact legs and sit down to read. Obviously, the other crewmembers are less oriented to wildlife conservation and do not share my concerns. They are sound asleep and beginning to snore.

I continue to look longingly through the rain at our dry, clean aircraft sitting, all alone, on the runway…

After a few minutes, the rain slows to a steady soft drizzle on our tin roof. The only other sound is the occasional dripping of rain from the roof onto the floor of our Crew Lounge. I ritually scan the pages of the Reader's Digest. The words bounce off my retinae and progress no further to a higher level of comprehension. I am leaning back in my chair toward the screen wire window behind my head. Progressively, I feel more and more uncomfortable, with the sensation that someone is watching me. This sensation increases until; finally, I turn around to look through the screen and into the rain outside. As I do so, I find that a small Vietnamese girl of fourteen to sixteen years is standing beneath the eaves looking in at me. Her face is less than three inches from my head. Her small round face is framed by the large round straw hat that is customarily worn by these people. As our eyes meet, she gaily laughs out loud and says, "You, Numbah One!"

This is an expression gleaned from American G.I.s, where everything is graded in terms of 1 to 10. Number 1 is the highest accolade, while number 10 is the lowest. I'm sure this is probably the only English she knows and I return her smile. Then, I return to my reading. After a while, noting a lack of interest on my part, she disappears as silently as she appeared.

I admit to being a bit dense and slow on the uptake in matters of human interchanges and sex. I will never know if she was simply being friendly or if her mother had sent her out to earn a few piasters from the Americans. I only know that she was very young.

Finally, after what seem many hours, we offload our aircraft and fly back to Cam Ranh. Here we load another large batch of steel matting for runway construction at An Khe.

An Khe is the home of the division headquarters for 1st Cavalry. Located between Pleiku to the west and Qui Nhon to the east, An Khe is a combat hotspot.

The runway is no more than strips of aluminum matting that interlock over the dirt foundation. When wet, it can be extremely tricky to land on. This is validated today by the forward halves of two former C-130 fuselages that adorn each end of the runway.

Despite the austerity of this location, war has a tendency to blind one to the natural beauty of this mountainous region. The air is dry and a cool breeze seems to always blow. The steeple of a small church can barely be seen over the hill from the airstrip.

We return to Cam Ranh and make another trip to An Khe with the same type of cargo. By the time we return to Cam Ranh, it is approaching 6 p.m. and we chock the wheels to finish the day's work.

Total flight time for the day is five hours.

CHAPTER 9

Wear and Tear

FLYING COMBAT IN THE F-4C PHANTOM IS STRESSFUL, not only mentally, but also physically. The forces of gravity are both relentless and unforgiving. Increased G-Forces are present with every takeoff and with every flight maneuver. During a dive bomb mission, the steeper the angle of dive, the more accurate will be the bombing. But, the steeper the angle of dive, the steeper will be the angle of pullout and the greater the number of G-forces imposed on the pilot.

With development of high-speed monoplanes in the late 1930s, forces of acceleration, incurred during combat, became democratically more hazardous to both friend and foe. As early as 1940, some German aircraft were equipped with footrests above the rudder pedals to allow the pilot's legs and feet to be raised in combat. This minimized blood pooling in the lower extremities during high-speed maneuvers. Being able to cut inside the turn radius of an opposing aircraft without blacking out was a definite advantage. Continuing modifications of these early methods have led to the reclining seats used by modern astronauts during stages of launch and recovery.

During World War II, dive bombing was performed by propeller-driven aircraft. Many of these planes were fitted with "dive brakes" or "dive flaps" to avoid building up excess speed during the dive. These were metal flaps that were lowered to increase air flow resistance and, thereby, reduce dive speed. This permitted accuracy afforded by a steep dive angle without exceeding the red line, or maximum safe speed for the aircraft. Without these devices, buildup in velocity of a steep dive angle would tear the wings off the aircraft and implant the pilot in the target alongside his bomb.

Examples of aircraft emplying these measures were the Douglas SBD Dauntless for the United States and the Junkers JU 87 for Germany.

Advanced jet-propelled fighter bombers such as the the F4-C Phantom II are tolerant of greater speeds and G-forces than their World War II ancestors, but they also have their limits. For the Phantom, the G-meter will peg the highest number of Gs encountered on a mission. If 9 Gs are registered, the airframe must be inspected for structural integrity.

It is generally recommended that dive angles not exceed 70 degrees. However, in actual practice, this limit is frequently exceeded. Pilots that fly them are of the same flesh and blood as in WWII, but they have increased their tolerance to G-forces by using G-suits and learning to perform G-straining maneuvers. G-straining maneuvers require tensing of the abdominal muscles to exert pressure on the blood vessels within the muscles. This retards the blood from draining to the lower extremities. The maneuver is performed by forcibly exhaling against a closed glottis. (The glottis is the flap of cartilage situated immediately behind the roof of the tongue. It covers the larynx during swallowing to prevent food from entering the lungs.) It is the mechanism activated during a sneeze, cough or strain to have a bowel movement. To perform this usually evokes an exclamation of "grunting." During dogfights, the pilot's life depends on violent muscular efforts to combat G-forces. Audio recordings of pilots in combat are filled with the sounds of "grunts" as they labor to tolerate G-forces while striving to outmaneuver enemy aircraft.

Even with a G-suit, high G-forces are not comfortable and may be accompanied by significant physical pain. If blood is allowed to pool in the veins of the lower body, less blood will be available to provide the brain and heart with sufficient oxygen. Hypoxia is a condition of decreased oxygen being available at the tissue level. Initially hypoxia results in decreased visual acuity and may result in "greyout" or "brownout." Further oxygen deprivation to the brain results in "tunnel or gun barrel vision," as described below. Without reversal, continued oxygen deprivation may result in complete loss of vision with blackout and loss of consciousness. This condition is known as "G-Loc." The danger of G-Loc to pilots is magnified during the relaxation or recovery period, in which disorientation may occur before full sensation is regained. Typically, a G-suit will add one G of tolerance to that limit. While increasing the threshold for tolerating G-forces, an equally important function is to allow the pilot to sustain high Gs longer with less physical fatigue. The resting G-tolerance of an average person varies from 3-5 Gs, depending on the physical condition of the person.

Six Gs was considered a high level in fighter aircraft.

Because of the increased weight from G-forces, turning the head or twisting the neck to better observe your foe is nearly impossible. Mother Nature's gravity is relentless, but it is also unwaveringly democratic. The same effects are visited on the enemy pilot!

My personal experience with the effect of raw G-forces on the brain and central nervous system occurred on a dive bomb mission. As we were pulling out of a steep dive, I noted the sudden onset of progressive, concentric narrowing of my visual fields to a degree that I was looking down two gun barrels. The black boulders on the hillside were growing larger and larger and clearer and clearer through a smaller and smaller visual field. Recognizing these as the first signs that precede a loss of consciousness and blacking out from G-forces, I strained to maintain consciousness while at the same time groped for the fitting where my G-suit links with the aircraft air compressor. To my dismay, I found that the hose from my G-suit had become unplugged from its fitting with the aircraft. I no longer had a functioning G-suit.

In flight, the solution to this problem involves more than simply plugging the G-suit back into the aircraft fitting. Movement in the cockpit is too restricted for such contortions. However, with this knowledge, I began performing G-straining maneuvers until we pulled out of the dive. This restored my visual fields. When we were out of the dive and back up to altitude, and before our next run on the target, there were no G-forces to hinder me. I squirmed around and finally reconnected my G-suit to the aircraft. This was no small feat since there is very little "wiggle room" in the cockpit after you are strapped into the harness and seat. But, once accomplished, I experienced no further difficulties.

Pulling Gs imposes demands on the autonomic nervous system as well as on every other organ system. This is reflected in both subtle and overt ways. During the year that I flew in these high performance aircraft, I was twenty-eight-years old and had the physical advantages of youth on my side. But, youth or no youth, after each mission, I was physically wrung out. Since I flew fairly frequently, it was not simply a lack of practice or poor physical conditioning that exhausted me.

Flying is my first love, but my primary duty is to command and administer the flight surgeon's office. I confess that there were many times when the hassles of administration and the routines of paperwork seemed more formidable than defying death on a dive bomb mission. I have always lived an active life. For me, repetitive and routine paperwork is a special type of cruel and unusual punishment that leads to death from boredom.

However, at least the obligatory paperwork imposed a break for me from the daily risks of flying combat. But, the rated pilots who fly daily missions have no choice of duties. Flying is their primary mission and there is no paperwork option. The pilots I have encountered consider flying their reason to exist. One of the pilots with whom I frequently flew turned down promotion to colonel and then later to general on three occasions. He said: "I joined the Air Force to fly airplanes. I have no desire to fly desks." I concur.

However, the stress of flying two missions daily and standing alert all night for on-call missions, in response to demands of the battlefield, impose enormous stresses on the pilots. Fortunately, I did not participate in flights against MIGs or SAMs, but for those pilots who did, I have the greatest respect and sympathy for the demands placed on them.

I have always professed that there is no such thing as useless knowledge. Nearly a half century later, while practicing medicine in Santa Barbara, California, I was interviewing a long-term friend and patient. He was in his eighties and continued to function as a very successful international businessman. During our conversation, he commented that he had recently had some difficulties with his vision. He noted that a recent evaluation by his ophthalmologist revealed only small cataracts, insufficient to account for any visual impairment. Thus reassured, he drove home with his grandchildren in the back seat.

At an intersection, he nearly collided with a car approaching from the side. This was the second time that this had happened while driving with the grandchildren. They thought that it was funny and simply the deficiencies of an elderly grandfather. They responded as children frequently do with laughter, "Whoops, Pop, here comes another one!"

When I heard this story, my mind flashed back to my non-functional G-suit while dive-bombing in Vietnam. Loss of peripheral vision is not a sign of cataracts. Constriction of the peripheral visual fields is the first sign of insufficient blood flow to the brain and occipital visual cortex of the brain. I promptly referred him to a radiologist for a Doppler ultrasound of his carotid arteries. Sure enough, he had 90-plus percent narrowing of the right common carotid artery. After a successful endarterectomy to open the artery, he has continued to do well as he now approaches his 100th birthday. Without the surgery, the odds of a massive stroke occurring in the near future would have been nearly certain.

CHAPTER 10

==

End of My First Month

30 June 1966

The month of June 1966 has now ended. No other month of my life has been filled with such changes in lifestyle and high adventure. In less than a complete month, June 1966 has provided enough adventure to last for the rest of my life. Compared to an equal period of time in the practice of medicine, this has been the most satisfying month of my life. To a degree, exceeding all of my hopes and expectations, I have performed satisfactorily in flying combat missions in our most advanced supersonic fighter. I cannot predict what the remainder of this year will bring, but I can envision nothing to compare with this first month. If I am fortunate enough to live through the year, this month of June 1966 will remain the high-water mark in my lifetime search for adventure! Life is exciting!

Jack London verbalized these emotions in a single sentence: "I would rather be ashes than dust!"

1 July 1966
5th Phantom Mission
Pilot in Command: Capt. Owens

After awakening at 4 a.m., I plow through the ubiquitous sands of Cam Ranh toward the dining hall for a leisurely breakfast. Afterward, like a conditioned laboratory rat, I stop by the yet-to-be-awake flight surgeon's office. There is no specific task awaiting me here, and I do not delay in this ritual visit for more than a few minutes before walking the few remaining steps to Base Operations for our pre-flight briefing at 0500.

Today's mission is to provide support for our ground troops in the Tuy Hoa region. An air strike has been requested for close ground support of U.S. Marines and Republic of Vietnam soldiers in the area. I am more than happy to be flying with Capt. Owens as aircraft commander. He is a friend and a very fine pilot of the 391st TFS.

Our F-4C aircraft are organized to function at the squadron and wing level. At the squadron level, there is usually little appreciation for the overall military significance of assigned targets for our strike missions. 7th Air Force Command in Saigon informs our wing commander of a target that should be attacked. Subsequent delegation of the mission is rotated between the four squadrons at Cam Ranh. Wing intelligence provides information about the target to pilots who fly the mission. This includes target weather, location in latitude and longitude, local geography, type of target and possible opposition encountered in the target area. This information is the sum-total provided to the pilots. Not until many years later, while transcribing these notes, did I have the opportunity of obtaining the historical context of certain targets. The following information about our June 1966 Tuy Hoa target is the result of my research in 2012.

In 1965, Air Force interests were concentrated on the development of three airfields: Tan Son Nhut, Bien Hoa and Da Nang. Subsequently, three additional airfields were approved for construction by Military Assistance Command Vietnam (MACV) at Cam Ranh Bay, Phan Rang and Phu Cat. In early 1966, the Air Force required a fourth jet airbase to be operational by the end of 1966. The site selected was Tuy Hoa, a sandy delta on the coast of the South China Sea, 240 miles northeast of Saigon. By this time, the civilian construction firms were overcommitted and unable to respond to the demand for a base at Tuy Hoa. The Air Force assumed the task of planning and directing construction to assure that combat air missions would be flying out of Tuy Hoa by December. In June 1966, the first advance contractors and Air Force engineers arrived at Tuy Hoa. However, before any type of base could be established, the area had to be cleared of enemy forces. Our strike mission was to provide aerial support for our ground troops during the cleansing process.

During the pre-flight briefing, weather over the target region was reported to be fair, with very light cloud cover reported over the area. Our intelligence briefing emphasizes the ever-present possibility of ground fire. Fuel requirements are not an issue since the target was so close to Cam Ranh. The remaining few minutes of the intelligence briefing is spent in reviewing emergency conditions such as flameouts of the aircraft jet engines. Takeoff time is 0700. The TOT (time-on-target) is 0710. The ten-minute flight time from Cam Ranh to target reflects both the speed of our aircraft and the short distance to travel.

This is my fifth mission in the F-4C Phantom. One might think that after a number of missions in this very powerful aircraft, a takeoff would seem routine. But there is nothing routine about this aircraft. It is always new and exciting...and always a bit frightening. With each flight, it becomes more obvious that if you don't control the aircraft, the aircraft will control you.

Both pilots sit in tandem above and between the two jet engines. At takeoff, the deafening roar of the twin jet engines, throttled against the firewall in full afterburner, overwhelms you with a mixed sense of fear and exhilaration as you are slammed back into the seat when the aircraft leaps into the air. It is as if you have suddenly been locked into the saddle of a giant wild stallion that fights the bit and tries to tear the reins from your hand. The fear is that the stallion might win, but that emotion is quickly drowned in the exhilaration of being able to overwhelm and command the beast. With the stick in your hands, you now control the beast. Our ground troops have been in a running battle against V.C. troops embedded in the area. Our task is to deliver an air strike, armed with napalm and strafing of enemy troops with the Vulcan cannon. The Viet Cong encampment has been identified as the target.

After a routine take off, we climb to an altitude of 9,000-10,000 feet before establishing radio contact with the FAC. His risk is not inconsiderable since he makes a favorable target for ground fire by flying at this low altitude. I learned later that FACs are rarely fired upon since enemy fire would reveal the location of the enemy and invite the certainty of retribution from our bombs, napalm and anti-personnel weapons.

We descend to an altitude of 200 feet above the terrain and begin our strafing run. There is no time to sightsee. I am busy calling out altitudes to allow Captain Owens to focus on the targets. Each time we pull off target initiates a new approach for the next run. After we have dropped our napalm, I looked out of the cockpit to see multiple red, orange and yellow lights blinking from the jungle on both sides of the aircraft—muzzle blasts/flashes from enemy ground fire with AK-47s and automatic weapons. Fortunately, their aim was poor.

The first strafing run went well. "Well" meant we shot at the enemy and the enemy shot back at us…but without hitting us.

During the second low-level strafing run, our Gatling gun not only malfunctioned, but actually exploded. It may have been due to a round that did not leave the barrel. Regardless of the cause, it terminates any further considerations of strafing during the mission. Unfortunately, the equipment is often not equal to the man flying the aircraft...

We returned for our napalm drop. Other aircraft have arrived and the ground is obscured by roiling towers of flame and smoke. Everything moves so fast that it is impossible to see a single individual, friend or foe.

The napalm run was conducted at very low altitude. In Vietnam, the most frequently used container of napalm held about 130 gallons of gasoline with a solution of six percent napalm added. When dropped from "hedge-hopping"—meaning to fly at an altitude of about 100 feet—a single napalm canister is able to cover a surface area with flames 270 feet long and 75-100 feet wide. The object is not simply to drop the napalm canister on the enemy, but to "smear" or "splatter" the liquid petroleum jelly across as broad a swath of enemy troops as possible. The burning jelly sticks to anything that it contacts, namely human skin. The conflagration that erupts from the drop also kills by consuming all of the oxygen in the immediate air. It is a particularly nasty weapon that not only kills but also tortures the victim with horrible burns.

Frequently, when American military forces in Vietnam were in fear of being over-run, air strikes were called-in with napalm to stabilize an escalating situation. Other airborne explosives were cluster bomb units filled with metal fragments and explosive charges, to scatter the explosions over a broader area. However, the North Vietnamese Army (NVA) quickly caught on to this devastating weapon and would "dig-in," finding shelter underground in thousands of connecting tunnel systems.

Napalm was also sometimes delivered to its intended and unintended targets (a.k.a. "friendly fire") by flamethrowers mounted on U.S. Navy vessels plying the inland waterways of South Vietnam. Those boats are part of what was known as the "Brown-Water Navy." In Vietnam, napalm was as much a psychological weapon as a killing weapon.

Incendiary devices have been used as a tool of war since 1,200 B.C.E. Perhaps the most well-known of such devices was "Greek fire," a weapon said to have been invented in the seventh century A.D. and used by the Eastern Roman Empire. Napalm is an incendiary weapon invented in 1942. It is an extremely flammable, gasoline-based defoliant and antipersonnel weapon that can generate temperatures in excess of 2,000 degrees. A large napalm fire can create a wind system, a result of intense heat that is generated, causing vertical wind currents. Winds then feed more air into the fire, which increases the rate of combustion, thereby perpetuating itself. In some cases, the wind is called a "fire storm" and can sometimes reach up to 70 mph.

The product was conceived during World War I when gasoline was used in flamethrowers. The problem with gasoline was that it burned too quickly. During World War II, Harvard University researchers, led by Dr. Louis Fieser, discovered that mixing rubber with gasoline made it a longer-burning product. Rubber, however, was scarce at the time, so they had to find some other ingredient. They eventually mixed aluminum soap powder with gasoline (among other chemicals) to produce an extremely long-burning substance. The thickener turns the mixture into a thick jelly that flows under pressure and sticks to a target as it burns. Polystyrene and other polymers have since been used as a thickening agent.

That formula was used during the bombings of Germany and Japan. It was decided by the United Nations in 1980 that the effect of such a substance was too horrific. As a result, a number of nations signed an accord to no longer use it. Although the United States did not sign the agreement, the U.S. government claims to have officially destroyed its last canister in a public ceremony in 1991.

Pulling off target we regrouped to form our flight element and head back to base. Captain Owens turns the stick over to me. With each mission I am progressively improving in flying this incredible aircraft. I fly it down to enter final approach before returning control to Captain Owens. With completion of the mission, our return to base and landing is uneventful. It is the very best way to end a mission! Our gun will need major repairs or replacement by the ground crew.

3 July 1966 Sunday

Arising at 0600, I have breakfast at the Officers Club and walk over to the office. There are no patients to see, but the usual paperwork is waiting to try my patience. Finally after 1 p.m., boredom overwhelms me and I walk two miles to the beach in search of solitude. Unfortunately, others have the same idea. However, solitude is not their goal. The beach is so densely crowded with G.I.s that it would make Coney Island on the 4th of July appear deserted. I start walking in search of a quiet area away from the crowd.

My search is finally rewarded. After two to three miles, I find a small deserted cove with pristine white sand, washed by the sparkling blue water of the South China Sea. Overhead, seagulls soar on silent wings through a cloudless sky, while sandpipers compulsively stab the sand in search of small crabs and sand fleas. It is so perfect that it seems to fulfill Robert Browning's statement that, "God is in His Heaven and all is right with the world."

In this delightful alcove, I sit with my back against a large black boulder and dig my toes into the sand. To the dismay of a tiny yellow crab, my toe disturbs both his solitude and his meal. Obviously angry, it scurries away to seek a safer haven in the sand. I attempt to grasp him before he disappears into the sand and he promptly pinches my fingers. Apparently, I interrupted him while he was dining on the remnants of a small Portuguese man-of-war, which had been stranded on the beach by the tide. His anger was quite obvious to me since Elaine has informed me that I, also, become crabby if my meals are delayed or interrupted.

For these few precious moments, removed from the war and surrounded by my beloved Mother Nature, I am intensely happy, feeling a part of the grandeur that envelops me. I feel blessed beyond measure to simply bear witness to it all. This happiness is short-lived, for just as suddenly, I am overwhelmed by a sense of terrible loneliness, such as I have rarely experienced in life. My boyhood friends were companions, but there were always differences. Those who shared my lust for adventure did not share my insatiable thirst for knowledge. Perhaps I was attracted to them for their physical prowess and hell-bent-for-leather attitudes to satisfy my wild side. But this trait is only a part of me, whereas for them, it was their entirety.

And now, in this private place, removed from the insanities of war, for these few moments, I return to things that are dearer to me than life itself. The beauty of the waves as they break on crystal white sand…the tiny crab…the small sand dollar washed by the waves…the brilliantly colored fragment of coral that I find at the water's edge…seagulls soaring effortlessly through the intense blue sky…all of these beautiful things…and I want with all my heart to share them with the woman I love. I believe that Elaine would find as much delight in these simple, profound beauties of nature as I. Marriage is more than a legal bond between two individuals. It is the union of two souls to share experiences as both travel together down the wondrous journey through life. And now, more than any other time, I long for Elaine to be at my side, knowing that she would also laugh in delight at the tiny crab that indignantly pinches my fingers…and giggle as the froth of a wave swept over her toes…

(These notes were transcribed in 2011, forty-five years after they were written. Personal emotions and passions have been essentially expurgated from previous renditions of events that occurred in Vietnam during 1966-1967. In fact, while in Vietnam, I kept two sets of notes. One set represented a true rendition of daily activities and events. The second set of notes was written in letters to Elaine. I dared not inform her of everything that occurred, since she had basically "fallen apart" emotionally before I left the U.S. But, no writer can escape honestly recording the truth, whether it be expressed in terms of daily events or entered as a matter of record, despite a time lapse of more than a half-century. To do otherwise would compromise one's soul, and that, I cannot do.)

After walking back to base, I return once more to the flight surgeon's office to read and to catch up on chart notes. By this time it is evening and the office is quiet and cool, a perfect retreat from the constant cacophony of jet engines, either revving up for takeoff or with turbines winding down as they enter final approach to land. Far in the distance is the deep booming of artillery fire. But, here, in the quiet of my office, I can find a measure of silence. Churchill stated that, "wars are eternities of boredom, interspersed with moments of stark terror." By bringing a footlocker of classical literature and medical textbooks, I have successfully eliminated the "boredom" element. The "moments of stark terror" are yet to come.

Sunday Evening

The Officers Club doesn't usually serve meals on Sunday night, but there is always a party for something or someone that provides free steaks, hamburgers, drinks and all the other trimmings. Much of this very excellent food results from a time-honored informal exchange program between the Air Force and the Navy. The Air Force can easily buy all the liquor, beer, wine, champagne and other delicacies very cheap in countless places and fly them anywhere. On the other hand, the Navy has always had the finest food in all of the military services. The Navy has known for centuries that the isolation and conditions that exist aboard ship can create problems for morale in seamen. Good food is the easiest method of preserving domestic tranquility within the crew. Alcohol, however, unleashed on board ship may result in proverbial "drunken sailors" to jeopardize all military discipline. Its use is carefully monitored and severe restrictions are imposed on how much alcohol is allowed on board ship. This creates a relative deficiency in alcoholic beverages available to the Navy.

These facts create a perfect marriage. The best food in the U.S. military from the Navy is exchanged for first-rate but cheap alcohol from the Air Force. In exchange for a case of beer, we in the Air Force readily obtain a case of the finest steaks in the world from the Navy. Since I did not drink during those years, alcohol had no value to me, but I could certainly eat steaks. The alcohol was so cheap that it beggars description. Not being a drinker, I was totally ignorant of the virtues and values of fine wines and champagnes, but one night a pilot came by the office and left a bottle of Piper-Heidsieck champagne on my desk. I opened the bottle and took a small sip...and low and behold, it tasted good! Anyway, about once a month someone would drop a bottle off for me. I offered to pay them, but they laughed. It was less than $1.25 a bottle. Many years later in Santa Barbara, while purchasing wine for a social event at home, I saw the familiar name of Piper-Heidsieck on the shelf. The bottle that could be had for $1.25 in 1966 was priced at more than $125. Obviously, I didn't buy it. Sentimental reasons only carry so far.

Tonight, we had a party at the Officers Club to welcome the new hospital commander, Col. Wilbert McElvain. The process of welcoming a commander usually coincides with the exit ceremony for the previous commander. When I arrived in June 1966, the hospital commander was a certain Colonel Barnum. With the exception of an introductory handshake when I arrived on base, I had little acquaintance or subsequent contact with Colonel Barnum. He seems to relate more to the hospital and medical clinics than he does to the flight surgeon's office and the pilots. In short, his mind is that of a physician instead of a pilot. Anyhow, as the new kid on the block, with the relatively low rank of captain, I have been far removed from the 12th Air Force hospital commander with the rank of "Bird" colonel.

Working in the flight surgeon's office on the flight line, I am removed from the usual activities of hospital-based physicians. There is more communication between the flight surgeon's office and the Wing commander about pilots and aircraft than there is with the hospital commander and other physicians. I live in the same quarters as the pilots of my squadron and socialize with them during off duty hours. It is rare for me to even see the hospital-based physicians except during meals at the Officers Club.

I have far more in common with pilots and Wing combat support personnel than I do with other physicians at the hospital. This suits me fine. I am here to fly and support the pilots that fly. I provide medical care for the pilots. The pilots are a healthy bunch and are rarely ill. I have no desire to return to the closeted confinement of hospital medicine and the daily drudgery of clinical medicine. But, it is appropriate to add that the other hospital-based physicians consider flight surgeons to be "PlayBoy physicians" who are not seriously devoted to practicing conventional medicine. They are correct. I have no desire to confine my practice to the treatment of gonorrhea, pneumonia and sore throats. But, more appropriately, I couldn't care less what their opinions are! Compared to their lifestyle, I'd rather be FLYING!

But, I digress. Shortly after entering the reception at the Officers Club, I struck up a conversation with Dr. Hungerford, one of the oral surgeons from the hospital. He is a pleasant person whose acquaintance I had previously made at Wilford Hall Hospital during my internship. We were discussing the usual subjects of politics, the current war and various and sundry other things, none of which have any grave implications for any issue and are symbolic of the social exchange between two men. Col. Barnum, the outgoing hospital commander walked over to join our discussion. Dr. Hungerford made a few benign comments about having to learn the rudiments of dentistry all over again while visiting the local Vietnamese villages once a week to render dental care. Col. Barnum was well lit with Auld Lang Syne alcohol as he sailed into the conversation. He abruptly turned toward me. With somewhat of a challenge in his voice, he says, "…And what have you learned since you've been at Cam Ranh, Doc?"

I thought for a few moments before speaking, and looked him squarely in the eyes and replied, "Patience." Long pause… "And what do you mean by that?" he retorts. At this point, Dr. Hungerford immediately recognized the direction that things were taking and attempted to intercede. He tried to make a joke by playing on words, "Patience vs Patients… Ha…Ha…Ha."

But, the colonel didn't buy the diversion and pressed me more aggressively for a response. "No, I mean it. What do you mean by 'patience'?" I thought, hell, if he wants a response, I'll damn sure give it to him. I lock eyes with the colonel and reply, "By 'patience,' Colonel, I mean the ability to bear with a situation that I do not understand, and to view with tolerance, those above me who pretend to understand—yet, whom I know full well have no greater comprehension than I."

I continue, "And as far as the 'Big Picture' is concerned, I am convinced that no one in Vietnam, regardless of rank, has any concept of the direction that this war is heading—not to mention this base and this hospital. I don't believe that anyone except McNamara and LBJ has any inkling of forthcoming events—and I have grave doubts about them. The overall direction of this war was initiated from Hanoi and not from Washington, D.C. All that Washington can do is to react to Hanoi's aggressions."

"Not having the big picture" was the epithet applied to anyone of lower rank who did not have the celestial view enjoyed by the upper ranks. The absence of having the "Big Picture" became a cliché that was applied to soldiers in the trenches or to anyone lower than the rank of general, who have no concept of the overall war strategy possessed by more exalted ranks. But, of greater significance was the implication that the commanders in charge had a God-like perception of all strategy, as if they sat atop Mount Olympus with Zeus, Apollo and the other gods. Only from such an ethereal seat could one observe and fully appreciate the panorama of life, death, war, and peace as it unfolded beneath them.

The edge in his voice continued to increase as the colonel pressed me for specific examples. I used the case of Col. Buck Cantor, my mentor in hematology during internship at Wilford Hall Hospital in 1963-1964. Dr. Cantor is fundamentally a research-oriented hematologist. He is a gentle person and an excellent teacher. He loves his work. I also mentioned Col. Jerry Parker, who was chief of gastroenterology at Wilford Hall. My question to Colonel Barnum was, "How do such men with their super-specialized interests in medical research fit into a combat hospital, located in the jungles of Vietnam, where everything concentrates into the ultimate pragmatism that separates life from death?" His reply was, "We don't have fires every day, but we keep fire trucks in a state of readiness. We don't have crashes every day, yet we keep crash teams and rescue helicopters available at all times."

Unfortunately, I didn't have the wisdom to shut up and let him have the upper hand in terminating the discussion.

My response was, "Colonel, assuming the very worst of circumstances, say this war blows wide open and Red China invades Cam Ranh Bay...and we have 500,000 casualties...and then, someone drops an H-bomb...what purpose will be served by a research hematologist, who (1) has not performed a physical exam in twenty to thirty years, and (2) whose primary concern during those years has been (i) electrophoresis of plasma proteins, (ii) kinetics of erythrocyte metabolism, (iii) karyotype analysis of inherited orders of metabolism and (iv) electron microscopy of the red blood cell? How do you justify sending this specialist to a military field hospital in a combat zone?"

He was turning red in the face, while I obtained some perverse pleasure in watching him squirm. But, thankfully for both of us, someone interrupted the conversation and shortly thereafter, at an appropriate moment, I excused myself. Boy, am I ever glad he is leaving next week. Having to work under someone like this for a year would be worse than a year in purgatory. After all these years, I've lost any inclination to cooperate with academic idiots who mouth platitudes as their only substitute for intelligence!

As I transcribe these notes in the year 2011, I am somewhat ashamed at my behavior. In all likelihood Colonel Barnum was a decent human being and physician, who was swept up in events far beyond his control and far beyond the control of his superiors. I'm sure that he did his job as best he could in service to his country and in a manner that reflected credit upon his profession as a physician. I was twenty-eight when I arrived in Vietnam. I have possessed a lifelong streak of rebellion against all authority, especially when I perceive that the "authority," who outranks me, seems inferior in intellect, integrity and strength of character...all characteristics that I consider inappropriate for someone in his position. My rebelliousness is not without qualification, however. I yield authority readily to someone whom I perceive to be wiser and more experienced in life than I.

At the time of this encounter, I had not met the incoming hospital commander, Col. Wilbert McElvain, to whom I would yield on every issue. My greatest flaw is to possess the uncanny ability of sensing insecurity in a person who cloaks it with arrogance and is obviously overeducated for his/her intelligence, yet, who holds a superior rank based on tenure and not merit. It was not only in the military that I have had difficulties with such people. The academic world is populated by persons who are inadequate for daily life and who derive their authority from the institution that employs them. Academic medicine, in particular, seems filled with this type personality. The general public considers the medical profession to be the top of the intellectual totem pole. It grants instant commendation to one who holds the M.D. degree. This is done to an extent that is totally divorced from the character whose name is attached to that degree.

Now at this advanced age, I realize that I have probably overreacted to such persons. My genetic heritage is noted for rebellion against authority. My ancestors signed the Magna Charta in England and fought in wars of rebellion before modern Europe existed. They fought in the American Revolution against England and continued the tradition into the Confederacy during the American Civil War. My family has always been intolerant of authority. As my grandmother noted: There are two types of animals: Those that may be led and those that must be driven. Neither she nor I ever doubted the category into which I fell. And yet, in an effort to maintain perspective of this issue, a study of history makes it obvious that all freedom on this planet is the product of rebellious men and women who refuse to submit to unwarranted authority.

These musings and comments bring to mind one of my favorite quotes by Albert Einstein: "He who joyfully marches to music in rank and file has already earned my contempt. He has been given a large brain by mistake, since for him the spinal cord would fully suffice."

Today marks the beginning of my fourth week "in country." I close this note with a letter to Elaine. "How I long for you…for your bright eyes…your happy hops…your giggling sessions at bedtime…but most of all I treasure your warm, wonderful love that fills my heart with happiness, making every day of my life the most marvelous and joyful experience…."

CHAPTER 11

Tiger Hound Country

4 July 1966

Today's target is in one of the most active regions for infiltration of North Vietnamese troops, munitions and supplies, to be transported from North Vietnam to South Vietnam. As a neutral country, Laos is also officially out-of-bounds to North Vietnam. But these diplomatic niceties are ignored by all three countries. The United States is more concerned than North Vietnam about preserving its image of honoring Laotian neutrality. Because of this, all missions against targets in Laos are cloaked in the thin veil of anonymity and non-recognition. Prior to this mission, we receive the usual intelligence briefing concerning the target and anticipated resistance. The probability of ground fire against our aircraft spans a large breadth of uncertainties. The range of weapons directed against us includes small arms fire from pistols, rifles, machine guns, anti-aircraft artillery and the possibility of surface-to-air missiles. In short, today's target is a "hot area."

Our flight of four Phantoms is armed with the entire panoply of napalm, rockets, and guns. The target is fragged to be two trucks and a string of pack animals, all laden with weapons and war materials. While at first glance this may appear to be a paltry target for such massive weaponry, this is a war in which the majority of supplies are trekked down jungle paths and dirt roads, in hand-pushed/pulled carts, on the backs of pack animals, in the saddle bags/baskets of bicycles and occasionally on the backs of elephants. Since the enemy works night and day to transport supplies by all means, the small quantities add up to massive infusions of munitions and supplies that can be turned against our forces.

When we arrive in the target area, radio contact with the FAC is established. The FAC directs our strikes, which from our altitude appears to be a brown thread interlaced in the green jungle. In fact, it is barely visible from our altitude. This brown thread is a small dirt road, off to the sides of which are two trucks loaded with supplies and a string of pack animals.

After several passes have been made by each of our four planes, the area is burning and pockmarked by our explosives. No one in any of our aircraft ever so much as catches a glimpse of a truck or, for that matter, anything except trees and a dirt road. After we reform our aircraft at altitude and are preparing to return to base, the FAC gleefully reports that we were 100 percent on target and that we have killed three pack animals and damaged one truck. While this might be considered a successful strike by the United States Air Force, I have a slightly different perspective. This is one helluva price to pay for endangering the lives of nine men and five aircraft (four Phantoms and one FAC). The average value of each F-4C Phantom is more than $3 million, while the expenditure of ordnance is in excess of $10,000. And, all of this is required to kill three jackasses and damage an old truck! The cost of killing these three donkeys is prohibitively expensive when the costs of efforts and armaments required to kill them are considered. However, from purely a historical perspective, other jackasses may have been more valuable. After all, Sampson slew 1,000 Philistines with the jawbone of only one ass!

But there is more to war than the value of tactical targets destroyed. The issue is political, based on inter-service rivalry. The number of flights during this war against trivial targets must be considered in the perspective of the ongoing competition between Naval aviation and Air Force aviation. The number of sorties or flights against the enemy is a carefully monitored tally for the annual allocation of federal resources. In other words, the military service that flies the most receives the most money. A strange war indeed, but probably no different from other wars in other times.

6 July 1966

Today's mission is a C-130 flight from Cam Ranh Bay to Qui Nhon. The aircraft commander is Capt. Richard Prater. Total anticipated flight time is four hours thirty-five minutes, with the total number of landings being six.

After my previous rides in the supersonic Phantom F-4C, traveling in the cargo bay of a C-130 is comparable to riding in a cattle boxcar. Qui Nhon is a town with a small U.S. Army military base, where my cousin, Johnny Kaiser, is stationed. I had hoped to see him on this jaunt. Unfortunately, for multiple reasons, I was unable to contact him. However, a delay at the airport provides time for me to explore the local environment. The town is interesting. The Vietnamese township is composed of old French buildings, which abut the operations of the burgeoning U.S. Air Force base.

In the town of Qui Nhon, the squalor is appalling. Garbage is dumped along with raw sewage into the narrow streets while children run naked everywhere, using any available space as a toilet facility. As I walk down a side street, a young person, of perhaps sixteen to eighteen years of age, strolls casually out of a doorway into the alley, carrying a pail of water. In full view of all, the person removes all clothing above the waist and proceeds to toss cups of water alternately over the shoulders, back and chest, while rubbing to cleanse the area with her hands. After bathing the upper extremities, she rolls her pajama-type breeches up to the groin and meticulously bathes each leg. Only during this late period of observation do I discover that the person is a girl. These women are so poorly endowed in breast development that it was only after she has finished and her hair fell down that her gender became evident. Throughout this public bath, people continued to stroll past her and paid no attention as she performed her toiletry. No one even glanced at her, and she seemed totally unconcerned about privacy.

My impression is that these people have so many terrible problems to cope with, in terms of daily survival, that modesty has no significant role. They live from day to day, simply trying to stay alive in order to live another day. Americans have no concept of this marginal existence. There have only been two times in American history where elemental survival played such a predominant role: The American Revolution and the Civil War for the Southern States.

After we off-load cargo in Qui Nhon, we continue the next leg of our mission. This route places us over the mountains. At an altitude of approximately 3,000 feet above the jungle mountains, a squawk on the radio informs us that an aircraft has crashed in our vicinity. The pilot of the downed aircraft is requesting aid. We circle several times above the area without finding any visible evidence of the mishap. Since other rescue aircraft are present, and we are low on fuel, we continue our flight to Duc Tho. Duc Tho is a very small Special Forces camp in the Central Highlands of Vietnam, only eighteen miles from the Cambodian border. The camp is nestled in a small valley between two mountain ridges, adjacent to a

Montagnard village. It is protected by entrenched howitzers and mortars surrounding the base. The 3,000-foot runway is barely adequate for handling the heavily laden C-130. But utilizing a short-field-landing technique with reverse props, we come to a halt barely fifty feet from the end of the runway. This camp is composed solely of pup tents and small canvas shelter halves, all clustered about the runway. The prop wash of every aircraft tears the tent stakes from the ground, thus eliminating any thoughts of permanency. Like swarms of dragonflies, helicopters, transporting combat platoons, fill the air.

The soldiers sit beside their tents with dull, listless and trance-like gazes as they robotically clean their weapons. They sit quietly, with the appearance of someone who is beyond every measure of physical fatigue and caring. Only an occasional person looks up as we walk by. Their eyes have the "thousand-mile stare," a haunted appearance beyond desperation. From reports, there are several Viet Cong battalions hiding only a few miles from camp. Daily encounters with the guerrilla units are sporadic since the enemy quickly melts into the jungle or vanishes over the border to seek refuge in Cambodia. Small O-1E Bird Dogs and other types of reconnaissance planes slip in and out of the tiny camp as they survey the jungles and mountains.

We unload four large 500-gallon bladders of gasoline and return to Qui Nhon for another load. On our second and final trip to Duc Tho, the aircraft is jarred on landing by the sledgehammer blows of howitzers and the smaller thump of mortars, firing at intervals toward the surrounding hills. As we begin our takeoff roll, one explosion rocks the runway and throws our aircraft skidding sideways. I don't know if it represents return fire from the enemy or simply the concussion from our howitzer along the runway. But, regardless of whether the pitcher hits the stone or the stone hits the pitcher, it still bodes ill for the pitcher. And, this evening, our aircraft is the pitcher. It is obvious that a battle is not only imminent, but has already begun. One lucky hit will cripple our aircraft or damage the runway, making takeoff impossible. Ramming the throttles to the firewall, we shove the last of our cargo out the back ramp. Finally, after a rocky take-off roll, we lift off and climb out of the valley to escape being trapped by incoming mortars and shells. Passing above the site of previous F-4 strikes at Tuy Hoa, we sight a Navy destroyer stationed offshore, belching smoke and fire from its large guns as it hammers at targets on shore. After that, things settle down. We continued on to a smooth landing at Cam Ranh Bay, thus ending an otherwise uneventful day.

7 July 1966
F-4 C mission number 7, with Capt. Caughill as aircraft commander
Time: 1 hour 20 min.

After the usual intelligence briefing, we take off from Cam Ranh. Armed with two 500-pound, low-drag bombs[15], we proceed to an area approximately forty miles due west of Saigon. I fly in aircraft number two. This is the third strike mission for our squadron today. The aerial call sign for the 391st Tactical Fighter Squadron is "Hammer." The current mission, therefore, is designated Hammer 3 and each plane within the flight reports in as Hammer 31, Hammer 32, Hammer 33, and Hammer 34, respectively. The weather conditions are optimal at Cam Ranh, with clear skies and unlimited visibility. After takeoff, however, the conditions progressively deteriorate to suboptimal over the target area, where the ceiling

---

15 Low-drag, general-purpose (LDGP) bombs are used in most bombing operations. Their cases (bomb body) are aerodynamically designed, relatively light, and approximately 45 percent of their weight is made of explosives. General-purpose bombs may use both nose and tail mechanical or electric fuses and conical or Snakeye fins. These fins slow down the bomb to permit the aircraft to avoid the blast and fragmentation of its bombs.

is approximately 800 feet. Such a low ceiling leaves minimal leverage for dive-bombing. The entire target area is a swamp, which seems impossible for human habitation. However it is reported to be teeming with Viet Cong. Our target is a Viet Cong supply depot. The FACs direct the air strikes under this exceedingly dangerous low ceiling area. All is complicated by ground fog that merges with the clouds to a degree that it becomes impossible to establish a horizon or to visualize the ground. From our four aircraft, not a single person actually sees the target. The bombs are dropped in the direction indicated by the FAC, who flies at treetop altitude. When our fourth aircraft pulls off target, the FAC happily reports that our bombs have destroyed 100 percent of the target. After pulling 5-6 Gs during the dive bomb runs, I am weary. With marginal weather conditions and the usual prospect of ground fire, my adrenaline level must have "red-lined."[16] All of this for bombing a target that was never seen! For some reason, I am less enthused about the results of our bombing than is the FAC.

Resuming formation for the flight back to base is complicated by the fact that one of our aircraft has a hung bomb. In this case, the 500-pound general purpose high-explosive bomb does not separate from the bomb rack. Usually when a bomb does not release on target, the aircraft is flown over the ocean or other open, non-populated area, while the pilot attempts to throw the bomb out of the bomb rack by violent maneuvers. Frequently, this works. This bomb has a chemical long-delay fuse attached to an anti-withdrawal device. If the fuse is forcefully removed by wrenching it from the nose of the bomb, the bomb will detonate. Since the aircraft had flown an attack mission and the bomb remained "hung," the ordnance

---

16 "Red-line" is an expression taken from the tachometer of an aircraft, in which the normal range of operation terminates with a red line to establish the recommended safe speed of an airplane. Another definition applies to a function that is "off the chart."

must be considered armed. In our landing approach, the crash team of the fire department and ambulance stand in readiness by the runway. But, all's well that ends well. After a gentle landing, and evacuation of the crew, a demolition team stands by to deactivate the bomb. This is successfully accomplished. All crews of the strike aircraft are too fatigued for small talk. After a short debriefing at Base Operations, we head to the Officers Club for dinner. I make a short stopover at the flight surgeon's office to check for mail or other pertinent matters. After becoming absorbed in other matters, I lose all subsequent contact with the fate of the errant bomb. Since I heard no explosion, I presume all went well.

8 July 1966
Elaine's birthday

The flight surgeon's office received a new tech sergeant today. He received fourteen days' notice before debarking from the United States to Vietnam. His wife is chronically ill with renal disease and they have three small children. He asked for a compassionate extension of his port call to allow time to make arrangements for his sick wife and children, but his request was denied on the grounds that his position was urgently needed in this office. We have so many personnel in this office already that there is neither enough work for them to do or chairs/desks for them to sit. They sit around writing letters, playing cards and talking. This drives me nuts, but I am not the chief of this office yet. Things will change when I become chief. My feeling is: Don't hang around the office. If there is not enough work to keep you busy, get out of the office, but remain on call, if circumstances change.

We even called 7th Air Force headquarters in Saigon to request that no more personnel be sent to this office. But, that is equivalent to calling city hall to complain about a water bill.

9 July 1966
F-4C Skyspot Mission over Tiger Hound
Aircraft Commander: Capt. Caughell
Mission Duration: 1 hr. 40 min.

"Sky Cap" is a mission in which the F-4C Phantom fills the role of a platform bomber. The four aircraft are vectored to the target area by a FAC and subsequently "electronically talked into position" over the target. For today's mission, the target is 250 miles from Cam Ranh, in Tiger Hound Country (Laos). When we are over the target, a countdown is initiated by the ground coordinator. At the end of the count down, the ground coordinator calls, "hack," and all bombs are released, or "pickled." Each aircraft carries two 500-pound, multipurpose bombs. This is all accomplished from an altitude of 24,000 feet. The electronic sensors on the ground have been placed in areas of high foot traffic for delivering arms and supplies to the enemy. It is an extraordinarily boring mission for the pilots who must fly the mission. For me, it is all too reminiscent of the twelve- to twenty-four-hour B-52 missions I flew from Bergstrom, AFB. You are at high altitude and never see the target. You have no sense of movement. Bombs are dropped on electronic signal. After dropping your ordnance, you return to home base. This is a case of "No Guts…No Glory!" It takes no guts to fly the mission, and there sure as hell is no glory in it.

The only complication encountered on today's mission is a hung bomb on aircraft No. 2. After multiple attempts to jettison the bomb over the South China Sea, we return to Cam Ranh for landing and turn the hung bomb task over to the demolition experts.

CHAPTER 12

Comes the Monsoon

10 July 1966

It is raining lightly this morning when I awake. Since this is the first rain that I've seen at Cam Ranh, my first thought is, "Boy, this is a welcome relief from the heat."

A short time later, the rain stops and it remains cloudy. However any sense of relief is misplaced. Now it is utterly miserable. The humidity is stifling. You can wave a handkerchief through the air and wring the water out of it. Over half the construction on base has foundations below the water line. This means that toilets don't flush or the sewage backs up into the living areas. Most of the outhouses are overflowing and the smell is beyond description. When I rounded on a patient in the hospital this morning, the odor inside was terrible. One positive result, however, is that there are no malingerers here!

The 12th Air Force Hospital is projected to receive 150 additional personnel next month. I have no idea what the breakdown will be between

M.D.s, R.N.s, corpsmen, technicians, etc., but it is a huge influx of people. From my perspective, the entire medical establishment here is already bloated and over-staffed.

If I had the temperament for it, I would go into politics. There is so much to do in improving the policies and practices of our country. It wouldn't displease me at all if a future son or daughter chose this for a profession. Every one decries the corrupt politicians. They note that an honest person couldn't survive or succeed. My answer to such pundits is that if good men and women do not enter politics, the profession, by default, will be left to the scoundrels…much as it is today!

12 July 1966

I've spent the better part of today giving lectures on medical issues of battle casualties and how to treat them to men of the 391st TFS. This means that the fundamentals of first aid, triage and medical management are discussed in lay terminology. Al Aleckna did the same for his squadron. Al is so funny…he's a natural wit and stand-up comic. I asked him how his lectures went. He said over and over again, "They just laughed…every damn one of them…they just laughed…I don't understand it!"

His humor is the brightest spot of my assignment. He has a very dry, wonderful sense of humor. But he doesn't have to say a single word. It is enough to look at the twinkle in his eyes and his handlebar moustache and you want to laugh.

I'm informed that in September the monsoon season begins. It rains all day, every day for three straight months. At least it will be a change.

13 July 1966

Today I received a letter from my previous hematology/oncology professor at Wilford Hall Hospital, Dr. Buck Cantor. It is worded in general terms of inquiry as to what types of aircraft we have. And then he states, rather apologetically, "As you know, I did volunteer for Vietnam."

He also notes that he knows that he will not be able to practice his subspecialty of hematology. It was not until later that I learned that his daughter had died of leukemia. He further noted his desire to return to general clinical medicine. He states his desire to participate in MEDCAP (Medical Civic Action Program provides health care to the local Vietnamese villages).

I'm afraid that providing medical care for the local Vietnamese will provide little satisfaction. The majority of health problems in the native villages result from poor sanitation, inadequate personal hygiene, contaminated water and malaria from mosquitoes. Sanitation of the water supply and mosquito nets would play major roles in improving the villagers' health…and so would soap and water baths/showers. Treating individual cases of infection, diarrhea, malaria and countless other maladies are exercises in futility, comparable to pouring penicillin in a septic tank.

Today, Al Aleckna received his order for two to four weeks "temporary duty," or TDY, at Binh Tuy, a small base in the Vietnam delta region, about sixty miles south of Saigon. Most of the delta region is nothing but swamp. But this swamp is also the breadbasket of Vietnam since it provides the ideal situation for growing rice. Although there are a few American advisers there, the majority of the base personnel are Vietnamese. This is not a "highly sought after" assignment. It is simply the result of local delegation by 7th Air Force in Saigon and the new hospital commander, Colonel Mack. Probably, my rotation will be next.

Today, Colonel Mack noted that he might allow flight surgeons the privilege of an occasional weekend off to fly out-of-country. This would add a bit of spice to our life with an occasional trip to Japan, Malaysia or Bangkok. None of the other physicians at the hospital will be able to do this, and as hospital commander, he must appear impartial. There are definite advantages to being a flight surgeon!

I have had several opportunities to talk with men passing through Cam Ranh whose duties have involved the ground war in Vietnam. They live and fight in the rice paddies, jungles and swamps, with death constantly tugging at their heels. Their lives are pure, unadulterated hell!

13 July 1966

F-4C Mission

Aircraft Commander: Major Chico Solis

Mission Duration: 1 hr. 30 min.

This morning the sun is not shining at Cam Ranh Bay. In fact the flying conditions are lousy, with fog alternating with light drizzle. Even the seagulls are walking on the sand. The cloud ceiling at Cam Ranh is only thirty feet and visibility is less than a quarter mile. It is raining on take-off. According to our intelligence briefing, the target is a Viet Cong supply depot on a mountainside in Tiger Hound Country. I am flying in the lead aircraft with Major Chico Solis.

Today's flight is complicated by thunderstorms throughout our entire flight path and the fact that the front-seat radar is out of order. Fortunately, there is a duplicate radar scope for my rear-seat position, just as there is a stick and throttle for the pilot in the backseat to fly the aircraft. However, the 'master radar scope' is located in the rear pilot position, for my management and control. This is not visual flight rules (VFR) weather. It is 100 percent instrument flight rules (IFR). During takeoff, visibility of the runway is less than 100 feet. Nearly blind, we maintain our heading and roar down the runway, climbing into the fog. There is no clearing as we climb out. We are in dense soup from the moment of our takeoff roll. Radar is the only method of avoiding storm cells that lie in our path. Since the radar for Major Solis is out of order, the task of navigation by radar falls entirely on my shoulders. Under these conditions, the options are few. One option is for me to take control of the aircraft from the rear seat, while another option is for me to interpret the location of thunder cells on my radarscope and call them out to Major Solis in the front seat. I elect the latter option. I call out their location and advise a course correction to thread the flight path of our four aircraft through a vast myriad of storm cells. Since I am very new in flying this aircraft, I do not feel competent to fly it under instrument conditions. Overall visibility is poorer in the back seat position than in the front seat. (One might note that with overall visibility outside the aircraft being zero, the ability to see from the backseat position is irrelevant.) But, one thing is for sure. I am not qualified to lead three other aircraft flying through thunderstorms at 600-plus mph.

In the Navy version of the Phantom, the rear cockpit does not have controls or a "stick" to fly the aircraft. The GIB is strictly an electronics warfare operator (EWO). In contrast, the Air Force Phantom can be flown from the rear cockpit. But, as noted, the visibility for the back seat pilot is much poorer than the front seat offers. However, this is war and missions are not canceled because the weather is not perfect. During this flight, the most severe storm cells are indicated by fuzzy green patches on my radarscope. This location and avoidance of storm cells is accomplished while flying at nearly the speed of sound, while simultaneously being bounced around the cockpit by the up and down drafts surrounding and within these storm cells.

At this speed, there is only a fleeting moment for me to appraise our position relative to the position of storm cells on the radar screen. By the time that I note the location of the storm cell on the radar scope and call it out to Major Solis, we have already flown past it, while I continue searching for the next and the next and the next… I call out the location of the cells, with their distance, size and intensity, while, at the same time, estimate the number of degrees deviation necessary to avoid them. It is all consuming for two persons. It would have been much easier for one person to fly the aircraft and alter the course as required by looking directly at the radar-scope. All in all I am intensely focused on the radarscope as we thread the four aircraft through the masses of storm cells hidden in the all-enveloping "soup."

As we approach the target area at an altitude of 12,000 feet, radio contact is made with the FAC, whose call sign is "Hound Dog-21." Hound Dog-21 advises us to begin our descent to 6,000 feet, where we should break out of the clouds. It is significant that multiple mountain peaks in the region extend to over 6,800 feet. And, these heights are not to be trusted. These maps and elevations are of ancient vintage and have not been recently measured with sufficient accuracy. It is also significant that our air speed throughout all of this is approximately 600 miles per hour. When we finally break through the cloud layer, we are in a valley, surrounded on all sides by mountain peaks. We are now flying below the tree line at 600 miles per hour. We drop down further until we are approximately 100 feet above the ground. This is the optimum altitude for dropping napalm. Our target, reputed to be a weapon storage depot, is nestled in a small clump of trees, precariously balanced on the side of a steep cliff. Hound Dog-21 fires two Willie Pete rockets to mark the target and withdraws.

Swooping down at 650-700 mph to drop napalm canisters on a cliff-side location is sufficient to raise your adrenalin to a red-line level. The activities demanded to fly the aircraft, drop the ordnance and avoid crashing into the mountain allow no opportunity for sightseeing. Our pull-out is tenuous, at best. The mountain seems to erupt in our face as we apply full after-burner, to stand the aircraft on its tail in order to avoid smiting the granite before us. The ordnance is dropped on the target area in a single pass as we continue climbing out of the valley to resume our formation and fly back to base.

The return flight is no easier than the flight to the target, with hard-core soup all the way. As we approach Cam Ranh, the air traffic approach controller warns us that the tarmac (tarmac is a type of aluminum matting used to create runways in combat environments) runway is wet and slippery. On final approach, the runway is not even visible until we are about thirty feet from touchdown. We make a ground controlled approach to landing. "Wet and slippery" are understatements. As we touch down, there is none of the usual deceleration expected to occur after landing. I would almost swear that we sped up!

The Air Force Phantom has different landing gear and tires than the Navy Phantom. The Navy has heavier landing gear to absorb the shock of carrier landings. To compensate for this increased weight, the tires are smaller and inflate to 225 pounds. On the other hand, the Air Force Phantom does not need the added weight of the landing gear. Without this weight the Air Force tires are larger and are inflated to 150 psi. The Air Force Phantom has "no skid" brakes, which provide better stopping performance than the Navy Phantom. The higher pressure of the Navy tires means that it will not hydroplane on wet surfaces below 135 knots. These facts apply to our current situation. At their lower pressures, the tires of an Air Force Phantom lose traction above 110 knots.

Our speed at touchdown is about 130-140 knots, which means that we are going twenty knots faster than the tires are capable of obtaining traction. Ordinarily, this would be of little concern since on a routine landing, the drogue chute deploys promptly to drastically slow the aircraft down.

But, today the drogue chute does not deploy, and the aircraft continues to hydroplane down the relatively narrow runway that terminates in a cliff overlooking the South China Sea.

From my perspective, there seems no appreciable decrease in our speed as we continue hurtling down the narrow runway at 130-plus knots. With the thin coat of water on the tarmac, the aircraft is virtually hydroplaning down the runway. Later we learn that the drogue chute failed to open and simply dropped in a neat bundle onto the runway.

We continue screaming down the runway with no sign of slowing down. Using the brakes is not an option since it will only increase our chances of skidding out of control off the runway. From the forward cockpit, I can hear Major Solis mumbling profane intonations under his breath!

The length of runway ahead of us is rapidly being consumed as the plane continues to hurtle unleashed through the rain and mists. Over and beyond the runway, I can see the froth of waves from the South China Sea rising from the beach and rocks below. In a kaleidoscope of motion, the end of the runway rushes faster and faster toward us. The distance from the end of the runway to the ocean is a straight vertical drop of 200-250 feet. If the aircraft cannot be stopped, we have no other option but to eject before it goes over the cliff.

Suddenly, there is the calm, crisp voice of Major Solis over the intercom, "Okay, Doc, lock your harness…we're taking the barrier!" The "barrier" is a one-inch steel cable crossing the runway that can be engaged by dropping a hook from the tail of the aircraft. It is the court of last resort to keep the aircraft from plummeting over the cliff. Before that gesture fails, however, both of us will have ejected from the aircraft.

The Phantom is designed in such a manner that the rear pilot must eject before the front cockpit. I wait until the instant that Major Solis is no longer able to control the aircraft, and on his signal, I will eject first, and he will follow.

With these few words from Major Solis, I secure my harness and drop the visor of my flight helmet in preparation for ejecting. I prefer to use the ejection rings above my head since there is more trauma to the spine incurred from using the alternate ejection handles beneath the seat. Bracing myself against the seat, in preparation for ejecting, I am elated to feel the sudden deceleration of the aircraft. The wire has been snagged! The barrier has held!

Suddenly, there are swarms of fire trucks, crash ambulances and maintenance men surrounding us. I pop my canopy and gratefully feel the cool, moist ocean mists on my face. Before unlocking my harness, I wait until one of the ground crew climbs up a ladder to my cockpit and places a cotter pin in the ejection mechanism to avoid it accidentally firing while I climb out of the cockpit and down to the ground. Before I climb down, I glance through the mists over the nose of the aircraft and for a moment see waves breaking on the beach below. The nose of the aircraft is hanging out over the cliff's edge.

A tow truck arrives to tow the aircraft back to the hanger. A crew truck is also present to transport Major Solis and me back to Base Operations for debriefing.

This mission only lasted one and half hours, but that was the longest one and half hours I have ever spent. I can imagine that someone in the maintenance department or the ground crew will catch hell. Two major failures (squawks) of radar in the forward cockpit added to failure of the drogue chute to deploy.

In reflecting on these events, I clearly recall that my mind assumed a nearly extracorporeal state. It seemed as if I were outside the cockpit, looking in as an impartial observer of my performance as an airman. If death were to strike my corporeal state inside the cockpit, then my extracorporeal state would not be harmed. I experienced no fear and was fully aware of what duties were required for me to survive. It is difficult to explain.

Perhaps, it is a method of self-preservation to permit calmness and efficiency of effort without panic leading to self-destruction. To confront your mortality while remaining calm in the presence of events seems an involuntary occurrence that does not fit into any medical texts. Later, some of the rescue personnel commented on my apparent calmness and detachment during the affair.

14 July 1966

Fifteen new physicians are scheduled to arrive next month. Included are seven to eight general medical officers, one orthopedic surgeon, one ear nose and throat specialist, one psychiatrist, one flight surgeon, one opthalmologist and two internists.

The new flight surgeon and chief of aerospace medicine is a major who has recently completed his residency in aerospace medicine. I have no idea what his job will be.

Orville Langford is the radiologist and the only doctor here who puts in a full day's work. He was at Wilford Hall when I interned there. Of course, the psychiatrists are usually busy. That's to be expected since so many young men over here are away from home for the first time. When you look around and view things objectively, it makes you believe that if you don't develop some type of neurosis in this place, you definitely need a psychiatrist!

14 July 1966

F-4C

Aircraft Commander: Captain Saltsman

Mission Duration: 1 hr. 50 min.

Our preflight intelligence briefing informs us that today's target is a Viet Cong supply depot in Tiger Hound Country. Located on a hillside in a very deep mountain valley, it is considered to be heavily defended by small firearms, machine guns and anti-aircraft artillery. Our ordnance for the mission is napalm.

On our approach, the FAC is already in the valley. He has located the target within a grove of trees and marked it with two volleys of Willie Pete rockets. As soon as these are fired, he slips his small plane out of our flight path and we roar in. With our first napalm pass, it is obvious that something more than trees is present in the target area. A huge column of white flames leaps into the air and continues to grow. On our second pass, we fly through the flames to drop our ordnance on the designated target.

After expending all ordnances, we regroup for our return to base. The FAC reports that we demolished two large buildings filled with supplies and two bunkers filled with explosives and ammunitions. The flight back to Cam Ranh is smooth and uneventful, as is our landing. It is satisfying to strike a target of significance in such a difficult location.

A new doctor arrived on base today by the name of Walker. He was formerly a flight surgeon, but he's been stripped of this rating and sent here as a last resort before he is either court-martialed or given a dishonorable discharge from the Air Force. We were forewarned before he came. A number of the physicians here have had previous contact with him. I met him previously in a single meeting for about twenty minutes while he was passing through Cam Ranh. I am amazed at the animosity expressed against him. In fact, I've never seen such intense hatred for any one person as these doctors direct against him. I have no idea what he has done to merit such distinction and don't want to know. Since he will be a general medical officer in the outpatient clinics of the hospital, I will have very little contact with him. He reminds me a great deal of one of the doctors with whom I interned at Wilford Hall Hospital.

It seems to be the day for military personalities…

There is a corpsman in the flight surgeon's office who should be a standup comic or in the movies. Airman Third Class Andrews is thirty-five-years old. The fact that he is this old and is still an airman third class means he has been busted for certain reasons or that he cannot progress beyond this low rank. His overall appearance is the stereotype of a Chicago hoodlum, but he is actually from "Redneck" Mississippi. I believe he is the dumbest person I've ever encountered in the Air Force. He has no duties other than working here in the office, but he carries a large hunting knife strapped to his waist as if he plans to encounter a bear at every turn. He has a squash nose, cauliflower ears and a vegetable brain. The ludicrous thing is that he is so terribly affected.

He comes to the doorway of my office, stands rigidly at attention, clicks his heels and clears his throat until I recognize him. He then clicks his heels again and braces into a more rigid stance of attention before announcing in a stilted voice with a feigned British accent, "Sir, I have a gentleman who desires to see you."

I say, "Okay, send him in."

Well, the "gentleman" is usually a big burly sergeant in aircraft maintenance, with a seventh-grade education who is dressed in dirty fatigues and is sweating like a horse plowing a wet field. I neglected to say that, when I tell him to send the man in, Anderson replies in a supercilious manner, "Most certainly, Sir."

Honestly, by this time, I don't know whether to laugh or cry. He leads the same burly sergeant into another room to check his vision. "Sir, will you kindly be seated," he gravely requests. "Now sir, before you are several rows of letters…" The sweating sergeant blows his nose on a greasy, sweaty handkerchief and looks into the machine. "Now then, Sir, would you be so kind as to read line number 21." The sergeant mumbles the letters and Anderson replies in his most British manner, "Very good, Sir." His manner is a caricature of the perfect British butler. At first, it aggravated the daylights out of me, but now he is one of the few points of amusement I have in the office on a daily basis. The ironic thing is that Al and I are the only ones here who appreciate the situation. Everyone else thinks he is no different from anyone else, except through some cruel hand of fate he has been forced to remain an airman third class for almost twenty years.

16 July 1966

F-4C Mission

Aircraft Commander: Captain Russell

Mission Duration: 1 hr. 15 min.

With each of four aircraft loaded with two canisters of napalm, we start out for another target in Tiger Hound Country. About forty miles south of Binh Tuy we are informed that because of weather, we are being diverted to an area twenty miles northwest of Binh Tuy, where a battle is raging. We are informed that "Charlie" (nickname for the Viet Cong) is out in the open. It was also demanded that we "come and get him!" We arrive and orbit the area at an altitude of 24,000 feet, while waiting for the FAC. After about ten minutes he appears over the radio to state, with tremulous voice, that the VC have automatic weapons and .50-caliber machine guns. "I'll be damned if I am going any closer," he says. And so, he keeps his distance and directs us in. Each plane makes two passes from an altitude of fifty feet to scorch the earth with napalm. Flying in excess of 600 miles an hour affords no time for personal observation during our descent to target. There is no sign of life noted in the trees where we have made the strike.

However, just as we pull out of our dive to regroup, I twist in the seat to view the scene of destruction and see several figures darting about on the periphery of the flames. From both sides of the cockpit I also see a multitude of winking red, orange and yellow lights sparking from all sides of the jungle - muzzle blasts from small arms, automatic weapons and .50-caliber machine guns shooting at us. After we pull off target, a very excited FAC radios that on the last pass our aircraft was the target for a huge barrage of .50-caliber machine gun fire. Neither Captain Russell nor I was aware of it. No damage was detected on inspection of aircraft after we land. This represents my second time under direct fire, of which I am aware. Captain Russell is extremely courteous and turns the aircraft over to me to fly home. Having control of the aircraft breaks the monotony of simply being a navigator and copilot.

CHAPTER 13

―――――――――――――

Close Calls

17 July 1966

F-4C Mission

Aircraft Commander: Major Chico Solis

Mission Duration: 1 hr. 35 min.

In the northeast corner of Cambodia is a hook of territory wrapping a small portion of Laos in scrubby forests and mesas. Within this area is our target, a truck depot, reported to be in a grove of trees. Our ordinance is two 500-pound, low-drag bombs. When we arrive in the target area, the FAC marks the target. It is not a difficult target to dive bomb since the terrain is reasonably flat and non-mountainous. The mission is accomplished in short order and we regroup for our flight back to base. We neither see any enemy activity in the area nor receive any return fire from the target area.

On the return flight to Cam Ranh, Major Solis leads the four aircraft to an altitude of 20,000 feet. This placed us in the midst of towering masses of cumulus thunderheads that reach up to 50,000 feet. These huge cloud pillars tower above and around us in all their magnificence against a fiercely blue sky and contrast with the azure blue of the distant ocean. Here in this ethereal world, with ample fuel and ample time, we luxuriate and soar through this domain of the gods. We execute a leisurely series of acrobatic maneuvers, during which we soar between the towering columns of clouds…and then lazily roll over into an inverted position, as earth and sky interchange positions. The pace is as leisurely as a porpoise or dolphin frolicking in the breakers. We are consumed by the ecstasy of having broken the bonds of earth-borne life and having entered a glorious new realm of existence. I didn't want to leave! I want to preserve and continue in this realm for the rest of my life! At no other time have I experienced such euphoria in flight. I feel a pity for anyone who has never had this experience. Later, I reflected on the poem, "High Flight"

> *Oh! I have slipped the surly bonds of earth*
> *And danced the skies on laughter-silvered wings;*
> *Sunward I've climbed, and joined the tumbling mirth*
> *Of sun-split clouds - and done a hundred things*
> *You have not dreamed of - wheeled and soared and swung*
> *High in the sunlit silence. Hov'ring there*
> *I've chased the shouting wind along, and flung*
> *My eager craft through footless halls of air.*
> *Up, up the long delirious, burning blue,*
> *I've topped the windswept heights with easy grace*
> *Where never lark, or even eagle flew -*
> *And, while with silent lifting mind I've trod*
> *The high untrespassed sanctity of space,*
> *Put out my hand and touched the face of God.*

— Pilot Officer Gillespie Magee, killed 11 December 1941
No. 412 Squadron, Royal Canadian Air Force

Obviously, I am not alone in my emotional experience or feelings.

16 July 1966

Last night, after finishing a letter to Elaine, I picked up my pistol belt to go to the post office and then to the barracks. It seemed awfully light. On all of my missions, I carry my knife, ammunition and pistol on the same belt. I generally use a G.I. holster when I fly since the shoulder holster gets in the way of the parachute and restraints. Well, tonight the holster was empty – someone had stolen my pistol. I'd laid the gun in the chair by my desk since several of the corpsmen were still working while I went out to eat. Sergeant Calindine, who is the non-commissioned officer in charge of the flight surgeon's office, left the office for about ten minutes to use the latrine. Naturally he didn't lock the door for the short period he was out of the office. However, this short period was the only time that the gun could have been taken. I have accounted for everyone here in the office and really do not believe any of the corpsmen took it. The flight surgeon's office is in the Base Operations Quonset hut, with people constantly going in and out of the building. I am convinced that it was either someone from the Weather or Intelligence Section, who has observed our habits at all times. I have one person in mind, whom I am trying to check out, but my hope of regaining the gun is slim.

Finally, I replace my initial anger with reasoning. If five years from now someone is killed with that gun in the United States, and they trace the serial number to me, it is prudent for me to report the theft to the air police and go on record as no longer being the owner of the pistol. I have written to Elaine to pull the receipt of purchase at Oshman's Sporting Goods store in Austin and to send me the serial number. The air police were extremely courteous and did not even question why I did not turn the gun in initially when I arrived in country. They came over to the building and interviewed practically everyone. It is more than a little ironic that Cam Ranh Peninsula is secure from the Viet Cong and North Vietnamese, but it is not secure from our own troops.

19 July 1966

This morning, our squadron is called upon for an early mission. During the pre-flight intelligence briefing, all crews are astounded by the quantity of bombs, napalm and rockets loaded onto each aircraft. Each is loaded to full capacity. The armament capacity of each F-4C Phantom exceeds the bomb loads of the B-17 Flying Fortress and B-29 Super Fortress Bombers of WWII. The pilots are walking on air all the way to the planes. No previous missions have had this much ordnance for many months. When they arrive in the target area, the FAC informs them: "You lucky men are going to be in the movies. There is a spot on that hill that you are to bomb, strafe and napalm. There are no enemy forces present, and there are no friendly forces present. And, there is no danger of ground fire."

No enemy troops…no friendly troops…no ground fire! There is simply one damn, dumb hill to consume over $75,000 worth of ordnance for some politician's propaganda purposes. In the entire time that I've been here, I've never seen such bitterness or such a violent reaction from the pilots flying the mission. For a while, they are on the verge of mutiny! The vast disconnect between the politicians in Washington and the combat personnel in this war seems to increase by the day! Most of our missions are flown with inadequate arms and ordnance. The politicians want to disprove any adverse publicity about a "bomb shortage" with the film.

19 July 1966
F-4C Mission
Aircraft Commander: Major Chico Solis
Mission Duration: 1 hr. 30 minutes

Our pre-flight intelligence briefing informs us that today's target consists of several buildings within a small village of Quang Ngai. The buildings are reported to be supply depots of the Viet Cong. For our flight, the first three aircraft are loaded with napalm while the fourth is loaded with four 250-pound, general-purpose bombs. I am flying in the lead aircraft with Major Solis. Approaching the target area, we establish radio contact with the FAC. He advises that he will fire his Willie Pete rockets in a direction that is remote from the target. The usual procedure is to mark the target directly. But, under the circumstances, the white phosphorus is fired at some distance from the target as a feint to deceive and entrap the enemy. Our strike aircraft are given directions to the target, taking our bearings relative to the drift of the smoke, to drop our napalm.

In the lead plane, we immediately dive to tree-top level, roaring in at 600-plus mph, at less than fifty feet above the ground, over the buildings, before release. A multitude of people are seen fleeing from the fiery wrath about to descend on them. Just before we are certain to collide with a tree at this speed, we release the silvery canisters of napalm... ram the throttles full forward to apply full afterburner...while bringing the stick all the way back, to stand the airplane on its tail and climb straight up. With each pass, many people are seen fleeing in terror. The last aircraft is loaded with four 250-pound bombs, of which two are duds. But, regardless of the duds, this finishes the job.

Rarely is it possible to see the results of a bombing, strafing or napalm air strike. The mission is usually flying to coordinates on the map, at which points you drop your bombs, napalm or shoot at targets you rarely see. The explosions cannot be heard when traveling at our speed while flames and smoke that follow the strike make visibility of anything or anyone nearly impossible. The speed of this aircraft and the tasks required to deliver the ordnance leave no time for observation. It is only after you are far removed from the target that the FAC reports the results by radio. Thus far in my experience, it is only on an occasional mission that enemy troops are seen. But this time is different.

From the moment of dropping the ordnance, our climb out is so steep and so fast that for a few moments, we are inverted and look directly down on the target. It is a moment of glorious isolation from the other three aircraft that provides a rare panoramic view of the target area as well as a chance to observe the other aircraft dropping their ordnance.

A huge column of flame roils up from the target area as people flee in every direction. I watch as the other two aircraft drop their silvery canisters of incineration on the hapless victims. With each pass, more and more people are swept up and sucked into the conflagration. From our orbit altitude of 3,000 feet, the entire target area looks like a giant ant bed that has been kicked by a mischievous child and then sprayed and torched with lighter fluid. It is difficult to relate the ants to humans. We see only ants as they flee in all directions. But, even as a mischievous child, I could not do this to an ant bed. It would be too terrible for me to contemplate.

Ten large buildings have been destroyed. There are several smaller secondary explosions, indicating that ammunition and explosives have been stored within the structures. The FAC said the target area is merely a bed of ashes. Flying at low level, he reports a KBA (killed by air) body count of five Viet Cong. Of course, this could not include the countless number of individuals within the target area that were instantaneously vaporized and incinerated by the holocaust, whose remains were beyond all recognition, and will forever remain so.

Flying at such speeds and altitudes is fortunate. The soldiers and Marines who fight this war on the ground are not so blessed. They must kill other men and women to avoid being killed. We, on the other hand, only kill ants fleeing from their torched ant bed.

After dropping our ordnance, the four aircraft regroup and climb to an altitude of 20,000 feet for the flight back to base. By this time of day, the usual afternoon thunderheads are forming over the jungle. To relieve some of the previous stress, we take advantage of the opportunity to again cavort, like dolphins, weaving back and forth at 600-700 mph, between the giant thunderheads towering more than 40,000 feet above the jungles. Finally, our approach at Cam Ranh is standard and uncomplicated. After reporting to Base Operations for routine debriefing, I walk the short distance to the flight surgeon's office to apprise myself of any new regulatory issues. Finding none, I shower in my quarters and then slog through the sand to the officer's mess for a steak dinner. I suddenly realize how tired I am. With the steep climb out from target, we were pulling nearly 6-7 Gs. I have found that pulling Gs is extremely fatiguing, despite having a G-suit to maintain adequate cerebral blow flow.

After eating, I return to my office, where I write to Elaine and enter today's events in a separate diary.

After this, I read a short passage from Marcus Tullius Cicero's letters to his son. They were written in October-November 44 BCE at age 62, during Cicero's last year of life. Cicero states that for purity of intellectual thought, one should be removed from the necessities of daily reality, and think only on higher principles. Only with this isolation can one preserve pure intellectual integrity and philosophical insight.

When I first encountered Cicero during my freshman year of college, I stood in awe of his wisdom and abilities to express himself. Now, after living in the world beyond philosophy texts, I am not so overwhelmed by his sagacity. My impression now is that Cicero was obviously divorced from reality when he wrote these comments.

Throughout the year, Elaine and I have shared various books and discuss them as best we can in letters to each other. In many ways, I regarded my assignment in Vietnam as a sabbatical year to catch up on reading many of the literary classics that I had missed in my formal education. I particularly remember Dr. Strozier, a professor of Latin and Greek at Emory University. He was a kindly, elderly gentleman, who must've been in his eighties. I remember that he always entered the classroom with a sports jacket draped over one arm. His favorite saying was, "Don't let them hand you that diploma until you have read such and such..." I always left his class with a feeling of intellectual inferiority, since I had not read many of the books he cited. Vietnam was a time to compensate for my ignorance. I had filled an entire footlocker of neglected classics and shipped them to Cam Ranh Bay. The selection for this month was Turgeniev's *Fathers and Sons*. Today when I picked up this book, there was an air of familiarity that I had trouble placing. Then it dawned on me that I had read all but 100 pages of this book during the humdrum of activity that preceded my leaving for Vietnam. As part of the processing for Vietnam, I had received a multitude of immunizations, such as typhoid fever, yellow fever and others. I experienced quite a febrile response to these with temperatures varying from 104-105 degrees. Elaine and I spent a few days in Carmel, California, before I was assigned to Hamilton Air Force Base for combat training. Many things that occurred during these days were blurred in my memory. Lost in this blur was my memory of having read Fathers and Sons. When I opened the book and noted the parts I had underlined and commented upon in the margins, it all began to come back. Now as Elaine commented on some of the same texts that I had underlined, I was impressed at the commonality of our thought processes and appreciations that link us.

Here are my thoughts after reading a passage from *Fathers and Sons*:

Upon arriving at adulthood, Bazarov left his two aging parents. He later returned for only a short time to visit them. His parents were old and feeble and of the serf generation that is forever rooted in the earth. After he left, his elderly father bewailed his leaving. "He's forsaken us, he's forsaken us," he began to babble. "He's forsaken us; he became bored in our company. I'm all by myself now, all by myself like a single finger!" He repeated this several times and each time thrust forth his hand with the index finger isolated from the others. It was then that his wife, Arina Vlassievna, drew near to him and, placing her gray head against his gray head, told him: "What can a body do, Vassya! A son is a slice cut off the loaf. He's the same as a falcon; he felt like it, and he came back to the nest; he felt like it, and he winged away. But you and I are like brown autumn mushrooms that grow on a hollow tree; stuck there side-by-side and never budging from our places. I alone will remain unchanged for you through all time, just as you will be for me."

This is what I wrote to Elaine:

"It is a wonderful thing to be able to write with such eloquence and with such passion. I can only imagine how magnificent it would be in the original Russian language, rather than in the English translation. While in medical school at Northwestern, I studied Russian in night school, but I never achieved the level of proficiency to read such great Russian literature. There is something about the great Russian writers, Turgeniev, Pushkin, Dostoevsky, and of course Leo Tolstoy, that triggers a sensitive nerve in my soul. Despite its Slavic origins, Russian literature does not seem nearly as foreign as does much of English, German, French, and, even some American literature. I wonder if there isn't, perhaps, a concurrence of experience between Russian literature and the old South of my heritage. The Russian aristocracy lived in a feudal system with serfs and peasants to till the soil. The Southern aristocracy also lived in a feudal system with slaves to till the soil. After the Civil War, the land remained agricultural.

The slaves and poor whites were employed or sharecropped the farms, which were owned by wealthier whites.

"But pervasive throughout both the Russian experience and the Southern experience is the wonderful language of an agrarian society of yesteryear, which is founded upon idioms, deeply rooted in the land and natural phenomena. When I read these works, I feel at home. There is a melancholy veil of tragedy that soars above both the Russian and the Southern experience. Both were worlds doomed to extinction by time and events. They were replaced by a new world of urbanization and mechanization, a world that is divorced from wind, snow and rain. The new world no longer centers on the grandeur of the seasons, migration of geese in the autumn, and the rejuvenation of life with springtime.

"The thousands that were slaves in the Old South and the tens of thousands of serfs who were nearly slaves in Russia have been replaced by tens of millions, all over the world, who are now enslaved by technology. Only in this new world, the Masters are not free. The Masters are heads of corporations, who are now enslaved by their own greed and indebtedness. All humanity of this new age is stricken with the fever of capitalism, in which some are enslaved by their acquisitions, no less than others are enslaved by their debts and poverty. The chains of ancient slavery are gone, but taking their place is something more vicious and more demoralizing. It feeds upon the Achilles' heel of human weakness. Man is never satisfied with his position, however exalted his status, or how vast his wealth. He is addicted to change, and in capitalism, the change must always be for greater wealth, more power and grasping without end.

"John Steinbeck once noted: 'It is more than a little ironic that the virtues treasured in their abstraction by nearly every culture are Honesty… Trustworthiness…Kindness…Charity and Love of fellow man. But those traits of greed, dishonesty and lack of personal integrity are rewarded, lauded and held in highest esteem for gathering wealth and power. We laud certain traits in their abstraction, but reward traits that are the direct antithesis of the laudable virtues.'

"It seems axiomatic that 'The further that mankind moves from the earth, the further he moves away from his God' (*War and Peace*). I do not feel at home in England, Germany and France, or even in America of today, except the South and West. I have a strange bond to Tolstoy's Russia that I really can't explain, except by the tenuous comparison with the Old South."

20 July 1966

Tonight, I am MOD (medical officer of the day). There are more than 12,000 Air Force personnel on this base. There are several ROK (Republic of Korea) units on the mainland that also are treated at the hospital. There is a large U.S. Army base up the peninsula, but they usually take care of their own. Our hospital (12th Air Force Hospital) is fitted for 1,000 beds, and hence, is the largest Air Force hospital in Vietnam. It is the referral hospital for all smaller hospitals and medical units throughout the country.

Tonight, I was called to the psychiatric unit, which is a large tent some distance from the air-conditioned Quonset hut hospital. The patient was a young airman who had tried to commit suicide by ingesting a large quantity of anti-malarial medication. When I arrived, he was in respiratory distress, cyanotic and gasping for breath. I told the corpsman to get him on a stretcher and to "run-like-hell" for the intensive care unit. By the time we arrived, he had practically stopped breathing and was becoming bluer by the minute. After I made a couple of unsuccessful attempts to insert an endotracheal tube, time was running out. I snatched a scalpel from a surgical tray to perform an emergency tracheostomy. Luckily, the surgeon on call arrived at that point. Working together, we finally were able to insert the endotracheal tube and connect it to a respirator. If the surgeon had been thirty seconds later, the patient would have received a tracheostomy, and I would have performed the procedure for the first time

21 July 1966
F-4C Mission
Aircraft Commander: Captain Harris
Mission Duration: 1 hr. 25 min.

Pre-flight intelligence briefing was initially fragged for a mission in Eastern Laos in Tiger Hound Country. I am flying in the No. 2 aircraft with Captain Harris. However, we are hardly airborne before being diverted to an area near Tuhy Hoa for a napalm strike against several "undefended buildings" containing Viet Cong supplies. We are vectored to the target area by the FAC. The "buildings" appear as rather ill-defined structures from the air. Hidden in a small grove of trees, they appear to be isolated from any enemy forces. We orbit the area, with each aircraft peeling off for the low altitude napalm drop. All goes without a hitch as we regroup after all ordnances have been expended. The FAC confirms satisfactory destruction of the target and we group for the flight home. Not until this time did I learn who is flying the lead aircraft. The strike leader is Colonel Chase, the 12th TFW wing commander.

On the return flight to Cam Ranh, the four aircraft receive a drill in tight formation flying. This is usually performed when a flight of four aircraft enters clouds. There is poor coordination in every maneuver as the aircraft jostle each other in alternating tight and loose formation. It is the most uncoordinated flying that I have ever observed. I am only glad that it is an exercise performed during conditions of clear weather. Either Colonel Chase has let his aerial skills slip as a result of too much desk work or the unit has never practiced together. I am very glad to feel the aircraft touch down at Cam Ranh, and even happier to climb down from the cockpit and touch terra firma.

CHAPTER 14

A Small Thing

22 July 1966

Yesterday afternoon a young 1st Lieutenant Zadra entered the flight surgeon's office carrying a small sandpiper he found injured on the beach. He asked me if I would take care of it. After all, the flight surgeon is responsible for caring for the injured and wounded. Inspecting the tiny gray and white bird, I found that the right wing tip had somehow been injured. It appeared to be in the primary stages of healing and only the delay of growth for the pinion feathers would delay its immediate return to flying and surviving. If we could keep the small creature alive until the feathers grew and matured, it should be able to return to his native habitat in the wild.

I spent a couple of hours this evening building a small cage for it. Afterward, I placed water and bread crumbs in the cage before I left for the night. The next day, I did not arrive at the office until noon because of an early flight. When I arrived, I was dismayed to find that one of the less bright corpsmen had taken the crippled bird and released him on the beach. By doing so, it marked the death of the small creature, since its ability to evade and escape predators was virtually non-existent. I was extremely vexed at this callous action by the corpsman and reprimanded him…all to the delight of the NCOs in the office, who believed that such concern over a small bird was utterly ridiculous. In the afternoon, Lieutenant Zadra returned to inquire about the wounded bird. Hearing of the bird's release, he flew into a rage. He slammed the corpsman against the wall and was on the verge of striking him.

I ordered the airman out to search for the bird. I was in disbelief that he was able to find it. But, find it he did. Unfortunately, however, despite very zealous attention to care for it, the bird refused to eat. We even used an eyedropper to force feed it with a mixture of milk and beef bouillon. But nothing worked. The tiny bird died. I believe that there were internal injuries in addition to the superficial wing injuries. But, who knows? Perhaps, he was simply not able to live in a cage. I have great empathy for that issue. I feel that I spent four years in a cage called Northwestern Medical School in Chicago, that is, until "I met a lovely girl with moonlight in her eyes."

I have previously observed Lieutenant Zadra while flying combat situations. He is generally calm and collected while flying some very hazardous combat missions. He takes tremendous pride in his flying skills and in a successful mission.

Later, I reflected on these issues. It is ironic that in a single mission, many enemy troops and civilians may be killed and mutilated by bombs, napalm, rockets and gunfire…and in the context of "war" this is considered both commendable and admirable. These atrocities are the language and the music of war in every age and every country. Men are decorated by such success. And, yet…

The mistreatment of a tiny, helpless bird is sufficient to completely shake the self-composure of this young warrior. I, too, felt as strongly as he. It is indeed remarkable that the human creature can reconcile such paradoxical philosophies within the same sphere of human reasoning. I have no answer, except to quote from the conversation of Jeremy and the Spider: "Life is funny," said Jeremy. "As compared to what?" said the Spider.

24 July 1966

Comments to Elaine after reading, *Absalom, Absalom!* By William Faulkner:

"After reading this, I realize now what you meant when you said that after reading Faulkner, you could more readily appreciate me and my family. The only things that I have previously read by him were several humorous short stories. But, now, his writings bring things to my memory that have been long forgotten or suppressed. A couple of times, a rather spooky feeling swept over me as I read it. His writings contain so much of the undercurrents that course through the subconsciousness of a person descending from the Old South. Of course, I am interpreting things in light of experiences with my own family—but so much of it is applicable that I have to force myself to continue reading. It is too close to home. I feel as if I were confronting ghosts of my own past. Of course, most of this is a result of my vivid imagination, combined with my family genealogy. As I read, I found myself attempting to block out my background, lest I become so ensnarled in the web of the past that I become incapable of dealing with the present or of facing the future. When I was growing up, I never considered the South to have a history that is so distinct or unique from the rest of the country, but it does. I'm glad that you enjoyed reading the book, but without an extensive experience with the innuendos and subtleties of Southern customs, I think it would be difficult reading.

"The boredom here is phenomenal. I certainly agree with Winston Churchill's statement that "wars are eternities of boredom, interspersed with moments of stark terror." It doesn't strike me as hard as it does some of the others, since I have an opportunity to read books that I have long treasured. Bill Simmons apparently doesn't care to read and I've never seen him pick up a book since I've been here. He spends most of his time at the officers club drinking with his squadron, and in his off moments, he is obsessed with the squadron softball game. On the other hand, Al Aleckna could easily be a standup comic, but most of his off hours are spent reading and studying French. It is a pleasure to be here with Al since he has a broad knowledge base and can discuss nearly any topic that is raised. In the case of Bill, however, if you ask him any question beyond baseball or medicine, he usually responds with a blank look on his face, and then tries to change the subject back to baseball."

A big battle called Operation Hastings is taking place near the demilitarized zone (DMZ) between North and South Vietnam. Apparently 8,000-10,000 North Vietnamese Army troops (representing an entire division) are involved in this battle. The DMZ was established by international agreement to be a fifteen-mile swath of "No Man's Land" between the two countries a few miles south of the 17th Parallel. Taking advantage of its neutral status, the Viet Cong have been using it as a staging area from which to attack South Vietnam. I strongly believe that our Cam Ranh aircraft will participate in this operation.

There is a regulation stating in effect that anyone flying twenty combat missions over North Vietnam will have one month deducted from his one-year tour of duty. If our aircraft and pilots participate in this operation, they will qualify for this exclusion since, technically, they will be flying over North Vietnam. To my knowledge, this policy does not apply to doctors (i.e. flight surgeons) who fly combat missions over North Vietnam.

First Mission over North Vietnam

24 July 1966

F-4C Mission Aircraft Commander: Major Sutherland

Mission Duration: 1 hr 55 min.

Pre-flight intelligence briefing confirms that our target is a truck depot in the DMZ. This is my first flight over North Vietnam. Intelligence reports that there is a division of 7,000-10,000 Viet Cong in this region. These are being countered by the U.S. Marines in Operation Hastings. Prior to this flight, we are given an unusually thorough intelligence briefing on the anti-aircraft, automatic weapons and surface-to-air missiles stationed around the area. In the event of an attack by North Vietnamese MIGs, we will have to utilize our superior speed to escape, while at the same time, calling in aid from other Air Force or Navy fighters. This is necessary because our heavy bomb load does not permit us to carry either air-to-air missiles (such as Side-Winder or Sparrow missiles), or our midline externally mounted Gatling gun.

Despite all of these warnings and precautions from intelligence, the mission is actually a bit dull. This is the coastal plain region. The FAC marks the target in an unobstructed group of trees. We dropped our 500-pound all-purpose bombs in ripple ("ripple" means that all bombs were dropped in one pass instead of one at a time in different passes). We have been cautioned about making more than one pass on the target since this increases our chances of drawing anti-aircraft fire. We see none of this activity, however. Had it not been for the intrigue of "flying over enemy territory," it would have been a rather ordinary and somewhat dull mission. The psychological effect, however, has been remarkable. After the mission, several of the pilots admitted that they had been slightly nervous about the mission. This was the second day that Cam Ranh Phantoms had participated in flights over North Vietnam. I keep hoping that with nineteen more of these missions, I might be able to go home a month early. After 100 missions of this type, you can return to the United States, regardless of your original assignment time.

A more sanguine statement about "flying over enemy territory" is that any flight, anywhere in Vietnam, may be described as "over enemy territory."

26 July 1966

Overstaffing seems to be the order of the day over here. We expect to get a new flight surgeon within the next two weeks. I have no idea what he will do. We only have two offices and there is barely enough work for one to two people. If the weather were more favorable, I would go to the beach, but the milder Western Monsoon brings a drizzle of rain for most of the day. I understand that the Western Monsoons let up in late August. In early September, the real monsoons sweep in from the East with their deluging rains.

At Cam Ranh Bay the first expeditionary airfield was constructed by a private contractor—Raymond, Morrison-Knudsen—in 1965, using laborers from South Korea. The runways continue to be maintained by them. Recently, the laborers have been on strike. The issues seem relatively minor, such as when meals are to be served, etc.; they recently traced the problems to four or five Korean agitators. The Korean ambassador to Vietnam was brought in to investigate the problems and issues. The investigation revealed that these four or five agitators were Communist inspired. The workers were deported back to South Korea; however, I doubt that they will actually make it back to Korea. They are sure to be killed along the way. The South Korean troops/Marines are extremely tough and the Viet Cong are terrified of them. With few exceptions, they never take prisoners. If they do capture two to three Viet Cong, they question them by taking them aloft in a helicopter. Interrogation begins while airborne. If the first prisoner doesn't answer their questions, they simply push him out of the helicopter and bring up the second man. By the time the third man is questioned, he is usually ready to talk.

The ROK (Republic Of Korea) Marines were the first troops to arrive at the Cam Ranh Peninsula, and they cleared the area of Viet Cong. I have heard from several independent sources that they captured two Viet Cong during the first few days of operation and skinned them both alive to set an example. The local villagers are terrified of them. They will grab any Vietnamese woman off the street and rape her with no qualms. They are very friendly and respectful to American G.I.s. In fact, they have formed a combo that plays popular dance music at the Officers Club one to two nights a week. They are really quite good...far better than any American musical groups that I've heard.

Of course, the Koreans are not the only brutal troops in this war. A U.S. Marine colonel leading a regiment in the Central Highlands offered $25 to any man who killed a Viet Cong with a hatchet. The regiment became known as the "Hatchet Brigade." Unfortunately, they always kill the Viet Cong with gunfire and that doesn't count. Finally, they caught some poor bastard (Viet Cong) in a swamp and about fifty men converged on him. When they emerged, they were carrying his head to present to the colonel. It just so happened that several news correspondents were embedded with the troops. After they finished vomiting all the way to their typewriters, their stories were sent out to the major wire services. This resulted in a minor revolution in the higher military echelons to keep this type of news away from the American public. It was finally hushed up. But regardless of how much it is covered up, this is the war in Vietnam today, and it differs little from other wars in other ages. The veneer of civilization is very thin. But lest non-participants judge the participants too harshly, who knows what he or she would do when subjected to comparable circumstances on a regular basis, from day to day?

This is not written as an apologia for the atrocities of war, but simply as a statement of conditions that impact the thinking of any human involved in the chaos that attends all wars. Actually, I am encouraged, in the midst of this eternal instability; I have found stability in two irrefutable facts:

In the morning at Cam Ranh Bay, the sand blows from east to west... in the afternoon, the sand blows from west to east.

26 July 1966
F-4C Mission
Aircraft Commander: Major Chico Solis
Mission Duration: 1 hr. 40 min.

This mission was originally fragged for a target approximately 320 miles northwest of Hue. Shortly after takeoff, because of weather conditions, we are diverted to support an operation approximately twenty miles northwest of Saigon. The "friendlies" have evidently trapped a regiment of Viet Cong in several patches of forest area, scattered over an immense swampland of wilderness and rice paddies. We are armed with a total of four 250-pound all-purpose bombs and napalm. To complicate matters, there is a very strong 25-30 knot crosswind and the "friendlies" are only a few hundred meters from the enemy. It is extremely difficult to place the bombs on the pinpoint target marked by the FAC. The bomb strikes are slightly off, but the napalm is dead center and accomplishes the objective.

No significant ground fire is encountered. The return flight to Cam Ranh is relatively non-eventful.

I note that Major Solis is a bit quieter than usual on the return to Cam Ranh. Before this flight, I was informed that on an earlier napalm strike, his plane had been struck by ground fire. One bullet had struck his cockpit at such an angle that had it not been for an intervening small temperature control box, he would have been shot through the chest. Upon hearing this, my thoughts, more and more, have been occupied with how to fly the aircraft from my back seat position—or at least how to land it. If I know that the aircraft commander is wounded, it will be a choice of my landing the aircraft or ejecting from the aircraft. If the aircraft is flyable, I could not abandon him. I began to focus entirely on taking control of the aircraft if the aircraft commander is incapacitated.

Our return to Cam Ranh is uneventful, but my subconscious continues to dwell on this issue.

27 July 1966
F-4C Mission
Aircraft Commander: Lt. Col. Jack Daugherty, Commander,
391st TFS
Mission Duration: 1 hr. 50 min.

This is my second mission into a region of the DMZ known as "Talley Ho." It counts as a combat mission over North Vietnam. Our flight consists of the usual four aircraft with call signs Hammer 41, Hammer 42, Hammer 43 and Hammer 44. Hammer 41 and Hammer 42 each carry four 250-pound, low-drag bombs plus the Gatling gun in the midline, under the fuselage. Hammer 43 and Hammer 44 carry two napalm canisters each. To approach our target, we penetrate approximately five miles into the coastal plain region of North Vietnam. Our mission was originally fragged to demolish several fuel storage tanks and to saturate a group of adjacent trees with bombs. Under the cover of these trees are food (rice) storage areas that are invisible from the air.

I am flying in the lead aircraft, Hammer 41. We initiated a steep dive bomb attack of approximately 700 mph from an altitude of 4,500-5,000 feet, with bomb release at 1,500 feet. There is a violent explosion that jars the aircraft as we climb out. This is more than expected simply from the bomb blasts. It is followed by two to three more explosions, with flames shooting at least 1,000 feet into the air. These secondary explosions confirm that we have hit something volatile, such as gasoline storage tanks.

As we regroup, after expending our ordnance, our FAC radios that we have successfully destroyed the target area. No enemy has been seen, but the bombing has been precise and on target...all in all, a successful mission.

27 July 1966

Letter to Elaine

"Al returns from Binh Tuy on Saturday and I must go down there for two weeks to fill our commitment. If you have that map of Vietnam, follow the easternmost branch of the Mekong River up from its entrance into the South China Sea. At this location is a town of Can Tho, which should be on the map. Binh Tuy is approximately ten to twelve miles upstream from Can Tho. I needn't conceal the fact that this assignment won't be as fine as Cam Ranh, but I can tolerate anything for two weeks. I am very impressed with Colonel Mack. He received orders from 7th Air Force in Saigon to send a flight surgeon to Binh Tuy for sixty-nine days. He refused and said that he would accept only four weeks and that he would split this between two men. He didn't want any single person to take more than two weeks off for this duty. Bill Simmons is chief of aviation medicine so he was excluded. This temporary duty therefore falls to Al and me. This has significance for me in the future. I am senior in rank to Al and will inherit the position of chief of aviation medicine when Bill rotates to his next assignment. Also, with new flight surgeons arriving at Cam Ranh, they will be more susceptible to temporary duties elsewhere than I. When I am chief, there will be very little chance of transfer from Cam Ranh.

"Keep in mind that Binh Tuy is more remote than Cam Ranh, and therefore the mail will be delayed both in my sending and your receiving (and vice versa).

"Today a doctor from the South Beach Area of Cam Ranh came by the office. South Beach Area is the U.S. Army Dispensary and not Air Force. He was going on his R&R and Cam Ranh is the major airport for debarkation in Vietnam. During medical school at Louisiana State University, he was Tom Robinson's lab partner. As you recall, Tom was one of my closest friends during internship at Wilford Hall. This man is single and a really fine person. I was very impressed that he is far above average for a physician. He was in general practice in San Francisco when he was drafted. He is so thoroughly versed in the arts and culture of the Orient that he put me to shame. He is extremely masculine, but he differs from most single doctors (and many married doctors) that I have encountered by not being obsessed with the flesh pot activities on his R&R and local leaves in country.

"I am more and more impressed by two types of single doctors. Most of them leave you in no doubt. They are the insecure, inadequate personality types. The others are exceptionally fine men whose sense of value and ethics will not allow them to settle for anything short of their ideals. They are anxious to get married, but only to the right person, and not simply to satisfy society or be a salve for their loneliness. I only spoke to this man for about twenty minutes, but I got that opinion of him. When I think of our relationship, my thoughts are, 'There, but for the grace of God go I.' As I spoke to him, I felt a simpatico that I haven't experienced with many married physicians.

"When I think of places for us to practice, my mind is still open, but there are definite advantages in Texas. There are endless hours of good weather for flying. I dream of our hill that overlooks the lakes and think how wonderful it would be for us to own a plane and look down on the peaceful green depths of our lost canyon. I dream of the time when we can forget that there was a place called Vietnam, a place where the air is filled with the constant drone of helicopters, the roar of jets, the pounding of artillery and men dying in muddy foxholes. I dream of nights that smell of honeysuckle and jasmine, when the silence is broken only by the melancholy whistle of a Whip-poor-will or the serenade of a mockingbird at midnight. With you I am the wealthiest and happiest man on earth. Without you, if I possess all the wealth in the world, I am poverty-stricken."

28 July 1966
Letter to Elaine

"For some reason lately our planes have been carrying full bomb loads, napalm and anti-personnel weapons. This is in stark contrast to recent times when an aircraft would take off with two 250-pound bombs for a mission. This is hardly the equivalent of two hand grenades. This armament is a pittance of the optimum ordnance for this aircraft. I understand that McNamara has argued that there is no bomb shortage. When aircraft take off, armed with ordnance that a foot soldier could carry, there is an obvious problem. Perhaps it is rooted in the competition between the Air Force and the Navy. Both have inadequate ordnance. Therefore, each must compete with the other in the number of sorties. As a result all air-craft are under-armed, but must continue to fly in order to compete."

28 July 1966
F-4C Mission
Aircraft Commander: Major Sutherland
Mission Duration: 1 hr. 40 min.

Today's target is about twenty-five miles southwest of Quang Ngai. Preflight intelligence notes that this is a small, fortified village reported to be an ammunition storage area. Hammer 31 and Hammer 32 aircraft are each armed with six 250-pound low-drag bombs, while Hammer 33 and Hammer 34 are armed with a mix of napalm and four 750-pound anti-per-sonnel weapon canisters, or cluster bomb units (CBUs). As we approach the target area, contact with the FAC is established. We dive bomb and destroy twelve to fifteen hooches and one gun emplacement. There are multiple secondary explosions as we pull off target, which indicates that our bombs, CBUs and napalm have struck ammunition and arms storage areas. As we scream through the target area at nearly 700 mph, there is no indication that we are being fired upon. However, the FAC, with a speed of 120-125 mph was struck several times by machine gun and small arms fire. No injuries were incurred, however, and the flight back to Cam Ranh was relatively uneventful.

29 July 1966

Tonight I am MOD. Tomorrow morning I leave for Binh Tuy. I have spent nearly an hour tonight with a patient, a twenty-seven-year-old air-man who has been married for six years and has four children. Recent letters from his wife expound upon her infidelity…going into great detail as to her affair with another man. He has been informed that he can't obtain a curtailment in his tour, which extends for an additional four months. He is so distressed that he is unable to eat or sleep.

What can I tell him? As far as I am concerned, a man with this problem is no different than a person who has had a death in his family. There are hundreds of other men in the same position. War destroys marriages no less than it destroys lives on the battlefield. This is certainly one of the largest psychiatric problems here. I saw the opposite end of the spectrum when I was stationed at Bergstrom. These were wives who admitted infidelity while their husbands were in Vietnam. As the impartial observer, I realize that there are two sides to every story. However, it goes against my innate sense of personal integrity for a woman to show infidelity to a man who is in a combat zone. It is to kick a person when he is down. I feel the same for the men over here who show infidelity to their wives. It is common for them to visit the office requesting a blood test for sexually transmitted diseases before returning home. They are concerned about transmitting syphilis to their wives. These problems are not simply confined to the lower ranks of airmen. My only conclusion is that these are common weaknesses and strengths of the human species. It is no solution to be judgmental. The pressure of daily life and events is sufficient to elicit these problems. People who are completely happy with their relationships are usually faithful to their spouses. If there are subliminal problems in relationships, the stress of circumstances and the absence of spouse may be sufficient to strain any ties of personal loyalty. Perhaps, these actions are an example of "any port in a storm."

29 July 1966

F-4C Mission

Aircraft Commander: Maj. Chico Solis

Mission Duration: 1 hr. 35 min.

After receiving the usual preflight intelligence briefing, we take off to form a flight of three aircraft. Major Solis and I are in the lead aircraft of Hammer 31. Our ordinance consists of four 750-pound CBUs. Cluster munitions are air-dropped or ground-launched explosive weapons that eject smaller munitions: a cluster of bomblets. They have much the same effect as multiple hand grenades. The most common types are designed to kill enemy personnel and destroy vehicles. Some of these "bomblets" are loaded with napalm, and thus offer a more controlled delivery of napalm. The other two aircraft carried six 250-pound low-drag bombs.

Our target is nested in a jungle valley. In this area, the jungle floor lies 200-300 feet beneath the treetops. In addition to this jungle climax growth of towering trees, there are multiple secondary canopies. All of these canopies offer protection for our target. Intelligence reports that it consists of several buildings for the storage of rice. The bombs have a chance of penetrating this foliage, but napalm isn't practical since it invariably explodes in the uppermost treetops and usually does no more damage than to burn out the upper canopy.

On approach to the target area, the FAC marks the target area with a Willie Pete. We drop the CBUs and bombs on his direction. Needless to say, no one of our strike force sees the target or any other sign of the enemy. After we have pulled off target, the FAC radios that our ordnance was exactly on target. One building has been completely demolished, but fallen trees obscure further surveillance of the area.

As I reflect on this mission after we return to Cam Ranh, the absurdity of this war and the futility of our efforts scream out. There are thousands of square miles of jungle like this in Vietnam. The enemy is ubiquitous and lives in these jungles like fish swim in the ocean. How many shrubs, trees, caves and other sequestrations are available to hide munitions, rice and all other instruments of war? To send three of the most sophisticated aircraft in the world with six highly skilled pilots on a bombing mission, during which each bomb costs $10,000-$14,000, is an exercise in futility. The ordnance dropped on this single mission is equal to $400,000-$500,000. This does not include the expense of operating the aircraft and the enormous infrastructure that coordinated this one small mission. Are a few bags of rice worth this? Or, more pertinent is the question, "Can the U.S. or any country afford to spend millions of dollars on these types of targets?"

This is the home of the enemy, no less than North America was home to the American Colonies. It was said of the American Revolution against England that the Colonists did not have to win the Revolution; they only had to not lose it.

The flight back to Cam Ranh offered some reprieve from the above issues of war. Major Solis turns the aircraft over to me to fly back to base. The weather at Cam Ranh is less than one-mile visibility with a ceiling of 1,000 feet. Under these conditions we made a ground controlled approach for landing. This is the first GCA that I have tried to fly in the Phantom.

In a ground-controlled approach air-traffic controllers guide aircraft to a safe landing in adverse weather conditions based on radar images. Most commonly, a GCA uses information from a precision approach radar (PAR), for precision approaches with vertical, glide path guidance. Technically, the term GCA applies specifically to the precision radar approach with glide path guidance. GCA requires close communication between air traffic controllers and pilots.

The air traffic controllers determine the precise course and altitude of approaching aircraft, then provide verbal instructions by radio to the pilots to guide them to a landing. Both rate of descent (glide path) and heading (course) corrections are necessary to follow the correct approach path.

Two tracks are displayed on the GCA or PAR scope: Azimuth, showing the aircraft's position relative to the extended runway centerline, and Elevation, showing vertical position relative to the ideal glide path.

By following both tracks, a landing aircraft will arrive precisely over the runway's touchdown zone. Controllers issue position information and/ or correction for both of them at least every five seconds. The guidance is stopped over the approximate touchdown point. However, to continue the approach to a landing, pilots must be able to see the runway environment before reaching the published "decision height," usually 200-400 feet above the runway touchdown zone and one-quarter to three-quarter miles from the touchdown point (the published minimum visibility and decision height vary depending upon approach and runway lighting, obstacles in the approach corridor, type of aircraft, and other factors).

Because of its labor-intensive nature – one GCA controller is normally required for each aircraft on final approach – and with the advent of new technology, GCAs are no longer in widespread use at civilian airports, and are being discontinued at many military bases.

The Phantom is designed for hypersonic speeds. It begins to wallow and be a bit unruly to handle at landing speeds of 140 mph. Attempting to maintain a strict heading while controlling my rate of descent by GCA exceeded my capabilities. I gladly turned the stick back over to Major Solis. I suppose I could excuse my deficiency by noting the poor visibility from the back seat cockpit. But, GCA is not a visual approach. It requires control of the airplane and compliance with instrument flight rules. However, I am very grateful to Major Solis for allowing me another chance to try my skills.

Later today, I had opportunity to review the medical records of Major Solis. What attracted my attention were the letters of commendation from previous commanding officers concerning his flying abilities. Every letter stated that without qualification, Major Solis is a one-in-a-million pilot. I certainly agree. This man lives to fly. Flight pay holds no sway with him—flying is his life. His persona is such that even a brief association with him arouses a very deep respect from his peers. He has treated me with the utmost courtesy, respect and friendship. I only hope that my neophyte status is not a burden for him on the missions that we share.

CHAPTER 15

Binh Tuy

30 July 1966

Before leaving for my temporary duty at Can Tho, I had a short session with the hospital commander, Colonel Mack. During the briefing, Colonel Mack informs me that Binh Tuy is a small Vietnamese outpost in the middle of the Vietnam Delta region, which is a treacherous miasma of endless swamps, waterways, rice paddies…all of which is infested with Viet Cong who delight in killing Americans. The last mortar attack on the base was two weeks ago. Primary control of the base is held by the Vietnamese Air Force. In his usual jocular manner, he said, "Guy, you will have a wonderful opportunity at this base to get your ass shot off!"

My droll reply was simply, "I can hardly wait…" He roared with laughter. I truly love this man! He is not the typical medical doctor. He is primarily a pilot with a doctorate degree in medicine. He flew P-51s during World War II. After the war, he went to medical school and rejoined the Air Force, but now serves as a physician and commander of the 12th Air

Force Hospital. When he arrived at Cam Ranh, there was instant rapport between the two of us. If I had to choose a surrogate father or Godfather, I would choose him. In reviewing these notes so many years later, my affection for this man continues to increase with each passing year.

I had duty as MOD last night and obtained about two hours of sleep between cases. At 1:15 p.m., I departed Cam Ranh in an Army U-8 aircraft. This is the militarized, sophisticated version of a Beechcraft Duke, and is standard air taxi for higher brass in this theater. I was lucky to get the flight. In fact, it was truly luxurious…soft seats, smooth flying and refreshments en route…Fat City!

When we arrived at Tan Son Nhut field in Saigon, it was raining in torrents. Since we landed at the Army end of the base, I needed to catch the next plane to Binh Tuy from the Air Force side of the field. I walked a quarter-mile before catching a ride the remaining distance to Air Force Base Operations. To my dismay, I found that I had just missed the last flight out and would have to wait until the next flight at 9 tomorrow morning. I caught a military bus to the base officers quarters (BOQ) to spend the night. Finally, I checked in for my overnight lodging. Ironically, my quarters were the same as those of the first night of my arrival in Vietnam.

This time it is different, however. This time, I am dressed like Wyatt Earp at the O.K. Corral, with pistols strapped to my waist and M-16 rifle in hand. With a small bandolier of ammunition across my shoulders, I feel more like a small boy who has been playing cowboys and Indians, but who must now come in out of the rain. My appearance must have been more like a wet rat than an American Fighting Man, wielding Death and Destruction.

My Australian style go-to-hell bush hat is supposed to keep the rain and sun out, but it only contributes to my buckaroo appearance…Ha!

The rain continues to fall in buckets all night, and having no desire to wade through mud to catch a bus going two to three miles to the Officers Club, I forfeit dinner in favor of sleep. There is a lullaby of background noise all night. The thump of mortars and boom of heavy artillery pound in the distance. I have been informed that there are a number of airstrikes taking place twenty to twenty-five miles northeast of Saigon. Supposedly, they have two to three Viet Cong regiments boxed into a corner. I couldn't help but wonder if some of the aircraft aren't from Cam Ranh. Occasionally, the night sky will flare up brightly at the place of destruction. The Air Force Base of Tan Son Nhut lives in constant fear of a serious, sustained mortar attack and tonight is no different. Rumors of countless attacks circulate freely, but tonight nothing lends credence to the rumor mill. All things considered, I feel very fortunate to have found space to bunk for the night. The quarters are spotlessly clean and are near the flight line for tomorrow morning's flight. Had the quarters not been available, the only other option would have been a hotel in Saigon. Quite frankly, I think that I would have slept on the floor in Base Operations before going into Saigon at night.

The bunk above me is occupied by an Australian Marine about my age. He is a most pleasant person. (Of course, I've never met anyone from Australia who wasn't pleasant.) He has been fighting in the jungle for the past year and tomorrow is going home to Sidney. He is nearly euphoric at the thought of leaving! He has a new baby daughter he has never seen.

31 July 1966

After a large breakfast at the Officers Club, and after waiting several hours at the Tan Son Nhut airport, I finally catch a C-123 flight to Binh Tuy at 11 a.m. By the way, this one flight by a C-123 is the only daily connection with the outside world. This is an enormous change from Cam Ranh, where in-country and international flights came and went in swarms on a daily basis, 24/7.

I have been assigned here as flight surgeon for two weeks. The entire region has been a frequent site for air strikes against a large endogenous population of Viet Cong. Recently, there was significant action here, and one of the local airfields was mortared by the enemy. This was reported in the military newspaper Stars and Stripes.

1 August 1966

A narrow single-lane road connects the base of Binh Tuy with Can Tho City. The surface of the road is hard packed with seashells, and God knows what else. The shoulders of the road are lined on both sides by impenetrable swamps and marshes of elephant grass. During daylight hours, this road is the epitome of capitalistic commerce, with menageries of Jeeps and trucks, chaotically mingling with wagons drawn by water buffalo and punctuated by weaving bicycles, rickshaws and pedestrians... all jockeying for position and the right of way. A rich cacophony of honking horns, whistling drivers, groaning water buffaloes, cackling chickens, quacking ducks and squealing pigs, mingles with sputtering engines and curses of all, to create a happy maelstrom of noisy commerce. The intersections are few, but each is filled with pedestrians hawking their wares at any who pass.

But toward twilight, a curtain is drawn on this commercial stage. As if orchestrated by a single stroke of the conductor's baton, the road clears of this hurly-burly daylight scenario. As night descends, the stage changes, and the actors may or may not be the same. The narrow road sheds it cloak of commerce and becomes the domain of the Viet Cong. Every turn in the road and every clump of elephant grass provides cover for an ambush.

It is probable that the characters of this drama simply change dress. The same friendly villagers who offered to sell fish to the wayfarer during daylight hours have cloaked themselves in black uniforms and armed them-selves with a multitude of weapons that include recoilless rifles, machetes and crude gasoline-wicked hand grenades (Molotov cocktails); attack the innocent traveler in wolf packs. The same elderly peasant woman, who smiled as she offered to sell you a tiny kimono-clad doll for 100 piastres, may now quietly slit your throat or slip a live hand-grenade into your pack or jacket pocket.

But, it is also valid to ask another question. Are we, who expect enemy encounters, missing the entire point? Perhaps those persons that we, in our paranoia, interpret as "enemy" or guerrilla forces are merely brigands that exist in every war-torn country that has been invaded by alien troops and hope to profit by raiding the rich foreigners? Perhaps these are simply poor individuals, spawned by generations of war and poverty, who struggle to survive in the chaos of war, and who are unrelated to guerrilla Communist forces or have any knowledge of political doctrines?

I find it virtually impossible to be both an observer and a participant in this conflict/war without drawing parallels between this war in Vietnam and that of the American Revolution when the colonies allied themselves against the tyranny of Great Britain. The average British soldier would have viewed passage through backwoods America with the same trepidation as U.S. military personnel now regard passage between Canh Tho and Binh Tuy. When a foreigner fears animosity of citizens in a region, one must question the righteousness of the foreigner's presence. Mao Tse-tung notes that the people are the ocean in which the guerrilla swims.

Allegiance of the common man and woman, of any country, to any cause is evidence that an alien military force is a "foreign body" to be expelled. Regardless of how different their ideas of government may be compared to ours, a democracy is determined by the will of the population.

The war in Vietnam is a civil war as well as a war of aggression from Communist North Vietnam. For many years, the American Revolution was a civil war between Tory Loyalists to the throne of England who were pitted against the population of Patriots, who wished independence. Not until excessive brutality from British forces impinged on Loyalists, Neutrals and Patriots did the people unite against the throne of England.

From my experience so far in South Vietnam, the average peasant has little loyalty to any government. He wishes only to be left alone with his water buffalo to grow rice for his family and to live without fear of oppression from any quarter.

Perhaps the type of government is less important to the average person than the intensity of intrusion of that government on the common man. I frequently find myself recalling the words of Thomas Jefferson about the American people during the American Revolution:

"One third of the people are for us.

One third of the people are against us.

And, the other third don't give a damn."

The first day I arrived in this war-torn country, I noted in my journal how much it reminded me of the American Revolution. I also noted one major difference. This time, we are the British.

The Can Tho Region is composed of a complex network of rivers and canals, in which the Hau River is considered to be the primary benefactor of the region. Yearly flooding of the Hau deposits large quantities of alluvia on the rice fields. This fact alone has earned Can Tho the title of "the green lungs of the Mekong Delta."

Mother Nature has positioned the marshy Lung Ngoc Hoang mangrove forest in a favorable position to escape the clutches of the occasionally threatening Hau River. This region and the waters near Bac Lieu also offer shelter for the many types of wildlife that thrive here. The ongoing conflict between mankind and the other creatures of Mother Nature is particularly prominent in these marshes. The terrains in which fish, crabs, tortoises, yellow boas and other snakes, seek their seasonal shelter are the same places where wartime troops often seek strategic refuge.

Cần Thơ's climate is tropical and monsoonal with two seasons: rainy, from May to November; and dry, from December to April. Average annual humidity is 83%, rainfall 1,635 mm and temperature 27 °C. The province is endowed with sunshine all year round as well as a high humidity. It is blessed by the fact that few storms hit the province.

Its location on the Bassac River makes Can Tho an ideal base from which naval forces can operate against Viet Cong supply traffic on surrounding waterways.

Another attractive feature of Can Tho City is its accessibility to logistic vessels deployed in the South China Sea. Before the current involvement of U.S. Naval Forces, there was an existing Vietnamese Navy installation here. The current favorable location makes it an ideal choice to accommodate the first increment of the U.S. River Patrol Force to be deployed here. For these reasons, Can Tho, as the largest city west of Saigon, serves as the headquarters for key Vietnamese naval and military commands.

Newspapers are a precious commodity here. The Stars and Stripes is our main source of news, just as it was during World War II and Korea. But even that is limited to one paper for every ten men on base, and it is usually three to four days old by the time you read it. Today I received a letter from Al Aleckna at Cam Ranh Bay about some paperwork he had forgotten. It took more than five days for the letter to be transmitted "in country" from Cam Ranh.

Elaine and I are reading *Uncle Tom's Cabin* by Harriet Beecher Stowe since neither of us has read it before (despite having known of its historical significance from high school and college). It represents a literary style from an earlier era. It is remarkable for its melodramatic and simplistic comparison to modern style and sophistication. But everything is an opportunity to learn. The term "Jim Crow" is the name of a quadroon boy in the book. A quadroon is the offspring of a Mulatto and a white parent; a person who is one-quarter black. I didn't know this.

Psychological warfare at Binh Tuy

Begun in 1963 and administered by the Joint United States Public Affairs Office after its formation in 1965, the Chieu Hoi Campaign resulted in billions of leaflets, millions of posters, magazines, and leaflets. It also produced thousands of hours of loudspeaker exhortations to encourage Viet Cong defection. The program is said to have been the largest propaganda campaign in history.

In addition to offering amnesty and good treatment, monetary rewards are offered and paid to defectors who turn in weapons. Rewards are offered to third parties who induce Viet Cong to defect, with special bonuses for mass defections.

There are a number of aircraft from Binh Tuy devoted to psychological warfare. The 14th Air Commando Wing was thus created in March 1966.

During the early days of the program, the psychological warfare C-47s flew only night missions. These were called "harassment" missions, during which the unarmed psychological warfare C-47s were escorted by an AC-47, equipped with three 7.62-mm mini-guns. The AC-47 instilled terror in the Viet Cong. The report of a defector speaks of "strict orders never to shoot a psychological warfare aircraft, because most of the time a 'gunship' will soon come to its rescue..." Each "PSYOP" mission is prepared with the cooperation of the psychological warfare staff of the U.S. Army. Each mission has stated themes and targets with provision of pre-recorded tapes for the Air Force units to broadcast. The impact of these messages was also reinforced by the "Earlyword" process, invented by Maj. Richard M.

Rowland. Earlyword consists of connecting the radio to the loudspeakers of the plane. These devices permit the immediate broadcasting of messages or statements made on the ground by Viet Cong deserters. During the whole Vietnamese conflict, the American military authorities had widely supported these actions. The program was found to be economical from a budgetary point of view and profitable for gathering information. Official reports in 1967 noted 24,000 surrenders, thanks to the common efforts of both leaflets and loudspeaker propaganda.

The Helio U-10 is frequently utilized to drop propaganda leaflets and to broadcast propaganda to the Viet Cong in the jungle below. Fitted with very powerful loud speakers, they play music to attract attention as they announce to large areas the wondrous alliance between the United States and the Republic of South Vietnam. They also announce the evils of the Viet Cong. While this acoustic tsunami sweeps over the terrain below, propaganda leaflets, in the tens of thousands, flutter out behind the aircraft. These leaflets praise the virtues of our side and damn the evils of the enemy. In this agrarian, non-technological country, these are frequently the only messages received by the common man from the outside world to contrast with the Viet Cong who invade their villages. Indoctrination of these rural people by fanatical Viet Cong and North Vietnamese personnel has been so pervasive that few local Vietnamese have ever heard any other side of the story.

Recently several Viet Cong prisoners were captured not far from this base. During the course of interrogation, they were asked about their reactions to the propaganda broadcasts and leaflets dropped. They stated that when these planes fly over, their superiors had instructed them to cover their ears and shout.

Of course the Viet Cong in this region are not so nearly well supplied and reinforced as those in the Central Highlands. Viet Cong from these latter regions are frequently reinforced through Cambodia and Laos, whereas the Viet Cong in the Delta region have been forced to utilize their own resources to a greater extent. Perhaps the strain is beginning to tell.

6 August 1966

Today is a BIG DAY! My tour of duty at Binh Tuy is half completed.

On this hallmark day, I begin to reflect on the situation at Binh Tuy. A summary description reveals it to be no more than a small fortress surrounded by a huge jungle swampland infested by the enemy. It is impossible to escape the confines of the small base without being challenged, either by our own security guards or shot by the enemy. Any desire to explore the adjacent countryside is squelched by the reality that it would be insane to trespass beyond the confines, even if it were not prohibited. I recall how the British and French had prisons for their most desperate criminals that were simply placed in the midst of dense jungles, filled with fierce natives. There were no walls or barbed wire fences around these prisons; they were not required since no man would dare trespass into the boundless jungle-swamp and hope to live. In all truth, how does this differ from that prison?

My duty schedule from 8-10 a.m. consists of only a few patients for sick call. That's it. The remainder of the day I stare at the wall, walk in circles like a dog looking for a place to take a dump, or re-read for the umpteenth time the few books that I brought with me. Honestly, my eyes are just about to go out from reading.

This evening, I propped a chair outside the door of my hooch to watch three shrews catching insects by the dim light. I remember studying them at Emory and have an outdated zoology text for reference. Shrews are small, mouse-like mammals of the family Soricidae, class Insectivora. They have large cutting, or incisor teeth, similar to those of a mouse. But unlike a mouse (which is a rodent and thus has teeth that continually grow), the teeth of shrews must last a lifetime. Also, their snout is narrower and more pointed than that of a mouse. Shrews are more primitive (i.e., with an older evolutionary lineage) than most mammals as evidenced by the presence of a cloaca. This is an external opening into which both the genital and urinary tracts empty. Reptiles, from which mammals evolved, also have a cloaca.

Shrews digest their food very rapidly, so quickly, in fact, that much of it is not fully digested. Consequently, some shrews re-eat their feces, to capture the undigested nutrients. Having a large surface/volume ratio, and a very high metabolic rate, shrews must eat almost continuously to obtain enough energy to support themselves. This is particularly true for the smallest species. They are approximately 8 inches long and can consume enormous quantities of insects. I remember reading somewhere that their basal metabolic rate is so high that they must consume a quantity of insects equal to their total body weight several times an hour.

Shrews have poor vision and therefore rely more on smell, touch and hearing to avoid their enemies. Sound is very important in the life of shrews. Squeaks, squeals, and high-pitched clicks are made on various occasions. For the most part, though, shrews of the same species avoid each other, except at mating time. Their territories rarely overlap, and if they meet, they chitter loudly at each other until one gives way. Some shrews can apparently use their high-pitches squeaks as a kind of sonar; the noises echo back from objects, helping the shrews to define their local environment. Many shrew sounds are so high pitched they cannot be detected by human ears.

Some shrews have poison in their salivary glands that allows them to prey on animals much larger than themselves. Some water shrews with poisonous bites can kill large fish. The poison has been known to cause an inflammatory response in the skin of humans that persists for several days. These little creatures are extremely fierce in their own environmental scale.

Their course through life is torrid, at best. They usually do not live longer than one to two years, but they have one to three litters per year with two to ten young per litter.

I have spent a large portion of tonight watching these fierce little creatures as they gorge themselves on moths, beetles and worms that crawl from the darkness into the light.

The toilet in the dispensary makes me laugh. It has an honest-to-God chain pull. Elaine has spoken of this before, but this is the first one I have ever seen. Elaine has been talking for years about "pulling the chain," and I have never comprehended what she meant. This reflects her childhood in Chicago. We underprivileged Southerners know about toilets that flush and outhouses that don't, but this is the first chain I've seen firsthand.

There is a guard tower approximately twenty yards from my window. It is manned all night by U.S. Air Police with machine guns. At times when their radios click on with the transmission in Vietnamese, I feel like I'm in the midst of the proverbial "Chinese Fire Drill."

7 August 1966

Today is Sunday, a day of rest. That is amusing since I haven't done anything since I've been here except rest. Honestly, it's terrible. I'm taking two to three naps a day just to escape and pass the time. I've never done this before in my life. I sit down to read and it is so muggy that sweat drips from my forehead and chest onto the pages. Each page is stuck to the next as if the entire book has been dunked in water.

The main duty of each day is sick call from 8-10 a.m. and it drives me to distraction. It is a thousand times more tedious than at Cam Ranh.

It is similar to MOD duty at Bergstrom minus the children. The officers are no problem. The enlisted men, however, are a different breed of cat. They report for minor complaints such as "my muscles are sore after I exercise." Now, what should be my response to this? They don't need a doctor. They need their mother. The isolation here is so profound that they simply want attention. Fifty to 75 percent of the cases relate to venereal diseases. They are terrified at the prospect of having syphilis, but their fear doesn't prevent continuing indulgence in the pleasures of the local flesh pots. Each presents with their sad story of indiscretion. These are young men raised with the puritanical ideals of America, now exposed to biological temptations beyond any previous experience.

Today I toured the perimeter road that surrounds the base. At frequent intervals are small, wire, chicken coop structures of approximately 18 inches high and 36 inches square, with a mud floor. This is the place where South Vietnamese incarcerate Viet Cong prisoners. The space is inadequate for one person, yet frequently they place as many as four prisoners into it for as long as a week, without food, water or sanitation. I have also been informed that the Viet Cong prisoners are not exclusively assigned to such incarceration. The South Vietnamese also place their own men into these structures for disciplinary purposes. After a survey of these structures, I am sure that incarceration would convert me from a loyal South Vietnamese patriot to an active Viet Cong rebel.

The war is so terribly indiscriminate, perhaps by necessity, as are all wars. If South Vietnamese are informed that Viet Cong are in a small village, the entire village is bombed and strafed, with subsequent attack by ground troops. Usually out of twenty-five to thirty people killed, there may be one to two Viet Cong suspects killed. In order to avoid persecution for killing civilian, non-Viet Cong, the ground troops walk from body to body, stuffing anti-government literature into the pockets of the dead. Thus, they can justify killing innocent civilians. What a war!

It is remarkable how little regard these people have for lives of their own kind. A South Vietnamese hospital is not far from the base. It is staffed by Vietnamese doctors who treat all the Vietnamese on base. The United States is trying to establish a program of medical aid for the outlying villages. Many of the places are totally isolated in the middle of the surrounding jungle. There are no roads to them, only single file trails that villagers travel to market their wares or to trade with other villages. The only practical method of reaching them is by boat or helicopter.

Dr. Wuta has responsibility for the Medical Civic Action Program (MCAT) on this base. He is a general medical officer and one of his duties is to coordinate medical assistance to the villages with the Vietnamese physicians from the local hospital. There is one big problem. The Vietnamese doctors don't have any evangelistic zeal to play missionary in the jungle. Most are extremely well trained from medical schools in Paris. They work hard in the hospitals and serve an enormous number of patients. I've spoken with a number of them about this jungle crusade for Christ and Washington. The answer is always the same, "It's too dangerous." Quite frankly, I agree with them. For one to two physicians and two to three corpsmen to march into these Viet Cong-infested jungles with their only protection being two pistols is not dedication. It is tantamount to insanity. In this war, there is no respect or diplomatic immunity for physicians, especially American military physicians. There are many places in the Vietnam Delta that I wouldn't go into without a division of U.S. Marines, fully combat ready.

The program in Vietnam is purely voluntary for U.S. military personnel and I have no intention of volunteering. I had a short discussion with Dr. Wuta when he inquired about my participation. From my limited experience over here, the majority of medical problems are based on poor sanitary practices, lack of screens on buildings/huts and lack of antibiotics. To make a personal crusade for public health measures makes more sense than to place Band-Aids on wounds that will get infected if not kept clean. Since I originally committed to medicine with a missionary goal, these facts do not set easily with me. But neither does the concept of pouring penicillin into a septic tank.

I have five more days on this base and I look forward to returning to Cam Ranh Bay. However, compared to the average G.I. serving in this war, I have no complaints whatsoever.

8 August 1966

Today began with the tedium of Air Force meetings. There are several visiting high-ranking officers/"Brass" from Saigon, including a number of higher-ranking M.D.s. Because of the latter's presence, I was dragged into it. It began with an intelligence briefing in a room barely large enough to accommodate twenty-five to thirty people. The room itself was bare, with the exception of a large table covered with maps. During the briefing, everyone stood with their backs against the walls. Approximately halfway through the briefing, there was a sudden crash of shattered glass as an unknown object hurtled through the window into the room. A dark round object rolls under the table. This is a war zone, permeated by Viet Cong infiltration. The most likely object should be a hand grenade or small bomb. There was an indescribable look of terror in every eye…especially since all knew there was no place to seek cover. Several men dropped to the floor and covered their heads with their hands, but most simply stood paralyzed and looked panic-stricken. I was in the process of diving behind a map case directly behind me, knowing I would have four to eight seconds before the grenade detonated. Just before I leapt, someone outside shouted, "Baseball, baseball." Whew! Several G.I.s have been playing baseball outside and had knocked one through the window. I thought some of the men would break into tears with their new lease on life. I am also sure that I had a tachycardia of at least 150 beats per minute. Boy, what an experience. This is only one more indication of the subconscious tension that exists from day to day on this base. It would have been a perfect opportunity for a grenade: A small room filled with senior Air Force officers and no ready escape. No one would have left the room alive.

First flight with "Spooky" the AC-47D
Aircraft Commander: Maj. Charles Ozmore
Total flight Time: 6 hrs. 15 min.

Our intelligence briefing predicts a quiet night, and so it was from 1900-2400 hours (7 p.m. to midnight). After five boring hours of flying in circles over the jungle, we receive a call for assistance from a small village (fortress) approximately thirty-five miles north of the Mekong River. The area is under heavy mortar and recoilless rifle attack by the Viet Cong. Our aircraft is the first to arrive on the scene. Below us the darkened jungle is broken by orange-white flashes and streams of orange tracer fire going back and forth from jungle to the village fortress. We began to orbit above the action in a left bank of 15 to 20 degrees. Major Ozmore sights in on an area of most intense enemy fire. It is important to realize that Major Ozmore's tasks are many. This is a relatively unsophisticated aircraft. There are no infrared devices for night flying or fire-control computers. There is no night observation sight. There are only the pilot's eyes and his ability to calculate the many variables of "Kentucky Windage" to "Bore-Sight" the target. Those variables include the aircraft's airspeed. One knot of wind displaces the bullet 1.69 feet per second that the bullet must travel. Another factor is the recoil of the Gatling gun. Since the guns are mounted from the left aft side of the fuselage, firing the guns causes the aft fuselage to drift toward the right, thus causing the bullets to fall short and toward the rear of the target. There is the factor of target saturation or how many bullets must fall within the target area. A four-second burst from one minigun fired at a slant range from 4,500 feet will place 400 bullets within a circle of 32 feet in diameter.

After the target has been acquired, the pilot maneuvers the aircraft until the target is in a position that is approximately 100 degrees relative to the gunsight. Then when all of the above variables have been worked out, the pilot rolls the aircraft into the appropriate amount of left bank and begins a firing pass. Since each firing pass creates new variables from the recoil, corrections must constantly be made for wind conditions and changes in target area. Because of the variables listed above, the overall flight path of the aircraft is elliptical.

These battles are very close encounters between Viet Cong forces and friendlies, whose locations relative to each other may be a hundred yards or less apart. Night flying at an altitude of 3,500-4,500 feet makes all estimates of who-is-who nearly meaningless without some method of target identification. Since the Viet Cong usually wear black pajamas, the difficulty is compounded. In the Delta region, the isolated hamlets/fortresses are most often guarded by Army Republic of Vietnam troops. For this reason, each Spooky flight always has a Vietnamese interpreter on board to talk with the ground contact. If there are Americans or English-speaking FACs on the ground, the pilot communicates with them on an FM radio net.

The pilot then identifies himself as "Spooky 1-99" overhead with flares and miniguns. He requests that the Friendlies mark their position and the position of the Viet Cong. This may be accomplished by firing tracers toward the enemy position or by using flares for identification.

Anytime that an AC-47, or any other aircraft in the Mekong Delta region, fires on the enemy, clearance to fire must be issued by "Pawnee

Control" at Bien Hoa, 7th Air Force in Saigon, U.S. Army commander of the region or by the regional ARVN commander. This regulation contains the inherent delay of locating the proper authority for authorization. During the delay, men, women and children may be dying from Viet Cong fire. The only time that an aircraft is permitted to fire without permission is when the aircraft is receiving fire from the target area. There have been times that such delay is intolerable. Allied forces shortcut the bureaucracy by firing a burst near Spooky and report that it was "Charlie," or the pilot "imagines" he has been fired on. This allows Spooky to fire on the enemy while maintaining legalities of procedure. Tonight, none of these subterfuge measures are required to legalize our return fire. The enemy begins to fire on us…and we return his fire!

I am thoroughly startled by the intensity of noise when the Gatling guns begin to fire. I can only compare the sound to the noise produced by a giant dental drill that needs oiling. The combination of sound with vibrations is so loud that I plug my ears with my fingers in an effort to shut out the noise. A stream of liquid fire spews continuously from the six rotating barrels. Since every fifth round is a red tracer, they unite to create a stream of liquid fire that sears the fabric of night like a hot cautery that burns through the darkness and is oblivious to all in its path.

Suddenly the jungle directly beneath us erupts into a conflagration of crisscrossing red lines and explosions. It is virtually impossible to determine their source of origin. Some of the fire seems to ricochet off the black molasses surface of the Mekong River. Other streams of fire surround our aircraft, as if the jungle itself were probing the sky to find the source of its torment, inflicted by our miniguns. These streams of tracers pass over us and disappear into the dark sky above. The intensity of the anti-aircraft firepower aimed at us is unsettling. One hit can convert our aircraft and all aboard into a flaming meteorite. Over the intercom comes word that helicopter gunships have arrived on scene to further reinforce the besieged fortress. By this time the entire jungle beneath us is erupting into a bright thatch work of orange streaks from automatic weapons, punctuated by the white flashes of mortar fire. The air around our aircraft is surrounded by red and yellow fingers of molten lead, probing for a weak spot to destroy us.

The gunners work feverishly to keep up the fire and to assure that the guns continue shooting without jamming. After 2,000-3,000 rounds, each gun has to be reloaded. This involves hand-cranking many feet of belted cartridges into empty magazines, an extremely arduous task at any time. But effort has little meaning now. The only "meaning" is survival, and the only method of surviving is to destroy the enemy before he destroys us. This is no drill on the gunnery range in Texas or Arizona. Elemental survival of the villagers and our troops below, as well as of this aircraft, provides no slack in the urgency of combat.

There is no time to think or to consider what provocation led us into this war. Are we in the right or are the Viet Cong a civilian militia fighting righteously for their country? All such questions are moot. On the battlefield, on the seas and in the air, individual survival is all that counts. Politicians have the luxury of pious decisions from their leather chairs and mahogany paneled air-conditioned offices as they send men, whom they have never met, off to die. The soldiers, sailors and airmen that serve on the battlefield, sail the seas and fly the skies have no option beyond fighting to survive, regardless of foreign policy. It is ironic that the direr the circumstances, the easier the decisions become. When the only question is, "Do you wish to live or die?" the decision is easy. It is a truism that the length of foreign policy debates is inversely proportional to the lethality of the immediate threat.

There is no sound or conversation between crewmembers. The thunderous outputs of bullets from these three Gatling guns are, and will be, the first and last words spoken by this aircraft. The pilot maintains the plane in a tight bank to orbit around the point of a small village outpost, but his purpose is almost secondary to the gunners. The only purpose of the pilot is to keep the guns firing. With this realization, all is subordinated to the feverish activity of gunners, loading and reloading the miniguns to maintain the roar of bullets leaving the aircraft.

Finally after exhausting our ammunition and fuel, we withdraw from the fray and start back to base. Before, though, we radio the next AC-47 in line to fill our space and to maintain the fire. Not until after landing, when we step out onto the tarmac at Binh Tuy, is there any conversation among the crew. Here safely on the ground, and without the desperation of survival, we are able to finally admit what we had subconsciously realized but not verbalized in the air: The streams of tracer fire that issued from the jungle to surround our aircraft were fired by .40- and .50-caliber machine guns aimed at us. Compared to the F-4C Phantom, the AC-47 is a large slow target, whose only defense is the enormous volume of fire that it expends on the enemy.

Later recalling the feverish intensity of the gunners sweating blood to keep the fire up, I fully appreciate its capabilities. As the fastest fighter in our military arsenal, the F-4C Phantom is smaller, faster and more deadly. It is a strike aircraft, capable of rapidly delivering an enormous amount of destruction in one or two passes. At nearly twice the speed of sound it can deliver the same bomb load as the B-17 dropped on Germany during World War II. But tonight, to defend this small village, the ability to orbit above the village for an extended period of time and to maintain a continuous stream of fire against the enemy made this old, slow Gooney Bird the better weapon.

It is 2 a.m. before I get to bed. Sleep does not come easily. But I can only imagine the horrors that remain in the region surrounding that small village.

Finally I fall asleep, only to be awakened at 3 a.m. by a rag-tag chorus of chanting and/or singing in Vietnamese on the road across from my window. An Air Force guard tower is between my quarters and the road, which is jointly manned by a U.S. Air Force air policeman (AP) and an equivalent Vietnamese Air Force air policeman. The metallic clicks of both guards cocking their pistols and rifles are audible in the otherwise quiet night. In lockstep with their actions, I roll out of bed and onto the floor behind the sand bag wall beneath my windows. Simultaneously, I switch my M-16 to full automatic. Suddenly all is quiet until the Vietnamese air policeman challenges the noisy crowd. After an awkward moment, the chorus is replaced by drunken laughter and Vietnamese profanities that defy translation. This 'alert' is simply a group of Vietnamese Air Force pilots who have imbibed a bit too much beer during the evening and are trying to navigate their way back to the barracks to sleep it off.

I am now convinced that Cam Ranh Bay is the most beautiful spit of sand in the world. We have previously joked about Cam Ranh by renaming the base, "LBJ's Cat Box." But compared to the Delta region and this base, it seems like heaven.

Only three more days before I can leave this place! In all honesty, nothing disastrous has occurred while I have been here. It's purely a mental thing. Surrounded by an overwhelming number of enemies in the adjacent jungle, with infiltration of the base by enemy sappers that perform the menial tasks of maintenance, you can never be sure of surviving another minute. I realize this is luxurious compared to the Army and Marine troops in the bush, but it is quite enough for me.

One final note: One of the corpsmen in the dispensary received a notice today from the Red Cross stating that his "former wife just had an 8-pound baby girl." Since he didn't know that he had been divorced, he's in a state of shock/hysteria, not knowing if he or another man is the father.

I have recently seen articles in the Stars and Stripes about Martin Luther King Jr. and his marches throughout the country for equal rights and racial equality. I am somewhat bemused that he noted the hatred encountered from whites in Chicago far exceeded the animosity of the whites in the Deep South, such as Mississippi and Alabama. Elaine's parents live in South Side Chicago and I anticipate nothing but continuing racial conflict for that region of the city.

9 August 1966

Today has been relatively uneventful. Daytime routine of sick-call and paperwork in the morning yielded to inspection of flight line and central supply emergency equipment.

Another flight in the AC-47 takes up the entire evening. Aircraft commander was Captain McDermott. Flight time was five hours, forty minutes of airborne standby, orbiting the Delta region over jungle and villages, awaiting any call for assistance. The evening and flight were uneventful and reminded me of Winston Churchill's description of war as, "eternities of boredom, interrupted by moments of stark terror." Finally, just as I settled into bed for sleep, every alarm on base sounds to warn of impending mortar attack. This continues for an hour or so. The remainder of the night was spent curled up in a sandbagged bunker, clutching my M-16 and pistol, as I lie protected from the mortar attack that never materialized. I am very tired.

10 August 1966
7:30 a.m.

Today is Wednesday, "Hump Day!" I will leave Binh Tuy on Friday, heading back to Cam Ranh Bay. Hallelujah! I have almost given up writing at night since the temperature and humidity is so oppressive that my dripping sweat smears the ink on the paper. Mornings are cooler.

I am at the office a few minutes before sick call. There is humor wherever you find it. An airman just dropped in with a large bulge in his pocket. Somewhat secretively he pulls a carefully folded newspaper from his pocket and magnanimously asks if I would like to have it. He says that it is the very latest edition of Stars and Stripes. Obviously, he had gone through considerable effort to obtain it. I graciously thanked him and unfolded the treasure. It is a three-day-old issue of Stars and Stripes. Whereas, one man's treasure may be another man's trash, all is relative to time, place and circumstances. It was very thoughtful of him to bring me the gift.

Later this morning, Dr. Wuta came in to ask if I wished to make another MEDCAP (Medical Civic Action Program) visit to the Catholic orphanage. Since I have a list of things to do in clearing base and wrapping up my assignment at Binh Tuy in one to two days, I promptly replied, "No, I don't."

He said, "Why don't you go anyway?"

This response places the issue on an entirely different level of discussion.

I look him directly in the eye and say, "I thought I had previously made it clear that I'm not going." He is a general medical officer and has no authority over me whatsoever. I outrank him in every way, but choose not to play this card. He immediately drops the subject. He had previously made the comment that a doctor should visit the orphanage every day. I informed him that my primary duty is to render medical support to United States military forces in Vietnam and aircrew members in particular. I further said I had no compunction to spend taxpayers' money—either in terms of my time or the expense of medical supplies for a program that the native Vietnamese physicians will not support. The area of the orphanage is not secure from the enemy. This is why the South Vietnamese physicians will not go there. For a U.S. physician to enter this enemy-infested jungle without armed escort is foolhardy. Perhaps Dr. Wuta is seeking sainthood through martyrdom, but I have no such aspirations. Wuta is not primarily motivated by the humanitarian purpose of caring for the needy so much as he is devoted to the "Catholic" sponsorship of the orphanage. He has refused to participate in other non-Catholic and less sectarian efforts. I certainly endorse any assistance that we can render to the citizens here, regardless of religious consideration. But my primary commitment is to airmen of the U.S. military and not to the Catholic Church.

11 August 1966
6:30 a.m.

Life here is cyclic. The routine boredom of the day seems to yield to the chaos of night on a regular basis. At 7 p.m. last night an explosion rocked the base. Everyone took cover in the belief that it was simply round number one of a forthcoming mortar attack. In truth, it was only an airman of the Vietnamese Air Force who failed to unload a 20 mm cannon (aboard an airplane) and a shell went off with no damage to anyone. After this incident, all was quiet until 1 a.m. when two large explosions and jolts, typical of a mortar, nearly threw me out of bed. This turned out to be one of the outlying Vietnamese garrisons, in the neighboring jungle, having a "practice alert." Again, I returned to bed and had hardly dozed off when I was awakened at 3:30 a.m. by someone screaming; "Help me, Oh my Lord, help me!"

The sound came from an area of the perimeter road around the base. Guards in the watchtower outside my window were pacing back and forth, muttering in confusion—obviously not knowing how to react.

I go outside and find no one else around. Having no desire to be a one-man rescue force for a drunken airman or other, I return to my quarters. Occasionally the Viet Cong have captured an American serviceman and tortured him, leaving him to suffer in a place likely to attract attention. This poor soul is bait for a trap that is set for all who attempt rescue. Since the sound comes from the perimeter road, which is encircled by the jungle, this is a very real possibility. However, shortly after all is quiet again. Neither the guards nor anyone else made any effort to investigate. The following day, I inquire of the guards and those on duty in the local hospitals, all to no avail. To this day it is still a mystery. Perhaps it was someone having a nightmare and calling out in his sleep.

This entire night has been like a page from Dante's Inferno.

11 August 1966
7:30 p.m.

Today at lunch, I spoke with an RMK engineer who has been in Vietnam for almost two years. He is a very fine person, in his early thirties, and is divorced. After twelve years of happy marriage, his wife's mental status progressively deteriorated until she was diagnosed with schizophrenia. She required several years of institutional psychiatric care and consistently demanded a divorce. Ultimately, at the advice of multiple psychiatrists and ministers, he granted her divorce for the sake of the children. It is a very sad case.

I ask when he plans to return to the States. With a very blank expression, he replies that he has nothing to return to. He was vague about the disposition of the children during these events. He noted only that his family was his entire life and now he has lost it. He is making excellent money over here, but it has no meaning for him. He is a very unhappy man. My heart breaks for him.

In the course of the conversation, he spoke of a Chinese witch doctor in Can Tho who treats back pain by inserting burning bamboo slivers into the paravertebral muscles, "to lead out the evil spirits." He performs this by heating bamboo stakes in the fire until they are in flames. He then stabs the paravertebral muscles to a depth of 1-plus inches with ten to fifteen of these flaming slivers.

His "office" is on a street corner in downtown Can Tho. Apparently the patients bleed profusely, which enhances the treatment. Since there is little spice in life on this base, or in Can Tho, I have to see this for myself. Driving to Can Tho, I position our Jeep on a corner that affords observation of the "doctor's" practice.

Sure enough, there he is, with a bundle of bamboo sticks, a small hibachi-type fire and a pan of bloody water, all arraigned on the street corner. No patients present after an hour. While we watch, he steps back about three paces from his "instruments" and squats to have a very large bowel movement. After which he pulls up his trousers and resumes his "office duties" of fanning the fire and waiting for patients.

There is also a Chinese dentist with his "open office" about a block from the above noted Chinese surgeon. But, pulling teeth on the street doesn't hold a candle to therapeutically stabbing people in the back with flaming bamboo ingots to cure their back pain. During the 1990s, a program of "sclerotherapy" for back pain was initiated in the United States. It involved injecting hypertonic glucose into the paravertebral muscles. Hypertonic glucose is an irritant that results in the formation of scar tissue in the ligaments and paravertebral muscles. Scar tissue and fibrotic changes contract and thereby correct the "ligamentous laxity" that contributes to low back pain. The use of burning bamboo fagots, thrust into the paravertebral muscles, would accomplish the same purpose. The cauterized and injured tissue creates scar tissue, no less than the hypertonic glucose that contracts and counters the ligamentous laxity creating low back pain.

This morning, I participated in a training flight and exercise mission, flying around Can Tho and local area in a Huey, H-43-D helicopter. Flight time was 1 hour, 45 minutes with aircraft commander Maj. J. Kays. During the flight, I photographed the aerial layout of the Binh Tuy base and Can Tho region.

I can't wait to leave this base. Cam Ranh has spoiled me. My usual escape from adverse circumstances is found in reading or writing. But, it is impossible to either read or write at night in this Delta location. It is worse than the swamps of Florida for bugs. It is impossible to sit in my room at night and read without the myriad of insects buzzing around the light and falling onto my book or writing. Despite spraying insect repellant liberally throughout the room, there is little alleviation of the bugs, but near asphyxiation of myself.

However, I must maintain perspective that despite all of these "inconveniences," Can Tho is considered one of the most secure bases in Vietnam. Its remote and isolated location has rendered it free from the frequent terrorist activities that are so often found in Saigon. My intention is to return to Cam Ranh Bay tomorrow, but I may have to stay overnight at Tan Son Nhut Air Force Base in Saigon, depending on flight connections.

CHAPTER 16

Leaving Binh Tuy

12 August 1966

All Air Force flights from Binh Tuy have been canceled because of weather. However, I am determined not to spend another night in this place. If the Air Force is incapacitated because of weather, the U.S. Army may not be. At the Army side of the field at Can Tho I am fortunate enough to catch a last-minute helicopter flight to Saigon. The flight is 1 hour, 30 minutes via Army helicopter from Binh Tuy to Tan Son Nhut in Saigon.

When we arrive at Tan Son Nhut, it is raining in torrents. Since we land at the Army portion of the field, I must walk approximately one mile to the Air Force portion of the airport. Presentation at Base Operations of the Air Force reveals no beds are available on the field. I catch a bus to the Base Officer Quarters, approximately two miles from the airfield.

As I enter the building a captain approaches me and asks if I have just arrived from Binh Tuy. I say yes. He is a physician who introduces himself as Bill McDuffy. He has been in Vietnam for approximately two

233

weeks and is still in an assignment holding pattern at Tan Son Nhut. He still doesn't have a definite base assignment. He has been informed that he will go to the base that I didn't want, i.e. Binh Tuy versus Cam Ranh Bay. He said the surgeons' office of 7th Air Force is asking whether I wish to stay at Binh Tuy or return to Cam Ranh Bay. Well, I am blown away! Then I recall a meeting two days ago with Colonel Barnum, the wing commander at Binh Tuy.

Barnum had requested a meeting with me in his office to inquire about a rather vague accident supposedly involving a Vietnamese civilian. I had absolutely no idea what he was talking about and informed him so. He then became quite chatty with questions such as, "How do you like it here at Binh Tuy?" and "Isn't it more pleasant than all the sand at Cam Ranh Bay?"

Politely, I inform him that I much prefer Cam Ranh Bay because I have already established friends with pilots of the 391st TFS and with other squadrons of the 12th TFW. I cite my long-term friendship with medical school classmate Al Aleckna. I didn't dwell on the fact that flying as a crew-member in the F-4C Phantom II is vastly more satisfying than being an observer in an AC-47 Spooky. He drifted away from these pointed questions with comments on the weather, etc. The informality of our conversation should have alerted me.

This encounter with Dr. McDuffy suddenly brought it all back. I realize that the true reason for Colonel Barnum's conversation was to feel me out on my assignment preference. In talking with this new man, I realize that I should be cautious. If I tell him my true feelings about Binh Tuy, he might protest assignment there and force me back to that miserable place. Yet, if I praise it excessively, then it would be logical for me to return to such a "pleasant place." I inform him that Binh Tuy is a nice small base in the Vietnam Delta region near Can Tho. It offers multiple opportunities to see local Vietnamese culture, etc. I explain that I had already settled in at Cam Ranh and preferred not to transfer. He accepted this in good grace and offered no protests or qualms about being assigned to Binh Tuy. On this note, we parted.

In consideration of these issues, I appreciate the Air Force giving me first option on assignment. The hierarchy of seniority prevails in the military. I have been "in-country" longer. Application for advancing my rating from aviation medical officer (AME) to flight surgeon (FS) is in process. I even outrank Bill Simmons in this respect. If I can ride out this transition period, my chances of being designated chief of flight medicine at Cam Ranh Bay are excellent. With that established, I don't believe that Colonel Mack will permit my transfer from that position. Another flight surgeon or flight medical officer is scheduled for assignment at Cam Ranh Bay this month. I wonder if this man is the person under consideration. To cinch the issue, I call 7th Air Force in Saigon to inquire about my status. It is reassuring to hear that there is no change in my assignment at Cam Ranh.

13 August 1966

After my encounter with the good doctor, I finally locate an empty room with an empty bed and crash. I sleep from 7 p.m. to 4 a.m. today. This is the first decent night's sleep I've had in weeks. I subsequently catch a bus over to the "In Country Passenger Terminal" of the Air Force. The flight to Cam Ranh Bay is scheduled to leave at 7:30 a.m., but it is filled with people who have waited all night (in this stench-ridden place) for a seat. I am placed on stand-by for the next flight, which is scheduled to leave at 2 p.m. I have pulled every string that I know to find an earlier flight, to no avail.

This flight is not limited to military personnel. It is comparable to the passenger station of a Greyhound Bus Station in the slums of Chicago. I sit on a couch with stuffing oozing out of every seam between two Vietnamese soldiers who smell like rotten fish. Every now and then a spider drops into my lap from unknown origins. Another Vietnamese soldier sitting across from me has a transistor radio, whose sound is deafening. The "music" is twang-twangy; with a vocal accompaniment that can only be compared to psychotic cats fighting in a back alley over a sexy mouse. It is difficult to see how a human being can consider this "music" enjoyable!

The entire room is packed with Vietnamese soldiers and American G.I.s, all awaiting a flight to somewhere else and creating odors that are comparable to a men's locker room in a cheap gym. I can't leave the room for a breath of fresh air without losing my flight call position. It will be good to return to Cam Ranh Bay, with the clean sand and the breeze from the South China Sea.

Finally, at 2 p.m., I board a C-130D at Tan Son Nhut, heading back to Cam Ranh. The flight is 1 hour, 45 minutes, a "milk run" linking Saigon to An Khe, Quinhon to Nha Trang and, finally to Cam Ranh. We arrive at Cam Ranh Bay around midnight.

After landing at Cam Ranh, I finally off-load on the flight line in front of the flight surgeon's office. As a matter of habit, I visit my office. On my desk is a set of orders for me to attend Jungle Survival School in the Philippines. Apparently Lt. Col. Jack Doerty, squadron commander of the 391st TFS, must also attend, and he has specifically requested my company in training. Every pilot who flies over the jungle terrain of Vietnam must attend Jungle Survival School. As Colonel Doerty is squadron commander, he probably wants to assure that I can survive if we go down in the jungle. I am a bit flattered that he specifically chose me as partner. He was shot down and captured twice during the Korean War. He escaped both times and has a silver plate in his skull as witness to previous injuries. On talking to him, I learn that an Air Force regulation prohibits any previous prisoner of war from returning to duty in the same theater of conflict (Asia) in which he had previously been a prisoner of war. Colonel Doerty had to

Sharkbait

sign a declaration that he was returning to the Asian theater of operations of his own free will and understood all risks of recapture, etc. I learned later that he has turned down promotion to general rank on two separate occasions. He simply stated, "I am in the Air Force to fly airplanes, not to fly desks."

There is a small clipping on my desk from the Stars and Stripes about a recent air strike near Can Tho. Although I was not involved, I was aware of this because of the number of casualties that flooded into the hospital on that night. There was quite a public uproar about the civilian casualties that resulted from the strike with bombs and napalm. The Air Force is desperately trying to close off publicity on the incident. The hospital is staffed by an Air Force surgical team, consisting of one surgeon and another, by name of Jerry Baughn, who has just finished his first-year surgery residency at Charity Hospital in New Orleans. It just so happens that he is from Austin, Texas. They had a very busy night.

In the rush of events, I neglected to mention that Binh Tuy has been mortared twice in the past six months. The last attack occurred the week before Al Aleckna arrived there for his temporary duty. I feel blessed to have missed all that action and even more blessed to be back at Cam Ranh.

15 August 1966

Colonel Mack sponsored a steak cookout on Sunday evening. This consisted of the usual hospital staff with drinks and steaks. Al and I tried to time our entrance so that we could sneak in and sneak out, appropriately to the social situation. We arrived approximately fifteen minutes early. The drinks were flowing freely and I simply stood aside and observed.

A colonel is nibbling at the neck and ear of a large red-headed nurse. It is more than I can tolerate. Perhaps I could sympathize more if the women were attractive. When women this ugly attract you, it's time to go home, war or no war. I retreat outside where I strike up a conversation with the black staff sergeant who is cooking the steaks. Al and I eat and leave the party.

I am inside the fighter pilot system and see only the relative frailties of the pilots around me. There is little macho or braggadocio that I observe in these men, who are exposed to death on a regular daily basis. Too many times, pilots have knocked on my door and asked somewhat petulantly if I could fly for them today, even though I am not on the schedule. They are tired or have a slight cold, or drank too much last night, and the thought of charging off into the sunset or sunrise is the last thing on their mind. They do the same work day-to-day, repetitiously performing the monotony of any daily routine.

But, here again, they relate to me as an equal, a friend, or perhaps as a weary son might relate to an indulgent father or a brother. These young men are the cream of America's manhood. I see extraordinary young men performing life-threatening tasks day in and day out in this boiling cauldron and inferno of war. It is an honor and a privilege to work with them and to have their friendship.

I've seen other examples of aberrant behavior in individuals who have been removed from their familiar environment and sanctions. I well remember a doctor who stopped by the flight surgeon's office at Cam Ranh Bay. He was dressed like an enlisted man and had bandoliers of ammunition strung across his chest. He told me that he was practicing very little medicine, despite his assignment as a general medical officer in an Air Force facility. Instead he assumed the role of a side gunner in Huey helicopters. This is an extremely dangerous position in which the individual leans out of the helicopter, restrained by a single chest strap, while he fires an M-60 machine gun at any available target below. Then he proceeds to tell me about waterskiing on the Mekong River, while towed by one of the gunboats of the Brown Water Navy. Both sides of the river are controled by Viet Cong.

On another occasion, an Air Force general medical officer I encountered in Saigon informed me proudly of the number of cases of gonorrhea that he had contracted while being in country.

I wonder now, and will continue to wonder, what motivates such insane behavior by reasonably intelligent individuals, when they are removed from familiar physical surroundings and know that no one is watching. I could continue with multiple other examples of risk taking, simply for the thrill. Perhaps they were denied the experience of "raising hell" during their youth, and were attempting to recapture it.

In war, where all things of value are threatened, strange thoughts arise from the depths of your subconscious during the terrible hypnotic grind of day-to-day monotony. Contrary to all reason, at times there emerges a yearning for action, as terrible as it may be… anything to bring things to a climax of termination. These thoughts are constantly balanced by the terror of imminent disaster. This ambivalence of hope and fear are all too often constant obsessions.

This is not a modern phenomenon. How well I remember the passage in Tolstoy's War and Peace about Prince Andrea, who has wealth, is of noble birth and is a Russian officer fighting against Napoleon. He mused that for all his wealth, his beautiful wife, family and magnificent home, he would give it all up in an instant for a moment of glory on the field of battle.

Man is a strange creature who seems destined for unhappiness when he arrives at any goal. His happiness is derived from the search, the quest to realize hopes and dreams that forever lie beyond his grasp.

These sentiments have been more eloquently expressed in "Ulysses" by Lord Alfred Tennyson.

> *I am a part of all that I have met;*
> *Yet all experience is an arch wherethrough*

Gleams that untraveled world, whose margin fades
For ever and for ever when I move.
How dull it is to pause, to make an end,
To rust unburnished, not to shine in use!
As though to breathe were life!

In his book, *Democracy in America*, Alex De Tocqueville poignantly described Americans as "forever restless amidst their prosperity." Perhaps that is only true when life is assured.

Bill Simmons is a very gentle, congenial person. He is a pleasant, competent, dedicated officer and I respect him for this. Simmons has a wife and three children in Mississippi. He has been trying for some time to spend several days in the Central Highland region with Special Forces of the Army or Marines performing "search and destroy" missions. These teams patrol remote jungle areas to seek out the Viet Cong in the wild. Our troops who engage these guerrilla forces are in constant danger, every hour of every day in kill-or-be-killed warfare. It is comparable to the Indian type warfare utilized by American Colonials during the 1600-1700s against the French during the French and Indian war, and later against the British during the American Revolution. I am comfortable in the jungle, but I see no reason to look down the throat of a dragon, just for a thrill.

In discussing Bill's passion for exposing himself to danger with Al Aleckna, the junior flight surgeon in the office, I commented about Bill's behavior, citing his obligation to his family at home. Al is tall, handsome and slender, with a subtle air of European accent, sophistication and culti-vation. Sporting a meticulously groomed handlebar moustache, he spends many evenings in the office next to mine, practicing his French pronun-ciation. In fact, his efforts to accomplish the proper French inflections of "Uhn" and "Ahh," prompted me on one occasion to request that he close the door while having such a satisfying bowel movement. After separating from the Air Force, he plans to become a "ski-bum" in France, removed from the rigors of practicing medicine.

His family origin is Lithuanian. Al's father was professor of surgery in Lithuania until the Communist takeover. In the middle of the night his father and mother fled with Al and his brother to avoid execution or imprisonment for political reasons. A member of the Lithuanian intelligentsia and upper crust, his family had been very wealthy. This all ended during the early morning hours of the night, when they were forced to flee the country only minutes ahead of being arrested and/or imprisoned. They left all behind, with their only possessions being the clothes on their back.

They obtained political asylum in the United States, where his father became a general practitioner in Chicago, albeit, with lifestyle far less grand than in Lithuania. Both sons became physicians. My acquaintance with Al began my second year in medical school at Northwestern. I was a sophomore and Al was a freshman. We were fraternity brothers in the Phi Chi medical fraternity in Abbot Hall at Northwestern Medical School. Al could easily have been a stand-up comic with his unsurpassed sense of humor and trace of European suave. Over and above the fraternity brother level, I have grown to love him like a brother. (In fact, if I could choose a brother, I would choose Al).

Al commented that Bill was nuts to take such insane risks of exposing himself so unnecessarily to danger for simply the lark of adventure. I responded that if Bill didn't fear for himself, then he shouldn't impose the burden of his irresponsibility on his wife and children. For a moment, Al looked at me wide-eyed and rolled his eyes in disbelief. Obviously quite flustered, he then stammered, "wha...what do you mean...? Well, hell, man, I've got obligations, too...I've got girlfriends..." Apparently my statements about Bill were interpreted as an implication that Al had nothing to lose, being foot-loose and fancy-free. This was not my intent at all. But Al took it personally and I was surprised at his interpretation of my sentiments. His demeanor was so serious, and his consternation so genuine that I nearly convulsed in laughter. And to make it more humorous, he wasn't sure why I was laughing so hard!

I should be laughing at myself. My only reason to choose medicine as a profession was to obtain backdoor entry into space exploration. Unable to pass the 20/20 vision requirements for military pilot training, I decided that medical school was my best second option. Space exploration is in the embryonic phase. Human tolerance of the space environment is a totally unknown field. Only with background training in medicine could I be qualified to participate. Entry as a doctor would place me on the ground floor for all future endeavors. Parenthetically, I thought, "If the mission demands are such, it will be much easier to teach a doctor to fly than to train a pilot to be a doctor."

And so finally, now in Vietnam, I am able to experience the high adventure that I've craved all my life. This would have been impossible without a medical degree that allowed me to become a flight surgeon. I am flying in the fastest aircraft that has ever been used in combat. And, I am doing this on a daily basis in actual combat situations. Before Vietnam, at Bergstrom Air Force Base, I flew in the B-52 with the hydrogen bomb on board. I also participated in the air-to-air refueling missions of the KC 135 for multiple aircraft types. None of these experiences would have been possible without a doctor of medicine degree. The only difference between Bill Simmons and me is that he has a family with children. I do not. I have a wife, but no children. Should something happen to me, Elaine is very bright and will continue her life. The shadow of my death will pass very quickly. There are no children to suffer from my actions. Elaine has known of my passions and future plans from the time of our first meeting in Chicago. I am the risk that she accepted with marriage.

I read in the Stars and Stripes that Senator Russell from Georgia is urging a call up of the military reserves for Vietnam duty. Senator Russell is chairman of the Senate Armed Services Committee. I remotely know his family since the Clarks and Russells are long-time residents of Georgia. I have mixed emotions about this. It seems a terrible shame that a nation as powerful as the United States is unable to cope with this "dirty little war" by using its first string military to settle the problem and therefore must resort to its second-string reserves. Psychologically, it seems a poor reflection on our country. However, there are many who serve in the reserve forces positioned by political influence to avoid the risk of active duty. Perhaps, these are the ones that Senator Russell is trying to put to work. But reserve or no reserve, I see no easy solution or victory in sight.

I learned through a newspaper article forwarded by Elaine that a "hunger strike" had taken place at the Civilian Construction Camp on Cam Ranh Peninsula. Construction of bases and airfields in Vietnam has been contracted out to a U.S. based outfit of RMK. The working conditions are not always pleasant and the reimbursement to laborers is probably very poor. There was a "hunger strike" in August for better working conditions, pay, etc. Since Cam Ranh is a favorite resting spot for reporters, I'm not surprised that it got extensive coverage in the newspapers back home. Despite the construction camp being only one to one and a half miles away from the base, I only learned about the issues when I read them in a newspaper. The press can inflate any issue, all out of proportion to its significance.

14 August 1966

After Binh Tuy, how good it is to return to the cockpit!!

F-4C Mission: Time 1 hr. 05 min.

Aircraft Commander: Maj. Chico Solis

This mission is very short. Pre-flight intelligence informs us of the target coordinates. There has been considerable Viet Cong activity in the region of the target and the possibility of ground fire is likely. Approximately three miles from target our flight of four Phantoms contacts the O-1E FAC, known affectionately as "Bird-Dog," to mark the target with Willie Pete rockets. We approach 2,000-3,000 feet above him and "Tally Ho" to establish recognition. The little Cessna looks like a small butterfly wafting above the jungle canopy. Immediately after firing the rockets, the little plane flies clear of the area as quickly as possible so that we can begin our run on target. On this mission, the target is a Viet Cong storage area approximately ten miles west of Nha Trang. Since our ordnance is napalm, we fly at treetop level or lower. Napalm must be spread or "smeared on the landscape" from low altitude.

Why were we called upon for this mission? Apparently, Cam Ranh is the nearest source for close ground support missions in this area. Approach altitude is 9,000-10,000 feet, with napalm drop to be accomplished at what seems to be within ten to fifteen feet of the ground. (It is difficult to determine altitude when screaming above the ground at 500-600 plus miles per hour. I only know that I looked up to see the trees!) Despite the warning by intelligence, we encounter no ground fire. Our flight back to base is uneventful.

16 August 1966

F-4C Mission Time 1 hr. 45 min (Mission #21)

Aircraft Commander: Lt. Colonel Doerty

I am flying in the GIB pilot position with Lt. Colonel Doerty as pilot in command.

In contrast to the usual four aircraft, today's mission is a flight of three aircraft. Each plane is loaded with eight 500-pound, high-drag bombs. One of the aircraft, a camera plane, is also loaded with four canisters of napalm.

Initially, we proceed to a fragged target area near Tay Ninh, when we receive the radio message to divert immediately to an area approximately fifteen miles northwest of Saigon. Between us and the directed target area is a huge weather system of thunderstorms and turbulent air space.

To fly formation in heavy clouds, the aircraft close ranks to the point that there may be only a matter of inches between wing tips. Col. Daugherty and I are in the lead aircraft. The other two Phantoms orient themselves with our wing tips. One of our aircraft is piloted by a former member of the U.S. Air Force aerial demonstration team, the Thunderbirds. It is a thing of beauty to see our three supersonic Phantoms as they maneuver with precision in unison, while flying at 500-600 mph, with only inches between wing tips. Finally, after being battered by vicious weather, winds and thunderstorms, we emerge from the clouds to arrive at the target. The target area is already under attack from a flight of 4 F-100s (Super Sabers). I believe that they are from the 614th TFS out of Phan Rang.

We orbit the area at an altitude of 10,000-12,000 feet until the F-100s have expended their ordnance. Beneath us the entire terrain appears as a solid mass of water and flooded rice paddies that extend for hundreds of miles. It is impossible to discern where the rivers begin or end and/or where the rice paddies begin or end. Since it is the seasonal monsoon deluge, with its characteristic flooding, all blends into one. After the F-100s leave, we are diverted by our FAC, Cobra-4, to a cluster of red-shingled stucco buildings. These are rapidly demolished by our napalm and bombs. According to intelligence, these quarters were considered to be a Viet Cong headquarters and supply depot.

We are unable to disengage one of the bombs, but no difficulty is encountered during our return flight back to Cam Ranh Bay. After a few minutes of attempting to "sling the bomb loose" with violent maneuvers over the ocean, we give up and land with the retained bomb hanging precariously from the bomb rack. Disarmament of the "hung bomb" is accomplished without incident on the ground.

Returning to the flight surgeon's office, I receive notice from the Air Force powers-that-be that I have been awarded a ribbon for Marksmanship with the M-16 at Hamilton Air Force Base, before I came to 'Nam. Apparently, out of a perfect score of 360, I scored 358 in the target zone. This was accomplished at 300 yards, and thus is not bad shooting. For this success, I give credit to my years of hunting during my youth in the South.

18 August 1966

Letter to Elaine

"Tonight I am MOD. For my idle hours, I bought a paperback copy of Joseph Conrad's *Nigger of the 'Narcissus'* and *The End of the Tether*. Both are sea stories and both are excellent. Conrad is an eloquent and poetic author. He writes a wonderful introduction, which he concludes with a statement of his goal as an artist and writer. The following is a quote from it:

'To arrest, for the space of a breath, the hands busy about the work of the earth and compel men, entranced by the sight of distant goals to glance for a moment at the surrounding vision of form and color, of sunshine and shadows; to make them pause for a look, for a sigh, for a smile…such is the aim, difficult and evanescent, and reserved only for a few to achieve. But sometimes by the deserving and the fortunate, even that task is accomplished. And when it is accomplished …Behold! -- All the truth of life is there: a moment of vision, a sigh, a smile… and the return to eternal rest.'

"For me, this is a statement of exquisite beauty. Joseph Conrad was from Poland and immigrated to England at the age of seventeen. He was a sea captain until he was forty years old. At age of forty, he wrote his first book, Almayer's Folly. So much of his writing touches my soul.

"After reading such a passage, one may ask, 'what the hell?' 'Who cares?' To answer these simple, mundane questions, one must realize that Conrad's writing is the expression of a man's soul. I can say this because his sentiments are also mine.

"It is difficult for a person immersed in more civilized matters to appreciate the simple expression of sentiments that are universally relevant to all people in all times. Modern lifestyles are so busily engrossed in getting, spending and in dancing the metronomic cadence of daily dictates, that we forget the eternal and meaningful things that supersede paying the bills and disposing of the trash. It is tragic that only here, in the maelstrom of destructive warfare, that we are finally able to appreciate life as an end unto itself, and as a moment of existence that is so precious that sunsets, shadows, smiles and all other simple pleasures are finally recognized for their true value. These simple things that are so easily neglected during the humdrum of modern life are not merely the spices of life. They are the very essence of life. Only when these things are threatened, does one find majesty in their truth and simple beauty.

"During war and all dire circumstances, all else is extraneous and superfluous. So much of this majesty and grandeur is lost in a more civilized world, drowned in the fervid tempo of daily activities. Perhaps, proximity to death is required to lift the veil that blinds us during lives of comfort and convenience. How tragic that the magnificence of living existence cannot be recognized until it stands on the cliff's edge of destruction. When all things are considered, wealth, position, status and power fade into insignificance. The more 'progressive' and 'facilitating' that modern life becomes, the further we distance ourselves from the elemental universal truths that render one moment of joy more valuable than all the power, wealth and status that we so fervently seek.

"I have spent most of my life alone in the swamps and woods of Florida, Georgia and Alabama. The wilderness is my home. I have never found a companion to share my joys of this natural world. My writing is a compulsion…perhaps an attempt to share my love of the world with someone else…an invisible reader…some distant muse… It is difficult to explain…"

If nothing else, the practice of medicine provides the physician with a "front-row-center" seat to observe humanity, with all its blemishes and nobility. The blemishes are no deterrent for me. Man is a biological creature who struggles to survive, no more or less than any other creature. But, if observed for a sufficient period of time, there is another irrefutable trait that emerges to set the human species apart from other creatures. The occasional glimpse of this intangible and unexpected trait is a constant source of wonder and inspiration for me. The "Gods," chosen by our species to be worshipped or feared, have generally fallen short of expectations when measured against time. Centuries of experience with "Gods," "demi-Gods," priests and saints have universally and predictably demonstrated that most of these exalted types have clay feet. Any discussion of kings and politicians about personal integrity, generosity and honor is usually an exercise in futility.

It is, therefore, somewhat ironic that throughout my life I have found more majesty and nobility in a few individuals of my fellow men and women than I have found in the more exalted creatures ascribed to inhabit the heights and depths, above or below us, respectively. These statements and beliefs are based on personal observations of how men react under dire combat situations, when no one is present to record their cowardice or valor. (I consider myself to be an unrecognized observer under these circumstances.) Yes, there are knaves, cowards, thieves and all manner of scoundrels, but this herd cannot detract from the "common man/woman" who emerges from the flames of life and gives his/her all for another. This is not meant to glorify the individual who falls on the hand grenade or steps into the line of fire to shield another. Animals and humans generally act in their own self-interest. But I find exception in the adage that "a dog is the only creature that loves his/her master/mistress more than self." I have observed inherent nobility in some members of our human species that supersedes any expectation of personal gain. Whether during war or peace, there are certain men and women who give without expectation of reward or return, and this action is based on the one simple reason that he or she cannot act differently. Under the same circumstances, others make other choices, to flee, to cower, to deny... but for a few individuals, there is no choice beyond that of nurturing, assisting and succoring a fellow creature in need.

Today, I met such a man.

A young pilot was seen in the flight surgeon's office today to request my endorsement for emergency leave of absence. He is twenty-six-years old and a first lieutenant who flies daily combat missions in the F-4C. He was extremely personable and congenial in both speech and gesture. Movie-star handsome, there was a clean-cut all-American appearance that any casting director would seek to portray in the role of an American fighter pilot. He has a master's degree in engineering and loves to fly.

His parents have been separated or divorced for ten to fifteen years, and he has no idea where his father is. He's been married only twenty months himself, but during that time he has only been with his wife for five months or less. His request for leave is in behalf of a fifteen-year-old sister who has been drifting from family to family, free of all moorings as she wanders from one bad situation to another. He and his wife plan to more or less adopt this sister in an effort to get her over the trials and travails of her teenage years.

It is difficult to imagine the impact that a rebellious adolescent girl will inflict on his fledgling marriage, a union that is hardly airborne. To have lived with the new bride for only five of twenty months imposes extraordinary stress on both him and his wife. To compound his already strained marriage by bringing a rebellious teenage sister into their home, a sister of which he knows little, and of which his wife knows nothing, is a task of Herculean proportions. The impact of these decisions on his career and marriage are beyond measure. And yet, he is willing to risk it all by accepting the responsibility of an older brother for a younger sister whom he hardly knows, fully recognizing that all may end in vain. Needless to say, I did the best that I could in his behalf. But more than that, I consider it an honor and a privilege to have known men of this caliber. My encounters with the human species continue to reinforce my belief that mankind is the most noble of God's creatures!

August already appears to be a full month. The next item on the agenda is Jungle Survival School in the Philippines.

CHAPTER 17

Jungle Survival School

19 August 1966

Dear Elaine:

Tomorrow, at 0600, Lt. Col. Walter L. (Jack) Doerty Jr. and I will depart Cam Ranh Bay via C-130 on a long, circuitous flight to Clark Air Force Base in the Philippines. As the crow flies, the air time between CRB and Clark is only four to five hours. Unfortunately, the way of the Air Force is not the way of the crow. Crows are far more intelligent. The aircraft will stop at every dirt landing strip of every jungle outpost between Vietnam and the Philippine Islands to deliver supplies and ammunition, in total disrespect of my important personage and critical mission.

Presumably, we will arrive at Clark AFB in the Philippines before midnight on 20 August. The singular advantage of this excursion is that I am removed from the combat zone of Vietnam and thus am able to call home through civilian telephones lines."

It has been a major obstacle to call Elaine from Vietnam. I can hardly wait to hear her voice.

We are lucky enough to catch an unscheduled direct flight on a C-141 from Cam Ranh Bay to Clark. This is a marked improvement over our originally scheduled flight. It is direct and only three hours in length. We arrive at Clark at 1 p.m.

Upon arrival, we are escorted to the billeting office for on-base officers quarters (BOQ). The duty officer informs us that he has room available for only one field grade officer (this translates to rank of major or above). At this point I collide with the principle that rank has its privileges. Colonel Doerty promptly says, "I'll take it." He tells me to find lodging in one of the nearby motels off base.

All quarters on base are occupied except for a couple of doubles and triples, which don't appeal to me. As a physician/flight surgeon I have previously been nearly immune to the usual regulations of military protocol. For officers, the cut point for discrimination in ranks begins at major. Thus, the lower ranks from second lieutenant to captain are "company grade" ranks. Since my duties as flight surgeon are with pilots, rank is rarely an issue. In fact, this is my first encounter with such blatant segregation by rank. Welcome to the Air Force!

I suppose what took me off guard was the alacrity of Colonel Doerty's response. He is my squadron commander and one of the nicest persons I've ever met. He and I fly together frequently and I think very highly of him, both as a fine human being and as a very capable officer and pilot. Ah well, as Dr. Anson, my anatomy professor at Northwestern, used to say, "Live and learn…die and be dissected."

Two other pilots from Cam Ranh were on the plane with us. Both are captains. They have contracted for a three-bed suite in an outside motel and have already called for transportation. They ask if I would like to share it with them. Being tired, hot and ready to settle for anything with a shower and bed, I say, "Okay." Well, let me describe that "suite"!

The room rate is $12/night or $4/person, and it is drastically over-priced. The lights are at least two candlepower and the air-conditioning doesn't work. The humidity in the room is 95-plus percent and the ambient temperature is over 100. When I enter the room, the activity of giant cockroaches reminds me of being on an aircraft carrier when all planes are revving up for takeoff. Only, in this case, the aircraft are cockroaches. They rev up their wings, preparing for takeoff, and then zoom through the room until they crash land on the opposite wall. Their immediate increase in activity is an obvious expression of displeasure at our intrusion. On visual inspection, it is difficult to distinguish the cockroaches on the wall from the crud that has accumulated in heaps on the walls and floor. The deciding factor is that the crud doesn't move when you approach. Everything smells like urine. If this is preparation for jungle survival school, I can hardly wait until I get to the jungle!

Philosophically, there are certain advantages to living in military quarters. The officers quarters are usually air-conditioned, except when it doesn't work. There are, however, inherent problems in living dormitory-style with other officers. Each room has the capacity for four people. At present, there are only three of us. One of the other men is scheduled to move out shortly. This leaves me with a second lieutenant to occupy the space.

Finally, in the homogenous military environment at Clark AFB, I must conform to the discipline and routine of barracks duty imposed on every "junior officer." I have had little experience with military protocol. My first experience in the Air Force was during my internship at Wilford Hall Hospital at Lackland AFB, Texas. It was a sheltered introduction, where doctors were generally exempted from the routine drill and military protocol usually required of officers with comparable rank. I have been totally spoiled. As a doctor, and especially as a flight surgeon, I have never been treated as a "junior officer." With the exception of Bergstrom AFB, full colonels and three-star generals have addressed me as "doctor," and not by my rank. But here, my flight from military reality has come to a screeching halt.

As Irving Berlin said: "This is the Army (insert Air Force), Mister Jones! No private rooms or telephones. You had your breakfast in bed before. But you won't have it there anymore."

The second lieutenant with whom I share the room is a most affable and pleasant person. There is no problem there. But Air Force regulations are Air Force regulations. Every morning at 0600, there is room inspection for neatness, to ensure that beds have been made and floors swept. To make beds up in proper military fashion, effectively precludes sleeping on that bed the night before. The bedspread and sheets must be made up and stretched so taut that a quarter dropped on them will bounce. It is all purely cosmetic. I am not accustomed to such nonsense. Initially, I said, "To hell with it," and continued the day. None of my roommates said anything. But suddenly I realize that they are receiving demerits because of me. Before this, all personnel have gone out of their way to help me. They had requisitioned lockers, linens and toiletry for me...all without request from me.

My conscience and sense of right vs. wrong intervene. I cannot drag them down because of my own lack of military discipline. But the longer that I live with it, the angrier I become. At this age and stage of life, the thought of someone checking on me, as if I were three years old, and penalizing my colleagues because I am too stubborn to cooperate, becomes intolerable. Since we are about to move into the jungle, I endure the situation for another twenty-four hours. The independence offered by life in the jungle looks far more inviting than this life of surveillance and constant micromanagement.

While going through these machinations, I visit the Officers Club. I am impressed. It operates on the scale of a first class nightclub. The food is excellent and at reasonable prices. Each evening there is a first class floor show with live entertainment. There is usually a Filipino band with male/female vocalist, both of which are of good quality.

Initially it is a bit awkward. Remember that I have arrived from a combat zone…where nearly anything goes. But here there is a dress code that requires sport coat, tie and trousers. I have none of these. (I planned to attend jungle survival school…right?) The club provides a generic sports coat, tie and even trousers for us Vietnam types. But, they do not have shoes. The combat boots are my own. To sneak through the club entrance, I have polished them to a mirror-like shine. Somehow, things always seem to work out.

What I have thus far seen of the Philippine Islands and Clark Air Force Base is impressive. The landscape is very verdant and plush in contrast to the desert island atmosphere of Cam Ranh Bay. The heat and humidity are about the same as Vietnam.

Stopping by the Base Exchange, I purchase a paperback version of Studs Lonigan by James Farrell. It is about growing up in Chicago. Hopefully, it may provide insight for me into Elaine's background, just as William Faulkner's writings have provided insight into the South and my Southern background for her. It is written in three parts, totaling 800 pages. I'll take this with me into the jungle and hope to have a little spare time to read it.

22 August 1966

10 p.m.

Today was devoted to classroom instruction on general aspects of camping and surviving in a jungle environment. I find it all a bit boring and highly repetitious. The entire day from 6 a.m. to 5:30 p.m. is spent in a sweltering classroom receiving instruction about things I learned and experienced in Florida as a Tenderfoot Boy Scout. I have to realize that the majority of these pilots have been raised in urban environments and life out-of-doors is entirely foreign to them. I am comfortable in the jungle, but they are not.

The story of a previous survival class is related to us. During one of the nights camping out in the jungle, a flight surgeon was awakened by an "unfamiliar noise." He suddenly panicked, and in his terror, ran off a cliff, breaking his neck. Such things are beyond my understanding. However, for most adults today, urban noises are their background noise. Traffic noise, sirens and honking horns drown out all noises of nature. The thousands of unknown voices and calls of insects, frogs, lizards, night flying birds and predators are completely foreign to city people. Since I spent my boyhood in a Florida swamp, the jungle is no less than a surrogate home for me. For me, the jungle is what the briar patch was for Brer' Rabbit.

The flight surgeon at Clark looked me up. He was one year behind me at Northwestern Medical School and in Al Aleckna's class (graduated 1964). I recognized his face, but didn't know him well in medical school. He is single and rotates two months at Clark, with two months at Da Nang in Vietnam. He was very affable and informed me that there are a number of NUMS (Northwestern University Medical School) graduates in the region. He named five more Northwestern doctors who are stationed in Vietnam.

An assignment in the Philippines is a vacation spot compared to Vietnam. I can understand why. The island is beautiful, but the accommodations are average. For most of the military personnel here, guards must be hired for their houses. Life is so impoverished for the average Filipino that they will steal anything at the first opportunity. This presents a ticklish political situation. Military personnel are instructed to ignore most infractions by Filipino housekeepers. Even if they catch a Filipino in the act of theft, they cannot shoot him/her. It is better to let him/her steal. Evidently, the Air Force walks a tight rope with the Philippine government. All water for drinking and cooking must be imported from Clark since tap water is not potable. It all makes you appreciate the ole U.S. of A. more and more.

26 August 1966 Midnight Letter to Elaine

Dear Elaine,

When I think of telling you that I will write notes to you on a daily basis while in the jungle and then mail them to you all at once, upon my return to base, I can only laugh at my naïveté. What follows are summaries of my experiences. I'll let you draw your own conclusion as to the amount of spare time that I have had to write…

Tuesday

At 7 a.m. we check out ponchos, canteens and machetes at the school and board buses, transporting us to the jungle.

The route we travel passes through a valley framed by mountainous jungles and green pastures on both sides. The fields on each side of the road are lush, green and completely pastoral in appearance. One of our instructors points out that this peaceful road was the former path taken by American prisoners of war on the Bataan Death March. He points to a beautiful, peaceful mountainside on the left side of the bus and says more than 10,000 Americans who died on the Death March are buried there.

Then turning to the right, he points to the other mountainside and says another 7,000 Americans are buried there.

I am nearly speechless. For me this is Holy Ground. The Bataan Death March has haunted me since childhood. As one of the citadels of American sacrifice, it is one of my strongest memories of World War II history. It stands on a par with Valley Forge, the Alamo, Wake Island and Guadalcanal. I have known only three survivors from the Death March. One was a college physics professor from Emory-at-Oxford, who had sought the seclusion of teaching in junior college after World War II. Another person was an Army doctor who was captured and later wrote of his experiences. (Batan Diary by Dr. Paul Ashton. Library of Congress Catalogue Card No. 85-192945. 1984). The third was a patient, Jack Garcia, from Santa Maria, California.

The Bataan Death March was a seventy-mile forced march of 72,000 American and Filipino prisoners of war captured by Japanese forces. American forces were under the command of Lt. Gen. Jonathan M. Wainwright IV. Faced with starvation and no ammunition, they were forced to surrender to the Japanese Army after their defeat in the grinding, three-month-long Battle of Bataan (January 7 - April 9, 1942). The Allied soldiers had not been resupplied for a couple of months, and most were sick and malnourished.

All survived, clinging to hope of "The Return," a mythical concept when the mighty United States of America would send fleets of ships with thousands of soldiers to rescue them from the Japanese. Unknown to them at the time was the fact that for all practical purposes, the Philippines and all American forces had been written off by Washington. Prior to this, Gen. Douglas MacArthur had been commander of all U.S. forces in the Philippines. He was smuggled out of danger in a motor P.T. boat that took him to Australia. MacArthur was sufficiently prominent with the American public that the consequences of him being captured were not politically palatable to the Roosevelt administration. While others of his command surrendered with their troops to Japanese atrocities, he fled to safety with his family and pet dog. Rightly or wrongly, this action was interpreted as an act of cowardice by many enlisted men in all branches of the military. Because of this episode, he was nicknamed, "Dug-Out-Doug." Gen. Jonathan M. Wainright, his second in command, faced the humiliation of defeat by the Japanese in the largest surrender of military forces in U.S. history.

The prisoners were placed in prison camps remote from Bataan. Despite the poor condition of the prisoners, the Japanese command calculated that it would take them only three days to march seventy miles through the jungle. Japanese officers took this order to heart, driving the wounded, ill, and emaciated prisoners relentlessly through the tropical heat, while depriving them of food and water.

Anyone who fell behind, muttered a complaint, or had a souvenir previously taken from a fallen Japanese soldier, or even looked at one of the Japanese in a wrongful manner, was bayoneted or shot. Some prisoners were shot for stopping to fill their canteens at a roadside ditch. Beating a prisoner with the butt of a rifle was commonplace for offenses such as helping a faltering comrade. Many prisoners were bayoneted for no apparent reason, other than for the fun of inflicting pain. Filipino civilians along the path who offered food or water to the prisoners were also summarily killed by the Japanese.

A total of 18,000-20,000 of the POWs died during the first week of the Bataan Death March. Many simply collapsed and died of illness or starvation, but most were murdered. For those who survived the march, a large but unknown number of the POWs died shortly thereafter in the internment camps as well.

After Japan's unconditional surrender in 1945, the Japanese commander in charge of Bataan, General Homma, was put on trial for war crimes and atrocities, which included the Bataan Death March. He stated that he had been unaware of the high death toll from the march until some time later. Nonetheless, he was convicted and executed in the Philippines on April 3, 1946.

But now, looking out on the peaceful green fields that stretch quietly on each side of the muddy road, it seems nearly impossible to think that more than 17,000 Americans are buried beneath the grass. These were American servicemen, no different from me or any of the other men on the buses. It is like a pall suddenly cast over me to think that only twenty-four years ago this path was one of unmitigated horror, suffering and death.

In the eyes of history, twenty-four years is the blink of an eye. It all seems terribly surreal. And later, when I look back, it continues to haunt me. How could I sit in an air-conditioned officers club, surrounded by the decadence of polished wooden floors at a table with white tablecloth… and listen to the sugary crooning of a young Filipino woman singer…without thinking of this? It is comparable to having a carnival in a cemetery.

I readily admit being a sentimental fool, but I make no apologies for feeling humbled in a place where brave men have died and are buried. Most people simply push such terrible times from their memories, as if such a gesture removes them from any responsibility and assures that the atrocities never occurred. In social discussions, during better times, the very suggestion of these atrocities and hardships raises eyebrows of distaste. It is more socially acceptable to smile all the time and to speak only of more positive issues.

But I am not this person. The debt that all Americans owe to the soldiers who paid the ultimate price can never be repaid, and their memories should never be erased. We continue to live in a free country because of men who placed their lives on the line to defend our way of life.

After we continue driving for more than two hours, the dirt roads progressively narrow and worsen, ultimately forcing us to stop. At this point, any thought of a "road" has faded into mud and ruts. What continues is more appropriately called a narrow muddy path. Whatever you call it, for our current mode of transportation, this foot path has rapidly changed from impassable to non-existent. We transfer from buses into large troop-carrier trucks with four-wheel drive. We ford streams and climb nearly sheer cliffs to follow what is little more than a rabbit's path.

Finally after another ten miles of groaning engines and straining gears, the going becomes impossible, even for these combat-hardened trucks. We leave the trucks and shoulder our packs and other gear to begin our long trek on foot into the jungle. It has been raining continuously all day. But now the heavens open up to reveal the full potential of tropical rainstorms. The rain falls in sheets, not only from the clouds above, but also horizontally in sheets that merge into waves, flowing in from the fog that begins to envelop us. The deluge is so heavy at times that I consider swimming rather than walking through it. There are other times during which we fall rather than walk into the jungle morass. The ground drops precipitously before us and we grope for vines to slow ourselves from skidding downward into invisible quagmires. Arriving at the bottom, we grope blindly for roots and vines to pull ourselves up and out of the cavern.

Progressively, the trees grow taller and taller as their trunks grow larger and larger in diameter, sending their rope-like roots across our path in every direction. The waning sunlight under the canopy of the trees is progressively blocked out as we stumble on through the stygian darkness like a chain of drunken blind men.

As soon as the brush closes to embrace us, we are attacked by myriads of leeches, mosquitoes and legions of other biting insects and creatures, while we are slashed by briars of a wondrous array. Then we fall, slide, stagger and splash our way farther into the blackness before us. There seems to be no solid ground. The mud is like syrup as it quickly fills our combat boots. With each step our feet sink into the muck and squelch under foot.

When one foot sinks, there is no traction for the other foot to pull you out. I later learn why the natives go barefoot. It is easier to flex bare toes for leverage in breaking the suction of the mud than to struggle with the smooth contours of our boots. The sound generated by the sucking mud is considerable. This is particularly important during escape and evasion situations, where the sucking noise created by extracting a foot carries far in the silent forest and may reveal your entrapped presence to the enemy. Meanwhile the rain continues, descending in drops and dripping from billions of leaves overhead. It runs down our collars and necks to mingle with sweat and soaks through our packs and down to our waists.

Finally, the terrain's incline begins to plateau, while the path remains invisible. The only certainty is the direction…up. Grasping vines and tree limbs, we struggle to keep our footing on some of the roughest terrain I have ever faced. I have seen more briars, vines and potholes many times in the South as a boy. But never have I faced the extraordinary combination of all these obstacles.

There is no concern about keeping anything dry. That is a laugh! But, I know from previous experience that I won't melt in water. The "path" before us is a trough of mud that courses up cliff sides of 70-80 degrees inclination. The effort of moving is all consuming, as we grope for handholds and footholds, constantly gasping for breath, and further weighed down by our packs.

I hadn't realized just how poor my physical conditioning had become. My breaths are no more than short gasps as we plod on. And then, suddenly, after about an hour the going suddenly becomes easier. I realize that I've finally found my "second wind." I couldn't help thinking that if I did this every day, I wouldn't have to wait so long for my "second wind" to kick in. Unfortunately, a number of the other pilots don't get their "second wind," and they are truly in agony. A few of them drop out of line and I hear them vomiting on the sidelines with dry heaves. By now, I am too tired to stop or care. It is almost dark because of the cloud cover, which deepens as we continue for another two hours until total darkness is upon us. We are tired beyond caring. The fatigue is so all consuming that no man admits to another how tired he is... each person thinking subconsciously that, if he can make it, then so can I. And so we continue plodding on through the mold-smelling wet tangle of jungle web...military automatons on the march!

We try to maintain our line of march, but it is impossible to see beyond the man in front of you. You are either blinded by the rain, when looking ahead, or blinded by sweat dripping into your eyes while looking down at the mud, searching for a root to grab. The rain continues in torrents.

At last, we finally reach our campsite, which is on a plateau high in the mountainous jungle.

We have been previously instructed on how to construct individual shelters from native materials before the darkness becomes absolute. I remember this with a faint smile, since it is less than one degree from absolute darkness. The description has an academic ring that is totally divorced from reality.

Construction of our shelters for the night is supposed to be the result of individual effort, with no cooperation between the men. Responses are variable. Some of the men simply collapse on the soggy ground, groan in resignation and pull their ponchos over their heads. They simply plan to ride out their misery on the ground, enduring rain, mosquitoes, snakes and whatever else emerges to torment them throughout the night. The types of equipment that we are allowed to carry are: 1. A panel of silk parachute that we would have after ejecting; 2. Multiple strands of silk parachute lines; 3. Two matches; 4. Hunting knife; 5. The usual survival vest that is standard issue for pilots. In addition, I smuggled a bit of mosquito netting contraband inside of my boots. This is standard equipment when I camp out.

I have no desire to be devoured by swarms of mosquitoes. Drawing upon my childhood in Florida, I lash three logs between three trees with parachute lines to form a triangle arrangement. I next lace a portion of the parachute panel into the triangle. This forms a triangular parachute hammock about four feet off the ground. (It is necessary to get above the ground because of the large number of snakes, rats, and other animals that roam through the jungle at night.) It also allows a person to stay above the ground where puddles of water abound. I lash three poles above me with vines, and overlay them with bamboo and banana leaves to form a roof.

As a boy in Central Florida, I have gone through similar exercises, on countless campouts, under many of these same conditions. I am well aware of the suddenness of nightfall in the tropics and have had a great deal of practice in speedily constructing a shelter for the night. In fact, my boyhood campouts in the swamps of Florida render these activities rather routine procedures, which I accomplish rather easily.

Now, at least I have a dry bed with a roof over my head. There is only one thing missing…and I am prepared for it. The worst things about camping in a jungle or swamp are the clouds of mosquitoes that descend upon you. Whether they whine around your ears or bite you is almost irrelevant. Both features will drive you to madness. Wrapping my contraband mosquito netting loosely around my head, I am in "Fat City." I have a safe dry bed, out of the rain, and above the snakes and vermin, plus mosquito netting over my head. I eat my C-Rations and go to bed. My clothes are soaking wet, but this does not concern me. I know that as I sleep, the heat of my body will dry them out, while at the same time shielding me from mosquitoes.

Ah! Life is good! God is in his heavens and all is right with the world! My stomach is full. My bed is high and dry. Mosquitoes can't reach me. The rain continues in sheets all night, but I sleep well. I fall asleep, smiling at the sound of raindrops on my roof of leaves, a steady drumbeat all night.

CHAPTER 18

═══════════════

Surviving Survival School

IN THE MORNING, MOST OF THE OTHER PILOTS ARE huddled in misery, squatting over a smoky little fire. Their hammocks have either collapsed or never worked at all, and they have had little or no sleep. In general, they appear to be miserable. I feel slightly guilty to be in such chipper spirits. I do recall many similar experiences as a boy when I was hunting and camping, just as wet and just as miserable. During my youth, I loved every moment of it. But, this is a new experience for 90 percent of the other men. They have been raised in urban environments and the jungle is a foreign world to them. For me it is déjà vu all over again.

But, I can't say that it is the same. Now it is rougher. As a boy, this was all part of a wondrous adventure, with little thought being given to personal comfort or inconvenience. So why is it different now? The rain is no wetter and the mosquitoes are no fiercer, but somehow, now, it is a shade more miserable and a little less fun. Is the difference only due to my years of softer living and long absence from the elemental conditions of survival, or is it simply a matter of being older, beyond the horizon of youth that once reveled in any new adventure? I don't know… I don't know…

The next morning (Wednesday) is spent trudging through the hills following our Negrito guides. There are many different tribes that dwell in the Philippine jungles. All are separated by time, religion, custom and languages. The Negritos are of unique stock and customs. They are black, nomadic aborigines of near-pygmy proportions who construct no homes and live in no dwellings, but who live and hunt through the forests. They have no permanent shelters and simply sleep in nests of leaves on the forest floor. In fact, it is believed that they were the first human inhabitants of these islands. They are nomadic hunters who have lived their entire lives in these jungles and know the paths, flora and fauna better than any other people. They continue to hunt with bows and arrows. Their dress is no more than a breech cloth over their loins and they follow the custom of filing their teeth into sharp points.

They earned their place in American history during World War II. When the Japanese conquered the Americans in the Philippine Islands, the peaceful Negritos were maltreated by the Japanese. During the Japanese occupation, the sole purpose of the Negritos was to exact vengeance on the Japanese for the cruelty inflicted on their people. Stories abound about their feats against the Japanese. One example is:

A group of Japanese soldiers captured several Negritos and tied them up. The Negritos are a peaceful tribe dedicated only to feeding their families by hunting and fishing. And since they had no animosity towards the Japanese or anyone else, they were surprised when the Japanese captured them and treated them poorly. On one occasion, the Japanese took several unknown fruits and vegetables from either the jungle or from local natives. As they cooked them, the Negritos tried to warn them that a particular tuber was poisonous unless prepared in a special manner. Not comprehending the Negrito language, the Japanese became angry at the interference of these "savages." After beating them, the Japanese ate the tuber. All Japanese soldiers died from the poison tubers and subsequent blame was placed on the Negritos.

The Negritos were incensed at many comparable situations. In many subtle ways, they became very antagonistic to the Japanese. A typical approach was to sneak into the gardens of the Japanese to plant various local poisonous plants that resembled familiar, non-poisonous vegetables. They continued to set traps for ambushing the Japanese and harassed their activities throughout the occupation.

At the end of World War II, in appreciation for their guerrilla-like tactics, General MacArthur awarded lifetime commissary privileges to the Negritos. Now, some thirty-plus years later, the Negritos are used by all branches of our military as jungle experts to teach our pilots and seamen techniques of jungle survival. Usually they are rewarded well (by standards of the local economy) for their services.

We spent most of our time learning about edible roots, tubers and leaves from the Negritos. The jungle has become steamy, and the steam rises from the ground to conceal the faint paths through the vegetation. Nothing is dry. Finally I accept the inevitable wetness and mildew. As the survival manual states, this is an exercise of escape and evasion in a jungle environment. The only purpose of this course is to teach the downed aviator how to survive long enough to be rescued. Deal with it and suck it up! Your life depends on it!

On our second day in the jungle, we are shown how to cook wild rice in bamboo culms. After cooking, we pour the rice out onto banana leaves and eat it for lunch. During all of this, I notice that Col. Doerty eats with a pair of chopsticks he has fashioned for himself, while the rest of us whittle small paddles out of palm fronds to use for "spoon-fork" utensils. I watch Colonel Doerty eat with the chopsticks and greatly admire his dexterity.

I also note that he hesitated a moment before starting to eat. He simply stared quietly at the rice, as if in contemplation. I said nothing.

Later in casual conversation I smile and tell him of my admiration for his dexterity. It is then that I learn the truth. He was shot down twice during the Korean War and served more than two-and-a-half years in a North Korean prisoner of war camp. During his imprisonment, his only food had been a daily small ration of rice and occasional dried fish head. He escaped several times but was always recaptured and tortured for his efforts. He does not speak of any of this readily, and I did not force the conversation. Truly, it must have been hell on Earth. I gained a new respect for the man. To have escaped not once but twice was no small feat …and now to continue along the same path!

This is fine for him, personally, but, with a family, his decision becomes a bit more complicated. I can fully appreciate what his wife and children went through during his years of captivity. But this is his career and his choice.

The rains begin anew each day and continue through each night. The following day is devoted to practice being picked out of the jungle by helicopter. In this exercise, the helicopter hovers above the jungle canopy and a jungle penetrator is dropped about 200 feet from the helicopter. Our familiarity in using the jungle penetrator is critical for being extracted from the jungle during escape and evasion from combat situations. The technique requires some practice and is not as easy as it seems. The jungle penetrator is a weighted device that is wedge-shaped to penetrate the jungle canopy. It features a collar that must be fitted appropriately before the winch on the helicopter activates and pulls you out of the jungle.

Unfortunately, too many downed fliers have been so panic-stricken to escape from enemy territory, that in their haste, they fitted the collar inappropriately and fell to their death while being extracted.

During the afternoon of Thursday, September 1, 1966, we are to be dropped off in pairs throughout the jungle. Each pair is to survive, escaping detection by the Negritos, who have been hired to "capture" us. Each person is given two "chits" or tokens. If captured by the Negritos, we are honor-bound to give our captor one of the chits. The Negritos will later redeem the chit at the Base Commissary for three pounds of rice for each G.I. captured. The Negritos are expert hunters and trackers. They are able to track you like a dog, by sight, sound and by smell. We have been informed that it is virtually impossible to escape their detection. The valid assumption by our military is that the ability of the average Viet Cong or North Vietnamese soldier in jungle tracking is grossly inferior to that of the Negritos. We are therefore pitted against the best stalkers and trackers in this part of the world.

I must say that this project is my cup of tea! Having spent my youth playing hide and seek with others in the swamps and woods of Central Florida, I am well-prepared, mentally and talent-wise. I am the exception, however.

We trek across streams and marshes to another rendezvous point, where we are loaded into trucks for a journey to "strange jungle areas." The rain continues in a constant downpour as the trucks wind their way through river bottoms and swamp areas. Just as we pull out of a marsh area and head for a small jungle plateau, we hear the "egg-beater" flop...flop... flop of helicopter rotors. A few moments later, the trucks stop abruptly. Everyone is rather bedraggled in appearance. Besides being sleep deprived and physically exhausted, we are soaked through to the skin by the rain, hungry, unshaven and filthy dirty. No one is in a sociable mood. Groaning, we pile out of the trucks onto the soppy ground. The helicopter lands in a small cleared area downhill from some small trees. To my utter amazement, Arthur Godfrey steps out of the helicopter!

For those who may read this in future years, Arthur Godfrey was a number one celebrity of the very early days of radio and television from 1950-1960. He was an American radio and television broadcaster and entertainer who was sometimes introduced by his nickname, The Old Redhead. He was at the helm of a ubiquitous CBS-TV series and a daily ninty-minute mid-morning television show through the decade of 1950-1960. His TV shows became our family gathering point. He came across as a congenial television personality who played host to many celebrities. He was also respected by my father as a veteran of World War II.

Godfrey holds the rank of captain in the U.S. Navy Reserve, and is on active duty as a helicopter pilot during the Vietnam War. He steps jauntily from the helicopter and makes the rounds on our bedraggled group, shaking hands and chatting with each person. It is drizzling rain and the mosquitoes are beginning to tune up for their early evening orchestration and assaults.

I notice that he is breathing a bit hard with short breaths. I then remember that he has previously sustained surgery for cancer of the lung. It is significant for me that there are no reporters or cameras available to record this encounter for future publicity purposes. Because of this, I truly appreciate his efforts. Obviously, he is not here simply for a photo opportunity with "our boys in Vietnam." He is a personality type with no particular talents, such as singing or dancing, but he obviously thought enough to make an unpublicized visit into this damn rainy jungle, just to shake hands and to chat informally with each of us. My appreciation is shared by all the other men of our class.

A transition period occurs when all pilots are out of the trucks, and Godfrey is departing in his helicopter. Colonel Doerty prods me to follow and we both duck into the bushes beside the road. Now, free of the group, he and I spend the next several hours, sneaking and crawling, worm-like, through head-high elephant grass and bushes, attempting to conceal our path from the Negritos.

We decide to spend the night on a hilltop, surrounded by elephant grass. This offers a 360-degree field of view to observe anyone trying to approach us. It is here that I again appreciate my foresight in smuggling the mosquito netting into my boot. Draping the netting over my "go-to-hell" Australian style bush hat and tucking the ends under my collar, I can ignore the clouds of mosquitoes that swarm over and around us. All is quiet, except for the chorus of jungle sounds as we settle in for the night.

Sometime later during the night, as I am dozing off to sleep, something nudges my foot. Since I still have my combat boots on, I pay little attention, believing it to be a mouse, rat or other small creature. I continue to lie motionless but the characteristic winding movements of a snake soon becomes evident as it finds a rip in my trousers and proceeds to crawl inside my trousers and up my leg. I know that it is attracted by the heat of my body and is exploring the heat for a source of food. I do not believe that it will bite, solely on the basis of my body heat. It continues to crawl all the way up to the level of my groin, and then, having satisfied its curiosity, it slowly begins to backtrack out, coiling and uncoiling as it goes. I know that if I simply do not move, the odds are that whatever the type of snake, it will tire of a path that leads nowhere and leave. Ultimately, this proves to be the correct course of action. After fifteen to twenty minutes of intense "focused immobilization" on my part, the snake crawls out the hole in my trousers and returns to the jungle. Since the darkness is absolute, I am unable to identify this curious reptile.

As we lie in the elephant grass, the constant chorus of frogs, crickets and other jungle noises is reassuring to me. In my boyhood, these noises had been punctuated by the hoot of a great horned owl (in Southern collo-quialism…a hoot owl), the distant grunt of an alligator or a whippoorwill with its melancholy strains drifting on the warm summer breezes. I loved it all. Any interruption, falter or sudden termination of this jungle chorus, was an auditory cue to warn that an intruder had entered the scene. The intruder might be any large creature…such as a man. As a child, I always considered the wilderness as being an exclusive club of different creatures, noisily conversing with each other until a stranger entered the room. When this occurs, the club members will suddenly fall silent at the intrusion. With this background serenade, I fall into a shallow sleep.

Several hours later I am suddenly awake. It is about 0200. I am immediately aware of what wakened me. It is the sudden silence. The intrusion is either by a large predator or human. I know that there are no large predators in this part of the Philippines.

I am now awake and fully alert as I lie motionless, waiting for the intruder to give himself away by either sound or motion. I am reassured to note that Colonel Doerty is also awake and alert to the cues that have awakened me. Very slowly, I moisten my raised finger to discern the wind direction. Peeking through the blades of elephant grass, I see the silhouette of a man approximately 150 yards from us, with his face turned upward to sniff the wind for our presence. We are downwind from him and therefore safe from a scent track to detect us. The most sensible option is to remain totally quiet and motionless, in the hope that he will eventually turn to another path and leave. But, he doesn't!

Very slowly, he turns in our direction and methodically begins walking directly toward us. Obviously, this is a master of his trade, a professional tracker, skilled in the ways of the wilderness. I watch in silent admiration as he slowly continues to stalk us. We have to move. With a gesture, Colonel Doerty and I slowly begin to worm our way through the elephant grass, heading downhill toward a small flowing stream. At our slow pace, we finally reach the banks of the stream in about an hour. Quietly, we slip into the water and silently work our way upstream to a group of logs and bushes that have fallen into the water. Nearly submerged, except for our mouth and nose for breathing, we hide within the brush. The gurgling water provides excellent sound cover.

The decision to go upstream is mine. It is based on the fact that for a person being pursued, it is contrary to the expected route of flight, somewhat like fleeing toward the police station to avoid arrest. Because of this, we expect that he will search for us downstream. We are correct. Slowly and stealthily he comes to the stream bank and pauses. He is within two feet of us and so close that his breathing is audible. After a few minutes, he turns away to follow the stream away from us and then eventually fades into the night. We wait for an hour or so and then slowly work our way further upstream until we reach a sandbank and slowly creep from the water. So far, the coast is clear. By making a circular detour out and away from the stream, we follow our compass to the pre-arranged extraction point and wait there until sunrise when the helicopter will pick us up.

The helicopter is a bit late, but just after dawn, we hear the familiar flop-flop of the helicopter rotors. We have partially dried out from our water adventure. At this point, it is simply a matter of popping a flare to signal the helicopter. Sighting our flare, the pilot flies toward us and hovers about fifty feet above us. From this point, the loadmaster drops a cable with a jungle penetrator to extract us from our hiding place. The loadmaster reels us in, one at a time. Climbing into the helicopter is a relief beyond measure. We have made it!

We have successfully "escaped" and "evaded" capture. Finally when we reach the central camp, we learn that out of 300 airmen in the class we are the only two persons who have evaded capture by the Negritos. We turn in our "chits," and are proud of our achievement. In retrospect, I could easily have done without the previous night of misery, but there is a strong sense of accomplishment in having outwitted the Negrito trackers during this period. Perhaps they are so accustomed to the amateurish efforts of city bred Americans that they did not expect the challenge that we presented.

Later, I questioned Colonel Doerty about his previous experience. He seemed as much at home in the jungle as I throughout the entire adventure. His previous two captures as a POW and two escapes during the Korean War made him comfortable with anything. And so, we were a perfect team. He had previous experience from the reality of survival in enemy territory, while I had the background of childhood games in the swamps of Central Florida.

We return to Clark Air Force Base. After turning in our equipment, the things that I want most are a shower, a shave and a good night's sleep. The clothes that I wear have not been changed for more than a week. My fingernails are stubs from digging roots in the jungle. And, for the first time in my life, I obtain a manicure at the Officers Club barber shop. The cost for this by a Filipino woman is 25 cents. I check into a room at the Clark, AFB motel. There is a desk and carpet on the floor. It is spotless and the sheets are crisp. Compared to the Filipino economy models, it is plush. Since I have eaten nothing for the past four days except berries, roots and leaves, I am starving.

I change into a clean, newly starched uniform. After supplementing my dress with sports coat and tie borrowed from the Officers Club, I begin to feel human again. I order Chateaubriand for two persons. It is one of the best pieces of beef I have ever eaten and the serving for two is the correct order for this one starving person. I accompany my meal with a bottle of Piper Heidsieck champagne.

Colonel Doerty has friends at Clark and we pay them a visit. His friend is a colonel in the Air Force who served with him in Korea. This is a very nice family by any measure. Of medical interest is one of the housekeepers, a young woman with a huge goiter. The goiter is so large that she must turn her entire body, and not just her head, to look to the side. On closer inspection, she has obvious, persistent branchial cleft cysts of her neck. These result from failure of the second branchial cleft to obliterate during fetal/embryonic development. I am informed that goiter[17] is endemic in these islands.

After refreshments, we excuse ourselves to prepare for our return to Vietnam.

Before leaving the Philippines, we were scheduled for a trip to Manila and Baguio. Unfortunately, flights were not available for either of those places. Instead, I spend the morning doing laundry, shining boots and attending to the usual toiletries of life. The rest of the day is spent taking a nap. I shop to obtain a small wood carving of flowers for a table centerpiece. It has to be dismantled for mailing. I advised Elaine in a short note: "Please let me know what it looks like after you reassemble it. Its first appearance is that of a Chinese puzzle, but it seems attractive on my cursory inspection." I also obtained a mother-of-pearl tissue box. I told Elaine: "If you don't like it, we can use it as a gift. I only wish that you were here to help with my selection of gifts. I'm sure that we can obtain better in Japan."

Before we leave the Philippines an amusing incident occurs. Shortly after we arrived, one of the pilots had his wallet picked from his pocket. When we return to Clark Air Force Base to catch a flight back to Vietnam, a group of pilots walks through a large open-air market. One section has black velvet paintings of nude women vividly displayed. This type of thing

---

17 Goiter is the term used to describe an enlarged thyroid gland. Large goiters can make it hard to breathe or swallow and can cause a cough and hoarseness. Goiter occurs much more frequently in women than in men. Worldwide, the most common cause of goiter is iodine deficiency, which can be prevented by the appropriate intake of food rich in iodine (salt-water fish, crabs, shrimps, squid, seaweeds) and others; and by the regular use of iodized salt in daily diet. Iodine deficiency is the cause of Goiter in the Philippine Islands. The Philippine Thyroid Council has been organized to deal with this public health issue.

is commonly sold to enlisted men, but I never observed officers buying anything. That is until now! Apparently, someone had found the picture (headshot) of the pilot's wife in his stolen wallet. They used her picture as a model for their black velvet nude painting! The lieutenant was speechless. Needless to say, he promptly bought the painting to get it off the market.

While strolling through the market, I was approached by street vendors carrying a tray, comparable to vendors who sell hot dogs during baseball games. The tray is filled with duck eggs, called baluts. A balut or balot is a fertilized duck embryo that is boiled and eaten in the shell. Others are not boiled. It is commonly sold as street food. Balut eaters prefer salt and/ or a chili, garlic and vinegar (white or coconut sap) mixture to season their eggs. The eggs are savored for their balance of textures and flavors; the broth surrounding the embryo is sipped from the egg before the shell is peeled, and the yolk with young duckling inside can be eaten.

My understanding is that the embryos are half rotted or fermented to provide their unique flavor. I found this interesting, but not so much to entice my tasting it.

It was not until later that I learned of injuries sustained by many of the pilots during their course of jungle survival. These included machete cuts, torn cartilages, lacerations and back injuries from falling over cliffs. After we returned to Cam Ranh, eight pilots were hospitalized with bronchitis, flu and various febrile complaints from exposure and sleeping in the rain.

CHAPTER 19

─────────────────

Return to Cam Ranh

AFTER LAST MONTH AT BINH TUY, FOLLOWED BY Jungle Survival School in the Philippines, the return to my routine duties at Cam Ranh Bay is somewhat of a relief. With the exception of continuing expansion of the facilities at Cam Ranh Bay, nothing dramatic has happened while I was away.

1 September 1966

The song, "I Left My Heart in San Francisco" as sung by Frank Sinatra, was played at dinner tonight in the officers' mess. I was struck by a wave of homesickness…

2 September 1966

F-4C Mission

Aircraft Commander: Major Strickland

Time: 1 hr. 20 min.

The mission is fragged[18] for a Viet Cong ammunition depot in the mountains about fifty miles east of Cam Ranh. The weather at Cam Ranh is clear and visibility is unlimited. Our takeoff and approach to target are without a hitch. We climb to an altitude of 9,500 feet to form up and fly to the target area. As we approach the target, the FAC is contacted and surprisingly enough, shortly thereafter we locate him visually. It is not always this easy to spot the tiny plane against the background of jungle. Floating over the treetops, he marks a target in the dense jungle by firing two Willie Pete rockets.

Each of our four planes dive-bombs the area with two five-hundred-pound general-purpose bombs. After pulling off target, we regroup for the flight back to Cam Ranh. Throughout the entire attack, the actual target was never seen by any pilot of our group. We simply bomb the area of jungle marked by our Bird Dog with his white phosphorus rockets. The FAC reports that the target was destroyed. It is nice to have confirmation of our efforts since none of our pilots saw either the target or the results of our dive-bombing.

On our return flight, Major Strickland turns the aircraft over to me. I am slowly gaining proficiency in flying the F-4. This is such an extraordinary aircraft. Nothing else can compare to flying it! The return flight to Cam Ranh and subsequent landing are uneventful. This completes my twenty-second strike mission in the Phantom.

---

18 Abbreviation for Fragmentation Order (Frag Order), a portion of the entire mission directive that defines a specific mission of the day without stating the entire mission directive.

3 September 1966

This morning in the flight surgeon's office has been uneventful. From 0700-1200 hours, I saw a few patients with minor problems and continued wading through the usual mountain of paperwork. At noon Bill Simmons and I went to the Officers Club for lunch. On our way to the club we stopped by the Post Office. I received a letter and small package from Elaine. Bill complained about not receiving mail from his wife, Marilyn, in several days.

During lunch, Bill and I discussed some of the problems of the war, my plans for future residency, as well as Bill's plans for moving his family to his next assignment in Bitburg, Germany. He spoke enthusiastically of rejoining his wife and children in approximately three months before proceeding to Germany. I was particularly impressed by his words of affection for his family and noted somewhat subconsciously that he is the friendliest of individuals, and how it would be impossible not to like him.

After lunch we head back to the flight surgeon's office, and, on Bill's insistence, we again stop at the Post Office. He notes that this is the third time today that he has checked on the mail; he has not received any mail from his wife in about five days. He says this is the longest interval in which she hasn't communicated. Because of this, he is going to mail her a letter, "Slightly fussing at her," but he wanted to make sure he didn't make a mistake by overreacting. He mails the letter, and before returning to the flight surgeon's office, we walk over to the hospital area for a meeting with Colonel Mack in his office.

Those who have never been in an isolated position, duty station or combat zone (or, perhaps prison) can never understand the significance of something as simple as a letter from home or a loved one. It is difficult to appreciate the value of letters from loved ones when you are totally removed from them and immersed in a combat situation. The success of each day is measured in terms of the number of letters received from family, wives, children and friends.

A letter is the link that binds you to the sanity of a civilized world and all that is dear to you. A "care-package" is always appreciated but no more so than a letter or card. Relationships with other people are bonds that not even war or oceans can breach.

But there is always a dark side of the coin. Removed from family and friends, a progressive paranoia frequently intrudes on the subconscious when someone does not write with a certain frequency, or when events trigger the ever-present free-floating insecurities that isolation seems to breed. Isolation from one's family, friends and the world from which we were birthed exacts a toll on the depths of one's soul. I'm sure Bill was aware of this when he spoke of "not wanting to overreact."

At Colonel Mack's office we discuss plans for expansion of the flight surgeon's office as well as various and sundry housekeeping problems. From there, Bill and I return to the flight surgeon's office. Since no patients are waiting to be seen, I go to my desk to continue my study of cardiology. This self-imposed study program is in anticipation of the internal medicine residency that I plan in one year after leaving the Air Force.

Sometime shortly thereafter, Colonel Mack comes into the office to see Bill. Bill subsequently comes to my desk, asking that I join them in a discussion about new air conditioners for the office and several other minor problems. I remember at the time being pleased at Bill's invitation for me to participate in the conference. In three to four months after Bill rotates to his next assignment, I will be in command of the office. I muse that this action is worthy of his gentle person.

I appreciated that he asked my input for a situation that would involve change in the flight surgeon's office, of changes that would impact me far more than him during the short time that he had left on base. There were no earthshaking issues to discuss, but nevertheless, Bill was a big enough person to include me in the discussion—and personally secure enough in his position not to be threatened. It just so happens he is from Mississippi. Our personalities were in sync.

Maybe Southerners have mutual simpatico of cultural commonality from birth.... who knows? I can only state that it is a pleasure to work with one of my own people.

At 1315, Bill left the office to attend his 1330 preflight briefing at Base Operations. At approximately 1400 hours Bill stuck his head into my office to say that he had a strike mission in the F-4C and would return to the office around 1700 hours. I acknowledged this with a nod and a wave of my hand and continued studying. Little did I know that this would be the last time I would see him alive.

The afternoon passed slowly. No patients presented for care. The temperature outside was 114 degrees. The air conditioner was not functioning in the flight surgeon's office, where the inside temp was nearly 100. This is a recurrent problem. Yesterday, the sewage lines overflowed into the office. Raw sewage under your feet changes the atmosphere of a professional office by exuding its very distinctive odor. It also increases the humidity. It is best described as a fecal sauna. It is better today, but, like the song "where the melody lingers on," in this office, the odor lingers on. Because of these issues, I can hardly stay awake to study or to work through the mountain of paperwork on my desk. But, more important, I am afraid to fall asleep since I might be asphyxiated and never wake up. I envy Bill as he is now flying in the sterile, air-conditioned splendor of altitude, above these earthbound concerns of temperature, odors and humidity.

As 1700 hours approached, I began to close out my paperwork and prepare to leave the office before going to the O-Club for dinner. However, at approximately 1645 hours, one of the office corpsmen drifts by to say he had just overheard news about an F4-C being "lost."

This immediately gets my attention! Knowing that it is about time for Bill to return from his mission, I grab my cap and bolt for the door, heading toward the Command Post next door. Just as I open the door into the hallway, I collide with Colonel Mack, who is coming in as I am going out. Neither he nor I say a word. We simply look each other squarely in the eyes and nod. No words are necessary. We walk briskly to Base Command in the Quonset hut next door. Usual access is granted only through voice or facial recognition of familiar personnel. Tonight all formality has been lost. The control room is packed with personnel from Bill's squadron, the 557th TFS. Higher echelon types of all service areas are also present, representing the multiple tiers of search and rescue personnel with directors.

The flight of four Phantoms was returning to Cam Ranh Bay after a rather "routine napalm run." Capt. Clifford S. Heathcote of the 557th TFS was pilot in command, with Bill flying in the backseat position.

Heathcote and Bill's aircraft was in the number four position when they were approximately twenty nautical miles due northwest of Cam Ranh Bay. The flight was straight and level at an altitude of approximately 9,500 feet as they began a gradual descent toward base. The mountain peaks in the region extend to 4,500 feet. During the instrument penetration of one cloud layer, the backseater of the lead plane, flown by Capt. Marvin M. Gradert, noted that all four aircraft were in formation position. A large thunderhead was noted to the left of Heathcote's plane. Continuing the approach, a small stratus cloud layer was penetrated by the flight of all four airplanes. However, only three planes emerged. Aircraft number four was never seen or heard from again. The remaining three aircraft returned to Cam Ranh Bay and landed without incident.

Rescue choppers were immediately dispatched from Cam Ranh Bay and from Nha Trang. These were supplemented by six to eight armed Hueys from the Army. By this time, it was dark and the distant mountains were shrouded in the evening rain, fog and towering cumulus clouds that are so constant at this latitude. Under these conditions, the mountain peaks are cloaked in clouds while the ground is obscured by both clouds and ground fog. The land itself is treacherous, with dense jungle glades and trees that may tower up from the ground to 300-350 feet above the jungle floor. This umbrella of towering vegetation is dense enough to conceal an entire city from aerial detection. The fact that every inch of the land is controlled by the Viet Cong has already been validated on multiple previous occasions by bullet holes in reconnaissance and rescue helicopters, flying over the area.

Outside of Base Operations, the flight line is uncharacteristically silent tonight. The usual sonic pandemonium of jet aircraft... turbines screaming to take off... merging with the decrescendo of jets on final approach, desperate to land... is absent. Instead there is an unearthly hush, drawn like a curtain over the giant base... as all eyes and ears strain, hoping against hope, that the stillness will be ruptured by the whistling roar of the lost aircraft and its crew winging home.

Toward twilight, at these latitudes, the relatively cool moisture-laden air blanketing the South China Sea blows westward toward land, creating an updraft to collide with the warmer air from the jungles of the coastal mountain range. At the same time, when the sun goes down, the warmer humid air from inland jungles and rice paddies rises in the cooler atmosphere, creating an updraft. The collision between the moist, cooler air masses from seaward and the warmer moist air masses inland gives birth to towering spires of cumulus clouds that extend 30,000-40,000 feet above the mountains.

Usually with approaching darkness, the noisy traffic of landing and departing aircraft quiets down for a few hours, as if to usher in these more celestial events. Every evening at this time, a cosmic switch is activated and this meteorological conflict erupts with shards of lightning and peals of thunder that flash and rumble. This daily drama, in all its grandeur, is reenacted each day with the metronomic regularity of a maestro, who suddenly waves his baton or draws a curtain on this giant stage.

Many days in the past, after leaving the office, I would stand alone, looking across the flight line and over the barren sands of Cam Ranh Peninsula toward the mainland, enthralled by the unfolding drama, power and magnificence of these natural events. I often wonder if such phenomena must not have inspired astronomers of ancient Greece to picture Immortal Gods, living in their Pantheon on Mount Olympus, swathed in clouds to conceal all from human eyes. Drawing upon my limited knowledge of Greek mythology, my mind wanders easily to imagine a jousting match between giants, performed for the amusement of Zeus, Apollo, Poseidon and other Immortals. From their collisions, lightning flashes through the clouds while the thunder of their concussions rolls across the mountaintops.

But, tonight…tonight is different. Instead of flashes of lightning and peals of thunder, there is only silence and Stygian darkness. It is as if the Gods of Old renounce the frivolity of jousting in the presence of these grave current events. The usual Greek drama of these special effects has been replaced by silence as all stand in muted reverence for the tragedy evolving before us.

This Twilight of the Gods, this Götterdämmerung, has now merged into dense darkness, while the interior of the Command Post becomes clouded by murky shadows of personnel moving through a veil of cigar smoke with microphones and chalk to mark the positions of the search aircraft. The silence is broken only by the crackling staccato of electronically transmitted voices, stretching through the blackness across miles of trackless jungle, from the fluttering helicopters to the map-encased room. An electronic cacophony of curt phrases cuts through the smoke and ranges through the room.

"Roger, Dustblower 4, your next quadrant for search will be tracking outbound from the 020 degrees radial to 045 degrees..." "Dustblower 3, your next pattern will be a dogleg, tracking outbound on the 060 radial to 084 and then..." etc.

As the night grows darker, it becomes obvious to all that the search must soon be terminated. With progressive darkness the attendant risk increases for search aircraft to collide with each other.

Al Aleckna enters the room. He doesn't speak. Sinking into a chair, he stares blankly at the acoustic tiles embedded in the ceiling. Finally he looks at me, and with a deep and mournful melancholy in his eyes, says, "He's had it."

We both know this, but it still hits hard. Only the day before I had flown that same route, as had Al only two days prior. The three of us were partners, a triumvirate, in all of this, and we had discussed the odds before.

Only the day before, in idle conversation, Bill and I had noted that if we continued to fly with our current frequency, the odds were overwhelming that one of us would have to punch out. There have been over 10,000 sorties flown from Cam Ranh since its opening. But now that it has happened, why did it have to happen to Bill?

All three of us have been flying with the same frequency of two missions a week. Yes, Bill's odds were 33 1/3 percent; my odds are 33 1/3 percent and Al's odds are 33 1/3 percent—one chance out of three—Russian roulette; the cylinder spins, the trigger is pulled, and one of us loses the game. This time it is Bill. All of these thoughts intrude into our subconsciousness. It would be hypocritical to say that we did not think of these matters.

Out of the darkness of our suppressed emotions, reality dawns. These are not twenty-five-cent rides on the roller coaster at the State Fair. This is war, and not the "Vietnam Conflict," defined by Congress. Regardless of what Congress may call it. The price of performing your daily duty is the constant threat of death...and now, that threat has become Bill's reality.

Death is the same in a "conflict" as it is in a "war." The Sword of Damocles swings continuously, every day and every time that we fly, but tonight it has struck.

I could not also help reflecting on the following issues: The 12th Air Force Hospital at Cam Ranh Bay is the largest Air Force Hospital in Southeast Asia. It is staffed by medical and surgical specialists of every type, offering a quality of care that is equivalent to any medical school or university hospital in the United States.

However, the doctors that work in the clinics and hospital live in their cocoons of professional conformity, embraced in aseptic procedures and white sheets, while nurses take orders and provide therapy; and to perform duties that are neither more nor less than the same duties performed in any civilian institution in the U.S.

And yet, these doctors have no concept of this war or of matters that involve the lives of pilots every day. They have never heard a shot fired in anger, never seen napalm incinerate a hillside village and all of its inhabitants. They have never experienced the terrors and elations of combat. For them, the only difference between military medical duty and medical duties of civilian life is the location of the hospital; Vietnam, instead of the United States; 12th Air Force Hospital at Cam Ranh Bay, RVN, instead of Parkland Hospital in Dallas, Charity Hospital in New Orleans, Grady Hospital in Atlanta, Bellevue Hospital in New York or Cook County Hospital in Chicago.

For those physicians who have been drafted, Vietnam will be a distant memory …an inconvenient interruption of personal plans…a disruption in practice routines that forced them to travel to a primitive country, to serve in an unpopular war and to work in a relatively austere environment. Vietnam service will be remembered for inconveniences, compared to the superfluous lifestyle assumed by physicians in the states. For them military service will be measured in terms of personal deficiencies and inconveniences but not in memories that scar your body and haunt your soul.

Regardless of any personal disaster or tragedy, the war and military duties continue. On this particular night, I am medical officer of the day at the hospital.

However, tonight I delay reporting to the emergency room. I remain in the Command Post for several hours... serving no useful purpose... remaining for reasons that I cannot explain. Voices from the search helicopters are silenced, not to be heard again until the next morning. A paralysis or numbness has seized and immobilized me... beyond any conscious control.

Finally, I slowly rise and walk toward the hospital, stopping by the darkened flight surgeon's office to pick up my stethoscope. The lights are out in the office. Al is sitting at his desk, enveloped in darkness, staring at the wall. I say nothing and enter Bill's office. Turning on the desk lamp, I sit down at his desk and look at the picture of his wife, Marilyn, and their children, smiling out from photos on his desk.

I close my eyes and suddenly I am in the cockpit of Bill's plane. I feel the throb of jet engines under my seat. The enormity of their power is full-throated, and smooth. By now, I know the instrument panel blindfolded. I hear the electronic crispness of voices over the intercom and the usual amenities that are spoken. I hear the lead aircraft conduct his radio check as we switch channels and tighten our formation for penetration of the cloud layer: "Sharkbait 41, check, 2, 3, 4." All is well. The tally is correct. All aircraft are accounted for. All is well.

From our cockpit cocoon, the towering cumulus clouds to the left are magnificent and beautiful, silhouetted against the night sky. The formation of four aircraft is the perfect picture of modern science -- aerodynamically styled to perfection. With a top speed approaching 1,600 mph, the F4-C Phantom is the fastest combat aircraft in the world. The security of my harness locks me into the back seat as the cloud layer is penetrated. I watch entranced as its veil of filmy whiteness envelopes the cockpit in gentle foam. G-suit plugged in… still confident of my instruments – the flight, still under the control of Heathcote, the aircraft commander in the front seat…all is well…all is well…

But, when did it happen? -- was there any warning of impending disaster? Did Heathcote, or Bill in the back seat, have any forewarning? In the few seconds during which the meteor sped to Earth, what happened? I can explain it only by attributing it to momentary spatial disorientation that developed while in the cloud.

Finally I receive a call from the dispensary that saves me from further agony of my thoughts. I leave the flight surgeon's office and plod through Cam Ranh's sand, toward the hospital.

CHAPTER 20

After the Crash

PATIENTS ARE USUALLY FEW AND THE TEMPO OF WORK is rather slow. But tonight is different. Between answering multiple telephone calls concerning Bill's missing aircraft and responding to the usual medical conditions, I am busy, very busy. Most of the medical problems are minor respiratory illnesses, lacerations and occasional injuries from various types of equipment. Finally, near midnight, both the telephone and the number of patients quiet down. It is good to be busy…too busy to think of other things.

At midnight, I am awakened by one of the corpsmen, who asks me to see a staff sergeant who seems rather blasé about his complaint and apologizes for disturbing me. He is thirty-six-years-old, muscular and appears in no apparent acute distress. Having just gotten off duty, he has casually dropped by the hospital, on the way to his barracks. He complains of a rather vague substernal chest pain, which is intermittent in nature, and which radiates into his left lower jaw and molar region. He is extremely athletic in appearance, walks vigorously and is very polite. Further history reveals that his symptoms have been present for approximately three days.

His vital signs of blood pressure, pulse and temperature are all normal. I initially examine his TMJ as a source of pain. His ears are clear and there is no obvious dental problem to account for his symptoms. Percussion and auscultation of his chest is within normal limits. Cardiac exam is also within normal limits. The remainder of the physical examination is completely unrevealing.

After these exclusions have been made, I consider his symptoms to be compatible with most textbook descriptions of atypical angina pectoris or cardiac pain from insufficient blood flow to the heart muscle. However, I am also aware that, statistically speaking, very few otherwise healthy men without family history of heart disease have heart attacks at age thirty-six.

I brought a footlocker of medical textbooks with me to Vietnam, preparatory to a residency in internal medicine. This is my month to study cardiology and I haven't seen an EKG in more than six months. The sergeant provides me with an excuse to order one. EKGs are ordered so rarely in this population of healthy young adults that my request disrupts the usual routine of the emergency room. I have to wait another two hours before the machine can be located and the tracing performed.

I never learned to read an EKG in medical school or during my internship. It was not a subject taught in medical school, being deferred to the postgraduate level of training. My internship provided excellent backgrounds in general surgery, obstetrics-gynecology, neurology, pediatrics, gastroenterology and emergency care. But, there was simply no room in the curriculum for cardiology, and certainly not for learning to read EKGs.

Because of this, I always felt deficient in my knowledge and skills in electrocardiography. And, because of these deficiencies, I considered the ability to interpret an EKG as mandatory for any physician…especially for an internist. Feeling quite self-conscious, I searched for a method to compensate for my ignorance. Therefore, while stationed at Bergstrom, I took a nine-month correspondence course through the mail from the University of Southern California on how to read electrocardiograms. I also asked the internist at the Bergstrom Hospital if he would allow me to read all EKGs from the clinics and hospital I further imposed on him to review all of my interpretations He was more than happy to diminish his workload by agreeing to my requests. He had been drafted into the Air force after only two years of internal medicine residency. He was an honest man and sensing his own insecurities, replied about being my tutor: "While you are on Page One of reading EKGs, I am only on Page Two..."

Finally, tonight, the EKG machine is retrieved from the medical ward of the hospital and the leads are attached to the patient. After the tracing is finally obtained, the corpsman brings it across the hall and hands it to me. I can hardly believe my eyes! The pattern of the EKG tracing is a classical, textbook pattern of a recent and currently evolving anterolateral myocardial infarction. As I was taught in medical school, regardless of how slim the odds are for a patient having a particular disease, for the patient who actually has the disease, the odds are always 100 percent.

The sergeant is promptly admitted to the intensive care unit, to remain there until he is stable enough to be air-evacuated to Tachikawa Air Force Base in Japan. Under ordinary circumstances, someone this age, with these symptoms, in a combat zone, would have been given a few antacid pills and returned to duty.

He is lucky that cardiology is my current study topic and that I needed the practice of reading an EKG. It was lucky for both of us.

Next morning the hospital cardiologist reviewed the case and the EKG. The electrocardiographic evidence for diagnosing the heart attack is irrefutable. But, the cardiologist seemed befuddled as to how a flight surgeon could have made the diagnosis, with or without an EKG. He stated categorically that not only would he not have obtained an EKG but he would have sent him back to duty. My reply was, "When you are behind, you run faster." I did not provide background or elaborate on my answer.

4 September 1966

Just before the search and rescue efforts were terminated last night, a fire or semblance of a burned area was noted by aircraft flying over the mountainside across from the base. Because of darkness and deteriorating weather conditions, it was not possible to investigate further. When the search resumed this morning, yesterday's area of concern is determined to be only a brush fire and irrelevant to the plane crash.

I release all corpsman from duties in the flight surgeon's office to other duties except those persons to be held on-call for helicopter duty in the search.

The entire day has been consumed with screening reports of possible crash sites, but the search today again failed to discover the crash site. It is anticipated that the search will continue for the next two days. If the crash site is not found by that time, the search will be officially called off, with Simmons and Heathcote listed, officially, as MIA or "missing in action." There is little hope of either man surviving the crash. If the crash site is found and the bodies are positively identified; it will be easier for his wife, in terms of insurance proceedings, and, of course, the awful suspense will end. The Air Force cannot officially state that they were KIA or "killed in action," since this implies positive identification of the bodies.

The Accident Investigation Board met at 1400 hours today. The board concluded that the most likely cause of the crash was, as I noted earlier, vertigo due to spatial disorientation.

5 September 1966

The search for the crash site continues. Helicopters begin flying at daylight and stop at sunset. They will fly again tomorrow. I personally doubt that they will ever find the crash site. Any low-altitude aerial search over this jungle is dangerous. Already, several of the helicopters have been shot at by Viet Cong. The jungle is incredibly dense with a triple layer canopy of trees. A plane can easily penetrate the first layer of canopy without exploding while continuing through the second canopy until it finally explodes on the jungle floor. The immediate effects would be to scorch and destroy the vegetation below the second and third canopies. Since the uppermost canopy of leaves would be untouched, evidence of the crash would be completely invisible by air until sometime later…if ever. Trees of that region not infrequently reach a height of 250-300 feet tall. Since the weather is bad in the area, it is commonly impossible to send helicopters into some of the valleys where the entire jungle may be engulfed in clouds.

An awful suspense and helplessness looms over us at the realization that all of this has happened so close; and yet it is so far, in terms of ever being able to locate the crash site or to render assistance. It only makes you realize just how terribly wild this country is. The area involved is supposed to be swarming with Viet Cong, so even the search planes can't be too daring. The risk of being shot down while searching for the crash site is great. I doubt that they will search for more than the next two to three days.

My friendship with Bill has been unique, and I treasure it. Bill and I did not always agree on questions of office management, but he was always open to other ideas and considerations. He never tried to foist his ideas on me or any other person that I know of. He respected another man's opinion even though his might be different. There was never any question of confrontation or antagonism. He seemed happy with himself, knowing that he had made the best decision based on the conditions and circumstances.

He was forever optimistic in his plans for the future and respected me for mine, as fulfillment of my wishes. It hurts me to see him go.

6 September 1966

Last night, the search for the crash site was "officially terminated." Thus far, no evidence of the crash site has been found. Despite this, there are plans to take aerial photographs of the region for a more detailed evaluation. I believe this is likely to be more of a formality than fruitful.

7 September 1966

Today a flight of three Phantoms was returning from a mission when they were contacted by Cam Ranh tower. A C-130, flying over the Cam Ranh area, had radioed that they had picked up an emergency radio beacon south of the base. One of the Phantoms diverted to investigate. In the process, an intermittent signal was picked up on Guard Frequency. By tracking the sound on Automatic Direction Finder)[19], the pilot finally located the signal on top of a small mountain. Running low on fuel, the Phantom pilot called the tower to report the location.

The emergency locator beacon is a small survival radio carried by all pilots in a pocket of their survival vest. The same type was carried by Simmons and Heathcote. An emergency localizer beacon (ELB) is also

---

19 ADF or *automatic direction finder* is one of the older types of radio navigation or non-directional beacon (NDB). NDB is a radio transmitter that does not include inherent directional information. It is used when line-of-sight transmission is unreliable, such as dense jungle terrain. NDB follows the curvature of the earth, allowing it to be received at much greater distances at lower altitudes. ADF is used to identify positions, receiving low and medium frequency voice communications, homing and tracking.

carried onboard each aircraft. It is automatically activated on impact during a crash.

With the sound of the ELB, hope is revived that one or both of the pilots might still be alive. If either or both pilots were able to escape at the last minute, their emergency beacons would be their only method of communication.

There is another more sinister possibility. Perhaps one of the two had tried to eject at the very last minute but was killed before the parachute could open. In the latter circumstance, his radio might still be intact. The Viet Cong are noted for taking these radios and signaling distress calls to attract rescue planes and helicopters to the scene. Any planes that respond become targets of the Viet Cong ground forces. The enemy is very cognizant of the desperate emergency measures to rescue downed pilots. The result is that all rescue efforts become targets within their shooting gallery.

Of course, there always exists the one out of a million chance that the men have been able to stay hidden for these three and a half days and continue to signal, but the likelihood of this is extremely slim.

As part of the search efforts, an Army Mohawk helicopter has been parked on the ramp in front of Base Ops. While the above events were being reported, the pilot of the helicopter intercepts the radio transmissions and heads out to launch his chopper. However, before he reaches it, he is intercepted by Dean Cooke, another Phantom pilot of Bill's squadron, who wishes to go along. The chopper pilot hands Dean two bulletproof vests, one to wear and another to sit on. They take off with no support from any other aircraft.

As soon as they arrive over the beacon, and are about ten feet above the treetops, the Viet Cong open fire. The helicopter is caught in a crossfire of bullets. A round penetrates the floor of the chopper and continues through the protective flak vest that Cooke is sitting on. The bullet enters Cooke's posterior gluteal muscle region and terminates in his left hamstring muscle. Al and I meet the helicopter on the ramp and transport him in the crash ambulance to the hospital where he is immediately taken to surgery for removal of the bullet. There is no severe vascular, neurological or bone damage. I heard later that he was okay when discharged from the hospital five days later, but I also heard later that he nearly bled to death on the medical evacuation flight back to the States. He is okay. He is lucky. It's simply another reminder that the country out there belongs to the enemy and not to us.

It is well known that the Viet Cong in this part of the country don't take prisoners. If the pilot is dead, they mutilate the bodies. If they are alive, they torture them to death. Since these enemy forces live in jungle isolation from their higher commands they have no justification to exploit prisoners for propaganda purposes. These guerrilla forces are usually isolated from their supply lines and frequently do not have sufficient food for themselves. They certainly do not have extra food for any captured enemy prisoners.

In contrast, pilots captured in North Vietnam are treated as prisoners of war and exploited for propaganda purposes. They receive some form of food and enough medical attention to allow them to be paraded through the streets of Hanoi to be cursed and spat on by Jane Fonda and others who believe that "anything from the Communist left is sacred." They may spend several years in Hanoi, imprisoned and tortured, but rarely are they killed outright. They have more propaganda value alive than dead.

For Bill's sake, I hope that he was killed in the crash, or was able to commit suicide if he were about to be captured. Tomorrow morning, armed aircraft and a company of Army soldiers have been ordered to search and clear the area on foot. I do not believe they will find our men alive. The Viet Cong trap/ambush with the radio is further evidence against that.

It is a terrible feeling to be here, in a relatively secure location, looking across at those mountains, knowing that less than twenty miles away, those little yellow bastards have found the wreckage, taken the radio off a dead man, and are now using it to lure our rescue parties into an ambush. The radio beacon today is like a voice from the grave.

12 September 1966

Ground troops have been looking all week for the crash site. The entire region is infested with Viet Cong. For the ground troops involved in the search, staying alive has become a priority that is equal to finding the crash site. This is the second plane crash in the past month or two into this region and as of this date, neither has been found. This particular crash is an unusual situation for the Air Force, since it involves a doctor flying on a combat mission over hostile territory. The incident is being officially hushed to avoid undue publicity.

For the past five days, for twenty-four hours a day, an armed air police guard has been stationed around our Quonset hut. Evidently the Viet Cong have threatened to assassinate United States officers all over the country during the Vietnam elections. Officer's quarters have been cordoned off by this special guard detail.

Over the past several days there has been an increased intensity of fighting in the mountains west of Cam Ranh. The clashes at night are visible as mortars and howitzers respond in kind to attack. The attack today is probably twenty miles from Cam Ranh Bay, but in a direction away from the crash site. All night a cacophony of dull thuds, wump, wump, wump from mortars and boom, boom from howitzers shake the buildings on base. Their white and yellow muzzle flashes are visible in the distant mountains.

It makes you thankful to live on this peninsula, since it is nearly an "island fortress."

13 September 1966

2100 hours

The search for the crash site and wreckage has been severely hampered by monsoon storms, mountainous jungle and enemy fire. Multiple efforts to discover the location of the survival radio "beep" have been unsuccessful. One of the helicopters did pinpoint the sound and distance to within several hundred feet of the jungle canopy. But the helicopter was caught in a scorching crossfire from enemy ground forces.

14 September 1966

This morning, an Army helicopter was shot down while searching for the crash site. Fortunately both pilots were rescued. Approximately thirty minutes later, in an area three miles from where the first chopper was downed, another Army H-43B helicopter spotted the site of the Simmons crash. It is on the mountainside of Cam Ranh Bay, approximately twenty miles northwest of Cam Ranh. The plane evidently crashed into the jungle and cut a swath of approximately 350 meters long before it exploded. I reviewed the photographs taken from the Army helicopter, and there is nothing but a cleaned out swath in the midst of huge trees. A single landing gear is visible in the photograph. From all the evidence, it appears that the aircraft struck the mountainside while in straight and level flight or with less than 5 degree climb in altitude. The site is almost invisible from the air since the jungle virtually swallowed all evidence of it. This explains the failure of numerous search missions over the area to detect it.

This delay in finding the crash site provided adequate time for the scorched leaves of the uppermost canopy to die and be shed. Loss of this uppermost canopy uncloaked the lower tree levels and jungle floor to reveal the crash site. Now, from the air, only a brown swatch of scorched leaves is seen to contrast with the deep green of the surrounding jungle. The burned swath extends approximately 200 yards up the mountainside. Since the entire area belongs to the Viet Cong, entry into the crash site will be delayed until the area can be neutralized by ground troops. Only after this has been accomplished will an investigation team enter. From the looks of the jungle, this may take some time. Obviously, the Viet Cong have had ample time to booby-trap every fragment of the wreckage, as well as to arrange a warm reception for curious investigators. Today, hostility of the region is further emphasized by another helicopter flying approximately three-fourths of a mile from the site. It was severely shot up by ground fire and crashed. Fortunately, the crew escaped and all were rescued by several heavily armed Hueys.

Tomorrow, a team of Special Forces men will be dropped into the crash site area by helicopter. Of course, we won't know anything for sure until the survey is able to confirm that any remains are those of Simmons and Heathcote. I honestly hope that they were both killed in the crash and not captured. There are many things over here that are worse than death.

It is my understanding that Bill's wife, Marilyn, has received a telegram confirming that Bill is listed as MIA. I have also been informed that several men of his squadron, who were good friends of Bill and his wife, are returning to the United States. They plan to visit her. They wanted to emphasize the futility of any hope.

Maj. (Dr.) John Bettancourt is the new director of aerospace medicine on base. He has replaced Major Chubb as chief of aeromedical services. Major Chubb has been transferred to Da Nang AFB as hospital commander.

CHAPTER 21

===================================

Taking Over—Dealing with Grief

15 September 1966

With the death of Bill Simmons, the full burden of command of the flight surgeon's office is on my shoulders.

In 1965, Bill Simmons did a fine job of building this office from scratch. But in many ways, Bill was too nice. Discipline among the corpsmen is virtually nonexistent. When Bill was here, I didn't interfere. But now that it is my job, I'm cracking down a bit. The office is grossly overstaffed. We have about fifteen corpsmen. Bill wouldn't let them work anywhere else other than in the flight surgeon's office. As a result, they all sat around in the waiting room, playing cards, joking, writing letters, or engaged in various and sundry things to amuse themselves. There was reason for Bill's attitude. These are specially trained medical personnel, with an Air Force Service Code (AFSC) related to aeromedical activities and duties. This rating is only preserved if they remain on duty in the flight surgeon's office.

But it is my job to preserve the efficiency of this office rather than to shelter overly redundant personnel. Therefore, I informed Sergeant Calendine that I want four and only four corpsmen in this office. The remainder can be sent to the hospital personnel pool for reassignment to any appropriate function or duties. It is unprofessional to have excess personnel cluttering up a doctor's waiting room. I have also made myself further unpopular by requiring that the office be swept and mopped daily, with all furniture to be cleaned daily with a damp cloth. It is unprofessional to have a dirty office, even in Vietnam. I informed Sergeant Calendine that I am not here to win a popularity contest, but to get a job done. In spite of Vietnam and in spite of sand, heat, and the overflowing septic system, the flight surgeon's office will be operated in a professional manner.

Another thing has happened to send my head spinning. Major Bettancourt volunteered to go down into the jungle to inspect the wreckage of the F4-C. Initially, I considered his proposal to descend into the jungle on a rope from a helicopter to be a melodramatic gesture to provide him with a medal. I cannot believe that the life of another doctor will be risked to investigate the crash site when there is virtually no chance of finding living survivors. However, these statements reflect my naïveté about Air Force regulations. Since Vietnam is not a formally declared war, it does not fall under the regulations or usual rules of wartime combat. I've been informed that regulations state: "Except in a declared war, the crash of any military aircraft, for any reason, must be investigated by a flight surgeon and by a senior pilot, who is appropriately rated in the performance of that aircraft."

Last night, I left the office at approximately 1700 hours to get a haircut. Since Al was on call he remained in the office. In popped Colonel Mack, who looked Al in the eye and said matter-of-factly, "I need a volunteer to go into the jungle tomorrow."

Al said he gave him a "Have-you-lost-your-GD-mind, Colonel?" look.

Recovering from his shock, Al replied that Dr. Bettancourt had already spoken for that "privilege." Colonel Mack simply stated, "Okay, but if he can't go, I will go." We were all in total ignorance about the official Air Force policy of investigating crashes during any "non-declared-war" situation. Al and I both consider it an idiotic procedure to risk the life of another physician by lowering him on a rope into the Viet Cong infested jungle -- not to render aid -- but to search for human remains. The office corpsmen are aghast at the prospect of losing another doctor.

And so, early this morning at 0500 hours, Maj. John Bettancourt presents on the flight line, looking for all the world like an overgrown Boy Scout prepared to lead the "Beaver Patrol" on its first hike. I'm sure he has camera and film for the occasion, bird-identification hand book, survival kit, snake bite kit, M-16, and of all things, he is wearing a white helmet with red cross painted on it (according to the Geneva Convention). He will be a perfect target for a kid with a slingshot. A bit later in the morning, he returned to the flight surgeon's office with a morose, dejected expression. He had dressed up for the occasion, but due to poor coordination with the Army helicopters, the event was called off for the day. Tomorrow morning, he will try again. My only comment is, "Good luck!"

16 September 1966

This afternoon an Army Special Forces sergeant attempted to lead a platoon of thirty-two men into the Simmons crash site to neutralize the area. Since the terrain is extremely dense, the team had to be inserted from helicopters by hoist with jungle penetrators. In an overly ambitious gesture of enthusiasm, one sergeant strapped himself to the "tree penetrator" hoist. Before adequate supervision and instructions could be given about methods of descent, the sergeant leaped through the open door of the helicopter, hoist and all. The latch on the hoist cable slipped and the man rode the steel bomb-like jungle penetrator down, plummeting 150-200 feet into the trees. I've heard that members of the Army Special Forces feel invincible and bullet proof…but even Army Special Forces troops can't fly!

How he lived to tell the story is still a mystery to me. True to form for the Special Forces, he calmly gave himself an injection of one-quarter grain of morphine and then radioed to the chopper that he had internal injuries and compound fractures of both legs. After a considerable bit of effort, he was retrieved. I met him and the helicopter on the flight line. On examination, he had sustained a compound fracture of the left tibia and fibula. Despite these significant injuries, he appeared stoical and never uttered a single protest. His only other injury was a fractured lumbar vertebra, later detected on X-ray. It is regrettable that his brainpower didn't match his physical courage, else he wouldn't be in this predicament. Nevertheless, it was a remarkable example of stoicism under fire. I wouldn't go so far as describe it as "bravery under fire." "Stupidity" or "reckless abandon" would be more descriptive of his behavior.

It never stops! Shortly after this incident of 16 June, I receive word that while making a strike in the DMZ; one of our F-4Cs was struck by ground fire — probably 20 mm. The pilot in command was 1st Lieutenant Giere and the back seat pilot was 1st Lieutenant Knoch. The hit occurred just as they were pulling off the target. Immediately the left engine went out and the instrument panel revealed a fire in the right engine.

Every attempt was made to gain altitude. Lieutnant Giere headed for the sea. Suddenly, the instrument panel lit up with warning lights indicating that all hydraulics and controls were out. The agonal aircraft pitched into a sharp dive. Lieutenant Giere ejected without difficulty. Lieutenant Knoch was jammed into his seat by the excess negative G forces and was unable to activate either the primary ejection handle above his head or the secondary ejection handle beneath his seat. Finally and frantically grasping between his legs, he succeeded in clutching the secondary ejection handle and departed the airplane. Attempts by both pilots to deploy the seat survival packs failed. The "parachute landing falls" (PLF) of both pilots were successful in cushioning their landings. They hit within several hundred yards of each other, but each had no knowledge of the other's presence or whereabouts.

On the ground, they were surrounded by voices of enemy troops. Only the speedy use of the survival radios vectored the armed rescue helicopters in to extract them. Ultimately, they escaped and were flown by helicopter back to Da Nang. By the time that they were finally flown back to Cam Ranh Bay in a Gooney Bird (C-47), it was 2300 hours. Meeting them as they climbed down from the airplane, Aleckna and I examined both pilots for injuries. A more complete exam was accomplished several minutes later in the flight surgeon's office. Their injuries were limited to minor contusions, abrasions and mild ligamentous strains.

It is remarkable that Lieutenant Knoch did not sustain a compression fracture of the spine despite the fact that he was in a position of complete truncal flexion when he ejected.

This is the third ejection from the F-4C by Lieutenant Knoch and the second ejection for Lieutenant Giere. This event sets a record for ejections from the F-4C aircraft in Vietnam. Neither of the two pilots has quite finished his Vietnam tour of duty, but Colonel Allen, the deputy wing commander, is sending them home. They have had enough war. They are both in their early twenties and fortunate to be alive.

As Al and I were examining the pilots, Lieutenant Knoch noted that it was "usual and customary" for the flight surgeon, namely me, to provide a surviving pilot with a drink of first-rate whiskey. He asked, "Where is it?"

This was the first time I have heard of this particular custom. As a matter of office policy, I won't allow alcoholic beverages of any kind in the office. This request was obviously an exception to my previous rules. To compensate for my lack of sensitivity, I offered to buy him a drink tomorrow at the Officers Club. I explained that the only thing in the office that I had to offer containing alcohol was cough syrup, elixir of terpinhydrate with codeine (ETH). For years, it has been dubbed, "G.I. Gin." It tastes awful! He seemed hurt and offended that we couldn't comply with the customary ceremonial libation to celebrate his survival. But I am sure he will survive the omission.

Inclement weather continues to prevent further evaluation of the Simmons crash site. I hope that tomorrow this issue may be cleared up. But, thus far, compounding the tragedy of the original crash, is the price of reconnaissance aircraft destroyed near the crash site:

One helicopter has been shot down during the search.

Two other helicopters have been shot up during the search.

One pilot has been wounded in the leg from Viet Cong ground fire.

Extreme injuries were experienced by the Special Forces sergeant as he attempted to descend by jungle penetrator into the region.

It is pouring rain outside, and the next opportunity to enter the crash site is currently in limbo.

The standard tour in Vietnam is twelve months. For every twenty combat strike missions that pilots fly, one month is deducted from their tour of duty. Twenty combat missions also equates to the award of an Air Medal. After flying 100 combat missions, a pilot may be transferred back home. I suspect that these rules will be changing to increase the maximum number of missions on a single tour. The Air Force desperately needs pilots and retaining them to fly more combat missions is the most readily available solution to the personnel shortage. Flight surgeons also earn Air Medals on the same basis, but there is no deduction from the twelve months tour of duty. The death of Bill Simmons on a combat mission may close the door on physicians flying combat missions. I hope not!

17 September 1966

I am shuffling papers at my desk at 2100 hours when a muffled detonation shakes the room. Since mortars and howitzers on the mainland have been maintaining a rather constant barrage lately, I pay no attention and continue wading through the paperwork. A few minutes later the crash phone rings. There is a message, "to stand by... There has been an explosion off the north end of the runway, which may have been an aircraft."

Grabbing the crash radio, I run to the Jeep parked in front of the office. Since I have no idea what has taken place or exactly where, I head up the hill toward the north end of the runway that hangs out over the South China Sea. This hill is highly restricted since it houses the Hawk Missile Battery sites and Anti-aircraft Artillery (AAA) that protect the entire military establishment of Cam Ranh Bay and Peninsula. As I approach the summit, the usual clues of emergency situations, such as fire trucks and scrambling rescue helicopters, are conspicuously absent. In fact, the entire base seems unusually placid and as I speed up the hill, I become even more certain that some error has been made.

Finally I see some activity at the summit. At the top of the hill, the Air Police sergeant on duty recognizes the flight surgeon Jeep and frantically waves me through. Parking the Jeep, I run to the small lookout point overlooking the ocean, where several Air Policemen are clustered. One of them says, "Yes, a plane has just crashed."

I see a flare of the type carried in a personal survival vest, beaming from a distance of one to two miles off shore. While I am watching, a helicopter is just arriving and begins to circle overhead. From past experience,

I know that a man is down in the water, and that he will soon be brought back to base by the helicopter. I continue to be completely ignorant of the nature of the situation. How many aircraft? What type of aircraft? How many personnel/casualties might be involved?

While driving, all attempts to contact Cam Ranh Crash Control were futile, since all radio transmissions are garbled. The Hospital Emergency Response Center also failed to respond. While I am driving rapidly back to the flight line, the helicopter, returning from the in-water pickup, approaches overhead, passes me and I follow it. I continue to wonder if there has been some mistake. Parking the Jeep at a respectable distance, as soon as the chopper touches down, I run to it. Special care is taken to approach the helicopter from "head on" to avoid the whirling blades. By this time I see the lights of a crash ambulance approaching the flight line from the rear of the chopper. This is strictly taboo since it is the most dangerous area of approach to a helicopter. The blades have greatest clearance from the ground in front of the chopper. Firemen on the scene frantically run over to me and shout, "Keep those damn fools out of the way."

I respond by nodding and dismissing him to search for other survivors. Simultaneously, I motion with my arms in a circular pattern for the ambulance to drive around to the front of the helicopter to remove the injured man.

At last the ambulance cooperates and approaches the helicopter from the front. Al Aleckna, my associate, is driving. I later learn that Major Bettancourt was in the ambulance and had ordered Al to approach from the rear of the helicopter…since it was closer. Al told me later that Bettancourt cursed up a blue streak when I waved them to the front of the helicopter. Fortunately, Al followed my directions and did not yield to Bettancourt's superior rank. This man has completed a residency in aerospace medicine and is board certified in aerospace medicine. Apparently his whole life had been spent taking examinations on paper, with no practical experience in life-as-it-is. As a result, it took a great deal of persuasion by Al to explain that you could not enter from the rear, even if it did look closer. I told Al later that he should have gotten out of the ambulance and let Bashaw continue his approach…

The helicopter contains a single injured person. A cursory physical examination reveals that this pilot, who ejected, has a probable compression fracture of the lumbar spine but is otherwise not critically injured. Al and I load him into the ambulance and drive to the hospital. The area is deserted. I grab a corpsman as we remove the patient from the ambulance and transfer him by gurney into the intensive care ward. Examination under the lights reveals that he has experienced burns, and probably a lumbar compression fracture, but is otherwise not critically injured. He is Captain Browning, an F-4C aircraft commander who on this mission was flying in the backseat pilot position. I tell the nurse to activate the Medical Emergency Recall plan for hospital disaster situations. I still have no idea as to the extent of the accident or the number of casualties that might be involved. For all I know, a C-130 with as many as 75-100 people may have been involved. Al and I drive the ambulance back to the flight line to wait the arrival of more casualties.

By now the entire sky above the ocean is aglow with continuing bursts of parachute flares dropped from C-47s, both from Cam Ranh Bay, Phan Rang and other bases. H-43 rescue helicopters are also called in from Phan Rang to assist our two rescue helicopters. The Army sends three LARCs (landing and reconnaissance craft), to enter the water and transport any wreckage and/or human remains back to land.

By bits and pieces the story begins to come in. On approach to landing, two F-4Cs collided in mid-air. One of the aircraft had a hung bomb. Captain Browning was flying in the back seat of one aircraft. He said he bent over to pick up a dropped pencil when he saw a blinding flash of light and felt an explosion. By reflex alone, he pulled the secondary ejection seat handle beneath his seat. This reflex action saved his life. The three other pilots died in the explosion, which was primarily from the hung bomb.

The helicopters dart in and out of the illuminated areas, fluttering like moths in the candlelight, to inspect the ocean area of the crash more clearly. These activities consume the next two to three hours, but the time passes rapidly. It is now 12:30 a.m. and thus far no other survivors. Hope is waning.

At approximate 0200 hours, the amphibious vehicles begin to bring in pieces of bodies; lungs, intestines, limbs and other human debris. My personal observation of these tissues begins with a grotesque form looming out of the shadows. It creaks and groans as if it were alive. Water drips from its dingy body, and I think that surely giant aquatic dinosaurs must have looked like this when they lumbered out of the ocean depths eons ago to search the darkened earth for prey. The monster is a LARC.

This amphibious behemoth has been scouring the surface of the sea, searching for remains, both of the aircraft and of the men who flew them. As it crawls clumsily from the water, the flat deck is covered with dripping, twisted, charred fragments of the broken aircraft. Looking closer, small bits and pieces of tissue are also scattered and draped over the greasy metal. A piece of lung is plastered into the honeycomb aluminum of the fuselage. A fragment of intestine morbidly cloaks the piece of auxiliary tip tank. A sufficient amount of blood is obtained from a fragment of lung to yield a single blood type. It is AB positive and matches with the other aircraft commander.

The Army men pull out a plastic bag and say, "Doc, you'd better handle this," thrusting it toward me. I am overwhelmed with nausea, since it reeks with JP-4 fuel from the fractured aircraft and the odor of fresh human tissue. I climb down from the landing craft onto the tarmac. In that bag, no larger than two fists, are the remains of three men. These same men had been strong and healthy less than a few hours ago. These were men who had hoped, dreamed and loved; men who were husbands, fathers, brothers and sons; men who had laughed and wept for their personal joys and sorrows. Now all of these emotions and bodies have been reduced to fragments of tissue, soaked in seawater and tainted by JP-4 fuel.

I am overwhelmed by a sense of complete inadequacy. Al and I examine the pieces, which are now termed, "tissue specimens," under flashlight. There are portions of human lungs, aorta, transverse colon and rectum with prostate attached. My corpsman, Airman 1st Class Frank Sabourin, mixes a 10 percent solution of formalin to preserve the tissues.

Two tasks now confront us:

To find evidence for positive identification of three pilots

To determine as best we can the manner in which the crash occurred by noting the significance of tissue on various portions of the aircraft fragments.

By now all hope of finding other survivors has vanished. Confronted with the problem of identifying the three pilots from the meager tissue pieces, I asked Colonel Mack to call Dr. Guillebeau, the pathologist, (Guillebeau was chief of pathology at Wilford Hall Hospital where I interned) to advise us. Colonel Mack complies immediately by telling a corpsman to "tell Dr. Guillebeau to get his ass out of bed and out here, immediately."

Guillebeau arrives in a semi-stuporous state, capable of responding to questions only in monosyllables. Finally, realizing that he is of no use, I dismiss him. Colonel Mack insists that he remain on the flight line to assist us, rather than vice-versa. He specifically says he wants Al and me to assume complete responsibility for the work. By now, it is 0300 hours. Colonel Mack returns to his quarters. I tell Al to get some sleep and I will cover for the remainder of the night. He can take over in the morning. I doze for intervals of thirty to forty-five minutes in the crash ambulance, between incursions of the LARC. Two or three more times the LARC lumbers in with its grisly cargo and each time I conduct the gory task of processing tissues.

The night seems endless. But finally, as always, the dawn arrives to herald a new day. Helicopters and planes continued to swarm over the expanse of vacant sea, but there is nothing to find. By now, myriads of fish have removed even the scant remnants of human tissue from the water. Al comes to relieve me and I return to the Quonset hut to sleep. Despite my exhaustion, I cannot sleep. Each time I close my eyes, the amorphous hulk of the LARC rises groaning out of a primeval sea, dripping dark waters as it rolls awfully toward me.

The final details of the incident will be determined within the next two days by the Accident Investigation Board. According to the board, the aircraft were not yet under the control of Cam Ranh Control Tower. Since they were on final approach to land, I can't explain how they were "not under control of the tower." Events happened so quickly that not even the single survivor is sure of the sequence of events that resulted in the mid-air collision. Thus, much remains unknown.

From my personal and very mundane point of view, there is now enough paperwork to occupy me for at least another year of active duty. Al has been a godsend. He is an extremely hard worker, and he has one of the finest senses of humor that I've ever encountered. Circumstances such as these demand that you find humor in the non-humorous, if only to prevent weeping. He takes great delight in calling me "boss" since he knows how much it irritates me.

CHAPTER 22

═══════════════════════

Accident Investigation Board

19 September 1966

This afternoon was spent with the Accident Investigation Board. At this point, it may well require four to five additional meetings before any answers or conclusions can be made as to the cause of the crash.

This is what we know:

On September 17, 1966, three F-4C Phantom aircraft took off from Cam Ranh Bay air base, responding to a call for air support during a night-recovery rescue of a downed helicopter. After a successful mission, the three Phantoms landed at Da Nang Air Force Base for service and refueling. The three F-4s of the 558th TAC Fighter Squadron then took off from Da Nang AFB for the flight home to Cam Ranh Bay AFB.

As the two lead F-4s prepared for a formation landing flying side by side, the third F-4 trailed behind a few miles and maintained visual on the lead aircrafts. Suddenly, everything seemed to go wrong: in seconds the two Phantoms slammed together and a hung bomb from one exploded, killing

Captains Rocky and Surwald in the first F-4, and Captain McCann in the second F-4. Captain Browning, who flew as backseat pilot with Captain Rocky, instantly ejected and from his parachute watched helplessly as the two burning F-4s plummeted in balls of fire into the South China Sea. The trailing F-4 Phantom pilot saw the brilliant explosion only seconds ahead of his flight, reacted to possible shrapnel and debris and took evasive action, then immediately called for search and rescue efforts from Cam Ranh. Captain Browning flew over the explosive falling debris and the airbase, before looping back to maintain surveillance over the crash site.

I find inconsistencies in this report. After dropping ordnance to rescue the downed helicopter, one of the aircraft had a hung bomb. The report states that this aircraft and the other two F-4Cs then landed at Da Nang for service and refueling. The hung bomb should have been defused and removed from the aircraft at Da Nang before it was cleared for takeoff back to Cam Ranh Bay. And yet, the report notes that the hung bomb was retained on the aircraft, only to explode during the mid-air collision on final approach to Cam Ranh.

If it is possible to be philosophical about death in any form, it may be stated that the death of these three pilots was nearly instantaneous with no attendant suffering. They were all honorable young men who died in performance of duty to their country. They died in the peak years of their lives and were not forced to suffer the indignities, humiliations and degradations of spending years in nursing home beds, dying by millimeters each month in protracted agony. As Jack London noted, "It is better to be ashes than dust." The meager remains of their bodies have now returned to the ocean, ancestral home of all life on this planet.

Considering the options that separate life from death, there are worse ways to die.

Apparently, the isolated pockets of Viet Cong in the region observed the entire panoply of war from a distance. The initial event was the F-4C crash of Heathcote and Simmons. Following this event were various helicopter flights over the area to reconnoiter the crash site. The next event was the mid-air collision of the two F-4Cs with the bomb blast. They observed the enormous explosion of colliding jets with bomb blasts, followed by hundreds of parachute flares, lighting up the ocean for miles around. They had previously observed the small ground team of thirty-two men, who were introduced to investigate the Simmons crash site. This team had been put on hold for two days because of the midair collision activities. From the Viet Cong perspective, it seemed that we were launching a full-scale land, sea and air invasion based on the extraordinary activity of flares, airplanes, ground troops and all the other accoutrements of the Normandy type "D-Day" invasion of Europe. The enormity of these events progressively put the fear of God in their hearts. Better to surrender than to be run over by a steam engine. Rapidly the small encampment of American Army Special Forces began to fill up with Viet Cong who wanted to surrender. The latest count is 240 Viet Cong, a number expected to shortly increase to 275… and all without a shot being fired.

More and more this is beginning to sound like a soap opera war. No campaign in Vietnam thus far has ever resulted in this number of prisoners. It is believed that these Viet Cong were stationed here about a year ago to fight off our inroads into the Cam Ranh Bay region. Unknown to the enemy, the Air Force had no intention of launching "search and destroy" missions into the surrounding mountains. Having established a safe perimeter of defense around our bases at Cam Ranh, all local efforts have been completely focused on defense, with no offensive military incursion or search-and-destroy advances into the mountainous region.

In the meantime, the war shifted from the coastal region of Vietnam to the Central Highlands Region. When this happened, these disparate pockets of Viet Cong were left stranded, cut off from their supply lines and getting hungrier by the day. In short, they had no one to fight and no food to eat. They were hungry, and in general, "fed up" … so, they finally said, "To hell with it" and surrendered. It will be interesting to observe how the Army and Air Force characterize this "glorious victory" in the newspapers. I'm sure there are many generals in the United States with red faces. If the military is true to form, they will send in a large number of ground forces to study the situation and to observe the results. This type of thing simply does not happen over here. Perhaps, it represents a new strategy to win battles without firing a shot. Finally, today, our helicopters are able to gain access to the region of the crash site and locate the remains of Simmons and Heathcote. Evidently, when the plane crashed, they never knew what hit them. Their bodies were scattered over an area of about 300 yards. When I met the helicopters and received the body bags, I routed them to our pathologist, Dr. Guillebeau, for his disposition. I did not want to go over the bodies. The total weight of the bag containing the remains of Simmons was fifty pounds. The weight of Heathcote's remains was forty-five pounds. The only positive identification was a particular type of boot that Bill wore and an I.D. found on Heathcote. Evidently there were no recognizable features or whole limbs obtained. It is not at all pleasant. Since we have Dr. Guillebeau, it eliminates the need for Al and me to perform autopsies on the remains. Thank God!

For his wife's sake, I'm glad that some portions of the body were found. As terrible as it seems, a definite answer is always easier to live with in the long run than a gnawing doubt/hope, which is impossible not to have. This finally closes the case of Bill's death, and I'm glad. It has been a terrible episode, dragging out as long as it did. I'm sure that had not Bill been such close friends of Colonel Chase, the Wing commander, such a heroic and prolonged search would never have continued for this long.

20 September 1966

A Wing memorial service for Bill and Cliff was held tonight. I did not attend. I have no more tears to shed. My esteem and affection for Bill Simmons will remain for the rest of my life. I've always abhorred public mourning…but that's my problem. When I remember Bill, I think of the quote from Shakespeare's Julius Caesar Act III, sc ii: Mark Anthony as he stood over the body of Brutus:

"His life was gentle
And the Elements so Mixed
That Nature might Stand and Say
To All the World,
This Was a Man."

Toward the end of my tour of duty on 10 June 1967, I placed a mahogany plaque on the wall in the flight surgeon's office to commemorate his death. It was engraved to recognize Dr. Simmons as Chief of Aviation Medicine for the 12th Tactical Fighter Wing from 1965-1966. It was hand-carved in mahogany with the insignia of the 12th Tactical Fighter Wing and a plaque dedicated to Bill.

On the reverse side, I appended a note that, when this office or base is closed, the plaque should be forwarded to his wife, Marilyn, with the then current address in Meridian, Mississippi. I had hoped that it would be meaningful to his family. It was with regret that I learned many years later that his family never received it.

Major Bettancourt will be transferred from Cam Ranh around 20 November 1966. He will probably clear the base on 17-18 November. At present, no one is scheduled to replace him. This means that as chief of aviation medicine, I will have to assume the duties of director of preventive medicine and public health and every other aspect of aviation medicine that he had previously covered. This will definitely end any consideration of a combined one week leave plus two weeks R&R with Elaine. So much for personal plans. As General Sherman said, "War is hell!"

24 September 1966

Colonel Mack's son arrived two days ago for a short visit with his father. He just graduated from the Air Force Academy and is now enrolled in a master's degree program at UCLA. He is a very handsome young man, the very image of his father. He returned to the States today. Colonel Mack accompanied him back as far as Tachikawa in Japan.

The weather is actually quite pleasant now on the days that it doesn't rain. Temperatures are in the 80s. I understand that it won't get any cooler… just wetter.

Had an informal discussion with the base psychiatrist about the incidence of emotional problems in the troops. He noted that 15-20 percent of the troops in Vietnam have fairly severe emotional problems. At least, this is better than during WWII where the incidence was over 20 percent. He noted that a large number of these became full-blown psychoses. He also stated that on the average, the fourth month is usually the most difficult.

25 September 1966

Rain, rain, rain, all day and night. This is payback for the recent pleasant weather. I try to pass time by studying medicine, but I spend more time staring at the pages than I do in absorbing the content. I spend a significant amount of time applying for residencies in internal medicine. I prefer the West Coast, i.e. California. San Francisco vs. Los Angeles is the final round. This is complicated by coordinating my choice with Elaine's application to medical school in the same area.

When Al leaves Vietnam in December, he will go to Lowry AFB near Denver for eight months, after which he will separate from the Air Force. After the Air Force, he plans to go to Paris, live on the Left Bank of the Seine for two years, and become a ski bum!

26 September 1966

The death of Bill Simmons while flying on a combat strike mission had further repercussions. While I am not privy to all that happened at different levels of command, certain bits of scuttlebutt circulated around the hospital. As I have noted previously, 7th Air Force regulations stated that physicians, i.e. flight surgeons, were not to fly on combat missions except by special authorization from the Wing commander. In Bill's case such authorization was given. That authorization extended to all flight surgeons assigned to the 12th TFW. Sometime later, a congressional investigation team from Washington arrived at Cam Ranh to conduct an inquiry into the circumstances of Bill's death. I was not invited to these discussions, but I heard later that Colonel Mack was called on the carpet. He later came to me requesting that I write a letter of defense to justify flight surgeons flying on combat missions with the aircrew members that were under his care. From my perspective, nothing changed. I continued to fly strike missions from two to three times a week.

Comments to Elaine:

"As I look at many offices of medical and non-medical personnel, there are pictures of the officer's children mounted on each desk and the pictures of girlfriends mounted on each desk, but rarely is a picture of the person's wife present. A number of people have spontaneously commented on your beauty, Elaine. In fact, one man was totally surprised to learn that you were my wife. It is expected to have pictures of children and girlfriends, but never a wife."

In a combat zone, it is routine military policy to post an evacuation priority list for personnel. This means that if disaster is imminent and the base is threatened with being overrun by the enemy, certain critical personnel must be evacuated; this list dictates who must be given priority for evacuation. 12th USAF hospital is a 1,000-bed hospital with 100-plus doctors. It is the largest military hospital in Vietnam. Only two physicians are listed for priority evacuation, Colonel Mack, the hospital commander, and me, as chief of flight medicine. During communications on base, the flight surgeon's call sign is "Band Aid-2." The call sign for the hospital commander is "Band Aid-1."

Thus ends a very eventful month. I have completed three and a half months' duty in Vietnam. I look forward to the "eternities of boredom" that Winston Churchill promised.

1 December 1966

The month is starting with a BANG! No pun intended! I am medical officer of the day for the hospital dispensary tonight and have just met an Army helicopter transporting a patient to the hospital. The patient is a G.I. who attempted suicide by shooting himself in the head. Apparently, earlier in the evening, he had attempted a less drastic self-inflicted wound to remove himself from a combat situation. While being air-evacuated by helicopter, he feared that this previous attempt was inadequate. Therefore, during the process of evacuation, he found a gun and decided to finalize the issue by a more focused bullet to his brain.

By the time I arrived at the landing pad, his brains were splattered throughout the helicopter. The hole through his skull and brain is about two inches in diameter, which means that he shouldn't last very long. He is in surgery, but I can't conceive how he will emerge alive.

This event brought back memories of my childhood in the South. War and hard times bring out different responses in people. The South was defeated in 1865 by the North. From that defeat the South lay nearly moribund until the 1960s, when it began to recover. Like a stricken animal, the southern states turned away from their enemy and learned to endure that which it could not defeat. Withdrawing into the lair of its geography, the South became oblivious to the outside world. For nearly 100 years, the eleven states lay morosely licking their wounds and growling at any intervention, while all the while sinking lower and lower into the mire of poverty, ignorance and frequent hostility against outside intrusion.

When the only norms of life are poverty and hard times, depression and despair reign. Under these circumstances, each individual responds in his or her own manner to survive and to cope with life. Some drown themselves in the anesthesia of alcohol while others become morose and non-functional. Others may turn to crime as a diversion. But mankind's spirit is not so easily destroyed. There are other, less self-destructive methods of weathering the storm. Self-deprecation and humor provide rescue from circumstances that would otherwise be intolerable. Rather than flounder in the pits of despair, another path may be taken. A person may subvert personal disasters into collective victories by developing a humorous interpretation of oppressive and hopeless circumstances. This is known as "gallows humor." Typically, Southern humor is gallows humor. Its origins are traceable for as long as mankind has suffered on this planet. In times past the humor was expressed by men/women who were condemned to die on the gallows. Gallows humor is the ability to look death in the eye to recognize the futility of opposition, all the while smiling and thumbing your nose at the confrontation.

I recall a story I heard as a child. It seems that the "ne'r-do-well" of our small, rural Southern community was an alcoholic who had failed in every enterprise of his life. One day, chronically and morbidly depressed, he crawled beneath a bridge and soused himself with moonshine liquor. In his drunken despair, he held a pistol to his head and pulled the trigger to end his misery. But his hands were so unsteady that he missed and only succeeded in blowing off part of his left ear. Later, when he was discovered, bleeding and in greater misery, his story became a community joke that spread like wildfire. The conclusion was that Ole' Tom was so incompetent he couldn't even kill himself..

Tragically, the young American G.I. who was air-evacuated today was not so incompetent.

The weather at Cam Ranh has changed from the usual torrid sun and sand to the monsoon season. The word "monsoon" means wind, and now I understand why. The wind has been blowing constantly every day with velocities of 50 mph or greater. The terrain of Cam Ranh Peninsula is nothing but sand. Driven by these winds, the blowing sand stings your face and nearly blinds you. Frequently, the wind is intermixed with torrential rain. Logically, you would expect the rain to moisten the sand and keep it from blowing, but Mother Nature does not abide by human logic. The sand shrugs off the rain instantly and dries so quickly that little respite is gained from the added moisture.

2 December 1966

I just learned that Capt. Ken Cordier, a young Phantom pilot I've known for some time, was shot down today. It grieves me. Last month, when Elaine and I were in Hong Kong on my R&R, we encountered Ken at the Hong Kong Hilton Hotel. He was on leave and sitting in the lobby, looking very forlorn and depressed. After introducing him to Elaine, I returned later to chat with him. He informed me that in a recent flight over Hanoi, both of his wingmen had been shot down. I later learned that he was flight leader for the flight. It must be terrible to lead four men into battle and when it's all over, only you survive to fly back alone. My God! What a burden to bear!

And now, today, while flying fighter escort for B-52 bombers over Hanoi, he too went down. Ken is assigned to the 559th TFS at Cam Ranh. Since I know most of the pilots in the squadron, I tried to obtain information about Ken. The reports are all the same. Today was like total war in the skies over Hanoi. The air was filled with MIGs, SAMs (surface-to-air missiles), heavy flak from artillery and every known type of ground fire. A number of planes from Cam Ranh Bay, as well as from other bases, were involved in a continuous melee of dog-fights with MIGs, while flying cover for the Thuds[20] (F-105s) who carried out the bombing runs. A number of these planes were hit and/or shot down. The consensus is that Ken's plane "simply disappeared." One of the men thinks that he saw it explode, but he

---

20 "**Thud**" is a term that refers to the **Republic F-105 Thunderchief**, a supersonic fighter-bomber used by the United States Air Force during the Vietnam war. Capable of flying at Mach 2 (twice the speed of sound), the **F-105** conducted the majority of strike bombing missions on Strategic Targets during the early years of the Vietnam war. **F-4C Phantoms**, with their greater agility, and Tactical capabilities, usually flew **MIG CAP** to protect the **F-105** bomb runs. The **F-105** has the dubious distinction of being the only U.S. aircraft to have been removed from combat due to high loss rates. Because so many of these planes were lost, the **F-105** was nicknamed, "**Thud**" by its aircrews.

is unsure. At that moment, everything around Ken and the pilot reporting the incident seemed to be exploding. Whether Ken was able to eject and survive to be captured is unknown.

Earlier, I had seen 1st Lt. Mike Lane for a minor skin problem. Mike is Ken's usual back-seat pilot and was Ken's back-seater today. His fate is also unknown. Ken and I both arrived at Cam Ranh in June. This really hurts. Ken was one of the finest men I've ever met.

As an addendum, a more complete report of the battle of that day says the U.S. lost a total of six to seven aircraft in that area on that day. Reported lost were: three F4-Cs, two F-105s, one F-104 and a Navy aircraft that I'm unsure of the type. The other two F-4Cs were from Da Nang. This represents an enormous amount of losses in highly trained men and high tech aircraft...and for what purpose?

Happily, I learned many years later that both Ken and Mike survived the SAM explosion of their aircraft. They were captured and served six years in the hell of the Hanoi Hilton.

When I learned Ken had been shot down and was presumed to be KIA (Killed in Action), the entire war in Vietnam hit a raw nerve in me. It is more than frustrating to be a citizen of the most powerful nation on earth and see the cream of our young manhood being destroyed in a futile war. I am not privy to the highest decisions of our government as to why we are fighting here. What is true and what is vented for public consumption are two different matters. I truly doubt that any definition of "truth" exists except in a relative context. More and more, I believe that Vietnam is a civil war between North Vietnam and South Vietnam. For our propaganda purposes, we are assured that the invasion of South Vietnam is instigated by the Communist regime from North Vietnam. I do not doubt that. But we are attempting to fight a high-tech war against guerrilla warriors of an agrarian society. It will not succeed.

There is no question but that the war materials for our opponents originate in Hanoi, or that Hanoi and North Vietnam receive them from Russia, Communist China and other Soviet Bloc countries. To win or even stalemate this war, we must be willing to place an embargo around North Vietnam to prevent resupply from other countries. We must be willing to issue a warning to Hanoi, Haiphong Harbor, and all other ports to evacuate their civilian populations within 24-72 hours. At the end of which time, we should blast the city of Hanoi and the Port of Haiphong into oblivion, just as we did in Germany and Japan. Will Russia then enter the war? Will Communist China enter the war? Possibly...probably...I don't know. Am I recommending these measures? Hell, no. Regardless of whether you are in North Vietnam or in South Vietnam, Americans and our allies are considered invaders. When you have to be concerned about old men, women and children dropping hand grenades into your backpack or under your bed every night, you are conducting war against the civilians of a country and not simply the military forces of that country.

In all my years of schooling, I have never encountered such a high quality of American manhood as the pilots who fly these missions. Students that I have encountered in college and medical school do not hold a candle to the strength of character, dedication and personal integrity of these men. They are the finest pilots who fly the finest aircraft in the world. It breaks your heart to watch them take off in the morning, knowing that some of them will not return. And, for what... the destruction of an oxcart or a donkey burdened with ammunition, or perhaps, a straw hut filled with ammunitions?

As a child, I struggled for survival against "white trash" schoolmates in the South. I learned one thing. You do not back up to a bully! But, neither can you oppose a river in flood stage. The manner in which this war is conducted reminds me of a doctor whose patient is suffering from pneumonia. As the patient becomes progressively more toxic, appropriate antibiotics are withheld, while the doctor continues to prescribe nostrums, "Take an aspirin and call me in the morning."

The manner in which politicians are conducting this war is abominable. The Russians fight their wars by using the manhood of other nations as surrogates. We fight wars for other countries by laying our finest manhood on the chopping block and reelecting the remaining dregs to Congress.

The method that Washington is conducting this war prostitutes both our country and the men who die in defense of it. There is an old aphorism that, "The old men start the wars and young men fight the wars." Perhaps, this explains why the quality of "old men" leading us is so derelict. Qualified, young men never live long enough to become qualified old men… and we wind up with dregs for the politicians… Whew! I simply needed to vent my spleen.

We received a new flight medical officer today by the name of Lon Kerry. He went to the University of Illinois Medical School and interned at Presbyterian Hospital in Chicago. He was married only three months before being assigned to Vietnam and is very depressed about everything. He is a nice person and I'm sure he will be okay, but he is very green and naïve about many realities of life and all things military.

4 December 1966

The more I see of this war, the happier I am to be stationed at Cam Ranh Bay. Located on a peninsula, it is about as safe as you can be in Vietnam. I can't say that about other bases. Tan Son Nhut is the next largest Air Force base. Located in Saigon, it is surrounded by Viet Cong cells, which consider the Air Force base and any U.S. military establishment high-priority targets.

Intelligence recently reported a suspicious buildup of the 1st Company, 2nd Battalion of the Viet Cong moving into hamlets of Thong Tay Hoy village. This village is about ten kilometers west of Tan Son Nhut. The following events confirm all suspicions.

At approximately 2045 hours on 3 December 1966, maximum security posture was achieved in expectation of a mortar attack on Tan Son Nhut. It is openly acknowledged that our defenses for the area were undermanned and inexperienced. The initial alarm that Viet Cong had penetrated the base came by radio at 0110 when a sentry dog handler on a perimeter listening post, Alpha K-19, immediately reported from the north side of his post. Reinforcements were sent, while explosions and small arms fire immediately ensued.

At 0114 hours, post Delta 15, a soldier in the main line-of-resistance bunker reported that Viet Cong were coming through the Delta Sector. After firing at this group his weapons jammed. The Viet Cong assault force, estimated at eight to nine individuals, entered the taxiway from between the concrete revetments, which contain RF-101 aircraft. There were con-current penetrations from a group of thirteen Viet Cong, who attempted to access the aircraft parking area. An M-60 machine gunner intercepted this group and was credited with killing nine VC. Two Air Policemen in a nearby bunker killed the remaining four VC with M-16s. An unconfirmed number of VC sprayed a 180-degree area with automatic weapon fire and grenades after mortars had bombarded the area. Multiple explosions and sporadic gunfire occurred throughout the area. Ultimately, they were driven back by a combination of small arms, automatic weapons, rocket launchers and hand grenades.

On last report, I heard that two Americans had been killed and twenty-one injured. Considering the congestion of troops in this area, this casualty report is unexpectedly low. In addition to Tan Son Nhut, another base, Bien Hoa, about twelve miles outside of Saigon, was also hit. I don't know the details of this attack.

Most of these attacks were based on information provided by Vietnamese employees who work on the bases. I am informed by the intelligence section here at Cam Ranh that it takes a minimum of two years to perform an adequate security check on these people…as a result it is an exercise in futility.

The Vietnamese employees at Cam Ranh are primarily women who serve as maids and perform housekeeping for some of the higher-ranking officers. Most of these people are filled with diseases that range from tuberculosis to hepatitis and parasitic infections. I've written this up in multiple public health reports, but all to no avail.

Our new flight medical officer, Lon Kerry, lost a watch in Saigon before he came to Cam Ranh. A group of small children swarmed around him and began to tug at his arms and clothing. Suddenly, they dispersed and he realized that his wristwatch went with them. You can't help admiring such smooth thievery. I'll bet that you can't find that type of finesse even in Chicago!

It has continued to rain day and night here with no respite. In spite of the heat, I much prefer sunny days to this perpetual overcast.

The knowledge that Al Aleckna is leaving impacts me more than I care to admit. Al has been a friend and Phi Chi fraternity brother since medical school at Northwestern. Rarely have I found someone with whom I am so simpatico. Al is studious, but knows how to have a good time. When he speaks, it is because he has something to say. As if silence were a void to be filled, the new younger flight medical officers chatter all of the time. When I am engrossed in some paperwork or simply reading for pleasure in off hours, someone is constantly interrupting me and wanting to talk about something. They remind me of a bunch of women or a bunch of magpies.

As I write, there is a big puddle of water forming under my desk, despite numerous towels to soak it up. With all of this rain, and since we are only a few feet above sea level, there is no drainage. I shouldn't complain. Troops in the field have to sleep, eat and die in the mud all day and all night.

At present, there isn't enough work for five flight surgeons, but at the rate that things are increasing around here, the increased manpower may eventually be appropriate.

CHAPTER 23

Another Loss

6 December 1966

We lost another Phantom today.

The crash occurred in Ninh Thuan Province during the approach to landing at Cam Ranh Bay. The aircraft commander was Maj. Lee A. Greco of the 559th TFS and its back seat pilot was 1st Lt. John M. Troyer, of the same squadron at Cam Ranh Bay. Major Greco's aircraft, Boxer 02, was in the number two position of the two aircraft in the Boxer flight.

The weather was clear with visual flight rules (VFR) conditions as the flight passed over Phan Rang. Approximately twenty miles out of Cam Ranh, the weather worsened. Boxer 01 requested a straight-in approach for Boxer 02. This was granted. Boxer 01 turned east to 0900 while Boxer 02 was cleared to 5,000 feet for a straight-in approach. Boxer 02's radio transmission appeared to be weak and variable at several points. At eighteen miles southwest of Cam Ranh, both radar and radio contact were lost with Boxer 02. Multiple attempts to re-establish radio contact on guard frequencies were unsuccessful. At approximately 1252 hours, Boxer 02 was declared missing in action. Boxer 01's return was an uneventful Radar Ground Controlled Approach (GCA) and landing.

The weather is atrocious with overcast skies and sullen clouds that glower from horizon to horizon. Monsoon winds blow continuously out of the northeast and the rainfall is non-stop. Throughout all of Southeast Asia, the Northeast Monsoon prevails between November and March, while the Southwest Monsoon prevails between May to October. This weather is rather typical for Northeast Monsoon weather in December, but regardless of which direction that the wind blows, these conditions virtually eliminate any and all attempts to conduct an aerial search in the mountains for the crash site.

Boxer 02 was at an altitude of 3,000 feet when all radar contact was lost. It is important to note that mountains in this area extend from 3,500 feet up to 4,000 feet. These recorded heights, however, do not accurately represent the safe clearance required for aircraft. An additional 150-300 feet of jungle canopy extends over and beyond the heights printed on the aviation regional and sectional maps.

It seems likely that Boxer 02 attempted to maneuver through this "soup," of rain, clouds, fog and indefinite mountain peaks. It does not require a stretch of the imagination to think that the aircraft most likely flew into the side of a mountain swathed in clouds. The aviation aphorism applied to a mountain, so enveloped in clouds, is best described as a cumu-lo-granite cloud.

This is fundamentally the same situation in which Bill Simmons was killed in September. The pilots of Boxer flight were not rookies. However, both pilots were relatively new to flying in Vietnam. The aircraft commander was thirty-three-year-old Maj. Lee A. Greco of Gilroy, California. His reputation is that of an exceptional pilot, having won a number of awards on previous assignments. He had been in Vietnam for six days.

The back-seat pilot, 1st Lt. John M. Troyer, from Beach City, Ohio, had been in Vietnam for less than a month. Both of these men are from the same squadron as Ken Cordier and Mike Lane, the 559th TFS. This squadron has had a devastating record of losses.

There is nothing for me to do now except wait out the weather until we can conduct an air search of the area. I will eventually have to go down to investigate the crash. But when, I don't know.

I am MOD tonight. When I arrived at the hospital, I was introduced to a new general medical officer. Initially, I had trouble understanding him. He mumbles in one breath and snorts every word in his next breath. For a few moments, I wondered if he had a speech defect or other problem. A few minutes ago, he came in to introduce himself and to talk a few minutes. He is a graduate of Harvard Medical School and was in general practice for one and half years before he was drafted. He hated Harvard. He noted that the attitude at Harvard is that if you don't go into research or academic medicine you are considered a traitor. There is certainly no Boston affectation about him, that's for sure. I understand what he is saying. Northwestern Medical School also had a certain arrogance or hauteur against anything that didn't reflect glory back on the medical school. The private practice of clinical medicine is hard work, with precious little glory, for either the physician or his medical school.

7 December 1966

The Preliminary Accident Investigation Board meeting about the crash of 6 December 1966 was conducted today from 1-2:30 p.m. This is a routine procedure after every crash or aircraft accident. Chairman of the Investigation Board is Col. Norman C. Gaddis, assistant deputy commander of operations of the 12th TFW. Other departments that are pertinent to aircraft safety are represented: aircraft maintenance, wing intelligence officer, aircraft safety officer, flight commander, and chief of flight medicine for the fight surgeon's office (me).

For ninety minutes, all possible causes for the crash were discussed. These ranged from "shot down by enemy gunfire" to the possibility of a sudden heart attack experienced by the pilot.

As a matter of background information, all aircraft crashes or incidents in the U.S. Air Force may be allocated to one or more of five explanations:

Pilot error or judgment -- Since the pilot is frequently dead, he all too often falls heir to blame that cannot be attributed to other factors.

Aircraft or instrument failure -- The maintenance record of every aircraft is carefully scrutinized. After every flight, the pilot notes any problems or glitches that he encountered in operating the aircraft. These notes and/or comments are collectively referred to as "write-ups." The maintenance log is a compilation of these "write-ups" and the corrective actions or repairs made in response to them. After an aircraft accident or crash, the maintenance records are reviewed to assure that no "write-ups" were left unattended. Later, all instruments and fragments of the aircraft recovered from the crash site will be carefully analyzed for inflight malfunction.

Air traffic control by the control tower -- All facets of pilot-control tower communications are permanently recorded. If the aircraft is under Radar Approach Control by the Control Tower, every word exchanged between the pilot and the air traffic controller is recorded for posterity, with little left to the imagination.

Parenthetically, it should be stated that Air Traffic Controllers represent some of the youngest enlisted men and non-commissioned officers in the Air Force. Their formal education beyond high school is not extensive.

I have always been sobered by the enormous responsibility imposed on these young men and women. From my perspective, they are the unsung heroes of aviation.

Aeromedical -- After every aircraft accident, the first items to be scrutinized are health records of the aircrew. Subject to review are: recent medical events, medication or conditions that might contribute to a compromise in performance of aerial duties. Psychiatric traits and/or paranoid ideations are quickly ruled out.

In the attempt to establish cause and effect, and therefore to affix blame for an aircraft accident, the fondest hope of every Accident Investigation Board is to attribute the crash to that rarest of entities known as "sudden medical death" of the pilot. Here is an explanation that is not subject to the usual routes of redress by superior officers and congressmen. As an act of God, sudden medical death has no competition for responsible factors. There is no one to blame. Not even the flight surgeon is privy to the crystal ball and dice throws of the Almighty. The exquisite finality of "sudden medical death" precludes follow-up investigations, truncates paperwork and preserves the integrity of all present. It is a delicious solution for all Gourmets of Disaster.

My response to queries about the possibility of "sudden medical death" for the pilots involved in this event:

Yes, it is within the realm of possibility for a massive stroke, heart attack or arrhythmia to instantaneously incapacitate a person and render him incapable of performing his duties and responsibilities as an airman.

But, the odds that any of these circumstances would spontaneously occur in an unusually healthy young pilot, with no previous known risk factors, is somewhat less than the odds of being struck by lightning on a clear day. And, furthermore, since there are two pilots in the F-4C, the chance that any of these events would happen simultaneously to both pilots requires the same lightning bolt…odds that beggar the mathematics of infinity.

Unlike other physicians, the flight surgeon is constantly haunted by his dual allegiance to the pilot as a patient versus his allegiance to the mission. I personally have never known a flight surgeon to protect patient confidentiality by jeopardizing the mission. During combat, the F-4C Phantom aircraft, the pilots and the mission are inseparable. What affects any one of these elements affects the entirety and the mission is the "all."

My medical report methodically listed the lack of all evidence supporting a medical role in the present tragedy. The report was submitted and accepted… with regret, judging by the expression on many faces.

Enemy action -- Despite the fact that Congress and President LBJ have not declared a state of war between the U.S. and anyone else, flying in Vietnam continues to be dangerous. Our strike missions bomb villages and incinerate both people and pigs. It is unreasonable to think that some irate farmer won't shoot back. After all, this is their country and we are the intruders!

The crash occurred behind enemy lines. None of these coastal mountain areas have been secured by our military and allies. But, for the Air Force, that is irrelevant. Air Force regulations require investigation of any crash site. Vietnam is not an "Official, Bona fide, Certifiable" war. It is "simply" a conflict! Only if there is an official congressional declaration of war, are regulations such as this waived. But, after all is said and done, this crash will receive the same scrutiny and deliberations…and generate as much paperwork as any plane crash into a farmer's barn in an Iowa cornfield.

7:00 Returned to office to find ankle-deep sewage overflow with feces and toilet paper drifting throughout entire office.

7:05 Moved my paperwork to intelligence department across the hall. No sewage here.

11 December 1966

F-4C Mission

Aircraft Commander: Captain Tom Ross

Time: 2 hrs. 10 min.

This is our first clear day in three weeks. Our target is a bridge, located thirty-five to forty miles north of the DMZ in Tally Ho Country[21]. The bridge is in the Quang Binh Province of North Vietnam. The area is bordered on the south by the demilitarized zone (DMZ), on the east by the coastline and South China Sea, on the west by the Laotian border and on the north by an imaginary line drawn from the coast to the border thirty miles north of the DMZ.

Today's mission was originally fragged/scheduled as a Sky Spot mission. Sky Spot is ground-directed radar bombing. It is employed in dense jungle areas, during nighttime attacks or when the weather prohibits dive-bombing a target. From the perspective of being the pilot who flies these missions, I can only state that these are rather boring missions. You simply fly to the target area and on a prearranged radio frequency, contact the ground observer. The ground observer directs you to drop your bombs, based on radar guidance. Usually, we are above the clouds and weather. Rarely is the ground visible and almost never is the target area visible.

Today, however, at the last minute, the mission changes. The Sky Spot mission is canceled and we are ordered to dive-bomb the target. Our pre-mission intelligence briefing about the target area said no defenses were recognized in the target area. Weather of the target area reports a

---

21 **Tally-Ho** is an air interdiction program initiated on 20 June 1966 in the southern part of North Vietnam. Its purpose was to slow the infiltration of North Vietnamese troops, equipment and supplies through the **DMZ** or **Demilitarized Zone** into South Vietnam.

cloud cover ceiling in the target area of 3,000 feet with scattered clouds and five miles visibility.

Our flight to the target area is uneventful. The FAC is easily recognized over the target area and radio communication is readily established. He fires two Willie Pete rockets to mark the target and then swoops away out of our path. Despite the favorable description about "no expected ground fire over the target," we know that very heavy AAA (anti-aircraft artillery) has recently been reported in this area.

Employing the usual "wheel formation" for dive bombing, we push over in squadron order to pickle (release bombs) three 500-pound general-purpose bombs in ripple (random bomb drop) at 4,500 feet. Our aircraft is the only one of our three aircraft to retain a hung bomb. Because of the explosions, smoke and debris that overlay the target, it is impossible to determine how successful our strike has been.

The INS (Inertial Navigation System) of the F-4C Phantom II is the computer that permits our aircraft to navigate in a trackless jungle and land without land-based navigational aids. This is the first use of this technology to be employed in combat for any U.S. Aircraft. During the Vietnam Air war of 1966-1967, there were no computers to assist pilots in performing missions of dive-bombing, dropping napalm, and strafing enemy ground forces, from altitudes that varied from 50 feet to 2000 feet above the ground. There were no computers to assist the pilot in avoiding heavy ground fire at these low altitudes. These feats were accomplished solely by human pilots... Men who risked their Asses and their Aircraft, day in and day out, to accomplish their Missions...The supersonic speed of the Phantom was advantageous in avoiding ground fire, but this same speed had to be violently reversed to pull out of a dive before you collided with the mountain in front of or beneath you...or were within range of enemy ground fire during the critical moment when you reversed your dive and began to climb out of a dive…

Pulling off target, we rejoin other members of our flight at an altitude of 15,000 feet, climbing out on a heading of 90 degrees to an altitude of 30,000 feet. At this altitude, we rendezvous with a KC-135 Stratotanker. It is one of those exceptionally clear and beautiful days. The sky above us is pale blue and the South China Sea below us is azure blue. Small cumulus clouds float above and below us. The result is a complete loss of horizon. Sky and sea are one and we are suspended somewhere between the two. Without our instruments it would have been impossible to distinguish up from down.

After refueling, we head back to Cam Ran. I fly most of the distance to base. This provides more valuable practice for me in flying the Phantom. Since our plane has a 500-pound bomb that wouldn't release, we fly out over the empty ocean for radical jinking maneuvers in an attempt to sling the bomb off. Unfortunately, the hung bomb persists and we finally give up.

Thankfully, we land softly and without incident. After we roll to a complete stop on the runway, the bomb is disarmed without complications.

13 December 1966

The office is becoming very busy.

Earlier this year, C-130s from the 315th Air Division squadrons, based in Japan and Okinawa, began shuttle missions out of Cam Ranh Bay. C-130s and C-123s from Tan Son Nhut and Nha Trang made pickups at Cam Ranh. In October 1966, the 483rd Troop Carrier Wing was activated at Cam Ranh under the recently activated 834th Air Division. Aircraft of the 834th Air Division are former Army CV-2 Caribous that were transferred to the Air Force. A new ramp on the west side of the current runway will serve these transport aircraft. All of this escalates Cam Ranh Bay into the primary airlift base in South Vietnam.

In addition to all of these changes, in July 1966, the 9th Aeromedical Evacuation Squadron was elevated to become the 9th Aeromedical Evacuation Group. Aeromedical evacuation flights will be flown from Cam Ranh Bay to medical facilities in Japan and the Philippines. The group flies C-9 Nightingale aircraft as well as Douglas C-118 Liftmasters.

Thus aircrews that present to the flight surgeon's office are not only from the 12th TFW with F-4C Phantoms. Now, there are transient aircrews of C-130s, Caribou, C-141s, C-54s, C-47s and a multitude of smaller courier aircraft of both the Army and Air Force.

My previous complaint of "too many doctors for too few patients" is no longer an issue. Even with the added number of doctors, the flight surgeon's office is always overflowing with patients. I understand that we are approaching 500,000 military personnel in Vietnam. As with all things military, there are more meetings, conferences and non-medical issues to fill every day and parts of most nights.

Every day has some laughs. We have an outstanding corpsman in the flight surgeon's office by the name of Ripp. (I can't recall his true name. Everyone calls him Ripp.) Today, Airman Ripp walked by Lon Kerry's desk and then did a doubletake. Airman Ripp was staring at the picture of Lon's wife on his desk. Rip said, "My God, what is that?" Being in another room, I had no idea what he was referring to. I simply muttered, "I don't know… what are you referring to?" Airman Ripp didn't really answer me. He simply kept talking. "My Lord, anyone with that much nasal septal deviation shouldn't be out on the street." I responded jokingly that he should be careful saying such things…he might get into trouble. When I looked at the picture, I smiled, but didn't say that I had to agree with him.

This is the same person who walked into my office, looked at the picture of Elaine on my desk and gasped. Then he said: "I can't believe it.

She looks so much like my wife that I was shocked. My wife is also beautiful!" Ever since then, on his clean-up duty in the office, he lingers over Elaine's picture and lovingly wipes the dust off the frame. I told him that obviously we both have good tastes in women…ha! He is an airman first class and apparently comes from a very wealthy family. He is extremely well-educated and articulate to a degree rarely seen even in officers. During his boyhood, he and his sister traveled all over Europe with their parents. His sister is now studying at the Sorbonne University in Paris. He can wield words like a sword and is clearly head and shoulders above the other airmen in intellect. It is a pleasure to have someone so bright in the office.

CHAPTER 24

First Attempt to Enter Dec. 6 Crash Site

13 December 1966

At 0900 hours this morning, I am notified by the wing command post that the wreckage of the recent F-4C crash has been found and that I should report immediately for a briefing prior to being inserted into the crash site area with Maj. John Clayton, assistant chairman of the Accident Investigation Board, for the purpose of evaluating the wreckage and collecting any remains of the two pilots for positive identification.

The crash site was discovered this morning by an H-43B Huey helicopter flying at low altitude over the area. It is located on the 45- to 60-degree slope of a mountainside, approximately fifteen miles south of Cam Ranh. Intelligence reports that the entire area is infested with both Viet Cong and North Vietnamese Army troops. I am also informed that an Army Special Forces platoon has been called in for ground support. They will be inserted with us into the crash site area. Whether this will happen is still open to question, not because of the Army, but because of the manner in which the Air Force is trying to hurriedly organize this venture. The Air Force cannot simply request the U.S. Army Special Forces to drop whatever they are doing and come running to assist! In addition, the four F-4Cs on alert status at Cam Ranh have been warned to stand ready for immediate aerial support if we encounter enemy opposition. Additional cover and support will be provided by an A1E Skyraider circling above us.

All of this happens very fast, almost before I can catch my breath. When I enter central supply, a staff sergeant meets me at the door and thrusts an M-16 rifle with six clips of ammunition into my hands. Next follows an extra survival vest, a .38 pistol and two rubberized body bags. The only thing missing is my camera and I grab it, too. Major Clayton and I are the only people other than the crewmembers to board the H-43B helicopter and head due south. The side doors are open and I lean out to search the sky for other aircraft.

Where are the other helicopters with the Army Special Forces to protect us? Nowhere in sight! Where is the A1E Skyraider that will fly low cover for us? Nowhere in sight!

Beneath us, the sea and mountains shimmer in the morning sun. Small fleecy clouds float serenely past the green, craggy peaks, while waves bathe the white sands with opalescent waters. If I were not so heavily armed and were it not for the deafening thump-thump of the helicopter rotors, it would have been all too easy to forget the gruesome task confronting me.

Below us, the mountains are cloaked with tall rain forests, which stretch skyward from 100-300 feet. This green blanket is only intermittently broken by sparse savannahs of elephant grass. From our altitude of 3,000 feet, the elephant grass and jungle below present a picture of pastoral tranquility. From this altitude, the patches of elephant grass have the appearance of well-groomed meadows and putting greens of a golf course, nestled into the verdant green mountainsides with enticing nooks of darkness that invite exploration. However, a casual observer would little realize that each blade of grass extends above the height of a man's head and has razor-sharp edges. Nor is it obvious that the verdant, green quilt of jungle conceals crevices and morasses of impenetrable briars, vines, tendrils, roots and brush. From this altitude, no human presence is evident, but Intelligence from ROK (Republic of Korea) Marines on the ground report a heavy enemy presence throughout the entire area.

While scanning the horizon from the open side of the helicopter, my eyes pause momentarily to focus on a small brown smudge, a scar, on the south side of the highest peak. Subconsciously, I look away. But, again my gaze returns to that small brown scar… that blemish on the green mountainside. Involuntarily, Major Clayton and I look at each other. His gaze is also rigidly fixed on the same brown smudge. For a moment, our eyes lock in silence, as if this action will shut out the emotions evoked.

In an attempt to locate and to further define the area with greater geographic accuracy, I refer to my regional aviation map. A wave of slight nausea washes over me…no question now remains. This brown blemish on the southern slope of that green, jungle mountainside matches the image that was seen and photographed during our recent fly-overs. This is Mountain 3410.

Our aerial surveillance ends abruptly as the bottom falls out of our lofty aerie. Without warning, the pilot noses over into a gut-wrenching plunge down toward the scar of burned tree trunks on the mountainside. Previously lost in my thoughts, the sudden abrupt change in pitch to a lower flight path focuses all of my attention on the ocean of trees that is rushing up to meet us.

There is no semblance of a smooth, controlled descent. We have flown into the maw of severe aerial turbulence, a maelstrom of winds and crosswinds from interlocking canyons now entrap the Huey, like a foreign body to be expelled…determined to wrest control from the pilot. Our flight path is comparable to the path taken by a drunken horse on loco weed, with a burr under the saddle. The helicopter is progressively slammed into a series of contortions...pitching up and down, while rolling, nearly to inversion toward the right. The pilot strains against his seat harness, desperately attempting to retain control for an orderly and gradual descent to hover over our insertion site.

For an instant, we strike a smooth river of air and cruise serenely downstream to the happy hum of turbines and rotors... until, the aircraft slams into a cataract of crosscut air with a WHAM! that nearly inverts us and continues to bulldoze us, like a toy, toward the rocky ledge projecting from an adjacent cliffside. The previous happy hum of the turbines has suddenly turned into a howl of outrage as the Huey claws for air, ricocheting off another blast, only to collide headfirst with a larger wall of air that surges in from the opposite direction. The tortured groans of the turbines rise out of this chaos and are transferred to the blades while they claw desperately through the turbulence, rasping like a dull crosscut saw through the cross-grain river of air.

The situation continues to deteriorate until it is no longer an issue of flying or landing the helicopter. Now, all attention is devoted to simply avoiding a crash. The pilot frantically attempts to regain and maintain some semblance of control before the chopper is thrown, hurtling out of the chaotic air to crash into one of many giant boulders, protruding and beckoning from the jungle floor. And, it continues to worsen, as we are tossed about like a leaf in a cyclone...pitching, rolling, jolting and hurtling from one gust, only to slam into another...

The chaos of this turbulence is generated by hot sundown winds rising from jungle canyons as they rush to mate with cooler ocean breezes... and spawn rip currents of air to engulf us and anything that flies in their path. These manic energies are controlled only by the chaos of winds that propel them...and send them brawling like drunken sailors, crazed by drink and blind to all reason. The rotors and blades chatter like the wings of a thousand dragon flies in a summer mating frenzy…SLAM! Again, we are thrown against another wall of wind that sends us ricocheting toward another rock outcropping. Full left rudder and nose down throws the chopper away from the rocks, with rotors missing the granite outcropping only by inches.

Bouncing beneath us is a small plateau, covered with elephant grass and surrounded by towering jungle cliffs. As the crow flies, the plateau is only one to two miles from the crash site. But for anyone knowledgeable of the jungle, the same distance on foot will be considerably greater. Abandoning the original landing zone, we make several efforts to approach the crash site from various directions. One low swoop reveals that, indeed, the brown scar on the mountainside is composed of charred, truncated tree trunks that stretch grotesquely upward. The ground can be seen, but no evidence of the wreckage is visible from this height. By now, the clouds and fog have begun to roll in from the sea until even the treetops are rapidly becoming obscured from sight. The pilot's energy is no longer devoted to hovering or to landing. He focuses entirely on avoiding a crash against the cliffside or into the jungle below.

"ENOUGH!"

Unstrapping my seat harness, I grab any hook or strap available for support, to prevent being thrown out through the open sides of the bucking and gyrating aircraft. Feeling like a loose cannon on a ship's deck during a typhoon, I lurch forward, slam into the bulkhead and continue trying to reach the pilot. Tossed like a chip on the stream, I swing on straps and harnesses, ricocheting off one side gunner and onto the other…colliding against bulkhead and seats, gradually weaving a path to the cockpit and the pilot's seat. I continue bouncing and slamming against the bulkhead that separates the cockpit from the rear bay…banging from one side to the next, while my helmet rams again and again against the top of the helicopter…my head drumming out an irregular staccato against the fuselage

344

wall. Finally, I reach the cockpit and insert myself between the pilot and co-pilot. Struggling to hang on, I lean over, and at the top of my lungs, yell into the pilot's ear, "Major, break it off …let's get the hell out of here before we add more corpses to this mountain. We aren't going to kill ourselves for the stupidity of this mission…"

He is too busy to answer…until a moment later, when, with a short, grateful nod, the pilot wrenches the controls, yawing hard to the left, while simultaneously pointing the nose downward and adding full throttle… desperately seeking enough airspeed to swoop back up and penetrate the millrace of winds that cascade around, above and below us. Finally and desperately, we break through the invisible barriers of air to soar up; clawing and groaning out of these devil canyons, and up into the open sky… finally to escape the psychotic winds of this witches caldron.

No one speaks. Silence is the unexpressed relief to be out of this place and still be alive. We turn south, heading back to Cam Ranh. Again, I note that we are the only aircraft in the sky.

And, again, I ask myself, "Where are the other helicopters with Army Special Forces to protect us?"

The psychoses of these winds are matched only by the idiocy of the Air Force in non-planning this mission!

I have no desire to be dropped into that jungle morass, armed with an M-16 and a pistol. Major Clayton and I will be forced to spend the night far behind enemy lines, surrounded by enemy forces, and with only the nebulous hope that the weather will clear sufficiently in the future for us to be extracted. These mountains are nearly encased with fog now. If it is impossible to insert us, how much more difficult will it be to extract us?

Without ground support, two lightly armed men, dropped into that vast ocean of jungle—surrounded by enemy sharks—would have little chance of survival. Any thought of depending on aerial support from F-4Cs or other aircraft as they orbit 9,000-10,000 feet above us with guns and bombs is ludicrous at best. Perhaps Major Clayton and I could survive the night, but behind enemy lines, without support, it would only be a matter of time before we would be annihilated. And, for what?

What purpose our death? Have they considered that dead men cannot write an accident investigation report?

The only purpose of this insane gesture is to fulfill a regulation that requires crash site investigation, to salvage the two-week-old fragments of two dead pilots during this period of "non-war"…this Vietnam conflict.

All future efforts for insertion and extraction into and out of the crash site must hinge on the local weather and terrain conditions. This is monsoon season. As we are witnessing, the weather changes from hour to hour and sometimes from minute to minute. If the weather closes in, after we are inserted, another month might pass before aircraft would be able to extract us or reinforcements be inserted to protect us. Any thoughts of an orderly, planned insertion and/or extraction by helicopters or other aircraft are not "plans." These "plans" are not even illusions; they are delusions, divorced from any and all reality. The crash site on Mountain 3410 has remained inaccessible by air for weeks. Weather conditions might easily deny access for another month or longer.

After arriving back at Cam Ranh, we are informed that if weather permits, plans are to make another attempt in the morning…

Now, in the year 2011, as I read my handwritten notes of these events, I remain incredulous that anyone would seriously consider inserting two lightly armed individuals behind enemy lines, with photographic evidence of a large enemy presence, less than two miles from the crash site with no reasonable hope of extraction or reinforcement, for the single purpose of identifying the remains of two corpses and completing a check list for the Accident Investigation Committee.

However, in deference to the military authorities that issued those orders, I am less amazed at their lack of wisdom in ordering this mission than I am confounded at my own stupidity in complying with the mission without objection.

14 December 1966

Another attempt to gain entry into the crash site is planned for today. But, without progressing to the idiocy of yesterday, this same attempt to insert Major Clayton and me is aborted by the Army helicopter pilots, due to deteriorating local weather and winds. And, again, without any support from friendly troops! The futility of pitting a helicopter against the maelstrom of winds in these jungle canyons is obvious. I consider this refusal by Army pilots as testimony to their sanity. The request to make another attempt further validates the insanity of the Air Force. You don't have to be a rocket scientist to recognize that a different approach to the problem is needed.

The Air Force requests a team of Army Special Forces to enter the area for pictures and to make observations. The Army Special Forces, in turn, conclude that the only proper manner to approach the crash site is by landing a Chinook Troop-carrier Helicopter on the northern side of the mountain. This would permit a sufficient number of troops to be inserted and trek more than twelve hours through the jungle, cross the peak and then trek down into the crash site. As part of this arrangement, plans are for Major Clayton and me to be lowered, on the following day, by rope from a hovering helicopter into the area of the crash site, and rendezvous with the ground forces. This plan will require the two of us to descend, dangling 150-200 feet by rope, into the area using a jungle penetrator. I can't even imagine swinging from a 200-hundred-foot rope in winds with turbulence comparable to our recent experience. Every Air Force revision becomes more farcical than the previous.

15 December 1966

For a while, the crash site investigation is placed on hold for "more important considerations": The visit of Air Force Surgeon General Lt. Gen. Douglas Brady.

Today seemed an endless chain of meetings in a war of words about military policies and materials that is beginning to exceed the intensity of the conflict in the field. The entire morning is consumed by a "disaster control meeting," where a long-winded colonel takes full advantage of his captive audience. The colonel has read about combat in books, but has never heard a shot fired in anger or seen a drop of blood shed on the battlefield. Probably, he has also seen John Wayne movies of WW II. This is part of the staff preparation for Lt. General Douglas Brady, surgeon general of the Air Force.

At 11:30 a.m., the general enters the hospital auditorium Quonset hut with an entourage of officers, in a procession usually reserved for the ceremonial level of audience with the Pope. The time spent in meetings with General Brady is exceeded only by the hours spent in preparation for these meetings. As the "command structure" drifts down, the next level is Colonel McElvain, commander of 12th USAF Hospital and my boss. Little love is lost between Colonel Mack and General Brady. In light of that, I thought Colonel Mack did a masterful job of biting his tongue when he introduced the general. After all of this official flappage, the entire entourage departed from the hospital and proceeded in caravan to the flight surgeon's office for Colonel Mack to "show off."

There is justification for this. On a recent 7th Air Force inspection of all medical facilities in Southeast Asia, the flight surgeon's office at Cam Ranh was deemed the "most outstanding flight surgeon's office in Southeast Asia." It received the highest accolade for any department of the

12th USAF Hospital. I'm not sure how my flight surgeon's office came out so well, but I am grateful for this gift to Colonel Mack.

Certainly, the flight surgeon's office at Cam Ranh is one of the plushest medical offices in Vietnam. Bill Simmons and I had comfortable furniture flown in gratis from Japan and the Philippines by multiple pilots. It exceeds the opulence of many executive offices found in the States.

This is not my first encounter with General Brady. I first met him while stationed at Bergstrom in Texas. The rank of lieutenant general with three stars is the highest rank a physician can achieve in the Air Force. He is the perfect picture of political compromise, a person who does not offend enough to provoke opposition, yet does not accomplish enough to stimulate support. He is a political figurehead in a high office. On his previous visit at Bergstrom, the man seemed totally detached, as if he were forced to fulfill a distasteful obligation to "visit the troops." Now, at a different time, in a different place, he presents with the same obligatory perfunctory disinterest that defines D-U-T-Y.

Here, just as at Bergstrom, he mechanically states, no less than ten times, in as many minutes, that: "I'm very glad to be here. You are not forgotten in Washington…we're still thinking about you…"

He spouted the same words verbatim at Bergstrom and no one paid any attention. But over here, things are a bit different! His words have more than an empty impact, not only on me, but on the career medical officers who surround me. There are numerous murmurs and cynical comments from multiple voices in the back row, that say in effect, "Well, he has paid his courtesy call and is now eligible to collect his combat pay and apply for his income tax deduction…Ah, what the hell; forget it! This bullshit is over with…"

16 December 1966

I was MOD last night. At 2 a.m. two badly burned civilian patients were brought into the dispensary. The patients were Vietnamese men who work for the RMK construction company. While refueling a generator with diesel fuel, one of the two lit a cigarette...the explosion was huge. One of them, an old man, a Papa San, was burned over every inch of his body. It even burned his shoes off. When I saw him, I knew that he would not live long as assessed by the extent of his burns. I spent the next few hours trying to hustle up a helicopter to air evacuate him to the burn unit of Provence Hospital in Nha Trang where his family lives. The other person was burned less severely and should recover.

As I looked down at the old man, I am absolutely overwhelmed by grief with pity for him. He lies quietly and asks only for his family in an even tone. He is so severely burned that the pain receptors in his skin have all been destroyed...a tender mercy! I turn away so that the corpsmen do not see my tears.

I can only think how terrible it must be to have lived a Sisyphean existence in the squalor and degradation of this war-torn country, suspended by a thread between the Scylla of unfounded hope and the Charybdis of bottomless despair...or perhaps even worse, with no hope or not even a dream of something better in the future. His entire life has been consumed by eking out a subsistence level of existence to support his family.

All of his life he has lived in mud and filth...and knows nothing else...and, now, surviving to a relatively old age, he must perform manual labor, with an intensity that youth can barely tolerate, until he is finally and horribly destroyed. The tragedy of this single human being transcends and dwarfs all political considerations, nationalities, race, religion and ethics. The simple dignity of being human deserves better than such degradation.

There is a point or degree of pain and suffering beyond which no man should have to go. Too much pain is unjust! But, life is unjust...

I am truly amazed that this incident involving the old man has impacted me so profoundly. During this war and in the practice of medicine, I have seen and dealt with human tragedy and desecration in countless degrees and occasions. Indeed, with recent exposure to episodes of mass and individual slaughter, I have begun to question my own humanity. War reduces the value of life to a price so cheap that mere existence becomes of questionable value. Life begins to seem cheap when it is squandered so readily. But, there is no price to be fixed on the suffering of this poor individual...there is only pain, suffering and degradation beyond human understanding.

I cannot speak for the masses, but I continue to hold an abiding faith in the integrity and worth of each individual. The peasants who farm the rice paddies with their water buffalo know little and care less for the political nuances of centralized government leadership. Most are simple men who desire only to be left to tend their crops, care for their families and be respected for their efforts by their family and within their villages. The universality of man is little changed by politics.

On an individual basis there is probably no man or woman anywhere, of whatever political persuasion, that I would not be comfortable with at the dinner table. Nations, like religions, divide mankind.

And yet, I find some small solace and relief in my response to this one person, this Papa San. The very fact that I find myself so overwhelmed with grief by the old man's tragedy, and experience such angst in my pity for him, has to mean that I have not become totally insensitive to human tragedy.

If I am still capable of experiencing such an emotional response to the misery of another human, is that not evidence that despite it all, I have not totally lost my humanity and compassion for others less fortunate than me? My response brings me back to reality of life on this Earth. It is a reminder that I too am human, no less nor better than this old man, and no less nor better than these poor people We are all of one blood…we are all family.

Since I must cover the hospital for emergencies tonight, I am unable to leave Cam Ranh to accompany the old man on the short helicopter flight to Nha Trang. But, competent medical corpsmen from the air-evacuation unit will escort him to the Province Hospital there. I accompany him to the helicopter pad for transport and stand silently as it takes off and fades into the night.

18 December 1966

The best made plans of mice and men…

Amateurish attempts by the Air Force to "sneak" Major Clayton and me into the crash site area have failed. Apparently, pressure from higher levels of command, demands that the Air Force "do something" even if it is wrong. But the plot has thickened. Now, if a larger team effort is attempted, we must obtain permission from the Chief of Ninh Thuan Province to enter his domain. Permission to introduce our investigation team with troops into the area has thus far not been granted by the Province chieftain. He was contacted early this morning and promptly refused permission. He may be under pressure and penalty of death from Viet Cong in his village, or he is holding out for more money. He may or may not be a Viet Cong sympathizer. The operation remains on hold until we can obtain permission from higher Vietnamese authorities.

The request will have to go up the chain of command in the South Vietnamese government. The chieftain may have done this to obtain a fat bribe from the Air Force or, more likely, he and his province may be under

Viet Cong control. Judging by the confirmed number of enemy troops in the area, the latter option seems likely.

However, other local and remote politicians have become embroiled and now the whole venture is up for grabs. But, regardless, I'm willing to bet that we will ultimately pay him off in order to investigate the crash site. If we don't pay him off, we will pay off a higher official for a higher price to force the local chieftain to permit our entry. In fairness, it is difficult to be judgmental. There are other issues that influence the indigenous population. This entire region is infested with North Vietnamese Regular Army troops and Viet Cong. All political structures of the Province are probably in the grip of these forces. Judging by other locations and circumstances, officials, families and entire villages are held hostage by these forces. Any action that involves our entry must be approved by these enemy forces.

I am sure that it has always been this way in other wars, in other lands and in other times, throughout history. However, this is my first personal experience with war and it is very easy to lose all perspective or to remain objective. I have no other standard for comparison.

Al leaves Cam Ranh at 0600 tomorrow. He will lay over for one night at Tan Son Nhut before taking a flight the next day to Yakota AFB, Japan. From there, he will return to the States. His attitude was a little better today, but still not his old self. I will probably never know the truth of what happened to him. I only hope that my worst fears are not true. I will miss him.

December 18, 1966
F-4C Mission
Aircraft Commander: Capt. Tom Ross
Flight Time: 1:30
Ordnance: Rockets and Anti-personnel weapons

Today's weather is excellent, both on takeoff and in the target area. Our mission is to provide close ground support for Marines in the Mekong Delta region. After contact with the FAC, we spread our ordnance over the area marked by his Willie Petes. During our approach, we see no enemy troops and encounter no ground fire, either when dive bombing the target or when pulling off target.

Captain Ross is kind enough to let me fly back to Cam Ranh. I continue to improve with each mission. I am grateful that Captain Ross and the other aircraft commanders put up with my amateurish efforts to fly this incredible aircraft. The return flight to Cam Ranh is uneventful and VFR conditions prevail.

CHAPTER 25

===

Changing of the Guard

19 December 1966

The first generation of fighter pilots to arrive in Vietnam is now rotating out to other assignments. These are men of the 391st TFS, with whom I have flown on multitudes of dangerous missions since my arrival in June. Major Solis and other pilots of the 391st TFS introduced me to the extraordinary F-4C Phantom II and opened a world of flying for me that exceeded all of my dreams. I had never considered myself a "team player" before these experiences, but the bond that I established with them has been engraved indelibly in my brain. It will endure for the remainder of my life. Daily exposure to death from the same enemy forges a bond between men that defies description. You know their reaction patterns, in dive bombing, in flying formation, and in drinking beer.

They are all good men!

They are all strong men!

They are all honorable men!

They are the cream of American manhood!

I am deeply honored to have served and flown with them!

When these men arrived, they were one year younger and had never flown in combat. Now after a year, they are many years older. They have faced death day in and day out, day and night. And, yet, they have continued to fly and fight the good fight even as they watched their roommates and wingmen explode around, over and under them after being struck by ground fire, SAMs and MIG's. They hail from the small villages with only whistle stops, the small towns and the large cities of America. As children, they played on dirt roads, sidewalks and city streets. They attended small colleges, large universities and postgraduate schools.

As young adults, they left parents, wives, children and sweethearts to fly in a thankless war, in a distant land. Now they have finished their current tour and will rotate out to another assignment. I did not know them before June. But now they will always occupy a place in my memory. I can never forget them.

They are very different from the younger pilots who are arriving. Perhaps the difference will vanish after these new, younger pilots have faced the tedium of daily missions and the stark terror of aerial combat. We shall see.

The older group is more symbolic of the Snoopy cartoon, hell-bent to shoot down the Red Baron. They have a flair for wearing white silk scarves and yellow kid gloves, a flare that is absent from their younger replacement pilots. The older group fought hard, played hard and consumed enormous quantities of alcohol…before arising at 4:30 a.m. the following morning to fly two missions that day and then stand alert duty all the next night!

The newer, younger pilots drink Cokes and go to bed promptly by 9 p.m. before an early morning mission. They are the stereotype of the All-American male, handsome and clean cut. In the "hooch" or Quonset hut where we all sleep, the nights are much quieter. I am no longer awakened by the swaggering braggadocio of drunken voices describing the intensity of flak over Haiphong Harbor. Nor does the slurring tongue of bourbon guide the hands of the new pilots as they describe their maneuvers for getting on the 6 o'clock position of a MIG over Hanoi, and to proclaim triumphantly about "burning his ass" with a side-winder missile up his tail pipe! The first group of men were the prototypes of "fighter pilots," which seems absent in the new arrivals.

If I live to be 100 years old, I can never forget flying with Maj. Roland X. Solis, or "Chico," as he carefully donned a yellow silk scarf around his neck and ostentatiously thrust each hand into a yellow kid-leather glove before climbing into the cockpit in front of me. Nor will I ever forget screaming in to a dive at more than 600 miles per hour to level off only a few feet above the ground to drop anti-personnel weapons or splatter napalm on enemy troops attacking our Marines. And then hurtling straight up in full afterburner to barely avoid the mountain that was erupting in front of us. These were fighter pilots! And this was combat flying! Sending enough adrenaline flowing through your arteries to scorch your eyeballs!

Without reservation, I know Major Solis is the finest pilot I've ever met and I'm sure that if the World War I Flying Ace, Manfred von Richthofen (The Red Baron), were still flying; Major Solis would be a most worthy adversary.

There are "good" pilots and there are "not-so-good" pilots. There is also a special category of pilots that defies all description. These pilots do not simply fly their aircraft. They are part of the aircraft. They are the consummate union of man with machine that is so rarely seen in peace or in war. Major Solis is of this exceptional category of pilots. It has been an honor and a privilege to fly with him and to be taught by him. With the exception of Colonel Mack, there is no person that I hold in higher regard! For me the departure of these pilots marks the passage of an era! I salute them!

20 December 1966

F-4C Mission 4 Aircraft

Aircraft Commander: Major Tom Ross

Flight Time: 1:40

Ordnance: Each aircraft is armed with four, 500-pound general-purpose bombs, with Gatling gun in midline under the fuselage.

This mission was initially fragged for close air support of troops near Can Tho. We had just performed the pre-flight check as we sat in the cockpit with chocks under the wheels, when the call came for us to scramble (take off immediately). After we are airborne, radio informs us that we are to fly cover for an Air Force C-130 aircraft that is involved in some type of secret mission in the Delta region. The C-130 is receiving a considerable amount of ground fire while flying at low altitude. We contacted "Paddy Control," the regional air traffic control that vectors all aircraft in the Delta Region. Paddy Control, in turn, vectors our flight to the harassed C-130. As we passed over Binh Tuy, I couldn't help recalling the uneasy two weeks I spent in this tiny marshland outpost. A grove of trees near the river is the source of automatic weapon fire on the C-130. We break into elements of two aircraft for our strafing run on the position. After two passes, the ground fire is suppressed. Having finished this part of the mission in such short order, we attempt to contact the FAC for the initial mission. Having four 500-pound bombs under the wings of each aircraft, we are fully capable of fulfilling the demands of our original mission. However, multiple attempts to contact our FAC through Paddy Control are unsuccessful. We have no choice except to "Bingo" and return to base. ("Bingo" is the Air Force term for the point in a flight in which there's only enough fuel remaining to return to base.) The weather is excellent and we have an uneventful flight back to Cam Ranh where all four aircraft land, fully armed with their loads of bombs.

21 December 1966

Bob Hope with his entourage of beautiful women arrived at Cam Ranh today. He gave his "stand-up" comedian show at South Beach, home of the U.S. Army Base at Cam Ranh. I couldn't make the show, but standing in front of the flight surgeon's office, I watched him depart from Cam Ranh.

21 December 1966

Today, Army helicopters, flying low-level reconnaissance over the F-4 crash site area, report enemy trenches and earth works fortifications within one-half mile of the crash site.

22 December 1966

Permission is finally granted by the chief of Ninh Thuan Province for our entry to investigate the crash site.

23 December 1966

The weather continues to be atrocious and a continuing obstacle to our investigation of the crash site. Today I took a short walk to the beach and noted that not even the seagulls are flying. Under these conditions, there is no chance of getting into the crash site. Triple canopy jungle foliage in this mountainous region prevents any meaningful aerial observation of the crash site.

Somehow, it seems ironic how our military...empowered with the most sophisticated and technically superior forces in history... must huddle, cowering in the sand before the elemental furies of wind and water... no less than the legions of Julius Caesar or the Mongol Hordes of Genghis Khan.

As senior officer in the flight surgeon's office and member of the Accident Investigation Board, I must investigate this crash. Regardless of the weather, it is simply a matter of time before I will have to go into the jungle, hopefully with troops, to investigate the crash site. So far all plans for entry into the crash site area have been thwarted by weather and by failure of the Province chief to grant us permission to enter his domain. During our requests for permission to enter the area, we have emphasized that our mission is limited and goal directed. We wish only to collect the remains of our two dead pilots before leaving the area. But, until yesterday, all plans for entry into the crash site area have been thwarted. Today he granted permission for our entry. The extended haggle with the province chief for permission to enter the site has left no doubt about our intentions. To expect secrecy on the chief's part would be a flight from reality.

The most current plans are that we will be accompanied and guarded by 70-plus ROK (Republic of Korea) Marines. There is no intention of conducting a search and destroy mission against any residents or persons who are indigenous to the region. This was been emphasized on several occasions to reassure the Viet Cong and North Vietnamese Regular Army troops that we don't want a fight...

Reports of Viet Cong activity in the crash area have been conflicting. ROK Marines, who patrol this region on a regular basis, report that as many as 1,000 or more North Vietnamese Regular Army (NVA) soldiers are in this immediate vicinity. Our Air Force Intelligence says, "No. Perhaps, a few hundred North Vietnamese Troops may be present, but no more...."

Of course, since Viet Cong are indigenous to the province, their number must exceed the number of North Vietnamese Army Regulars by several fold. I prefer to trust the on-site intelligence reports of the Korean

Marines. These Marines operate on the ground and are capable of personally observing enemy troop strength and activities. But, I can't say that either or both intelligence reports are reassuring for the upcoming venture.

Two days ago, Army helicopters, flying low level reconnaissance over the area, reported trenches and fortifications within a half-mile of the crash site. While that may seem a rather paltry distance in most places, the 'paltry' epithet does not pertain to this jungle. Here, advances are measured in feet, not miles. The crash occurred in an area considered by friend and foe, alike, to be the heart of a great coastal rainforest that marches down the mountains to meet narrow savannah precipices, all of which are cloaked in elephant grass and punctuated by massive black rock formations. It is generally acknowledged that the terrain in this area represents some of the most remote and densest jungle in Vietnam. The majority of this region is not inhabited and has not been explored in modern times.

My thoughts return again and again to the reality of our present situation. After sixteen days of exposure to torrential rains, heat and the ravaging of jungle creatures, any human remains can only exist in a state of advanced decomposition. But, these are not ordinary times. A more pertinent consideration is that sixteen days provides ample time for the enemy to booby-trap every scrap of human remains and every scrap of twisted metal. Sixteen days has also allowed the enemy adequate time to accurately register their artillery and mortars on the crash site in anticipation of our entry.

It is inconceivable that the numerous fixed and rotary wing reconnaissance flights over the area have not focused enemy attention on the crash site. Certainly, any enemy forces in the area have had adequate forewarning of our interests in the area.

I later learned that considerable discussion has taken place at wing headquarters concerning the necessity for a physician/flight surgeon to actively participate in investigating the crash site. However, the Rule Book is quite firm on the matter. Regulations require a flight surgeon and a senior Air Force pilot to conduct and appraisal of the crash site.

As the senior pilot, Major John Clayton quickly informs all interested parties that if any tissue remains are found, he, as a pilot, "Would be unable to distinguish human meat from goat meat…!"

This declaration of "medical inadequacy" is sufficiently blatant to discourage any consideration of an alternative for a flight surgeon. That matter being settled, Wing Commander Colonel Jones E. Bolt queried Major Clayton about my physical wherewithal to survive the rigors of such an operation. Since physicians are rarely a paradigm of battle-hardened physical prowess, it was not an unreasonable consideration. Major Clayton's reply is brief and straightforward, "Colonel, I have no reservations about Clark. If anyone can make it, he can. Quite frankly, I'm more concerned about whether I can make it or not."

By this time, myths of what other pilots perceived as my success in Jungle Survival School have been amplified and emboldened with accolades from Major Solis about my flying abilities in the F-4C Phantom. Senior pilots are the equivalents of chiefs who lead their clans into battle. Major Solis is the most respected and talented pilot, not only in our 391st TFS, but also in the 12th TFW. The principle of "Follow and Protect the Chief" is sacrosanct. Since I fly only with Major Solis or other senior pilots, any positive trait perceived in me is amplified beyond all reason as it filters down to the younger pilots. Since aerial combat is teamwork, it naturally follows that they wish their flight surgeon to be a hot pilot of tempered steel, just as they consider themselves to be. If their flight surgeon doesn't boast, they will do it for him…

In general, a person sees what he wants to see. Young fighter pilots are not noted for modesty around non-pilots. They are noted for their macho personalities, swaggering attitudes and braggadocio. These traits are consummate parts of a cultivated self-image that they wish to convey to the non-pilot population, as well as to themselves. This persona validates their role as "Knights of the Air." The assumed role is not merely the shallow egocentric vanity of self-flattery. It is an extension of the age-old chivalric, quixotic theme of combat that embodies a man in a standard theme of personal courage to assure the triumph of such brave individuals over adversity.

It is this "cloak of invincibility" that permits them to assume risks and court death to a degree impossible without it. It is the armor that protects them from the enemy, while isolating them from their own insecurities and admission of their personal mortality. In their daily jousts with death and destruction, their assumed persona is the talisman that allows them to risk all and to survive. As fighter pilots age, the adolescent emotions of "Dering-Do" are gradually transformed into mature talents and skills that ensure mastery of their trade and distinguish the mature warrior from his adolescent novitiate.

Without these attitudes, the combat risks experienced by these men would otherwise be intolerable for a reasonable person. (On second thought, however, no "reasonable person" would be a fighter pilot.)

The other member of the investigation team is Maj. William Boucher, a staff officer at wing headquarters. He flies four hours a month in a C-47 Gooney Bird to qualify for his flight pay. He is handsome and is happiest when being photographed. However, he only permits a photo when the proper angle of his jaw is exposed...

Although he has no true function to fill on our mission, he has prevailed on higher brass for permission to go with us. This has finally been granted.

On the afternoon of 21 December 1966, I report, as requested, to the office of Colonel Mack. Initially, Colonel Mack seems his usual cordial self. We chat for several minutes about minor, inconsequential matters concerning the flight surgeon's office, none of which have any pertinence to the upcoming crash investigation.

Our conversation begins to lose steam and eventually he seems lost for words. At last, he clears his throat and seems unusually ill at ease. Then with a facial expression of having something distasteful to discuss, he suddenly appears very sober and refers to the accident investigation mission. Without any tone of conviction, he begins to cite the usual, official reasons as to why a flight surgeon is required to participate in an assault helicopter landing behind enemy lines to retrieve portions of corpses that have been rotting in the jungle for sixteen days.

He informs me about the continuing pressure that he receives from the wing level of command, demanding that a flight surgeon play an integral role in the crash site investigation. He explains that since Vietnam is a "conflict" rather than a bona fide "war," declared by Congress, a standing Air Force regulation declares that any aircraft crash must be investigated by a flight surgeon and a senior pilot. On the other hand, if a plane were shot down over Hanoi, the crash would be considered a combat loss and no investigation would be necessary.

While Colonel Mack is speaking, I observe his eyes and I weigh his attention and dedication-to-duty mannerisms…as they waiver, wane and progressively dwindle with each word of official justification. Finally, his words run out…

For a few moments, he says nothing, and then clears his throat, "At this point I have no choice."

He has the same reluctance and reservations about this mission as I.

After a significant pause, he says softly, "There are only two doctors on this base who are capable of performing this mission and surviving… you and me.

"You are the only doctor here who can go down into that jungle and come back out alive... But, I want you to know that this is not an order. I won't order you to do this... If you don't want to go, I will go..."

At first, I didn't reply. I am twenty-eight-years old and he is over forty. I have never known a man for whom I have greater respect or whom I hold in higher personal regard than Colonel Mack. I can't allow that. My reply is simple and direct, "No, colonel, I don't want to go, but under the circumstances, I don't seem to have a helluva lot of choice, do I?"

He doesn't respond. Our eyes meet for an instant. He thrusts his hand forward to grip mine until his knuckles are white.

"Be careful!"

"I will..."

I turn and walk briskly to the door. Then, for reasons that I can never explain, I stop and turn around. Colonel Mack is still standing. I come to attention and salute him. The flicker of a smile touches his lips. He easily comes to attention and returns my salute. I turn and open the door to leave.

"Guy..."

I pause to look back...

"Guy, don't get your ass shot off!"

Facing him, I can't suppress a grin,

"Colonel, of all the asses on this earth that are worth defending, I consider mine to be Number One...and will defend it to the death!"

I can still hear his roar of laughter as I adjust my cap, close the door behind me and plow through the ubiquitous sands of Cam Ranh Bay. Walking to the large inflatable warehouses known as "White Elephants," I enter Base Supply. Here, I quickly check out my gear of jungle fatigues, survival rations for three days, poncho, M-16 rifle, ammunition, steel helmet and two canteens.

Night before last, Weather reported a break in the dense cloud and fog cover that perennially cloaks the coastal mountain peaks and valleys.

Timing for our enterprise is most critical. Within any interval of clear sky, an assault landing of troops with our investigation team must be accomplished by "Slick" Huey helicopters[22], which in turn, will be escorted by Huey gunships.

The choppers must be able to hover above the elephant grass long enough to insert troops[23] and the investigation team from a height of 15-20 feet. The number of risk factors increases geometrically with each minute spent in execution of our insertion. The area chosen for insertion is a small mountain plateau, bounded on the west by a rocky escarpment that stretches up to the jungle and towers above it.

Obviously, entering the site is only half of the problem. The weather and conditions have to remain stable and clear, for a sufficient period of time to permit our extraction after we have finished our mission. With this information, Maj. John Clayton of the Accident Investigation Board and I will be inserted by helicopter into the crash site. We will be accompanied by approximately sixty-five Korean Marines. I never knew why the Army Special Forces did not accompany us on our previous attempt...or what had happened to plans for trekking across the mountain and the 200-foot insertion by rope for Major Clayton and me? However, quite frankly, if I had to choose companions for a do-or-die combat situation, I can think of no one on this planet, better suited or in whom I have more confidence, than the South Korean Marines... the ROK Marines!

Things always seem to work out. Consideration of all of these different plans reminds me of a favorite quote from Winston Churchill:

---

22 A "Slick Huey" is a Huey helicopter that has been stripped of heavy armament and weaponry to allow more room for hauling troops. "Slick" is the term to describe relative absence of weaponry. A "Slick," however, continues to have two door gunners, armed with M-60 machine guns.

23 Insertion is the term for inserting combat forces into a combat zone. Extraction is the term for extracting them.

"You can always count on Americans to do the right thing...after they've tried everything else."

These preliminary plans reveal that since no suitable landing site can be located near the crash site, the closest point for our insertion will require a hike of three to four days through the jungle to reach the site. The Korean Marines veto this plan immediately. Progress through this miasma of jungle swampland and cliffs is measured in inches and not by miles. The time consumed in this agonizing trek would only allow the Viet Cong and North Vietnam Army (NVA) regular troops more time to organize and plot our destruction in ambush. This would represent a classic example of "guerrilla warfare and how not to fight it."

Instead, the ROK Marines propose an alternative plan. This involves the sudden assault of a remote pass about one to two miles from the crash site. The helicopters cannot and will not attempt to land. In this area of jungle, the terrain and wind conditions are so rugged that all pilots agree that flying and landing in the area is impossible. Beneath the elephant grass, the terrain is riddled with innumerable crevices, fissures and caves that scarify the plateau and spell disaster for any landing attempt. Terrain to the East of the insertion point terminates abruptly into a ravine that plunges more than 100 feet into an impenetrable morass of vines, smaller ravines and cliffs. All of this geography finally tumbles into the South China Sea. Accompanied by the Korean Marines, Major Clayton and I will be inserted suddenly, by jumping from the helicopters while they hover ten to fifteen feet above the ground.

No choreographer for an Old West movie could have fabricated a more ideal ambush site. The plateau is swept by vicious crosswinds and turbulence, generated by cooler sea breezes colliding with warmer jungle winds...all of which cascade through myriads of canyons and mountain passes, increasing in wind velocity and turbulence at each intersection...

When a helicopter pilot thinks of hell, LZs (landing zones) such as this must come to mind. An assault landing into a jungle island, where it is virtually impossible to hover because of chaotic winds and turbulence… an LZ, where the enemy sits, ensconced in stone fortresses, with weapons preregistered and sighted in range for the landing zone below.

For the helicopter pilots, the primary goal of this mission is to safely insert troops into this cauldron; their secondary goal is to avoid sacrificing their aircraft and air crewmembers.

All plans are based on weather being favorable, as predicted. In this narrow swath of transition between jungle and ocean, local factors, ultimately and unpredictably, determine air-to-ground accessibility and ground-to-ground communication. The local variability is so volatile that in a few minutes, several square miles of jungle mountainside may be transformed from "clear and visibility unlimited" to zero visibility around you and zero visibility above you… and …all by a small cloud/fog bank moving in from the ocean. The rapid formation of morning or evening fog may quickly conceal several hundred square yards of a drop zone, either before or after insertion of troops. Only the local Muses are privy to the schedule of these happenings.

I am well aware that if the weather deteriorates rapidly after our insertion, it will be impossible for aircraft, at any altitude, to fly protective cover for the men on the ground. Ultimately, extraction by hovering or landing helicopters will be impossible. Under these conditions, the ground forces will then be at the mercy of an entrenched enemy that is fighting on home ground. The sequestered ground troops, with limited rations and ammunition, can then be leisurely sniped out of existence.

My duty is to identify and extract sufficient remains of the pilots to permit positive identification. Any tissues that I bring out will be forwarded home to their families for interment. Procurement and identification of the remains will also allow the Air Force to certify that an Expert

Witness (Namely, me as a physician) has identified the remains and thus can certify to their deaths. All of these procedural matters are considered necessary and of value for legal purposes, as well as for any questions that might arise in the future.

But despite the rhetoric, my subconscious returns time and time again to "The Charge of the Light Brigade" by Alfred Lord Tennyson"

"Into the Valley of Death rode the six hundred..."

This entire endeavor progressively smacks of an expedition that approaches sheer suicide. The plane crashed sixteen days earlier, in enemy-infested mountains and jungles. Each pilot carried a radio in his survival vest, but all have been silent. From my perspective, the enemy will use the crash site as bait for us to enter the area of preregistered artillery, mortars, automatic weapons and booby-trapped crash relics.

We are scheduled to depart by helicopter at 0600 on December 22, 1966.

CHAPTER 26

The Search

22 December 1966

I awaken at 0500, dress, collect my gear and go to the mess hall for breakfast. It promises to be a clear, pleasant dawn, with a slight refreshing breeze wafting in from the South China Sea. The temperature is pleasantly cool for Cam Ranh.

After breakfast, I walk to the flight line in front of the wing command post. In front of the building, I meet Air Force Majors John F. Clayton and William (Bill) A. Boucher. The 12th TFW Army Liaison Officer, Captain Tom Strickland, will also accompany us to coordinate ground forces with air support measures.

Traveling by jeep we cross the Cam Ranh runways to a pontoon bridge that connects Cam Ranh Peninsula to the mainland. Once on the mainland, we follow a narrow gravel road through the small village of My Kah to Highway 1. My Kah is a tiny Vietnamese fishing village through which we must pass before reaching Highway 1. Highway 1 is the "Street

Without Joy," which was immortalized in Barnard Fall's 1961 book of that same title. The book's theme is spun around the final ouster of the French Colonials from Indochina. The events culminated with defeat of the French in the Battle of Dien Bien Phu in 1954 by Viet Minh. It seems no little irony that the last French troops in Indochina left from Cam Ranh Bay in July 1956.

Now, in 1966, every village and hamlet in Vietnam, regardless of size, is suspected of hosting Viet Cong. At this time, this squalid little fishing village of My Kah is considered to be "Secure," but this morning, I see little evidence that My Kah is secure from anything…nothing in its appearance presents evidence of any exception to the rule of Viet Cong occupancy. Before departing Cam Ranh, we loaded our weapons. Rolling slowly into My Kah, we slip a round into the chambers of our M-16s.

But all is quiet. It is early morning, before sunrise. As we drive through the village, the only evidence of humanity is an elderly Vietnamese mama san, who squats to urinate beside her doorstep. After a few minutes of further driving, scattered remnants of the village melt into the ground fog and finally vanish into muddy ruts of the narrow road, leading to Highway 1.

Continuing down Highway 1 for an uneventful three miles, we finally arrive at the encampment of the White Horse Regiment of the Republic of Korea (ROK) Marines. (ROK 30th Regiment, ROK 9th Division… Infantry).

Major Paik Un Taik and Captain Shin Mal Up, company commander of sixty-five ROK Marines, are in charge of conducting the assault landing and for clearing and securing the crash site. They will escort our team into the crash site area.

The ROK Marine camp is nearly invisible to anyone without a knowing eye. As we approach, there is little to distinguish the camp from the stunted bushes, scrawny shrubs and dwarfed trees that populate the adjacent surroundings. The entire Korean encampment site is extremely austere and Spartan in every respect. In contrast to Western military encampments, the usual military accoutrements of tents, latrines, command posts, etc. are removed from sight. In fact, there is so little evidence of human habitation that a casual passer-byer would hardly pause at the way-stop. There are only smattering bunches of stunted trees and scruffy shrubs that protrude starkly out of the barren reddish sand.

Suddenly, a human form emerges from the anonymity of the fog and void. As if a product of spontaneous generation, Major Taik stands silently alone beside the road to greet us. A few words of recognition are exchanged between us. After a short time, in response to an unspoken signal from Major Taik, out of the shadows, quietly emerge these singularly tough ROK Marines from holes in the earth that have previously been covered with brush and canvas shelter halves. These men sleep in small dugouts or foxholes, covered by a tarpaulin, which lies flush with the ground. Their camouflage is so perfect that when we drive into camp, there is absolutely no evidence of life, in any form.

Major Taik is a man of short stocky stature. Compactly muscular, he conveys the image of a powerful, coiled spring, and moves with the graceful agility of a great cat. Immaculately dressed in creased fatigues and wearing spit-polished combat boots, he carries a stick in his right hand that, I initially interpreted as a "Swagger Stick." It is not. There is no "swagger" in this man. He carries a stick of highly polished wood, against which he performs isometric calisthenics, straining muscle, tendon and bone against its seasoned rigidity. After our introduction and during a discussion of the mission, he continues to exercise with the stick. Finally, content with his efforts, he hands the stick off to his aid.

The adjacent parade ground has silently filled with phantom-like, moving forms of Korean Marines, as they perform their daily drills and organize for the day's activity. Despite the intensity of their physical exertions, relative silence is maintained. They speak in hushed tones and communicate only in sign language. This Silence stands in marked contrast to the Pep-Rally drills of the military in Western Nations. Throughout past centuries, Western Civilization, Africa and countless other cultures of war, have incorporated chant and cadence counting with professed ferocity, to enforce coercive unity or to stir the soul before death. But, Silence has far greater power than sound or music to instill fear in the enemy. Death is silent... Nothing exceeds the power and unspoken ferocity of silence...

Now, silence cloaks and envelops these smaller warriors with a portent of ferocious lethality and ominous power that has long been lost in the circus arena frenzy of noise, maintained by other armies, both ancient and modern. But silence has never entirely left the field of battle. Regardless of the age or of the civilizations in conflict, the ultimate validation of victory over the vanquished is proclaimed by sudden silence, that moment in time when life leaves one body to permit the other to live. Beyond silence, nothing else remains. Silence is isolation from life...and isolation is the death knell for mankind.

Abstractions of philosophy aside, regardless of training style, no one can contest a single determinant of military fitness. The absolute test of a warrior is decided by confrontation on the field of battle. And, this I know as a fact: The North Vietnamese Army (NVA) forces and the Viet Cong of South Vietnam have no reticence about attacking the Armies, Navies, Marines and Air Forces of the United States and their allies, but they desperately try to avoid conflict with the Korean Marines whenever possible.

These ROK Marines have a reputation, acknowledged and recognized by friend and foe, as the toughest of the tough. The Viet Cong are terrified of them. What sets them apart from the Troops of Western Nations is self-discipline, inurement to pain and the absence of Christian ideals of compassion, mercy or fair play that are so deeply embedded in American troops.

For centuries, the history of Western Civilization has been dominated by wars between kings and kingdoms…. wars have always been the sport of kings. And, no less than a game of chess, Western warfare abides by rules of chivalry, fair play and conquest, mirrored in the current Geneva Convention of warfare. Whether fought for Fortune, Fame, Glory or Religion, they have the same infrastructure to seek power over the enemy.

Unburdened by such conventions, Korean Marines fight in the manner of their Asiatic heritage. For them, the enemy is to be killed by any means. It has been rumored that they eschew killing the enemy from afar with gunfire. Western nations fight with long-range artillery and high-flying aircraft to spare the lives of our troops. This implies that we wish to save the chessmen without concern for the chessboard.

Asian warfare has little concern for either. It matters little whether the enemy is destroyed, ravaged or enslaved. The results are all the same. In contrast to the remote high tech warfare of the United States, the Koreans much prefer closing with the enemy and killing him in hand-to-hand combat with knives, bayonets, or better yet, strangling him with their bare hands. The Koreans are fully cognizant that there is only one elemental immutable truth between combatants of any war:

"Destroy the enemy before he destroys you!"

During and after the Korean War, the South Korean military was introduced to the high-tech methods of American and European nations. Quickly learning the Western military skills, the Koreans adopted improvements in their methods of warfare, but they did not forsake their Asian heritage. Combining the methods and technology of the West with the primeval ferocity of the East, the Korean Marines have now excelled and surpassed their previous tutors.

These men train by chopping bricks with their bare hands. I have seen any number of fifth metacarpal fractures in the dispensary to bear testimony for this practice. There are stories of them actually skinning captured Viet Cong alive in front of other prisoners to "encourage" them to talk. They generally prefer to take no prisoners. In battle, no quarter is either asked or given.

Once, when I was on MOD duty, a young ROK Marine was brought in with a bullet wound through his foot. I initiated first aid before calling the orthopedic surgeon to render more definitive care.

Before I could proceed, I was interrupted by a young ROK lieutenant who politely saluted me and introduced himself by rank and unit. He asked if the patient with the foot wound were present. I acknowledged that he was receiving treatment at the time. The officer firmly requested that I turn the young man over to his care. I complied, without comment, since I have no authority over the Republic of Korea Marines. I thought no more about it until one or two days later, when I learned that the wound had been self-inflicted to avoid combat. The young Marine was taken back to the ROK camp where he was executed for cowardice, while witnessed by other troops.

Dawn is beginning to break. And, for a brief moment, my attention is diverted from the horrors of war to watch the sunrise. The sun begins to rise majestically out of the South China Sea…catching the reflections of mountains to our back and melting away the tiny patches of ground fog that cling tenaciously to the low places. There is a gentle, southerly breeze blowing, while a white heron floats silently over the distant blue of the sea. The silence of the Koreans seems an appropriate expression of muted reverence for the grandeur of these earthly events.

Lt. Colonel Hastings of the U.S. Army Special Forces appears to coordinate the various stages of our mission. He appears startled after the first few sentences of conversation. The Koreans have a penchant for closely guarding all information about a forthcoming mission. This translates to the fact that, up to now, details of the entire mission have remained a closely guarded secret, even from the U.S. Army. For the Koreans, surprising the enemy is more than a fetish. It is a way of life. It is survival. Only now is the U.S. Army Lt. Colonel informed of the mission details.

And, with this newly received information, he turns to brief us on the mission. His original jocular smile has faded, replaced by a very sorrowful expression. His dejected mien is so profound that he now appears depressed and in mourning. The details of this mission have obviously taken him completely by surprise.

Initially, the area of our insertion will be prepped with a 45-minute artillery bombardment by 105mm howitzers of the Army. A U.S. Navy Cruiser, off shore, will then bombard the LZ area and remain on station to assist us if we meet heavy resistance. Immediately, following the seaward and artillery preps, two waves of helicopters and helicopter gunships will insert us into the LZ area.

Suddenly, reality strikes me in the head. My God! I've become part of a full-scale invasion…and, not simply a part…I am the PRINCIPAL participant in a mission whose only purpose is to identify and extract the remains of two pilots!

After fifteen to twenty minutes the first wave of U.S. Army Huey helicopters begins to approach. Shortly thereafter, the whoomp-whoomp-whoomp sounds of the helicopter rotors fill the air. Six Hueys settle, fluttering into the dust of the parade ground.

Immediately, the Army flight commander of the Hueys expresses his trepidations about the entire mission to insert us. On multiple previous occasions, while flying over this same area, his aircraft have received significant amounts of ground fire…along the same flight path chosen for our insertion. His reticence is not subtle. It is blatantly obvious. Before starting this mission, he wants to reconnoiter the insertion area once more. He and Major Boucher take off in a Huey that is especially protected by reinforced steel armor and is heavily armed with rockets and machine guns. After approximately thirty minutes they return.

There is a rush out of the helicopters by their pilots. They are all talking in angry tones to each other. I can't hear details of the discussion or of the issues involved, but soon they break up and the Army flight commander approaches us. Addressing Major Clayton, Major Boucher and me, he states in rather heated tones that, unequivocally, he does not want to fly into the area. It is simply too dangerous. Without waiting for a reply, he abruptly turns away to call his superior. The next twenty minutes is spent haggling with his superior over the radio as he vigorously protests this mission assignment. I overhear parts of his discussion. He emphatically wants no responsibility for taking his aircraft and crewmembers on a mission into an area of known heavy enemy concentration and firepower. He states, summarily, that he considers such a mission as being tantamount to suicide. When he returns, it is obvious from the expression on his face that he has been overruled. The mission will continue…

Now, I really have very serious questions as to what in the hell we are walking into. This man has been flying combat missions in the Huey, at tree-top level, in Vietnam, for almost a year…and from his experience; he has trepidations about this venture! He is no neophyte to combat. He has participated in some of the bloodiest battles, thus far fought in Vietnam. Now, with objections that border on mutiny, he expressly states, "I hope that I won't lose all of my choppers!"

But inter-service rivalry intervenes. With all the enthusiasm and naiveté of a frustrated Boy Scout, afraid that an exciting campout may be canceled, Major Boucher steps forward to insist that we continue. It is worth repeating that Major Boucher is a thirty-four-year-old Air Force pilot, and not a foot soldier. He has never been in ground combat, or for that matter, slept in the jungle (except during jungle survival school). He is a graduate of West Point. He is handsome, debonair and slick of speech. Officially he is the Training and Plans Officer with the 12th Tactical Fighter Wing at Cam Ranh Bay AB, South Vietnam. All of these vainglorious traits combine to lead him in search of something to distinguish him from other officers in his class. Vietnam could provide the perfect windfall of opportunity for him.

As I noted, the first assault wave of Marines will be inserted by the helicopters, immediately after termination of the artillery prep. This first wave of Korean Marines is to "hit hard and secure" the area for the next assault wave, in which we are to be transported.

Thus, at approximately 0800 hours, the first wave of thirty Korean Marines departs and disappears in a chain of whirling rotors speeding southward. Time passes at a snail's pace. I am sure that they have run into trouble or else they would not be taking this long to return.

The Army Special Forces lieutenant colonel reappears and watches the departure with a mournful expression. Finally, he walks over to us, stating that he must go to supervise the artillery. He vigorously shakes my hand and says: "Good luck! You're going to need all that you can get."

After this short encounter, thoughts of "What the hell am I doing here?" continue to race through my mind. This is no war movie. This is not a war game. This is the "real thing." These experienced and battle-hardened Army pilots expect to encounter heavy resistance and a savage fight…simply to salvage their aircraft, while attempting to insert our team into the jungle… and ultimately hope to get some of us out alive!

And, yet despite the eloquence of my Aristotelian logic, I stand, milling like a dumb beast, and continue ruminating on these thoughts until they are finally interrupted by the muffled approach of throbbing rotary blades. Louder and louder, the whoomp-whoomp-whoomp increases until, like giant dragonflies, the helicopters settle into the dustbins they have created beneath them.

Before I can digest all of these events and thoughts, I am running, bending over and heading into the prop wash, to climb in and strap myself into the chopper. Seconds later, we are airborne, as the ungainly beaters thrash the air, clawing for altitude. And finally, we lift off, soaring above the land and over the coastline, sounding like a dragonfly with valve problems.

In the absence of courage, passions prevail. Looking down and around, I find it easy to suppress the noisy rotors, engine sounds and even thoughts of our insertion as I view the panoramic, breathtaking beauty of the countryside beneath us. In the early morning light, the mountains above and below us are blanketed in deep, rich, green colors, over which shafts of sunlight filter through scattered clouds. Waterfalls peek through ravines and secret canyons, before their waters cascade downwards, in sparkling crystals and leap through the morning mists, towards the azure blue of the South China Sea. At our altitude of 1,200-1,500 feet, over and below us, flocks of waterfowl wheel and sweep synchronously in formation. For these few moments birds and man are fellow travelers above the eternal union where land and sea come together.

The supersonic combat missions that I have flown in the F-4C Phantom miss much of this grandeur. Modern warfare demands efficiency of destruction...efficiency does not permit sightseeing, in or above the countryside. Efficiency converts weaponry into mechanical instruments of death, with no consideration for what we are destroying in the process of delivery.

But, war and destruction are not necessary ingredients for blindness. It happens daily in the United States, when we travel on freeways and turnpikes to arrive sooner at points on a map...destinations that can never equal the charm and intrigue of countryside hamlets, orchards, streams and farming communities. We delude ourselves in believing that we are richer in peace than we are in war!

But, whether during war or peace, mankind has lost its moorings... now sacrificed on the altars of peacetime efficiency or wartime destruction. Even Roman Legions of antiquity, as they marched to their death through forests, mountains and plains, could not remain oblivious to the grandeur of the world around them. The Elysium that beckoned from beyond life's horizon had already been tasted on the march. They knew what they were leaving behind and hoped to regain with death. But in 1966, spiraling downward through the sky at 600-700 mph, in a dive bomb attack or napalm strike, there is no luxury of time to appreciate what you are going to destroy or time to remember what you are leaving behind.

Today's slower, more leisurely helicopter approach to battle may achieve the same end, but the journey is more pleasant...regardless of our destination.

I continue to be mesmerized by the beauty that spreads beneath, above and beyond us. Occasional patches of golden elephant grass, sprinkled with huge black boulders, accentuate the surrounding jungle. This is wild, jungle country, far removed from the flat chessboard of manmade rice paddies that consume the Mekong Delta region. No dwellings, roads or paths are visible. Removed from the contamination of mankind and isolated from commercial pollution, it seems a travesty of justice that only during wartime is its virginity exposed. Despite recent Intelligence reports, it seems at that moment that we and our noisy helicopters are the only intruders. Of course, we know that hundreds and perhaps thousands of other humans lurk in the shadows of that verdant green jungle carpet, waiting to kill us. But not even that knowledge can diminish the grandeur of all that rolls before and under us.

As I watch the panorama unroll, I wonder if this has not always been the case when men go into battle, with death so near. Perhaps, it is only at times like this that life seems so precious and vibrant... when the world around us is so painfully beautiful. At these times when the grass is always greener, when the ocean is always bluer, when streams and rivers are clearer and the sun always shines brighter! And, it seems that you can see forever.

I become aware of a deep ache in my chest. It is all too much...too much! It is not sorrow at the possibility of losing all of this in death. There is no fear of death. It is not even regret for previous blindness. It is to be in the presence of something so magnificent...so beautiful, that all efforts to define it or describe it are woefully inadequate. It is to exhaust body, mind and soul attempting to describe ripples on the surface of the sea, yet all the while knowing that beneath the ripples lies an eternity of infinite depths through which flow mighty rivers. It is the shattering inadequacy of religion...of human worship...in the presence of Something...some Power, so omnipotent and omnipresent that it can only be recognized and acknowledged by silence.

There is no thought of "capturing the moment," any more than a minnow thinks of capturing the ocean or a gnat thinks of capturing the air. Quite to the contrary, the moment has captured me, it has assimilated me, incorporating every atom and molecule of my being into its own substance...and now...we are one. All of that is in me and I am a part of all that.

My revere ends abruptly as the Huey dives into a knap-of-the-earth flight pattern, skimming over treetops and darting below treetops... through chains of ravines and mountain valleys...ever downward, but always toward the crash site. As winds and cross winds funnel through these valleys, the air grows progressively more turbulent. The artillery prep from sea and land has ignited fires in the elephant grass. Now, whipped into frenzies by the winds, the fires generate their own vortices and drafts to blend with winds from the sea and crosswinds from the canyons.

There are moments when the pilot struggles to control the pitching chopper. Beneath us, the ground is fissured between huge black boulders. Ordinarily, the ground is concealed by dense elephant grass, but the down wash from helicopter rotors has plastered the grass down to the ground to reveal the hazards beneath. The insertion point is a small meadow. From altitude, this appears smooth and as manicured as a putting green on a civilized golf course. But, as we drop lower and lower, it becomes obvious that any thought of landing is a flight from reality. We will have to jump from the helicopter while it attempts to hover 15-20 feet above the ground. I stand in the open door of the Huey. To my right is the side gunner, nervously swinging the barrel of his M-60 machine gun back and forth over the terrain. With his finger on the trigger, he constantly scans the terrain beneath us, inspecting every nook and cranny, every bush and every blade of elephant grass…anything that might harbor the enemy.

From the perspective of the Army helicopter pilots, this is officially considered to be a "Hot LZ," even if we do not land or touch down. Before and during my jump from the chopper, my plan is to hit the ground and run or crawl like hell for cover, any cover. My only concern is to avoid being shot, either by a hidden sniper, or by a machine gun, nesting on the surrounding hill. But, before I can evade the enemy, I must first survive jumping from the helicopter and land without injury.

Taking a deep breath, I hold the M-16 away from my body and over my head. Momentarily as I look down, the ground seems an eternity away. That thought is quickly dispelled when I jump. The ground rushes up to meet me… I hit rolling, with a PLF (Parachute Landing Fall) to absorb the shock. Happily, it is a good jump. More important, I land on solid ground without falling into a crevice to twist or break my ankle on the rocks. Surrounding me is sea of five- to six-foot-tall elephant grass with razor sharp edges, now pressed flat against the ground by the helicopter prop wash…looking for all the world like hair on a wet dog.

On hitting the ground, I roll, clambering on all fours, while at the same time, clawing, crab-like to retain my gun and helmet. Less than ten feet away is a huge black boulder, also surrounded by elephant grass. Stooping to maintain a low profile and avoid being an easy target, I run through the prop wash and over the elephant grass to the boulder…diving to flatten myself on the ground so hard that it nearly knocks the breath out of me.

I remember the expression of my Confederate ancestors when fired upon. They advised, "Grabbing a root." I would do the same if there were any roots to grab. But here, there are no roots...there is only burning elephant grass and this gargantuan, black boulder that I can neither embrace...nor tunnel under...

Since I have absolutely no idea from which direction an attack might come, I back up to the boulder and face outward, with my M-16 ready to fire. For a few moments, I watch the other choppers fly in, hover and quickly disgorge the ROK Marines. With each subsequent pass, the choppers hover higher and for a shorter period of time. The maneuvers reflect the attitude of their pilots to "Stay high and get the hell out of here as soon as possible." The drawn expression on one pilot's face seems to partially relax as he gratefully pulls off the LZ and departs. How, I envy them...

I recall the prodding of my high school football coach who thought me a bit shy during scrimmage. I can still hear him grunting aggressively over clenched teeth, grinding the ever-present cigar in his mouth, "Get down amongst them!" Well, he should be happy to know that I'm sure as hell "down amongst them!"

The last Huey slips and claws precariously for altitude in the turbulent air as the pilot desperately attempts to hover... in this maelstrom of smoke, fire, crosscurrents and vortices...each agitating and begating others. But, hovering becomes progressively impossible. In order to remain flying, slight forward motion is required. From the helicopter's open side doors, men jump, while others cling reluctantly to the doors, blocking efforts of others who try to crawl back in. Some hang onto the skids, halfway between heaven and earth, in desperation borne of exhausted options.

Just as the last chopper hovers to release its troops, I look up from my plastered position against the black boulder, and for a moment, as the

Huey pitches downward, rolling to the left and before it soars away, I peek quickly through the side door, into its cabin. Plastered on the bulkhead panel, between the two waist-gunners, is a large flag, the "Lone Star Flag of Texas." Abruptly, my trance is broken. A wave of nostalgia and homesickness washes over me at the sight of that flag. Soon, both the helicopter and its flag vanish into the smoke. But, before it disappears completely from sight, the adolescent enthusiasm symbolized by that "Lone Star Flag of Texas" has ignited a ray of hope that focuses all of my energies on elemental methods of surviving this progressively grim situation. Unconsciously, I shake my head in bemused pride and wonderment at the sheer audacity of the Forever-Adolescent American Spirit... And, for the first time today, I smile…

As the final chopper pulls out of the LZ, there is the tortured din of full throttle applied to the rotors as the pilot struggles to maintain altitude and to control the inherent instability of a helicopter through interactions of the throttle, collective, cyclic and anti-torque pedals. All of this activity blends with the muted shouts of men thrown into the wind…and then, it too is gone. Now, except for the sound of wind and fire crackling through the grass, the world is silent.

I am left with the sun beating against the boulder behind me to radiate its own warmth of life. The smell of burning grass is delicious and soothing, bringing back memories of happier, more peaceful times…times of childhood and camping with my dad.

I stir the coals and throw another oak branch into the fire. It soon begins to blaze and blister my face…I begin to push my blanket away from the campfire…The chill of the nights dew has finally burned away…

"Boy, oh, boy…Nothing holds heat like oak. Pioneers and frontiersmen used to bury their coals beneath two feet of dirt. When they returned two weeks later, they'd dig 'em up and start a new fire…"

The small boy digs idly into the coals and nods his head knowingly. His dad has told that story a hundred times...yet, it never seems to grow old. Now, here again, he pushes back from the glowing coals and the flames. But, something keeps him from moving. The fire is getting hotter. Again, he pushes.

Suddenly, I realize that the campfire is gone...the hounds, sleeping by the fire, are gone. My dad is gone... there is only a giant black boulder, against which I am plastered. The fire is still there...an ocean of burning elephant grass is flowing toward me, as inexorably as the incoming tide...

After the helicopters have gone, the elephant grass springs upright to engulf us. Surrounding me the entire LZ area is literally alive and crawling with camouflaged ROK Marines. They are silently spreading out and regrouping into squads to sweep the area for enemy troops. They have reached the periphery of the LZ and are scouting the nearby adjacent jungle and bushes for enemy.

Throughout the area, radio antennae extend above the elephant grass and smoke, as Marine squads communicate with each other to coordinate their efforts. It is impossible to see their bodies, but their radio antennae protrude above them to validate their presence. A neutral observer might note that the area seems to be crawling with invisible giant insects, tunneling through dense vegetation; the only indications that Marines are present are the antennae, wiggling silently above the elephant grass.

In contrast to the usual Hollywood scenario, no voices are heard. The only sounds are the faint, diminishing sounds of retreating helicopters and the crackling flames of burning elephant grass. Fanned by coastal winds and their own energies, these flames are slowly gnawing their way through the ground cover and chewing through clumps of elephant grass, towards us. Since the furor of helicopter prop washes has vanished, they are slightly less aggressive, but the flames are relentless in their progression towards us. I feel a slight bump against my boot. Glancing down toward the ground, next to my foot is a small, terrified brown and grey rat that has been driven from its burrow by its ancient enemy, fire. With muted terror in his eyes, he peers at me and does not flinch. Fear of the flames has easily extinguished his lesser fear of this strange creature in his path. Desperately searching for a new path, he quickly darts over my boot to find refuge in a deeper subterranean cavern beneath the rocks.

Now, except for the wind and the crackling flames, the sky is silent. We are alone…I pause to look around me and observe the most beautiful, wild scenery that I have ever seen. We are in a small meadow of elephant grass. The grass weaves a carpet of rich greens, browns and golden colors that are broken only by huge ebony boulders. On both sides, the luscious green jungle towers above us to the east and west. To our south, the South China Sea shimmers blue in the morning sun.

But one and a half miles north lies the mountain of our objective… surrounded by a jungle of grotesquely rugged ravines and jungle valleys. The mountain rises like a verdant sepulcher from the valley floor, marred only by tiny brown scar about three-quarters of the distance up. A misty cloud clings lazily around the peak.

Yet, somewhere in that impenetrable jungle morass are the remains of two American pilots, men of my age who had given their most cherished possession…their lives.

I cannot dwell on these issues…between us is a jungle of indeterminate depth, concealing, God only knows, how many shadows, silently waiting for us to approach? I look around at the surrounding peaks and wonder how many eyes are peering at me now from the shadows, as they track me through the sights of their weapons…and, indeed, how many brown fingers are even now touching their triggers.

I must force these emotions aside as, involuntarily, a chill races through my body. I try to melt farther back into the rock, leaving only the steel helmet to mark my previous location. Suddenly I realize that I am clutching the M-16 with the intensity of a child squeezing a security blanket. If we are attacked in force, our chances of being overrun are almost assured. Facetiously, Huey gunships, armed with rockets and machine guns, flutter higher above us, like dogs with fangs bared, spoiling for a fight…but they will be useless. Here below, between the boulders and in the grass, their ferocity will be as impotent as that of dogs on opposite sides of a fence.

Farther above the Hueys is a tiny O-1E Bird Dog (FAC), ready to direct jet fighter bombers, at higher altitude, in an airstrike for our support. But my personal experience in flying over fifty combat missions disallows all naiveté. I know full well that from the altitude of a dive bomb pattern, the ground is far, far away from this ethereal weaponry… so far away that neither friend nor foe can be recognized by a pilot screaming down from 9,000 feet. Nothing, nothing can prevail or intervene to save me…in the end, there will only be the struggle between two, or more, men, as each tries to kill the other.

Mother Nature, however, harbors another foe that not only equals but exceeds enemy firepower. The vegetation that fills these crevices and jungle ravines is dense enough to swallow up our entire force before any retaliatory action can intervene. I feel terribly naked and alone…

I am not discouraged by an encounter with Mother Nature. I have lived with her in the forests, swamps and mountains of the United States, and through it all I have loved her and her world for my entire life. She can be terrible in her wrath, but it has forever been a matter of deep faith for me that she is completely democratic in all issues. Confronted by her challenges, I feel more than equal to my enemy.

If the enemy has any intelligence, he would know about our entry into his domain. He has had ample time to register mortars and rocket propelled grenades (RPGs) at hundreds of places between our LZ and the crash site. With his intimate knowledge of terrain and micro geography, the potential number of ambush sites is limitless. He can shoot down from the ridges and we will be the proverbial "fish in a barrel." All of the high tech air support in the world is useless to protect us. High technology holds little sway in guerilla warfare. High tech air warfare does not deter the elemental provisions of numerous ingenious devices or "man-traps" to explode beneath our feet or to hang suspended from a twig, and that require only a touch to set off a salvo of explosives from all sides.

After about thirty minutes an ROK Marine officer notifies me that one of the Korean Marines injured his ankle while jumping from the helicopter onto the crevice-riven and boulder-strewn ground. I run, crouched over, seeking cover from boulder to boulder, until I come to an area that is relatively open, yet somewhat protected by surrounding boulders. I signal them to bring the wounded man to me. Two Marines run toward me, bending low, as they carry their injured comrade and heave him to the ground in front of me. I look down on a rather small-boned young man, whose right foot is angulated nearly 45 degrees from his ankle mortise. His eyes are those of a frightened child, filled with terror and pain. His overall appearance reminds me of a frail and frightened young boy, who appears entirely too small for his uniform. While I acknowledge the tendency of Westerners to recognize the disproportionate appearance of youth in aging Asians, I find it irrelevant in caring for their medical problems. I smile and softly grip his shoulder to reassure him that all is under control and that he will be cared for. For a brief moment, the terror lifts from his eyes…he nods quietly before closing his eyes and lying back on the elephant grass.

The ankle is swollen and tender, but without bony deformity or palpable evidence of a fracture. His injury is compatible with a severe ligamentous tear that can be just as disabling as a fracture. Splitting hairs about a clinical diagnosis, without X-ray evaluation, serves little purpose. On a practical basis, it is obvious that this Marine cannot participate further in this operation. I advise that an air-evacuation helicopter be called in to extract him… This message is transmitted to the same helicopters that only recently inserted us into the landing area.

No more than ten minutes later, I am informed of a repeat performance by another Marine. Physical findings are virtually the same as in the first Marine. He also requires evacuation by chopper.

But, the screw has turned. Having safely departed the area, the Army pilots are reluctant to return and evacuate these men. They cannot and will not attempt to land. Therefore, they will have to hover low enough for two or three men to lift the injured Marines up into the hovering chopper. From the intensity of discussion between the chopper pilots and liaison officers of the ground troops, there seems to be progressive panic developing among the chopper pilots to get the hell out of the area and to stay out.

The second injured Marine has barely been lifted up into the chopper before the pilot terminates any serious attempt to hover and takes off. The Marine is left, suspended between heaven and earth, with his legs and lower torso left to swing in the air below the chopper. Only his chest and arms are desperately clinging to the floor, feebly grasping at the doorframe, attempting to clamber aboard. But, there is no concession or pause. The chopper continues its climb out to an altitude of thirty to forty feet. By this time the Marine is beginning to slide, slowly and agonizingly out of the chopper. The chopper continues its climb out. By the time that it achieves an altitude of 50-60 feet above the elephant grass, the Marine has slid down to the skids of the chopper and is now clinging desperately with both hands to the skids, as his body and legs dangle below. It seems that the chopper crew finally recognizes his predicament; crewmembers hang over the edge of the cabin and attempt to retrieve him.

This is my last glimpse of the situation. I think he made it but I can't be sure. I must focus on problems that face us here on the ground.

During these developments, both Major Paik Un Taik and Captain Shin Mal Up are gnashing their teeth in frustration at the "softness" of their troops. Both wounded Marines have been severely chastised for their "ineptness" and "stupidity."

Advance patrols signal the "go ahead" and we begin to move out. The elephant grass is still wet from the morning dew as we slide and skid down the mountainside with less control and coordination than the proverbial hog-on-ice. Weaving between large boulders, we flee the advancing fire, while, at the same time, attempt to shield ourselves from snipers that might fire down on us from the surrounding hills.

We descend the mountain, like ants in a small chain, with Marine scouts on all sides. I watch as the antennae of field-pack radios wiggle above the grassy horizon, to maintain the constant dialogue of communications required to maneuver between ground-to-ground, ground-to-air and air-to-ground.

Indeed, with the assist of Isaac Newton's gravity, our descent down the mountainside is relatively easy compared to what we encounter at the base. But at the base, the honeymoon is over. There is an occasional halt as point-men check out a suspicious element in the terrain, but it is only momentary. We continue our trek.

We enter the jungle, hacking our way, inch by inch, through walls and curtains of vines and thorns. Our perspective of life is now measured in terms of the time required to hack inch-by-inch with machetes through the morass of grasping vegetation. There is no solid ground. There are only heavily textured giant boulders, wreathed in tapestries of gnarled trees and roots, all of which, in turn, are cloaked with impenetrable vines and thorns. The only path available for us is that which we create by hacking and threading our way through darker and darker entanglements of these bottom lands. Our route is determined by the terrain and not by our choice. All attempts are dictated by the terrain. Boulders, too large to be climbed over are tunneled under. Smaller boulders are climbed over.

Chasms that seem bottomless are crossed by swinging over on vines, tethers or ropes. There is always the initial silent prayer that the vines will be able to hold our weight. Stretching, nearly endlessly below are the depths and walls of the ravines, coated with mats of impenetrable vines and briars, mosses, lichens and ferns…all of which slip beneath our boots and worsen the path with every step. Attempts to hack through this curtain of interlacing lianas with machetes are measured in inches. There is no firm ground. There is no path. There are only fissures and boulders, filled with morasses of vegetation to bog us down and physically exhaust us. The terrain underfoot has all the treachery of a cliff-side path in the high mountains, coupled with the invisible risks of wading through a snake and alligator infested cypress swamp.

On childhood fishing trips with my father in the Ocala, Florida, National Forest, we confronted swamps that were nearly impenetrable. My dad would gesture toward each side of the boat and solemnly state: "There are many areas in the Ocklawaha Swamp where no white man has ever been," and then after a dramatic pause, he would continue, "…and very few Indians."

I believe that this jungle also qualifies for such an epithet.

As we emerge on the other side, we bog down in a marsh of glue-like mud that sucks our feet down in a vice-like grip. Each step requires a supreme effort to simply pull one foot out of the mud, before it can be placed in front of the other for the next step. Finally, when the mud releases its grip, a loud sucking sound is vented… a sure audible tip-off to any enemy in the area. As you take the next step, the process starts all over again. As previously noted, I learned from U.S. Marines sent out on Long Range Patrols that it is better to remove your boots and walk barefoot. The bare foot is an irregular, flexible shape and surface that makes it less likely to form a tight vacuum, to be broken with the sound broadcast to the enemy. It can be removed from the mud without the sound announcing your presence to the enemy.

By this time I am rapidly reaching the end of my physical tolerance. My breath comes in short gasps and my knees have turned to rubber. My heart races like a trip hammer, seeming to pound a hole through my shirt. I can go no further…!

Suddenly, in the pits of despair and desperation, a terrible thought wells up to loom before me and grow larger and larger in my mind…until the phantom of these thoughts overwhelms me and renders all issues of the body totally irrelevant.

I am holding the Marines and all of our efforts up! I cannot be responsible for these young men…these young Marines, who have accompanied me into this Valley of the Shadow of Death…whose sole reason for being here is to protect me because I lack the physical stamina and conditioning to continue…The thought grows and grows with each step that I stumble until it becomes a burden that is heavier on my soul than any fear of the enemy…greater than the physical fatigue that overwhelms my body…The pall of these thoughts…and of this happening dwarfs all fear of death, ambush or extinction…as I feel it consume me…

But, I can go no faster and I can breathe no harder…regardless of the consequences… for myself or for them.

I take two swallows of water from my canteen and mental balance returns slowly. Reluctantly I look around at the Korean Marines who accompany me. The scene both reassures and dismays me. I stand watching as the younger Korean Marines are collapsing all around me. They lie supine and limp across rocks and boulders. They lie prostrate in puddles of water, unable to go forward or backward. Their bodies are scattered prone and half-buried in leaf piles…as they gasp for air, like fish out of water. There are no groans or sighs. There is only this multitude of young men, whose physical energies have finally been spent.

Why, they are in no better shape than I. These are Korean Marines, for whom physical conditioning is not simply a daily drill. It is a daily fetish…a way of life… and Now, even they are wilting and collapsing on the trail…

My past years of practicing medicine and desk work have obviously caught up with me…but what is their excuse? I continue to ruminate on these issues as my M-16 rifle becomes heavier and heavier with each step, and the steel helmet feels progressively more like a vise compressing my skull than protection from the enemy.

But, we cannot stop. At this point, we are now too far submerged in the jungle for airpower to find us and extract us. We are behind enemy lines. If we are ambushed, there will be no quarter asked or given by either side. When there is only one choice, the decision is easy…And, now the only choice is that we must go forward…out of this cavernous jungle morass…forwards toward the light.

I have spent my boyhood camping and fishing in the Florida everglades, the Okefenokee Swamp of Georgia and the swamps surrounding the Ocklawaha and Withlacoochee Rivers of Florida. I have climbed in the Great Smokey Mountains of North Carolina and the Rocky Mountains of Western America. I have always prided myself on wilderness survival, and on many occasions, have taught it to others. Even the more recent Jungle Survival School in the Philippines does not compare to this. I have never encountered any terrain, swamp, jungle or mountain ridges to compare with this. It combines the treacherous uphill footing of climbing mountains with the invisibility of undergrowth and marshland offered by the jungle. Of course, none of my previous experiences have involved enemy forces stalking me for the singular purpose of killing me. This is my first "forced march" through enemy infested jungle where time is of the essence. Today, there is no safe footing and nothing to cling to except your weapon.

This unfettered growth of vines, briars, roots and foliage has occurred for centuries without Man's intervention. The isolation from established paths is the merit of taking this route. Not even the enemy can conceive of any sane person approaching the crash site from this direction and by these means.

Finally, inch by inch, after another eternity, we exit this valley morass to find a mountain looming before us. From our location at its base to its peak of 3,500 feet is an inclination of 45-70 degrees. The summit is only partially seen since a circle of clouds embraces the peak. We pause, staring, without speaking, to survey the mountain...not so much by choice as by necessity.

No one speaks and the jungle is silent. No birds sing. No insects serenade. Even in the mud puddles and seepage, no frogs or other small creatures are heard or seen. No small creatures rustle in the leaves at our feet. Where are the lizards and snakes? I know that our intrusion into the domain of jungle creatures will send them scurrying and crawling into rocky nooks and hollow tree trunks for safety, but I have never observed this silence and absence of animal life in the wild. I have never seen forests, jungle or plains so devoid of sound as these. All of my life, I have loved the forests, swamps, plains and mountains...not so much for the geography as for the abundance of life in each environmental niche...but this is different. I can't explain it... There is only the gentle swish of the wind in the treetops above us.

There is something dark, sinister and evil about such profound silence in a fertile jungle world...a world that usually abounds with creatures scurrying, crawling, wiggling, slithering and flying... The Jungle is the incarnation and very essence of Life on our planet...and yet, here, there are neither bird calls nor sounds, either from the sky above or in the trees around. If nothing else, one expects to be tortured by the ubiquitous mosquitoes, gnats or flies that seem intent on driving a person to madness. But none of these wretched denizens are here. Can it be that this is one of the few wild places on this planet without insects that bite and sting? Is the Karma here so tainted that even the lowest of all creatures, the vermin, cannot or will not live here? There are no sounds of life. There is only the silence of death...

To reach the foot of the next mountain, we have to cross a fissure or ravine, with depths of 50-75 feet. Luckily, in the remote past, an ancient tree has fallen across the ravine. It now offers a precarious bridge for crossing. The tree is semi-rotten from age. The bark slips off beneath our feet to reveal an undercoating of wet moss and slippery lichens. Resorting to expressions from my Southern childhood, the bridge may best be described as "slicker than an eel in a barrel of snot."

At best, the crossing is treacherous. At worst, the crossing can be disastrous and even life threatening. It is impossible to see the bottom of the gorge beneath us, but sharp boulders protrude like giant stalagmites through tears in the vegetation. Attempting to maintain balance on flat and level ground with this degree of fatigue is difficult. But maintaining footing and balance on this wet, slick, round log with legs so tired that they refuse to cooperate, pushes everyone to the extremes of human endurance. Occasionally, one of the Marines slips and falls, with one leg gouging into the oblivion below. Frantically, his fellows, before and behind, grasp any available portion of his clothing or person, and struggle laboriously, to return him to the slippery path. The silence continues, only to be rendered by an occasional muted grunt, announcing that another Marine has fallen through the vegetation into the crevice. When found, he is rescued by his fellow Marines, as he clings precariously to a bonsai-like shrub growing from the crevice wall.

After another eternity we miraculously emerge on the opposite side in one piece, still alive...to face another mountain that now towers above us. The climb is now uphill, over ground that is laced by an infinity of invisible crevices and fissures, from which elephant grass protrudes to conceal the origin of its roots. Occasionally, someone breaks through this crust and drops into another crevice, calling to his fellows for assistance. This pace and struggle continues for hours until at last we reach the summit.

Here, we have to pause. There is no choice. Human endurance may be relative between individuals, but it also has absolute limits. Gazing down toward the other side affords little hope of an easier trek. In fact, the trek down portends to be worse than the hike up. The terrain is the same. But gravity intervenes to force us through giant thorns and through crevices that defy all description. Steep downward grades are interrupted by precipitous cliffs, at the bottoms of which are swamps and bogs, miasmas of rotting vegetation and the expectation of mosquito infested vapors…but here, there are no mosquitoes.

A Marine steps into a seemingly shallow puddle of water to wade across. In less than two steps, he is sucked under by mud of infinite depth until only his head remains above the surface. It requires four fellow Marines to cut saplings to bridge over and pull him out. By this time that he is finally pulled out, his nose is disappearing beneath the mud.

At one point there is a cliff-edge with a sheer drop of 60-75 feet that requires us to descend hand-over-hand, by rope. By the time I reach the bottom, I hardly have the strength to stand upright. I am too exhausted to consider that on the path out I will have to climb back up this same rope. In the desperation of elemental survival, considerations of anything beyond the present moment are beyond my horizon to consider or to appreciate.

Finally having arrived at the bottom of the mountain, we confront another jungle labyrinth, filled with streams, bogs and invisible crevices through which our boots fall through. Fording streams is accomplished by wading and swinging across their narrowest expanse. On the route across, vines with giant thorns, tear at your face and hands while shredding your clothes. It requires another hour to cover no more than 25 yards. Finally, we emerge and stare blankly at yet another large hill to climb.

Throughout these events I am painfully aware, on a subconscious level, that if we walk into an ambush, I will have little strength left to defend myself. I'm not at all certain that I could muster enough strength to even pull the trigger. The best that I can hope for would be to bury myself under a boulder and hope to catch my breath, while the bullets whine overhead.

I think again just how utterly useless is the armed gunship that flutters 2,000 feet above us. Except for the psychological effect on the enemy, his role in defending us would be an exercise in futility. But, it can also be used against us to mark our path. In this gloomy morass, I can barely keep the man walking one foot in front of me in sight. What perspective of our situation can an observer have from the ethereal altitude of two thousand feet? In the hand-to-hand combat of these jungles, intervention by gunship is a delusion of Pentagon mindsets... concocted before the waning hours of 5 p.m. while sitting in swivel chairs in air-conditioned conference rooms... surrounded by maps and half-drained coffee cups, delaying departure long enough for highway traffic to lessen....

As a postscript to these ruminations, however, I neglected to add another factor. There is a marvelous reinvigoration of the human body and spirit that occurs when the first shot is fired at you. The adrenal glands that have become progressively moribund now erupt into a survival mode... but I was too tired to think of this. Winston Churchill once commented that, "Nothing is more exciting than being shot at...and missed!"

After another killing climb, we reach yet another peak. And, from this peak, we look across another valley to gaze at another mountain... Mountain 3410, our objective, with the small brown spot, now appearing more like a scab than a scar...now closer and larger!

CHAPTER 27

===============

The Mountain

WE PAUSE TO ALLOW ADVANCE PATROLS TO RECON-
noiter the area for ambush, booby traps or whatever else might await us.

It is midafternoon and cooler mists from the ocean are beginning
to engulf the mountain and the crash site. Knowing what the brown spot
contains, the mist reflects the afternoon sun to cast a surreal atmosphere
over the mountain before us. As I stare, Mountain 3410 seems to transform
from a topographic location to a sepulcher for the two pilots.

The trek from our present location to the crash site trek will be no
less formidable than our previous paths, but it is no longer the terrain or
the enemy that I dread. Mountains, jungles and streams are adversaries for
any man who challenges them, but they are democratic adversaries. Rain
falls on the Just and Unjust with equal intensity. Now, what I dread above
all else will be found on the hillside in that brown spot…By now I have no
fear of enemy attack or even death, itself. If I die as a result of personal folly
or incompetence, it will be on the couch of Mother Nature and I will finally
return to my home. But what confronts me on that mountainside is neither

life nor death. I cannot define it. It is a spectre that haunts me and fills me with dread…a personal adversary against which I have neither defense nor method to counter. I cannot defeat it and I cannot flee from it…I must only confront it and try to endure.

Perhaps for the first time in my life I must confront the reality of myself as a man, no different from the tissue evidence of two men that lies silently waiting for me in that brown scar, on the mountainside above me. For the first time today, I am afraid. But it is more than mere fear that besieges me. It is stark naked terror…I am terrified. Yet, I cannot afford the luxury of either fear or terror. We can only go on…

It seems unrealistic to believe that the wreckage could have remained, unknown and untouched, by the enemy for this period of time. The metal fragments from the airplane and the fragments of human remains are all prime materials to booby trap.

But, there is no choice. We are well past the point of no return. Helicopters cannot land to extract us. If the fog rolls in to blanket the region, we will be cut off for several days or longer. As I stand, mulling over these thoughts, we receive a sudden signal from the forward observation party of ROK Marines. After a few minutes, the "All Clear" is given and we begin to move out for towards the final objective.

Descending into another jungle ravine, we are again forced to crawl on our hands and knees, tunneling through crannies beneath boulders, too huge for climbing over. The trek becomes progressively more rugged as we inspect each inch to avoid stepping into an invisible crevice or creating a landslide of rocks that will sweep us into the crevice. This is no place to break your leg…or even worse, your neck. The soles of my combat boots are worn relatively smooth and I have extreme difficulty in maintaining traction and footing on the slippery wet path.

At one juncture, it is necessary to traverse a ravine that is no more than six to seven feet across and twenty-five to thirty feet deep. The distance is so short that we only consider jumping across it. Now, any high school student can easily broad jump six to seven feet. But, that high school student isn't nearly as tired as I. Nor does he have the weight of boots, backpack and rifle to weigh him down. In my fear of jumping short and plunging to the bottom, I jump beyond my intended landing point. My right ankle promptly disappears into a crack of the ground between two jagged rocks. Immediately, there is a sharp pain and "snap" as my foot is hyperextended against the ankle. My first response is to utter an oath at my clumsiness while I attempt to extricate myself. Through my boots, I palpate my ankle and am reasonably certain that there is no break. The obvious diagnosis is a torn tendon or ligament. With hyperextension, the Achilles tendon will receive the force of injury. But, thankfully, this tendon seems intact. Without surgical repair, rupture of the Achilles is crippling. Anything else, I can live with.

Two things are certain:

(1) Regardless of the injury, I cannot remove my boot for closer evaluation. The boot lacing acts as a partial splint. If I remove it, there is a reasonable possibility that I will be unable to put the boot back on again.

(2) I must be extra careful with the ankle since it will no longer fully support my weight. If I have to jump during a future traverse, I must land on the left foot rather than the right. It is impossible to use a stick as crutch for partial support since the terrain demands both hands to grasp vines and climb trees over and around boulders. If I pause, the ankle will freeze up to a degree that renders me unable to continue the pace.

By the time that we finally emerge from the morass at the mountain base, my breathing bears little resemblance to respiration…each breath is more of a shallow gasp than shallow panting.

During these painful few hours, I realize that at age twenty-eight, I am no longer the young man of eighteen who blithely skipped across moss-covered rocks of the Flint River in Georgia. Nor am I the same person who could climb a 20-foot rope, hand-over-hand, in as many seconds as an Explorer Scout. During my boyhood, and through high school, I never excelled in football or team sports, but in the forests of central Georgia and in the swamps of Florida, I came into my element. Roaming these forests and swamps was like heaven to me. Returning to nature was nearly an "animal thing."

But, since those early times, the years of study and medical practice have demanded more mental and less strenuous activity. Behind the lines in enemy territory, my legs feel like lead and my coordination is gone. Never in my life have I reached such depths of physical exhaustion…and never have I needed physical strength and prowess more than at the present.

We trudge and shuffle on, up the mountain, as ROK Marine scouts fan out before us to look for Viet Cong ambushes, booby traps and other efforts to destroy us. At one turn, we receive word that the aircraft crash site has been located. After another 20 minutes of fierce hacking through the underbrush, we come to the first evidence… the shaft of a landing gear protrudes from the jungle floor. Overhead, the trees tower 150-200 feet above us, screening out all but a few rays of fog-diluted evening sunlight. From this point on our path increasingly becomes darker and darker. I feel as if we are being forced into an open grave.

Progressively, the odor of JP-4 (jet fuel) and decaying flesh fills my nostrils, drowning my senses, and overwhelming my brain. These are all too familiar odors that I immediately recognize.

My first impulse is to turn and run…anywhere…anywhere…and to keep running until I am far away from here. But I am too fatigued to run, and it is too horrible to stay. The gloom of that jungle mountainside and the odors of the crash site etch themselves into my brain. I know all too well what lies ahead, I hope and fervently pray that all human remains have been totally destroyed by fire from the crash…or…completely removed by animals of the jungle or completely decayed beyond all recognition. But I also know that if these fantasies were true, that damnable odor wouldn't be there. There is no trace of life here. It seems that even wild animals have fled from the scene, recognizing the taboo; imposed against all living things…a taboo that hangs like a shroud to isolate and remove this place from the living world.

As the fog continues to roll in from the ocean, shadows continue to darken and grow longer with the fading sun. Except for the soft jabbering of the Koreans, the area is ensconced in absolute silence.

At this point, Major Clayton calls out, "Hey, Doc, here's something for you!" I cringe at the words, but dutifully, I inspect what he hands me. With an audible sigh of relief, I realize that it is only a fragment of parachute harness. My relief, however, is short-lived. Approximately 20 feet away, draped in the fork of a small charred tree, hangs a piece of human thigh, still attached to the right ilium and pelvis. It is in an advanced state of decay.

I acknowledge and accept the fact that my job is to obtain tissue specimens for positive identification, but all I want to do is to run like hell away from this hideous place!

The aircraft crash site lies nearly 100 yards further up the mountain, and God only knows what else will be present. I unpack two rubberized body bags, and with a piece of metal from the wreckage, pick up one of the gory specimens and stuff it into the bag. Tying the mouth of the bag tightly, I walk over to Major Paik and request one of his men to carry the bags and assist me. As we walk progressively closer to the scattered wreckage, the odors of decaying tissue become more and more overwhelming.

Within a space of 50 square yards, countless fragments of various human tissues are scattered everywhere…all burned and in different stages of decay. I collect sufficient evidence to allow identification of the two pilots by inference and exclusion. I also collect the wallet of one pilot and an I.D. card for the second pilot.

This is sufficient evidence to stand in any court of law. I have no intention or desire to collect every scrap of human tissue scattered over this mountain, simply for the sake of academic fulfillment. Just as I am refusing to accept further bits of tissue offered by the ROK Marines, one of the Marines, quite excitedly, tugs at my shirt and points to something on the ground beneath the burned trunk of a small tree. Lying between the roots is the terribly charred and decaying left hand of one of the pilots, complete with white gold wedding band on the fourth finger.

There is something uniquely human about the hand. Its identity has no mimic in other creatures. Most surgical procedures drape human anatomy in sterile drapes to a degree that conceals and nearly cloaks human identity. But, surgical drapes can never conceal the identity of the human hand. The anatomy of the hand validates human identity, no less than the human skeleton defines our species.

This avulsed hand, with wedding band on the fourth finger, as it lies disembodied between roots of a tree on a jungle mountain, holds a terror of certainty that supersedes identification by dog tag, driver's license or any other legal document.

I am familiar with generic methods of receiving and processing raw human tissue. I know that the moment we return to base, the body bags and their contents will be taken from me and transferred to a laboratory science pathology assistant or "Diener." The credentials of this "Diener"[24] can't be predicted, but since this will be accomplished at Cam Ranh by Air Force personnel under the supervision of our pathologist, Dr. Guillebeau, I'm not concerned.

However, afterward the specimens may be subcontracted to civilian laboratories anywhere for further processing. In this case, the initial tissue

---

24 Diener [dē′nər] Etymology: German man-servant. An individual who maintains the hospital laboratory or equipment and facilities. The morgue diener may also assist the pathologist in performing autopsies.

transfer is the weakest link in this chain. There will be no considerations to establish the specific relationship between wedding band and the hand that wore it. Many of these laboratory assistants are low wage-earners, very poor and frequently illiterate. There is no method to monitor the system and no one to prevent one of these persons from slipping the gold ring off the finger, and selling it on the open market. I don't want to take that chance. Wedding bands do not fit under the coverslip of a paraffin section for microscopic analysis…

I tell the ROK Marine to remove the ring and give it to me. Turning my back I hurriedly walk away, not having the stomach to oversee how the ring is removed. The hand goes into the body bag with the other tissue specimens. Fingerprints will confirm its identity. Taking the ring, I place it in a small plastic bag, which in turn, is placed in a white envelope. I drop the envelope containing the ring into my pocket for safe keeping and identification.

Major Clayton is still measuring distances and angles while analyzing the wreckage. Evidently the plane struck the hill at the 3,000-foot level. It was on a bearing of 315 degrees in a 15-20 degree right bank with 5-10 degree nose-down attitude. A recovered air speed indicator had stopped at 300 knots. The plane had exploded instantly, destroying the two pilots, and virtually disintegrating over a 400-500 feet swath of terrain.

By this time it is 3:30 p.m. and we are having progressive difficulty seeing through the incoming fog and darkness. In another hour it will be completely dark and I have no desire to spend the night in this place. In a very short time, it will be too dark and dangerous for helicopters to extract us from this remote location. We are behind enemy lines and so far we have been so fortunate that we dare not think or speak about it. But every minute that we remain increases the risk of retaliation by allowing time for the enemy to find us.

I catch the eye of the ROK Marine Major Paik, who is in charge of the troops. As I approach, he is casually looking for a comfortable place to sit. I say, "Major, we have what we came for. Let's get the hell out of here before it gets too dark and foggy for the choppers to extract us."

He looks at me and smiles as he says quietly, "Yes, we must make haste…but slowly…"

He gestures to one of his Marines, who comes trotting over to face him, and, then just as quickly, does an about-face and squats down in front of the major. This exposes a large bulging backpack. The major unlashes the straps of the pack and smoothly pulls out a can of ice cold beer from his backpack, filled with crushed ice. With the inscrutable politeness that is characteristic of the Asian personality, he offers the first can of cold beer to me while reaching for another. I am too shocked to speak! The thought of leisurely drinking beer when you are far behind enemy lines and have no idea where the enemy is…while the darkness increases and the fog obliterates any hope of helicopter extraction!

I didn't reply, but he must have read the expression on my face as he quickly drained the can of beer and reluctantly got to his feet.

I've heard of "grace under pressure," but this tops anything I have ever seen. Later, when I recall the incident, I have to smile at his quiet confidence and admirable nonchalance.

By now, my ankle is throbbing painfully. The swelling is probably due to bleeding and a hematoma from the strain or torn ligament. I dare not remove my boot. I cut a walking stick from a tree limb and hobble as best I can. Although I carry injectable morphine in my kit, I would rather bear the pain than have my reflexes clouded by the drug on our path out. I believe the dread of being stranded in this loathsome place will drive me forward even if both legs were broken. Already, Major Boucher is being supported and partially carried by two ROK Marines. He has twisted his knee and is unable to bear weight on it. Two more Marines have sustained injuries and are supported by their fellows.

To leave this awful place, we must now return to our previous path and descend to the mountain base. We previously arrived at the base by rope descent from a rocky plateau 60-75 feet above us. There is no alternative. That same rocky plateau offers the only suitable LZ for the helicopter to hover, land and extract us. To reach that plateau, we must trek back down to the foot of Mountain 3410 and then rope-climb, hand-over-hand back up the cliff to the plateau above.

There is nothing to be gained by repeating the trials and agonies that plagued and cursed us on the same path back, except to note that, while the path is the same, and the rope may be the same, the humans that previously descended the rope are not the same as those who must now climb back up the rope. The energies of all men are beyond exhaustion. With every step we expect to walk into an ambush or to be sniped at from an invisible foe. Fear, however, is a powerful motivator that pushes you beyond the envelope of human endurance. We push ourselves back over and under the same boulders and traverse the same ravines and streams as before.

Compared to both the ROK Marines and the Air Force officers that accompany me, I am doing fairly well until we arrive at the foot of the cliff that we descended on our previous trek. Now, instead of descending 60-75 feet on a rope, we must climb that distance hand-over-hand with the rope. Since identification of the former pilots is the first priority of the mission, I am given first priority for extraction. I will, of course, carry the two body bags with the tissues and other materials out with me. My emotions border on despair as I look up at the cliff side. While I stand staring up, unwilling to accept what I must do, a pair of weary ROK Marines are sent ahead of me to test the rope and to make sure that it is anchored securely to a tree, rooted to the rocky outcropping above us.

Waiting until the first of the Marines is near the top, I sling the M-16 over my back and shoulder, bandoleer style, and begin the climb. The first of the Marines has barely reached the top and is having difficulty climbing the final few feet. The second Marine has lagged behind him and is only seven to nine feet above me on the rope. When I am about twenty-five to thirty feet up the rope, I look up to find that the second Marine is climbing progressively slower and slower. After I have climbed up another five feet, I again look up to find that the second Marine has not only stopped climbing, but is slowly sliding down the rope toward me.

When he reaches a point 4-5 feet above me, he stops. His labored breathing is audible and comes in short gasps. Slowly, very slowly, his grip on the rope loosens and in slow motion he falls past me onto the rocks below, cartwheeling as he crashes head-first into a soundless heap. Throughout the entire interval, he never uttered more than a soft sigh as he fell past me.

This single event provides the injection of adrenaline required to motivate me. Slowly...very slowly, I progress inch by inch up the rope... At this point, my M-16 has become a burden that I can no longer bear. Its weight seemed to increase with every inch that I climbed. Finally, unable to carry it further, I pause and with great difficulty, slide out of the sling, letting the rifle fall where it may on the ground below. At this point, I am in a complete survival mode. Finally, within 1-2 feet of the top I can go no further...I have no more breath or strength. I glance up and see the face of a young Korean Marine, bending over the edge. I am fading in and out of consciousness as he reaches down to grab my wrist. He gestures excitedly for me to grasp his hand, but if I release the rope with one hand, I will fall. I am barely conscious and his face begins to blur before my eyes. Obviously recognizing this, he is joined by another Marine, who hangs down over the cliff edge to grab my wrist and together they pull me to safety. But, I don't remember sliding over the cliff's edge. All I remember is lying face down in the wet grass, desperately gasping and sucking air into my tortured lungs… as I had done a few times in high school football after having the breath knocked out of me.

With my face buried in the grass, my mind seems to drift in and out of the scene. I remember watching a cavalcade of large red ants streaming between the tendrils of grass, beneath my eyes, winding their way around clumps of grass, as they hurry home or search for food. The tiny creatures seem impervious to these monstrous alien beasts that are now invading their domain with guns and explosives while crushing all beneath their feet. And for some reason, I remember thinking…

"If I were an ant, and lived here, I would be home now."

When I finally have the strength to raise my head and look around, there are few persons standing. The limp body of the ROK Marine who fell from the rope has been lifted to the plateau for air-evacuation. The stronger Marines have tied bowline knots and rope chairs to pull their injured and exhausted comrades from the black maw below. Because of injuries, Major Clayton and Major Boucher are being hoisted up by rope chair. All others of our expedition, both American and Korean, are lying face down, gasping for breath, like so many fish out of water. The only exceptions are several squads of Marines that have scattered around us as forward scouts to patrol for the enemy and to guard the perimeter.

With the exception of our heavy breathing, the area is intensely silent. With dread, I watch the sun sink lower and lower on the horizon while a dense bank of fog and clouds creeps inexorably in from the sea. If we are enveloped by the fog, clouds and darkness, it will be impossible for any aircraft to extract us. Despite being less than twenty miles away, as the crow flies, Cam Ranh seems a thousand miles from this miserable place. The thought of those barren, hot sands is as refreshing as the thought of an oasis for weary travelers through the desert.

In the darkening twilight, I watch as the fog blanket tongues its way up the mountain from the ocean and swallows the jungle below us. Without pausing, it relentlessly crawls up the mountain toward our position. The only sound is the wind. An eternity seems to pass before the silence is quietly broken by the soft, familiar whoomp-whoomp-whoomp sounds of helicopter rotors. Looking up and following the sound, a dot in the distant sky slowly enlarges as it approaches and is transformed into the familiar silhouette of a Huey, slowly approaching from over the horizon. Drawing closer, the Huey flutters overhead and then dips lower to fire a smoke grenade into an area one-quarter mile away. This signal and message is from the pilot to indicate that he can probably land in the area marked.

Calling upon strength and breath that I never knew existed; we rise to begin a shorter but no less laborious trek, hacking our way over to the designated area. The LZ marked by the pilot is at the top of a small knoll, less than a quarter mile away, that is covered with elephant grass. As we approach the hilltop, we stagger and stumble on the jagged shards of a huge boulder that has been shattered into a thousand pieces by a fortuitous hit from the previous artillery. The Marines immediately begin trampling down the elephant grass while chopping down small trees and bushes to establish a landing site.

With body bags filled with human remains, I am pushed forward and given first priority for extraction.

It is generally acknowledged that the greatest risk of attack from an enemy will be directed against the last choppers and troops to leave the area. With this in mind, the first Huey descends into a tight pattern to encircle the LZ. Immediately it unleashes streams of rocket fire into the green blackness of the surrounding jungle. When the rockets quit, another Huey gunship orbits the landing area, spraying streams of liquid lead with red tracers from the door gunner's M-60 machine guns into the periphery of the LZ. Overhead, two other heavily armed Hueys buzz in tight circles, like angry hornets whose nest has been vandalized.

Several laps of this circular fire saturate the periphery, and hopefully sterilize any concealed enemy troops and hidden fortifications. Finally, the gunship breaks off and our "Slick Huey" maneuvers in, darting between two hillocks, to finally slide into the LZ, about 20 yards away from me, not to land, but to hover 3-5 feet above the ground.

I am in no mood to wait any longer. Ducking my head and leaning forward into the prop-wash, I run to the helicopter as the pilot struggles to maintain the hover, fighting crosswinds that increase by the minute. As I approach the chopper, the side-gunner hangs on his harness and reaches down to pull me aboard. Directly behind me are the two Korean Marines with the two body bags. One is slightly injured and requires assistance in climbing on board. Major Clayton is behind me and is hurriedly dragged aboard while he still has a chance. Time is running out for the helicopter to hover. The winds are increasing in their efforts to expel this man-made foreign body from their domain. The pilot continues to struggle with the controls, fighting the turbulence that progresses to make further hover impossible. Finally the body bags are thrown in and secured in the open bay. And, not a moment too soon, before the pilot must break off to point the nose down and apply full throttle…desperately attempting to increase airspeed and gain enough forward momentum to fly back up into and through the turbulent river of contentious winds. There are bumps and jolts before we break out of these demon gusts… to enter…at last, the smoother air above us…above the fog-enshrouded canyons and above the treacherous jungle…where the air is calm…and the night is clear.

CHAPTER 28

Relief!

IT IS OVER... NEVER IN MY LIFE HAVE I FELT SUCH relief as when the chopper lifts off and I watch the darkening jungle melt farther and farther into the gathering mists below. We continue climbing out above the tree line and into the blessed sky above. Moving from the darkened sky above the jungle, we climb toward the mountain crest. When we top the crest, the darkness recedes beneath and behind us. Suddenly, the curtain on that darkened stage is drawn to reveal another stage of greater drama. The vast panorama of the South China Sea unfolds before and beneath us as it sheds its cloak of sunlight. Before us, onto the horizon a single star winks in solemn jest from overhead while a nearly full moon floods the ocean surface with a heavenly light.

I watch mesmerized, while, as if on cue from a maestro's baton, the off-shore reef in the distance suddenly bursts into a brilliant necklace of shimmering pearls, created by countless lanterns from countless fishing boats, manned by countless men, women and children, who continue the lives of their fathers, their grandfathers and their ancestors. They form a single stable human element in the midst of all of the chaos that surrounds them. The scene before me is a panorama of grandeur and pathos that has accompanied mankind through all of his journeys and time on this planet. It symbolizes the inherent nobility of a fragile creature who must struggle all of its life against cosmic brutalities, democratically visited upon him, to merely survive and live another day on our small planet. The painful grandeur of this scene will remain etched in my mind and soul for the rest of my life.

Ascending further, we whip through several small clumps of cumulus clouds; in the process, the rotor blades remind me of an egg-beater spinning meringue. Far above us in the clear sky are windswept skeins of cirrus clouds or "mare's tails." Leaving the clouds behind, we head west across Cam Ranh Bay toward the ROK Marine camp on the mainland. From our altitude, the runways and lights of Cam Ranh Bay Air Force Base shimmer in the distance. How I long to kiss those hot, barren sands once more!

At the ROK Marine encampment, the chopper lands smoothly and I assist one of the injured Marines off the helicopter. I have barely set foot on the ground before I see Army Special Forces Lt. Colonel Hastings running across the landing zone toward me. He is quite out-of-breath. Grabbing my hand he shakes it repeatedly, and gasping for breath, asks over and over again: "Are you all right? You aren't wounded?"

He seems as happy as I am for our safe return. He informs me that the helicopters that inserted us into the Landing Zone in the morning had been severely shot up. Up-dated intelligence reports of the area confirmed that we confronted not only large numbers of Viet Cong, but also a battalion strength of more than 1,000 North Vietnamese Army regulars. The most recent reconnaissance places them at less than a quarter mile from the crash site. And yet, we encountered no opposition and found no evidence of their prior to entry into the crash site.

Major Clayton and I silently collapse into the back seat of an Army jeep, driven by an Army private, and head back to Cam Ranh Air Force Base. From our distance, across the two runways, a fierce concentration of lights seems to rise out of the sand and suffuse the entire area in front of Base Operations. Driving closer, we realize that these are the headlights of numerous jeeps, fire trucks and crash ambulances, all gathered in front of wing headquarters to form our reception party.

Sergeant Xeras, the NCO (non-commissioned officer) in charge of the flight surgeon's office, is first to meet me. With a huge grin, he runs to pump my hand. Climbing stiffly out of the Jeep, I drop the body bags onto the ground and gesture their location to him. I pull the envelope with the enclosed ring from my pocket and pass it to him, along with the explanation to match the ring with the anatomic specimen in the body bag. When they are in his grasp, he instantly acknowledges the situation and promptly pulls a grease pencil from his pocket to nonchalantly inscribe the letters, "BTB," on the body bag. I ask him, "What is that?" He tells me BTB means "Believed to be..." I nod and turn away, heading toward my quarters.

I have taken less than ten steps before I am confronted with the figure of a tall man in my path. I stop and blink. He doesn't move. Finally, shaking my head to clear my vision, I recognize him.

It's Colonel Mack standing in the headlights.

Slowly, very slowly, I reel in the slack of my aching body and in slow motion, come to attention and salute him. He returns the salute. For a moment my hand wavers in fatigue and then drops to my side. But, he continues to hold his salute for a moment longer, before dropping his hand. He and I walk together back to his Jeep. No words are spoken. He sees from my shredded shirt and trousers that the going has been tough. When he shifts into first gear and turns to drive off, I see him in profile. As always, he seems the perfect example of control and self-assurance. By this time, it is almost midnight. It is late in the evening and I didn't expect to see Colonel Mack until tomorrow morning when I report on today's activities.

He didn't have to be here…he didn't have to be here…not at this hour of the night…

Opening the door into the hallway of the squadron hooch, I walk slowly to my quarters. When I enter the darkened room, the entire squadron of pilots is asleep and I must grope through the darkness for the familiar guideposts to my bunk. A hot shower is a must before I turn in. Groping my way through the dark, I gather my shaving kit, washcloth and towel before heading for the shower.

When I enter the shower area, I pause to stand in front of the banks of sinks and mirrors. I see a stranger peering back at me. His fatigues are shredded. His skin is bruised and scratched… his eyes are sunken into the sockets. Who is this person? The stranger is a detached spirit I must confront and reconcile with the image of another person…one in the flesh and the other in the mirror.

Afterward, I return to my bunk and close my eyes. I am tired, perhaps more tired than I have ever been. But sleep does not come. I can't shake the haunting sensations that attached to me in the jungle. Despite my fatigue, I am afraid to fall asleep… lest I slip back into that Stygian darkness of jungle and putrefaction…to remain forever trapped with the shattered airplane and the terrible apparitions of two pilots…

This is a new sensation for me. I have always been able to shut out unpleasantries of life, including the horrors of war, from my subconscious. Simply by being a physician it has been necessary to maintain a certain amount of emotional detachment in order to cope with so many human tragedies. Without this ability, all objectivity is lost. And without objectivity, it is impossible to help another individual. But, now, these defense mechanisms fail me… Perhaps, I have never before experienced such combined effects of physical and mental exhaustion…I don't know the answer… And, all of these events occurred within twenty-four hours. Only one day—a very small aliquot of time in a man's life. But during the past twenty-four hours I have experienced more of life than an average person does in an entire lifetime.

Finally, I lapse into a fitful sleep.

This narrative was written within 24-48 hours of my return to Cam Ranh. Writing of these events is a catharsis to close the chapter on the preceding events. Perhaps in twenty to thirty years I will read these notes and ask myself, "…so what was the big problem?" But years from now the events and narrative will be out of context, and therein lies the difference. Perhaps it is better to write when muscles continue to cramp and lacerations from briars and stones burn and sting. Perhaps it is better to write while your ankle still throbs and is painful to weight bearing. And perhaps it is better to write when your mind and your soul ache and while bruises are still blue and tender…I don't know…

In a year the "brown leaves" of scorched trees in the jungle will be gone. Dead vegetation will be replaced by fresh, newly sprouted greenery to heal old wounds. And in time, birds and small creatures will return… to this small portion of jungle, which will once more be a fountain of life.

Man, however, is less fortunate. The wounds that scar memories all too often remain, to be locked away in some deep recess of the brain… hopefully never to emerge…and hopefully to fade into the oblivion of time…but they will never be erased. For the remainder of my life, there will be future nights when I will awaken in the jungle…once more in the mist, surrounded by the remains of two men, who were friends… men, with whom I walked the path of life…and followed to their death… I know all too well that although I have left the jungle, the jungle will never entirely leave me…

When I was a boy in the rural South, my father was a storehouse of homespun, rural Southern and pioneer folklore. He treasured common sense as much, or more than academic prowess. Common sense relates to the world as it is. Knowledge untempered by the fires of life experience is an abstraction that leads to self-fulfillment akin to intellectual masturbation. Wisdom is knowledge tempered in the flames of pain and suffering. During my childhood, one of my father's favorite questions was to ask:

"How far can a dog go into the woods?"

The correct answer is, "Only half way… if he goes farther, he will be going out of the woods."

Over the years, I've had occasions to recollect the wisdom encompassed by those simple words… during times when I struggled in the turbulent rivers that flood every man's life; …desperately trying to survive in the rip tides that surge between the Scylla of Unfounded Hope and the Charybdis of Bottomless Despair. During those times, when the nights seemed endless and clouds forever hid the sun, I have asked myself, "Am I halfway yet?"

And if the answer is, "Yes," I have the consolation of knowing that things can only improve.

If the answer is, "No," then I have the hope that, if I can only survive a bit longer I can reach the halfway point…and from there, I can walk or crawl out of the woods.

And so, it was today, that by surviving a bit longer, beyond the halfway point, I left the jungle and the crash site.

My father served with the U.S. Coast Guard on Guadalcanal during WWII. Guadalcanal was known as The Island of Death by the Japanese. My father was a wise man, made so by pain and suffering…And, I am sure that there were many nights when he also asked the question, "Am I halfway yet?"

With reports of large enemy forces throughout the region, I continue to marvel that we went through the above ordeal without encountering armed resistance on the ground, either in the form of an ambush or by finding the crash site mined and filled with booby traps. When we entered the crash site, there was absolutely no evidence of previous human entry. However, even in the absence of actual entry into the crash site, if the enemy had knowledge of the specific crash location, they had plenty of time to register mortars, machine guns and bring all weaponry to bear on the crash area to greet us when we entered their "Kill Zone."

Not until the day of our insertion did the enemy finally recognize that we were invading their domain. However, they continued to be ignorant of (1) our exact insertion point or the (2) trek route through the jungle to the (3) unknown crash site location. At the end of the day, helicopters, flown in to extract us, finally focused the enemy's attention toward the crash site and directed their belated efforts to intercept us. Before our insertion, intelligence reported the enemy presence was one-half mile from the crash site. During and after our extraction, that same intelligence reported that enemy forces were now less than one-quarter mile from the crash site. This movement toward the crash site supports the premise that our activity had stimulated their interest to investigate further.

The efficiency of U.S. Army helicopter pilots in inserting us quickly and, more important, extracting us quickly, was a key element to our success. Not until later did I learn that they had been fired on again when they were extracting us. My definition of "bravery" does not apply to a person who has no fear. A "brave" person is a person who continues to perform his duty, regardless of fear, while fully recognizing that he may die as a result of his actions. Thankfully, none of the helicopters or their crewmembers were lost. By any measure, these U.S. Army helicopter pilots were all Brave Men…I will always be eternally grateful to them…I salute them! Nor can I ever forget the concern for our safety, expressed by U.S. Army Special Forces Lt. Colonel Hastings…both before and after our mission. I can only say, Thank You, from the bottom or my heart…Thank You…!

My observations of military operations and their execution in war reveal scant evidence of intelligent planning or logical considerations. (Exception to this was the planning and execution by the ROK Marines and their leaders.)

Momentums of energies develop spontaneously during war and these blind energies guide and drive reactions on the field of battle. Once unleashed, these actions provoke further actions and reactions until all events become dissociated from mortal control and consideration. Because of this, attempts to apply Aristotelian logic to the insanities of war are little more than exercises in futility.

If I live another hundred years, my weltanschauung or philosophy of life will be quite different than today. But that is of no relevance. I must react to life as I encounter it at the moment that it occurs. The fears of a twenty-eight-year-old man are not the fears of a sixty-year-old man under the same circumstances. The same is true for every human emotion. I am what I am and this is what I have recorded.

Perhaps in twenty years, Elaine I will sit on our hilltop overlooking Lake Travis and gaze across the lake, glistening in the evening sun... and hear the timid footsteps of deer that emerge to feed in the cooler shadows of sunset...And we will delight in the plaintive melancholy whistles of whippoorwills that lash the breeze... and remember Vietnam as only a slight interruption in our happiness. Perhaps, we will even look into each other's eyes and smile, thinking of how young and foolish we had been to let the events of this one year disturb us through the rush of years that followed.

Someday, perhaps, Vietnam will become a geographical location and not an emotion...and, then perhaps, we will be able to discuss it with an air of philosophical detachment, instead of pain. But Bill Simmons will never discuss it...nor will Lee Greco or John Troyer, now lying on that distant hill in a dirty brown spot, which has now overgrown with jungle vegetation...

No, Vietnam will never be a geographical location of latitude and longitude. We will think of it in future years, when time had dulled the edges of memory…when personalities and people have lost their distinctions … and when events have merged one into another to form only an anonymous blur of this year. Vietnam will always remain an emotion, like the bitter aftertaste that continues long after good food has been digested and bad food has been disgorged.

Tomorrow is Wednesday. If Elaine were here it would be Christmas Day. But, without her it is simply another Wednesday, like every other day… And as we say in Vietnam, "Every day is Wednesday…"

I have MOD duty today. It has been the day for fractures. By noon today, I have sent seven to eight various and sundry fractures to orthopedic surgery. It seems that orthopedists and radiologists are the busiest doctors over here.

CHAPTER 29

A Welcome Christmas Gift

26 December 1966

HOORAY! TODAY I RECEIVED APPROVAL FOR MY REQUEST TO SEPARATE FROM ACTIVE DUTY...U.S. AIR FORCE...EFFECTIVE 10 JUNE 1967!

MERRY CHRISTMAS, INDEED!

27 December 1966

This afternoon for three and a half hours I sat on the Accident Investigation Board of the crash. Another meeting is scheduled for tomorrow morning. I am so weary of this whole affair...

I don't understand why this event bothers me so much, but it does. I can't seem to shake it...!

There are now sixteen persons working in the flight surgeon's office. As chief of the office, my workload has increased considerably, but time passes faster when you are busy.

28 December 1966

The Accident Investigation Board has become the albatross around my neck! Today, from 9 a.m. to noon, I sat in this smoke-filled room, haggling over details of the angle of descent when the plane hit the mountain... what medical conditions could have impaired the judgment or consciousness of the pilots to allow this thing to happen...etc.

Again from 3 to 7 p.m., we convened in the same smoke-filled room to question Air Traffic Control about allowing the aircraft to fly into the mountain. It grieves me to see them trying to hang the twenty- or twenty-one-year-old airman second class who was air traffic controller on this thing. All efforts seem to aim at anything that takes the heat off the pilots flying the airplane.

29 December 1966

Thankfully, there are no meetings today. I went down to the beach for a break of a couple of hours, and just walked, inhaling the fresh air and the beauty of the sky and ocean. Except for the wind, it has been a very pleasant day. The only problem with the wind is that it creates the effects of a sand blast on the desert environment of Cam Ranh. But, all in all, it is beautiful. Exposure to nature always cleanses my soul.

I often wonder how men in the Pacific Theater during World War II could psychologically tolerate any assignment that had no terminal date, only a statement of "for the duration." That seems almost like a death sentence. Perhaps, under those terms, you simply give up all hope, with no expectation of return. But, I cannot think of life without hope.

The new doctors and corpsmen in the flight surgeon's office have asked me several times, "Why don't you gripe more?" Boy, that's a new twist on me! I feel like all I do is gripe. Their primary gripe is not against Vietnam duty, but duty at Cam Ranh Bay! I gripe about spending a year away from Elaine, but I've seen enough of other bases to realize how fortunate I am to be at Cam Ranh Bay. From all that I've seen, any move on my part would be for the worse. I simply hope that I can ride out the next six months on this "Devil's Island!"

One young corpsman preparing to return to the U.S. made a statement that seemed worth noting. He said, "When I came to Vietnam one year ago, I was eighteen years old. Now, after only one year, I will be leaving at age thirty-five."

So many of these young men have become old men overnight. A man of nineteen years, hospitalized on the psychiatric ward, told me in expressionless, flat tones and with a lifeless face, "Doctor, we were under heavy machine gun fire when my buddy was hit badly. I put him on my back and tried to carry him up the hill to cover. All the while, he kept saying, 'Sam, Don't let me die…don't let me die…' But, doctor, parts of his lungs and guts were hanging out."

He just stood and faced me with no expression on his face. Finally, he turned slowly and walked away. How can you respond to something like that? Should I have reassured him? And if so, about what? For the young men who survive this war and return home, how will they respond to a society that wallows in the trivia of Beatniks, Beatles and Berkeley…the gutless wonders that thump their chests and send blood and gifts to Hanoi?

I wonder if this young man will walk up to the effete of Haight-Ashbury to inform them that if it weren't for someone else 10,000 miles away, who had his guts shot out, there would be no country within which they might exercise that precious Freedom of Speech that is espoused so loudly? I don't know…I truly don't know. The same things have occurred in every war, but this is my first and only experience with it. My family has fought in every war of this country. I believe that freedom is not free.

One of my favorite quotes, relevant to this issue, is by John Stuart Mill:

"War is an ugly thing, but not the ugliest of things. The decayed and degraded state of moral and patriotic feeling which thinks that nothing is worth war is much worse. The person who has nothing for which he is willing to fight, nothing which is more important than his own personal safety, is a miserable creature and has no chance of being free unless made and kept so by the exertions of better men than himself."

30 December 1966

The Accident Investigation Board met all day today. Finally at 7 p.m. the investigation was concluded.

Learning later of the final conclusion, I must retract any praise for the Accident Investigation Board and its final assessment of the probable cause of the crash. The board members voted between the two most likely causes of the crash.

The first blame rested on radar approach control, meaning the personnel in the control tower were at fault for guiding the aircraft into the mountainside.

The second possible cause was instrument failure that resulted in pilot error.

Four members of the board, including myself, voted for the second option. This constituted the majority opinion of the board. However, Colonel Gaddis, chairman of the committee, voted for the first option. Supposedly, the majority opinion should prevail. But Colonel Gaddis had his mind made up as to the cause, before any evidence was presented; indeed, before the crash site was discovered. His decision cannot be supported by any evidence obtained or by any factor except his political bias.

At the last minute, before the final draft for our signatures, someone turned up an arcane Air Force regulation that specifically stated that the final decision would be that rendered by the committee chairman.

Major Clayton, who accompanied me to the crash site, did a superb job of collecting evidence, and after he worked long and hard to objectively evaluate all possibilities, voted the same as I. After his conscientious analysis of the data, he was really crushed by the verdict.

The entire Accident Investigation Committee was no more than a Kangaroo Court in which a single colonel decided: "My mind is made up. Don't confuse me with facts." From the colonel's perspective, there is a vested interest in immunizing the pilots from any fault. Errors by pilots reflect poorly on their superior officers for allowing them to have responsibility for flying the aircraft or for not providing adequate training to excel under any and all circumstances.

From my perspective, the pilot in command is responsible for flying the aircraft under all circumstances. Air traffic control is to assist and direct the flight. However, if the plane descends behind a mountain and is lost to radar 10-20 miles from base, there is no logic to blame air traffic control for the pilot descending below and out of radar range.

Air traffic control is the logical whipping boy, since it falls under an entirely different division of responsibility. And so, probably an enlisted man or NCO is blamed for the aircraft vanishing off the radar screen. But it does not end there. All of the agonies experienced during the trek to the crash site, the Korean Marines who were injured and the risk of disaster for the troops, helicopter pilots and helicopters…i.e. the entire undertaking… not to mention the expense of the artillery prep to set the woods on fire… and all to no avail!

I suppose I should rejoice that the entire chapter is officially closed. But, "official" closure for the Air Force does not wall it off into oblivion in my mind or from my conscience. Unfortunately, I am still naïve enough to believe that the Air Force, as well as the other Armed Services, represents me and my country. If I damn the Air Force, it is comparable to damning the family business. The Air Force is an arm of this country. This country was founded by my ancestors, including Sam Houston in Texas. The first English Colony at Jamestown, Virginia, was financed by my mother's ancestors. In 1637, my ancestors in New England and Connecticut fought in the Pequot war. While I am not so proud of warring against American Indians, it is still a part of Early America. Ancestors on my mother's side of the family and ancestors of my father's side fought in the American Revolution. This country is me and I am this country.

General Joe Stilwell of my mother's family was the bastion of strength for the United States in China during World War II. In that same war, my father fought at Guadalcanal. I can no more turn away from the instruments of the United States than I can reject my parents or future children. This is my Air Force, just as much as it is the country of the Puppet Colonel in this Kangaroo Court. This is a part of me and what affects my country affects me. I realize how chauvinistic I sound, but this is how deep my emotions flow about this country.

But, as all passions lose their fire, perhaps I am experiencing the pains of transition, known only to an Eagle Scout as he confronts the world of reality…rather than the world of his ideals.

And yet, through it all…the war goes on….

F-4C Mission 4 Aircraft
Aircraft Commander: Captain Wayne
Flight Time: 2 hours

We are originally fragged to bomb a Viet Cong staging area in Tiger Hound Country. However, because of early morning ground fog, we are forced to divert for another mission. This mission is a Skyspot or Combat Skyspot Mission. Our flight of four F-4C Phantoms joins up ("marries") with a flight of two Marine A-4 Skyhawks for precision bombing.

This marriage of our flight with the A-4s is successfully accomplished at 28,000 feet. Precision bombing with ground control radar guidance is readily performed. The results of our efforts on this mission are unknown. Usually Skyspot missions are quite boring, but, thanks to Captain Wayne, this mission was fun. Captain Wayne turned the stick over to me as soon as wheels were up and I flew to the target area and back to base. Initially, my flying was rather sloppy, but I am finally getting a feel for flying the F-4C and my flying improves with each mission. I can now maintain formation with the other aircraft and set up a smooth approach to landing.

This is a very powerful aircraft. With propeller-driven aircraft, the pilot responds with the controls to changing factors of flying, such as air speed, attitude, engine sound and countless other indications. This response is commonly referred to as "flying by the seat of your pants." But, in flying the F-4C, if you wait to respond to a change in the aircraft, it is too late. In this aircraft, you have to know and anticipate any change before it occurs or suffer the consequences. In aviation jargon, this is known as "staying ahead of the aircraft." The inexperienced pilot frequently loses control of a high-powered aircraft by letting the aircraft "get ahead" of him. I can only compare it to riding a high-spirited and powerful horse. If you don't control the horse, the horse will control you.

On this flight, I am encouraged by my improvement in flying. Actually it has improved so much that by the end of the mission, I can maintain descent formation as we make a ground controlled approach (GCA) to Cam Ranh. As we approach, we enter a large cloudbank off the south end of the runway. Despite being under radar approach control, I am unable to suppress my apprehension at descending through those clouds to 3,000 feet. This was the same altitude that Troyer and Greco crashed into the mountain, five to six miles away. A tremendous sense of relief sweeps over me as we break through the clouds and the blue ocean lies beneath us. I continue to have nightmares about flying into a cloudbank in that region and crashing into one of the mountains. I know full well that if you see the mountain in front of you, it's too late.

I recently received a clipping from The New York Times extolling the Christmas spirit in Vietnam and Cam Ranh Bay in particular. Pictures of Christmas trees, angels and stars of Bethlehem seem to dominate the landscape. Is this to reassure the American people that the parentally instilled values of Christianity prevail in a war zone? This is a perfect example of showing the average person what he/she wants to see, rather than reality. My first response is to ask, what stage was constructed to display the Yuletide scenes? I have been over every inch of this damn sand box and I haven't seen more than a few tiny Christmas trees anywhere except in the bars. The profusion of decorations described are figments of journalistic creativity. I can only wonder what they have been smoking...or what brand of yule cheer have they been drinking.

31 December 1966

Despite December being only thirty-one days long, this December seems to have lasted ten-plus years.

In a few hours it will be 1967. My tour of duty in Vietnam officially ends on my DEROS of 10 June 1967. I am halfway through the woods. From now on, I will be heading out. I hope to survive long enough to see it happen...

3 January 1967

As part of Operation "Red Leaf" the U.S. Army transferred 133 CV-2s to the U.S. Air Force. This was completed December 31, 1966. The Army designation, "CV-2" will be changed to the Air Force designation, C-7. Whether the designation is CV-2 or C-7, the most common name applied to these aircraft by all services is "Caribou." As part of this transfer, the newly formed 483rd Tactical Air Wing (TAW) will be located at Cam Ranh Bay. Two squadrons out of 6 will be at Cam Ranh Bay. The 457th TAS (Tactical Air Squadron) and the 458 TAS will be at Cam Ranh, while the other 4 squadrons will be home-based elsewhere. The 459th and 537th TAS's will be assigned to Phu Cat, RVN. The 535th and 536th TAS's will be assigned to Vung Tau, RVN. All squadrons were activated on January 1, 1967.

The Caribou is a twin-engine, short takeoff and landing (STOL) utility transport built by De Havilland Aircraft of Canada, Ltd. It is used primarily for tactical airlift missions in forward battle areas with short, unimproved airstrips. It can carry 26 fully equipped paratroops or up to twenty litter patients. As a cargo aircraft the Caribou can haul more than three tons of equipment. The Caribou's STOL capability makes it particularly suitable for delivering troops, supplies, and equipment to isolated outposts.

The addition of this new wing at Cam Ranh has increased the workload of the flight surgeon's office considerably. Almost overnight, more than 200 pilots reported in for processing and medical clearance. Generally speaking, these pilots are older men than the younger, fire-eating fighter jocks. The younger fighter pilots live to fly. The older transport pilots fly to live, i.e. to earn a living. These are older men, like the B-52 pilots and the KC-135 pilots at Bergstrom. Their lives are spent in the monotony of twelve to twenty-four-hour missions at altitudes above the weather, where the terrain is no more than an inanimate map beneath you. At these altitudes, you have no sensation of movement unless you are climbing or descending through clouds. As such there is no thrill of high performance that dive-bombing gives. No, these are older men, with the complaints of older men, who gracefully accept a DNIF (duty not involving flying) medical decision to be grounded. This is in contrast to the younger fighter pilot, who becomes angry with the flight surgeon for grounding him despite the fact that his leg is broken.

Case in point: The first lieutenant who fractured his fibula when leaping from an airplane that was likely to explode. When I declared him DNIF, his eyes widened and with a hurt expression on his face, said, "And, I thought you were my friend!" I quietly reminded him that during any strike mission, he might have to eject and then escape and evade enemy troops in a dense jungle environment. With a broken leg, your chances of survival are markedly diminished. He thought for a moment and then nodded in agreement.

In short, every day is busy from before sunrise to after sunset. Since we are still in Monsoon Season, the winds of 60-70 mph with rain and blowing sand combine to make it less tempting to go to the beach for a swim.

4 January 1967

This evening, an Air Force general visited the base. I don't have any idea concerning the purpose of his visit. But apparently he wished to tour some the facilities. He proceeded to the BOQ mess hall, where we all eat. Eating at the officer's mess is no longer a matter of passing through the line cafeteria-style to obtain food. The base population has increased so much in the past few months that it is necessary to stand in chow line for 20-30 minutes in order to eat. I usually take a book.

The 12th TFW wing commander was chagrined by the length of the chow line. Not wanting a visiting dignitary to consider the long line an indication of administrative inefficiency, he ordered the dietician, a registered nurse, to cut the line off and terminate meal service. This resulted in twenty-plus pilots being denied food. Many of these pilots had been flying in and out of dirt landing strips and fishing villages since 5 a.m. without having time to eat. The dietician became so upset that she began to weep. Quite obviously, the pilots were all bitching about this...and rightly so!

For a while chaos reigned. Several of the pilots came to me, in the flight surgeon's office, to request that I intervene. Driving over to the kitchen, I discussed the matter with the cook and requested food for all of the hungry pilots through routes other than standing in line. This solution seemed satisfactory to the pilots. It quieted the dietician's concern and finally solved the problem. Colonel Bolt was not available for me to consult. He was too busy chaperoning the general around the base.

Apparently, higher echelons of military are not aware of Napoleon's Dictum: "An Army fights on its stomach."

The same is true of airmen, sailors and Marines. The insanity of such an order, issued to avoid consideration of administrative incompetence, is beyond description!

Lt. Colonel Buck Cantor has insisted on spending an hour a day working in the flight surgeon's office. He hasn't seen a single patient in the past thirty days and I have politely informed him that we have adequate staffing and very few desks. But, evidently, this fulfills some deeper need of his. He just sits quietly in the chair beside my desk and writes or reads. Since I am usually very busy in the morning with paperwork, I stay at my desk and continue working while he simply sits there. Ah, well! As Thoreau said, "We all march to a different drum..."

Otherwise, conditions on base are unchanged...another day of wind, rain and sand...

5 January 1967

Last night at 11:30 p.m., Tom Robinson came into the office while I was writing at my desk. Tom is one of my favorite people. We interned together at Wilford Hall Hospital from 1963-1964 and were in the same class at flight surgeons school. He had just returned from Emergency Compassionate Leave in the States. His youngest son has had multiple complications from congenital ureteral strictures that necessitated surgery. Tom noted that his daughter has also had congenital problems with the urinary tract. I feel for him. It must be devastating to be stationed this far from his family.

I spent the next two and a half hours trying to find him a place to bunk overnight. This morning, I drove him to the new runway on the opposite side of the base in order to catch a flight back to Vung Tau. Tom is the only Air Force doctor at Vung Tau. He is so funny. He is like a friendly, old alley cat that can just wander around and be at home anywhere. He will never get an ulcer. He takes life in stride, as it comes; regardless of the conditions. His brother is twenty-eight years old and a professional football player who makes $24,000 a year. Since Tom is over here, his brother is considered exempt from the draft. Tom is also very athletic and a formidable tennis player.

7 January 1967

I have flown enough missions in the Phantom to achieve a reasonable level of proficiency as back seat pilot. It has become more and more common for "back seaters" to search for a substitute on repetitive daily missions. Knowing that I like to fly, I am frequently sought out to fly as substitute for the back-seat position on missions. The usual line is, "Hey, Doc, I know that you are not scheduled to fly today, but I'm a bit hung over… could you fill in for me?" There is also another angle to my flying. By this time in my tour I have flown more combat missions in the backseat pilot position than many of the newly arrived, younger pilots have flown in the front seat pilot's position. As far-fetched as it sounds, both the squadron and wing are scheduling me to fly more frequently with these younger pilots to give them the benefit of my experience on strike missions. For most of my tour, I have flown only with the most senior and experienced pilots in the front seat. Now, they seem to forget that I am not a military jet-rated pilot and are placing me in a position of responsibility over these younger pilots for reasons based solely on my on-the-job training. I am not comfortable in this role!

The following mission was flown under some of these circumstances.

F-4C Mission

Air Craft Commander: 1st Lieutenant Terald Osborne

Time: 1:30 hours

Lieutenant Terald Osborne's back seat pilot is a relatively new man, whom I have encountered only casually when he checked into the flight surgeon's office at the time of his arrival. For some reason that I can't recall, he had some excuse for not flying the next day and Osborne asked me to fill in for his backseat position.

I awoke at 5:30 a.m. to attend a pre-flight intelligence briefing at 6 a.m. This timing permitted breakfast before our 8 a.m. takeoff. The mission consisted of a flight of three F-4C's, each of which is armed with four 750-pound general-purpose bombs plus the undercarriage Gatling gun. The weather at Cam Ranh is poor with a ceiling of 900 feet and three miles visibility with rain.

The target is originally fragged as a Viet Cong supply depot in the proximity of Pleiku. Pleiku is under a state of siege. Between 0130 and 0200 hours this morning, a communist sapper unit struck the Camp Holloway Complex of Pleiku with mortar, satchel charges, grenades and small arms fire. This attack was one of the most concentrated mortar barrages in the history of the Vietnam conflict. Troop casualties were considered to be light by official sources, but extensive damage was done to the supply center maintained by the 88th Supply and Service Battalion. Damage to the Holloway Airfield and aircraft was light. This was the second major attack on Camp Holloway in almost two years. Holloway is home base for the 52d Combat Aviation Battalion. On February 7, 1965, Holloway was subjected to the first major enemy assault on U.S. troops during the war. On that same day, American planes were ordered to bomb North Vietnam and shortly afterward U.S. troop deployment escalated.

Our mission today was requested to provide aerial support for our ground troops; however, the ceiling was too low in the Pleiku area for us to accomplish this mission. We were, therefore, diverted to a "combat proof" mission.

"Combat proof" is another name for Ground Directed Bombing (GDB). Aircraft are remotely guided from the ground with the assistance of height and direction-finding radar. In mature versions of the system, bomb release is controlled from the ground for precision. This enables delivery of unguided bombs in poor weather and at night, under conditions when pilots are unable to see the ground and identify targets. Until the introduction of GPS (Global Positioning System) guided bombs, this remained the primary method of bomb delivery in poor weather conditions. Over 75 percent of all bombs delivered in Vietnam, in particular, all Operation Linebacker sorties, were performed with GDB. The United States Air Force developed the AN-MSQ-77 Radar System to guide the aircraft to the target. The radar portion of the AN-MSQ-77 is capable of tracking aircraft anywhere within 200 miles of the radar system.

On our current strike mission, the bomb release altitude is 23,000 feet. Our four bombs are pickled[25] in ripple[26]. While flying the aircraft to the target area I experience difficulties in the yaw damper. Because of this, I ask Lieutenant Osborne to take control and he also has difficulties with the yaw damper. The F-4C Phantom is a high performance aircraft and with 3,000 pounds of bombs plus the Gatling gun under the fuselage, the control is a bit sloppy in this platform-type of bombing mission. After dropping our ordnance, the difficulties with yaw are alleviated. But the behavior of the aircraft under these circumstances is a bit unsettling. The target is hidden by the cloud layer far beneath us, but there is no question our bombs hit the target. This semi-automated bombing is not something I relish!

On the route back to base, we are entirely in the soup of heavy clouds. As we approach Cam Ranh, we execute a Ground Controlled Radar approach to landing. There are several critical occasions on the approach in which radio contact with the control tower is lost entirely. Having flown with such outstanding pilots as Major Solis, I am impressed by Lieutenant Osborne's ability to control the airplane under the circumstances. It was under similar conditions that crashes have occurred on the approach to Cam Ranh. It goes without saying that I am extremely relieved to feel our

---

25 To Pickle Bombs: To release bombs

26 Ripple: To release bombs in an almost random pattern.

wheels safely touch down. Next time I will be a bit more selective and fly with a senior pilot to cover my weakness in flying this aircraft.

This represents my 37th combat mission in tactical aircraft.

I jumped at the chance to fly because I enjoyed it, but I also flew to escape the boredom of my administrative duties in the flight surgeon's office. And I realize I had become nearly addicted to the adrenaline rush of dive-bombing at 700 feet per second, dropping the ordnance and pulling out before colliding with the mountain rising in front of us...before rolling inverted at 500 mph to make another run on a target. With napalm or anti-personnel weapons, it was not unusual to fly at 400-500 mph at an altitude of only 50 to 100 feet above the terrain. While flying at this low altitude, it was a frequent occurrence to have the jungle light up from all sides, like a Fourth of July celebration, with muzzle flashes from enemy ground fire. Since we might be flying at nearly the speed of their bullets, there were few hits on our aircraft. Fortunately for us, the enemy shooters were not duck hunters who were accustomed to leading with their shots. In the words of Winston Churchill, "Nothing is more exciting than being shot at and missed...."

8 January 1967

The number of patients passing through the flight surgeon's office continues to increase. Many of the newly arrived older pilots have a multitude of psychosomatic complaints that prevent them from flying. I have no privacy...just people surrounding me all day and night with their complaints. This is very difficult for me. I must have some element of privacy and isolation from the world to maintain my sanity.

9 January 1967

Today was another very busy day in the office…to the extent that I had lunch brought to my desk and kept working.

In addition, there were an unusual number of "routine flight line emergencies," which add to the harassment. For instance, the cockpit canopy of one F-4C blew off about 100 miles from base. Luckily, the pilot had his visor down and no injuries were incurred.

In another incident, during takeoff, an F-4C dropped 750 pounds of napalm plus two 500-pound bombs onto the runway. The napalm exploded with a huge fireball that spread the burning, jellied gasoline all over the north runway. Luckily, the two bombs did not explode and no one was injured. Of course we must respond immediately by sending a crash ambulance out to the scene. By the time we returned, patients were backed up in the office. Today, chaos reigned supreme for a while!

For various reasons, I had difficulty sleeping last night. Finally I got up at 5 a.m. and went to the flight surgeon's office. I immersed myself in paperwork, but finally ran out of steam at 2 p.m., and had to take a two-hour nap in the squadron Quonset hut.

More of our missions are going up North and every pilot on base has "MIG fever." I believe when one of them finally shoots down a MIG, he will be sainted on the spot.

In closing this note, the wind continues to blow at Cam Ranh and the sand continues to blister your face…

10 January 1967

Today, I spoke with Colonel Mack about the Accident Investigation Board and its decision. The wing commander is responsible for all decisions on this matter and Colonel Mack is not part of the decision-making process.

F-4C Mission Hammer 11 flight

Aircraft Commander: Major Dearborn

Time: 1:50

The fragged target is in close support of ground troops in Mekong Delta region. Ordnance is four 500-pound general-purpose bombs plus Gatling gun for strafing. Target weather is VFR. A normal dive bomb pattern is established with a wheel effect and bombs are released in singles. The target area is thickly wooded and the FAC is unable to provide an exact battle damage assessment. Guns were not used. Return to Cam Ranh was uneventful.

CHAPTER 30

<hr>

Politics and Policy

11 January 1967

The daily routine drags on. This alternates between sick call and mountains of paperwork. The multitude of trivial complaints is beginning to shorten my temper on a daily basis.

The quality of food in the Officers Club is degenerating daily. It was really quite good when I arrived, but they changed cooks. Now we have a woman, a professional dietician, and it is intolerable. Each day for lunch and dinner we have big green peas, pickled beets and meat loaf or spam. This is the same from day to day.

12 January 1967

Today the secretary of the Air Force arrived on base. Everyone was "invited" to attend a conference presented by him. Frankly, I can't even remember his name…I have long learned the standard line of these types.

With such an exalted position, it is easy to expect some magnificent and enlightening exposition about the course of the war or future policies, but it is predictably and invariably the same: "We, in Washington, are thinking about you, etc."

The numbers of in-country F-4C missions out of Cam Ranh have decreased considerably. More flights are flying north over Hanoi and the Haiphong area than are flying the shorter hops in South Vietnam. Of course, this change in policy does not affect the Caribou flights. Their missions are short hops to ferry supplies and armaments throughout our bases in South Vietnam.

15 January 1967

Recently, Cam Ranh has been swept with high winds and sand storms. Most personnel wear goggles when outside. The sand fills your eyes and plugs your nose and ears. The sand storms are so dense that in mid-day trucks on base must drive with their headlights on. There is at least an inch of sand on the dining room floor each day. Tables are dusted in sand and sand is mixed in your food. It seems impossible to screen it out.

A number of corpsmen in the flight surgeon's office are finishing their tour of duty. Five or six of them are leaving this week. At this rate we will be short-handed unless we receive replacements. The food is progressively worsening in contrast to when I arrived last year. I don't blame any formal policy decisions for these changes…probably, no more than the inherent variability in any large system over time.

17 January 1967

F-4C Mission

Aircraft Commander: Captain Swalm

Mission Time: 1:20

This mission is to provide close air support for U.S. Marines operating in the Iron Triangle Region, northwest of Bien Hoa.

The Iron Triangle is a National Liberation Front (NLF) stronghold 20 miles northwest of Saigon. Its origins date back twenty years, when it was built by the Viet Minh in the war against French colonialism. It served as a supply depot and staging area with an immense underground complex that includes command headquarters, dining halls, hospital rooms, munitions factories, and living quarters. It was never cleared by the French, nor was it successfully neutralized by the United States or ARVN (Army of the Republic of Vietnam).

Located between Saigon, Tay Ninh, and Song Be cities, the Triangle comprises about 125 square miles and includes portions of Bien Hoa, Binh Duong, Phuoc Long, Long Khanh, and Hau Nghia provinces. It is bounded by the Saigon River, the Song (river) Thi Thinh north of Bien Hoa, and the Than Dien Forest in Binh Duong Province. The entire area is thickly forested, consisting of jungle and rubber plantations, and contains a few small villages and hamlets. The most strategic village is Ben Suc, which has been under Viet Cong (National Liberation Front) control since 1964.

In January 1967, the United States and ARVN mounted the Vietnam War's first major combined operation and the first U.S. corps-size operation. Operation Cedar Falls deployed 32,000 troops against the Triangle. Its "search and destroy" objective was to engage and eliminate enemy forces, destroy base camps and supplies, remove all noncombatants along with possessions and livestock to strategic hamlets, and completely destroy four principal villages. Vast underground complexes were found, and large quantities of supplies and papers were captured. The complete U.S. arsenal was employed—intensive bombing, flamethrowers, chemical warfare (defoliants and the first authorized major use of CS, or tear gas), and land-clearing Rome plows (i.e. fortified Bull Dozers). Units participating in Cedar Falls included the 173rd Airborne Brigade, the 196th and 199th Infantry brigades, elements of the 1st and 25th Infantry divisions, the 11th Armored Cavalry Regiment, and the ARVN 5th Ranger Group.

There was little fighting as the NLF fled to sanctuaries in Cambodia until the operation was finished. However, the destruction, chronicled in Jonathan Schell's The Village of Ben Suc, was considerable. About 7,000 refugees were created and the region was made uninhabitable to anyone other than NLF-NVA forces. The operation's magnitude increased NLF utilization of Cambodian sanctuaries; however, they did return to rebuild camps, which became springboards for the assault on Saigon during the Tet Offensive in 1968.

Our strike was one of many other air strikes in the area. The scenery far below had the appearance of a Hollywood production, filled with explosions, bomb blasts and artillery, all occurring on cue. Different types of aircraft were stacked at variable altitudes, waiting their turn to intervene with bombs, napalm, machine guns or anti-personnel weapons. The air was filled with F-100s, F-4Cs, A-4s and various helicopter types, from Chinooks to Hueys.

And out of this cauldron of chaos, jet fighters and bombers scream upward after delivering their ordnance, desperately clawing for the safety of a higher altitude to escape this blanket of fire, smoke and death. Even from our altitude, it is evident that ground fire is intense. As we dive into the fight to deliver our bombs, every nerve is strained to avoid a mid-air collision with other aircraft, including the slow and tiny FACs that float beneath us. To avoid flying and diving in a straight line, we jink from right to left and then from left to right in an effort to prevent enemy ground fire from drawing a bead on us.

At 10,000 feet, we push over into the dive. Captain Swalm focuses all of his efforts on hitting the target. My job is to watch for other aircraft, comment on tracers of ground fire that reach out toward us, and most important of all, call out altitudes so that we don't dive to an altitude that is so low as to make pull out impossible. The altimeter unwinds at a dizzy pace as we pass 9,000, 8,000, 7,000 and 6,000 feet. Between 5,000 and 6,000 feet we pickle four 750-pound, low-drag bombs and then swoop upward, clawing our way back up to safety.

I call out to Captain Swalm that we are taking heavy fire as tracers stream past both sides of the cockpit as we pull off target. The FAC in the area radioes that much of this ground fire is from a large marsh area in the target area. With this knowledge, we make two strafing passes with Gatling guns to eliminate the sources of our harassment. It is satisfying to hear the FAC radio back that no further firing from Viet Cong comes from the marsh.

Finally, as we regroup at 20,000 feet, and have the luxury of looking down on our previous target area, the decimation of the landscape seems complete. The entire area is pockmarked with bomb craters that overlap with other craters, and extends as far as the eye can see. What had once been extremely fertile rice paddies that gave life has now been replaced by bomb craters and death.

Like a patient who has been mutilated by extirpative surgery for cancer, the neoplasm of human conflict continues to flourish, until the patient dies of the disease or is destroyed by the surgery to eradicate cancer.

Regardless of the cause or justification for any conflict, the people who bear the burden of its horrors will rarely be the same people to benefit from victory.

18 January 1967

Today, memories of Bergstrom and the Strategic Air Command (SAC) have returned to haunt me. Colonel Mack came to the office this morning to introduce Major So-in-So, who is a regular Air Force M.D. I was informed that he was here "to inspect." I spent all morning acting as chaperone to this "doctor" while he looked at latrines, read reports and looked at inventories in the personal equipment shop. He is stationed at Norton AFB, California, and does nothing except this type of work full time, all the time. I have difficulty believing that any semi-intelligent person would perform such duties. He has completely abandoned any medical accomplishments to assume a position that is no higher than a stock clerk in a large organization.

When my behavior is compared to the other physicians in my office, I feel like a monk who returns to his cloister every evening. This is my quiet time for reading, writing and contemplation. I have considered it my only sabbatical for reconciling myself with the world at large. And I truly treasure it.

Sam Hyde is very sociable and joins other doctors and officers in the club by having a few drinks. He will soon go to Jungle Survival School in the Philippines and be out of the office for two weeks.

David Byron goes to every third-rate movie, regardless of rain, wind or how sandy the night. He frequently tries to engage me in esoteric ethereal discussions about human morality, ethics and subjects, such as, "wondering what the Gods are doing tonight." I frequently react by blurting a caustic or cynical comment to thwart conversations, devoted to the fate of the universe and other matters, or I crack a joke that takes him an hour to think through before he realizes that I am toying with his intellect. These are questions that I asked in junior high school. When he notes that I am not enthusiastic about the discussion, he withdraws and sulks.... Oy vey, Oy vey ... How long, O' Israel?

Lon Kerry sits in the far office with his head resting on the desk, sulking because his wife won't send him enough money to buy food. Apparently, in neo-marital enthusiasm, he signed his entire paycheck over to his wife as an automatic allotment. She has to send him money for expenses! When not involved with these activities, he is writing letters to relatives, former classmates, ex-professors, internship attending physicians, maiden aunts and all other previous acquaintances, all to reinforce how tough things are in Vietnam. The other portions of the day are spent with his head on the desk or sitting in the chapel. He attends every prayer meeting, choir practice and Bible study group. He is definitely a "Jiner." (This is Southern slang for a person who joins anything and everything, simply to be part of a group of something.) I told him today that if I didn't know he was from Illinois, I might think he is a Baptist from Georgia. He is more of a fundamentalist than Billy Sundae or Oral Roberts.

After these statements, I must look in the mirror at myself! Buck Cantor told me that one of the internists at Wilford Hall Hospital, where I interned, considered me to be "pathologically introverted." When I heard this, I burst into laughter! I think that is delightful! I wanted to respond, "As compared to whom?" But, I didn't.

This evening, an Air Force consultant in internal medicine, a Dr. Grollman, presented two conferences to the physicians. He hails from Texas Southwestern University in Dallas and is a specialist in renal and electrolyte disorders. He is considered a leader and prominent author in his field, but when these accolades were being written, someone omitted the fact that he is past his prime! In fact, from his presentation, I would go so far as to state that he is walking the razor's edge path between sanity and senile dementia. The lectures were gauged for lay persons or nursing students, with no new information being imparted. In fact, they were rambling bits of tedious information that one might overhear being discussed over a cup of tea by two nurse's aides and two Grey Lady volunteers.

The monotony of the sand storms was broken today. To add variety to the environment, it began to rain. Now instead of sand in your ears, nose, throat and eyes, there is mud. By my count, I have 133 more days in Vietnam!

20 January 1967

The sand continues to blow and the rain continues to fall...

Tonight there is a squadron party. Being sociable and drinking beer are not my strong points, but they also have STEAKS for dinner! Therefore, I decided to endure the social gauntlet as a path to the steaks. As I have said so often, "You pay a price for everything you get..."

I purposely arrived a bit late to observe the other members of my species. Most of the brass on base was present, from Colonel Mack to Colonel Bolt, the wing commander. It was a bit ludicrous watching these "mature" senior officers ogling these very ugly nurses. If these women were attractive, the younger lieutenants couldn't date them for fear of treading on the toes of the colonels. However, these women are so homely that they are their own best defense from being approached by handsome young fighter pilots.

25 January 1966

An old acquaintance, Sergeant McNeely, called tonight. He arrived at Cam Ranh about three days ago and will drop by tomorrow. His first statement was, "Gee, you're a short-timer now, aren't you?"

Anyone with less than six months of active duty remaining in Vietnam is considered a "short-timer." I replied, "Four months doesn't seem too damned short to me."

I am eternally grateful to have Colonel Mack as my hospital commander. He lets me run the office with absolutely no interference. During the past five to ten years, the U.S. Air Force has undergone extraordinary changes in organization, temperament and philosophy. The Air Force in which Colonel Mack made a career no longer exists. He is an honest man, and from his perspective and my perspective, the Air Force has lost its way. In so many ways, he is a victim of the circumstances that have now entrapped him. He has too much time invested to quit, and philosophically he cannot conform to the changes.

Realizing that once I also considered the Air Force as a career choice, his fate is a mirror that reflects my own. I hope that he makes brigadier general, but I don't believe he will. He has a strong personality that stands on principle. The politics of military hierarchy is no different from any other political situation. The only principle is relative to what advances you. That principle demands obeisance to those who have power to promote you. He bows to no one. This is why he was sent to Cam Ranh as hospital commander while Colonel Barnum was made surgeon of the 7th Air Force in his place.

I have read recent passages from Representative Government by John Stuart Mills that are very apropos to this discussion:

"Plato had a much juster view of the conditions of good government when he asserted that the persons who should be sought out to be invested with political power are those who are personally most averse to it, and that the only motive which can be relied on for inducing the fittest men to take upon themselves the toils of government is the fear of being governed by worse men."

I presume that this passage was taken from Plato's Republic, but I cannot be specific about that. Nevertheless the statement is a very valid concept that position and rank in life demand integrity of character to fulfill the responsibilities of that position.

26 January 1967

Dinner on the U.S. Navy seaplane tender, USS Currituck (AV-7)

This afternoon at approximately 4 p.m., David Byron, Lon Kerry and I take the office Jeep and drive to the naval end of the peninsula. From there, we board the officer's skiff and travel about a mile into Cam Ranh Bay where the Navy seaplane tender USS Currituck (AV-7) is anchored. We have been invited for dinner by the dentist, Don Morris, who went to high school with Lon Kerry. The ship has one general medical officer, one dentist and one flight surgeon on board.

It is such a relief to see the cleanliness of this ship. It seems that all activities, including meals, are extremely formal in the Navy. There is a very definite distinction between officers and men that is generally lacking in the Army and Air Force. The officers dining hall is immaculate, with tablecloths, silver service and personalized place settings. The food is superb, filet mignon, and of course, everything is served Driskill Style (referring to the Driskill Hotel in Austin, Texas).

My gawd, I look around and compare this setting to the mess hall at Cam Ranh Bay. The Naval officers are all attired in cleanly pressed, starched khakis, to a degree that I felt like a clod in my clean, pressed-under-my-mattress fatigues and "polished combat boots." The doctors all have private rooms with baths, desks, and all the amenities of civilization, including real honest-to-goodness rugs on the floor of each room. The ship has a crew of about 700 men. Such confinement would, I'm sure, get old after a length of time, but it is a welcome change from our usual environment. The Air Force really has no couth compared to the Navy and its traditions. The Navy is hell for enlisted men, but it is by far the finest for officers. That is, if you are single and don't mind being at sea for long periods of time.

All in all, it was a wonderful mini-vacation away from our desert sands of Cam Ranh.

CHAPTER 31

Nha Trang...and the South

27 January 1967

I am convinced that the "default mood/temper" of the human creature is unhappiness. If the top of the scale is total despair, then he improves by sliding down to his lowest level of unhappiness, which he calls "happiness." As Thomas Jefferson said, "...the pursuit of happiness..." is the best that man can hope for.

What triggers this discussion is my observation of the other physicians in the flight surgeon's office. Since we live with the pilots and share their quarters, we have hot showers while other physicians assigned to the hospital have only cold showers. The water of the showers is almost red with the iron salts that are dissolved in it. The water also has a terrible odor because of the chlorine that has been added. But the result is clean and uncontaminated water. I am grateful for it. In contrast, combat troops who have bathed in nothing except rivers, creeks and rainwater for an entire year are admitted daily to the hospital.

I have no grounds for complaint. Yet despite all of this, other doctors in the flight surgeon's office are constantly bitching, not about being in Vietnam, but about being assigned to Cam Ranh Bay. They don't realize just how damn fortunate they are. Thousands of American troops in Vietnam sleep in muddy foxholes with mosquitoes or in canvas tents that are infested with rats, and all the while must contend daily with the Viet Cong attempting to kill them. There is little room for anyone to complain about being assigned to Cam Ranh Bay. I only hope that I can remain here for the rest of my tour.

The majority of my patients today were young men who work in aircraft maintenance and other ancillary fields that keep aircraft flying. Most are enlisted men, who are much younger than the average pilot. They seem to be divided into two categories.

Those who fear they have venereal disease, but have not been diagnosed, and those who have been diagnosed and treated for venereal disease, but continue to fear they are carriers of the disease and might transmit it to their wives.

Even in front of a physician, they act secretively and are remorseful, regardless of how many episodes of disease that they have experienced. As my grandmother, Laura Mae, used to say about people who hang around low-life individuals, "If you lie down with the dogs, you're going to get up with the fleas."

I treat them when warranted and explain how contagious diseases are spread. My primary question, however, is less about diseases and transmissibility than it is: "How can a man sink so low as to look for comfort in a septic tank...or is it a flesh pot?"

Leper Colony at Nha Trang

This morning between 6:45-7:00, Buck Cantor called to ask if I would like to accompany a small group of doctors from the hospital to the Leper

Colony near Nha Trang. Colonel Mack has obtained a special C-47 to fly us up and back. In fact he will fly it himself! Nha Trang is a small town about twenty-five miles up the coast from Cam Ranh.

Nha Trang is the closest village to Cam Ranh that is available for the enlisted men to visit. It, therefore, follows that Nha Trang is the venereal disease capital of Central Coast Vietnam. A saving grace is that Nha Trang is considered "secure" from a military point of view. As such, it poses no problem for short visits. From my perspective, Nha Trang is simply another sad, dirty, little Vietnamese fishing village that has been corrupted by this war. The major sources of civilian commerce are bars and bordellos. Both the U.S. Air Force and the Vietnamese Air Force have large bases here.

Nha Trang has a large Province Hospital, which is equivalent to a county hospital in the United States. Formerly, all facilities and equipment in this hospital were very primitive. Quite frankly, they still are. But, finances from the U.S. and other countries have injected new life into the aging facility.

I find it ironic that three U.S. Public Health Service physicians have been assigned to work here. For doctors during the Vietnam War, joining the Public Health Service was equivalent to an Underground Railroad to avoid being drafted. But, these docs must have had the shock of their lives when they found themselves in a Vietnam combat zone rather than on a Navajo reservation...ha!

In addition to the Province Hospital, Nha Trang has a leper colony, located on the outskirts of town, as well as a "hospital for old people."

The United States has only two leper colonies. One is in Kalaupapa, Hawaii, while the other is in Carville, Louisiana.

Colonel Mack really went "all out" for this excursion. The C-47 Gooney Bird is waiting for us at 0745 on the runway in front of the flight surgeon's office. With the exception of Colonel Mack, the only other physicians going are Dr. Cantor, Dr. Farber (a dermatologist), Dr. Doug Smith (a radiologist), and me. Three registered nurses are also on board to attend to administrative matters for a U.S. aid program. Despite the fact that Nha Trang is considered to be a "secure area," Colonel Mack requested an escort of five Air Policemen with flak vests, who are armed with M-16s and full combat gear.

At the Nha Trang Air Field we are met by "a personal representative" of the area, with a special bus to transport us wherever we wish to go. The first stop is the Khanh Hoa Province Hospital. By average U.S. hospital standards, the conditions are primitive. However, compared to my experience as a medical student at Cook County Hospital in Chicago, I have seen comparable, if not worse conditions, in the United States. We are informed that an infusion of large sums of money over the past six months has greatly improved conditions here. Before this, all buildings, from operating rooms to patient care areas, were constructed of bamboo sticks, with no screens over windows or doors, no fans, poor lighting, and meager toilet facilities and plumbing.

The hospital was little more than a cluster of thatched huts. Now, most of the thatched huts have been demolished and are being replaced, through U.S. financing, with permanent stucco structures.

The U.S. Public Health Service physicians assigned here are amazed and amused at our entourage with armed guards. Somewhat facetiously they ask if there is a war going on. Evidently, with the exception of isolated civilian atrocities, they have felt little to no impact of the war. This hospital serves a vast segment of the eastern Central Coast of Vietnam.

I presume that the nonchalance of these Public Health physicians is a mere reflection of their perspective of the war. The battles are being fought and war is being waged in the Central Highlands region, North Central region and the Mekong Delta region. There is little to describe of the hospital interior that cannot be found in Cook County Hospital in Chicago on a larger scale. Patient beds are contained in open-bay wards for variable numbers, depending on ward size. The setting is austere, with no frills. Each ward has its own plumbing and toilets.

There is, however, one significant difference between this hospital and its counterpart in the United States. There is neither a hospital kitchen nor any formal type of food service for the patients. All food is provided by relatives. If the patient and family live in the area, each meal is delivered to the patient as directed by the nursing/medical staff. If the patient and relatives live remotely, the families will camp out on the hospital grounds and cook for the patient.

The Vietnamese physicians have, for the most part, received their medical training in Paris. They began practice here immediately after graduating from medical school without additional training as interns or residents. Doctors simply "plunge into major surgery," learning as they go. I believe it would be overwhelming for a young man from Vietnam to pursue the typical path required for a physician in Paris or the United States.

For an individual who has had the benefits of advanced approaches to modern medicine with advanced technologies and instruments...in modern aseptic hospitals...to return to Vietnam with its grinding poverty, marginal hospital facilities and non-existent public health measures would be stifling.

This is exemplified in our own society by extracting very bright black students from the ghettoes and providing them with federal grants for higher education. Very, very few of these young black physicians return to the slums or economically depressed areas to practice. Few humans have such messianic zeal to return to the farm after they've seen "Paree" (Paris).

The Khanh Hoa Children's Hospital was first established by 1st Battalion, 3rd Marine Regiment as a clinic for MEDCAP (Medical Civic Action Program) patients in December 1965. The hospital grew to become a seventy-bed wood-and-tin building in 1967. By that time the children's hospital was staffed by Vietnamese nurses and aides under the supervision of Force Logistic Command. Hospital corpsmen and doctors were filling a definite need by providing sound medical treatment to thousands of children from Chu Lai to the DMZ. Since February 1967, an average of 1,200 children have been treated each month, and about 120 in-patients are hospitalized at all times.

The ever-increasing need for medical care and a growing acceptance of the hospital by the Vietnamese people has inspired the present structure. With the help and supervision of FLC Marines, Navy Seabees and the donations of many contributors, civilian and military, local Vietnamese have constructed a new 120-bed facility. This building is constructed of brick, handmade by refugees of Hoa Khanh village, completely lined with ceramic tile, and is valued at $300,000.

To ensure that free medical care is available to the children when American forces leave the Republic of Vietnam, the World Relief Commission (WRC), the overseas relief arm of the National Association of Evangelicals, is assuming co-sponsorship with the Marine Force Logistic Command. The WRC, working in half a dozen areas of the world to relieve suffering, will eventually replace all military personnel at the hospital with South Vietnamese and Free World doctors, nurses, aides and technicians.

I don't know the source of the funds, but I would guess the money came from America. If so, I am heartened by the fact that we have contributed to improvements in medical care for the Vietnamese civilian population. It is of great importance to me that American interventions in this poor country provide something to ease the suffering of the common man beyond the devastations that are imposed by and are inherent in all wars.

Eventually, we will leave this war-torn country. In our wake will be a destroyed economy, displaced families and countless orphaned children. While there is no doubt in my mind that the magnificent resiliency of the Asian people will triumph over time, transitions between war and peace are traumatic in every age. Perhaps Vietnam will eventually return to an agrarian lifestyle of meager subsistence, where farmers only wish to be left alone to till their rice paddies with water buffalo and raise their families in peace. But win, lose or draw, future generations of Vietnamese must not view the heritage of America's intervention as simply a legend of destruction, death and war.

From the province hospital, we went to the ARVN (Army of the Republic of Viet Nam) Hospital. This is simply the military hospital for Vietnamese active duty military personnel and their dependents.

From Nha Trang, we board a bus and proceed several miles out of town to the leper colony. It is quite isolated at the foot of mountains and surrounded by self-supporting agricultural fields and activities.

A Catholic monk is the sole attendant. He serves as physician, nurse, administrator and agronomist, despite having no formal education in any of these fields. My initial response at meeting him is to salute him, not in the military sense, but as recognition of his devotion to suffering humanity.

The entire campus is spotless and by far the cleanest area that I have seen in Vietnam. Everything is immaculate. The hedges are clipped and all lawns are mown to perfection. The stucco buildings are spotless.

The patient population is a heterogeneous mix of all age groups, with entire families present. The clothing of patients is clean and the children are well-scrubbed. Everyone seems to take great pride in the grounds, orchards and buildings. All work is accomplished by the patients and their families. The entire scene is far removed from the horrors associated with leprosy during the European Middle Ages. When Dr. George Farber, the dermatologist, examined a patient, a bottle of alcohol was immediately brought forth for him to wash his hands.

Many of the patients exhibit mild to moderate deformities of the face. The limbs, however, are the most seriously affected areas of the body, with loss of digits and contracture deformities. In children, the earliest sign of infection is a flushed or erythematous color of their cheeks.

Leprosy is a chronic infection caused by the acid-fast, rod-shaped bacillus Mycobacterium leprae. Leprosy is a chronic infectious disease that primarily affects superficial tissues, especially the skin and peripheral nerves. Initially, a mycobacterial infection causes a wide array of cellular immune responses. These immunologic events then elicit the second part of the disease, a peripheral neuropathy with potentially long-term consequences.

The social and psychological effects of leprosy, as well as its highly visible debilities and sequelae, have resulted in its historical stigma.

To minimize the prejudice against those with leprosy, the condition is also known as Hansen's disease, named after G.A. Hansen, who is credited with the 1873 discovery of Mycobacterium leprae. This mycobacterium grows extremely slowly, and thus far, has not been successfully cultured in vitro.

Contrary to popular belief, this disease is not highly infectious. Regular physical contact is required for its dissemination. Children frequently develop the rash on their buttocks by being carried sidesaddle on their mother's hip. The social stigma is so strong that it is virtually impossible for a patient to obtain employment, even in the absence of disease. They either continue to live at the colony or are given positions as helpers and attendants at several state-owned and operated nursing homes for the aged.

The next part of our tour was to the Province Hospital for Elderly Citizens. The conditions that we encountered are rather grim. The patients live in filthy hovels with little evidence of attendance or care. The concept of screens for doors and windows is totally unknown. As a result, all sorts of vermin, flies, mosquitoes and other creatures fill the hovels. The conditions are very poor. However, in all honesty, I have seen comparable situations in the United States.

Nha Trang is noted for its seafood all over this region of Southeast Asia. We go to a restaurant in Nha Trang for lunch. It caters to U.S. troops and military personnel, and is routinely checked by Air Force and Army doctors, but I only ate well-cooked food. Prices are approximately the same as in the U.S., as I have noted in other places in Vietnam. The lobster that I ordered was $3, but the serving was more than I could eat. It was all meat and no stuffing. It was delicious. The only other dish that I tried was fried rice. In addition, I had a bottle of "Bear La Rue," a local beer with alcohol content one-quarter that of American beer. For obvious reasons I drank no water. This beer originated during the French domain and is used as a beverage with meals, as a substitute for wine.

Shortly after lunch, we are driven back to the airfield, to be met by Colonel Mack, with air transportation back to Cam Ranh Bay.

It has been a very interesting day, and I'm glad that I was invited. After seeing the level of hygiene in Nha Trang, I am doubly thankful for my assignment at Cam Ranh.

30 January 1967

The following discussion with Elaine involved my disgruntlement with the election of Lester Maddox as governor of Georgia. I consider him to be a bigot and that his election is a step backward for the state. He was selected by the state legislature for the simple reason that he was a Democrat. I don't understand these people…this man served his purpose as a symbol of resistance to an unpopular law. I agree that he has the right to turn away anyone that he desires, for any reason. This doesn't mean that I believe him to be right. I merely respect his rights and independence as a proprietor. These statements refer to events of July 3, 1964, when Maddox and his supporters chased away three black Civil Rights activists from his Pickrick Restaurant with the help of pick handles and a 9 mm revolver. Maddox's segregationist beliefs are so strong that he closed his cafeteria rather than serve blacks and abide by the provisions of the Civil Rights Act of 1964. I am not a segregationist, but I believe that an individual has the right to refuse service to anyone he chooses.

Elaine, you married a strange animal who is sometimes at a loss to explain himself. I like to think that I can divorce myself completely from my Southern heritage, and that I have no real attachment to any geographical location except the USA. It is only at times like this that something stirs within me. During these times, I become nearly chauvinistic about the South. I stop and try to think…am I overplaying a role? Am I really disturbed, or do I simply believe that I should be? Unfortunately, I am not simply playing the role. I am truly angry and disturbed. I feel like a hounded refugee from William Faulkner's novels.

Regardless of where I go, I have to accept the fact that Georgia and the South will always seem like home. The roots go too deep…long before there were thoughts of separating from England. It is beyond my control and I'm not even aware of the emotions until times like this when I see her fall. It all rushes upon me like a wave, and I know that I must simply ride it out. It seems impossible that any non-Southerner could understand what I am talking about, since I'm not sure that I understand myself. My reasoning and intellect prevents me from establishing some "mystic" bond with a geographical region. In all likelihood, my generation will be the last to have these schizophrenic emotions of identity. Perhaps you are privy to observe a species struggling with the prospects of extinction. Perhaps I am experiencing the emotion the anti-bellum Southern patriots experienced, who survived the Civil War, and watched the glorious South succumb to carpetbaggers, while watching illiterate former slaves and prisoners rise to legislative prominence. There is, however, one difference. Those conditions were imposed upon the defeated South by a conquering nation. What we are observing now is a direct result of the choice of people who lead the state in the Twentieth Century. If there were a figure comparable to

Maddox in the ante-bellum days, he would be no higher than a sharecropper, taking out his vengeance on a slave or a mule, and his chances of being elected to any office would be no higher than those of his mule.

I am sure my outbursts on such matters are totally bewildering to you, Elaine, a non-Southerner. The moment I believe such things have been buried and I know my inner workings, I realize how much I have been fooling myself and must start all over again. And, if you are a bit bewildered by my outbursts, don't be alarmed. I am also bewildered by my outbursts. Perhaps I should either go into politics or quit bitching about the decisions of other people.

Well, enough of venting my Southern spleen. In another generation, that Southern influence will be "Gone With the Wind."

Today, I received a letter from Miss Julia Elliot, my high school speech and dramatics teacher. Outside of my family, two teachers have been instrumental in changing my life. She was one and Dr. Edward T. Martin, professor of English at Emory University, was the other. "Miss Elliot" never married and never had children. But she overcompensated by instilling principles in students that have carried throughout their lives. The influence of a teacher transcends the generations and its impact can never be measured.

She saw more in me than I did in myself and challenged me to fulfill my potential. She taught me how to express myself verbally. Dr. Martin also recognized potential in me than I didn't. He taught me how to express myself in writing. It is ironic that for all the professors, teachers and instructors I have had in over twenty-one years of formal education, a high school speech teacher in a small southern town and an English professor at Emory University are the persons who influenced my life the most. Both inspired me to be more than I am. I will be forever grateful to these two teachers!

31 January 1967

It is the end of January. Nothing new…same ole sand and wind…

CHAPTER 32

===============

Return from R&R

1 March 1967

I have been away from Vietnam for two weeks' annual leave plus one week R&R with Elaine. I met her in Tokyo and we traveled to Hong Kong. After this we went to Bangkok, Thailand. It was a wonderful reunion, interlude and vacation for both of us. But now I must return to the reality of Vietnam.

When I checked into the flight surgeon's office upon my return, my desk was littered with paperwork, not the least of which were Temporary Duty (TDY) orders assigning me to Vung Tau, South Vietnam. I am to spend thirty days there. Ostensibly, the reason for this TDY is to fill in for their flight surgeon, Tom Robinson. One of his small children experienced renal failure and Tom was granted a compassionate transfer back to the States. My orders for a one-month assignment provide time for the Air Force to search for Tom's replacement...or so they say. I am haunted by the idea that my Temporary Duty Assignment might be extended to a

461

Permanent Change of Station (PCS) that would keep me in Vung Tau for the duration of the war and not allow me to return to my beloved Cam Ranh Bay.

This thought provided no solace for me as I departed Cam Ranh Bay this morning at 0700 via C-130. One hour and fifteen minutes later, I arrived at Vung Tau, or what is popularly known as the "Riviera of Vietnam." Everyone I encounter congratulates me on being assigned to this highly sought after "In Country R&R" city. It is the dominant in-country R&R center for U.S., Australian, Korean and Filipino troops in Vietnam. While interesting, from the perspective of local culture, I am less than enchanted with the assignment. There is little to interest my thirst for flying. I will sorely miss flying strike missions in the F-4C Phantom.

I have now been in Vietnam about nine months and have "settled into" a reasonably comfortable lifestyle at Cam Ranh Bay. Cam Ranh is the largest base in Vietnam. It is isolated from the Vietnamese population because of its location. It is a U.S. Air Force base whose total commitment is to support American pilots and American aircraft. Any and all privileges and amenities are for pilots.

I have nearly total freedom to fly anywhere in Southeast Asia, both as a crewmember and/or as a passenger/tourist. By this time in my tour, there are five flight surgeons under my command in the office, more than enough to cover all duties whenever I choose to be absent. Being chief of the flight surgeon's office, I have a very nice, private, mahogany-paneled office in air-conditioned splendor that is cool and quiet for reading, contemplation and study. I even have the only gyn examination table on base. Just how this happened, I will never know. The only women on base are nurses and Red Cross workers. But somewhere in the vast bureaucratic process of resource distribution, the soft, luxurious examination table arrived in my office, where male pilots are the only patients. I never advertised its presence. But it was wonderful for taking a daily noontime nap, and I used it on a regular basis.

Cam Ranh Bay is the primary interface between the Navy and Air Force, as well as being the main port of entry/departure from the Continental U.S. If I need anything, I have only to snap my fingers and it will happen, whether it is to import something from the U.S. or from any region in the Southeast Asian Theater of Operations. If the Air Force were unable to comply with my request, the U.S. Navy could. Reciprocity in scrounging between the Navy and Air Force is chiseled in granite. Frequently, freshly baked sweet rolls from the base bakery would be smuggled into my office with a cup of hot coffee on my desk to greet me each morning. In short, life was good! In fact, it was so good that I arrived at my Vung Tau assignment in a grouchy, cynical and hypercritical mood.

In 1966 the 61st Army Aviation Company of the 12th Combat Air Group at Vung Tau was converted to the U.S. Air Force 536th Tactical Airlift Squadron.

The primary facility is under the domain of the U.S. Army. The Air Force is a tenant service that pays monthly rent to the U.S. Army. Although, there is an Army flight surgeon stationed here, I am assigned to provide aeromedical services to Air Force personnel and to serve as aeromedical liaison between the Air Force and Army.

The main medical facility for Vung Tau is also the domain of the U.S. Army. The aircraft flown out of Vung Tau are mostly U.S. Air Force Caribous (C-7) of the 535th and 536th TAS (Tactical Air Squadron). Overall, this assignment will be a step down for me, compared to flying the F-4C Phantom II at Cam Ranh. I have no responsibility for Army personnel. They are treated by Army physicians.

This is my first opportunity to interact with physicians from other military Services. I am the only Air Force physician in a dispensary with three to four U.S. Army physicians. My first impression is that one of these physicians, Dr. Pendleton, borders on the razor's edge of mental incompetence. This was not simply a personal observation. I have since been informed by the other Army physicians that Dr. Pendleton is probably the most incompetent physician in all of Southeast Asia. I spoke to the Army physician who is in charge of the outpatient clinic here. He spontaneously began to discuss Dr. Pendleton. Apparently Dr. Pendleton took six years to finish medical school. He was asked to leave after his second year for gross incompetence. He was placed on two years' probation, during which time he obtained a master's degree in zoology. It was only after his father pulled some financial and political strings that he was readmitted. Many of the stories about him seem far-fetched to me, but other physicians who joined our conversation swear that they heard the stories from medical school classmates who were contemporary with Pendleton. Supposedly, one of the classic stories involved Pendleton's experience in obstetrics. While the gyn resident was delivering an anencephalic baby, the baby was handed off to Pendleton, who was assisting. Pendleton took one look and then blurted out, "Hey, look! No Head!" Since spinal anesthesia was administered to the mother, she was fully conscious. It was a disaster of the first order. But the stories of Pendleton's incompetence at this assignment pile higher and higher. The other Army physicians are collecting funds to award him a trophy for "Idiot of the Year." Apparently, he has just applied for transfer to a unit in the field. This would allow him to wear the "combat medic" badge. His wife participates in local politics in the States, and is now doing "social work" work in Chicago. One guess as to what he expects to specialize in… yep, psychiatry.

He wants to take his residency in Washington, D.C., in order for his wife to do social work and where they can both go into politics. All of this would be humorous if it were not so near the tragic truth that idiots such as this are making policies in Washington at this time.

And, I thought the U.S. Air Force had its share of kooky doctors!

Some of the personalities I have encountered in Vietnam are beyond "colorful." If I had the talent of Ernest Hemmingway, a short story or novel could be spun for each of them.

Finally I learn the background issues that led to my assignment. Shortly after Tom left on his Compassionate Leave of Absence, the Air Force sergeant in charge was also directed to duty in the States. I had previously encountered this sergeant at Cam Ranh Bay. 7th Air Force Headquarters in Saigon had asked him who he thought was the most qualified flight surgeon at Cam Ranh Bay to come to Vung Tau and fill Tom Robinson's slot.

Without hesitation, the damn fool volunteered my name. This explains why the pharmacy and all medical personnel welcomed me so profusely and treated me like Hippocrates arriving in Darkest Africa.

The command situation is very awkward here. The dispensary is under the authority of Army physicians. This places the Air Force in the position, noted in the Ole South, of "sucking hind teat." As a result, I have only one small office for everything, both for patient examinations and administrative works. It is not a comfortable arrangement.

Since there are no quarters on base, I am to be quartered in a large hotel in the middle of town. The Palace Hotel was built by the French during their previous occupation of Indochina (today's Vietnam). The complex is surrounded by a barbed wire fence and cordoned off with sand bags. Entry to the grounds is through a kiosk manned by two Air Policemen armed with M-16s.

The building is poorly maintained and reminds me of delivering babies in the slums of Chicago. The Bong Lai portion is the domicile of pilots and high-ranking officers stationed here. The lobby of the ex-hotel has been converted into a bar with multiple tables for playing cards, drinking and shooting the bull. The walls are a dingy white plaster that flake and hang like scabs on a wound. The lighting is poor and there is a certain moldy odor throughout the entire room. So far, none of this has scored points with me since I do not drink and I have never been tolerant of playing cards.

But, the officer who conducts the tour for me is extremely proud. Pointing to the bar area, he comments that, "This is real living, such as one would not find at Cam Ranh Bay." I heartily agreed that Cam Ranh has nothing to compete with it. It takes some effort on my part to conceal my sarcasm, but they accept my reply as a self-evident complement. I am subsequently escorted to my "room," which has been recently vacated by Tom Robinson. I share the sleeping area with a major whose intellect I can only compare to a kindergarten dropout. It is on the ground floor and compares to any skid-row hotel or flophouse in Southside Chicago. The walls are bare and bleak, with chipping plaster. The shower offers the option of "cold water or water that is cold." The walls are sufficient to warm the heart of an ardent biologist with the abundance of flora and fauna that encase them. The major keeps trying to move Robinson's clothing around to facilitate my "settling in." I politely assure him that I prefer to leave my personal belongings in my duffle bags and suitcases. However, he insists that "one cannot feel comfortable and relaxed" if he continues to live out of a suitcase. I restrain myself from informing him that I have no intention of ever becoming comfortable and relaxed in this Gawd-awful-place, even if he finds enough space for me to place a sock in each drawer.

The thought of wasting my time by sitting around a table in a dark room, drinking myself into insensibility while immersed in boring conversation is an anathema to me. It reminds me of countless similar bars that I have seen in the slums of Chicago, filled with the dregs of humanity, ne'r-do-wells and end-stage winos finding collective consolation for all their failures in drunken conversation.

If one has any spare time, he goes into the nice club (that's what they call this dingy little bar) and drinks until he falls asleep. From an objective point of view, I can see why they drink. This place would drive you to any-thing. It may be the only manner to avoid insanity. An Air Force colonel showing me around points to the blocks of apartments that are populated by prostitutes. This bordello extends for many blocks. The colonel brags about never having a "security problem" with the Viet Cong. The only "security problem" here is with the G.I.'s... Ho! Ho! Ho! Big joke! By now I should know that when American men brag excessively about any loca-tion, it is for three reasons:

Liquor is readily available in a bar-type environment.

Women and sex are readily available.

The location is an environment of loud music/noise and dim lights.

I ask the colonel if there is some area where I might have a desk light and a desk for reading and writing. He looks at me as if someone has hit him in the head with an ax! In addition to the living conditions, I inquire about my flying duties. The response nearly blows me away. My only flying duty will be to satisfy the minimum requirement of four hours a month in any aircraft, to qualify for flight pay. I will be limited to flying milk runs in a Caribou, the clunkiest aircraft in the Air Force inventory. There is no fighter contingent at this location.

For a flight surgeon and chief of aviation medicine for a wing of F-4C Phantoms, the flying duty offered by the clumsy, cargo aircraft known as a Caribou is a definite demotion. Any flight time in the Caribou would be as a passenger, which is equivalent to another type of freight in the cargo sec-tion. This is comparable to driving a Ferrari and then being downgraded to ride in the back of a dump truck. Thus far, my flight time in Vietnam had seemed a reasonable trade-off for my previous astronaut aspirations. But this assignment at Vung Tau had thrown me back on the farm to ride a tractor or to plow with a mule. The thought of conjuring a hundred creative ways to treat gonorrhea and syphilis for wayward airmen and then flying four hours a month simply for flight pay, to pick-up and deliver garbage and rice to a village, is more than my inflated ego can tolerate…

My personality has two distinct sides. One is I crave high adventure, which I am fulfilling at Cam Ranh by flying combat missions in the F-4C Phantom. There is a quieter side of me that likes to read, write and reflect on life in general. Cam Ranh is the perfect assignment to satisfy both requirements. In childhood I preferred to roam the woods, fields and swamps of the great outdoors alone far more than I did playing ball with other kids.

It is obviously impossible for me to study or to write in the darkness of this filthy hotel; therefore I must obtain transportation back and forth from the office at night, when all is quiet. At least, in the office, I have a desk with a light for reading and writing.

I certainly don't have concerns about gaining weight. At lunch today we had dehydrated corn beef and cabbage, with dehydrated potatoes. Once a week, I plan to hook-up to an I.V. with glucose and multivitamins. The water here is not potable. It boggles my mind how anyone can brag about the amenities of Vung Tau. I would rather live in a tent at Cam Ranh Bay than have a suite in this hotel at Vung Tau.

2 March 1967

Today, I received some clarification about the medical condition of Tom Robinson's son. One of the Army flight surgeons received a letter from Tom. Apparently, Tom's son did not have glomerulonephritis as I originally thought. He had a complete ureteral obstruction at the site of a previous ureteral transplant. Naturally, he developed a very severe hydronephrosis, which has been treated by nephrostomy. He has been quite ill and further surgery will depend on his progress. Tom is seeking a compassionate reassignment in the United States.

After hearing this news, I feel like the proverbial cat-on-a-hot-tin-roof. The situation is ripe for my being permanently reassigned to Vung Tau for the remainder of my tour of duty in Vietnam. It seems that I have been on the receiving end of a perfect disaster. Not only can I not fly in the Phantom F-4C, but I have to fly in the hull of this cargo aircraft as just another type of cargo. My practice of clinical medicine will be to devise 1,000 creative treatments of venereal disease. Add these facts to my inability to study and write and my misery index soars off the chart!

Finally at noon, I sit down to consider all of this. I say to myself, "You idiot, you can't endure thirty days of pacing up and down and griping... either do something about it or stop griping!"

I travel over to the Navy portion of the base and hitch a C-47 flight to Saigon. When I arrive at Tan Son Nhut Air Force Base, I head directly to the surgeons office of the 7th Air Force. I have known Colonel Barnum from past acquaintance at the School of Aerospace Medicine in Texas. Unfortunately he is not usually involved in in-country assignments. This means that I will have to confront Major Larry Johnson. Major Johnson is board certified in Aerospace Medicine. At the time of my visit, it could be fairly stated that he was the most universally hated Air Force medical doctor in Vietnam. Initially he was assigned as hospital commander at Da Nang. After he had been there for several months, I heard reports from several sources that the staff physicians working beneath him were on the verge of lynching him. Never have I encountered such personal acrimony and vehemence against one man. I also spoke with several pilots who had known him as flight surgeon back in the States. Every one of the pilots regards him with contempt.

As is usual in military and governmental bureaucracies, the more of a liability that you are, the higher the position of responsibility you are placed. Finally, he was removed from Da Nang and placed in the position of vice surgeon of the Seventh Air Force. In this position he exerts an inordinate amount of power over all Air Force medical staff in Vietnam. With this background, I find myself, a mere captain and flight surgeon, breaking ranks to protest my transfer to Vung Tau. I dread facing the son-of-a-bitch but I have reached the point of no return and feel that I have little to lose. I enter the office and inform the airman at the reception desk of my presence. Major Johnson is working at a desk in the next room. The airman announces me as "Dr. Clark." Immediately, Major Johnson rises from his desk to greet me, with a very warm, "Dr. Guy S. Clark?" I acknowledge that this indeed is the case. Before I can say anything, he begins to gush about how excellent my write-ups on aircraft accident reports have been. I am entirely taken aback when he states that my reports are by far the finest of any base in Vietnam. Reflecting on my emotions involved in writing about men killed in a crash, I mumble something to the effect that, "I hope to God that I never have to write another one."

This goes right by him and I simply say, "Thank you" and proceed to inquire about my TDY assignment at Vung Tau. I explain that as chief of aviation medicine at Cam Ranh Bay, I hate to disrupt the program there, by my assignment at Vung Tau. I had made plans for pilot education and safety programs and hate to see these canceled. He says that because of my seniority, he had specifically designated me as aviation medicine consultant to the U.S. Army at Vung Tau. He reassures me that there is no intention of keeping me at Vung Tau beyond the thirty days stated in the original TDY orders. He notes that he will delegate someone else to rotate through Vung Tau after my TDY expires. At his signal, an administrative-type colonel emerges from an adjacent room who asks when I arrived at Vung Tau and I tell him. He writes a memorandum to have orders cut on another person from 29 March on. During the discussion, he expresses appreciation for my "fine work" at Cam Ranh, then smiles and says, "Vung Tau was meant to be a reward by getting you away from the Sand Box of Cam Ranh Bay."

When I emerge from his office, I am vastly relieved.

On my walk back to Tan Son Nhut for a plane back to Vung Tau, I pass a Vietnamese street vendor, selling magazines, books and sundries. A textbook, Histologic and Histochemical Staining Methods by McManus and Mowry, was on sale for $0.97, compared to $10 in the U.S. I bought it for Elaine to use in her research. The price of this in Japan is 1440 Yen or $4. I have heard that the cheapest place to buy books of any kind is Taiwan. Apparently, Taiwan does not have a copyright program, nor does it honor copyright laws from other countries. The prices are dirt cheap.

Finally, back at Vung Tau:

Life is tedious, not only for the lack of flying, but also because of the work. There are few flying personnel here. I therefore see all Air Force enlisted personnel for minor medical problems. I've seen enough gonorrhea, syphilis and diarrhea in one week to last my lifetime. I usually work in the clinic from 0700-noon each day. There is rarely anything in the afternoon so I close the office. If I stay at the office, the two Army general medical officers assigned to care for Army personnel will leave and I wind up taking care of the Army personnel also.

Vung Tau is also headquarters for the Australian forces in Vietnam. They are some of the most amiable chaps here. I've always had a soft spot in my heart for Australia. I think of the people in Australia and the people who settled America as two brothers separated at birth from the parent country, England. The Australians remind me of Americans during the 1940s, just wholesome, hell-raising, good people with a "can-do" attitude. They are some of the fiercest fighters in Vietnam, but occasionally they appear quite ludicrous in their big, floppy hats and short pants.

3 March 1966

After attending sick call at the office from 7 a.m. to noon, I return to the hotel for a short nap. After this, with camera in hand, I begin an ambitious stroll through the marketplace and village for human-interest photographs. My nasal sensitivities are the primary limitation to my photographic safari. It is difficult to become enthralled by the quaint little ole lady, carrying a basket on her shoulders, while at the same time, slipping and sliding through the filth of the streets. On several occasions, my gag reflex overrules my enthusiasm for photography and I lose the shot.

An all-night Vietnamese cabaret is adjacent to the Palace Hotel, and more specifically, directly outside my room. It exudes a bastard mix of noise that lies somewhere between the mating call of a saxophone and the wail of a tortured cat. The background music is the terrible twing-twanging of Vietnamese string instruments. Oh yes, there is a drummer, who is not good, but he is compensates for lack of quality with quantity by being extremely loud. To top it all off is a Vietnamese female singer with accents ranging from South Georgia to Paris to South Vietnam. And to ensure that patrons like me who are not on the dance floor are able to appreciate the music, the entire cacophony is amplified to at least fifty decibels above the average hearing range. The walls of my room actually tremble while the springs of my cot vibrate as part of the syncopation. Imagine trying to fall asleep every night to the lilting refrain of, "I reft my heart in San Flancisco," while a gentle breeze bathes your face and irrigates your sinuses with the odor of rotten garbage, fish and fresh human feces. Also, remember that this occurs every night from 5 p.m.. until 4-5 a.m.. The Vietnamese Riviera…sure enough…

Ah well, so much for my impression of Vietnamese culture.

I am beginning to believe that France has been over-maligned in terms of colonialism in Indochina. It has been said that France made no contribution to culture, economic stability and health beyond that of converting Indochina into a vassal state. From what I can tell, France took Indochina as far along the road to Western civilization as was possible. I am no scholar of the subject, but I would willingly bet that the urban conditions in France and Vietnam are not too disparate.

None of the water is potable here. All drinking water is imported by the military. There has been a recent lapse in water replenishment. Despite the fact that I do not care for beer, I care even less for unquenched thirst. Tonight, I had to yield to beer from the hotel bar.

The weather is splendid here. The temperature is pleasantly warm and has not been unpleasantly hot since I have been here. The humidity is relatively low and there is always a gentle breeze. Except for the constant putrid odor, it would be perfect for sleeping without air conditioning. However, if I were assigned here for a year or longer, I would buy a small air conditioning unit, for no other purpose than to filter out the omniprescent smell of feces and sewage.

4 March 1967

Tomorrow is Sunday and I will not go to the office. Sick call will be covered by the Army doctors. Living conditions here are certainly better than they were at Binh Tuy. At least I don't have to worry about a mortar attack when I go to bed at night.

I learned today that this peninsula was originally an island. Only after construction of a road between the island and the mainland did it become a peninsula. During the fourteenth and fifteenth centuries, the cape that would become Vũng Tàu was a swamp visited regularly by European trading ships. The ships' activities inspired the name Vũng Tàu, which means "anchorage." The Portuguese navigators passed Vũng Tàu many times and named it after Saint Jacques. The French invaded Vietnam afterward and called it Cape Saint Jacques. The cliff of Vũng Tàu is now called Mũi Nghinh Phong (literally meaning "Cape of breeze welcome").

5 March 1967

Today has been fuzzy. I can think of no better word to describe it. It has been raining all night and continues today. Since I missed the last bus ride to the office; I call the clinic to be informed that I have one patient, who has canceled. I stay in my room and try to make the best of it by reading, but I have no idea what I read. It is simply to pass the time. At 2 p.m. the sun comes out and it seems a perfect day for taking photographs of the local scenery.

Finally, pushing aside my disgruntlement at being transferred from Cam Ranh and having no aircraft in Vung Tau to compete with the Phantom, I decide to enjoy what I have. Vung Tau is very picturesque. The waterfront is filled with women mending feathery white fishing nets and small boats, or caracoles that bring fish from larger boats in the harbor. These caracoles have not changed since ancient Egyptian times of Moses in the bull rushes. They are small round crafts of reed construction that serve as the major water taxi service from larger boats to the shore. Their main cargo is fish. As with any seacoast village, the waterfront is very active.

Vung Tau offers the usual amenities that attract men who have lived in mud and been shot at for months on end. Liquor is plentiful. The houses of prostitution are equally plentiful. The climate is temperate nearly all the year. Streets are lined with small, hastily constructed bars that appear identical, every thirty-five to forty feet, lining the parkways. Each of the bars serves beer and has at least one to two pictures of nude females at the entrance. Most have rather facetious names oriented to the American G.I., such as "Papa-San Ago-Go." Nearly all have a loud speaker from which a deafening eruption of Beatles-type music floods the street. The philosophy seems to be that the louder the music, the more patrons will be attracted. Amazingly, despite the odor of rotten fish and garbage at every step, all of these establishments seem to be flooded with customers. Across from the storefront are small cubby holes looking out on the opposite side of the street. These have equally absurd names and usually feature one or several girls that advertise by standing in a winsome pose within the threshold.

Approximately every seventy-five yards are stationed Military Police of the Army, Air Police of the Air Force or Shore Patrol of the Navy, all to prevent the frequent brawls that break out after dark.

The Vietnamese people are universally friendly and there is a remarkable dearth of street urchins and beggar children on the streets of Vung Tau. This is in marked contrast with Can Tho, where swarms of street urchins descend on you whenever you walk the streets. This was most evident when I sat down on a stone retaining wall that overlooked the harbor. I sat for thirty to forty minutes in an effort to obtain candid photographs with a telescopic lens. Not a soul approached me. This was in marked contrast to Can Tho, where it was virtually impossible to shake off the urchins who beg and tug at your clothing.

A Catholic high school is several blocks from the Bong Lai Hotel. Each morning the young women students pass me on the way to their classes. I marvel at their simple grace and beauty as they pick their way through muddy streets going home from school or sailing by in graceful chatter on their bikes. They seem to float like beautiful nymphs, above the mud and excrement in the streets. The Ao Dai flatters every figure. Its body-hugging top flows over wide trousers that brush the ground. Splits in the gown extend well above waist height and make it comfortable and easy to move. Although virtually the whole body is swathed in soft flowing fabric, these splits give the odd glimpse of a bare midriff, making the outfit very sensual. Pronounced 'ao yai' in the south, but 'ao zai' in the north, the color is indicative of the wearer's age and status. Young girls wear pure white, fully lined outfits symbolizing their purity.

As they grow older but remain unmarried, they move into soft pastel shades. Only married women wear gowns in strong, rich colors, usually over white or black pants. The Ao Dai has always been more prevalent in Southern Vietnam than in Northern Vietnam. The young women all possess a youthful beauty, characteristic of the classical Asian appearance. They appear as the prototype of maidenhood's innocence. It grieves me to know that this period of youthful beauty and innocence will be short-lived in this wartorn country. When I hear the idle chatter of American G.I.s and their sexual exploits with Vietnamese women, I nearly weep. It is comparable to crushing a beautiful butterfly.

In perusing the small shops, I am surprised to find that very few of these are under Vietnamese management or ownership. Several of the curio shops are staffed by Chinese women, others by women from Cambodia and a large number of the tailor shops are managed by Indian merchants. This pattern of Indian merchants in dry goods and tailor shops was also encountered in Hong Kong. Finding such international settings interesting, I asked one Indian owner of a small shop what his plans are for when the war was over. He promptly replies that he will catch the first airplane out of the country.

It is twilight and I have returned to my hotel room. The woman singer in the Vietnamese cabaret next door has just started singing, "I found my thill on Brue Belly Hill!"

With the exception of the above serenades, evenings are quiet at the hotel. If you stroll outside for a breath of fresh air, the barbed wire fence that surrounds the hotel bestows a feeling of imprisonment that is reinforced by the Air Police guards with M-16s standing guard over the entrances. Occasionally, I exit the compound and stroll down by the water-front simply to people watch.

6 March 1967

The marketplace cannot be compared to anything in the United States. It is composed of multiple stalls filled with anything and every-thing, from fish to large haunches of water buffalo. The fish are hardly fresh by American standards. They are covered with flies and have the odor of decay. There are quarter haunches of water buffalo, hung for inspection by housewives. There is no effort toward preservation of the meat, since white worms, 1 to 2 inches in length, crawl from the interior of the meat toward the light of the outside. This seems no deterrent to housewives, shopping for their families. Perhaps, they view it simply as additional protein, rather than decay.

Along the boulevards, the mid lanes are filled with men and women mending their fish nets.

Along the streets, women squat in the gutters, picking lice from the hair of young girls. Both men and women change their clothes in public view without our Puritan senses of impropriety.

7 March 1967

Today was an unusually busy day at the office. This means that I worked all morning and half the afternoon seeing mostly Army enlisted men. Their complaints are all minor. If I were in private practice, I could have seen them all in thirty minutes. The medical talent in the Air Force is poorly utilized, but compared to the Army; it is the height of efficiency. Nearly everyone in the Army has been drafted into service. Nearly everyone in the Air Force and Navy is a volunteer, to avoid being drafted into the Army. This makes an enormous difference in individual motivation and work performance. No one wants to be in the Army in the first place. But now that they are here, their only thought is how to get out of work. Sick call is a perfect opportunity.

In the Air Force, there is rarely a problem writing prescriptions since most medications are readily available. But sick call in the Army is fraught by shortages of even the most common medications. There is a shortage of surgical soap such as Phisohex. Sulfa for treating urinary tract infections has been "bread-and-butter" therapy since World War II. But even this is frequently unavailable. Since I am an Air Force physician at an Army base, I don't necessarily have to see the Army's complicated cases, but I do have to use their pharmacy in caring for Air Force personnel. It is quite frustrating. It is also interesting that in the Air Force, physicians, regardless of rank, are addressed as "doctor." But, in the Army, rank is the title of address. This has taken some getting used to for me. Every time a sergeant in the dispensary addresses me as Captain Clark, I have to restrain myself from correcting him. It's a small point, but a significant point from a morale point of view.

Elaine is working on her Ph.D. in molecular biology at the University of Texas in Austin. She is exposed to the growing anti-war rhetoric erupting from academia. Recently, she forwarded an article noting Linus Pauling's perspective of the Vietnam War. The following is my reply:

"My first response is, What in the hell does a chemist, physicist or whatever know or understand about waging any war at any time? How does a degree in chemistry convey authority in any field except chemistry? His Nobel Prize validates his credentials as a chemist, but it does not validate him as knowledgeable in anything else. On what authority or omniscience grants him the power to make an intelligent statement about the balance of world power…beyond the opinion of any private citizen in the USA? To stretch his authority from the level of Nobel chemist to that of a

World Seer is extrapolation beyond the confines of reality. I understand that Pauling has communicated personally with Ho Chi Minh. My opinion is that this is a treasonous offense, which in time of war, demands only one response: He should be hanged!"

Von Bismarck once stated, "Funf und zwanzig Professoren und der Vaterland ist verloren." Loosely translated, this means that if a government has twenty-five academics as part of the administration, the Fatherland is doomed.

I am happy to have been accepted at Wadsworth V.A. Hospital in Westwood, CA, for my internal medicine residency next year. Most of the resident physicians will be veterans and I won't have to listen to the usual left wing tripe flowing from the sophomoric wisdom of academic mouths, with their vast inexperience in combat and everything else in life beyond books.

But, I must add the following on a more rational basis. Linus Pauling's claim that bombing is not effective is true. I do not believe that we can win this war. If you recall my first day in country, I stated this and compared the Vietnam War to the American Revolution…only this time we are the British! I believe that this is fundamentally a civil war to unite South Vietnam with North Vietnam. The revolutionaries have attached themselves to the Communist movement, simply because it is the only organized body to overthrow Saigon. We are fighting in the style of high tech industrial warfare against a guerrilla movement that poses no single target. Whenever a foreign soldier, sailor or airman has to fear every child, man, woman, grandmother and grandfather, it means that we shouldn't be here. This is David vs. Goliath and David will ultimately win. The Asian mind has patience borne through centuries of struggle. We should recall World War II and the air war against Germany. Day and night bombing of Germany's cities and industrial centers did not reduce their capacity to wage war. Indeed, under Albert Speer, the production of aircraft and armaments actually increased. The factories went underground and were scattered throughout the countryside. The Germans were an industrialized nation and they were defending their home turf.

Americans have no patience for any protracted struggle. Americans are arrogant because of their industrial might. The Asians are humble because of their lack of industrial might. But history has favored the Asian mindset over Western tactics. The Asians have fought these wars against foreign aggression for centuries, long before the U.S.A. even existed. The Asian knows that a monster wind/typhoon may uproot a great oak, but a thin reed, such as bamboo, bends with the wind and springs back after the storm passes. For thousands of years before Western Civilization, the Asians learned the strength and ability of bamboo to persist. Ultimately, the bamboo will remain after the mighty oaks have been uprooted.

CHAPTER 33

Vung Tau

8 March 1967

Today one of the Army sergeants from the dental clinic borrowed a Jeep to provide a tour for me to see the peninsula. Vung Tau is probably the only place in Vietnam where it is safe to travel among the native Vietnamese without concern for security. Cam Ranh was safe but there were no Vietnamese on base.

The French influence is apparent. At the southeast end of the island, on the top of Small Mount is a lighthouse. It overlooks the South China Sea and provides a magnificent panoramic view of the area. It was originally build by the French in 1911 and subsequently passed into Japanese hands. Now under the control of the U.S. and South Vietnamese, it is managed by the U.S. Navy. From its summit, you have a commanding view of the entire "peninsula," to the extent that it obviously was once an island, connected to the mainland by a stretch of brackish water and swampland. There are about 5,000 Australian troops guarding the route to the mainland. The entire mountain is honeycombed with miles of tunnels built by the French to form a veritable fortress underground. Most of this underground fortress has long been abandoned, but the tunnels remain in amazingly good shape. The sergeant and I entered a single tunnel for a short distance and I was amazed by its construction and the labyrinthine network. During World War II, it was confiscated by the Japanese. Below us, in the harbor, are masts of both Japanese and French ships that rest on the bottom…all succumbed to the fortunes of war!

From the summit, the U.S. Navy lieutenant in charge directed us to an area downhill where four large-bore old French cannons stand guard over the harbor. The cannons are enormous in size with muzzle diameters over 10 inches. There is irony in their location. Vietnamese Buddhist quarters completely surround them. If you did not know the specific location of the guns, you would never see them. Yet, the guns remain anchored in steel and concrete revetments, unchanged since their placement in 1870. In further contribution to the irony of their setting, the concrete bulwarks that supported them are covered with flower pots or brightly colored flowers. Their massive barrels are covered with shirts and trousers, laid out to dry in the sun.

Our next stop was the outermost point jutting out into the South China Sea, which governs entrance into the bay between the island and the mainland. At this point was a massive concrete and steel turret that formerly housed a cannon that was far larger than those we had just seen. This also was built by the French and was directed to the entrance to the bay.

The French seem addicted to defensive warfare, and worse than that, inflexible defensive fortifications. The Maginot Line is a prime example of such folly. When the Japanese attacked the French in Vietnam, they simply attacked from the side opposite that which the guns faced. As George Patton observed, "A fixed fortification is a monument to the stupidity of man. When rivers, oceans and mountain ranges can be crossed, so can any fortification."

Since the French anchored their guns in concrete and trained them out to sea, the Japanese simply walked in from behind and captured them without firing a shot.

The entire island is pocketed with concrete bunkers. Obviously, these bunkers are quite age-worn, but their gun portals and crumbling stones serve as mute reminders of how long this land has been dominated and haggled over by foreign powers. I am engulfed by a sense of futility as I stand at the lamp in the old lighthouse, high above the land, and realize that only twenty-one years earlier, a Japanese soldier or airman had surveyed the same scene, from that same spot, and six years before him, a Frenchman had done the same. A date of 1939 was carved into the tunnels on the mountain. I assume that this was French, since Vichy France, under Marshal Philippe Pétain, did not fall to Germany until 1940. It was only during the latter part of that year that Germany walked into France and received the French surrender. I cannot recall specific dates. But after Germany conquered France, as an ally of Germany, Japan was free to invade French Indochina, which is now Vietnam. As we drive down the road that winds around the island, heading north, up the coast, on the South China Sea side, a small island of one-eighth mile in diameter is visible. Even at a distance, it appears to be a veritable underground fortress, since tunnel and bunker entrances with gun emplacement are visible over three-quarters of its circumference. It has evidently been deserted for the past twenty-five or so years.

On our return trip, we visit the site of a large Buddha that fills the side of the mountain. This is reputedly the largest Buddha in Vietnam. Unfortunately we are unable to stop for a picture.

At the base of the mountain is a small fishing village, clustered around the hills before they tumble into the sea. A number of fishermen are present with their recent catches. I wanted to stop to see their catch. There were baskets of large orange–striped shrimp, eight to nine inches in length. In addition there was a very small variety shrimp, only one to two inches in length. Many baskets were filled with small squid, varying in size from six to eight inches. Of course there were umpteen different kinds of fish and eels, which I could not begin to identify.

Several small boys were standing next to the bank, in water up to their knees, to scoop one- to two-inch minnows out of water with a net. Since I am fundamentally a biologist at heart, these minnows are fascinating. They had black and white stripes longitudinally throughout the body. As the children lifted them from the water with their nets, the minnows immediately inflated a large air bladder on the ventral side. I've never seen or read about them before. My biologic soul was so enthralled with all of these unknown species of fish that I would have gladly stayed in the village with these children and the fish. But we are running out of daylight and head back to the Bong Lai Hotel.

Entering the lobby, I enter into conversation with several pilots. A number of them have been stationed here for six to seven months, yet have never seen any of the sights that I have seen today. Their lives are spent flying day to day, carrying cargo from village to village. At the end of the day, they retire to the bar and drink until bedtime. None seem the least bit interested in the local culture or Vietnamese people.

After talking with one of the pilots, who is an Air Force captain of approximately my age, I learned that his wife is an Air Force nurse, a major who is stationed at Baguio in the Philippines. I said, "Oh, that's fine, at least she's close enough for you to see her frequently." I was astonished to learn that he hadn't visited her during the entire six months he has been stationed here. Initially, he noted the restriction that disallowed members of the same family being stationed in a combat zone. But, he added that after arriving here, he found that it could be arranged for her to be transferred to Cam Ranh Bay for work at the 12th Air Force Hospital. The hospital at Cam Rahn is the only base in Vietnam with Air Force nurses. He then added, however, that he preferred to leave things as they were. If she were transferred to Cam Ranh, it meant that he would have to fly out of Cam Ranh Bay and he didn't want to spend a year in "that God-forsaken hole." He said she was well situated and enjoys the golf course at Baguio with her friends. He was quite happy with the way things worked out. Well, I suppose, one man's feast is another man's poison. At this early stage in my marriage, I terribly miss Elaine. She is the only person with whom I can share my life experiences. At Cam Ranh, the correspondence between the two of us has been reasonably prompt. But at Vung Tau, there has been nearly total blackout in communications between us.

9 March 1967

Well, I must eat my words about the wonderful weather here in Vung Tau. As I've said many times before, "If I bought stock in hell, the fires would go out." The monsoons arrived last night. Today's constant rain represents the beginning of the entire season. I wouldn't mind it so much except there is inadequate light in my room for reading. When it is cloudy during the day I am forced to use this poor lighting for reading and writing, and it really makes a considerable difference.

The 400-bed Army 36th Evacuation Hospital is near the airport in Vung Tau. I can't believe that I actually volunteered to rotate internal medicine night call with the regular Army physicians. This occurs approximately one night a week and will help pass the time more quickly. It is strictly inpatient care, and from what I hear, the cases are not too involved. I must, of course, spend the night at the hospital, but it can't be any worse than my present room.

A terrifying thought occurred to me today. Suddenly I realized that I am unable to smell the stench of this place anymore. Even the marketplace, filled with rotting fish, rotting water buffalo meat and human feces, no longer smells so bad. It is amazing how your sense of smell can adapt to anything. I remember my first night here well. It was comparable to sleeping in a pit of garbage. I am not so much relieved by the change as I am terrified by the thought that I might become asphyxiated and not know it until it's too late for resuscitation.

As I am writing, a dark green lizard about six inches long stations himself on the screen only a few inches from my head. His long tongue shoots out to catch a yellow moth. Now he is ardently clutching it with his jaws and running back to his lair. I'm sure he thinks I will steal it from him. This is not as ridiculous as it sounds. After tonight's dinner of dehydrated soup, with submerged clotted noodles, he might truly be in danger.

The woman singer in the cabaret next door is singing, "When Ilish eyes are smiring." In addition there is a new musical attraction in the cabaret. They have a child singer, whom I've never seen, but her voice over the loudspeaker is very well known. She sounds like a newborn in respiratory distress who is having a catheter run down her nose for suction in an effort to stimulate her first breath. I'm sorely tempted to buy a small tape recorder just to have a record of all of this local color and sound.

10 March 1967

Clinic duties this morning were relatively routine and I left the office at 11 a.m. This afternoon, at twilight, the bars along the street across from the hotel began to liven up. I wandered into the streets with my camera to obtain candid photos of the women prostitutes hawking their wares. Armed with a 200-mm telephoto lens, I hoped to fade into the shadows and obtain photos of their activities. If any of these girls spot a camera, they hide their face and dart back inside. Hiding in the shadows, I was able to get a couple of shots, but that was all. Just as I arrived back at the hotel all hell broke loose in that area. It was little more than the usual G.I. brawls that take place over girls. Finally after the Army Military Police and the Vietnamese gendarmes' arrived in force, things settled down to the usual dull roar. I knew that any further photography would be an exercise in futility since the entire area is now gun-shy.

11 March 1967

As noted, to relieve the boredom, I volunteered to rotate call with the Army physicians at the Army hospital. Tonight, I am MOD at the Army's 36th 400-bed evacuation hospital in Vung Tau. Since there is also a surgical officer of the day, this takes the pressure off in tough cases.

My first night on duty, within ten minutes after I arrive, an ambulance rolls in with a sailor who has just been involved in a shipboard explosion. Both of his legs have been sheared off at mid-thigh level with the lower portions dangling by threads of tissue. His face and torso are badly burned. I start blood/plasma expanders in both arms and tried to stop the bleeding by clamping the major arteries. I called the on-call surgeon. He arrived promptly and took the patient to the E.R. and surgery. I lost track of him after that.

When not involved in patient care, my sleeping quarters are in a small room above the shack that houses the generator for the entire hospital. The sound of this generator is nearly deafening, but I much prefer it to the caterwauling of Vietnamese music from the cabaret at the hotel.

All of this year I have tried to restrain myself from kicking walls and cursing the Air Force, Vietnam, Mao Tse Tung, Ho Chi Minh, and the overall inefficiencies of everything military. My restraint is based on the simple fact that with an entire year ahead of me, I could not afford to conduct my private war against everything military. But, now that the end of this year approaches, I am becoming extremely irritable and reactionary over issues that only months ago I would have shrugged off as being "understandably idiotic, since it is U.S. Air Force policy."

Now as I observe the U.S. Army in action up close, the Air Force seems a paradigm of efficiency and competence. All of the volcanic temperament that I have suppressed is beginning to rear its ugly head. I am beginning to simply explode. An example of this involves the Army doctors at the dispensary. These doctors are the most irresponsible and incompetent bunch of "professionals" that I have ever observed. With every emergency situation, the corpsmen must spend nearly an hour trying to locate them. Even with the direst emergency, the doctors on call simply say, "To hell with it" and leave the premises. There is absolutely no discipline or sense of professional responsibility.

The dispensary is staffed by one physician on Saturday afternoons. Today, I go to my office an hour early to get a book. I have been at my desk less than ten minutes before there is a knock at the door. It is a corpsman who asks if I will see a patient. I asked him where is the Army doctor on duty? The response is: "I don't know. We can't find him." I ask if the doctor isn't supposed to be here to cover situations like this. When they answer, "Yes," I then ask what they would have done if I had not been here. All I got was a startled look and a stammered, "I don't know, Sir." I inquire about the patient's symptoms and learn they are minor. I apologize to the corpsmen for being short with them. I also say that I could not take responsibility for the U.S. Army Medical Corps if they have no sense of responsibility for patients. I advise that if they are unable to locate a physician, they should call the hospital commanding officer for assistance. The entire system fosters irresponsibility. It is morally and ethically wrong to place this type of responsibility on the back of a young corpsman. This particular patient is not sick. But, next time, it may be a life-and-death situation! In all my time in the Air Force, I have never observed such negligence and irresponsibility on the part of physicians.

12 March 1967

I finally got to bed at 2 a.m. Prior to that, I was immersed in treating a multitude of drunken G.I.s, all of whom had bizarre complaints. Unfortunately, you can't relegate the diagnosis to a corpsman when a man comes in complaining of "severe chest pain" or "paralysis" or abdominal pain.

I had one interesting conversation with one of the general surgeons who was on call for the night. He has only been in Vietnam for six weeks. Last summer, following his surgical residency, he decided to take a "trip around the world," which was evidently a gift from wealthy parents. As part of the trip he came to Vietnam and became acquainted with a surgeon in one of the provincial hospitals. He decided to work in the hospital for a couple of weeks, just for the experience, before continuing his journey. While there, he received a draft notice forwarded by his father. Now he has returned to Vietnam – ha! I sure hope he enjoys all of this experience. I believe this is a true case of poetic justice.

Today by chance, I happened to meet two physicians from a Navy ship in the harbor. One of them is a bit older than I am, perhaps age 32, who finished his internship last year. I didn't pry, but after he discussed his wife and three children and a few other things, I came to the conclusion that he had repeatedly been forced to interrupt his schooling for financial reasons. He was extremely intelligent and very likable. He went to medical school at the University of Washington in Seattle and interned at Harbor General Hospital in LA.

He asked my plans. I merely said I wanted to do an internal medicine residency in the LA area. I said this because I'm still trying to ferret out the reputation of various hospitals and training programs on the West Coast, without committing myself. He was interested in internal medicine, and I thought he would have some opinions based on his experience and impressions of the institutions along the West Coast. He praised the University of Washington program and was well satisfied with it. He discussed the residency offered by the University of California in San Francisco. In essence he said what everyone else has said. The UCSF program in internal medicine is extremely weak, but political intrigue continues to keep it weak, and the situation is not likely to be reversed. He considered UCSF to be one of the worst teaching programs in the West Coast. He said that Harbor General Hospital in Torrence, California, was an exceptional hospital for internship. It was a new facility, clean, and with full responsibility inpatient care for residency training. However, it was weak in internal medicine instruction. He noted that LA County Hospital was good, but you tended to work yourself to death in the mass of humanity. He also noted that the program suffered a great deal from deficiencies in the academic sphere. He said, quite spontaneously, "The hospital you should consider is the Wadsworth VA Hospital. It is probably the finest program on the West Coast. At Wadsworth you have the best-of-three worlds:

1) Private university academic medicine from UCLA; 2) County-type acute medicine from its affiliation at Harbor General Hospital and LA County Hospital; 3) The VA Hospital has excellent teaching. I was naturally delighted to hear him praise Wadsworth. His opinion so far tracks with other opinions I have received, which makes me delighted with my choice. He spoke very highly of UCLA's Medical School. Since Elaine will be attending this school, she will be pleased to hear this.

Today, while browsing through an old issue of National Geographic, I stumbled on an article about the Florida alligator. There was a large picture and several paragraphs about the Ross Allen Reptile Institute at Silver Springs. It features a large picture of Robert Allen wrestling an alligator under water. I had to think for a minute to realize that this was the same Bobby Allen who was my classmate during grades two through six while living in Ocala, Florida. After it dawned on me, I recognized him immediately.

When I was in the third grade, I swapped him a pocketknife for a horned toad. I placed the horned toad in a box of sand and positioned it in the sun. Well, the horned toad was a "she." She laid about twenty eggs, crawled out of my box and into the middle of the dirt road in front of the house. A car ran over her and killed her. I tried to get those eggs to hatch, but to no avail. So there I was; no pocketknife, no horned toad and no box of eggs to hatch. This was the beginning of my failure in entrepreneurship. If the eggs had hatched, I planned to swap ten baby horned toads for ten pocketknives and proceed to fortune and fame. But the stupid horned toad eggs wouldn't cooperate.

12 March 1967—Continued
MEDCAP Ly Nhon

I have become acquainted with two U.S. Navy officers. The first is Lieut. (JG) Jim McCloskey, an adviser to the Brown Water Vietnamese Navy. I expressed a desire to accompany him and his crew on a MEDCAP cruise upriver. MEDCAP is an acronym for Medical Civic Action Program. Lieutenant McCloskey is one of two United States Naval officers who are assigned as advisers to the Vietnamese Navy "Junk Fleet." These junks routinely patrol the mouths of major rivers and canals in the ongoing search for Viet Cong boats and cargo. The waterways are the main thoroughfares for commerce, smuggling and arms transport. The junks are manned by Vietnamese sailors and armed with 50-caliber machine guns mounted on the bow of each boat. They are slow and clumsy craft, but they have the advantage of having a shallow draft to accommodate the sloughs and mud reefs of the Asian rivers.

On this particular trip, Lieutenant McCloskey and Lt. Bob Travitts were the commanding officers on our U.S. Navy swift boat. Our destination was a small village by the name of Ly Nhon, which is approximately three hours up the Saigon River. Shortly after I boarded, we stopped at the harbor repair shop to pick up a rather large entourage of two Navy doctors, one Navy dentist and one Navy pharmacist and several Navy corpsmen. More and more, the excursion began to remind me of a Sunday afternoon excursion to look at native flowers and sunbathe as expressed in the popular tune of the 1950s, "Cruising Down the River on a Sunday Afternoon." Most of the Naval personnel live on ships with clean shoes, clean uniforms, white sheets and air-conditioned quarters. This offers definite advantages to life on land…

The weather is splendid. The bluish green water of the bay soon melts into a dirty gray color, where river silt converges to meet the sea. Various currents blend the tides and soils of the Mekong Delta Region to create a streaking effect in the water. The river is broad and the shore is distant. It is interesting to note the abrupt transition in color of foliage on the shore. Defoliation chemicals have neatly cut a brown swath along the entire shore. Ostensibly, this is used to destroy vegetation that provides cover to the Viet Cong.

It is also interesting to note the various fishing devices used by the natives. The fishermen have formed a simple V-shaped funnel, created by large wooden poles, jammed vertically into the bottom. This arrangement covers very large areas of perhaps one-quarter mile from base to the apex.

At various intervals houses are elevated on stilts above the water, while racks are covered with fishnets left open to dry in the sun. In season, these are homes of fishermen and their families. These homes are of fragile, stick-and-branch construction in mid channel, giving the appearance of being precariously suspended above the waterway. Apparently, fishermen and their families live in these hovels for most of the season. Communication and transportation of supplies is conducted by junks and smaller skiffs.

After a while the water changed drastically. It appeared to be almost pure mud. This continued for the next one to two hours. Overhead flew the intermittent passage of huge Chinook helicopters with 20-mm howitzers suspended beneath them. Apparently they are removing these from an area of operations about six miles from our destination. Lieutenant McCloskey points out a site to our left where, two days ago, he participated in an operation involving the deaths of twenty-five to thirty Viet Cong. Our troops and Vietnamese troops apparently captured a large quantity of stored arms and ammunition. These originated in communist China. In addition there was a large quantity of United States arms, including .45-caliber and .38-caliber pistols along with M-16 rifles.

The village of Ly Nhon is a small fishing village on the right bank of the Nha Be River. Behind the village is an expanse of mangrove swamps and jungles. We were unable to dock at the village, since the draft of our boat exceeded the water depths before the village. The muddy bottom was only two to three inches beneath the surface of the water. As we approached, we encountered an old fisherman and small boy in a shallow-draft boat. We asked them if they would assist in portage of our team from mid-river to the shore. There was a large fish of unknown type tied to their boat. Unfortunately, even their smaller skiff had a draft too deep to maneuver.

In the face of these obstacles, we were advised to take off our boots, roll up our trousers and climb out of the boats to wade ashore. I am the only one of the bunch who decides to wade ashore with my boots on. In far too many places, I have encountered punjii stakes that were meant to pierce your feet with bamboo splinters, coated with excrement. The mud, through which we wade, is like chewing gum, tenacious and creating a vacuum to capture your foot with every step. I am grateful for my decision to wear my boots. Several members of the group receive rather severe lacerations on their feet and legs from unknown objects buried in the mud. Since the village privy hangs out over the water only a few yards distant, the wounds are, for sure, contaminated.

Finally arriving onshore, we find the village a shambles. The Viet Cong mortared the village only two nights ago. There were no soldiers here and the village had no strategic or tactical military significance. This was purely and simply an act of terrorism to warn the villagers who they were and to emphasize the consequences of not cooperating with them.

At its best, the village of Ly Nhon is a squalid cluster of mud and wooden shacks surrounded by a hedgerow of stakes driven into the ground. Water buffalo wander aimlessly through the paths. We set up our medical dispensary under an awning. Everyone in this village and surrounding countryside turns out. There is little translation of Vietnamese to English or vice versa. With grunts and groans, finger pointing, head rubbing and stomach patting, we try to garner the problem and come up with some treatment. Except for obvious cases of lacerations and broken limbs, the medical diagnostics is more veterinary medicine than internal medicine. If a patient isn't given some type of pill or cough syrup, he or she becomes quite upset, feeling a great injustice had been done or that they are being intentionally deprived of care.

The two most common complaints are cough and knee pain. On a number of occasions, the cough appears to be feigned. When I examined their heart and lungs and found them normal, I gave them a bottle of cough syrup and they seemed satisfied. We have no X-ray facilities. Perhaps, many have T.B., but this can neither be diagnosed nor treated at this level of care. Occasionally, the same person will sneak back into line again, after drinking all the cough syrup, to request another round of medication. Obviously, they like its taste.

The other common complaint is knee pain, for which I could find no obvious explanation on physical examination of both the hips and knees. It seems likely that squatting in rice paddies all of their lives will result in mechanical derangements and osteoarthritis, but without further diagnostic measures, this can't be confirmed.

For children, the most common complaints are earaches and diarrhea. Since each of us is seeing more than fifty patients an hour, the diagnostic medical care is more a matter of educated guess work than diagnostic acumen. For diarrhea, piperazine is the universal therapy. Piperazine is a drug that belongs to the family of medicines called anthelmintics. These medicines are used in the treatment of worm infestations. These people are universally infested with round worms (Nemathelminthes).

Before we started our expedition, I was introduced to a Vietnamese physician, Dr. Don, who seemed quite erudite. His mother was German and his father Vietnamese. He was very handsome and intelligent. He studied medicine in Paris for many years and was fluent in French, German, English and his native Vietnamese.

It was through him that I met my first patient. One of the Navy lieutenants brought in a small Vietnamese boy of perhaps six or seven years old. Dr. Don was with the child and asked me to take a look at him. The child's face looked like it had been hit with a load of buckshot. While sleeping, a Viet Cong mortar round had exploded next to him. But facial lacerations were not his main problem.

His left eye had been traumatized. A shrapnel fragment had pierced his cornea and very likely there was a retained fragment in his eye. When I raised the lid, I saw that the cornea, and probably the globe itself, had been penetrated by shot and shrapnel. The interpreter, his mother, said that it had happened when the Viet Cong had mortared the village two nights before. The village was occupied solely by fishermen, farmers and their families. She did not understand why they had been attacked.

The child stood very quietly while I examined him. He was handsome, and otherwise appeared to be an exceptionally healthy boy. It broke my heart to see him! He had lost the left eye and there was a very strong possibility that through the reaction of sympathetic opthalmia, his chance of losing the remaining right eye was extremely good. When an eye is injured, proteins are released into the circulation to provoke an antigen-antibody reaction that results in an autoimmune process that attacks the remaining normal eye.

The injured eye is termed the "exciting" eye while the uninjured one is the "sympathetic" eye. The original eye injury always involves the uvea, specifically the ciliary body, releasing uveal pigment into the bloodstream. This triggers the formation of antibodies that cause inflammation of the uvea (uveitis) in the uninjured eye with gradual progressive loss of vision and eventual blindness. The symptoms are blurry vision and pain in both eyes. The time between the injury in the exciting eye and the onset of disease in the sympathetic eye is generally two weeks to two months. The disease then typically runs a chronic progressive course with periods of quiescence punctuated by renewed inflammation. Treatment is the prompt and aggressive administration of corticosteroids and, if need be, other anti-inflammatory drugs. Enucleation (removal) of the injured eye within fourteen days of the injury will prevent sympathetic opthalmia.

I discussed the case with Dr. Don. Yes, he recognized the problem, but failed to see why I was so concerned about the case. In fact, he was rather nonchalant about the whole issue. For him, it simply represented one more childhood casualty in a long war…a statistical affliction…

I spent a great deal of time arguing with one of the Army colonels, who was conducting the Sweep Operation against Viet Cong in the area.

After much persuasion, I convinced the colonel to requisition a MedEvac helicopter to evacuate this child to a hospital in Vung Tau. I know there is an ophthalmologist available to provide proper care.

More than any other single factor, this single encounter brought home to me just what war means to the average person. When you consider that life expectancy in this country is approximately thirty-five years, and that during this life, a person must live an animal-like existence, in the jungle and in this squalid muddy village…plagued by death and disease… it is almost beyond human reckoning. But now in addition to these conditions, this child will be rendered blind at the age of six or seven. When I consider what lies ahead of him in a short life…and all for no military purpose, except to terrorize…at any price.

On the way back, the Navy officers drape their obese torsos over the deck house to enjoy their daily suntan and speak of how good a hot shower will feel and how good the ice cream will taste after such a "strenuous day." But I cannot tear my thoughts from a small frightened child and his mother, flying for the first time in their lives, in an open helicopter, as they leave the village of their family, friends and ancestors and approach the city of Vung Tau, a metropolis of extraordinary size from their provincial perspective. I am sure that his young mother is more terrified than he is.

The water on our return voyage became quite rough, with brackish water spraying over the bow and gunwales; but there was a sense of cleansing from the cold water and wind, as the mud and odors of the village were washed away. By 6 p.m. we arrived back at Vung Tau.

I could barely believe my eyes. The MedEvac helicopter only just arrived at the base after we disembarked from the swift boat. Apparently, several diversionary missions dictated the delay. The Navy lieutenant and I boarded the ambulance taking the child to the Province Hospital. I know there is an Australian ophthalmologist there. But I also know the bureaucratic delays in having the child evaluated from an outpatient status. A poor Vietnamese child is very low on the priority schedule. Dr. Don is quite put out with me about all of this. He wants to simply deposit the child on the hospital doorstep and leave. All of this emphasis on one child is over and beyond any personal commitment he has for the child. Finally, I contacted the ophthalmologist and assured him of the urgency in seeing the child. He was in surgery at the time. I tried to comfort the mother, but I only felt miserably inadequate for my task. Feeling distraught, I went back to the Bong Lai hotel and lay awake for many hours before falling asleep. This child may survive with one eye. But, if he loses both eyes, what is his future?

My intellect tells me that in the future I will forget my muddy boots. I will eventually forget the odors of rotten fish, human excrement and water buffalo dung that permeate the air of Ly Nhon. All of these things will diminish in my memory with time. And with the passage of years, I will hopefully forget many of the horrors that I have seen in this war. But intellect will not allow me to forget this one small child, whose name I do not even know. In two months, I will return to the United States and resume a lifestyle of relative comfort, peace and happiness. In several weeks, this child will return to Ly Nhon, a tiny village, with privy hanging over a very large, muddy river…for a lifetime of what?

CHAPTER 34

Sex, Lies and VD

13 March 1967

The dispensary is overcrowded daily with G.I.s seeking treatment for various venereal diseases. The most common is gonorrhea. I've grown so weary of diagnosing and treating it that I have trained the corpsmen to manage most cases. Many of the Army, Marine and Air Force enlisted men have been in the jungles and base camps near enemy activity. Their isolation and the pressure of combat have stirred up their hormones. Vung Tau, with countless brothels, liquor and nightlife, is the perfect place to let off steam. Last month, the rate of gonorrhea in U.S. Air Force personnel was 1,200 cases for every 1,000 personnel.

But even in this remote location, capitalism is alive and well. The city of Vung Tau has a strict ordinance that a man cannot sleep with any woman other than his wife. But for a small fee, the mayor will issue a special Limited Marriage Certificate that is valid for twenty-four hours. It is renewable every twenty-four hours for another fee. In war and peace, commerce prevails.

14 March 1967

Bubonic Plague in Vung Tau

Today brings to mind a bit of verse from third grade. "Mighty Lak' a Rose" was written in 1901 by Frank Lebby Stanton:

This world that we're living in...
Is mighty hard to beat;
You get a thorn with every rose,
But ain't the roses sweet!

One might apply the above poem to the pleasures and consequences of visiting a brothel. After the pleasure of sex (the Rose), the consequences (the Thorn) are venereal disease and/or bubonic plague.

This evening, Colonel Owens (the Army hospital commander and senior medical authority) asked me to attend a meeting with him and all the higher military brass in this area.

The Vietnamese Province Hospital in Vung Tau has suddenly reported seven cases of bubonic plague, caused by Pasturella pestis from fleas of rats. This is the disease that wiped out more than a third of Europe's population during the Middle Ages. A mood of hysteria is sweeping the medical community and everyone seems to be chasing his tail. Innumerable public health officials from Saigon and the World Health Organization have been investigating. It is their opinion that the Vietnamese authorities have ignored the problem by burying the victims without reporting the causes of death. The local politicians are afraid that it will affect the local economy. In my role as director of base medical services for a thousand-plus Air Force personnel, I have been chosen to organize the program for immunizations, public health and sanitation in all base facilities. This effort involves all Vietnamese personnel who are employed by the Air Force, such as housekeepers, dishwashers and other service personnel. In all, there are about 125 people involved. This isn't a large number, but they are widely scattered throughout multiple organizations, locations and shifts. Military personnel are no problem. Their immunizations and medical care are all maintained up-to-date.

In the meantime, the city of Vung Tau has been declared "off limits" to all military personnel. This edict is primarily to keep the G.I.s out of the brothels, where rats with fleas and God only knows what other types of vermin run rampant. My problem is that I only have two corpsmen. Both are very good and highly efficient, but for a short time, they are going to be run ragged. As long as military personnel stay out of the brothels, any threat to the military is essentially nil.

When I arrive back at the hotel this evening, the entire fenced-off enclosure of the hotel and grounds have hundreds of B-girls clinging to the wire, looking in at business that has been lost. They are as thick as mosquitoes clinging to the netting of a jungle hammock hanging in a Florida swamp.

When I left Cam Ranh, there were a few cases of bubonic plague admitted to the hospital. I was glad to avoid this added complication to the practice of medicine. Now it seems that the plague has followed me to Vung Tau. As I've learned throughout all of my life, you can't run away from trouble! As far as Vung Tau is concerned, the G.I.s will be better off by avoiding exposure to the venereal diseases of the brothels.

With the plague issue under control, I can enjoy reading all of my back mail that has finally arrived from Cam Ranh. There are several food parcels from aunts and uncles, parents and grandparents. Multiple back letters from Elaine are read over and over as I try to catch up on news from a sane world in the United States. Elaine continues her Ph.D. research at the University of Texas in Austin. The doctorate will be in molecular biology, and therefore, a joint sponsorship between the departments of zoology and biochemistry. She is involved in electron microscopy for much of her research. Her letters are filled with the daily vicissitudes of university politics, vagaries of science and activities of daily living. I find her research to be quite fascinating and long to share it with her in the future.

We discuss the forty acres of land that we purchased near Lakeway, Texas, and the implications of the "oil lease" in the contract. Elaine has made it clear that she intends to finish her Ph.D. and then apply to medical school. Medical school is not a popular subject in the world of non-medical academia. There is intense animosity between the "pure science" of a Ph.D. and the applied science of medical school. A large number of Ph.D.s could not get into medical school and the ashes of defeat continue to be bitter in their mouths.

I received a letter today from Master Sgt. Calindine, my noncommissioned officer in charge of the flight surgeon's office at Cam Ranh. I recommended him for the Bronze Star Award before I left Cam Ranh. Apparently the nomination was approved, but he had not received the award yet. He has been an outstanding NCOIC at Cam Ranh and I was very happy to recommend him for this award. Hopefully, it will be of help toward his future career in the Air Force.

15 March 1967

The days are hectic as we travel from place to place immunizing the personnel against plague. Vung Tau has now been declared, "on limits" for military personnel. The reason for this escapes me. Immunization stations are on every street corner. All Vietnamese stand in lines to receive their immunization before they are allowed on base. There seems a total incomprehension of the problem. Yes, the disease can be transmitted from person to person by contact or inhalations of another's sputum from a cough, but this is not the dominant mode of transmission. The dominant transmission is by fleas from rats that run rampant in the brothels and living quarters. The town has been declared open for G.I.s who wish to return to the brothels, where rats and fleas are in abundance. All the vaccine in the world isn't going to prevent the disease until the source of rats/fleas is removed from the equation. Perhaps, this is the military method of maintaining favorable public relations with the civilian authorities.

A very old Vietnamese woman cleans our quarters. About six inches from my head is a window with an open screen. While sitting in bed, trying to read with a flashlight, I suddenly sensed that someone was watching me. I looked up, and there, with her nose pressed against the screen, was this hag. It really startled me. She let out a cackle, like the witches in "Macbeth," and disappeared. If I were anywhere other than in Vietnam, I would have notified security. It would be a simple matter for her to slit the screen and drop in a hand grenade. There has never been such an incident in Vung Tau, but I don't want to be the first example.

Today, after a short lunch break, I returned to the hotel to retrieve a paper that I had forgotten this morning. I walked in to find my roommate, an Air Force major and pilot, bedding down one of his Asiatic whores. Since this is my room as well as his, I was quite aggravated by the whole event. The experience is eventually diluted out by my duties in dealing with the plague situation throughout the city. Just as I was leaving the hotel and returning to the office, another pilot approached and asks if I'd like to have lunch with him. I said, okay. On the way to the club for a hamburger, he makes some comment about swapping rooms with me so that I can have some privacy. Since he also shares his room, I couldn't quite figure out what he was talking about and just shrugged it off. In the evening when I got back, the door to my room was locked up, windows were sealed and shutters were closed. I then realized that this forty-year-old major and father of three had another "date." I got so damn mad, I just walked around cursing to myself. Finally I called my corpsman at the office to come get me and take me back to the office. Since I was locked out of my room, I couldn't get my glasses, pens and notes. And since there are no other vacant rooms in the area, I have no guarantee that it won't be worse if I transfer elsewhere. I guess I'll simply grit my teeth for another two weeks and then get the hell out of this miserable place!

Early in the day when I was at the office, one of the older Air Force majors came in for a visit. He seemed rather despondent and stated that he's "about had it." This is his second straight year away from home and family. He was in the African desert last year and spent less than two months with his wife and family. As soon as he returned from Africa, he had orders to report to Vietnam. His wife is German and she is staying in Germany with their three children. He started explaining rather apologetically that he "just isn't worth anything without his wife." I said, "Hell, you don't have to be ashamed of it. That's the first normal reaction I've heard in quite a while."

I told him that I would help in any way possible to find a way for him to get two weeks' leave, by hook or crook, to fly to Germany and see his wife. The missions that he flies here aren't very interesting. They are consumed by transporting pigs, chickens and ammunition by air cargo from one squalid base to another. All in all, a job description not unlike a localized truck driver. I can't envision this as an issue of job satisfaction.

17 March 1967

Dr. Metz Wright is a lieutenant colonel and deputy hospital commander at Cam Ranh Bay. Metz is a thoracic surgeon in civilian practice and a USAF Reserve officer who volunteered for duty in Vietnam. On his way to Can Tho for a chest consultation, he was delayed at Vung Tau, en route to Can Tho. He is very personable and we get along well together. I spent the better part of today driving him around to see the local color. His arrival and tour has helped the day pass faster. I informed him of my visit to Saigon and meeting with Major Johnson. He warned me not to be assured by anything that issues from Johnson's mouth since he is a snake and not to be trusted. He is noted for speaking from both sides of his mouth, depending on the situation.

He commented that I was the last doctor to be allowed temporary duty (TDY) in my travel to the U.S. for any reason. Apparently, there is a turf battle in progress between Colonel Mack at Cam Ranh and Colonel Barnum at 7th Air Force Headquarters in Saigon. Colonel Barnum has issued an edict that that there will be no more TDY's outside Vietnam for any reason without the express approval and blessing of 7th Air Force Headquarters in Saigon.

Colonel Mack is fundamentally a fighter pilot who has an M.D. degree. He has the devil-may-care personality of a fighter pilot. Dr. Barnum is fundamentally a physician who follows the rules and thinks in a straight line. On an administrative basis, Barnum outranks Colonel Mack and it galls him to deal with the independent spirit of Colonel Mack. They can never comprehend each other and they will forever be in conflict. Colonel Mack is a pragmatist who deals with life as it is. Colonel Barnum follows the rules that define what life should be, according to Air Force regulations. As Rudyard Kipling stated:

"East is East and West is West and never the twain shall meet..."

I am grateful that I sneaked beneath the wire by getting in my bootleg flight to the United States.

Today one of the interpreters at the office, a secretary, had abdominal pains and I was asked to see her. She had been seen by a French doctor in

Saigon, and after spending a small fortune by Vietnamese standards ($6 per office visit plus $10-$12 worth of nostrums at each visit), I was surprised with her next statements.

She had tried to consult the American civilian doctor in Saigon, but he had a long waiting list and was more expensive than the French doctors. I asked her to repeat the last statement. The only American medical doctors in this country are military physicians, public health physicians or private practitioners who come to this war-torn country to render charity care. Since the public health service physicians are usually career zealots who believe that they carry the wonders of medical science to the heathen, and also believe that all earthly treasures are evil, I eliminated them rather quickly. Nor do I believe that physician volunteers would perform in this manner. Most of these physicians have left prosperous practices for two to three months to come here. Certainly, with these altruistic ideals, it would make no sense for these physicians to "moonlight" for extra money during their short stay in-country. The only remaining choice is that of military physicians, who moonlight by practicing with the civilian, Vietnamese population.

This is blatantly wrong. They are probably physician draftees who resent being assigned to Vietnam. They utilize military supplies to equip their off-base offices while locking-in to the full potential of military medicine for their own enrichment. Medications to treat patients and equipment to examine patients are stolen from the U.S. military supply depots. It is not right to ask American taxpayers to make them wealthier. The chances that they take are phenomenal. The entire war is such a glass house over here that the newspapers would have a party with an expose of these medical black marketeers. The entire medical profession would justly receive an enormous black eye. This is especially true since the physician has lately become the public whipping boy for all social injustices.

19 March 1967

The situation at the office is nearing the boiling point. Dr. Kabaka, the "otolaryngologist," of which I have spoken, gave one of my corpsmen a note to pass to me. It suggested that I stay in the office for longer hours. Since the Air Force has only one room in the Army dispensary, they feel that we owe them something. (The U.S. Air Force pays the Army up to $50,000 per month for additional medical support here.) In short, he wants me to work longer hours to see Army personnel to allow him more time off.

My corpsman noted that Tom Robinson, being very easygoing, acceded to his demands. But he added that Dr. Robinson became very angry on many occasions. Dr. Kabaka is not the smartest dog in the kennel or he would have realized by now that I am not Dr. Robinson. Since he doesn't have the guts to approach me personally, I will ignore his suggestion. When or if he has the guts to approach me personally, I will tell him to go straight to hell. He doesn't tell me anything. I will continue to run my office in the manner that I choose.

I have spoken with Colonel Owens, the ranking Air Force officer in charge here, and requested that he find more suitable quarters for Air Force medicine, to save the Air Force money. There is little question of what is right or wrong in this matter. I owe no allegiance to either the U.S. Army Medical Corps or to Dr. Kabaka. But this type of big city bully can make it unpleasant if you are working in adjacent offices. If my stay in Vung Tau is extended, I will move out. There is no love lost between the Air Force and the Army. The Air Force would be delighted by not having to pay $50,000 a month to the Army.

21 March 1967

My tour in Vung Tau has brought me face to face with the reality of general medical practice in the military. The flying that I love is non-existent in this assignment. As a flight surgeon, my patients are pilots or enlisted men on flying status. Staying away from doctors is a sacrosanct habit to assure your flying status. If they can't fly, they receive no flight pay. But aside from the financial aspect, most flying personnel love their work.

At Vung Tau, I see all Air Force personnel, from cooks to mechanics. Very few are pilots or aircrew members. The difference from this assignment and my duties at Cam Ranh is phenomenal. Most patients are young men who use sick call for a thousand ulterior purposes. For some reason it annoys me to have a husky twenty-year-old kid enter the office shaking like a leaf and complaining of "heart pains" or complaining of "vague tingly sensations all over." In the safest assignment in Vietnam, the incidence of hypochondriasis and free-floating anxiety is rampant. When I was that age, concerns about my health were nonexistent. I never had any desire to see a doctor about anything. Some of these kids seem to pride themselves on invalidism and seem upset that I, the physician, can find no physical problem. When informed of this, they get this wounded doe look in their eyes, as if to say: "You can't kid me. I know that I've got at least a little, bitty cancer somewhere in my body…even if you can't find it!"

After four or five of these patients in a row, I feel like locking the door to the office. These young men must spend their entire day concentrating on a minor sprain, just to egg it on and hope it will spread. These are the patients that the general medical officers see daily, one after another, and then have the moxie to comment to me, "Gee, it's too bad that you are a flight surgeon…you never see any real medicine!" Yeah, right! For this you went through four years of medical school and another year of internship!

The only readily available place to get a morning cup of coffee before work is the hotel bar. Several young Vietnamese bar girls who work there have learned that I am a physician. Whenever I approach the coffee pot, one of them will announce in a stage whisper, "Bac Sey." "Bac Sey" is Vietnamese for physician or doctor. It is rare that one will request medical advice about a minor ailment. However, this morning, I was approached by a very thin young woman, who asked me, "How I get fat?" Her phrasing of the question was so funny that I couldn't suppress smiling and a soft laugh. She said she weighs thirty-five kilos. My off-the-cuff response was, "Eat more fish and rice." She said she wanted to be, "big, like Americans." I told her that most Americans are too fat and need to lose weight. I told her that it was not healthy to be fat. None of my answers were any consolation. I was grateful when my bus to the office arrived and interrupted the conversation.

Her question raised many questions. I began to wonder just how these beautiful, tiny people must feel to see their country overrun by these giant Americans. They have previously been under Japanese occupation, but the average Japanese is also small in comparison to the average American. I don't believe that the average French man or woman is as large as the average American. Of course, the Australians are equal in size with Americans. But somehow, the Aussies seem to behave with more dignity than Americans. They don't make themselves so conspicuous all the time like the loud, garrulous American G.I. Presumably the differences in body size are due to dietary insufficiencies compared to Americans. There are many records of Asian children born and raised in America who exceed the height and weight of their Asian-born parents. Certainly, the Australians are equally nourished with Americans.

22 March 1967

Today, from 7:30 to 10 a.m., I saw fifteen patients with venereal disease. This means gonorrhea, since it has a short incubation period and is obviously present when it is too painful to urinate and pus drips from the penis. Treatment is simple, but it's like pouring penicillin in a septic tank. As soon as their symptoms clear, they will be re-infected during their next visit to the brothels. I obtain serologic tests for syphilis on each patient, but they are performed in a regional lab in Saigon. It is rare for me to receive the results during the time of my assignment.

The next part of the day was equally thrilling. From 10 a.m. to 2:30 p.m., I inspected septic tanks that have overflowed. Since I am the only Air Force physician here, I am, by default, chief of public health. I visited four different types of septic tanks bound together in the Brotherhood of Septic Tanks by oozing their fragrant contents out on the ground and even into the living quarters and work spaces of several facilities. I have never before truly appreciated the individuality that seems inherent in different types of septic tanks.

With only seventy remaining days in Vietnam, I am beginning to compare myself to the trials of Odysseus in Homer's "Odyssey." As Odysseus attempts to return to his native Island of Ithaca after the Trojan war, he passes through many tribulations and trials. One of his sojourns is to pass through hell along the way. I don't know what his hell smelled like, but I doubt that it could be worse than the septic dysfunctions of Vung Tau!

After my inspection of these odiferous elements, the base commander requests that I write a complete report of each errant repository, stating why, in my professional opinion, I consider it unhealthy to have raw feces floating through hallways and rooms. While he is speaking, I'm sure that my eyes opened wider and wider in disbelief of what I was hearing. The sarcastic side of my personality wanted to tell him that raw feces flowing through rooms and hallways exerts a delightful invigorating effect on human perception and performance. The malodors heighten one's mental alertness and physical agility by improving the sense of balance as one runs through the hallways... But I knew my humor would be wasted. Anyone who asks questions such as this could never understand the humor of my response!

Therefore, I give my reports to a sergeant, who types each of the four reports and submits them in five copies to the squadron commander. The squadron commander, in turn, endorses my report by confirming that there is indeed a problem as I, the Expert, have described.

After the reports have received the proper official sanctions, they are submitted to the base engineer. The base engineer then convenes a committee to decide if the request for corrective action is truly justified. If the civil engineering committee approves the reports in favor of corrective action, the next big decision will be what level of priority to place on the corrective action. This will entail deciding whether repairing the air conditioning unit in the colonel's office has priority over septic tank repair. And, finally, after priorities have been assigned, there is the ultimate and most critical decision! Since there are four septic tank failures, the committee must decide which septic tank should be repaired first! This last decision must be made in compliance with a separate priority being assigned to each unhappy septic tank.

All of this makes you think twice about past wars. If we won World War II over the Germans and Japanese, it boggles your mind to think how screwed up those countries must have been! After today, I'll be afraid to use the toilet for fear of running into an acquaintance when I flush it!

Tonight while I was going to a dinner of dehydrated cabbage in the hotel, I was introduced to a U.S. Navy physician. He and I are about the same age and, like me, he is interested in internal medicine. He is clean-cut and handsome, but here all attraction ends. During an introductory conversation, he is as curt and surly as a bitch dog with puppies. To open the conversation, I ask where he had trained. He spat out, "Medical School-University of Michigan, Residency-George Washington University in Washington, D.C." It was all spoken very curtly. I thought, well, I'll try one more time. I politely ask if he were going into practice when he returned to the States this summer. He said, "Yes, in Connecticut." I was somewhat surprised and replied how unusual it is to encounter someone from the Western U.S. moving to the Eastern U.S. Usually, it's the other way around. He said: "My home is in Connecticut. I went to school in Michigan. I like snow." By this time I began to wonder if perhaps he had not been standing out in the snow too long and developed permafrost brain. We finished eating at the same time. He abruptly got up, shoved his hand into mine and departed. With such an encounter, I wondered who had put grit into his pablum. Maybe this is simply a manifestation of standard New England personality. I was once informed that despite my Southern accent, I had the personality of a New England farmer. Perhaps, the combination confused him.

Ah, well, "Life is funny," said Jeremy. "As compared to what...?" replied the Spider.

I wrote to Elaine after I read Tortilla Flat by John Steinbeck. The setting is Monterey, California, and it is delightful, just as is Cannery Row. His characters are paisanos. At the very beginning, Steinbeck asks, "What is a Paisano?" He is a mixture of Spanish, Indian, Mexican and assorted Caucasian bloods. He speaks English with a Paisano accent and Spanish with a Paisano accent. When questioned about his race, he indignantly claims pure Spanish blood and rolls up his sleeve to show that the soft inside of his arm is really white. His color he ascribes to sunburn.

One of the characters questions the source of the money donated as tithe for Mass. The other replies, "A Mass is a Mass. Where a Mass comes from is of no interest to God. He just likes them, the same as you like wine."

Steinbeck's description of "fat ladies, in whose eyes lay the weariness and wisdom that one sees so often in the eyes of pigs…" is exquisite.

I would give anything to be able to write like that. It would be wonderful to know that merely by reading one's words someone has gained insight into life or found expression for thoughts that he/she has been unable to portray or express.

23 March 1967

Shortly after I arrived at the office this morning, Dr. Kabaker sent three corpsmen in to ask if I would start seeing Army sick call. I emphatically said, "No!" Finally I got so angry that I simply walked out. I left the clinic offices and returned to the hotel to cool off, but the longer I sat and stewed about the issue, the angrier I became. I don't like to carry that much anger, and I was determined not to get an ulcer about this or any other issue.

I learned long ago as a child that the best way to deal with a problem is to confront it head-on. With this in mind, I caught a ride back to the base. At the Army headquarters office, I obtained a copy of the official contract about the obligations of the U.S. Air Force, as a tenant unit, to the U.S. Army in Vung Tau. It clearly states that the Air Force is responsible for providing flight surgeon duties and nothing else. The Army is receiving pay from the Air Force for use of hospital, lab, X-ray and other facilities.

I know that an encounter with Dr. Kabaker will only be an exercise in futility. Therefore, I go directly to the Army colonel, who is commanding officer of the Army hospital and the entire U.S. Army medical unit here. I politely ask if he will please read the contract and interpret it for me in regard to the commitment of the U.S. Air Force and its obligations to the U.S. Army. I further note that I do not like to be imposed upon, especially under the pretenses that I owe anything to the Army or to anyone else for anything.

The colonel has never seen the agreement before. After reading it he confirms the obvious. The Air Force is merely a "tenant unit" and owes absolutely nothing to the United States Army. Any services beyond that of providing a flight surgeon have already been paid under terms of the agreement. I then ask if he would please make this clear to Dr. Kabaker. By doing this, I feel as if a stone has been removed from chest. I also state that I would prefer not to take these differences to a "higher level" of decision.

About two hours later, Kabaker comes into the office with an obsequious, nervous smile on his face. He asks me, "Have you been upset about anything?" I said, "Only for a short time, but I'm not anymore." He started to deny all of his previous statements. Unfortunately for him there were witnesses to his previous statements as well as to his notes to me. I call the witnesses in to verify the multiple times he has made statements to the effect that "I should earn my keep," etc. He becomes agitated and extremely upset. He launches into multiple explanations as he tried to hedge his words and intentions.

I listened quietly, as did more witnesses, a crowd of which has gathered outside the door. They are U.S. Army corpsmen who detest Kabaker. Sensing that he is wounded, they chime in on my side to refute his every statement. After a few minutes Kabaker begins to flounder and choke on his own sputum as his face flushes and he hurriedly leaves the room. I don't think I've experienced such intense satisfaction with any event since I arrived in Vung Tau. I just feel good all over watching that bastard crawl out the door, slipping and tripping on his own lies. I learned later that Robinson used to see as many as three-fourths of the Army patients. One of the corpsmen noted that he had overheard Kabaker saying: "No, I'm tired of seeing patients today. Give it to Robinson." Initially, Tom would get angry, but his primary concern was taking care of the patients…not passing the buck. This would happen over and over again. I continue to believe the best way to solve a problem is to confront it head-on. You can either be a hammer or a nail. I just don't think it's healthy, mentally or physically, to be angry all the time.

Tonight I had dinner with a young Air Force pilot and lieutenant who was exceptionally intelligent. He is separating from the Air Force when his military obligation is over. He is from Carmel, California, and we began to discuss John Steinbeck. He said that two to three months ago Steinbeck came to the officers club in Vung Tau. Someone asked Steinbeck what he thought of Vung Tau. Steinbeck paused for a moment, then said, "I think it's a town that never was." Only Steinbeck could encapsulate the city and the mood so succinctly!

Today I found a quote from Thoreau that was new to me. "A man sits as many risks as he runs. We must walk consciously only part way towards our goal, and then leap into the darkness for our success."

I can only reflect upon myself as I left Florida with $700 in my pocket to pay for four years at Northwestern University Medical School. Having been raised on a Georgia farm and in a Florida swamp, and having learned to read from comic books, I had nothing to offer except the fire in my belly. This was my "leap into the darkness."

CHAPTER 35

Leaving Vung Tau

24 March 1967

Tonight is my last night as MOD in Vung Tau. I am very happy to be finishing my assignment here, and even happier to end this dysfunctional marriage with the U.S. Army.

25 March 1967

Last night was busy. I only obtained about one hour of sleep. The cases were not particularly difficult, but the volume was constant all through the night.

Non-commissioned officers are the backbone of the Air Force. The officers get the recognition, but the work is done by the NCOICs. Master Sergeant Hendley is the NCOIC for the flight surgeon's office. He has been extremely helpful in obtaining wooden footlockers from the Army for me. I can use these in a couple of months when I leave Cam Ranh Bay.

26 March 1967

Today, I fly from Vung Tau to Tan Son Nhut in Saigon to shop for Vietnamese native handicraft for gifts back home. It is a futile mission. The carved woodcraft sculptures are attractive, but a number of people advised me not to buy them. They are frequently carved from green wood. Initially they seem okay in this tropical humidity, but when removed from this environment, they all split after they arrive in the U.S. I fly back to Vung Tau empty-handed.

I have been awakened at 3 a.m. for the past two weeks by the sounds of cats fighting outside my window. This afternoon I walk up to the second-floor balcony and discover the source of the noise. In the rain gutter of the adjacent building, a mother cat has given birth to four kittens. They toss and tumble in the leaves, totally oblivious to the world below. Just before sunset, I look up to see all four kittens as they venture out for the first time to explore the roof. They gambol and play precariously on the ledges...all under the watchful eye of their mammy. Every so often one will slip and tumble from the roof...only to be saved by the six-inch-wide rain gutter, in which they were born. I am delighted to watch those kittens at play. Finally, they returned to their nest of leaves. Since they have never touched the ground, those kittens are probably the cleanest animals in Vietnam.

This evening after dinner, I decided to take a short stroll through the downtown area. I looked up to see an Australian soldier approaching me. He was obviously very tipsy as he circumnavigated toward me. He politely removed his cap and said, "Pardon me, Mate Sir, could you tell me where the 'Honeymoon Bar' is?" It takes all my restraint to keep from laughing at such an incongruous name. I reply that I don't know the location, but there is a military policeman around the corner and I am sure that he would be able to direct him. He jumps back as if I had jabbed him with a hot poker!

"Thank you, no, Sir; I tries to stay clear of those types!" He continues on his circuitous path down the street. He is so funny!

28 March 1967

For Air Force purposes, the reason for my existence is to serve as flight surgeon. In order to qualify and to continue in this position, I must have four hours per month flight time. Since my assignment in Vung Tau has been remarkably inefficient in flying duties, I decide to spend the day flying with one of the Caribou crews.

The aircraft commander is Captain Piety. The mission is to shuttle "as required" out of Vung Tau. The missions are primarily in support of small United States Army Special Forces camps that are scattered throughout the Delta region. At Vung Tau, we receive a load of ammunition, food, blankets and various other items to sustain the men in these terribly isolated garrisons. We make a number of trips to camps that are yet unnamed, camps that are represented simply by a number designating their whereabouts on the map. The landing strips average 1,200 feet and have been laid off from the adjacent swamp and plains region. Ordinarily, these landings are rather routine and without incident.

At Vung Tau, a Green Beret sergeant is supervising the Vietnamese workmen in the unloading of the aircraft. The sergeant is a tall, gawky, redneck who obviously feels that these "supervisory duties" are not part of his job description. He has recently been assigned to this work, and is distraught about the mental challenges and decisions to be made. For example, "should the blankets for Camp No. 1 be loaded before the food for Camp No. 2, or should cases of C-rations with beans be off-loaded before the cases of C-rations with cheese & crackers?" He comments that he is at his best when fighting. His difficulties with the Vietnamese laborers are evident. Frequently one of the laborers will become upset over his orders and simply find a quiet corner to sulk. The sergeant's language is not flowery. And, since it is limited to one or two choice expressions of profanity, his vocabulary is not extensive. In fact, whether the topic of discussion is the U.S. Army, the Republic of Vietnam Army, blankets, guns, ammunition or runway materials, he has only one, hyphenated adjective.

He speaks of "Mutha-fukin airplanes, guns, ammunitions, wars, rivers…" and all other physical entities. As the loading and unloading progresses, he becomes progressively more agitated as he mutters about the stupidity of the Mutha-fukin Vietnamese while pacing up and down, the Mutha-fukin Heat and Mutha-fukin Life in general. After almost an hour of these expostulations, he turns a florid face to us and mutters, somewhat incoherently, "I've got to get out of the Mutha-Fukin job." He develops a querulous, wide-eyed look of self-pity, and taps his head with his index finger, stating, "This work is affecting my Mutha-fuking mind." He is obviously a very sensitive person who had been shunted into an insensitive job.

Our shuttle mission is to deliver several thousand pounds of cement to a small camp on the Cambodian border by the name of Chau Doc. Chau Doc is on the edge of the Mekong Delta. It is a stepping stone into Vietnam for travelers arriving from Cambodia and the opposite for Vietnamese entering Cambodia. I learn later that the region is being serviced by Air America, the aviation wing of the CIA.

From the air at this time of the year, the land beneath us appears as a desert-like expanse of brown soil. However, during the late summer and winter months, the entire area is submerged and affords some of the most fertile farmland for rice and other semi-aquatic crops.

As we approach, it is difficult to define a runway from the adjacent turf. Finally Captain Piety points the runway out to me. The landing strip is no more than a strip of dirt without demarcation or definition from all the other land around it. It becomes clearer as we descend that the runway is smoother than the adjacent land. The tires of previous, landing aircraft have smoothed out a narrow strip. While on final approach, I look out. For miles on every side, there is no vegetation to speak of...only miles and miles of sunbaked clay. Bordering the landing strip are dwellings that resemble "lean-to's." These bear a remarkable resemblance to the primitive huts of the American Plains Indians during the nineteenth century.

The aircraft has barely stopped when suddenly, as if on signal, hoards of small brown figures seem to bloom out of the anonymity of brown clay and stream toward us from every direction. They converge on the landing site and envelop the aircraft, like so many ants might capture an unwitting insect that has strayed into their domain.

By the time we reverse engines and stop, the aircraft has become completely enveloped by masses of humanity. The propellers are still turning and for their safety, we fire our M-16 rifles into the air as warning not to approach farther.

Nearly every inch of the wings, fuselage and tail section is covered with children, men and women, old and young, clinging to the surfaces of the aircraft. Their faces are a study of querulous humanity. Their voices and eyes are filled with childlike innocence of utter astonishment and fascination to be near this giant bird. From the masses of people arises a single chorus of universal utterances of awe, joy and fascination to suddenly realize that this aircraft was the embodiment of something they have seen flying high above them in the unreachable sky. The entire scene is extraordinary. Old men with grey beards grin with toothless mouths agape as they timidly touch the aircraft with their fingertips. Their expressions and eyes reflect the innocence and awe of children as they explore life and view its wonders for the first time. Entire families turn out. Small boys fight for position to get closer to the aircraft, while mothers with infants, suckling at their breast, crowd in fascination about the plane. Some lift their infants from the breast and hold them up to face the aircraft, as if to record in their memory this once-in-a-lifetime event. I stand in the doorway, point my camera down and snap a photograph. The crowding has become so dense that it is extremely difficult for us to climb out of the plane.

An acquaintance noted a similar response when he landed in a primitive portion of Laos. There, old men, women and children crawled under the aircraft to determine its gender.

Finally, after managing to climb down, we are engulfed by the crowd. They are extremely friendly as they gently touch our clothing with nearly religious awe. The dress of individuals is varied, with no great distinction between the sexes. The men wear ragged, blousy trousers without shirts. They frequently wear a turban on the head, presumably as protection from the sun. Women are clothed in very loose slacks with relatively close-fitting blouses.

We receive word that the arrival of the Special Forces team to unload the aircraft had been delayed. The heat of the sun is so intense that we decide to re-board the aircraft to find shade. As we began to move, there is a reflex response from the crowd, as a nervous sense of urgency seems to sweep over the multitude. They progressively tighten their encirclement around us. It mimics the tightening grasp of an animal that senses the struggle of its prey to escape...a giant snake that reflexively constricts its coils tighter as the victim's efforts to escape increase. The crush becomes greater and greater as more hands from more children tug at our clothing, desperate to maintain tactile contact with our bodies. By the time I reach the ladder, hundreds of hands grip my feet and legs, while other hands grab at my belt and shirt to immobilize me. Suddenly I realized how people are trampled and crushed in large crowds. There is no malicious intent. It is their overwhelming curiosity and friendly efforts to touch and grasp us that are rapidly becoming a hazard. The hands relentlessly tug at every available crease, flap and fold of our clothing until we began to be drawn backward and down into the maw of the multitude. My attempt to climb the ladder into the aircraft is impossible. My grasps on the rungs of the ladder are ripped free and I realize that if I trip and fall down, it will be nearly impossible to get up. Through it all, there is deafening childlike laughter and expressions of joy, all as gay and innocent as children clutching favorite toys. The combination of voices and emotions are approaching hysteria, as grasping hands and the torrid heat all seem to self-organize, and generate a vortex of energies from which there is no escape.

The loadmaster, who has remained on the aircraft, recognizes our plight. He shouts to the crowd, but his voice is drowned out and lost in the tumult. Finally, he fires several rounds from his M-16 into the air over their heads. The crowd disperses like frightened children and we climb back aboard.

After we are safely aboard the plane, the crowd continues to mill around the aircraft, but not with the same intensity as when actual physical contact existed between us and them. After approximately thirty minutes, two one-and-a-half-ton trucks arrive to relieve us of our cement cargo. The trucks are manned by Army Special Forces personnel, replete with newly pressed fatigues, mirror-polished combat boots and, of course, Green Berets adorning their heads.

Supervising these select warriors is a Special Forces major. I am instantly reminded of the Pennsylvania farmer described by Stephen Vincent Benet in *John Brown's Body*. His description of "a Ham of a Man" could never be applied more appropriately. Like most members of his proud corps, he considers himself to be endowed with superhuman attributes of strength and physical prowess. Leaping up the ramp into the cargo hold, he immediately begins to wrestle with 500-pound bags of cement while barking orders to his troops. When one of the trucks is not pulled up close enough to the ramp, he shouts an order to one of his sergeants, but the response is too slow for his taste. With impatience and disgust, he jumps down off the ramp, grabs a cable and strains to manually pull the truck up closer. He is in constant motion, ordering his men and moving tons of cement by himself. His florid facies and muscular jowls are accentuated as he puffs and bellows until his chest expands like a grouse cock performing a mating dance. It is obvious to all that he is enjoying himself immensely.

He treats all of our aircrew members with remarkable deference, as if to acknowledge his kinship with "these brothers of the air." After each bellow to his hapless subordinates, he pauses to look around with a disarming smile of bewilderment, tinged with childish delight at the frantic activity that he has provoked. He is in his early forties, but his purpose in life seems dedicated to proving that he is a better man than any of the younger bucks. And from my personal observation, this is a point well taken.

At the conclusion of unloading the aircraft, he becomes a host who sincerely hates to bid his guests farewell. He comes to each crewmember, pilot, co-pilot, loadmaster and me, grasping our hands in both of his massive paws, in appreciation for our visit and services. After fulfilling these social graces, he hurtles off the rear ramp in a gesture of grand farewell. When the propellers start, the resultant dust storm makes breathing impossible for any ordinary mortal caught in the prop wash. All of the Vietnamese flee before the cyclonic furies of the engines' wake. Even the trucks beat a hasty retreat out of its path. But, standing in the vortex of it all is the major, his feet planted in the clay like Atlas, defying all tempests. He grins handsomely as the wind and dust tear at his clothing and lash his face. With legs planted in broad-based stance and hands set in defiance on his hips, like a Titan of old, he gloriously defies the tempests. By now the plane has full brakes, full power and full flaps for a short-field takeoff. With the tons of concrete removed, it suddenly lurches forward, spewing tumultuous clouds of dust and speeds down the short runway before it vaults into the air. I am choking with dust that covers the interior of the aircraft and continues to ascend with us to a height of 500 feet. As we circle the field to begin our return flight to Vung Tau, I peer out through the open cargo door. The entire area is enveloped in the reddish-brown cloud of dust, but in my mind's eye, I continue to see a sun-burned "Ham-of-a Man," standing like the Rock of Gibraltar, with flashing blue eyes and a bright smile through gleaming white teeth…lifting his hand to wave a gallant farewell.

The flight back to Vung Tau is uneventful. When I arrive at the hotel, I am delighted to find my roommate had been transferred out and for my last night in Vung Tau, I have a private room. I have little time to relish this luxury since I have hardly taken a shower before I am called to the dispensary by three pilots who have relatively minor complaints. I arrive back at the hotel at 1 a.m.

I've just learned that the Air Force has an Aero Club at Tan Son Nhut Air Force Base in Saigon. I can't believe the foolishness of having small aircraft for sport flying in a combat zone. They practice on a small dirt strip outside of Saigon. That area is not secure by any means. Shooting touch-and-go landings in an unarmed aircraft, while being shot at, is not my idea of fun. Perhaps flight instruction is part of the new recreation program for enlisted men. Some things in life I will never understand.

Tomorrow, at 5 a.m., I leave Vung Tau for my flight back to Cam Ranh…hallelujah!

CHAPTER 36

Return to Cam Ranh Bay

29 March 1967

Finally, I am back at my beloved Cam Ranh Bay. What a relief to be out of Vung Tau! This morning when I walked into the flight surgeon's office, I couldn't believe my reception. Sergeant Xeras, the senior master sergeant and NCOIC, nearly fell at my feet. It was embarrassing. He kept saying over and over again, "Oh, thank God, you're back... Thank God, you're back!"

There is no question here about my authority in the office. In fact, the problem is that no one wants to accept responsibility for anything. Sam Hyde is an experienced flight surgeon. I expected that he would be delighted with my absence so that he could be chief, but he was overjoyed to relinquish my desk back to me. Major Gorman, who is director of aeromedical services and is technically my immediate boss, walked in during our discussion. With a look of relieved desperation on his face, he blurts out before Hyde and all of the office staff, "Whew! Am I ever glad that you're back...and I'm sure everyone else is, too!"

I must say it's nice to be appreciated!

It is now confirmed that I will remain here at Cam Ranh and not return to Vung Tau. Seventh Air Force Headquarters in Saigon called Colonel McElvain yesterday and requested that he choose an FMO1 for permanent change of station to Vung Tau. David Byron was selected. I personally like Dave and hate to lose him from the office, but in light of what follows, I'm not surprised at Colonel Mack's choice. While I was at Vung Tau, Sam Hyde assumed my position as chief of aviation medicine. Sam is experienced and has a good head on his shoulders. I would hate to lose him in transfer to Vung Tau.

Apparently Lon Kerry, another FMO, is on R&R with his wife in Hawaii.

David Byron, however, has been in one of his depressed states, drinking all night as an escape and not arriving for work until noon or later. In the past week, there have been three F-4C aircraft accidents here. There were no fatalities, but each aircraft sustained considerable damage. All of this generated the usual mountain of reports, accident investigation boards and enough bureaucratic trappings to choke a horse.

Ben Bevins is our new flight medical officer. He is a graduate of Emory University Medical School, and from all appearances is a very fine person. I liked him immediately. But, he is just out of flight surgeons school and is totally green as well as understandably unsure of himself. He will be just fine in time, but there are many important issues, now pressing, that need to be resolved.

Shortly after this introduction, I learned of other critical events that occurred while I was at Vung Tau. As I noted previously, Colonel Mack had issued orders for me to accompany a "critically ill" malaria patient who was being air-evacuated back to the States. These were trumped-up orders simply to cover me and to provide an excuse for me to travel back to the U.S. in mid-tour. While the "patient" and I flew back on the same airplane, I never actually saw the patient. This was Colonel Mack's kind gesture to ease the burden of this year-long foreign tour on officers of his command. (Actually, I was the only person selected.) My first impression of this event was to ascribe it to Colonel Mack's generosity. But, on later reflection, I may have been used as the canary in the coal mine to test the waters for Colonel Mack's visit home in the States.

Apparently, Colonel Mack had informed Colonel Barnum of his intent to travel to the States under the same circumstances enjoyed by me. In some manner, Gen. William Momyer, who is head of the U.S. Air Force in Vietnam, learned about Colonel Mack's sojourn to the States and asked Colonel Barnum about it. Barnum denied any knowledge of it. Evidently, in the middle of the Da Nang Officer's Club, General Momyer practically cursed Barnum out about this issue. Barnum then called Colonel Bolt, the wing commander at Cam Ranh Bay, to inquire about "Mack," all the while denying his whereabouts. By the time Mack returned, General Momyer had worked himself up into such a furor that he was on the verge of requesting a court martial for Colonel Mack. This is a hard blow for a man of his career standing and stature. Finally, things quieted down, but now any TDY out of Vietnam must have the approval of 7th Air Force. If the TDY pertains to anywhere out of Southeast Asia, it must have the approval of PACAF (Pacific Air Force) in Hawaii.

All of these machinations were revealed to me when I reported to Colonel Mack this evening upon my return to Cam Ranh. Colonel Mack said he had expected Johnson to keep me at Vung Tau. He further noted that by my going to Saigon and confronting Johnson directly, and face-to-face, I had been saved from the fate of being transferred to Vung Tau. After Johnson reassured me that I would return to Cam Ranh, he would lose face if he went back on his word and retained me at Vung Tau. Colonel Mack then added that Johnson is too much of a snake to be that forthright.

But, I weep for Colonel Mack. Now he appears to be a defeated man as far as his military career is concerned. It grieves me. I don't know what past personal issues exist between him and Colonel Barnum. But, I do know that Colonel Mack is one of the finest men that I have ever known, and I sorely hate to see him cut to pieces by this low-level political intrigue. Both the Air Force and our country are fortunate to have someone of his caliber in their services. But, his case is an example of why so very few men of his status stay in the military. This very dedicated man has spent his entire life in the service of his country. It is tragic to see him treated so cruelly.

1 April 1967

Lon Kerry, one of our new flight medical officers, has spent the last two weeks of R&R in Hawaii with his wife. Lon is from Illinois and has spent his entire life in that state. He is friendly and has a great sense of humor. He is also entirely smitten by his new bride. She also is from Illinois and this is her first trip outside the state. Lon returned to the office today. Lordy, Lordy, they must really be a pair. His wife's all-encompassing comment as she left Hawaii was, "Now, I truly understand the Oriental people!" Whew. And I thought that I was provincial when I arrived in Chicago from the South. I suppose if she visited Georgia, she would truly understand the English Colonials better…

The squadron had a cookout tonight. They said it was to celebrate my return to Cam Ranh, but I don't believe it. Any excuse is sufficient for a party and cookout. But, whatever the reason, I must confess that it was nothing short of OUTSTANDING! Fresh vegetables were flown in from

Japan. Sirloin steaks were scrounged from the Navy. Huge crabs, shrimp and lobsters were fresh from Nha Trang. There was French bread with garlic sauce. Rarely do I remember what I have eaten, but tonight was an exception. Aside from the food, I never cease to be amazed at the high quality of these young pilots. Truly, they are the cream of American manhood.

We lost another F-4C Phantom today, on a mission about forty-nine minutes west of Da Nang in Quang Nam Province. It was a Close Air Support (CAS) Mission. The crew and aircraft belonged to the 557th TFS from Cam Ranh. The flight path was a dive-bomb run from which neither pilot had a chance to get out. Reports are that the aircraft simply hit the ground and exploded. The aircraft commander was Capt. George H. Jourdanis, an excellent pilot, whom I knew quite well. He has two small children. I didn't know the pilot in the back seat, 1st Lt. Robert W. Stanley, since he is relatively new on base. Jourdanis was considered to be one of the finest young pilots in the wing. I don't know the details of the target. The original frag was listed as a dive-bomb mission for close ground support.

At this point of my tour, sarcasm is beginning to prevail in all matters. I cannot help wondering what target was worth the death of these two fine men. Was it a bamboo bridge over a creek, built by a couple of Vietnamese farmers, overnight? The bodies of the two pilots thus far have not been recovered...

This morning at 7 a.m., when I stepped out of the Quonset hut on my way to the office, a Boeing 707 was taking off. The first rays of the rising sun caught its wings and reflected off the mountains and clouds over the mainland. Its destination is San Francisco. Suddenly, I was swept with an enormous wave of homesickness. I've had enough of Vietnam. I'm ready to come home! Buried in my reverie, I almost walked in front of a truck as I stared at the vanishing aircraft, like a thunderstruck mule with the blind stomps…

I am completely perplexed about the recent change in Viet Cong tactics. Up to now, the Viet Cong have fought a typical guerrilla-type war. Classically, guerrilla warfare, as described by historians through the ages, is to attack and then retreat. The typical "set battle" of European history, when masses of French troops faced off masses of English troops, is never fought. Guerrilla war is fought in the shadows, usually by irregular troops and not by professional soldiers. It is the battle that weaker forces must employ against stronger, armed forces that oppose them. But recently, the Viet Cong have employed the human wave assaults comparable to the Japanese in World War II and the Chinese Communists in Korea. The concept of massive, human wave assaults against a superior force is an anathema for guerrilla warfare.

Despite this, 600 Viet Cong were killed yesterday during a "human wave" attack against American forces. In addition, several hundred were killed during President Johnson's visit to Guam. The huge losses of Viet Cong are in contrast to minimal losses of American soldiers. This is sheer stupidity on the part of the Viet Cong. Like the Colonists in the American Revolution, they don't have to win the war. But they can't lose it. This is their home turf. If they simply hold on long enough, eventually we will go home, just as the British eventually went home. The French also went home after many colonial years in Indochina. The irregular forces of the Viet Cong cannot compete with the technocratic warfare of the United States; any more than modern technologic warfare can compete with the guerrilla warfare of hit-and-run tactics in a primitive, jungle environment. If they stick to guerrilla warfare, they can't lose. Courage and purity of cause cannot compete with a fusillade of cold steel bullets, napalm, bombs and rockets. The Japanese learned this the hard way on Guadalcanal during WWII.

Their courage and purity of soul amounted to little against American air, sea and land weaponry.

Today, I drove over to the new runway on the opposite side of the field from Base Operations. I specifically wanted to visit the new control tower. I am impressed. It is extremely modern and, in many ways, plush, compared to any modern U.S. airport. I was also interested to see the new area of the base that has been set aside for Navy planes. I understand that the U.S. Navy will keep twelve reconnaissance-type, multi-engine aircraft based here.

It is difficult to describe the phenomenal growth of this base during the short time I've been here. Today, when I arrive on the opposite side of the base, I pause to look around, and am amazed at the beauty of the surroundings. The ocean is crystal clear and the beaches are, by far, the most beautiful that I have ever seen. Lon Kerry said that the beaches of Waikiki were second class compared to the beaches of Cam Ranh. All of this is framed by the magnificent, jungle-cloaked mountains in the background. It is ironic that this beautiful land is so torn by the chaos and desecrations of war. I wouldn't be a bit surprised if in twenty-five to fifty years, this peninsula doesn't surpass Hong Kong both in commerce and as an international tourist attraction. I can imagine my son seeing this area in fifty years, stating: "My dad must have been crazy to complain about this. This is beautiful and really nice."

While I was visiting the new control tower, we watched an air strike by F-100 Super Sabers from Phan Rang as they dive-bombed a region about eight miles away on the mainland. We had front-row, center seats to the entire spectacle. This is a grim reminder that those beautiful green mountains contain more than trees and streams. It always seems incongruous to see such beautiful and peaceful terrain being bombed and shelled. Philosophically, it is difficult to explain. It is also a grim reminder that the enemy forces that we avoided during the December crash investigation are still there and growing in force. Eventually the military facilities at Cam Ranh Bay will be subjected to mortar attacks. Hopefully, they will defer this until I have departed.

5 April 1967

Lon Kerry sold me a Montagnard crossbow that he obtained from someone in Pleiku in the Central Highlands. I've wanted one for some time. But I never had the opportunity to fly into that region and shop for souvenirs. Since he will be over here longer than I, he can always get another one. I think they're extremely attractive and will make a fine wall ornament in our library or study.

A specific order has just been handed down from PACAF prohibiting physicians from leaving Vietnam before their DEROS. At present, I must consider this to be a rumor since there has been neither written nor verbal notification of this to me from any authority. This is interesting since I have plans to leave tomorrow for Tachikawa AFB in Japan for shopping. I choose to ignore this edict and continue my sojourn to Japan. Besides, the C-130 aircrew members are all patients and my job as flight surgeon is to fly with my aircrew members!

7 April 1967
Tachikawa, Japan

Yesterday, I had lunch with a C-130 pilot from Tachikawa AFB. He was very congenial and asked if I would like to fly back with him to Tachikawa. I accepted his invitation since this will allow me a chance to call Elaine and to inquire about an FAA physical. The offer was too good to turn down.

We arrived without incident at Tachikawa and now I am staying at the BOQ (Base Officers Quarters) for $1.25 a night. The rooms are very nice. They are semi-private and have private baths. Japan is lovely in the spring. Cherry trees are blooming and the air is cool and crisp. Unfortunately, it isn't as easy to leave here as it is to get here. Even though as a flight surgeon I have orders that allow me to fly as a crewmember, there are problems. At the present time I'm supposed to leave tomorrow at 1 p.m. for Taiwan. However, things can change a thousand times between now and then, and I expect them to. Unfortunately, the Air Force is far from being an airline and nothing is ever definite.

8 April 1967

It is 8 a.m. and I am at the coffee shop next to Tachikawa's Base Operations, awaiting a flight out. The spring weather in Japan is delightful and so much in contrast to the monotony of the heat at Cam Ranh Bay.

On the way to Japan I finished reading The Grapes of Wrath by Steinbeck. It is quite unlike Steinbeck's other books, Cannery Row or Tortilla Flat. It has a note of his social evangelism throughout. After reading it I can easily understand why Steinbeck is considered the foremost American writer by the literary elite in the Soviet Union. It is very anti-capitalistic and even pro-communistic in portions. However, I do not believe that Steinbeck is pro-communist, in person or in his philosophy. He saw a tragic social drama and depicted it brilliantly. It is, rather, a commentary on industrialization and mechanization, and the consequences of these changes on the pristine pure American peasant (Southern rednecks/sharecroppers/farmers). Having known these types all of my life, it is fairly easy to empathize with his characters, but for someone who has never had contact with them, they must seem quite fictitious. The Cedar Choppers of Central Texas are another prime example of these types. In the Florida Keys, they are known as "Conchs." There is no question about The Grapes of Wrath being a classic American social novel. I regard it as a companion novel to Studs Lonigan…each portraying different and incurable problems. Well! So much for GSC's Literary Guild…

9 April 1967

After sitting on the ramp/runway at Tachikawa for most of the day, we finally take off at 7 p.m. The flight plan is scheduled to go directly to Ching Chuan Kang Air Base, which is a Republic of China Air Force Base located on Taiwan. It is about 100 miles from Taipei, where the parents of our friends at the University of Texas in Austin, live. Our flight has been delayed all day by bad weather from a typhoon sweeping through the Philippines. Forty-five minutes before we are to land at CCK, we are informed by radio that the field is closed because of the typhoon. We divert to Naha AFB, Okinawa. From Naha, we fly directly to Cam Ranh Bay. The opportunity to pay my respects to our friend's parents has been lost.

It is becoming progressively more difficult to travel under a flight surgeons blanket crew orders. There are simply too many flight surgeons over here flying under similar orders. I happened to meet a flight surgeon from CCK on the flight. He went to high school with Bill Anthony, who interned with me at Wilford Hall from 1963-1964.

I also ran into a B-52 pilot I knew at Bergstrom. He now flies C-130s out of CCK. Since CCK is considered to be an "Isolated Duty Station," his wife remains in Austin.

Elaine, it was so thoughtful for you to include a sprig of Wisteria in your last letter. You always know how to touch my heart!

10 April 1967

Back at Cam Ranh, the beat goes on...and on... At 3:30 a.m., we had a C-130 accident with seven people involved. Although no one was scratched, the incident consumed the entire night, and the paperwork will consume the next few days.

11 April 1967

I've decided that it is safer and I'm much happier flying combat strike missions than performing the routine garrison duty of paper work in the flight surgeon's office. Several reasons why...

For the past few days, the daytime temperature has averaged 135 to 140 degrees, and what better time for an office air conditioner to be out? The office is in an aluminum Quonset hut, with no windows. The temperature inside the office is more than 100 degrees and we don't have a fan. Superimposed on this is the fact that it is the fourth day that the sewage for the entire building has been backed up. The floors are submerged under three inches of sewage, while toilet paper, human feces and Lord knows what else floats through the office. I don't know what the famous "sewers of Paris" were like, but they didn't have this type of heat. Of course, to look on the bright side, no one is shooting at us; they don't need to, the environment is toxic enough to be fatal! My Jeep is broken down, meaning that I have to walk several miles over the flight line for various inspections.

I am required to write regular Officer Efficiency Reports on the other doctors in the office and I hate it! All of our flight surgeons are good doctors and good people. Thank goodness, we don't have any bad eggs! But I should stop complaining. The non-commissioned officers perform 90 percent of the office paperwork. I can't speak highly enough of them. Sergeant Xeras is my "right arm." The problem is me. I hate paperwork.

12 April 1967

More of the same…

At 6 a.m. we had a practice alert, during which we were timed for our response to a simulated aircraft crash on the opposite side of the field. How long did it take to get to the ambulance? How long did it take to drive the ambulance to the crash site? How long to transport simulated casualties from the crash site to the hospital?

By the time I returned to the office, the lights were out. I used a flashlight to find my desk. Suddenly, the sound of a loud burp bubbled up from the floor…it was my old friend, the sewer, overflowing again. Obviously, I can't see patients in this environment. My Jeep is supposedly repaired, but on the way to the hospital dispensary to see patients, the gears locked and I abandoned it. I then borrowed another Jeep from the hospital motor pool in order to respond to crash calls. I had driven no more than two blocks before the clutch on this borrowed Jeep gave out….

I returned to the office to find the lights on, sewer overflowing and no air conditioner.

13 April 1967
C-141 Starlifter Crash

Last night at 1:20 a.m., the night corpsman on duty woke me up to inform me that a C-141 Starlifter had just crashed into the South China Sea while attempting to take off from the north end of the runway.

The C-141 had arrived at Cam Ranh Bay after a flight from Yokota AFB, Japan. It was prepared for a night departure back to Yokota, after being loaded with ammunitions and explosives.

I arrived on the scene before the usual crash teams had time to respond. Not even the rescue helicopters had taken off. There were only a few air policemen standing on the bluff that overlooked the runway and the South China Sea. Immediately recognizing me and the flight surgeon's Jeep, they waved me through. Getting out of the jeep, I walked to the end of the runway, where it terminates at cliff's edge. Beyond us and from the surfaces of the water beamed a flashlight, presumably held by someone in a life raft. I tried to radio the hospital command post but transmission was blocked. (Probably the airways were flooded with calls.) Unable to contact the hospital, I ran back to my Jeep and drove back to Base Operations to coordinate rescue efforts.

The aircraft had a crew of nine. Immediately after the crash, only two people were pulled from the waters and rescued by helicopters. The remainder of the night is consumed in searching for other survivors and for the tons of explosives that are beginning to wash up onto the beach. The Navy sent a team of underwater demolition experts with scuba rigs to dive into the wreckage in search of survivors and to recover bodies that had been trapped in the wreckage.

The search for human remains is one issue. However, an equally important issue is implementation of very different recovery procedures for the ammunitions and explosive cargo. Much of the ammunition had been armed by the impact of the crash and presented a very hazardous and delicate recovery operation. Having been "armed," the ammunition is subject to detonation with the slightest touch. It is a tedious and dangerous task that extends through the night.

I take my position near the helicopter pad, beside the crash ambulance, which is parked on the runway in front of the flight surgeon's office. I asked Sam Hyde to ride in the boats that are now scouring the ocean area for survivors. Sam promptly became sea sick while attempting to perform this task and is out of commission. I then assign Lon Kerry to the search and rescue helicopters that fill the skies above the crash site. All of these efforts continue throughout the night.

Sometime after lunch today I am finally relieved from these duties, but only to confront the anticipated avalanche of paperwork generated by the crash and to attend meetings with Colonel Mack and other members of the Accident Investigation Board. I am informed that this is the first in-flight crash for this particular aircraft. The C-141 Skylifter is the premier cargo aircraft for the U.S. Air Force, and from the Air Force perspective, tonight's crash is comparable to the sinking of the Titanic.[27] Countless numbers of people are running in circles to investigate the crash. A special team from Military Airlift Command (MAC) is being flown in immediately from McChord Air Force Base in Washington State to participate in the operations. Navy divers find two intact bodies in the wreckage. Both of the persons died from drowning. The search will continue for the other five bodies tomorrow...

I am so tired...

The magnitude of this crash is comparable to the mid-air collision of two Phantoms that occurred last fall. However, in this crash there are

---

27 The crash of C-141 (Tail No. 66-0127) at Cam Ranh Bay on 23 March is recognized in later years as the worst ground aviation accident of the Vietnam War.

far more fatalities. All things considered, we are lucky. The C-141 is the major air-evacuation aircraft for all Vietnam casualties. How much more of a disaster would it have been if it had been loaded with 100-200 patients? The carnage of such an event would have been awful.

CHAPTER 37

Humanity Calls

14 April 1967

I have spent all of today signing death certificates and writing reports on the crewmembers killed in the crash. There are, of course, a myriad of other details involved in ushering someone out of this life. I often marvel that only four copies of a birth certificate are required to herald one's appearance on the earthly stage, whereas twenty to twenty-five copies of a death certificate are required to validate the vacancy... Life is strange...

A Short Reprieve...

Last night I was too tired to think. With no sleep for thirty-six-plus hours, I finally ran out of steam. At 3 p.m. today, I needed a brief nap and simply crashed onto my bunk in the squadron Quonset hut. When I lay down, none of my three other pilot roommates were present. I awoke about forty-five minutes later to find one of my roommates sitting at the table in the middle of the room.

Spread out over the table was an elaborate tape deck, with lights flashing and needles flicking to indicate the variations in decibels and a thousand other nuances of musical amplification. The honey-like voice of Eddy Arnold and the Tennessee Plowboys vented from two speakers he had just purchased in the Philippines. These wonders of auditory technology were the proud property of 1st Lieutenant Taylor, a Kentucky farm boy…simple, plain and as friendly as an old hound dawg. His hand was on the volume control dial, but he was watching me intently. When I showed signs of awakening, he peered very anxiously at me, with slight trepidation in his eyes.

After looking at my watch I say, "Hi, looks like I'd better get back to work." With those few words, his face splits into a huge grin as he emits an audible sigh of relief. He then turns the volume of Eddy Arnold up a few decibels and, smiling, says in a soft Southern drawl, "I've been waitin' for you to wake up…I shure didn't want to disturb you. I've got some new speakers…bought them for $7 at the Army BX."

As tired and depressed as I am, I can't help smiling. His face has the glow of a child who has awakened at 5 a.m. on Christmas morning to quietly rustle the packages under the Christmas tree, all the while attempting to avoid awakening his parents but hoping and praying that they won't be able to sleep through it. He knows that his efforts can't be too blatant or he might be scolded. At the sound of our voices, several other pilots in the hallway enter the room to admire the flicking needles and the winking lights…each praising his equipment and bragging on the quality of sound that issues from the bargain-priced speakers. Lt. Taylor's face beams in childish joy at each favorable comment. Before leaving the room and returning to the office I again compliment him profusely on the quality of his audio system.

As I walk to the office, I ruminate on these small human events. It is interesting how men differ from women on certain issues. Some of these young bachelors have audio/sound systems that run into hundreds and perhaps thousands of dollars. If they had been women, they could be divided into two groups: those who possessed no speakers/stereo decks and those who had better systems. Each group would have deemed it necessary to belittle Lt. Taylor's sound system, in order to satisfy their own envy or selfishness. His fellow pilots, however, know that Taylor has a wife and several children. Considering his monthly pay, there is little coin remaining each month for spending on non-necessities. This discounted system is all that he can afford. Their praise of Taylor's sound system is genuine. They make it obvious that he has a first class system and that he obtained it at a bargain price. In relative terms of global events, this exchange of pleasantries between friends is a small point, but it is a warm commendation on mankind and the inner workings of the human spirit. And, however small the event, this very human exchange provides the ray of sunshine and hope that I sorely need...

After nearly a year in Vietnam, I struggle to avoid being emotionally overwhelmed by the fragmented human bodies and lost lives that seem to occur on nearly a daily basis. I have difficulty in remaining "enthusiastically detached" from human misery and death.

I've got to deal with these things better!

For a few moments respite, two nights ago I walked to the beach, believing that the beauty of the open sky and ocean would clear my head. Suddenly, the odor of JP-4 wafted on the breeze from the flight line to flood my nostrils and my consciousness...and once again, I am awash with memories of Bill Simmons's crash, the mid-air collision with explosion of the two Phantoms with death of the crewmembers, and now this C-141 crash. I find myself suddenly wallowing in a quagmire of death and destruction.

I've got to get hold of myself.

(Forty-four years later, while awaiting the arrival of my daughter, Laura, and my three grandchildren at the airport in Santa Barbara,

California, the odor of JP-4 from an airliner that was being refueled wafted past my nostrils. My vision clouded momentarily as I was suddenly transported back through time and space to Cam Ranh Bay…the crashes, mangled bodies and the horrors of it all rose again to confront me. Nearly a half-century later, I keep telling myself, "Let it go…Let it go!")

15 April 1967

The Military Airlift Command flight surgeon sent to investigate the C-141 crash is Bill Hendrickson. Bill and I were classmates in 1964 at Brooks Air Force Base in the Primary Flight Surgeons School. He is a fine person and very competent physician. After separating from the Air Force, he plans on going into private practice in Ketchikan, Alaska, with a medical school classmate from Oregon. His description of Alaska borders on paradise. It is good to see him again, but I would have preferred different circumstances.

Crash of a Caribou

A Caribou from the 483rd Tactical Air Wing at Cam Ranh Bay crashed at Phu Khet today. It was loaded with thirty troops, but thankfully, there were no fatalities. Apparently, the aircraft was demolished. Ben Bevins is the flight medical officer assigned to the Caribou squadron and he was sent to investigate the crash at Phu Khet. I have my hands full here. I'm grateful to have responsible, competent physicians like Ben to whom I can delegate responsibility.

16 April 1967

Civilization has arrived at Cam Ranh Bay! Somewhere on the mainland, they have established a TV station. Now, everyone is rushing out to buy a TV set. The remarkable thing is that the troops here do not consider it to be a luxury; instead they accept it as a normal necessity of life. The programs are taped, of course, and there is the nightly news program. Actually the presence of television on base has accomplished one thing. Previously, in the evening, men simply drank themselves into a stupor. But now, they glue themselves to the magic box and drink. They state proudly, "It's just like the States."

Two Army helicopters went down in the South China Sea, a few miles off shore from Cam Ranh Bay. Apparently, one was shot down, while the fate of the other is unknown. Thus far, there is no evidence of survivors. We have had more than our share of these problems lately. Thank goodness, the investigations will be assumed by Army flight surgeons and not by Air Force flight surgeons at Cam Ranh.

22 April 1967
7th Air Force Surgeon General Critique

Today is the Summary, Review and Recommendations for the 12th Air Force Hospital at Cam Ranh Bay. Conducted by the 7th Air Force inspector general, the inspection is the ultimate appraisal of how the facility is performing its role in Vietnam. This inspection and critique consumed all of last week. It involves all medical facilities on base and was conducted by Major Larry Johnson, whom I encountered on my previous visit to his office in Saigon while I was at Vung Tau. This inspection allows

7th Air Force to expound on its grudges with our hospital commander, Colonel Mack.

This annual event strikes fear in the heart and gives ulcers to career Air Force medical officers. Promotions frequently ride on the results. Each department in the hospital is evaluated and ranked. Since the conflict between Colonel Mack and the higher ranks of 7th Air Force is well known to the higher echelons, this inspection is considered to be the arena in which differences will be fought out. The generic rankings of the inspection and critique are:

Unsatisfactory

Marginal

Satisfactory

Above Average

Outstanding

The entire hospital facility and all specialty departments of 12th Air Force Hospital were ranked as "Satisfactory," but hedged in multiple qualifications. Most of the criticisms were nitpicking, with little relevance to quality of patient care or institutional excellence.

I was a more than a bit surprised when the flight surgeon's office received the only "Outstanding" rating. Major Johnson even went further and declared it to be the most outstanding flight surgeon's office in Vietnam and all of Southeast Asia.

Prior to this, I had no specific expectations about the results. I find it difficult to organize and manage an office by standards that are acceptable to higher brass. We have worked hard to be efficient and to provide the highest level of support for our pilots and aircrew members. Anything beyond this is bureaucratic superfluidity. Any credit for paperwork is due to my NCOIC, Master Sgt. Xeras.

But, they did not stop with the commendation. The bastard continued to use the podium and my office as an anvil to hammer Colonel Mack.

They praised the exceptional quality of my flight surgeon's reports "despite the inertia over and beyond that office…" In other words, we had an exceptional office in spite of the incompetence and inefficiency of Colonel Mack.

I stood to accept the critique and award and asked my NCOIC, Sergeant Xeras to stand and deferred all credit to him. I thanked Colonel Mack for his continuing support of the pilots and their welfare at Cam Ranh Bay. Without his support, nothing would have been accomplished…

For me, it was bittersweet. I have the greatest respect and admiration for Colonel Mack and it galls me to see him slandered in any manner, but especially by using my office as a pawn in their game. They know that he is primarily a pilot with an M.D. degree and that I have an M.D. degree that allows me to fly combat missions as a flight surgeon. They know that his primary loyalty is to the flight surgeon's office and goad him by stating that in spite of his screwups, the flight surgeon's office excelled.

The reason that we excelled is because Colonel Mack is a wise man who has given me complete independence in running the office. He has never tried to micromanage me as 7th Air Force is trying to micromanage him.

Of course, none of these glowing appraisals endeared me with the other hospital physicians! But, any victory that I have realized is bittersweet when weighed in the balance against Colonel Mack's career.

23 April 1967

From a stray Time magazine, I've just read about movements to send pharmaceuticals to Communist China. The liberals are concerned about starving children and impoverished humanity. All of this hand wringing seems to ignore the fact that most of the weaponry that we are opposing in Vietnam comes from Communist China. Apparently they wish to keep

Chinese children strong and healthy so that we fight armies of strong and healthy Commies instead of weak and scrawny ones. Apparently China is experiencing a number of epidemics. Quite frankly, the more misfortunes that fall on these people, the better. This has nothing to do with humanitarian ideals. If everything happens at once, famine, pestilence, political suppression and tyranny, the people will eventually relate their misery to their present government. If everything is lovely, they will think, "What a blessing is Communism!" Hell, no! Let them realize that their circumstances are all part and parcel of a nation/government that burns books, commits atrocities and suppresses life as we know it today. It is unfortunate that, as always, the poor people must suffer the most. But if the "poor people" had taken a stand before now, they wouldn't be in the present predicament.

26 April 1967

I have finished reading *Of Human Bondage* by Somerset Maugham. It is not something to be skimmed over lightly. In many ways it has pertinence to many of my own musings. The protagonist is Philip Carey.

"It seemed to him that all his life he had followed the ideals that other people, by their words or their writings had instilled in him and never the desires of his own heart. Always his course had been swayed by what he thought he should do and never by what he wanted with his own soul to do… He had always lived in the future, and the present always, always had slipped through his fingers. His ideals? He had thought of his desire to make a design, intricate and beautiful, out of the myriad of meaningless facts of life… It might be that to surrender to happiness was to accept defeat, but it was a defeat better than many victories."

These lines seem pertinent to so many young people. The problem is to determine and to recognize and admit what you truly want…not what you want yourself to want. Unfortunately, finding the answer to these questions may take a lifetime. There are times when I know perfectly well that I would be content to settle down with a beautiful home in the country, practice medicine and write. At other times I become terribly restless and want to travel and live with other cultures…always with my wife and family at my side. And there are other times when I crave a life of high adventure, experienced by me alone. I am fortunate, for with a medical degree, I can do as I please and always earn a living. Perhaps children will stabilize some of this lability…I don't know. If that happens, then perhaps I didn't truly want some of the wilder dreams…but only wanted to want them. I simply want to live each day to the fullest. I am the world's worst example of living in the future. Perhaps this is a result of immaturity and dissatisfaction with the present or a product of too long extended medical education where your whole life is couched in terms of the future. Or perhaps it is a method of avoiding the daily horrors of war…hoping that the future, if there is one, will be better.

27 April 1967
AC-47 Crash at Cam Ranh

Just as I am completing the above note, the crash phone rings to inform me that an airplane, an AC-47, has crashed on the beach about six miles from base. Sam Hyde and I form a convoy of Jeeps, ambulances and trucks to approach the crash area. The crash site is terribly isolated. We see the burning wreckage on the side of a rocky cliff that overlooks the South China Sea. Initially, we consider the possibility of survivors, but the terrain is too rough for helicopters to gain access to the area. The beach is narrow and we hike on foot up the rocky cliffside as far as we can. Flares are constantly being dropped over the entire area to illuminate the crash site until it is nearly as bright as day. Finally we realize that the terrain is impossible to traverse on foot. We return to the cove beneath us and requisition an Army light amphibious resupply craft (LARC) to carry us around the point to an area that is closer to the crash site.

From this position, the burning wreckage is about seventy-five feet above us on a rocky ledge. There are two options for approaching the crash site: climb to it from below or land on the cliff above the crash and rappel down to the site. Since we are below the crash site on a narrow beach, it seems appropriate to approach from below.

Between us and the wreckage is a sheer cliff of rocks and crevices in which we must find hand holds and footholds. The cliff side is nearly vertical and offers no easy point to scale the cliff or to climb through the debris. I lead the climb, struggling for every toehold and grasping every rock and twig. We climb using any available crevices for toeholds and handholds. After a short distance, we find that the entire cliffside and its crevices are all filled with human body parts, fingers, hands, toes and assorted anatomic pieces. Using spotlights from below to assist our search, there is absolutely no evidence of either a survivor or an intact body.

As I climb higher up the cliffside, through the darkness, there is the expected dislodgement of pebbles and gravel that roll down the cliffside, until something different occurs. Suddenly, I notice that the pebbles and gravel are not being dislodged by me; they are falling past me. Pebbles, rocks and gravel are raining down from above. In the shadows and dim light, I see a giant boulder that has wedged itself between the burning fuselage of the aircraft and a small sapling. The sapling has been torched and is finally burning away to release the boulder, the size of an automobile, which will hurtle down the cliffside toward me in accordance with the laws of Isaac Newton. I have nowhere to move from its path except to plaster myself against the cliffside, clinging with all my strength to any and all available small handholds and toeholds. I have no time to utter a sigh of relief as the boulder tumbles past me before a fireball of the same size follows the same path and roars toward me. Thankfully, it also roars past me as the cliffside and I become one.

The fireball is a portion of the burning fuselage from the aircraft. Having escaped both of these disasters, my grip suddenly began to slip from both my handholds and toeholds. Inside the crevices, where my fingers have been clinging, I feel something soft and slimy. I simply grasp whatever it is as I try to support myself and cram whatever it is into a specimen bag that I carry over my shoulder. As I continue to slide down the cliff, my hands grasp at my former toehold and also find something slippery that is separate from the soil. Reflexly, I grab a handful and stuff it into my specimen bag. Finally, I wind up at the bottom of the cliff with the other personnel.

At this point, I call off the medical search. I see no purpose in risking the lives of doctors and corpsmen by trying to climb up or rappel down these cliffs at night, and all for the sole purpose of collecting fragments of tissue. On the way back to Cam Ranh, even the amphibious vehicles become stuck in the sand several times. Finally, at 4 a.m., we arrive back at Cam Ranh. I spend the next hour attempting to obtain fingerprints from the fragments of tissue that we brought back. The objects that I had blindly thrust into my specimen bags from handholds and toeholds are portions of human brain and human intestine, respectively. As I remove my boots before heading for the shower, I scrape particles of human brain off the soles. The total amount of human tissue that we recovered would have filled a large cigar box.

Finally, at 5 a.m., I run out of steam and go to bed.

The crash involved an AC-47 with seven people on board. The plane was out of Nha Trang. Further investigation of the crash will be accomplished by the flight surgeon from Nha Trang. Once I am satisfied that there are no survivors, and that I can offer no aid to anyone, I lose interest in further investigation.

As part of my duty as a physician, I will risk my life to save a patient, but I will not throw my life away for specimens of dead tissue or corpses. I have spent too many hours this year gleaning scraps of human tissue off the ground, from rocks and off the jungle floors. I see no reason to subject my staff to accidents and possible fatalities running up and down a cliff in total darkness when there is no hope of human survival. I am fully aware that all tissues must be obtained and preserved for identification, but that can wait another three hours until daylight.

When I have awakened, I learn that Major Gorman, my boss, has been climbing the walls because I am not out searching today. None of the corpsmen or other doctors in the office will awaken me and Gorman doesn't dare. I'm sure that he lodged a complaint with Colonel Mack about my dereliction of duty. When I spoke with Colonel Mack a few minutes ago, I sensed that Gorman had complained to him. Gorman is straight out of school. He commands from a desk, not from the field of reality. He continues to look at things through academic lenses.

The flight surgeon from Nha Trang arrives to investigate the crash. He is a major, and like Gorman is board certified in aerospace medicine. This is his first time out in the field. He comes across as the typical wizened, ineffectual, obsessive-compulsive paper shuffler who prefers to direct from behind the desk, where things are aseptically clean and orderly and from where life can be controlled. It is obvious that he considers my blasé attitude about this crash and collecting tidbits of tissue from a burning hillside to be deplorable. For a compulsive person, the chaos of reality must seem intolerable. I wonder what his attitude will be after a year of investigating these crashes. My mind is numb. I simply can't let these things get to me any more. I am so tired of this whole business. Only twenty-eight more days before I can leave this entire scene behind!

But, on a lighter note…

Today, a letter was circulated to all Air Force physicians that "strongly encouraged" each doctor "to make a contribution to pay for an oil painting of General So-N-So to hang in the office of the new surgeon general in Washington. The "suggested amount" was $3.50. I could hardly believe it. At first, I thought it was a sick joke, especially for physicians now serving in Vietnam. Multiply that amount by the thousands of physicians that are on active duty and it creates a tidy sum. I burst out laughing when I read it and tossed it into the wastebasket.

The flight surgeon from Nha Trang who is investigating the crash radioed for me to meet his helicopter. He had been scuba diving all day, retrieving human body parts from the crash. Good grief! He has two large bags full of very ripe assorted body parts. He smells like offal! This occurs while I am walking to the Mess Hall for dinner. It takes all that I can muster to avoid vomiting. For all of his academic accolades of board certification in aerospace medicine, he has lost his virginity on this mission!

TWO MORE MONTHS BEFORE DEROS!

CHAPTER 38

Hypocrisy and the Vagaries of War

1 May 1967

I see no end in sight for this war. Yet I find it difficult to believe that the protesting Beatniks in the U.S. are representative of national opinion. The number of protesters in New York's last protest was listed as 200,000. The population of San Francisco is listed as 75,000. This represents about 0.13 percent of the U.S. population. This is hardly a significant representation. However, it should be noted that about 15,000 Nazis took over Germany to start WWII.

Today has set an all-time record of 100 patients per day in the flight surgeon's office. A major offensive is taking place on the mainland, across from and in sight of the base. We are receiving casualties on the flight line that are less than ten minutes old. Standing outside, in front of the office, white puffs of artillery are visible as they erupt in the mountains. Since Cam Ranh is on a peninsula, water intervenes between us and the mainland mountains. This distance screens out the sounds of artillery explosions. Apparently, the jungle crash site area that I investigated in December is now controlled and overrun by both Viet Cong and North Vietnamese Army troops. I doubt that Cam Ranh can maintain its immunity from attack too much longer. Long-range Russian rockets have been used against Da Nang. Eventually, they will arrive south. I'm glad that I will be out of here when they arrive.

Sam Hyde was selected Air Defense Command Flight Surgeon of the Year from his previous assignment in Iceland. Sam does good work and is more representative of the typical flight surgeon than I or Al.

At this late date in my tour, I am becoming more paranoid. The Air Force seems intent on getting its last pound of flesh from me. This morning I was called out for a situation in which an F-4C, with eight five-hundred-pound bombs, became engulfed in flames while sitting on the runway. Apparently, during the takeoff roll, with the aircraft speed approaching 180 knots, the left after-burner failed to ignite. The wingman notified the crew that their aircraft was on fire and told them to abort. They backed off on the throttles and braked almost to a stop. The entire tail section of the aircraft was in flames. During the few moments required by the back-seat pilot to unstrap himself, the fire spread to the wings and nearly engulfed the aircraft. Both pilots jumped from the cockpit level to the ground, a distance of about twelve feet, and ran as if the Fiends of Hell were pursuing them. Finally I am able to catch up and examine them. The only injury was sustained by the back-seater, who suffered a fracture of the right lateral malleolus (ankle). However, this didn't slow him down. He ran nearly a quarter-mile before stopping. No other injuries were sustained.

The base has been in turmoil for the remainder of the morning and part of the afternoon as the full fuel tanks of the F-4 feed the fires until eventually the bombs begin to cook-off, exploding one by one. This prevents the firemen from moving in closer to extinguish the blaze and clear the runway. It was later determined that a fuel leak to the left engine had ignited at the time that the afterburner was applied. We are lucky that neither of the pilots was seriously injured.

As a result of these events, the new left concrete runway at Cam Ranh has been closed all day and will require some time to repair damage from the fire and bomb explosions. This runway handles the large cargo aircraft. As a result, flights of larger, cargo and air evacuation aircraft will be delayed in leaving Vietnam. The 707s and C-141 transport aircraft cannot use the right runway since it too short and not sturdy enough to support their weight. It may take up to a week to completely repair these damages.

I nominate Sam Hyde for the Accident Investigation Board to investigate and write reports on the F-4 disaster. He needs the experience since he will take over for me after I leave next month.

The smoke and dust have hardly settled on this event before an F-100 from Phan Rang is struck by enemy ground fire while conducting an air strike against the Viet Cong on the mountains south of Cam Ranh. This location is in proximity to the F-4 jungle crash site that I investigated in December. After enemy ground fire hit the F-100, the pilots managed to maneuver out over the ocean before they ejected at the entrance to Cam Ranh. Both pilots were promptly picked out of the water by helicopters. Thank goodness, the flight surgeon from Phan Rang will investigate this incident and write all of the reports.

I've been here too long. I am beginning to judge the gravity of a situation not by the number of lives lost, number of injuries or by damage to the aircraft, but by the amount of paperwork that the event generates for me to complete.

3 May 1967

Dear Elaine,

I have just finished reading a fascinating book, *The Perikovsky Papers*. This is a collection of notes by Col. Oleg Perikovsky, a Russian intelligence expert who revealed an enormous quantity of Soviet secrets to the West. I can vaguely remember the stir that his 1963 trial created in Moscow. He was considered a zealot and the cream of Soviet military and Communist Party life. At some point he became fed up with the injustices of Communism and became a spy for the West. I thought how ironic it is that a man is willing to give up status, family and every amenity of life offered by his government in a single act of betrayal. He did this because he believed that the Communist Party was merely a monstrous tool for exploiting the Russian people. He firmly believed that Nikita Khrushchev was leading the world toward nuclear holocaust. His actions provided the United States with its greatest espionage coup in Anglo-American-Soviet relations. This was a man who had greater fortitude and character than thousands of other Soviets. He was willing to die for his beliefs, and worse, to be accused of betraying his government. Because of this, he will be scorned by the Soviets and probably the U.S. as well, as a person who betrayed his country and government. He will be dishonored in both camps. The stigma of betraying your country is like breaking faith or failing to honor your father and mother. In the eyes of every society, regardless of the justification, betrayal is a cardinal sin. During World War II, as Adolph Hitler led the German people to destruction, the person who plotted to kill Adolph Hitler was Colonel Claus von Stauffenberg. He stated: "The worth of a man is determined by his beliefs and his willingness to die for them."

The purpose of this discussion is that it raised the question in me. Would I have had the courage of my convictions, under the same circumstances, to act in a manner that benefits mankind, yet predictably is treasonous to my country and is not respected by the enemy of your country or by my country? I don't know. But this is not to be written off lightly in evaluating a man's soul.

The same questions may be asked of the Vietnam War. While I believe the vast majority of the American war protesters have more frivolous and self-serving motives than Col. Oleg Perikovsky, I am sure that a small number have higher motives in their objections. It brings to mind the toast by Stephen Decatur in April 1816. At a banquet, he raised his glass and spoke the words in response to a previous toast that stated, "To my country, may she always be right, but right or wrong, my country!" Stephen Decatur's response was: "To our country! In her intercourse with foreign nations, may she always be in the right; but our country, right or wrong."

In 1872, Sen. Carl Schurz rebutted this with: "My country, right or wrong. In one sense I say so too. My country; and my country is the great American Republic. My country, right or wrong; if right, to be kept right; and if wrong, to be set right."

4 May 1967

The damaged runway has been repaired and flights are back to normal. Thank goodness, my flight out of here shouldn't be delayed. Apparently when the runway was closed after the explosions, the first plane to be diverted was the mail plane with 20,000 pounds of mail.

Last night, while serving as MOD, a thirty-year-old Army enlisted man was brought in after shooting off his big toe to avoid work. This man was stationed with the Army units in the northern part of Cam Ranh peninsula. At this time, the peninsula is as safe as any place in Vietnam. There is little to fear here. Why did he shoot himself?

Well, I hope he enjoys dragging that plaster-of-Paris cast through the sand in this 130-degree heat. Apparently, similar actions were fairly common during World War II. Usually, troops or draft candidates would shoot their trigger finger off to avoid the draft, or later to avoid combat. This is my first contact with this practice in American troops.

Sergeant Xeras came into the office today saying that Major Gorman had written a "fantastic officer efficiency report" for me. He noted that Colonel Mack stated that in all of his thirty-five years of military service, I am the most outstanding flight surgeon he has known. Sgt. Xeras asks if I want to read a copy of it. My reply is, "Hell, no." This was my same response in medical school when I refused to claim my grades and previous exams. I have served my country as best I can. What someone else feels about my service is irrelevant, whether good or bad. In medical school I gave it all I had. That's all any man can do. No threat of punishment or promise of reward could have made me work harder.

Tomorrow morning I will leave for Bangkok, Thailand, with a number of pilots from the 483rd Tactical Airlift Wing. The 483rd is composed of ex-Army CV-2B Caribou light transport aircraft. It is perfect for transporting troops and equipment into small jungle landing strips in forward areas of ground combat. As chief of aviation medicine, I try to fly with these aircraft and aircrews to maintain rapport with the 483rd Tactical Airlift Wing. The flights are not as exciting as those flown in the Phantom, but they provide a chance for me to see the war from the perspective of logistical support instead of actual combat. Attacking the enemy is only one part of modern warfare.

But, on a more informal basis, flying with these men is always a pleasure. Their pilots and crews are universally friendly and always seem happy to have me aboard. The trip from Cam Ranh to Bangkok may be unofficially regarded as a "boondoggle," which means that, in truth, it serves no actual military purpose except for the amusement of the pilots and crew.

Of course, there are official reasons for the flight, such as procurement of logistical supplies for the combat zone, etc. But that is a cover for the fact that the flight is primarily a shopping trip for their colonels. Whatever the reason, I am delighted when they invite me to accompany them. I will have the same accommodations of food and lodging as the pilots and other crew members. Since there are special military discounts for contract hotels and restaurant, the trip will cost me far less than if I paid for it as an individual. It is the closest thing that I can find to a custom trip in the Air Force.

5 May 1967

Taking off from Cam Ranh at 5 a.m., we encountered an unexpected layover at Tan Son Nhut and finally arrived at Bangkok about 4 p.m. Flying in the Caribou compares to flying in a Cessna-150, with two engines, but it is a little more comfortable to ride. En route weather worsened and required that we climb to 15,000 feet to avoid some of the cumulus build-ups. We maintained this altitude for more than an hour. Since this is a local "puddle-jumper" type aircraft, there is no oxygen on board. At this altitude, without oxygen, hypoxia occurs and persists as long as you maintain this altitude. Nearly all of the crew, including myself, developed severe headaches from the prolonged hypoxia.

Now at midnight, as I write this, my head continues to feel like it is being hammered by some unseen demon. We are staying at the Grace Hotel, which is the primary billet for our flying personnel in Bangkok. At $6-$7 per night, the accommodations are quite nice. On the drive from the flight line to the hotel, we passed the International Hotel, where Elaine and I previously spent a week together.

Finally, it is morning but the headache continues. I get a haircut and accompany one of the pilots to an open-air Thai restaurant. The food is good, and if I had not felt so rotten, I'm sure that it would have been much better.

I left the group to do some shopping around Bangkok. Bangkok remains the most exotic city I have ever experienced. It is enjoyable if you can accept the simple fact that compared to an American city, Bangkok is a den of thieves and worse. The sex trade is rampant as impoverished farmers sell their daughters into prostitution in the city. One of the English newspapers has an ad to sell a thirteen-year-old "virgin" for $15 to anyone. Any purchase, for anything, from souvenir to cab fare is made only after haggling over the price for as much as an hour. It is the customary practice of doing all business. I learn quickly that it is impossible to win any bargain unless you are willing to walk away from it.

I never tire of Bangkok. No city can match its architecture, enormous Buddha statues or khlongs/canals that flow through the city in the same manner that streets flow through western cities. The Chao Phraya River flows through the city, as khlongs from its tributaries bring commerce into and through the city. The original site where Bangkok was founded was on the Khlong of Thonburi – before King Rama I moved the capital's epicenter across the river to the Rattanakosin Island.

Finally I walk back to the hotel, where other crewmembers are congregated in the bar. We agree to have a joint dinner in a nearby hotel that is noted for its food. This seems benign enough. We are promptly seated and served with a delicious multi-course meal of Thai dishes that are all very spicy.

Toward the end of the meal, one of the pilots turned to me and said, "Hey Doc, follow me; there are some things that your education may have missed!" Having no idea what he means, I follow him across the dining room and into a darkened hallway. The wall on one side of the hallway is filled by large glass windows that look into a large bay area. He informs me that the windows are "one-way glass" that permits us to look in without being observed by persons in the room. I peer through one of the windows and what greets me is a scene that I could never have imagined. It is a large room broken only by benches situated at regular intervals for sitting. The entire room was crowded with women. Each is scantily but modestly clothed and each has a placard with a number around her neck. I feel as if the panorama of womanhood on this planet is contained in that single room. I estimate that the ages of these women are between fifteen and thirty years.

There are intensely black women, with typical Negroid features and physiognomies characteristic of African origin, standing alongside blue-eyed blondes with typically Scandinavian features. Every nationality and ethic representation of Asian woman is there. There are women with the olive complexion and Mediterranean features of Spain and Italy. The earmarks of beauty are universally present in all. There are women with the Alpine/Celtic features of a round head, broad face, light chestnut hair color, hazel-gray eyes, medium, stocky stature, and variable nose shape. Just as there are women with Mediterranean features of long head, long face, dark brown/black hair, dark eyes, medium/slender stature and slightly broad nose. There are women with very Teutonic features of long heads, long faces, very light hair color, blue eyes, tall stature and narrow/aquiline noses.

My companion explains that a hotel guest can choose a woman by her number and she will become his dinner partner. For this service, the guest pays a fee to the hotel. Any further interest or relationship between the two would be totally independent of the hotel.

I found this both tragic and fascinating. The stories that any of these women have to tell would fill a thousand novels. But, in fact, this is no different from a dating service with personnel contracted by the hotel in Western society. Agencies in Western cities have equivalent "escort" services for a fee. But these are more discreetly marketed. What impacted me most was the mass commercialization of these women, herded like cattle into that large room with numbers around their necks. Perhaps if each were presented as an individual candidate for a dinner partner, it would have been more acceptable. The mass effect homogenizes all individuality until the result is dehumanizing. Even by Western standards of etiquette, a dinner partner seems innocuous enough, but Bangkok's reputation of an international "flesh pot" raises questions. It defies all logic to consider such limited service as the end point of a relationship.

From my Southern background and knowledge of history, the scene raised phantoms of slave-trade auctions, from as recent as the American South and as remote as mankind's earliest years, when the vanquished were enslaved by the victors.

As I looked upon them, I became very sad. I wanted to remove all barriers and embrace them, not in a romantic sense or because of any sexual attraction, but in the same manner I would embrace a sister who had fallen on hard times. Presumably these women are daughters, sisters, mothers and sweethearts of someone who cares for them, as human beings, who are in turn, sisters, mothers and sweethearts to other human beings. It broke my heart to see them. It was more than I could handle and to conceal the expression on my face, I turned away. Since we flew out of Bangkok very early the next morning, I could never pursue the issue. But it has left a very lasting impression on me. At the table, I had a cup of coffee and called it a night. Our flight to Ching Mai leaves early in the a.m.

Driving to the airport, the temperature was over 100 degrees and the relative humidity must have easily approached 90 percent. The roadsides on the drive from Bangkok to the airport had small groups of water buffalo clustered in every mud puddle. I didn't recall seeing them with such frequency before.

Ching Mai is the largest and most culturally significant city in northern Thailand. It is the capital of Chiang Mai Province, a former capital of the Kingdom of Lanna (1296 - 1768) and was the tributary Kingdom of

Chiang Mai from 1774 until 1939. It is located 700 km (435 miles) north of Bangkok, and is among the highest mountains in the country. The city is on the Ping River, a major tributary of the Chao Phraya River. Chiang Mai's historic importance is derived from its strategic location on the river with access to major trading routes.

For tourists and military personnel, it is respected as an art colony and for its lack of modern contaminants. Located in the Teak forests it has been a haven for wood carvers and artists. This was my second visit to Ching Mai. My first visit was with Elaine. I remembered it as a multitude of small wood-carving shops that masterfully carve the native teakwood into any shape desired. It is a delightful respite from the world of automation, highways and internal combustion engines.

There is an agrarian attitude in the people and a provincial mood that stands in stark contrast to the urban metropolis of Bangkok. Ching Mai had recently become a recognized R&R center for American forces. I am sure that its pristine personality would not long endure in the face of this recent G.I. onslaught. Shopping is confined to a single product: teak carvings and wares. The merchants merely laugh at the mention of jewelry, silk or anything else associated with Bangkok. For the Ching Mai natives, Bangkok may just as well be a foreign country. Perhaps, this is an ancient holdover from days of the city states.

The co-pilot of the Caribou that I flew into Ching Mai is a captain by the name of Nick Evanish. He is one of the most delightful characters I have ever known. He is about 6'4" and weighs approximately 235 pounds. He is very handsome and superficially appears innocently dumb. It is impossible to dislike him. He is the high school football hero who will always remain thus. Going from shop to shop with him has been one of life's funniest experiences. He is a perfect stereotype of the American tourist who roamed the world twenty-five to thirty years ago. Like the United States was before World War II, he is the adolescent giant who likes everyone and expects everyone to like him. He is big, dumb and completely lacking in manners or discipline…refreshingly innocent and incapable of deceit. In addition to being a friendly giant, he prides himself on his prowess with women, despite the fact that he has a wife and two children. However, I learned in a few moments that this was all part of the act… he is as harmless as a big St. Bernard puppy. The streets, hotels and alleys are filled with prostitutes, thus there was no challenge for him. It was readily apparent that he had no interest in the kill…the sport was only in the chase. As I recount a few episodes, keep in mind this young, handsome giant, laughing and shadow boxing as he meanders through crowded streets, towering far above the smaller Thai villagers. He reminds me of a combination of Innocents Abroad by Mark Twain and the young Earnest Hemingway as he shadow boxed through the streets of Spain and France.

The wood-carving shops all have monstrous carved teakwood elephants at the door for advertisement. Some are the size of a standard American automobile and weigh hundreds of pounds. The first thing Nick did on entering a shop is to flash a big toothy grin at the tiny Thai female clerk in the shop. He proceeds to bargain with her over the price of the big elephant outside. He expressly wants a "white one." I've never seen such consternation, amazement and utter disbelief as shown in the eyes and expression of that tiny Thai girl. But on second thought, how could this smiling American giant do anything but request the biggest elephant in the town? He kept up the bargaining, quite seriously, with an occasional wink to another Thai girl, who has come to observe. When he finally states that the price is too high, there are no less than ten Thai girls, mothers and bearded grandfathers who have gathered to feverishly discuss why they have lost the sale. It is obvious that they have not totally pleased this American, but he did not seem unhappy when he departed.

The next shop is even worse. This shop exhibits carved utensils for salad bowls and for decoration. Outside of the shop is a pair of giant wooden forks and spoons for advertisement. Without cracking a smile, Nick towers above the proprietor and requests the salad bowl that goes with the giant spoon and fork. Utter chaos breaks out in the shop! Several clerks gather to chatter nervously in Thai that there is no such thing as a twelve-foot diameter salad bowl. He innocently asks, after all, why anyone would make a salad spoon and fork without a salad bowl. Since the dimensions did not seem too far off for his stature, the poor people are running in circles, trying to make arrangements for an entire teak tree to be carved into an appropriate bowl. After a great deal of bartering, during which he convinced them of the utter absurdity of having utensils without a complementary appropriate bowl, he breaks into a huge grin, thanks them very graciously and purchases the utensils. After we leave, I glance back to see a large crowd of people standing in the middle of the street, watching us. They are all smiling and talking rapidly.

The third shop is also small. An older Thai lady comes out to wait on us. Within minutes, she is smiling and laughing. He is throwing out one fantastic story after another and it is all quite obvious to her. At one point, she calls his bluff by asking just what he means by a statement. He replies, "I make joke…laugh…like you are doing now!" With this, he points to his own broad grin and down at her smiling lips. When we left, I'm sure that the old lady would have done anything for him…she seemed ready to adopt him!

Nick and I decide to take one of the cyclopeds to search for a place to eat. These are small rickshaw affairs, pulled by a man riding a bicycle. Usually, they are pedaled by old men and young boys. The increased weight of Americans is frequently a problem. But, they are cheap transportation and very efficient in the narrow streets. My driver is a strong young man, who has no difficulty with my weight. However, Nick's driver is a tiny, elderly man, who appears on the verge of developing a hernia with each pedal stroke, as he attempts to pull this young American bull. After a few moments, Nick tells him to take his feet off the pedals. When this is done, Nick stretches his gargantuan limbs out and takes over the peddling from the back seat. The cycloped suddenly speeds through the streets like an arrow. The old man is terrified since he had never been able to generate such steam. He tries desperately to steer in and out of the traffic, while maintaining a steady stream of Thai language, aimed at this demon behind him. I am sure that if he had the courage, he would have abandoned this wild machine. Finally, we arrive at the restaurant. The old man is so frightened that he is pale and shaking. In less than five minutes, he has been transported into the jet age and it terrifies him. The other drivers are laughing and finally, after a liberal tip from Nick, he too begins to laugh…but not very enthusiastically.

Major Omo, the aircraft commander joins us for dinner. Afterward, everyone wanted to stop by one of the two nightclubs in town. The first one wasn't much. We stayed for about an hour after listening to the combo and having a couple of beers.

From the restaurant, we took a small Libretta bus. This is no more than a motor scooter with a small platform behind it. It is enclosed by a tin roof and can accommodate six small people. A large luggage rack is on top. It is also very cheap transportation.

There are already three other people in the bus before it stops for us. Nick realizes there will not be adequate room inside for his large frame, and so he promptly hops on top to sit in the luggage compartment. The poor driver becomes semi-hysterical with this crazy American. For God's or Buddha's sake, there is this giant fool sitting in the luggage rack on top of the bus!

The police will surely stop him, and besides, he might fall off and hurt himself. The little fellow excitedly runs 'round and 'round, entreating Nick to come down. The driver finally states that under no circumstance can Nick ride up there. The driver, who is all of four feet tall and weighs less than eighty pounds, stands alongside the bus, entreating Nick to jump and he will "catch him." I am laughing so hard that tears are rolling down my cheeks. At last, Nick condescends to "get down like a big boy." The driver simply smiles and makes arrangements for Nick to sit up front with him so that he can stick his legs out in front and have enough room…and away we go.

When we arrived at the nightclub, a smiling Thai maître d' opens the door and bows to us. Since Nick is leading our group, he returns his bow… and very low. The Thai returns the bow, as does Nick…each time lower. The poor Thai considers it impolite not to reciprocate by bowing lower and Nick is damned and determined not to stop the competition. Finally, I play the kill-joy role, much to the relief of the Thai gentleman, and call a stop to it. We all have a bottle of beer while listening to a fair musical combo. But forty-five minutes to an hour is enough, and the hour is late for us older men. I am sure that Nick would have continued on this type of tour all night. Major Omo and I plead "we old men must have our rest."

On our way back to the hotel, the drivers are constantly trying to "fix us up" with a prostitute. Their enthusiasm is based on the cut that they receive for every liaison. The typical sales pitch is, "You want Number One Lady?"

After telling them "no" at least a dozen times, Nick finally stops them cold with, "Listen, I don't want any damn lady! I want a whore!"

This shocks them so much that no further discussion follows. I am sure that they have never had such a blatant encounter before.

When we arrive back at the hotel, I am exhausted. Someone like Nick is funny for a while, but he is so much like a hyperkinetic child that you tire of his constant interchanges. Later, in speaking with Major Omo, he noted that on several past occasions, attempts to promote Nick to aircraft commander have been turned down. Nick's attention span is so short that he simply can't accept the responsibility. He might not make the ideal aircraft commander, but from my perspective, for an evening's entertainment, Nick is "Numbah One!"

I had really hoped to travel north out of Ching Mai to visit the teak wood forests and observe the use of elephants to transport heavy branches and entire trees to the mill for processing. I have never seen anything remotely comparable to it. But it is monsoon season in Thailand and the roads north are all flooded. I even spoke with several natives about renting a motorcycle to ride through the backcountry. But everyone discouraged it. Perhaps, another time…

We got several hours sleep before our early morning takeoff back to Bangkok. By the time we arrived at the airport, an enormous storm had engulfed the area. Not until the afternoon were we able to take off. Thunderstorms and turbulence plagued our flight all the way back. I was very happy to feel the wheels touch down in Bangkok. I must say, however, that standing on the runway in Ching Mai, I had a magnificent vista of storm clouds with thunder and lightning sweeping across the mountain background. Great gusts of wind and rain only added to the drama. I looked up at the beautiful villa of the King as gusts of wind presaged the oncoming storm. How wonderful it would be to have a beautiful home on a mountain in a temperate semi-tropical climate! I love the drama of thunder and lightning!

On arriving in Bangkok, I was unable to obtain a private room, so I share a room with one of the pilots. I've been promised a place on a Caribou leaving for Cam Ranh tomorrow morning. I'll believe it when I see it.

9 May 1967

When I arrive at the Bangkok Airport the weather has worsened. There are very heavy winds on the runway that blow an Army Otter into our Caribou, with resultant wing damage that kills all chances of flying out on this aircraft. I spent the remainder of the day attempting to obtain a hop on a C-130, but each manages to develop some malfunction at the last minute. Finally, I catch a flight and we take off from Bangkok at 1 a.m. We fly directly to Saigon, off-load some passengers, and arrive at Cam Ranh at 5 a.m. I sleep until noon and spend the remainder of the afternoon reading back mail.

It is interesting. When I am out of the office, the other flight surgeons do well. But, the very moment they hear that I am back on base, they seem to regress and come to me for every trivial detail imaginable. There are times that I feel like the most prominent "father figure" on base. Since most of my energies are devoted to tying up the odds and ends at Cam Ranh before I rotate back to the U.S., it is a bit exasperating to have to wipe runny noses and listen to complaints about trivial matters. In accordance with the usual Air Force policy, I am allotted one week to clear base at the end of my Vietnam assignment. Therefore, I officially declare to the office that from after 18 May, my work at the office is finished. I AM OFFICIALLY FIGMO! (F... You. I've Got My Orders)

Toward the end of any tour of duty, there is a period of transition, during which you have received orders for your next duty station. Technically, this is interpreted by many airmen as meaning that they are now under the command of the next assignment, in the nebulous future. As such, they argue that they are exempt from orders from their current commanding officer. Therefore, when an order is given by their current boss, they plead exemption by FIGMO.

The following comments are in reply to a letter from Elaine.

It is obvious that we are in rather severe disagreement about the war in Vietnam. But since I will soon be home, it is ridiculous to discuss such a controversial topic in letters. From your comments, I assume that you are getting your facts from the anti-war demonstrators on campus. And who could ever doubt the veracity of "facts" that originated in the sophomoric minds of such sage military, tactical-strategic and diplomatic experts... who have the benefits of wisdom accumulated from birth to their present ages of 18-20 years? I refer specifically to your recent "quote" about leaders of this country who claim that we must exterminate Vietnam in order to protect ourselves from Red China. If you can provide me with a formal reference for such a statement by a responsible person in our government, I, too, will question our presence here.

Elaine has expressed frustrations in dealing with a certain personality in her laboratory environment. I wrote: In another year you will be a medical student and begin to see patients who are not as sick as the person in your lab. For a physician to be "shocked" at the behavior of a psychiatric patient is not exactly kosher. This response only reinforces the patient's aggressive tendencies and demeans your role as a physician. As a physician, you will hear and see a great many situations that involve patients. Many encounters will tax both your imagination and your patience. Despite the many internal reactions that are invoked in you by these encounters, you must maintain a certain element of detachment in order to remain objective.

Remember, the simple act of consulting a physician is an overt admission by the patient that he or she has a problem beyond their own ability to resolve. There are no fine lines between friends and non-friends or between patients and non-patients.

At one time or another we are all patients, even though we may not formally seek care or counsel. But, you must always be a physician, not just when on duty, but every day and night for the rest of your life. Your responses to the problems of friends can be no different from your response to patients. This is both the burden and the privilege of being a physician.

Privilege of any type is only one side of a coin. The opposite side of the "privilege coin" is the responsibility inherent with that privilege. The privileges are superficial, perhaps gaining recognition in society, financial success and enhanced professional status. But the phantom of responsibility will haunt you every hour of every day and night for the rest of your life. Responsibility toward another person who has entrusted him or herself to you with that responsibility cannot be measured. Nor can a price be affixed to it.

I well recall a professor at Northwestern my first year making the following comments in a lecture:

While interviewing a patient, you may find yourself uncomfortable and not know why. This will be reflected in your attitude and approach to the patient. When this occurs, politely excuse yourself from the interview. Go into the men's/ladies restroom and walk over to the sink. Then look into the mirror and ask yourself, "What's your problem, doctor?"

And in further comments to Elaine about injustices against women, I wrote:

If I must make the understatement of the year: A letter of grievance from me to the Zoology Department at the University of Texas-Austin would probably explode in your face. While I can defend the supposition that throughout history women have been grievously wronged and unappreciated, the facts of debate would damn me to defeat. Surely, since highly qualified women have not achieved the forefront of recognition by society, the burden does not rest on a Male dominated society or any other single faction. As Shakespeare expressed in Julius Caesar: "Our fate, dear Brutus, lies not in our stars…but within ourselves." If women are so much more qualified than society recognizes, they have had ample opportunity to break the bonds. We live in a pluralistic and capitalistic society. In the United States, women control sixty to seventy percent of the wealth. In a capitalistic society, wealth is power. There is, therefore, no excuse for women's failure to assert themselves under these conditions. Perhaps women prefer to cry about injustices rather than to correct them. I personally do not believe that the majority of women are capable of or desire to liberate themselves from this dependence on the male. My considerations are purely pragmatic. Seventy percent of the physicians in the Soviet Union are women, yet Russia continues to be dominated by male factions. The vast majority of men that I have known from childhood through medical school and residency do not prefer a strong woman as a wife. Perhaps their personal insecurities do not wish to be challenged. And, on the flip side, if a young woman is given the choice of education vs. marriage, she will usually choose marriage. Most intelligent women know that the kiss-of-death for them on a date is to come across as "too bright." It scares the hell out of most men. It is as frightening to a man for a bright woman to challenge him as it is terrifying for a fox to be suddenly pursued by a rabbit.

But, let's focus on a couple, closer to home, namely thee and me.

You have superior ambition and intelligence. I honor these features and want you to develop and fulfill every potential within you. If either of these were untrue, I would not have married you.

Most women do not have your abilities and most men do not have my desire for a wife to excel. When these facts are compounded by reality, it is easy to see why 99.44 percent of marriages are mediocre. The most beautiful rose will not flourish if planted in poor soil, and conversely, the richest soil will not convert a weed into a rose. You speak of women being stereotyped into what they are expected to be. But do not forget that for every caricature, there is a grain of truth that inspired the caricature; otherwise there could be no basis for the caricature.

For me to choose a woman of lesser intellect to be my wife reflects more on my insecurity than on any trait of yours. I would dishonor myself to choose a woman of lesser intellect or capability than myself.

CHAPTER 39

Saying Goodbye

11 May 1967

Today I received a letter of thanks from Sergeant Calendine. He received the Bronze Star for which I nominated him. I'm happy about this because when I commit myself to something of value for another person, I expect success from the venture.

13 May 1967

Yesterday, Col. Norman C. Gaddis of the 558th TFS at Cam Ranh was shot down a few miles south of Haiphong. Evidently, he was struck by artillery and then finished off by a MIG-17. Someone observed one chute and there is a slim possibility that both pilots ejected successfully. His back-seat pilot was Lt. James Jefferson. If Colonel Gaddis is captured, this will be a coup for North Vietnam. To the best of my knowledge, he would be the highest-ranking officer to have been captured so far. At the time of this writing, none of this information had been published in the United States. My closest working relationship with Colonel Gaddis was during the investigation of the F-4C crash in December. Colonel Gaddis was chairman of the accident investigation board for the F-4C crash in December. Many years later I learned that Colonel Gaddis was captured and spent a number of years at the "Hanoi Hilton" as a prisoner of war. His co-pilot did not survive.

Today, we have had our share of dignitaries on base, including the deputy ambassador to Vietnam, Eugene M. Locke, General Westmoreland and other generals too numerous to count. It was impossible to move around the base without running into an Air Policeman. An amusing incident occurred when a Vietnamese, clad in black pajamas, appeared in front of the officers club. He was carrying a cloth sack. Approximately ten Air Policemen converged on him at once. Apparently he didn't cooperate because two minutes later he was knocked for about three flips before he was pinned to the ground. It was probably one of the workers with a sack of stolen C-rations.

14 May 1967

All week, pilots of my squadron, the 391st TFS, have hounded the flight surgeon's office to ask if I will be at the squadron party. They are all too aware of my penchant for isolation and seclusion. I sensed that this related to my forthcoming transfer from Cam Ranh and assured them that I would definitely be present. Every pilot in the squadron was present. Food and booze were present in copious amounts. It was delightful to have so many of the pilots and friends that I admire in one place.

This is the farewell party for many members of the 391st TFS, including myself. DEROS is next week. On that magic day, I and twenty other pilots from the 391st TFS will leave Cam Ranh Bay and Southeast Asia. We will be replaced by others, for better or for worse.

The evening began smoothly as the melodies rolled effortlessly from the battered upright piano and floated over the crowded canteen area like hickory smoke wafting on the breeze of an autumn evening. The piano has been flown in as part of cargo on a C-130. Its origins will forever be unknown. There is no limit to Yankee ingenuity for obtaining contraband by air. As long as there is a pilot and an aircraft large enough to transport it, nothing is too remote or too large to obtain from somewhere.

Leaning back against the wall, I braced my bum ankle/leg against the edge of the piano. "DEROS," "DEROS." For the enlisted men, that acronym is like speaking of heaven while your feet are planted in hell. But for me and for many pilots, it is a mixed blessing. I remember smiling as Lieutenant MacFarland topped off my mug with Heineken beer. Tonight is a special night for which I have abandoned my rule about "no alcohol." Having been a tee-totaler all of my life, I have no tolerance for any quantity of alcohol, and I am aware of the flush in my cheeks and slight slurring of speech that accompany a pleasant warmth that pervades my body and mellows my emotions. I chat with other pilots of my squadron and sing the lyrics from English pubs in the 1940s and more raunchy tunes taken from the mosquito-enshrouded tents of Claire Chenault, somewhere in the depths of China during WW II.

"Praise the Lord and pass the ammunition...Praise the Lord and pass the ammunition...Praise the Lord and pass the ammunition and we'll all be free..."[28]

---

28 Reference: Chaplain, Lieutenant Howell Forgy, was aboard the USS New Orleans during the Japanese attack on Pearl Harbor, December 7, 1941. A bucket brigade of became fatigued while lifting ammunition by hoist. Chaplain Forgy later noted that as "the

Another World War II favorite, "Coming In On A Wing and A Prayer,"[29] was quickly picked up:

> *One of our planes was missing*
> *Two hours overdue*
> *One of our planes was missing*
> *With all its gallant crew*
> *The radio sets were humming*
> *We waited for a word*
> *Then a noise broke*
> *Through the humming and this is what we heard*
>
> *Comin' in on a wing and a prayer*
> *Comin' in on a wing and a prayer*
> *Though there's one motor gone*
> *We can still carry on*
> *Comin' in on a wing and a prayer*
>
> *What a show, what a fight, boys*
> *We really hit our target for tonight*
> *How we sing as we limp through the air*
> *Look below, there's our field over there*
> *With just one motor gone*
> *We can still carry on*

---

men were getting a little tired, I just happened to say, "Praise the Lord and pass the ammunition." The expression was picked up and converted into music. It was extremely popular after the attack on Pearl Harbor.

29 This phrase originated with the WWII patriotic song "Coming in on a Wing and a Prayer," 1943, by Harold Adamson and Jimmie McHugh, which tells of a damaged warplane, barely able to limp back to base: Adamson and McHugh wrote several patriotic songs in World war II and were awarded the Presidential Certificate of Merit by President Harry Truman

Comin' in on a wing and a prayer

These are the good songs from World War II, the last good war, I thought. Turning to Major Strickland standing beside the piano, I asked, "Strick, why do we always consider World War II as the Golden Age of Aerial warfare?" This serious, philosophical question seems somewhat incongruous, when spoken with slurred speech and alcohol-tainted breath. Strick pauses for a moment's reflection, but only for a moment. Without changing his placid expression, Strickland continues to stare at the slowly dissipating curl of smoke rising from his cigar. He is obviously thinking of a response. Slowly, very slowly, he lifts his beer to the light and sights through the amber liquid. I watch the narrowing of his eyes as he formulates an answer and swallows hard. Then the serious expression yields to one of relief.

"Hell, Doc, that's easy to answer. World War II was the only air war that we truly won!"

A look of great satisfaction fills his face as he downs his beer. Such serious questions at a party are difficult to answer.

"Korea was anything except a victory." Then he looks especially thoughtful.

"Of course, from an aviator's point of view, World War I was Nirvana. It was a gentleman's war...that is, if you were above the trenches. But we shared the victory with England and France. World War II had all the ingredients of a "good war." It was partly a religious war in which the Christian United States was smote a dastardly, cowardly blow by the heathen nation of Japan."

Now, his eyes began to glow as he warmed to the subject. "With the awful majesty of the Old Testament God, who is slow to anger but terrible in His wrath, we crushed those yellow bastards! It was clear cut...right versus wrong...good versus evil...white versus black..."

He burps and quickly adds with a grin, "Actually, it was white versus yellow! The victory was total and final! But in Germany's case, color was not an issue. You know this was the third time that Germany had declared war on other nations. What the hell is their problem? The first war was the Franco-Prussian war in 1870. The second was World War I and the third war was World War II. During WW II, fifty million people died because this psycho-country likes to strut in military uniforms and can't control its testosterone! Without American air power, the war with Japan and Germany would have continued for a long, long time. But, we brought them to their knees with air power...

"As Winston Churchill said… 'The Hun is either fawning at your feet or snarling at your throat'...or, (burp!) Something like that."

By this time a small crowd of equally inebriated pilots had gathered to cheer him on.

"After World War II, the United States stood over the planet like a colossus, with one foot on Asia and another foot on Europe. And then we looked down on the terrible death and destruction that lay at our feet… Christian pity and brotherly love replaced our terrible swift sword, as we extended the hand of fellowship to our former adversaries…"

He poured a drink from the bottle on the piano and quickly downed it. "The bombs that fell on Nagasaki and Hiroshima were fitting thunder-claps of finality, unleashed from our bombers on the infidel. And, after this, war was no longer fun. In those brief moments, mankind passed from adolescence into adulthood. Maturity…whatever that is, will take longer…

"And, so, here we are, a group of overgrown barnstormers with our wonderful flying machines, trying to make the most of what we've got in this dirty little Vietnam War…! It ain't much but it's the only war we've got. So, gentlemen, let's make the most of it!"

"Hey, Major Strickland!" The hail came from a more than slightly inebriated 1st Lieutenant Thompson, who stood several feet away.

"Major, have you heard how the brass from Clark AFB get their combat time and pay?"

He paused, savoring the drama of the scandal to be unleashed. When he had everyone's attention, he grinned wolfishly and slowly poured himself another drink.

"Well, here's how they do it!," Thompson said. "On the last day of the month, General Butt Head leaves that dreadful, air-conditioned officers club at Clark AFB. He is driven by his chauffeur in an air-conditioned limousine to Clark Field. He and his entourage of SAC colonels and other sycophants enter an air-conditioned C-130, with customized interior to assure the comfort of important personages. Shortly after noon, they land at Tan Son Nhut.

"Bingo! They have landed in a combat zone and are now entitled to combat pay for the month. After a sumptuous lunch at the officers club, they are so fatigued from their journey that they require a nap. When they awaken, they head directly for base operations. They commandeer one of those twin-engine Cessna-310 courier type aircraft and for the next two hours shoot touch-and-goes in tight landing patterns at Tan Son Nhut. Ever aware that they are in a combat zone, they wish to avoid undue exposure to enemy fire. After twenty touch-and-goes, they have qualified for an air medal during that month.

"Now, don't forget that the air medal is a combat medal, awarded for acts of meritorious achievements while participating in aerial flight. Twenty missions are required to qualify for the air medal. A combat medal works wonders for you when you face a promotion board."

Lieutenant Thompson surveys the crowd.

"Now, after a dreary night of booze at the officers club, they are ready to face the next day. It just so happens that the 'next day' is the first day of a new month. This establishes their second month in a combat zone as well as it qualifies them for another month of combat pay. After a sumptuous breakfast, they return to Tan Son Nhut for their twin-engine Cessna-310. And after a full morning of touch-and-goes, they have won their air medal with oak leaf cluster. In addition to two air medals, they have won the Vietnam service medal, flight pay for two months and combat pay for two months...all without straying beyond the traffic pattern of Tan Son Nhut, AFB.

"It has been a strenuous day. They have a quick lunch of light wines and cheeses at the Tan Son Nhut Officers Club. By noon, they are winging their way back over the Pacific Ocean to Clark in the Philippines. Before leaving for their combat tour in Vietnam, they promised their wives that they would be home in time for the floor show at the officers club and the bridge party afterward. Except for perusing their maps, they will not return to this war zone for another two months, when it will be time to renew their benefits! Now, who can disagree? War is hell!"

A cheer of appreciation erupted from the surrounding pilots. Lieutenant Thompson basked in the glow of their applause as he toasted his admirers with still another beer!

Earlier in the evening, there had been an awards ceremony. To my astonishment and chagrin, I was honored as "Most Outstanding Airman of the 391st TFS" and presented an engraved plaque with squadron insignia. I was truly honored. This was not the product of some bureaucratic ribbon committee whose job is to customize decorations for future promotion boards. The award is from the men who fly the missions, pilots with whom I have flown, while they put their ass on the line every day in countless ways. These are fighter pilots who day in and day out fly supersonic jets against MIGs and SAMs over Hanoi and then return to dive-bomb and napalm Viet Cong in South Vietnam... while flying only a few feet above the ground at over 600 mph. Why me? I don't deserve this... These men are the cream of American manhood. No one is finer. Why me? I'm not even an official Air Force pilot...

My thoughts are interrupted by the words, "Hey, Doc!"

At my side stands a young first lieutenant by the name of Poteet. He is one of the new pilots, straight out of flight school, on his first combat assignment. Sticking out his hand, he says, "Doc, I've heard a lot about you and wanted to meet you. Congratulations!"

I tried to smile in appreciation, but words did not come easily. I could only ask the question to myself, "Congratulations, for what?" My thoughts are interrupted by a chorus of the Air Force song that erupts from the crowd around the piano and resounds from the walls...

> *Off we go into the wild blue yonder,*
> *Climbing high into the sun;*
> *Here they come zooming to meet our thunder,*
> *At 'em boys, Give 'er the gun! (Give 'er the gun now!)*
> *Down we dive, spouting our flame from under,*
> *Off with one helluva roar!*
> *We live in fame or go down in flame. Hey!*
> *Nothing'll stop the U.S. Air Force!*

By this time, the combination of alcohol, emotions and memories began to tell... I know I am on the verge of tears, but cannot explain why. Scenes of past missions flood my mind. The mission with Major Solis in which our four aircraft cavorted like dolphins, flying at 600-700 mph, between cumulus towers that rose 40,000 feet above the mountains...The ethereal beauty of shedding all earthly bonds to soar like eagles over the mountains and through the clouds. I didn't want to leave this camaraderie...these unreal supersonic flights. I wanted to stay here and fly forever, fighting the good fight, against an enemy that I rarely saw. I had risked my life for these honorable men, no less than they had risked their lives for me. From the depths of my soul welled up the realization that never in my life would I find this again. I knew that I would remember this night and this year for the rest of my life.

I remained aware that Lieutenant Poteet was watching me closely and recognized the emotions that struggled within me. He smiled and said dreamily, "Just listen to that, Doc…Why don't you stay with us for another year?"

My response was a sense of profound embarrassment toward what I faced on my return to the U.S. I am going back to face the plastic life of California and leaving this…all of this…behind. Groping for words, I stammered several feeble excuses as to why I could not sign up for another tour of duty in Vietnam. Suddenly, I caught myself.

What the hell are you doing? I thought. *You really have had too much to drink. Here you are trying to apologize to this rookie pilot for your choice to get-the-hell-out of this dirty little war that he is trapped in, and of which he knows nothing. Time to hang it up, Clark. Get to bed. Sleep this one off before you really make yourself look more like a fool than you are…*

With that, I pulled my flight cap from my belt, smiled at the lieutenant and slapped him on the back and staggered out the door. I faintly remember Sergeant Xeras waiting for me with the crash ambulance parked outside. Collapsing onto one of the gurneys, I recall nothing afterward until I awoke the next morning on the examining table in my office. Sergeant Xeras was quietly grinning as he turned on the lights to begin daily sick call.

Hanoi Hannah was on the short-wave radio last night, gloating in her syrupy voice about the capture of Colonel Gaddis. The poor devil is in for a hellish ordeal. I'm confident that they will not hesitate to destroy him mentally and physically for propaganda purposes!

18 May 1967

I was awakened at 5 a.m. today. Civilian Vietnamese are transported daily onto base and then transported off base in the evening. This morning a very large tractor-trailer truck carrying a large group of Vietnamese workers overturned. The people are stacked like cattle inside and hang against the rails, packed like sardines. Apparently, when making a turn the railing came off. This occurred about three miles from base. Twelve people were killed and ninety-two were injured. Thirty of the injured were in critical condition. It was a very real catastrophe to strike these poor people. The hospital surgeons have been busy all day.

23 May 1967

This morning I am awakened, not by the thunderous roar of Phantoms taking off for their morning strike missions, but by the loud, boisterous voices of pilots singing in chorus:

Happy Birthday to You... Happy Birthday to You... Happy Birthday, Dear Buddha... Happy Birthday to You...

Aha! I had forgotten. Today is Buddha's birthday, and in honor of this, there will be no bombing...a truce for Buddha's birthday!

This short respite will give both sides time to rearm and reinforce themselves before the bombing and fighting resumes tomorrow...with increased vigor!

There is no little irony in this as the Allied Forces call upon Christ for support. The Viet Cong call on their forest gods for strength while the North Vietnamese call upon Marx, Lenin, Stalin and Ho Chi Minh for support. After all, without religions, who would mankind call upon to support its wars?

Last night a dinner party was given by a number of senior pilots and senior officers that represent the 12th TFW and all four F-4C Phantom squadrons. Wing officials were present. I couldn't believe it when I was informed that the party was specifically dedicated to Major McQuillen and me, since we are both approaching the end of our tour in Vietnam. In contrast to the recent squadron party by the pilots, tonight is a quiet gathering of perhaps 100 people, older senior officers, including Colonel Mack.

As usual, the food is the best that the U.S. Navy could obtain. There were huge T-bone steaks, lobsters and multiple wines and liqueurs. After eating, the liquor flowed freely, but things never got out of hand.

I have never been so personally featured in the spotlight as at this meeting. I was very self-conscious and a bit embarrassed by it all. How do you react when men who risk their lives daily in countless flights, spontaneously stand and applaud you? I don't know. I'm afraid that I only blushed and tried to smile in appreciation. Hell, what else can you do? Rather, it should be the reverse. It is I who should applaud them.

After we had finished eating and were standing in small groups for conversation, Colonel Mack walked over to where I was standing. I smiled. But, there was something more than simple pleasantry in his eyes. He looked very sober. He fixed his gaze squarely on my eyes, with an intensity that I had never seen before. Slowly and powerfully, he grasped my hand in a vice-like grip and said, "You know, Guy, your job here has taken guts of steel…and by God, you've got them. Yes, you've got them. You are quiet and don't advertise, but you have guts of steel!"

I was taken aback at the near ferocity of his expression and declaration. I have absolutely no idea what I've done to warrant such praise. Perhaps, he simply had had too much to drink, or perhaps he was referring to my defiance of PACAF and 7th Air Force ruling that physicians would not leave Vietnam except by the express permission of the Pacific Air Force Command. (I had only recently returned from my jaunt to Thailand…with total disregard for this injunction!) Or perhaps, it related to my confrontation with Major Larry Johnson in Saigon about wishing to return to Cam Ranh from "temporary duty" in Vung Tau. It was about this time that the sky had fallen on Colonel Mack, when he had conflicts with 7th Air Force. I will never know.

But, in the year 2011, as I transcribe these notes, I can honestly state that I have never met a man for whom I have greater personal respect and affection than I had and continue to have for Col. Wilbert H. McElvain. What touched me just as deeply, however, was another encounter that occurred several minutes later. One of the more senior F-4 pilots walked over and firmly grasped my hand. He had flown fighters in Korea and was only one victory short of being an ACE. Looking me straight in the eyes, he said, "Doc…It's wrong for me to say this…especially since it's in regard to this God-Forsaken-Place. But I wish that you were staying with us. You're not like the other flight surgeons…I hate to see you go."

Then he blushed, appearing somewhat embarrassed, and walked away. How can he say that to me? All too often, many of these pilots will never live to return to civilian life. And, yet, they keep going. These men aren't the old men of SAC and cargo aircraft who ranked lower in their flight school class and couldn't hack it as fighter pilots. They don't fly at 40,000 feet above the battle, relatively immune to groundfire, SAMs and MIGs. They don't fly into Saigon on the last day of the month and shoot touch-and-go's in the traffic pattern until the number of touch-and-go's qualifies them to receive an air medal for their valor for two months. And they don't leave Vietnam for their safe haven that lies far, far away. These men receive combat pay for their combat efforts, not for worthy paperwork.

Most of the younger men will separate from the Air Force and return to civilian positions. (I have recently learned that two pilots from the previous rotation have been accepted to medical school.)

As the evening waned and things quieted down, I stood in a darkened corner and watched them singing, dancing and drinking. I kept thinking over and over again, "Where do they come from? How can one country find so many fine men such as these to fight her wars? These questions were not prompted by the emotions of the moment. I have continuously asked these same questions throughout every day of the past year. The answers are they come from her cities, her farms, her ranches and her plains. They come from the bayous and farms of the Old South, from the communities of the Eastern seaboard, from the hardscrabble soil of New England, from the plains of Oklahoma, Nebraska and Kansas, and from the Western plains and deserts of Arizona, Texas and New Mexico. They come from the mountain states of Colorado and Montana as well as the Badlands of Dakota. They come from the Pacific Northwestern states of Oregon, Washington and Alaska. They come from America...they are America!

I hasten to ask why we have such lower classes in Congress and in the halls of power. Perhaps that question was best answered by Alexis de Tocqueville in his epic analysis, *Democracy in America*. From the perspective of an impersonal observer of America in the 1800s, he noted: "In America, the highest quality of men does not enter politics." For me, that is a tragedy!

I have never associated with men for whom I have greater respect than these pilots. Any one of them could pass for student body president or captain of the football team in any college of the land. Even if all the masculine and macho elements are discarded from the discussion, I have never encountered any one of them that did not have exemplary personal integrity and a sense of personal honor. If there is such a trait as "inherent nobility," I have found it to be universally present in these men.

It is important to understand that the brain of a pilot can separate the act of flying from all other sensory input and he can actually enjoy the flying element as distinct from the reality of the situation. While attacking enemy troops or defending friendly troops, it is not the vengeance of killing the enemy. The act of flying itself is the alpha and omega of action. The best flying that I have ever experienced or ever will experience in my life has been in Vietnam.

CHAPTER 40

Officially FIGMO

24 May 1967

I had hardly arrived in the flight surgeon's office before Colonel Mack stood in the doorway. He asked me to write a report to justify flight surgeons flying F-4C strike missions and how this activity contributes to the overall combat efficiency and performance of the 12th Tactical Fighter Wing. After some discussion, I wrote the report and delivered it to him before lunch. He seemed satisfied with it.

I was tempted to feign being shocked at his request since I am officially "FIGMO" at this short period before I leave country. But, I didn't. I don't think that he realizes I will be leaving in a few days. The only date that he recalls for me is my DEROS of 10 June 1967. His DEROS is 20 June 1967, and it seems that he will remain on station until then.

The heat has been atrocious. It is comparable to living in an oven. Officially, it is 103 degrees in the shade and 135 degrees on the runways and over the sand at head level.

Last night at 1:30 a.m. the entire Quonset hut was awakened by the sound of distant explosions that shook the ground. We climbed to the top of the Quonset hut to watch Republic of Korean (ROK) Marines barrage the mountainside on the mainland with artillery. The entire mountain range flashed and reverberated under the assault. Presumably, both Viet Cong and units of the North Vietnamese Army have infiltrated the jungles nearby. These enemy forces were building at the time that we investigated the aircraft crash in December. Presumably, these same enemy troops are now receiving the present recognition from the ROK Marines. I must say it is quite a display. I only hope that it stays on that side of the Cam Ranh peninsula a bit longer, until I am gone.

Lon Kerry is having a terrible time dealing with the corpsmen in the flight surgeon's office. For the past five months, he has been overly friendly with them by fraternizing, joking, partying and becoming altogether too familiar with them. I have warned him about the necessary separation between officers and men. Such elitism is counter to his concept of democracy. By his over-familiar behavior he has sown the wind. Now he is reaping the whirlwind. Recently, he asked them to perform certain tasks. They responded with lip by making a big joke of it, as if to say, "Ole buddy, who are you to tell us what to do?" If I weren't leaving, I would step in to correct the situation, but Kerry must learn an important lesson from this. Even now, despite my short timer status, a mere suggestion of something on my part has the authority of a direct order. Actually, I have never given a direct order. I have never found it necessary. The men are pleasant and cooperative regardless of the issue involved. I don't recall ever having to repeat a request.

Tonight, when confronted with their insubordination, Kerry exploded and informed Sergeant Xeras that, "Just because Dr. Clark is leaving, they have no right to not follow my requests," etc.

I don't envy him his last seven months here. It is difficult to reverse the order of command after it has been flaunted for so long. I feel fortunate in that I have never experienced this situation. Democracy is not an issue here. It is the age-old relationship between those who command and those who follow. Perhaps, being from the South, it is easier for me. I was raised in a society of past serfdom in the form of slavery. Even in my youth, working for my father and grandfather in the oil business, I frequently had men working for me who were ten to thirty years my senior. I have always treated those subordinate to me with respect and fairness. But I have never considered myself to be one of them; however, I have always considered myself to stand up for them. I have intervened many times both in their defense and in their behalf. This is the foundation of their respect for me and the foundation of my respect for them. This is the burden of all leadership. I recommended both of the non-commissioned officers in charge of the flight surgeon's office for the Bronze Star. They have both been outstanding. Both men received the award.

Tomorrow, I will spend the day clearing the base. This means closing out all of my records and cleaning up all loose ends. On Friday there will be nothing for me to do except sign out and climb on the Northwestern Boeing 707 big bird and fly home.

HALLELUJAH!

24 May 1967

Throughout this year, I have observed an interesting phenomenon. Perhaps it is a lesson in mass psychology concerning individual survival. I have noted it primarily in others while I have admitted it more begrudgingly in myself.

Death is frequent in war. It indiscriminately strikes anyone, whether best friend or worst enemy. Of course, the emotional response varies with the person who has been stricken.

Whenever death claims a very close friend or acquaintance, there are inevitably two responses:

A sense of relief that it is someone else other than me;

Normal sorrow that attends loss of anyone who is dear…

In several dozens of people, regardless of the psychological defenses, the sense of relief is quite subtle but definitely evident. I have watched the sincerest of men lead a flight of planes into battle and return home with the loss of a dear friend vivid in their memory. Upon the first interview, the sense of relief that they have escaped pervades the atmosphere. Their attitude of sorrow is not hypocritical. It is heartfelt and true. A perfect example is when Kirt Haderlie led a flight of F-4Cs over the Hanoi area. Kenneth W. Cordier was lost on this mission. Kirt was a very dear friend of Ken Cordier, but when I interviewed Kirt less than an hour after landing, his response was initially relief that he survived. This rapidly changed to sorrow at the loss of his friend. After twenty-four hours, Kirt's mind had entirely closed out the event.

It is interesting that not all individuals react in this manner. Only two weeks prior to this, Ken had led a flight of three F-4Cs into an area near Tchepone, Laos. He watched as his two wingmen dissolved in flames from anti-aircraft fire. He returned to Cam Ranh alone. He was a changed man. Several days after this, I met him in Hong Kong. He was severely depressed and there was no element of relief about his personal survival. There was only the terrible grief that he had led those men into battle and had not brought them home. I have known Ken and have respected him as a sterling individual who loves to fly almost as much as he loves to party. He is not of an overly serious nature, but his sense of responsibility is extremely strong. From the time he lost his wingman to the time that he also failed to return, Ken Cordier was a changed man. I am sure that psychiatrists will interpret this response as a "subconscious death wish" that resulted from a strong sense of guilt, but so what? The fact remains that his response was exceptional...why?

26 May 1967

In five hours I will leave Vietnam. Strange thoughts enter my mind. I am experiencing the same thought patterns that I had before coming here. At that time, the idea of shipping out for Vietnam seemed very remote. Even with my orders in hand, I clung to a belief that the Air Force had probably screwed up again in my orders and at some last-minute point, they would be revoked. I even stretched my delusion further. Even if I were sent to Vietnam, the orders would soon be revoked and I would be flown back to Texas.

Now I am experiencing the same chain of delusions. I am guarding against disappointment by refusing to accept the fact that within a few days I will terminate the Vietnam chapter in my life as well as five years of active duty in the Air Force. I am unable to let myself go or be excited by the prospect of ending several chapters in my life lest some spiteful God on Mount Olympus reverse the plan at the last moment.

Someone reading the above would swear that I dictated it while reclining on a psychiatrist's couch instead of while sitting at a desk.

9:30 p.m.

I have just returned from Colonel Mack's quarters.

With mixed emotions, I shifted the Jeep into four-wheel drive through the last few yards of sand in front of his aluminum trailer. Over the dull hum of the air-conditioner, a roar of laughter echoed from within. Removing my flight cap, I gingerly knocked on the flimsy screen door. Colonel Mack quickly opened the door and a grin of obvious delight flashed across his face.

"Guy, come in...come in!"

"Colonel, I hope that I'm not disturbing you..."

Before I could continue, Colonel Mack had wrapped his arms around my shoulders and pulled me into the small living room of his quarters. Seated around the room were several older senior officers in fatigue uniforms. Still with his arm around my shoulders, Colonel Mack led me before the small group.

"Gentlemen, I want you to meet Guy Clark, the finest and the bravest man in the whole damn Air Force!" For a moment, Colonel Mack's voice broke. "Guy is our flight surgeon...he went down into the jungle out there to find our boys and to bring back their remains."

Colonel Mack pulled out his handkerchief to blow his nose.

"Guy, what are you drinking?"

I tried to apologize for interrupting him and his guests, but he waved me off. I recognized the wing commander, Brig. Gen. Jones E. Bolt, and was introduced to another general from off base, whose name I can't recall. Another colonel, whom I didn't recognize, was there. They all rose very congenially to shake hands with me. Colonel Mack seemed surprised to learn that I would be leaving tonight. He said he had just made a formal request for the 12th USAF Hospital at Cam Ranh to be named the William P. Simmons USAF Hospital. He insisted that I sit down and have a drink.

"Colonel, thank you, but I can't stay. I've got to finish packing. You see, I'll be leaving later tonight. I wanted to stop by and say goodbye and to thank you. It's been a privilege working for you."

He growled, "Nobody works for me; I work with you."

For a moment, Colonel Mack's face bore the expression of a small boy who has been ordered to come inside before the baseball game is over.

He regained his composure and spoke softly, "Yes, of course, it's almost time to go. I'll be going too before very long."

He paused for a moment.

"I wish I could be present to pin that Bronze Star on you."

From my astonished expression, he grinned as I stammered,

"For what?"

I remember the soft smile and fatherly clasp of my shoulder. I remember his sandy red hair and freckles on his face, but more than anything else that evening, I remember the deep sadness in his piercing blue eyes. Bittersweet...everything in life that I've ever known or held dear has been bittersweet.

I respect Colonel Mack more than any person I have ever known, and any praise from him is heartfelt and appreciated...but tonight I think he overdid things.

But now, I must travel to the other side of the base to begin checking on my flight out. Somehow, it seems unreal to say this.

Now in the year 2013, I can foresee no time in the future without war. Conflict is part of mankind's inherent personality. However, there may well come the day when aircraft are flown as drones and not by pilots. A person sitting at a computer console a world removed from the enemy can delete another person or thousands of persons from earthly existence with the click of a keystroke or mouse. No one can see the blood or appreciate the misery inflicted by mindless keystrokes. From 1966-1967 in Vietnam, my combat strikes in the F-4C Phantom II probably represented the last vestige of direct warfare. By "direct" I mean the implication of adversary against adversary, man-against-man, whether by personal conflict with bayonets and rifles, or by ships against other ships, or by aircraft against aircraft, guided by pilots against pilots. The human element has been the first line of defense in all pre-history and past-history of warfare. Whether the weapons were sticks and stones or rifles with bayonets, it was always the same, until now. Of course, this will not completely change overnight in all conflicts or for all military services. But the trend is evident and highly unlikely to reverse itself.

We have entered a new era that makes warfare all the more terrible. This is the Era of Remote Warfare, whereby an unmanned aircraft can be guided by computer with satellite communications from a trailer in the Nevada desert to destroy a person, a village or another aircraft in the Middle East, 12,000 miles from Nevada. Even if we discount the use of nuclear weapons, the circumstances are the same. In a Democratic society, there are no embarrassing body bags to arouse rejection of war by parents, wives, sons and daughters. Financially, there is no fortune invested by the Armed Forces in training pilots to fly technologically sophisticated aircraft. The cost of manufacture for these technologically sophisticated aircraft is avoided by utilizing much cheaper unmanned drones. With no concessions required for human frailty in operating the machines of war, economy of manufacture and utilization will overwhelm and dictate all other considerations.

Ships and submarines can launch missiles from oceans afar against targets with no risk to either the vessel or its personnel. The public does not have to face damaged ships and sailors in body bags when they return to port.

If circumstances of nuclear warfare are considered, it can only be stated that a single nuclear explosion 100 miles above the USA would create a burst of radiation to produce an electromagnetic pulse that is sufficient to destroy many of our technological advantages. It has been esti-mated that a relatively small device exploded over Nebraska would knock out approximately fifty percent of all electricity generated in the United States. In essence, such an event would render all scientific wizardry out of commission for at least ten years. Its effect would primarily destroy our satellites by the heat generated. As a result we would return to "direct war-fare," where human is pitted against human, whether on the ground with rifles and bayonets or in the air with WW II dogfights. Perhaps this is affir-mation of the age-old adage that "the more things change, the more they remain the same."

There will be no need for flight surgeons, in particular, or even for physicians in general. The human element of warfare will be absent except for the poor souls who must endure the automated chaos of destruction that rains from the skies or radiates from the heavens. When that day arrives, wars will be more terrible than we can imagine. Pain can be inflicted but not perceived. Destruction will become impersonalized to the degree of a video game that pits inanimate symbols against other inanimate symbols to achieve a lifeless, deathless score of victory or defeat.

These changes will require a different personality type than today's fighter and bomber pilot. The person who sits in isolation at a keyboard in the safety and comfort of a protected haven will have more in keeping with modern youth who are adept at video games and joy sticks than the devil-may-care barnstormer-turned-fighter pilot. There will be no adrena-line rush with takeoff or in plunging to earth at the speed of sound to dive-bomb a target hidden in the jungle. There will be no thrill when flying fifty feet above the ground at 600-700 mph, while the jungle on both sides of the cockpit explodes into a volcanic eruption of muzzle blasts and tracers that stream past the Plexiglas canopy in their attempt to destroy you. All the while you are ramming the throttle into full after-burner to turn the air-craft on its tail, rocketing straight up, just moments before the mountain in front of you lurches toward you. And at the same time the pilot is attempting to maintain consciousness in the presence of crushing G-forces.

It seems only logical to ask, Why risk multimillion-dollar aircraft and highly skilled pilots when reconnaissance detects the enemy by unmanned satellites and drones with real-time imagery? Why spend millions of dollars to train pilots in the use of high-tech weaponry when robotic aircraft and remote-guided weaponry can be controlled from your back yard by a computer link?

The glory days during which knights on armored horses tilted against each other have been lost. So have the days of aerial knights tilting against other aerial knights for control of the air. From the armchair of a pacifist, these changes may evoke a rousing Hurrah!

But there will be neither mercy nor tenderness in this change. Destruction of the enemy by keystroke will be terrible beyond all imagination! By removing the human element from waging war, we will save the lives of our military, but lose our consciousness of what we are mechanically inflicting on the enemy.

When I left Vietnam in 1967, these changes were already beginning to evolve. Instead of risking life, limb and aircraft by visual contact and dive bombing, laser-guided missiles and bombs were being unleashed from high altitude in surgical strikes that offered little or no risk to the pilot or to his aircraft.

Nearly half a century now stands between my year in Vietnam and my home in Santa Barbara, California. During those years, I have aged from a young man to an old man. But what a life it has been! My lifelong quest for "high adventure" was more than fulfilled in Vietnam.

Now at the three-quarters of a century mark and from the security of my family, I turn to survey those other moments in life that stand like mountain peaks, towering to pierce the clouds of routine daily existence. With the exception of my marriage and family, no life experiences tower higher than the privilege of flying combat missions in the F-4C Phantom II during my tour as flight surgeon and chief of aviation medicine for the 12th TFW at Cam Ranh Bay.

Since 1966-1967, the roar and scream of jet engines in full afterburner have long faded into the humdrum background murmur of the 101 Freeway that connects Southern California to Northern California, and which is two blocks from my home. Over the years, many memories of Vietnam have faded, but memories are like old photographs, which may fade but never entirely disappear. What remain are remnants and relics from a different world, of a different time, from a different life and of a different person. Experiences of more than ninety combat missions, once savagely burned into my consciousness, are now little more than charred, cold ashes, archived into anonymity and buried in crypts within my aging brain. With the passage of years, memories of strike targets, originally defined as a bridge crossing a particular river, blends with the memory of another strike that involved another bridge that crossed yet another river, until memories of all strike mission targets, bridges and rivers fade into the anonymity of their commonality. Memory that the target for an afternoon is a weapons storage area, snuggled into a mountain cliff side has little to distinguish it from the memory of another weapons storage area that lies 200 miles due south and is in another valley that we had attacked earlier in the morning.

For all targets, the blasts of bombs and the flames of napalm are remembered only in a generic sense. Occasionally, a larger secondary explosion confirmed both the target designation and the accuracy of our aim and weaponry. The explosions and fireballs that bounced and destroyed aircraft, as we flew through the smoke and flames to begin another run on the target, are registered in a mental file of numerous similar missions of lost identities. And, as years pass, even large explosions fade and float out of memories, whether by choice or by chance…diluted and displaced by the daily floodtides of civilized trivia…getting and spending…adapting to this Brave New World of robotic transactions…the defining events that separate life during peace from events of life during war.

EPILOGUE

I SEPARATED FROM ACTIVE DUTY IN THE AIR FORCE AT Tacoma AFB, Washington, in June 1967. I flew to Austin, where Elaine was finishing her Ph.D. in molecular biology at the University of Texas-Austin. Since my internal medicine residency did not begin until September 1967, I jumped in to help Elaine finish her work for her Ph.D. Finally in late August, we left Austin for Southern California. Elaine became tearful as we drove away. I understood. Our years in Austin were happy and we were once more heading into the unknown territories of my residency and her freshman year in medical school at UCLA.

Overall, I experienced the predictable difficulties of every veteran who re-enters civilian life after a combat experience. I rejected the academic regimentation and kowtowing that is standard fare in the organized world of academic medicine. For too long I had flown like an eagle, free from the confines of hospitals, supervision and the censure of attending staff that were less qualified than I. However, I was fortunate to have other resident physicians who were also Vietnam veterans. We never discussed experiences or even mentioned our past lives. But there was some comfort derived from their presence, especially when we were surrounded on all sides by younger interns and resident physicians who were steeped in California counter-culture.

During war, you are judged by what you achieve and not by knowledge of some arcane topic from the latest medical journal. The seniority of knowledge claimed by my professors did nothing to impress me. I had known better men, who had died for something beyond their own interests. With few exceptions, I found few personalities in the academic medical profession to impress me.

Several professors were both sympathetic and empathetic, since they had served in WW II. I remain forever grateful to one of those few physicians, Doctor Gold, chief of endocrinology at Wadsworth VA Hospital. I will never forget sitting in the rear of a conference room during my first month of Medical Residency. The topic under discussion was endocrine influences on renal function. Even though I had studied these topics from textbooks while in Vietnam, the discussion was absolutely over my head. Toward the end of the session, Dr. Gold asked questions of the residents in the audience. I listened but comprehended little. Dr. Gold looked at me sitting on the window sill in the rear of the class and asked, "Dr. Clark, what is TRP (tubular reabsorption of phosphorus)? My response was prompt and succinct. "Dr. Gold, I haven't the foggiest idea what you are talking about!"

Someone else answered the question correctly and soon the conference broke up. As I was leaving the room, I felt a touch on my shoulder. Dr. Gold placed his arm around my shoulders and said kindly: "Don't worry. It will come. I had the same problem when I returned from World War II." I will never forget those kind words! Now, nearly a half-century later, they still ring in my ears.

As an aside, I am all too aware of a rebellious streak in my personality that abhors authority. Many persons today consider military service to be high on the scales of automated human behavior, but this was never my perspective. Recognizing my personal rebellious trait, I found it remarkable that the Air Force was never an object of my rebellion. I attribute this to my personal encounters with hospital commanders, department heads and pilots of daily association. I had no resentment of their higher rank or position because I accepted their leadership and respected them. But, even more important is that they reciprocated by respecting me.

From my perspective, life experience is the only purpose to live. The practice of medicine provides a front-row-center seat to observe humanity. But physicians who perceive life only from their activities on the aseptic wards of hospitals do not know life. I found this to be true of physicians that I encountered in Vietnam. Physicians worked in the same aseptic environments of hospitals, nurses, aides and technicians, all far removed from the realities of war and the outside world. Of course, they treated the casualties of war, but whether in Peoria or Vung Tau, a hospital is a hospital is a hospital. Gunshot wounds are the same in Chicago and New York as they are in Saigon. Catastrophic fractures are the same in Cleveland, Atlanta and Nha Trang. The human stories behind these wounds are lost in the standardized mechanics of medical treatment. Physicians in these environments become immunized from contact with the realities of life that provide patients for them to treat.

Today, after half a century of practicing medicine and observing the human species, in triumph and defeat, in laughter and in sorrow, my respect for the individual man and woman continues to grow with each passing day.

Despite these reservations, overall the internal medicine residency training program at Wadsworth V.A. Hospital was excellent. The saving grace for me was patient care, largely free of unsolicited academia. Being totally immersed in patient care at the hospital, my thoughts were primarily focused on making appropriate medical decisions and learning the intricacies of endocrinology, hematology, renal and pulmonary diseases. Responsibility for another human's life and health relegates all personal concerns to second place. There was neither luxury of time or desire to reminisce on past events as I returned to the academic aspects of internal medicine.

Things were different for Elaine, who was immersed in her role of freshman medical student at UCLA. Unfortunately, my preoccupation with duties of patient care made me unaware of the progressive discordances that were developing in our marriage. For me, a wife is not considered chattel. She is considered to be an equal in every sense, including her career and thought processes. On our wedding bands, I had inscribed in Latin: "A robure per armorem ad concordiem et unitas," or "From Strength through Love to Unity." I considered marriage to be a bond between two independent individuals to form a superior union. I was a strong individual. For me to marry an individual less strong than I would reflect on my personal inadequacy. At this stage in my life, I had no personal insecurities. I had achieved my personal goals, solely through my own efforts, and with no dependence or assistance from anyone. I expected no less of the woman I chose for marriage.

Since I provided all financial support, I assumed that her primary concern was devotion to her studies. And, since I had supported her Ph.D. studies, I also presumed that she knew of my dedication to her medical education. In short, I believed that she was happy. I felt satisfaction in my work and teaching duties at the hospital. But, years later, in reflection, I became aware of a fatal flaw in my personality. If I am happy and satisfied with my status and work, I presume that my wife must also be satisfied with her status and work...especially since I had never wavered in support of her. But for the first time in our marriage differences arose.

While in Vietnam, I had maintained two sets of notes, my personal diary and narrative of events and letters to Elaine. Because of this, she knew very little about my daily duties or combat activities in Vietnam. I only informed her of experiences in which I was not exposed to danger.

When I separated from the Air Force after returning from Vietnam, I never discussed my combat experiences with anyone, least of all with her. And yet, she now seemed to harbor some resentment for my time and ventures in Vietnam.

One day, a mid-air collision of two helicopters occurred near L.A. International Airport. Mid-air collisions in Vietnam were a personal horror for me. In most cases, the pilots were friends and acquaintances with whom I had shared life and flown in combat. I had to retrieve the remaining fragments of their bodies and care for the seriously injured who survived. I had previously communicated these emotions to Elaine from Vietnam in letters.

On the day of the L.A. incident, I arrived home after a full day of patient care to be met by Elaine. I had not heard about the L.A. helicopter crash. With an expression of angst, she informed me that the Los Angeles Regional Office of the FAA had just called for me. Because of my experience in Vietnam, they requested that I participate in the investigation of the helicopters' mid-air collision. Since I was no longer on active duty with the Air Force, I failed to realize any personal relevance or contribution that I could make. But, the thought of doing so impacted me heavily, sending me into a brief emotional tailspin before I recovered and saw that she was joking. I found no humor in it.

The more cynical I became toward academic medicine, the more difficulty Elaine had in adapting to the change that had occurred in me. We had been married for nearly six years and I considered the bond of marriage as solid and irrevocable. I had memories of my father returning from combat on Guadalcanal in the Pacific during WWII. Mother coped with his difficulties and suffered through his agonies. But the bond of marriage held against all odds. My Scottish clan mentality assumed that in the midst of a storm, individuals of a family unite to fight against common enemies.

From my perspective, marriage was a mutual defense treaty against all internal and external enemies. Thus my naiveté reasoned…

But, Elaine was exposed to California counter-culture on a daily basis. She was four years younger and accepted the current moods of society as the norm. My atavistic attitudes were totally out of sync. I was utterly intolerant of the sophomoric-straight-line utterances, mouthed by faculty and fellow residents, whose life experiences were gleaned only from books and classroom dogma, instead of the world of human experience.

Although, I considered Vietnam as part of my past, survival instincts embedded in responses to that environment never quite left me.

One day, while accompanying Elaine down one of the underground corridors of UCLA Hospital that led to the computer section, we turned a right angle toward the hallway leading to the printer division. The printers at the time were very noisy, dot-matrix technology that had a distinctive loud chatter. To my ears, it was the repetitive staccato of machine gun fire. I immediately dropped to the floor and knocked Elaine down with me, crawling down the hallway through the querulous crowds of other students. Rather sheepishly, I recovered by ignoring the event.

I finally finished three years of residency with a designation of "Outstanding Medical Resident." Based on this, I was accepted to the highly competitive Fellowship in Clinical Rheumatology at the UCLA School of Medicine. This was financed by a small stipend from the Southern California Rheumatism Association.

During the last year of my residency, my marriage to Elaine came to a crisis point and divorce soon followed. I was saddled with alimony that exceeded the $900 per month I received for my fellowship from the Southern California Rheumatism Association. I needed to make more money, and I had no outlet for my grief except to work harder. I sought positions in the emergency rooms of community hospitals. Ultimately, I assumed responsibility for nearly 100 physicians to staff five hospital emergency rooms in the Los Angeles Area.

All of these extra-curricular activities were considered "moonlighting" from the Southern California Fellowship in Clinical Rheumatology. My experience in the academic world of rheumatology and academic medicine in general became more onerous with each passing day. What I learned from personal study and patient care far outweighed any knowledge imparted by faculty and other fellows.

In the midst of my discontent loomed the launch of Apollo 11 to the moon. Since I entered medical school for the sole purpose of entering the infant U.S. space program, it seemed appropriate that I observe this culminating launch. It represented the first attempt by the United States to land a man on the moon. The launch site was to be from Cape Canaveral, Florida. It was also an opportunity to visit my parents in Tallahassee, Florida.

I flew from Los Angeles to Tallahassee, then drove with my parents and sister to Cape Canaveral the night before the launch on July 15, 1969. We camped out on the mainland, across the water from the launch site, which afforded an excellent view of the early next morning launch.

The stark magnificence of the flood-lit gantry, Saturn V Rocket, and Apollo 11 stood in contrast against the darkness of the night sky. My emotions were many…and all depressed. The entirety of my adult life had been aimed at participating in America's space program. After a year of flying combat in Vietnam, my craving for high adventure had been more than satisfied and I separated from the Air Force. Now, more than anything else, I wanted a family. With the divorce, I had lost my family too. The driving forces of my entire adult life were lost in these two events.

As I looked across the bay at Apollo 11 being ready to launch, I was overcome by a sense of profound sorrow. The following morning, Apollo 11 headed for the moon with three Americans on board. I was not with them.

Part of my reason for taking a rheumatology fellowship was that the additional year of training coincided with Elaine's senior year in medical school. But divorce made even this consideration a moot point. I returned to Los Angeles to work days and nights for money that had no meaning for me and to continue in a "training program" for which I had no respect.

In 1969, during two weeks' vacation, I flew to Anchorage, Alaska, to investigate opportunities for private practice. The frontier aspect of Alaska appealed to me. My next planned destination was to be New Zealand. I was weary of California's hedonistic, superficial, plastic society, filled with nouveau-riche and steeped in sophomoric wisdom and self-satisfaction.

Flying to Anchorage, I peered out the right side of the airplane to view the magnificent panorama of rugged snow-clad mountain peaks, rolling beneath our wings for hundreds of miles, all unmarred by evidence of civilization. It was too wonderful to describe. The air in Anchorage was as pure and sweet as any that I have ever breathed. Renting a car, I began the drive from Anchorage down the Seward Highway toward the Kenai Peninsula and Soldotna for a meeting of the Alaska State Medical Society. There was no other traffic on the highway. I was spellbound by the drive through miles of virgin wilderness. I had smoked a pipe since medical school, but now it seemed to contaminate the purity of the environment. I removed the pipe from my mouth and spun the radio dial. There was only neutral static. It took me a moment to realize that I was outside the range of radio contact with the world. Suddenly my eyes began to cloud with tears that increased to the extent that I had to pull off the highway. There was a small lake several hundred yards off the road and I walked toward it. Sitting down beneath a tree, I broke down into sobs. This pristine wilderness both overwhelmed and comforted me. I experienced a reverence for its magnificence that bordered on a religious experience. I felt that I was home at last. And for the first time in many years, I found personal peace and solace.

Returning to Los Angeles, I resumed my hectic, whirlwind lifestyle of work at the university, L.A. hospitals and outpatient clinics.

Nearly thirty-six hours had passed since I last slept. After two consults at UCLA Hospital, I rushed to St. Joseph's Infirmary in Burbank to work the 11 p.m. to 7 a.m. emergency room shift. From there, I ploughed through the freeways to Hollywood Presbyterian Hospital in L.A. for an additional twelve hours in that emergency room. Finally, by midnight, I headed for my apartment for a shower and sleep. I was running on fumes and I knew it. Finally at 1 a.m., I fell into bed and succumbed to a deep sleep.

My next awareness was of being airborne in the F-4C Phantom II. Only this time I was in the front seat as pilot in command while the back-seat position was empty. I was alone. The aircraft was flying through dense clouds and visibility was virtually non-existent. My instruments indicated that the wings were level and that I was maintaining a fairly constant course heading while slowly descending. But, it was quiet… too quiet! There was no response to movement of the control stick, or to my advance of the throttles. The awful truth dawned on me! At some point, I had experienced a double flameout of both jet engines. Without power there is loss of hydraulic systems to control the aircraft. But more awful yet was the fact that I was losing altitude. How I maintained any semblance of coarse heading and wings level attitude, I could not explain. The flight path seemed predetermined and divorced from any input that I made.

Breaking out of the fog, I found myself within the narrow walls of a steep mountain canyon, with mere inches of clearance for both wingtips from the granite walls. The earth was barely visible beneath me. Under these conditions, there is only one option! Eject! Eject! But, ejecting within this tight corridor would be like jumping from the frying pan into the fire! There would no place to land by parachute. Ejecting would free me from the stricken aircraft, only to hang by parachute from a rocky crag until I died. I turned to memories of past experience and flying instructors for answers...

This recalled my first flight instructor, who had survived the Pacific air battles of WWII against the Japanese. Regardless of what is happening, he said, "Fly the airplane!" But without hydraulics, the airplane could not be flown. As Major Solis noted on my first flight, after I commented that the Phantom "really moves out": "Yeah, it does Doc, but it comes down just as damn fast as it goes up!"

And, now, this Phantom was coming down. I watched the altimeter unwind, lower and lower... Just as all hope of survival was fading, there was a slight cough from the engines beneath me before they roared into a full-throated throb. At the same time, there was a faint quiver in the control stick to indicate the bird was still alive and could be flown. Easing back slowly on the control stick to avoid a stall, I advanced the throttles and they responded. The miracle occurred. I began to climb up into the clear blue sky...I would survive!

I awoke, trembling and dripping with sweat to sit on my bedside and peer around my small apartment. Now at last I could smile. Flying combat missions in Vietnam had quenched my thirst for high adventure. I no longer had the passion for space travel and I separated from the Air Force to have a stable family life. Now this had been lost through divorce. These two personal flameouts were mirrored in my dream. But from it all, I would survive in a manner that was presently beyond my horizon, just as the Phantom of my dream survived with an air-start of both engines.

My thirty-third birthday was approaching and I vowed never to be unhappy again. I wrote a letter of resignation to the Rheumatology Fellowship Program of UCLA and to the Southern California Rheumatism Association and began packing. The next morning, I flew from Los Angeles to Anchorage. The urgency of my departure did not allow for transfer of all personal belongings. I left a footlocker full of my military uniforms in the garage of my apartment. At this point in my life, all past was moot. The future was an open book to be written.

On May 3, 1970, I arrived in Anchorage to begin a new life.

Nearly a half-century after my tour of duty in Vietnam, memories of events have faded, diluted by intervening years of practicing peacetime medicine in clinical rheumatology, raising a family and paying the bills. In civilian life, one becomes immersed in taxes, bills and repairs of the dwelling. Children must be educated according to the norms of society and status becomes more important than accomplishment and intellect. In the primitive world of early mankind, the purest essence of intelligence was elemental SURVIVAL.

Survival in twenty-first-century civilian life is less absolute than relative, but more degrading. The price of enduring the less formidable and trivial challenges of peacetime exacts a different toll, payable in different currency. The more advanced a civilization becomes, the more removed it is from the essential commonalities of life and death. For civilian life in America, during the twentieth and twenty-first centuries, reality is relative. Wealth is not related to being alive any more than poverty relates to death. Materialism is the ultimate arbiter of life in "civilized society," and materialism is always relative. Individualism succumbs to relationships, where any individual's all is measured against others of society. And yet, regardless of how wealthy a person is in material possessions, if he or she feels poor, then he or she is poor. Materialism is an addiction for which there is never satiety. In civilian life, the joy of surviving death has been replaced by the comparative dissatisfaction of relative materialism. In the modern world, corporeal survival has been replaced by achievement, measured in financial statements, automobile ownership and membership in proper clubs. Life is measured against the rule of "quality," rather than compared to its ultimate antithesis of quantity with death. During peacetime in civilized societies, life is expressed in relative terms of "Lifestyle" and "Quality of Life." Lifestyle replaces life and becomes the essential goal, while avoiding death becomes more an affirmation of medical technology and accident avoidance than a certainty that terminates corporeal existence. Quality of Life replaces the essential element of being or not being. But, during war, life is not an abstraction any more than death is an abstraction. Each is naked, unvarnished reality.

Regardless of war or peace and regardless of material possessions, a person who is filled with reverence for the splendors of Mother Nature... a person who stands in awe at the sight of a beautiful sunset ... a person who finds solace and beauty at the wind dancing over the waves...a person who is worshipful of birds soaring in the magnificence of a blue sky and delights in the glories of nature... then by any measure, in peace or war, that person is wealthy.

A lifetime of medical practice has exposed me to both the weaknesses and strengths of humanity. And in both war and peace, I continue to be inspired by the common man and woman as they persevere through the hardships of life. I have thought long and hard on Rudyard Kipling's writings of India where the jungle overgrowth covers "forgotten temples, dedicated to forgotten Gods." These thoughts forever lead me to the same conclusions:

In the bowels of this planet are relics of thousands of forgotten temples dedicated to thousands of forgotten Gods. Man is the fragile creature that created both the temples and the Gods in his search for something far beyond his comprehension. And yet, this fragile creature endures and continues to search for something far beyond his horizon.

Which are greater, relics of shattered temples, lost numbers of forgotten gods or this fragile creature that persists, groping through the darkness, in search of something greater than self?

Despite all flaws, treacheries, deceits and weakness, I continue to believe that Man is the noblest of God's creations.

It has been long quoted that a woman is the sum total of her memories while a man is the sum total of his dreams. I can only state that now in my advanced years, my memories are the sum total of my dreams as a young man. After my father's death, my mother stated that my father once said, "Guy has achieved everything in life of which I have ever dreamed."

I humbly accept this as the greatest compliment that a father can pay to his son. I can honestly state that I have been blessed by having fulfilled all of my childhood dreams.

Working my way through college and medical school, I obtained a trade in the form of doctor of medicine that further opened doors to knowledge. The struggles of self-sufficiency required to obtain my education conveyed wisdom to temper my knowledge, and wisdom is only achieved through pain and suffering.

Another youthful dream was to have a family. Now, thanks to my wife, Ramona, of more than forty-one years, I have three extraordinary stepsons, my beloved daughter, Laura, and my equally beloved son, Warren. Laura has further extended my blessings with a wonderful son-in-law, Kevin Catron, and three grandchildren, all bright, independent spirits: Abigail, Alex and Avery. I have no more mountains to climb, dangerous missions to fly or passions to be fulfilled. The physical infirmities of advancing age prevent any delusion that I may have of climbing future mountains, screaming to earth at the speed of sound or hacking a trail through a blizzard with 50-below-zero temperatures to reach my cabin in Alaska.

Ninety combat missions were injections of adrenaline that left me hungry for the next higher adventure. For me adventure was a drug that was forever insufficient to relieve my craving. But with the completion of my year of flying combat in Vietnam, my craving for high adventure seemed satisfied. My desire for family prevented me from pursuing this to my death.

But with fulfillment of all goals, in this old age, I feel empty! With the exception of writing, I have no further goals beckoning from beyond the horizon and less than enough energy to pursue them if they were present. I have always believed that writing should stem from experience and experience may require a lifetime to accumulate. Creativity is the province of youth, but youth is the time to live, with no concession for time to record. Writing requires the temperance of years' experience to validate history.

I muse at my past life and attempt to reconcile memories with my present life. I realize that I have never learned to be happy with the present. My happiness has been derived from the quest for something that is forever beyond the horizon… the pursuit, the chase, the hunt for some idea, goal or philosophy. While I realize the satisfaction gained by personal achievement, I also recognize that satisfaction does not equate to the exhilaration of pursuit. Fulfillment of goals is different from "happiness."

I consider myself a wealthy man, not in material things, but in accomplishments and life experience. And, as Polonius said to Laertes in Shakespeare's *Merchant of Venice*: "This above all…To thine own self be true…And, it must follow as the Day follows the Night…Thou canst not then be false to any Man."

I am content. I have been true to myself as I have run my race.